BURNHAM

King of Scouts
Baden-Powell's Secret Mentor

by Peter van Wyk

© Copyright 2003 Peter van Wyk. All rights reserved.

No part of this publication may be reproduced, stored in a retrieval system, or transmitted, in any form or by any means, electronic, mechanical, photocopying, recording, or otherwise, without the written prior permission of the author.

National Library of Canada Cataloguing in Publication Data

Van Wyk, Peter, 1929-
     Burnham : king of scouts / written by Peter van Wyk.
ISBN 1-4122-0028-8
     1. Burnham, Frederick Russell, 1861-1947. I. Title.
DT1851.M87V35 2003   968.04'5'092   C2003-904428-9

TRAFFORD

This book was published on-demand in cooperation with Trafford Publishing.
On-demand publishing is a unique process and service of making a book available for retail sale to the public taking advantage of on-demand manufacturing and Internet marketing. On-demand publishing includes promotions, retail sales, manufacturing, order fulfilment, accounting and collecting royalties on behalf of the author.

Suite 6E, 2333 Government St., Victoria, B.C. V8T 4P4, CANADA
Phone   250-383-6864   Toll-free 1-888-232-4444 (Canada & US)
Fax   250-383-6804   E-mail   sales@trafford.com
Web site   www.trafford.com   TRAFFORD PUBLISHING IS A DIVISION OF TRAFFORD HOLDINGS LTD.
Trafford Catalogue #03-1270   www.trafford.com/robots/03-1270.html

10   9   8   7   6   5   4   3   2   1

EX LIBRIS

Ode to a Thorny Hedge

When I depart this range to rest,
Beyond that Great Divide,
Just plant my frame somewhere out West,
That's sunny, lone and wide.

Let cattle rub my tombstone down,
Let wild critters mourn their kin,
Let mustangs paw and tramp the mound,
But don't you fence me in.

—*Anonymous*

THE West wasn't won by the white man who killed the bison to deny the red man an ambling commissary. True, an army of hunters did do battle with the great herds of American buffalo. But it took more than the killing of these prairie beeves to win the West.

Came the cattlemen with their gangs of line riders, tally books and great cow hunts. Came later the railroad makers. That seemed a fatal coming, but still the West was almost all open range, free and unpenned. What won the West was the closing of the range, because barbed wire took from the land those virtues so dear to the minds of men: freedom.

Thorny hedge. Sticker fence. For cattle, the finest enclosure on earth. Lighter than air, stronger than whiskey and cheaper than dirt. The critter ain't been born that can get through it.

Within five years, the open range was penned with bob wire and the West was won. It then belonged to the cattle ranchers, fence stretchers, cow pokes, sod busters, plow chasers, hay slayers, hen wranglers and churn twisters. Thus marks the passing of our frontier freedom — what the Free Rangers cherished most in the old West.

Major Frederick Russell Burnham, DSO, 1861-1947

At the turn of the century, when Richard Harding Davis was writing Real Soldiers of Fortune, *he heard a report that Burnham could turn around on his horse, Indian style, and shoot a pursuer out of the saddle. When he asked Burnham to verify that, Fred replied, "Not really. But I can shoot well enough to convince him that my pony is much faster than his pony and it doesn't pay to keep following me."*

How Others Felt ... about Fred Burnham

"There is no other man so worthy of the mantle of Kit Carson."
— *Los Angeles Times*

"...King of Scouts..."
— *Pearsons Magazine, London*

"I know Burnham. He is a scout and hunter of courage and ability, a man totally without fear, a sure shot and a fighter. He is the ideal scout."
— *Teddy Roosevelt, Oyster Bay*

"...World's greatest scout..."
— *Scarborough Post*

"Bullets, assegais passed your body within a fraction of an inch. Teeth, claws, horns of dangerous animals were powerless to harm you."
— *Willie Posselt, Africa scout*

"He was a wonderful little guy, tougher than a boot."
— *Cy Rubel, chairman, Union Oil of California*

"It may not be too much to claim for him a considerable if indirect share in the Boy Scout movement."
— *London Times*

"He is the Sherlock Holmes of all out of doors."
— *Richard Harding Davis, Real Soldiers of Fortune*

"Sir Robert Baden-Powell felt like a tenderfoot before this American scout."
— *James E. West, chief scout executive*

"He is quiet, courteous, extremely modest."
— *Richard Harding Davis*

"You watch Burnham. He has forgotten more (about scouting) than I shall ever know."

—*Johann Colenbrander, Africa scout*

"Lt. Gen. Baden-Powell, in his famous book on Scouting, gratefully acknowledges that not a little of his information came from Burnham."

—*Pearson's Magazine, London*

"It would be nothing short of a crime to leave your life story unwritten."

—*Samuel F.B. Morse, Pebble Beach*

"Those eyes apparently never leave yours, but in reality they see everything behind you and about you, above you and below you."

—*Richard Harding Davis*

"His eyes are of an amazing blue, and they fasten upon you when you come into his presence and never leave you, nor miss a shadow of your expression. They make you feel terribly naked."

—*Colliers magazine*

"Those blue eyes of his would knock a man down."
—*Rolfe McCollom, chief geologist, Union Oil Co.*

"The eyes of the man were what most impressed beholders. They were the all seeing eyes of the hunter, the eyes that let not the quiver of a twig escape. They were clear and bright, trained to gather swift impressions for the reasoning brain behind them."

—*Fritz Duquesne, Africa scout*

"There is one who is of the same stamp as you, who has the same pluck, the same courage, who faced all the hardships and danger, who traveled with you in the wilds of Africa. That is your wife, Blanche Burnham. Of her, I can say a marvelous, wonderful lady."

— *Willie Posselt, Africa scout*

In June 1896, Colonel Robert Baden-Powell made the original sketch for this watercolor. Fred Burnham and Bonnar Armstrong were escaping from angry Matabele warriors. Burnham had just slain the M'Limo oracle at Njelele in the Matopo Hills south of Bulawayo.

In This Biographical Novel

Adventures in Arizona 1
   Jeff Clark at the Tip Top 3
   Chief of Scouts 11
   The Christmas Gift 16
   Hunkey-Dorey Holmes 23

The Call to Monomotapa 30
   Cecil Rhodes 32
   London, Paris, Rome 42
   The Pungwe Is in Flood 48
   Trek North Rapidly 55
   Trapped at Fort Vic 63
   Oof Bird at Zimbabwe 71

The Matabele War 79
   Marching on Lobengula 81
   The Ridgeback 88
   Treachery in High Places 94
   Maxims at the Shangani 103
   Hotchkiss at the Bembesi 110
   Lo Ben's Konza Kraal Aflame 115

Wilson's Last Stand 123
   Chasing King Lobengula 124
   Burnham Breaks Out 132
   The Shangani Retreat 138
   Forced Night March 144
   Burnham Meets Rhodes 152

Chasing Rainbows 158
   The Birth of Rhodesia 159
   Zimbabwe & Dhlo Dhlo 166
   Rider Haggard and Lo Ben's Seal 174
   The Northern Coppers 180
   Chasing Rainbows 184
   The Jameson Raid 191

The Matabele Rebellion 199
   The Battle for Colenbrander's Farm 201
   Scouring the Insizas 209
   Turning Bullets into Water 216

Scouting with Baden-Powell 224
  Mapping Mineral King 225
  Slaying the M'Limo 235
  At War with Fleet Street 245
  Metamorphosis of Baden-Powell 254
  Walk Softly and Carry a Big Stick 263
  Baden-Powell, the Scout 270
The Call of the Klondike 276
  Ploughed by the Good Old Boy Net 277
  Race for the Riches 285
  Oof Bird on the Klondike 292
  Teddy Roosevelt 303
The Boer War 311
  Summoned to Africa 312
  Richard Harding Davis 320
  Scouting for Kitchener 327

Ambush at Koorn Spruit	336
Captured by the Boers	346
Behind Enemy Lines	**350**
Aylmer Hunter-Weston	*351*
Kempton Park Attack	*359*
Winston Churchill	*366*
Delagoa Bay Railway	*374*
Promoted to Major	*381*
King of Scouts	**392**
The Baden-Powell Letters	*393*
Queen Victoria	*398*
Distinguished Service Order	*407*
The Kenia Colony	*414*
Oof Bird at the Magadi	*422*
The Return to America	**428**
The Strangler Fig	*429*
Haggard & Hammond	*435*
Water for the Yaqui Delta	*443*
The Birth of the Boy Scouts	*453*
Came Scouting to America	*463*
Wealth & Honors	**473**
The Dominguez Air Show	*474*
Howard Burnham	*481*
Burnham Ex	*486*
Courtin the Union	*492*
The Shell Game	*500*
Union-Callendar No. 1	*504*
Hollywood Land	*510*
Scouting on Two Continents	*518*
Trail Dust	**525**
The Return to Africa	*526*
Mount Baden-Powell	*535*
The Bighorns of Arizona	*545*
Stabbed in the Back	*551*
The Last Outspan	*555*
Epilogue	**562**
Mount Burnham	*562*
Cecil B. De Mille	*564*
Hemingway's Hero	*564*
For Historians	*565*

Adventures in Arizona

The 1st Chronicle

Fred Burnham's Arizona

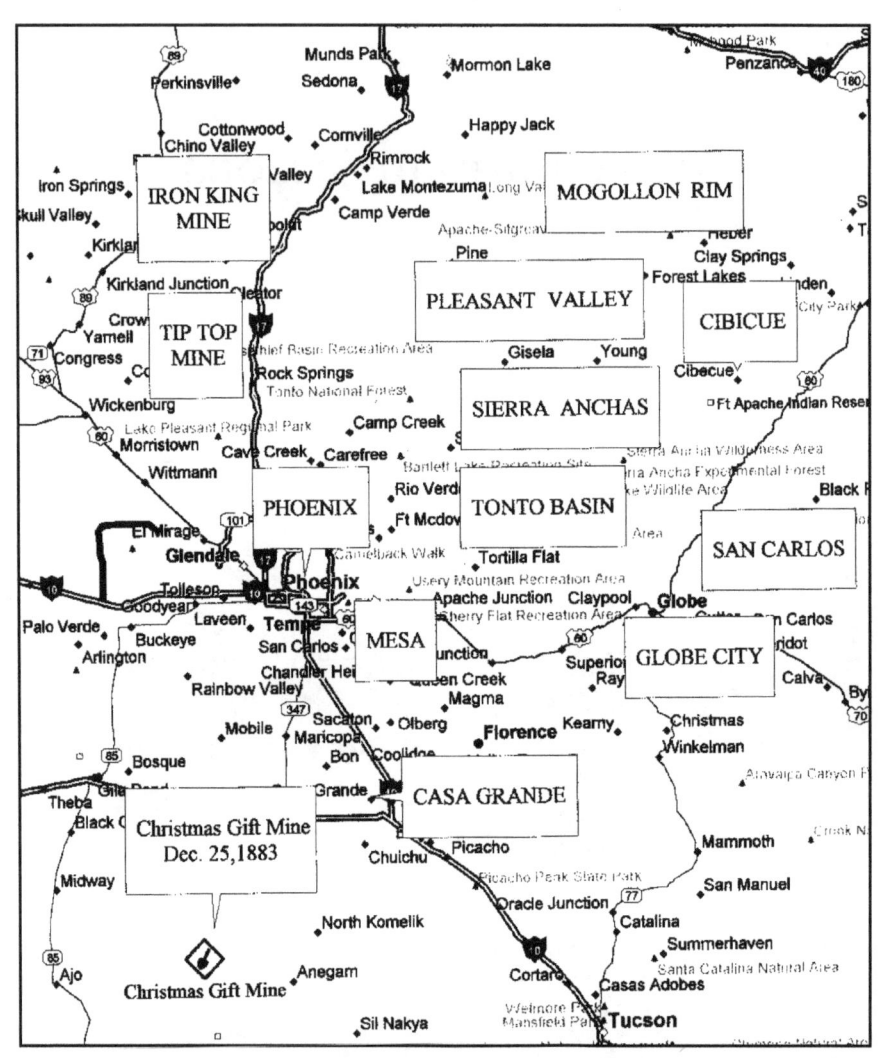

This is Fred Burnham's Arizona in the late 1800s. In 1876 he hunted game at the Tip Top Silver Mine south of Prescott. After attending a year of school in Clinton, Iowa, he returned to Arizona. From a cowboy-poet, he learned scouting in the Sierra Ancha Mountains north of Globe (page 1). On Christmas Day of 1883, Burnham and the Chilson boys discovered gold in the parched deserts of Papago Land southwest of Casa Grande. After his marriage to Blanche Blick, Burnham settled in Pasadena, but soon moved to Mesa, east of Phoenix where he became a banker. In later life, he bought Iron King.

1

Jeff Clark at the Tip Top

For decades, Stephe Baden-Powell galloped over the plains of India and Afghanistan playing polo and hunting tigers in the Kashmir. Only reluctantly did this dilettante soldier come to know the Indians of southern Asia — inferiors whom he dismissed as Worthy Oriental Gentlemen or WOGs. Nor did he come within a thousand leagues of a real red Indian from America.

Yet in the eighth year of the Twentieth Century, this gentleman general gave birth full blown to the Boy Scouts. And his scouting movement was based not on the Hindoos of south Asia, but on the red Injuns of America. Not on the Niggers of Lucknow, but on the Bantus of Africa. Explaining these riddles takes a real tellin, cause truth is stranger than fiction.

BLACK LAVA CANYON, ARIZONA • 1876

AFTER THREE DAYS clip-clopping south on horseback as Vulture Creek trickled through the Bradshaw Mountains, the lone rider with cinnamon-brown hair and cobalt-blue eyes entered the inky lava deposits of Black Lava Canyon. It was a hundred five degrees in the shade, but there was no shade.

"Would you look at what I'm seeing," said a gangly redhead standing by the headworks of a silver mine. He looked to be ten years older than the horseman, and his toothy grin stretched across a lean but friendly face. The rider wore the stalwart look of one who had just discovered fire.

"This here the Tip Top Mine?" the lone rider asked. Seated astride his brown gelding, the young man seemed as limber as rawhide belting. A Winchester 1873 carbine rested in the scabbard and a Remington 74 Army revolver was holstered at his right side. The rider looked a bit narrow at the equator

"Sure is the Tip Top," replied the host. "You look a sight indecent, sweet pea. Had a look at yourself beneath all that trail dust?"

"If it's the same to you, I'm not wearin my Sunday-go-to-meeting duds," the horseman retorted.

"Jeff Clark here," the redhead said offering a paw.

"You the job shark?" The rider dismounted to shake.

"Job shark? Uh, yeah. Guess that's me," the lanky manager said. "Looks like you could use some vittles. We got nothin fancy, but you're welcome to share."

The rider studied what seemed to be the world's supreme optimist. Clark was happy-go-lucky, a strip of sun-tanned muscle and sinew that harnessed reserves of strength.

"Feed your horse while I rassle up some grub."

As Clark fried thick slices of salt pork, he studied the young man: hair unkempt, an oval face that framed a cleft chin. His jaw, though firm, was covered by peach-fuzz. The young man was blessed with good looks, but at five-foot-six, he was just a runt — somehow his arms and legs seemed more than ample for the compact body. The most amazing features were those fierce cobalt-blue eyes — eyes that sparkled like icy diamonds and pierced the core of a man's very being. Jeff winced.

While the rider lined his flue with salt sowbelly and whistle berries, Clark asked about the latest news, always a priority in remote areas of the West.

"What's happening back East?"

"Fella named Bell's been talkin over a string of copper wire," the rider allowed between bites of food.

"Like the Western Union telegraph?" Clark asked, filling a tin mug with Arbuckles java.

"No, not that dot-and-dash stuff," he replied. "Real talk." He had overheard the news in Alvord Aitken's Cigar Store in Prescott. "Got any more of that sow's bosom?"

"Sure," Clark said. "By the way, I don't believe I heard you say your name."

"Didn't," the youngster grunted. In the West, it wasn't always polite to ask.

"You walking backward to throw me off trail?" Clark asked sharply. "Weren't you asking about a job? You're pretty bantam-sized to wear a short fuse."

At that moment, the lone rider learned that the man who has the gold makes the rules.

"Burnham's the name," he said. "Frederick Russell Burnham. The middle name comes from Ma's side."

"How long you been out West, sweet pea?"

"Five years. An don't call me sweet pea."

"You got kin?"

"Pa died three years ago. Last year Ma took my kid brother, Howie, and went to Iowa to live with my uncle Josiah Russell. The town's above the rapids on the Mississippi."

"Why'd you stay out West?" Clark looked puzzled.

"No wampum for the iron horse," Fred said. "I found work shootin game at the Cerro Gordo."

"I hear Cerro Gordo's closed."

On the Panamint Mountains, on the east side of the Sierra Nevada — that Great Wall of California — a lawsuit had closed the fabled Cerro Gordo Silver Mine. Burnham, a game hunter, was thrown out of work. The action caught him without a nest egg so when a pair of Cousin Jacks boasted of Arizona's silver lodes, Fred decided that was good enough. In Prescott, Fred learned from the owner of Aitken's Cigar Store that the richest silver strike was at the Tip Top mine. Alvord Aitken had given him the directions to Black Lava Canyon.

"Cerro Gordo got shut down by a claim jumper," Fred said. "Left me feelin like a skunk in church."

"You must be a real source of pride to your family," Clark said disparagingly.

"I'm as smooth as a tomcat pissin on velvet," Fred said. "I came here to hunt game for hungry pick pushers, not to start a church."

In the West, Cousin Jack Cornishmen wielded a lock-hold on the mining jobs. Recognizing a Cousin Jack was easy. Horsemen wore real ridin pants: tight at the waist and loose of leg, made at the Oregon City Woolen Mills. Cousin Jacks wore poor man's clothes: Levi's with orange thread and copper rivets. The frayed knees from kneeling on the mine floor was a dead giveaway of a pick pusher.

"Tell me, Freddie, how old are you?"

"Name's Fred," Burnham objected. "I'll be sixteen next month." *That was fudging only a year.*

After Burnham ate his fill, Clark invited him for a horseback ride to show him the lay of the land.

"Know how to hunt wild game?"

"Learned from Shacknasty George, a Shoshone hunter. Taught me to use an eagle-bone whistle too."

"Sheepeater from Cerro Gordo, eh?" Clark scoffed. "They eat anything that flies, hops or crawls."

"He has more guts than you could hang on a fence," Fred said. "He learned me how to track bighorn sheep." *Everyone knew that tracking the wary bighorn sheep was an accomplishment.*

"You're sharp enough to stick into wet sand," Jeff observed tersely. "But you're still green, young man."

"I'm as wise as a tree full of owls," Fred said smugly.

Crikeys, this kid is just a tenderfoot, lacking moral anchors, a confused orphan tilting between chance and anarchy, and he's fated for an early grave.

While they rode, Clark was surprised to see the egocentric youngster was virtually born to the saddle. He displayed a rare ability to be *at one* with his mount. Before the ride was over, Jeff had decided that Fred was pure magic on a horse. When they got back to the Tip Top, Jeff said Fred was free to shoot all the wild game he wanted.

"Pay you a penny a pound, dressed weight."

Back on California's Cerro Gordo, where it was all open range, Burnham had prided himself on being a skilled tracker of open-field game, the kind that grazed on the broad shoulders of the Panamint Mountains. But hunting in these close hills and valleys of Arizona called for a different technique and Fred returned from a day's outing empty-handed.

"In the Territory, you have to move in and shoot fast," Jeff said. The next day he agreed to train Burnham in the new Bogardus school of western snap-shooting. They approached downwind of wild game, dismounted, ran up and fired snap-shots until they downed an animal. The method would have been futile on the open range, but here in the Arizona hills it was just the type of hunting that kept meat on the table.

In the weeks that followed, Fred began to provide the Cousin Jacks with a dependable supply of venison and antelope. Except for occasional pangs for a real grease-feed from a fat bear, the miners came to be a contented crew. Burnham came to be grateful to Clark. Stalking the bighorn took skill, but here in the brushy hills snap-shooting was important. Now he knew how to earn a living anywhere.

In the following weeks, Fred came to enjoy the solitude of the Arizona desert, and he fell in love with the fleecy pink-cloud sunrises and sunsets. But his greatest pleasure — one that would last a lifetime — was to relax after dinner and yarn around the glowing coals of a campfire.

One night, Jeff Clark read news from a paper newly arrived in the jackass mail. "Over in Wyoming, Bill Cody has been boasting of scalping the Cheyenne chief, Yellow Hand."

Adventures in Arizona

"I seen scalpin in Los Angeles," Burnham said. "Tain't purty." He put another stick of wood on the fire and stirred the coals.

"Yellow Hand hasn't shown himself, so people are beginning to believe Buffalo Bill's claim."

"Ma went to school with Mr. Cody's big sister," Fred said. "That was in Iowa, at the rapids on the Mississippi."

Clark frowned, nodded a curt good night and curled up in his bedroll to sleep out under the stars.

• • •

FOUR WEEKS later, on a hot, sunny Saturday, Fred shot a brace of long-eared Arizona jackrabbits. The next day Jeff spit-roasted them for a potluck, inviting Fred to join him.

"These four-legged chickens will be done when Sunday services let out," Jeff said.

"Count me out for prayer meetin," Fred said. "Pa was a sky pilot. I was raised on prunes and proverbs an I don't need no more."

Sounds like the squawks of ravens echoed from the throats of faithful Cousin Jacks, but Burnham held firm. "While you're talkin to God, I'll mend Turk's bridle."

"Fred, what do you plan to be doing with your life when you're thirty?" Clark asked running a hand through his copper hair and eyeing Burnham closely.

"If it's any of your business, Mr. Know-It-All, I calculate to be a U.S. Senator."

Like a bolt, Clark's right fist caught Burnham on the jaw, knocking him to the ground.

"Don't get your bristles up," Jeff warned. "You might have gravel in your gizzard, but when it comes to the three Rs, if you don't get yourself some book learning, you'll end up familiar with the blister end of a manure fork."

"Why'd ya hit me?" Fred asked, rubbing his jaw.

"To get your mindfulness. You can't read. When it comes to doing sums, I could cheat you and you wouldn't know it."

Fred tossed the bones into the fire and stalked off.

Ritornello • Interlude

London • 1876

IN AN IVY-COVERED manse in Kensington Gardens, pencil-necked Robert Stephenson Smyth Baden-Powell, nineteen, celebrated his graduation from Charterhouse School. Though Stephe was only run-of-the-mill in academics, he was a good shot. He drew clever caricatures and made precise sketches.

He failed the orals for Oxford. Then during one of those periodic war scares, he took an exam for a commission. To his everlasting amazement, he received a passing grade and was gazetted into the British Army without the hindrance of a Sandhurst education. Sub-Lieutenant Baden-Powell was assigned to the Thirteenth Hussars, a light cavalry unit at Lucknow in Uttar Pradesh. It was the largest state in India. Stephe hated it.

Counterpoise • Equilibrium

Tip Top • 1876

STUNG BY JEFF'S CRITICISM, Fred began to hunt wild game for the other mines in Black Lava Canyon: Silver Museum, Eldorado, Foy and Lane. For the next month, he seldom saw Clark. In time, though, Burnham began to suspect that Jeff had told him something important. When he shot an antelope, he gave it to the mine manager for the Fourth of July barbecue. Jeff invited him to join with the other Cousin Jacks for a Western hoe-down and fandango.

During that Tuesday repast, everyone talked about the Big News. Nine days earlier, up on the Little Big Horn River in the Montana Territory, Sitting Bull's braves and Crazy Horse's cavalry had ambushed Lieutenant Colonel George Armstrong Custer. The slaughter of the Seventh Cavalry Regiment was a defeat that shocked all Americans — especially during the celebration of the Centennial.

After the meal, Clark told Burnham he was a grandson of Lieutenant William Clark.

The name meant nothing to Fred.

"Seventy years ago, Captain Meriwether Lewis and Grandpa Clark explored the Louisiana Purchase."

Fred had never heard of the Louisiana Purchase.

"President Thomas Jefferson appointed Captain Lewis as his secretary," Jeff said. "Jefferson sent Lewis to study botany, zoology and celestial navigation."

"Why did he study that celestial stuff?" Fred asked. At precisely that moment, it occurred to Fred why Clark was named Jefferson.

"So they could map their overland journey," Jeff said. "Grandpa Clark was the expedition cartographer, the map-maker. The stars in those constellations are the benchmarks of the evening skies."

Fred blinked at that bit of enlightenment. While Clark continued talking Burnham poured Arbuckles. *Benchmarks in the night skies, eh?*

"By reading the stars," Clark said, "Grandpa was able to draw maps as they crossed the continent. They followed the Columbia River to the Pacific at Fort Clatsop and returned to St. Louis. In four thousand miles of travel, Grandpa's charts erred by only forty miles."

Fred added that new bit of lore to his knowledge box.

"Lewis and Clark reported on the customs of the twenty-five Indian tribes they met," Jeff said. "They appraised the commercial opportunities, recorded plant and animal life and studied the topography and mineral deposits."

The midday sun blazed relentlessly and the talk trailed off to drowsy silence. Fred and Jeff scrambled into the shade of a greenbark paloverde tree for a holiday nap. When at last they awakened, Clark said. "By the way, the reason I told you about Grandpa Clark was not to boast. I was trying to impress on you the need for some book learning."

"What's all that botany and cartography stuff got to do with me?" Fred groused.

"More than you think, sweet pea," Jeff said sharply, "unless you'd like to spend the rest of your life pushing a plow and staring at a mule's ass."

Taken aback, Fred stalked off into the solitude of the saguaro cactus where he remained all that night. For some time after that Fourth of July powwow, he avoided Clark.

Lagniappe • A Little Extra

BUCKINGHAM PALACE • 1876

ALL OF ENGLAND chuckled when Queen Victoria's eldest daughter announced her engagement to the Emperor of Prussia. Good heavens, daughter would outrank mother. It wasn't seemly. Then that handsome opportunist Benjamin Disraeli shinnied up the greasy pole, winning appointment as Prime Minister. A great flatterer, Dizzy introduced a bill in Parliament to add Empress of India to the Queen's vast collection of titles. Parliament approved, making Victoria equal in rank to her eldest daughter. For that favor, the good Queen with the toddy blossom nose — mother of nine and lonely widow of fifteen years — showed her gratitude by elevating Dizzy to the peerage. As empress, the Queen engaged Hindu servants and set out to learn Hindustani.

Counterpoise • Equilibrium

TIP TOP MINE • 1876

A MONTH later, Fred timidly asked Jeff to learn him the stars.

Surprisingly, the kid proved to be an apt pupil. Before anyone knew it, Fred was familiar with the heavens. At night as they shared a campfire, he gazed upward to study the night skies. The Little Dipper was pouring into the Big Dipper. It was 9:30 p.m. The blue-white Summer Triangle of stars — Deneb, Vega and Altair — had ebbed into the western skies, signaling the end of summer.

As time passed, the sharing of Sunday dinner at the Tip Top came to be a weekly ritual, with Jeff serving as Fred's mentor on a variety of topics from the mountain men of the Tetons to the pioneer scouts.

Fred got up to add more wood to the fire, wondering why the smoke always followed him, stinging his eyes.

"The mountain men were the first scouts," Jeff told him. "Then beaver hats went out of style and the Oregon Trail opened. They scouted for the covered-wagon trains. Later still, during the Injun Wars, they scouted for the Army. They were good scouts for their time, but their scouting was based on learning the landmarks. In the future, scouting will depend on scientific principles: cartography and stuff."

For a couple of weeks Fred said little. He seemed caught up in somber thought. Then one chilly autumn morning he rode over to the headworks of the Tip Top and found his boss supervising the loading of silver ore for shipment to the San Francisco Mint.

"Mr. Clark, I think it's time to get acquainted with a couple of those three Rs you been palaverin about. Would you like to buy a well-kept carbine?"

"Why don't you keep it?" Clark replied. "I suspect that where you're going, you'll be pushing the reins real hard. You might need Old Reliable before you join your family."

Fred returned the carbine to its scabbard, a round in the chamber and the safety locked on. He nodded a tearful farewell to the copper-headed man who had been so good to him. Then he spurred Turk and rode into Black Lava Canyon. At that time, neither of them knew that one day they would meet again half a world away in a place called Monomotapa.

2

Chief of Scouts

Globe, Arizona • July 1882

GLOBE HADN'T CHANGED—still Hell's Forty Acres—angels plus misfits from Tombstone gathered in a valley surrounded by a green blanket of pine trees that covered the Pinal Mountains. Fred walked into the office of Judge Aaron Hackney, the editor of the *Arizona Silver Belt*. He read his mail, wrote a reply and repaired to the house in back to eat a hot meal at Mrs. Hackney's table. Judge Hackney and Uncle Josiah in Clinton were long-time editorial collaborators who exchanged news via the mails. The judge looked after Fred's mail in Globe.

"Yes, General Crook is back from the Department of the Platt in Nebraska," Hackney admitted stroking his long white beard. "And yes, Al Sieber is chief of scouts again — though I don't think that fact will change things much."

"It has to," Fred said. "I'm gonna be a scout."

He said good-bye, laid in provisions at Kellner's Mercantile Store and rode east toward the San Carlos Indian Agency. *Now that General Crook is back, things will be better*. On crossing the Pinals, the greenery of Globe gave way to the San Carlos Desert, a tawny field of sand waiting for someone to run out of water so it could swallow them. The aroma of desert sage was everywhere.

More than anything, Burnham wanted to enlist as an Army scout so he could train other white men as scouts. He believed that in the years ahead scouting would be more important than ever to the Army. After the Civil War, the repeating rifle had replaced the muzzle loader, giving each soldier greater firepower. So did the Gatling gun. Future scouts would have to be trained in reading the stars, Morse codes, signaling, electricity and cannon ballistics.

In the past, the chiefs of scouts in Arizona hadn't seen fit to use

11

white men as scouts. The Apache scouts knew the land like the backs of their hands. Burnham's scouting principles allowed him to penetrate unknown country, carry out his mission and come back unscathed. Burnham felt that Al Sieber—a kindred spirit from Minnesota—would listen. Fred knew he could convince General Crook's chief of scouts of his ideas.

To Burnham scouting was more than a craft. It was his life's calling. His own introduction to the outdoors began as a child in Minnesota. Fred's father, the Reverend Edwin Burnham, taught him to fell trees, build a log cabin, hunt, fish and survive a Minnesota winter. Fred's outdoors education continued in the sloughs of Dominguez Mesa south of Los Angeles, in the California Panamints at Cerro Gordo and in the inky lava deposits of Arizona's Black Lava Canyon. Most of all in the Sierra Ancha Mountains north of Globe.

But his deep, undying love for scouting did not become central to the core of his being until he went to live in Clinton, Iowa. There his mother set about tutoring him until he could catch up to the classroom studies at Clinton High School. At night, Uncle Josiah Russell apprenticed him as a printer's devil at the *Clinton Herald*. Fred thought newspaper work as akin to knitting lace. He wanted to study the stars and learn about navigation.

Clinton, the home of the world's largest sawmill, was a few miles north of the Mississippi Rapids. The rapids at Le Claire was where Fred's mother and uncles had studied in a one-room school with Martha and Julia Cody. Fred hated every minute of his stay in Clinton. He and Homer Blick, a lanky limber Jim who lived next door, were building a raft to float down the Mississippi River when the news arrived that Buffalo Bill was coming to town. That was more thrilling than if Barnum & Bailey showed up with elephants.

Cody was on an excursion to childhood haunts at Le Claire. Then he discovered his ancestral home no longer had a newspaper. So he rode a few miles north to Clinton where he gave an interview to Josiah Russell, the editor of the *Clinton Herald*. Cody then learned that Fred's Uncle Edward Russell was editor of the nearby *Davenport Gazette*. After that Cody began paying attention to Fred and Homer. He escorted them with a group of boys on a jaunt to Beaver Island southeast of town. Cody was thirty, tall with a square beard and a rat's nest haircut. He had given up the West and taken the lead role in a stage play based on his buffalo-hunting adventures. The boys were oblivious to his swashbuckling, seeing only a hero to venerate.

That day Buffalo Bill regaled the boys with a lesson in outdoors lore — coaching the boys in tracking and trailing, sign language and the use of wood and bone. Cody urged them to listen faithfully, as none of this information was available in books. He told them the great scouts of the past performed even minor tasks uncommonly well. Often when a trifling detail was overlooked, it could doom a person to the Happy Hunting Grounds. Cody didn't teach the lads much useful lore, but he did infect Fred Burnham with a first-class case of scouting fever. When the lads returned to Clinton, Buffalo Bill declared, "The things I tell you must never be forgotten. When I was a boy, my father made me swear I would pass on to the boys of the next generation all that he had passed on to me." The young men solemnly swore that when they became great plainsmen and scouts, they would pass on what Cody had imparted to them. From that moment, Fred's goal in life was to be a scout.

• • •

SIX DAYS BEFORE Christmas in 1879, Fred and Homer Blick ran away, floating down the Mississippi River in a raft to Jackson, Mississippi. There they struck out west to Texas, where they joined a cattle drive to Missouri. When the drive was over, they split up. Homer returned to his family in Iowa. Fred bought a pony and drifted west. In the mountains outside of Santa Fe, someone stole his horse and he was forced to walk four hundred miles cross-country to Globe.

There he came under the influence of a Texican named Bill Holmes, a cowboy-poet. People said that at the drop of a shot glass Holmes could compose a poem on any topic. His most celebrated bit of iambic pentameter was called "Hunkey-Dorey" and it became his nickname.

Holmes sort of adopted young Burnham. In the rugged Sierra Ancha Mountains north of Globe that summer, Hunkey-Dorey introduced Fred to the sweaty, tiring and unvarnished facts of scouting. The young man mastered following a faint trail where the territory's best trackers confessed bafflement. He learned to cope with the wily Apache and come back with his scalp intact. Under Holmes' tutelage, Fred distilled these finely honed skills until he could match his abilities in the out of doors with anyone. Armed with this knowledge, Fred was sure that General Crook's chief of scouts would be happy with his talents.

As Fred rode eastward, he saw the San Carlos Indian Agency really was a reeking sand-flat just like they said. The country duplicated the destitute land around Castle Dome Mountains and the bleak Harquehala Range over by the Colorado River. The presence of Apaches made Fred a trifle uneasy, but when they paid him no mind, and he entered the reservation as spirited as the day he had met Buffalo Bill.

"Howdy, there," Fred said to the subtler. "Lookin for Mr. Sieber. Know where I can find him?" Apache squaws wrapped in woolen blankets squatted in the cool interior of the log trading post. The place smelled like a slaughterhouse.

"Al took some scouts on patrol up the San Carlos River," said the owner, a sloth with tobacco juice dribbling over his chin-stubble. "He's on a punishment raid on the Natanes Plateau. Should be back in a day or two."

Fred studied a flyspeck-stained map tacked to the wall and picked out a route to the Natanes Plateau.

"Guess I'll just mosey up there and meet them," Fred said.

"Ain't you gonna buy nothin, you cheap little shit?"

• • •

AS HAD BECOME HIS custom when traveling in unfamiliar territory, Fred turned in the saddle every few hundred yards and committed the scene to memory. It helped speed him along on his return journey. Hunkey-Dorey had taught him that trick in the Sierra Anchas. Taught him to smell out Apaches too.

The Sieber party left a trail any tenderfoot could follow. Within two miles, Fred had figured out the patrol's composition. The big horse was well shod—that would be Sieber's mount. A smaller hoof-print was left by a burro. *Sieber has a packer to carry provisions.* The Apaches with their unshod ponies took a bit longer to puzzle out.

On the second day, Fred awakened at the dawn of a buttermilk sky. He got a whiff of smoke from a campfire. The aroma of Arbuckles drifted toward him. Food scent didn't travel well in the mists, so Sieber's camp was nearby. Fred saddled Fergus, his sandy buckskin, and led him through several thickets of burro brush until he spotted a circle of men seated on the bank of Big Bonito Creek. The men were concentrating on their breakfast.

A tall, thick man in a sheepskin coat and wide-brimmed hat strained coffee through a walrus mustache. *Sieber, no doubt.* Fred felt himself attracted to this big, rawboned frontier scout. The others sat cross-legged around a campfire. They were a turbulent, desperate, disreputable looking lot. They talked quietly, eating greasy Indian fry bread and sipping coffee. Next to Sieber was a pig-eyed troll frying sow's bosom and Injun bread. *The German packer with the jackass*, Fred guessed. Six Indians with red headbands—the sign of friendly Apache scouts—completed the fireside circle.

One scout held up his coffee mug and asked for *shug*. Another proffered his tin plate and said, "*hogga meat*." Fred was about to ask if he could join them. *Wait a second*. He saw the other Indian, no headband, wrists bound with rawhide thongs. He asked for *bisukit*.

The eerie silence was ample warning. Fred sensed—rather than heard—something awry. At that moment, Sieber tossed the dregs of his coffee. The subtler handed fry bread to the prisoner. Sieber snorted. In a split second, he picked up his carbine, laid it on the shoulder of the cherubic packer, aimed at the prisoner's head and pulled the trigger. The rifle exploded and the bullet entered the man's skull behind his right ear, blowing off the top of his head and scattering strips of skin, shattered pieces of bone, matted hair, custard brains, crimson blood and shredded flesh in all directions. Sieber laid down the carbine, reached into his overcoat and withdrew a pint of Taos lightning.

"I said no prisoners."

"Al," the packer drawled, "if I'd knowed you vas gonna do dat, I wouldn't haf giffed him so much bread."

"You're a cheap son of a bitch."

The stench of burned hair and bloody flesh reached Fred—Fergus whickered an alarm. One of the Apache scouts leaped up, stumbling over his carbine and sprawling awkwardly in the campfire. Sieber spotted Burnham and his face took on a troubled look.

"Stranger, what you doin in these parts?" Sieber demanded. He pulled back his sheepskin coat and fumbled for his blue lightning.

"Just hunting strays," Fred blurted out. "Didn't know I was on government property." He leaped onto Fergus and spurred the horse to a gallop, seeking the protection of the pinion pines. Three shots barked and three slugs thudded into trees on Fred's left and right, too close for comfort. One thing he knew instantly. So long as Al Sieber was chief of scouts, Fred Burnham would never work as a U.S. Army scout.

3

The Christmas Gift

ARIZONA TERRITORY • SEPTEMBER 1883

RED BURNHAM rode out of the Tonto Basin — an inaccessible lair of thieves — and into the verdant mountains around Globe. Twenty feet ahead of him, a white and brown skewbald sorrel pony carried a weasel-faced youth whose wrists were lashed to the saddle horn. The young man's holster was empty and he looked as unkempt as a barber's dog — the rat's nest under his hat suggested a prolonged absence from civilization.

For most of the summer, Fred had ridden shotgun for Wells-Fargo, but this week he was working as a deputy for Gila County Sheriff Glenn Reynolds. These days his pockets jingled with silver and he was feeling good about life. A carbine at the ready across his saddle said he didn't trust this prisoner.

At the Salt River, Fred paused to water the prisoner's sorrel and Fergus, Fred's handsome sandy-beige buckskin with a fancy all-black mane and tail. He ignored the man's thirst — prisoners didn't count for much. As he remounted Fergus to take his prisoner to the Gila County Jail, two riders hailed him.

"Hey, Gumbah, got yourself some reward money?" Gyp Chilson inquired. Fred nodded, automatically keeping his horse and the prisoner's out of line of the two riders. Fred's hands closed over the carbine in case there was any suddenness.

"Chilly enough for you?" brother Esme Chilson said. "We're heading to Papago Land for some winter prospectin. Care to tag along?"

"Okay, if I'm in for pee-wees, aggies and cat's eyes," Burnham replied. "A full share this time. Got nuff wampum now to grubstake myself." The Chilsons nodded and they blended into a foursome for the ride into Globe.

"If you wanna go now, I can shoot this guy," Fred offered.

"We're not leaving until next week," Esme said.

• • •

Judge Hackney had introduced Burnham to the Chilson brothers, stocky young men a few years older than Fred. Until that time, Fred had shown no interest in prospecting. But after his encounter with Al Sieber, he had decided it was time to search for a new goal — and prospecting proved to be a good choice.

A week later, Burnham accompanied the Chilsons as they rode out of Globe bound for the Fryers' outfitting station down south at Casa Grande. Fryer Station was near an ancient Pima Indian ruin in the Sonora Desert, between Phoenix and Tucson.

At Casa Grande, Fred was greeted by Pauline Fryer, a striking blonde six feet tall, a woman who would never experience the humiliation of rejection. Beside her was Jerry Fryer, her debonair husband, also blond and taller still. Even in linsey-woolsey, they were as comely as newlyweds on the cover of the Sears Wish Book.

Over spit-roasted spareribs that night, Jerry told the trio of the latest rumors from Papago Land.

"A few months ago, Alex MacKay struck a rich vein west of Tucson," Jerry said.

"In total secrecy," Pauline added, "MacKay staked his discovery on the tip of Quijotoa Peak. By June, it was too hot to work in the desert so he was forced to postpone development until the weather cooled. But he organized the Peer Mine and that news got out to the public."

When Pauline revealed that MacKay's silver discovery was made on May 11, Fred's eyes grew as round as onions.

"I'll eat hay with a horse," he blurted out. "That's my birthday." Fred had just turned twenty-two. On hearing this mixture of rumors and speculation—which Gyp, Esme and Fred accepted as cast-in-bronze gospel fact—they would scarcely have cared if the desert was covered with cholla cactus and with an armed Apache lurking behind every bush. They were gonna be rich.

In the corral behind the outfitting station, the Fryers had built a replica of a mine works where, for a modest fee, they taught lessons to would-be prospectors.

"You'll learn a lot here," Jerry said, lighting a pipe. "Arizona is the world's best school for prospecting. Its sands are a geological laboratory. Nature has deposited an improbable variety of minerals here and it will pay you to learn how to search for them."

Burnham nodded, beginning to realize deep in the gut that in addition to scouting, there existed something in life that was

17

potentially rewarding.

"Prospectors from elsewhere," Jerry said, "are often perplexed by the array of strange lodes and outcroppings found here. But Arizona-trained prospectors who go elsewhere are seldom stumped when putting their knowhow to use."

"In places where there's lots of water like the Mother Lode," Pauline said, "prospectors use the gold pan to sift the sands of stream beds. In Papago Land, the gold pan can't be used because of the lack of water."

From a wooden box, Pauline lifted out what looked like a foot-long piece of bull's horn that had been carved into a shoehorn. "In the desert we use the horn spoon," she said. "What you must do is carve a horn into a long spoon. It's the gold pan of the desert."

Curious, Fred picked up the spoon to examine it.

"Use black horn," Pauline said. "You can see the gold better." .

After a hearty dinner of organic son-of-a-bitch stew, they retired to the sitting room where Jerry explained to them how to assay ores. "You pulverize the quartz," he said, "then you wash it out with the horn spoon. If there's gold, it will be a yellow streak as fine as flour."

"Gold is scarce as hens' teeth in Arizona," Fred said. "How do you test for silver?"

"Good question," Jerry said. "Silver takes a more elaborate test." He spent the next half hour demonstrating to the young men the fine points of testing for silver.

That night as Fred drifted off to sleep, he concluded that the Fryers had more prospecting wisdom than you could cram into a mail-order catalogue.

As he slept he dreamed of pretty Blanche Blick, Homer's younger sister who was teaching school back in Iowa. Fred got sweet on her in 1876, soon after he arrived in Clinton. He was only fifteen then and she was a gawky twelve, still in the awkward age. But by 1879 when Homer and Fred ran away, Blanche was fifteen. Then Father Blick quietly forewarned Fred that he would not approve of anyone carrying on with his daughter until she was older and until the gentleman caller could support her in style.

After breakfast the next day, the prospectors stabled their horses with the Fryers and rented burros for the journey into the destitute land to the south.

"We know all about you Hopeful Bills," Pauline teased. "If you gain nothing else by your journey, you can console yourself in the knowing that nothing is there."

"And if you do find silver," Jerry added, "you'll start digging a tunnel into the heart of the mountain, thereby creating the world's longest lunatic asylum."

Ritornello • Interlude

LUCKNOW, INDIA • OCTOBER 1883

STEPHE BADEN-POWELL — he insisted it rhymed with maiden and noel — finished an eight-month-long course in military tactics, and he made good marks in surveying and fortifications.

Stephe hated India. For four unending years, he had written letters to Mother Henrietta Grace, urging her to use influence to get him transferred to England. Then overnight, Stephe's aversion was transformed into delight. The turnabout coincided with the arrival of cherubic Kenneth McLaren, nineteen, a peach-faced graduate of the British Military College at Sandhurst.

When McLaren arrived at Lucknow, he looked like a wee-laddie of fourteen and Stephe nicknamed him The Boy. Stephe and The Boy palled together in target practice, singing barrack ballads and playing practical jokes. Baden-Powell soon stopped begging Henrietta Grace to have him sent home.

Counterpoise • Equilibrium

PAPAGO LAND • NOVEMBER 1883

THE PROSPECTORS struck out to the southwest, descending into the broad Santa Rosa Wash en route to the Vekol Mountains. They left behind the tall and stately saguaro cactus and got to know the organ-pipe cactus, which had no central trunk. Its collection of green stalks made it look like an outdoor pipe organ.

On a calm autumn day the prospectors found themselves shogging along the soft sand in Bitter Well Wash. Seemingly from nowhere a stiff breeze blew up. Fred looked west at Table Top Mountain. A silvery shimmer appeared along the gloomy, blue gray horizon.

"Gyp, Esme, look," Fred cried. As they watched, wispy cirrus clouds coalesced into roiling, prune-colored cumulus storm clouds. Within minutes the prospectors were laced by sheets of stinging rain, followed by crashes of thunder and bolts of lightning. So quickly did the storm appear that they were soaked before they could to don ponchos. *How could there be so much rain? Could the sands absorb all this water? Would it be followed by drought?*

A faint noise from behind them grew to a roar.

"Flash flood," Gyp cried out. "Ride for it."

Gyp's warning roused Fred to action. He threw his arms around his burro's neck as it galloped to the safety of high ground. Quick as a rattlesnake, a wall of water three feet high roared through the ditch.

One moment the dry stream bed was empty. The next it was a roiling, tumbling, raging body of angry-brown water transporting tumbling rocks, broken branches, shattered brush, broken cactus and kicking jackrabbits. Fred watched in morose fascination as the flood carried out its deadly rampage. Within minutes, the waters subsided and the only evidence of the deluge was the moist, hard-packed, dark-brown sand in the empty stream bed.

"A close one," Gyp said, unbuttoning to take a leak.

They camped that night on high ground.

The next day Fred saw that the spindly, grotesque ocotillo plants had blossomed into clusters with bright green leaves and crimson flowers. The ocotillo looked like cactus, but wasn't. Esme said it contained rosin and produced a hot campfire. *A good thing for a scout to know.*

For the next several weeks, Burnham and the Chilsons prospected and drifted along a low, monotonous desert valley, always searching, sifting and examining the traces with their horn spoons and magnifying glasses. Wherever they looked, they found nothing, and they never did get anywhere close to the Vekol Mountains where the western sun set each night.

As the autumn days expanded into winter weeks, the weather grew chilly and Fred wondered if these desert deposits held any promise. Never a living soul crossed the land. Not that he minded all that much. He enjoyed the solitude, the glowing pink sunsets and the small talk around the evening campfire.

By the end of ten weeks, provisions began to run low. Gyp suggested they draw straws to see who would take a burro back to Casa Grande to stock up on fresh stores. Esme broke open the last box of tinned peaches and tomatoes — crisis rations saved for lean times. The last box wasn't quite full and it had been stuffed with crumbled newspapers. Esme flattened out a sheet and began to read.

"Come on," Gyp groused. "Get a fire started. I want some Arbuckles java."

Burnham, absorbed in assaying an ore sample, paid little attention to the two muttering brothers.

"Jest a minute," Esme said. "There's some news here from the *Tombstone Epitaph.*"

"That's old news," Gyp said, anxious for his java.

"Not old to me. It says Buffalo Bill has started a Wild West show. And here it says the Jurgins Company exported forty thousand tons of margarine to England. What's margarine?"

"It's lard," Esme replied. "Now start a fire, dammit."

Adventures in Arizona

"In Tombstone, the Grand Jury indicted Buckskin Frank Leslie for backshooting this trail-rider outside the Oriental Saloon. Seems Leslie claims he was a rustler."

"Oh?" The sound came from nowhere.

"It says Billy Claibourne worked for a mining company out of Dripping Springs south of Globe. They reported the loss of some stock."

Fred stiffened and his hands froze on the horn spoon. Esme tossed the newspaper in the fire, but not before he saw Fred's cobalt eyes piercing him.

"You know thet Claibourne fella?" Esme taunted.

"Met him once," Burnham said, continuing his assay.

"Git that fire going, Esme, and fix some grub," Gyp growled. "I'm so hungry I could eat the ass out of a gila monster."

Half an hour later, they finished a badly burned breakfast. Gyp cut straws into uneven lengths. Esme and Fred would draw the man with the longest straw would win the right to visit the Fryers for provender.

"Draw," Gyp commanded.

Burnham's face burst into a glow and he dropped his assay tools.

"Did ja win?" Esme demanded.

"What day is today?" Fred asked, ignoring Esme.

"It's Tuesday," Esme said, examining at a straw that seemed too short.

"No, no, no," Fred snapped, ignoring the straws. "What's today's date?"

Gyp looked at Fred. Then a grin crossed his face.

"By golly, Fred, it's the twenty-fifth."

"Hey, that's right, guys," Esme chimed in. "Today's Christmas Let's knock off and celebrate."

"Not yet," Burnham shouted, his voice all business.

"Why?" Esme implored, as if deprived of an excuse for some hoopty-do.

"Remember that unpromising chunk of quartz we shot this morning?"

"What about it?" Gyp asked, examining the straws.

"I assayed that rock while you were making breakfast," Fred said. "And unless I'm way off base, we just found the haystack needle. This ore will pay a couple of thousand dollars a ton."

"How much?" Esme bellowed.

"Two thousand," Burnham said, looking like he was on the verge of inventing fire. "Boys, this stuff is gold — not silver. Hot damn,

21

we're rich!" He leaped into the air to do a jig, but his legs got brockled and he fell on the sand. As he sat there, he thought, *Now I can go back to that brick house on a tree-lined street in Iowa and marry Blanche.*

"Jeez," Esme peeped, "we'd better hire some guards."

And so on Christmas Day of 1883 was born the fabulous, money-gushing Christmas Gift Gold Mine, the only gol-dang, gee-whiz, genuine gold mine in all of the silver lodes of Papago Land.

Clinton, Iowa

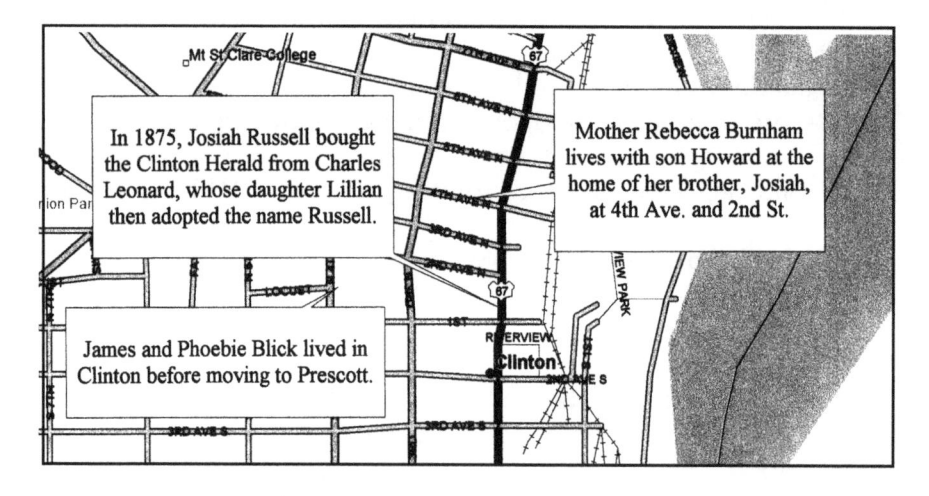

In 1875, Josiah Russell bought the Clinton Herald from Charles Leonard, whose daughter Lillian then adopted the name Russell.

Mother Rebecca Burnham lives with son Howard at the home of her brother, Josiah, at 4th Ave. and 2nd St.

James and Phoebie Blick lived in Clinton before moving to Prescott.

Clinton, Iowa, is on a low bluff overlooking the Mississippi River, just above the rapids. Fred Burnham criticized Clinton as a combination of religious intolerance and commercial greed. In the 1870s, it was the lumber capital of the United States. At night, no respectable woman would go closer to the river than Second Street. By day, the Catholic and Protestant boys fought it out at the Paper Mill using .22 pistols. Later, it became the junk mail capital of the United States. Le Claire, where Rebecca Burnham and Buffalo Bill's sisters attended primary school, is twenty miles south of Clinton.

4

Hunkey-Dorey Holmes

ARIZONA • AUGUST 1892

EIGHTY MILES northeast of Phoenix, the American who would inspire Baden-Powell to found the Boy Scouts was leading a gray burro into the Sierra Ancha Mountains. Fred Burnham, thirty-one, faced a vexing problem. If he didn't approve a bank loan, his oldest friend might starve. Fred stopped by a water hole and studied the trail where it disappeared around a bend, his cobalt eyes missing nothing. On both sides, sandstone rose a hundred feet. The hoofprints he was following were safely crossed by insect track — no one had passed in twenty-four hours. A whiff of mine tailings reminded Fred he was here to appraise a claim.

The Texas poet-scout Hunkey-Dorey Holmes wanted to develop a silver claim, and he had applied for a loan from the Western Investment Bank. Fred was employed by the Phoenix-based bank for his ability to assess the value of mineral deposits. Despite a lengthy obsession with scouting, Fred owed his financial success to his skill at evaluating mineral claims.

Burnham stood alert, holding the reins, listening, not breathing. Moments later, the aroma of jack rabbit roasting over coals told Fred he was near to Holmes' camp. Hunkey-Dorey's claim was at the end of the trail in a box canyon.

"Hy-dee, Burnham, yo're a grand sight for these sore old eyes," Holmes called out. He tried to conceal the chagrin of not hearing Fred's approach. Holmes still wore a long beard and hair to match. "This four-legged desert chicken'll be done in a jiffy. Hobble that flop-eared Arizona nightingale and pour yo'rself a cup o java."

Fred hoped Holmes had found a valuable silver vein to secure the needs of his declining years.

"Like my ja-mocha?" Holmes queried. Well-boiled coffee was

always refreshing.

"It has kick," Fred allowed. Holmes studied his visitor with a mixture of worship and greed. Fred's voice was a pleasing baritone that commanded respect. The two men drank in silence, each pondering the other's thoughts.

"You gonna approve my loan?" Holmes asked. Fred saw his friend had aged considerably since 1882 when they had last crossed paths. That had been in Tombstone. At that time, Fred was twenty-one and Holmes had seemed ancient, maybe almost fifty. Now his hair was silvery and he had added a layer of tallow around the equator.

"Depends on the quality of your ore," Fred said.

"Oh, it's a bonanza, Mr. Burnham," Holmes said, offering Fred a hind leg of campfire rabbit. Burnham's eyes fixed on Holmes. It was the first time Hunkey-Dorey had called him Mister. When they'd originally met twelve years ago in Globe, Holmes had called him Tenderfoot Freddie. Two years later, in Tombstone, his mentor had called him Fred, but never mister. *Hunkey-Dorey was growing desperate. Funny how easy it was to read a man's mind when he was in need.*

Fred chewed slowly on the stringy jackrabbit. It needed salt.

"You owe me a lot," Holmes said, trying to mask his anxiety. "I learnt you scoutin when you was wet behind the ears. Taught you to read sign so you can follow a tick in the dark of the moon. You're in debt to me."

True. It was here in these Sierra Anchas that Holmes had taught him scouting. In all of his travels, there was nothing to compare for ruggedness and challenge with these mountains north of Globe. So smooth were the vertical sandstone monoliths that the walls provided no foothold to gain purchase. So deeply cleft were the canyons that sunlight penetrated their depths only at midday. No trees or shrubs grew here. Only the hardiest of bushes found roothold. Yet Holmes taught him to scale these very cliffs.

Ritornello • An Interlude

VALETTA, MALTA • AUGUST 1892

STEPHE BADEN-POWELL'S career had taken a strange twist. While posted in India, Stephe wholly lacked experience in tracking and trailing. Yet here he was now writing articles about reconnoitering for the *British Cavalry Journal*. He did it by plagiarizing the works of other European military authors—calling it research.

Captain Baden-Powell, thirty-five, had accumulated sixteen years of military service without distinguishing himself. He was now assigned to Malta, living in the walled city of Valetta on a Mediterranean island a stone's throw from Sicily. San Antonio Palace,

Adventures in Arizona

the sun-bleached official residence of the governor, overlooked Grand Harbor. Stephe was responsible for the governor's social calendar, in charge of planning dinners, banquets and musical balls. At other times, he dispensed hospitality to the exalted owners of luxury yachts. As a matter of fact, Stephe worked for Uncle Henry.

General Sir Henry Smyth had commanded British forces in Cape Town at the tip of Africa before coming to Malta as governor general of the British island. Henry's sister, Henrietta Grace Baden-Powell, had arranged Stephe's appointment as aide-de-camp. Henrietta Grace, a woman of resolute determination, wielded considerable influence over her younger brother.

For Stephe, Malta was splendid duty. The palace served as a stately setting for his theatricals. When not occupied with social chores, he played polo and netted butterflies. During furloughs, Stephe traveled to Italy and North Africa, where he developed an interest in military intelligence. During these journeys, Baden-Powell also discovered the visceral excitement of the firing squad. He soon came to regard executions as a fascinating sport.

Now B-P faced a problem. To qualify for promotion he must attend the British Staff College, but his math was abominable. Despite extensive tutoring by The Boy McLaren, Stephe flunked the entrance exam. With that avenue blocked, combat service remained as his sole route to career progress. His only hope for promotion was to be mentioned in dispatches from the front.

That meant Captain Baden-Powell had to wheedle a transfer to an active military campaign. Stephe's best bet lay with Colonel Sir Frederick Carrington, who now commanded the native forces in Zulu Land. A few years ago, Colonel Carrington had been commandant of the Bechuana Border Police where Stephe's older brother, George Baden-Powell, represented the high commissioner for southern Africa. The recently knighted Sir George became a potential source of patronage for Colonel Carrington. Under the terms of the Good Old Boy Net, the colonel might be expected to do a good turn for Stephe.

Colonel Carrington had, in fact, promised Stephe a combat command if, as seemed likely, King Khama of Bechuana Land and King Lobengula of Matabele Land went to war. That could rescue Stephe's career.

Counterpoise • Equilibrium

Arizona Territory • August 1892

FRED AROSE, tossed the rabbit bones and turned to examine the ore body. Holmes had dug an exploratory shaft into the underlying copper vein wide enough for one man. He lowered himself to the bottom. In less than fifteen minutes, Fred's shirt was soaked with sweat. During the afternoon, probing revealed that Holmes' lode was a thin blanket vein, horizontal and difficult to develop. By the time the sun dipped in the West, Fred knew the ore would play out long before the cost of shoring up the veins had been recovered.

"We'll need to do a cupeling, just in case you may have found some gold," Fred said. "After we get the results, I'll make my recommendation to the bank."

"You can't do no better'n thet?" Holmes asked, his voice rising in anxiety. "Your report better be favorable. I'm gettin' on in years, you know, too old for hard labor."

"Old friend, let me tell you the cold facts of modern life," Burnham said. "Two years ago, President Harrison signed the Sherman Silver Purchase Act,"

"Yep," Holmes said. "Good news for silver miners."

"Not so," Fred replied. "Bad money drives out good. Have you noticed that gold is disappearing? It was chased away by silver, then silver was replaced by cheap paper money. Today a gold dollar buys two greenbacks."

"What's that got to do with me?" Holmes asked.

"Two things," Fred replied. "People are hiding gold under their mattresses. Paper money is almost worthless. The other thing is a collapse in the price of wheat during a period of high interest rates. Back in Kansas, the farmers are hurting. Wheat that commanded a dollar a bushel ten years ago now gets fifty cents. Three out of four wheat farms are mortgaged at twelve percent. Banks have foreclosed on a third of those farms."

"Two classes of thieves: railroads and banks."

"I travel a lot and I see what's going on. Thousands of covered wagons are crossing the Mississippi River. They are headed east, not west. Painted on the canvas of these prairie schooners are the words, 'In God we trusted. In Kansas we busted.'"

"Tha's what I sed," Holmes cried. "The bankers and the railroads are ruinin this country."

"What I'm trying to tell you, Hunkey-Dorey, is that the nation faces a financial crunch, a depression. Before my bank can lend you money, your ore has to be rich enough to pay twelve percent interest on the loan and then earn some money for your own profit. If the ore isn't rich enough, you'll go broke like those wheat farmers."

Lagnappe • A Little Extra

SAN FRANCISCO • AUGUST 1892

Adventures in Arizona

JACK HAMMOND, scarcely a decade out of the Royal School of Mines in Freiberg, Saxony, Prussia, decided to open an engineering office in New York. He had just rescued a treasure trove of silver from bandits in Mexico and Jack's name was in all the newspapers.

"It will be expensive," he said to wife, Natalie. "We'll lose the advantage of our California connections, but New York is where capital is. If I succeed there, my reputation will be national."

After completing his undergraduate school at Yale and his engineering studies at Freiberg in Prussia, the world's best mining school, Hammond had spent six months in California inspecting mines for the U.S. Geological Survey. On that assignment, mine operators were compelled to show him their earnings statements. In time Jack developed a detailed knowledge of mining costs.

As a consultant to the Vigorite Powder Company, he discovered that miners wasted a lot of blasting powder. He learned how to use it advantageously. And as an engineering consultant to the Union Iron Works of San Francisco, Hammond had the rare opportunity to study the production costs of mining machinery. He devised ways of delivering machinery to remote mines in South America that were accessible only by mule. No bundle could weigh more than the three-hundred-pound capacity of one pack animal.

Born on San Francisco's Nob Hill, Jack Hammond was well connected socially. He was the son of an Army colonel who had distinguished himself in the war with Mexico: that great practice for the Civil War. During the heat of combat at the Battle of Cerro Gordo, the backbones slid right out the rectums of a score of Army captains. They were cowering when Colonel Hammond used a few well-timed pistol shots to instill spizzerinctum into these chicken-hearted officers.

During the Civil War, these captains rose to become the generals for the blue and the gray. After the war, these men, now senators, presidents and diplomats who couldn't afford a scandal, showed their gratitude to the father by helping the son. As if the fig-nosed little tough needed help from anyone. From the start Jack Hammond had an ego like Napoleon.

Natalie agreed to the cross-country move and Jack leased space in Manhattan's Mills Building. Darius Ogden Mills struck it rich at the Comstock Lode by building the Virginia & Truckee Railroad. The trains made it possible to bring to Virginia City the hundred ton pumps and other mining apparatus needed to make the mines pay. Mills then bought the Bank of California and made western mining a legitimate industry in the minds of Eastern capitalists. Mills backed Hammond to the hilt, promising to put his own money into any enterprise that got a favorable report from young John Hays Hammond.

Jack called on Senator George Hearst, another Comstock Lode king. Hearst had taken a stake in the Homestake Mine in the Dakota Territory. He bought a seat in the Senate to protect his investment. During lunch, Hearst portrayed himself as a practical mining man who scoffed at college-trained engineers. He bluntly told Hammond to go out on his own and make some mistakes.

"Only if you make mistakes can you make successes," Hearst counseled. "Schools make you conservative. The conservative engineer lacks the daring spirit essential to success."

"Senator," Jack said, "I know more than most of those practical miners you rate so highly."

"Dammit, you're a forthright pup," Hearst shot back.

The support Hammond won enhanced his reputation so much that he soon commanded higher fees and attracted new customers. Before long, he had so many new clients in California that he reopened his office in San Francisco and moved his family back to California. He retained his New York office, adding extra engineering staff, and he became a railway commuter.

A few months after that, Hammond was back in Mexico, where he solved a mining problem that brought him to the attention of President Porfirio Diaz. Once again he won headlines around the world. Within a week, he received his first cabled offer from London to take charge of Barney Barnato's gold mines on the Witswatersrand: the fabled Ridge of White Waters in Johannesburg.

Counterpoise • Equilibrium

ARIZONA TERRITORY • AUGUST 1892

HUNKEY-DOREY scowled to hide his embarrassment. He walked over to feed the burros while Burnham built a fire to cook dinner. Whatever differences had come between them, Fred knew that he had to paper them over to hold up the social graces. Tonight they'd bed out under the stars as they had done in the summer of 1880 when Holmes taught him scouting. Fred was troubled by his feelings, more so after dinner when Hunkey-Dorey tried to flatter him.

"You know," Holmes said, "you're probably the best scout in the West. Better'n Al Sieber ever was, and every bit as good as Kit Carson and the rest of Ashley's Men." Hunkey-Dorey poured a cup of white mule, but Fred declined an offer of grog. He didn't smoke or drink.

In the shadows of the campfire, Fred tried not to let the flattery go to his head. *Holmes must need that loan badly.* The coyotes were yipping, making Fred's city-bred burro nervous.

"Here's another downright fact," Holmes said after downing a noggin of stagger sauce. "When we first met, people might not take much notice of you, cept for your eyes. Oh, you had sand in your craw, all right, but you had the sharpest, most piercin blue eyes I ever seen. Those eyes take in everthin without seemin to see, yet they miss nothin. That's why I decided to larn you scoutin."

Fred had trained himself to see in the dark, at first by moonlight, but later by the light of the stars alone. Through concentration, he had made himself a man of the night. He believed that darkness was the scout's greatest friend, a cover from enemies and protection from the sun.

His pint drained, Hunkey-Dorey dozed by the fire, and Fred covered his friend with a blanket. He was troubled by thoughts of Holmes' future, but what could he do? That night the coyote kept up a steady chorus of yipping and whining and Fred slept poorly.

Hours later, a fiery dawn the color of a smithy's forge proclaimed the arrival of another smothering August day. After a nearly wordless breakfast of sow's bosom and cackleberries, Fred packed his gear on the jackass.

"When'll I hear from ya?" Hunkey-Dorey asked.

"In about ten days."

"Say my greetins to Mrs. Burnham and young Rod."

Fred rode south toward his home in Mesa. The green bile bubbling in his gut made his mouth taste like he'd shared breakfast with that yipping coyote. It was going to be tough to say no to an old friend. That's what Fred hated most about being a banker.

The Call to Monomotapa

The 2nd Chronicle

The Boers called them koppies.

The Call to Monomotapa

Blanche Burnham

Blanche Blick Burnham (1862-1939)

5

Cecil Rhodes

Mesa, Arizona • September 1892

AS SHE PREPARED dinner, Blanche Burnham concluded something was in the air. Her intuition told her so and Blanche's intuition was not a matter to be lightly questioned. The big secret might have something to do with Fred's trip to Colorado. The Western Investment Bank had sent him there to lease mining properties in the Rockies. Before coming back, Fred would stop in Denver to record the deeds and attend a brush-up course in geology. In Denver, he had mailed a postcard to Blanche.

While walking to the office on Seventeenth Street, an explosion blew out the window of a building a hundred feet ahead of me. I wasn't injured. Be home Thursday. Love to both, Fred.

Here it was Thursday already. Blanche was making dinner: roast beef in a dutch oven and apple pie in the cook stove. Fred loved the aroma of butter and cinnamon-sugar. For the third time, she checked herself in the looking glass. She patted down wavy, golden hair that framed a gentle, puckish face. When the sun shined, her hazel eyes were flecked with nuggets of gold. As she smiled her lips, sweet, inviting, sensuous lips, completed the invitation.

When Blanche wore a dress, you'd need a good imagination to appreciate her striking figure. The billowing Victorian clothing hid the full breasts, a thin waist, well-turned hips and slim legs. But in a light corselet and doeskin pullover, the clothing poured over her body like a rivulet of water.

Blanche regarded Fred as a splendid husband, and herself as a natural complement. She was proud to be a skilled cook and an able seamstress. She could tan a hide, shoot a gun and make soap from hog lard and wood ashes. She enjoyed doing these things well. But what Blanche loved best was traveling. She was a born explorer. Sug-

The Call to Monomotapa

Burnham Manor in Pasadena

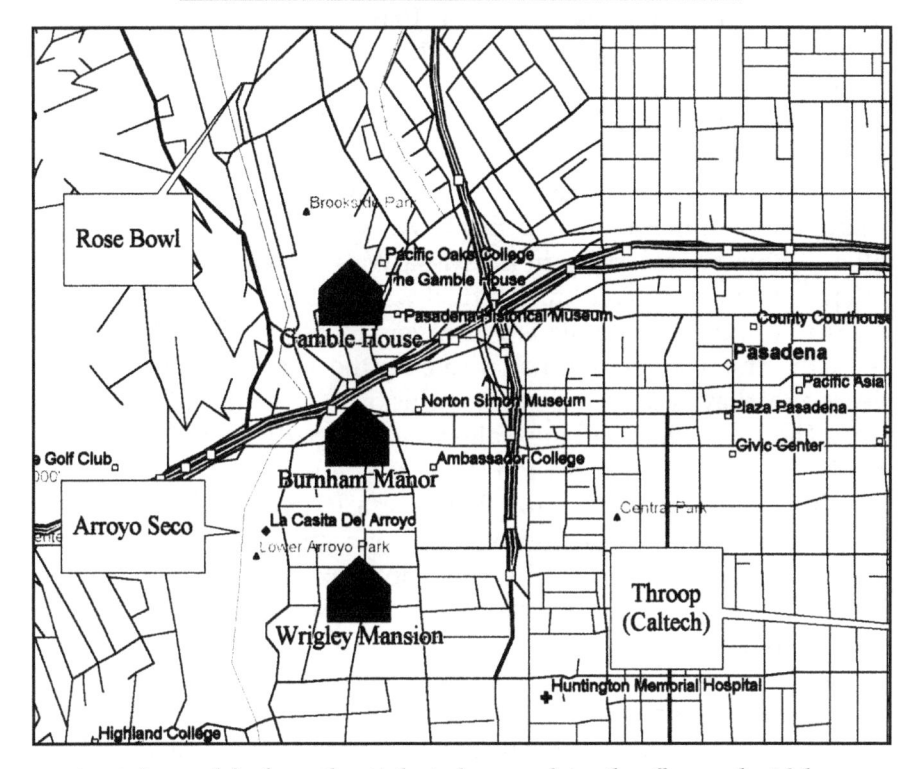

gest a trip and before the ticket dropped to the floor, she'd have a steamer trunk packed.

Though the Burnhams lived in Mesa, their home was in Pasadena, California. They had been married in Iowa on March 2, 1884, sixty-eight days after Fred discovered the Christmas Gift. They came west to Pasadena, where Fred built a manor home on a ten-acre plot at the corner of Orange Grove Avenue and Colorado Boulevard.

She had proudly written home to say it was a good neighborhood. A couple of blocks to the north was the spacious residence of soap king David Gamble. America's chewing gum king, William Wrigley, was building a Grecian mansion south of Burnham Manor. To the west was a cliff-side view of the Arroyo Seco, the huge, dry riverbed separating Pasadena from Los Angeles.

Early in her marriage, Blanche came to accept Fred's shortcomings. He was a great tease, a wil-o'-the-wisp, always chasing rainbows. He spent money—and gold—like it was water. Unless he was in the thick of the action, he grew bored. After building the manor house in Pasadena, he planted ten acres of fruit trees and settled back to become a gentleman citrus farmer. Watching leaves grow for a whole summer bored him so much he consigned Burnham Manor to the care of his widowed mother, Rebecca. Taking Blanche, Fred packed off to Arizona and settled in Mesa, a suburb of Phoenix peopled by Mormons.

There Fred got caught up in local affairs. He was fascinated by the farming methods of the Mormons, who wrestled a living from the desert. He wanted to learn how to grow oranges in a place where it seldom rained. In Phoenix, he met G.W. Sirrine, a civil engineer who offered him a partnership in the Mesa Water Company. When Fred offered payment in gold dust, a deal was struck.

Sirrine and Burnham made a discovery that stirred Blanche's pride. Since the first white settlers had arrived in the Salt River Valley twenty years ago, they had unearthed the ruins of an ancient Indian civilization. The local Pima Indians called their departed cousins the Ho-Ho-Kams, the Pima expression for *all used up*.

While digging laterals for their Mesa Irrigation Canal, Sirrine worked out how the Ho-Ho-Kams had once made the desert bloom. Hundreds of years earlier, they had done exactly what Sirrine and Burnham were doing: dig irrigation canals. It was Sirrine, the engineer, who recognized the ancient gradients for what they were—having laid unused for many centuries. Over the months, the two men unearthed a vast network of canals.

Despite Sirrine's engineering skills, he was unable to gain an inch in drainage over the ancient Ho-Ho-Kam designs. Sirrine told Fred the principles of designing irrigation canals dated to Julius Caesar's time. The Romans had built sewers and irrigation canals throughout Europe. If the water runs too fast, it erodes the canal bed. If it moves too slow, it silts up the bed. Judging gradients takes a keen eye.

Sirrine taught Fred to be a surveyor. The engineer described how the Mormons had designed Salt Lake City: a town set in a grid of north-south and east-west streets. The boulevards were wide enough that a span of eighteen oxen drawing a covered wagon could make a U-turn.

Blanche was proud of her husband.

When the Western Investment Bank offered Fred a chance to evaluate mining properties, he jumped at it. After that, he was often away for weeks at a time, so Blanche began to teach at the Mormon School. Then in the spring of 1886, after three years of marriage, Blanche learned she was with child. Fred was in pure rapture.

"We're taking you back to California," he declared.

"For goodness sakes why?" Blanche said. "Women have been

having babies on the frontier for thousands of years."

"In case of complications, I want you to be under the care of a competent doctor," Fred said. "A sober one. Most of the sawbones in Arizona are walking whiskey vats who came here because they couldn't hold a practice back in the East."

Blanche knew better than to argue so they returned to California. There Doctor H.J. Macomber, a teetotaler, attended the birth. Blanche's time came on a lazy summer Sunday, August 22. Doctor Macomber presided over the delivery of a cinnamon-haired, husky male child with cobalt eyes.

When Fred confirmed the infant was healthy, he opened the leather-bound *Burnham Genealogy* that Mother Burnham kept. The editor of the family record was Roderick Burnham, so Fred decided to name his son Rod. The book dated the family to the Norman Conquest of England in A.D. 1066. It said that one William de Burnham had served as an aide to William the Conqueror.

When it came to the American branch, the record placed the arrival of Thomas Burnham on colonial shores in 1635, fifteen years after the Pilgrims landed. The patriarch of the American branch had settled in Hartford, Connecticut Colony, and since then seven generations of Burnhams had been recorded.

Blanche had indulged her husband's preoccupation with this silver thread to the past. One rainy day she had opened the big leather-bound volume, glancing here and there. What she saw was breathtaking. During the French and Indian War, Michael Burnham had commanded the Connecticut Provincial Navy. Charles Burnham served under Ethan Allen at Bunker Hill and Ticonderoga. Half a dozen Burnhams marched in the Lexington Alarm of 1775. A score of Burnhams served George Washington in the Army of the Potomac.

Isaac Burnham served in the Connecticut Convention that ratified the Constitution. In the Mexican Wars, General Scott cited Colonel James Burnham for bravery. After the Treaty of Ghent, Hiram Burnham surveyed the U.S.-Canada boundary. During the Civil War, two dozen Burnhams answered the call to the colors.

Howard Burnham was killed at Chickamauga. Fred's younger brother, Howie, was named for this hero. Fred himself had scrawled the note in the margin. Hiram Burnham was killed at Chancellorsville. Edwin and Needham died at Vicksburg.

The Burnham roots touched every corner of American history. Some day, Blanche decided, she'd look into the reason why the family was so fascinated with its lineage. All the Burnhams were Congregationalist, not Mormon, so the search for a seat in heaven had not prompted this bizarre interest in the family past.

Shortly after Rod was born, the Santa Fe Railroad completed its southern route to Los Angeles, touching off a rate war with the Southern Pacific. The rivalry for passengers grew so intense that the price of a ticket between St. Louis and Los Angeles plunged briefly to five dollars. That was too much for the tourist in Blanche.

The Burnhams made a leisurely journey to the ancestral family homes in the East. Using the *Burnham Genealogy* as a travel guide, they visited Carrollton, Kentucky, where Fred's grandparents, Dr. Frederick and Harriet Burnham, had lived and died. They traveled north to Madison, New York, where Fred's own father, the Rev. Edwin Otway Burnham, orphaned at age five, had been reared by an uncle, a puritanical Congregational minister. Fred's father had grown up on prunes and proverbs too.

In Hartford, Connecticut, they learned that Thomas Burnham's colonial farm at State and Main Streets was now occupied by the home office of a big life insurance company. Next they journeyed west to Minnesota, but found no trace of the frontier village of Tivoli near Mankato where Fred was born on May 11, 1861. Tivoli had been abandoned after the burning of New Ulm and the Sioux massacre of 1862 when 750 whites were butchered in the largest Indian uprising ever recorded.

The Burnhams took a train south to Iowa to show off young Rod to Blanche's parents, James and Phoebe Blick. Father James, tall and gray, and Mother Phoebe, tiny and motherly, couldn't take their eyes off The Kid. They wondered what they'd do when Fred and Blanche left.

On a whim, Fred invited them to come west. There was space at Burnham Manor for the Blicks to live out their years. To the delight of Fred, James and Phoebe agreed to do just that. Blanche's heart swelled.

• • •

"SOMETHIN SMELLS larrupin good," Fred called out, walking briskly into the kitchen. "That horse thief's special in the Union Pacific diner tasted like machinery belting. I'm eager for some throat ticklin grub from the best cook this side of Paree."

"Oh, Fred, you're pulling my leg," Blanche cooed as they kissed. Then he smelled the apple pie.

"Well ain't she a huckleberry," he said happily. Fred's suit was wrinkled, but to Blanche he might have been wearing a new eight-dollar tux. As usual, Fred brought gifts for her and Rod.

The Call to Monomotapa

"Where's The Kid?"

"Out doing his chores. Get cleaned up. Dinner'll be ready soon."

As Fred disappeared into the bedroom, young Rod walked into the kitchen with an armload of kindling. He saw the packages and cried out with delight, knocking the newspaper off the table.

"Can I open my present now, Mama?"

"After dinner, Rod. Come and eat, Fred."

Half an hour later, Fred pushed his chair away from the table and rose.

"Papa, tell me about the explosion in Denver."

"Sure son."

"Fred, what was the name of that man who taught you scouting?"

"You mean Hunkey-Dorey?"

"Yes, that's the man."

Fred, dressed Rod in pajamas.

"Gee, Dad, tell me about the explosion."

It was an hour before Rod fell asleep and Fred was able to rejoin his wife.

"Blanche, why were you asking about Holmes?"

"The paper says he's dead. Glenn Reynolds too."

"What was he doing?"

"He was killed by the Apache Kid," Blanche said.

"Murdered? By Al Sieber's best Apache scout?"

"According to the paper, he was working as a deputy for Sheriff Glenn Reynolds. While escorting the Apache Kid to Yuma Prison, they came to that long grade south of Riverside."

"I know place well. Everyone gets out to ease the burden on the horses."

"Well, the Apache Kid drew a gun and shot Glenn Reynolds. According to the paper, Hunkey-Dorey was carrying a carbine and a pistol."

"He was a crack shot," Fred said.

"When the bodies were recovered," Blanche read, "Holmes' head was crushed as if by a vicious blow."

Ritornello • An Interlude

S<small>AN</small> F<small>RANCISCO</small> • O<small>CTOBER</small> 1892

JACK HAMMOND studied the two cables laying on his desk. Barney Barnato had renewed an offer to hire him as manager of his gold mines in Johannesburg. The other summoned Hammond to Edinburgh to deliver a report to the board of directors of the Arizona Copper Company, for which he served as consulting engineer. The

37

two requests, coming together, induced Hammond to travel to London. At dinner that night, he told Natalie about the invitations.

"You know," he said, "it is a geological marvel of the first magnitude that the greatest known deposits of diamonds and gold should occur in southern Africa within three hundred miles of each other."

"Will you take up Mr. Barnato on his offer?"

"Now may be a good time to leave the United States. President Harrison's high tariff policy combined with the silver purchase act will create a depression. I'll carefully examine the possibilities."

Counterpoise • Equilibrium

Mesa, Arizona • October 1892

ON A RAIN-DRENCHED autumn day marked by flashes of lightning, Fred paced the floor. The sound of footsteps on the porch told him Blanche had arrived from school. How could he tell her that he was caught in his own loop? He felt like Satan himself had come to visit.

"Bad news, Dear?" She stood by the table, her clothes dripping.

"All bad. First, the Mesa Irrigation Canal isn't making any money. Then the Hassayampa Dam burst, burying our new silver mine under a thousand tons of mud and silt. Now there's bad news from Pasadena."

"Is someone ill or injured? Mother Burnham, Mother Blick?"

"No, it's money. Deacon Clapp decided to save money by not buying fire-fighting equipment for the Alvord Mine." Alvord was a gold mine in the Mojave Desert that Fred had purchased to assure an income for his mother. Deacon Clapp was Fred's new stepfather, a penny-pinching real estate developer who had married Fred's widowed mother. A layman in the Congregational Church, this owl and the widow Burnham had been drawn together by a interest in religion.

"So Deacon Clapp saved some money," Blanche said. "Is that bad news?"

"There was a fire at the Alvord Mine and the stamp mill burned. Unless the insurance covers the loss, there's no money to build another. Our investment may be a total loss. Never again will I trust a skypilot preacher man."

Mesa Canal, Hassayampa and Alvord -- all at once? These were major financial blows. She needed to put on a brave face to bolster Fred's spirits. "We still have Burnham Manor in Pasadena," Blanche said.

"The citrus harvest was a bust," he said. "After totaling expenses, the oranges cost a nickel apiece. If carefully packed, they bring a penny each."

The Call to Monomotapa

The gravity of their long-term financial situation began to dawn. Blanche sat down. Her income as a teacher and Fred's salary as vice president of the bank would feed them nicely. Burnham Manor and the house in Mesa were paid for, so there was no immediate cause for alarm.

"What shall we do?" she asked. Then, behind his grim countenance, Blanche saw a tiny twinkle in her man's eyes. *Was he pulling her leg again?*

"We're leaving," Fred said suddenly, waving his arms. There was a new spirit of enthusiasm in his voice.

"Not now, Fred. Dinner will be ready in an hour."

Blanche walked to the kitchen to prepare the meal.

"Blanche," Fred declared from out of the blue, "we're going to Africa." He leaped into the air and kicked his heels together.

"Africa?" Blanche cried out in astonishment. "Africa? How'll we live?"

"I'm a scout and prospector. The American frontier is gone. The West is won. But the whole continent of Africa remains to be civilized. It's wide open for the taking and we'll clean up a fortune."

"Have you been reading adventure books, Fred?" She knew he didn't drink.

"Yes," he said and a wide grin appeared on his face. "Everything I read tells me it's time to leave."

When letters and other written material arrived by stage or train on the Arizona frontier, people pored over it endlessly, even the *wish book* from Montgomery Ward. Much of the news reaching American shores from Europe suggested the continent was preparing for a great conflagration. The war scare was a legacy of the 1871 Franco-Prussian War, a conflict that had placed Germany on the map.

Americans were consolidating the West in their quest for Manifest Destiny. This was the era of the Robber Barons, where railroad empires were being staked out. Americans cared little for Europe's age-old rivalries.

Still there was legitimate news from Europe to command the attention of Yankees. In 1888, newsman-turned-explorer Henry Stanley electrified continents with the news that he had found the Mountains of the Moon. That discovery solved a two thousand-year-old riddle about the headwaters of the River Nile. It concentrated world attention on Africa. It touched off a scramble among Britain, France, Portugal and Germany to carve up the Dark Continent.

The next year, a remarkable book arrived in Arizona. It was a novel about Africa that had found great popularity in England. *King*

Solomon's Mines was the story of two Englishmen who hiked into central Africa where they discovered a treasure trove of riches. The hero was a dashing daredevil named Allan Quatermain, who was aided in his efforts by a faithful and brave Zulu porter named Umbopa. Together they guided Sir Henry Curtis and Captain John Good to the kingdom of Kukuana Land, the site of forbidden diamond mines.

The author of this novel, Rider Haggard, was a civil servant who lived in Natal, a British Colony in southern Africa. While reading, Fred was smitten by Haggard's descriptions of the elephants and giraffes, and specially by the lions that made a *woof-woof* sound on the trail to Inyati. Newspaper articles said the fictional Allan Quatermain was patterned on the life of Frederick Courtney Selous, an English white hunter who had lived for many years in central Africa.

Haggard's high veld of Africa sounded to Fred like the open range of the American West—before the arrival of the hated barbed-wire. Added to the freedom of the veld, there were other exotic words to learn. When Quatermain spoke of an African *indaba*, he was referring to something like an Indian powwow. The war chief of Africa was an *induna* who led a battalion of warriors called an *impi*. Jerky went by the name *biltong*. Many of the place names could be found in the atlas.

At the library, Fred learned that Inyati and Shiloh were missionary stations in a place called Matabele Land, a native kingdom in central Africa. Haggard had changed the name to Kukuana Land. In an encyclopedia, Fred found that cruel King Twala had a living counterpart. He was Lobengula, the ruler of the Matabele tribe, a savage of three-hundred pounds who presided over a harem of a hundred wives.

By the time he had finished reading *King Solomon's Mines*, Fred had contracted an incurable case of Africa fever. The experience rekindled a flame in his heart that had smoldered since childhood. When he was a child in Mankato, he listened to bedtime stories about the Dark Continent read by Katy Boardman. Fred recognized that Africa was still primitive, savage, undeveloped. There would be a need for scouts to tame the land. His skills would be in demand.

About that time, a real hero began to claim the attention of the world. The British financier Cecil Rhodes was putting southern Africa on the map. The image of Rhodes burst forth on the world as the Colossus of Africa, an empire builder, a man who thought in terms of nations and entire continents. Fred wanted to participate in that grand spectacle.

Before Fred read *King Solomon's Mines*, the power of Cecil Rhodes

The Call to Monomotapa

had been a wisp on the political horizon. In a matter of twenty months, the name mushroomed into a billowing cloud. In newspapers and magazines, Fred had followed Rhodes' rise to power with keen interest. The more he learned of Rhodes' aims, character and his achievements, the more engrossed he became. A thrill of excitement sluiced through his veins and he felt he had never been so much alive. Fred was thrilled to the core of his being. His case of Africa fever was incurable.

"Yes Blanche," Fred confessed. "I've been reading books. Newspapers and magazines too. Half a world away, I've been watching the glory of Cecil Rhodes' splendid vision. It is leading him to rescue vast areas of Africa from the grasp of savages. It's a colossal dream of empire."

"I see," Blanche said simply, her hands clasped at her throat. Fred was always chasing rainbows, but this—it was altogether something else to fly off to Africa.

"Blanche, I'm summoned by an irresistible call," he declared, pacing the floor. "A hero worth worshipping is so seldom found that a journey to the ends of the earth to find and serve him is an honor. Rhodes has burst forth as the lion of Africa. He has one foot planted on the Cape of Good Hope and the other on the great Zambesi River."

Blanche thought Fred looked like an osprey eyeing its prey. She found nothing to say.

"Beneath Rhodes' loins is Kimberley, the great diamond pit that has bred his strength. His eyes are on Egypt, far to the north. Rhodes' feet might be on the ground but his eyes are in the clouds. I'm determined to go to Africa and cast my lot with this man who has so fired my imagination. I believe that with my knowledge of scouting, I can be of value to him. Blanche, I must go to Africa and serve Rhodes."

Fred wasn't given to grand speechifying and Blanche gasped. The mere mention of the word Africa had sent a twinge of fear through her. Yet she loved travel so much that the lure of visiting far-off places stirred her profoundly. Deep in her being, she recognized that this time Fred was responding to something more compelling than mere wil-o'-the-wisp. He was being called to some greater purpose than he could define. Only by pursuing his destiny could he achieve his goal.

"If that is your choice, Fred, we shall go."

Fred had no way of knowing that his life was just beginning.

41

6

London, Paris, Rome

A bard, dear muse, unapt to sing,
Your friendly aid beseeches;
Help me to touch the lyric string,
In praise of Burnham Beeches.

O'er many a dell and upland walk,
Their sylvan beauty reaches;
Of Birnham Wood let Scotland talk,
While we've our Burnham Beeches.

—Henry Luttrell

NAPLES, ITALY • FEBRUARY 1893

THE FREIGHTER *Reichstag* of the *Deutsche Ost Afrika Linne* glided out of Naples Bay while a peach-blossom sun announced a splendid Thursday and an East African itinerary with ports as far south as Durban in Natal. As the vessel sailed through the Tyrrhenian Sea, The Kid watched the wisp of smoke fade from Stromboli volcano in the northwest. The voyage on the Mediterranean gave Fred time to catalog the many impressions gained since leaving Pasadena.

Shrouded against the ocean chill in a blanket marked PULLMAN, Fred wondered why they hadn't made the break sooner. They sold the house in Mesa and their interest in the irrigation canal. Next they sold the land in Pasadena, keeping only Burnham Manor and a parcel with the villas that the Blicks and the Russells occupied. Uncle Josiah Russell sold his newspaper and moved out from Iowa to join them.

The Burnhams' leave-taking on January 1, 1893, was as solemn and final as the Pilgrims who had set sail on the *Mayflower*. Fellow

The Call to Monomotapa

Burnhams, Blicks and Russells gathered in Golden Gate Park in San Francisco for a great blowing of horns to usher in the New Year. Not a soul believed they'd see Fred, Blanche or Rod again. No one had any idea that in the next thirty years this departure scene would be repeated as many times.

The travelers took the Southern Pacific Railroad, traveling north through the Willamette River valley of Oregon. In Vancouver, British Columbia, they boarded the Canadian-Pacific Railway and crossed the Canadian Rockies and the open prairies.

In Ontario, they reentered the United States to visit the 1893 World Columbian Exposition in Chicago. March king John Phillip Sousa had just launched his civilian band at the exhibition. For Rod the highlight of the World's Fair was a ride on the Ferris wheel. Civil engineer George Ferris had created a colossal amusement ride that rose twenty-five stories above ground. Ferris' goal was to surpass the cast-iron tower built by Alex Eiffel for the 1889 Paris Exposition. Fred decided they had gone about as far as they could go. Before they left Chicago, Blanche packed away a wish book from the Sears Roebuck & Company store and a package of the new Aunt Jemima flour.

From New York, the Burnhams sailed on the *Sarvia* for Liverpool, where the Mersey River empties into the Irish Sea. In Liverpool, Fred learned that the name Albion may have been the Celtic name for England. In Latin, it meant cliffs. He also learned that a pound sterling was equal to five American dollars.

The matter of foreign exchange settled, the Burnhams boarded a train for Hatfield, Hereford County. There Fred led Rod on a search for the ancestral Burnham home described in the family genealogy. The Dad and The Kid scoured crumbly ruins, searching for any stone marker that might bear the family crest or coat of arms. If any existed, it had long since been ravaged.

While her boys were fossicking ruins, Blanche did a little detective work. In a trip to the library, she discovered that in 1694 one Benjamin Burnham died in London and reputedly left an estate in Regency Street, Westminster. The inheritance was said to be valued at one hundred sixty million dollars. In the 1870s, the American branch of the Burnham family sued in London and during a lengthy court case the plaintiffs introduced the *Burnham Genealogy* into evidence. During the trial, the Benjamin Burnham Estate was proved to be nonexistent.

In London, Fred was so proud of his British ancestry that he became a walking interrogation point. He sought information on a grand

43

uncle, William H. Russell. During the Crimean War, newsman Bill Russell had served as the world's first war correspondent. His reports on the Charge of the Light Brigade in 1854 brought down the British government. In Clinton, Fred's newspaper editor uncles, Edward and Josiah Russell, had told him the story, saying Russell had later covered the American Civil War.

The Burnhams toured Hyde Park, St. James' Park and the Palace Gardens that surround Buckingham Palace. They walked along The Mall and through Admiralty Arch to see the Horse Guards on parade. Rod chased the pigeons in Trafalgar Square. At Piccadilly Circus, the nation's meeting place, The Kid's legs gave out and they took a carriage back to their hotel in Westminster.

They next visited Westminster Abbey, St. Paul's Cathedral, Parliament and London Bridge. They sailed The Thames, looked in on the Stock Exchange, Parliament, the Science Museum, Madam Tussaud's and picnicked at Burnham Beeches. That public park, thirty miles west of London, was six miles north of Windsor Castle and closer still to Eton College. It was one of the few bits of primeval forest remaining in the United Kingdom.

Though he wore a smile, Fred was privately appalled by the filth, the poverty and the squalor of London. The streets were filled with orphans, whores and families trudging off to factories. Smoke stung the eyes and nose.

The London newspapers devoted major attention to military affairs. Queen Victoria was at the peak of her power. The British Navy had ruled the waves since 1805 when Admiral Horatio Nelson, sailing northwest of Gibraltar, defeated Napoleon's fleet at Cape Trafalgar. The Royal Navy was the world's most feared instrument of military power. The British people were patriotic and it seemed unremarkable that the Union Jack should fly over London, Ottawa, Gibraltar, Cairo, Jerusalem, Aden, Cape Town, Calcutta, Rangoon, Sydney, Singapore, Brunei, Sarawak and Hong Kong. It was the era of Pax Britannia.

If was true that women in American West existed on a higher moral and cultural plane than men, that vogue was magnified in London. Retribution for molesters was most terrible.

At the same time, the British had a vast appetite for stories of the mysterious East, for music-hall songs depicting British soldiers in action and for news of events in the far-flung empire. The two dominant military figures in the British Army were Field Marshal Lord Wolseley, the Africa general, and Field Marshal Lord Roberts, the India general. Roberts was known as Lord Bobs. Lord Wolseley had

The Call to Monomotapa

spent most of his career in London, but Bobs, the more colorful of the two, was returning from a forty year career in India, and that was big news. Years ago, Bobs had won the Victoria Cross for his pacification of the Afghans at Kandahar. Even though Roberts stood only five feet six inches, he was the hero of the Empire. Fred found himself attracted to Lord Bobs.

It was time to resume the journey. Fred fell in love with Paris. "The city of cities," he declared. "There is none like it in the world. What a country is France. No wonder its citizens seldom emigrate. I thought Americans loved their country, and they do, but these people fairly worship theirs. Cleanliness, art, patriotism and politeness are the refreshing characteristics of this nation. The Americans are well-liked over here and well treated."

At the Louvre, Rod was fascinated by the paintings of the lions creeping up on the Christians as they knelt to pray in the Coliseum. At The Kid's repeated urging, they visited the nine-hundred-foot Eiffel Tower erected with seven thousand tons of cast iron. It had three hydraulic elevators, one built by Otis of New York.

Fred decided the Alps needed but a short visit.

"Twenty Switzerlands could be carved from the wilds of the American Rockies and you'll still have scenery to spare," he wrote home.

He enjoyed the Italian landscape. "The clear blue skies and hazy mountains are like our own California," he wrote to Mother Burnham-Clapp. "Such a delightful contrast to dull, somber England." He approved of the handsome countryside and the fawn-colored cattle, but the farms were walled with stone and fortified. Every house was guarded by spikes or glass cemented into the walls. The women worked in the fields while uniformed men lolled about in the cafés sipping CinZanzo.

Rome would be different: Fred knew it. It was from Rome that the law, the arts and sciences radiated out to the civilized world. A quarter of the western world's cultural patrimony was concentrated in a city that gloried in two thousand years of history.

"The Eternal City," he declared. "What a place for inspiration."

The Kid wanted to see the Coliseum. "What a monument," Fred cried aloud when they inspected the formidable structure. "A mile around, solid and massive, yet built in such fine curves as to give grace and beauty to all."

"Is this where the Romans fed the Christians to the lions?" Rod asked.

"The very place," Fred replied. "Nine thousand animals and three thousand men fell in combat in that arena. One thousand days of the fiercest play an audience ever witnessed. What a crucible of human passion. The tears that were shed would turn this arena into a lake. No wonder the flowers grow so profusely. The soil drenched in blood again and again. It would have made a desert fertile."

Back at the hotel, an article in an English language newspaper told of financial troubles in the United States: railroad failures, brokerages folding and gold reserves slipping. Europeans were dumping American stocks. Fred told Blanche they had been wise to sell out when they did and get their assets into cash. Their capital was safe in Pasadena National Bank.

They toured temples, triumphal arches, handsome sculptures and beautiful piazzas with sparkling fountains, marveling at the Sistine Chapel and Michelangelo's ceiling frescos.

"The Baths of Carcalla prove that the classic Roman was vastly superior to the modern Italian," Fred wrote to Uncle Josiah. "But this city of marble palaces. How grand and splendid it is. In comparison with them, the great cathedrals of modern Europe and St. Paul's in London seem cheap and tawdry."

On the train to Naples, Fred said, "Rome, the city of medieval and renaissance churches, the capital of all Christendom. The bright light of the Christian religion has shown on it for hundreds of years. Yet it has left the inhabitants as despicable a lot of vagabonds as could be imagined. Even the supposed upper class is dishonest."

"Are you pulling my leg?" Blanche asked.

Fred thought that Naples, Italy's second largest seaport, was the most beautiful city in the world. That night he and Blanche celebrated their ninth wedding anniversary at a candle-lit Neapolitan restaurant. The light of sunset cast a veil of purple over the crescent-shaped city and the mountain top became ablaze with light.

"What a beautiful bay all dotted with sails," Blanche said.

"It's the magic Isle of Capri, a pearl in the Bay of Naples."

"Since the days of the Roman emperors, it has been a holiday favorite of the Italians," Blanche said, her tour guide at her side. "Let's visit it tomorrow."

"It's pure poetry to spend an evening on the bay and watch old Vesuvius catching the last glow of the evening," Fred said.

"Nature has done much to make this a land of enchantment."

"In three days, Blanche, you'll be thirty. Why not celebrate now?"

"Nothing on the ship can equal this."

While they toasted, Fred said, "M'love, there is one thing here that I like. It's the historical ruins of Pompeii."

"Pliny the Elder died and his nephew reported on Vesuvius' destruction," Blanche said. "For a day and a half, it rained down a foot of ash and white pellets. The entire city of Pompeii was entombed in forty feet of ash."

"Here the veil is lifted," Fred said, "and we can look back two thousand years at daily life during the Roman Empire. They began excavating the year I was born."

The next day from atop Capri's sheer cliffs, they looked upon a splendid view of the toylike ships in the Roman harbor and Mount Tiberious in the distance.

"Oh, Fred, an isle of dreams cloaked with vegetation and honeycombed with sea caves. It's a floating fairyland of purple and gold. Every color and shade is in harmony. There's nothing to offend the senses. I'm truly happy."

To Fred and Rod, the highlight of their visit to Pompeii was a tour of the church of Santiago della Madonna del Rosario. The tour guide showed the visitors an underground passage. Here the bishop slithered up into the statue of the goddess Isis to speak through her mouth: the oracle commanding the people. Roderick was amazed to hear the padre's voice so momentously amplified by echoes and reverberations.

"What lungs!" Fred said. "He's a one-man Mormon Tabernacle Choir."

The next day they boarded the *Reichstag* for the month-long voyage to Beira in Portuguese East Africa. To Fred, the most striking difference between British and German ships was that meals on the *Reichstag* were announced with a bugle, like a cavalry charge.

When the ship anchored at Port Said at the north end of the Suez Canal, Fred was supremely happy. As he stepped off the gangway onto Egyptian soil, he forgot St. Peter's Basilica, the Coliseum and the Isle of Capri.

"How my eyes have longed for this moment, this land of my dreams. After these years, I'm on Africa's shores, bound for an expedition into the unknown. Now I can die content."

7

The Pungwe Is in Flood

PORT SAID • FEBRUARY 1893

FOR THE BURNHAMS, it was a whole new world: Arabs, bazaars, veiled women, strange *dhows*, grotesque camels, everything queer. The Kid stood out in his white linen sailor-suit, blue collar and cuffs trimmed in white braid. On his head sat a sailor hat with gilt anchors and a streaming blue ribbon. A group of Egyptian donkey boys, spotting tourists from a German ship, invited Rod to take a ride on a donkey named Caprivi or his long-eared cousin, Bismarck. The Kid didn't seem to understand these names, but Fred did. Three years ago, Count Leo von Caprivi had succeeded Bismarck as the chancellor of Germany. It was Caprivi who had traded disease-ridden Zanzibar to England in return for some odd shaped pieces of African geography, stuff that nobody thought they wanted.

The donkey boys decided the tourists might be British, so they offered up the Prince of Wales. "We're Americans," Rod cried out. For a moment, the Egyptian lads seemed stumped. "Here," said one boy. "Verra good donkey, Ben Harrison."

"A good ass," Fred agreed. In a few weeks, Benjamin Harrison would give up the presidency to Grover Cleveland who would retake the office as president, after losing it in the 1888 election. It was Harrison who in 1890 had signed the now-unpopular silver purchase and high tariff acts.

South of Suez, in the Red Sea, the headlands were rimrock, reminding Fred of the Rocky Mountains. The Red Sea itself seemed to be some kind of liquid rift valley. The *Reichstag* called at Suakin, opposite Jidda, Arabia. There a contingent of stiff, bristling German officers boarded the ship, accompanied by a company of Soudanese recruits: tall, slim, fierce-looking fellows. As the recruits poured onto the deck to the shouted commands of their German officers, their

The Call to Monomotapa

jabbering made Fred think of roosting time in a poultry coop.

"They're dressed in every imaginable color," Blanche said.

"They'll get regular uniforms at Dar-es-Salaam," Fred said. "One of the crew told me."

"Poor things, I wonder how many will get killed."

They sailed down the Red Sea and through the rocky constriction called the Mendab Strait between Arabia and the French Soudan. Then they turned east, entering the harsh and forbidding red-rock cliffs of the Gulf of Aden. Fred wanted to examine the great naval cannons that dominated the harbor fortifications, but on arrival he was curtly rebuffed by British military officers.

Before departing Aden, another group of soldiers boarded the ship. In contrast to the Soudanese, these squat, trim men moved in split-second order in response to commands spoken in curt tones by their British officers. Fred guessed these turbaned soldiers hailed from India. What a contrast to the tall, slender Soudanese. Fred soon met their commanding officer.

"Leftenant Geoff Edwards at your service," he said. Fred extended his hand to a man of about twenty-five who wore an ibex-horn mustache waxed to spear-points. His urn-like ears and picket fence teeth produced a faintly comic look but his military uniform was impeccable.

As they strode along the deck, Fred asked, "May I ask what the soldiers are doing? Or is that a military secret?"

"No secret at all, old chap. We'll join forces against Arabia's Wahabi slave traders on Lake Nyassa. We'll attack from the south and the Germans will come from the north. We expect to box them up once and for all."

"Until now, I had always regarded Gibraltar as the universal joint of the seven seas," Burnham said. "After visiting Aden, I suspect the British regard Aden as more important."

Edwards nodded his confirmation, but said nothing. The next morning they passed the Cape of Guardefui: the graveyard of ships.

"Why do they call it the graveyard of ships?" Rod asked.

"In the last four years," Lieutenant Edwards said, "seven ships were wrecked here and their crews and passengers were killed by the Somalis: vicious people."

The sea was smooth and lovely. Flying fish, like a constant flight by flocks of swallows, populated the waters. At night, millions of tiny electric lights dotted the sea. After dinner, Fred took The Kid to the fantail to study the northern stars.

"The shapes of the constellations are the yardstick of the night skies," he told his son. "Old familiar stars drop away and we see them no more. Each night, the North Star gets lower in the sky. Before we reach Zanzibar, it should be gone. At the same time, the Southern Cross looms higher."

They walked to the prow of the ship to study the southern stars, but the shapes of the constellations were strange. Fred asked the navigator if he could study the star charts. He found it was difficult, without having seen the stars in their seasons, to recognize the faint patterns of the constellations. He decided that until he had a season or two of field experience in the southern hemisphere, he'd rely on Hunkey-Dorey's memory system to back track on the veld. Turning in the saddle to memorize landmarks wasn't a good way to find true north, but it did help get you back to friendly territory alive.

By day the tropical sea was alive with dolphins, flying fish and the sailing nautilus. The Kid, still wearing his sailor suit, spent hours peering over the rails, enthralled by the diversity of sea life.

The travelers soon learned that in the tropics when the sun sets, darkness quickly follows. One night, while the water was in full phosphorescent glow, they smelled the faint aroma of spice. Lieutenant Edwards told them the clove harvest was in season at Zanzibar. The reason for the aroma of cloves was because of a British law forbidding their adulteration. When an Arab *dhow* was discovered with a cargo of adulterated cloves, it was run ashore and set afire. As the cloves smoldered, the pungent aroma drifted out to sea.

In due time, the *Reichstag* anchored off the British island of Zanzibar. Their arrival was announced by the boom of cannon, but the port facilities were so primitive that passengers had to be carried ashore by blacks. A pompous German officer, wearing full regimentals, pistol, monocle and field glasses, was stripped of his dignity while perched astride the back of a huge, grinning black. Blanche rebelled, but when Fred paid two Negroes to cross hands and wrists to form a makeshift seat, she relented.

Zanzibar, its bay ringed in coconut palms, was a splendid collection of pink and peach buildings. The candelabra aloe, with its crimson candlestick flowers, looked like it belonged in Arizona. So did the naboom, which resemble the organ pipe cactus down by the Christmas Gift Mine. The graceful, lateen-rigged sails of the Arab dhows reflecting in the waters made a picture as beautiful to Fred as any painting in the Louvre.

Leftenant Edwards led the Burnhams on an afternoon tour of Zanzibar Island. Fred was introduced to the weird sound of the tom-

The Call to Monomotapa

tom and African melodies, which he found pleasant.

"Tis a pity this coast is not healthy for Europeans." Edwards said.

"What's unhealthy about it?" Blanche asked.

"Fever, the blackwater fever."

In a man-to-man aside, Edwards whispered to Fred that blackwater fever was a virulent form of malaria that turned its victim's urine black. Then he spoke to Blanche as well, "The fever is worse than gunboats and firearms. It's more deadly than rum. It's always lurking, always fatal and it ultimately claims ninety percent of the pale-skinned people in Africa."

Blanche drew Roderick to her side.

"See that graveyard?" Edwards continued. "British civilization on this island is three years old, yet there are a thousand tombstones over there and only a hundred and twenty British subjects living here. Beware the fever."

An easy three hours' sailing brought the ship to Dar-es-Salaam, Germany's new East African capital and its colonial crown jewels. The Soudanese soldiers noisily debarked to the shouted commands of their German officers. They looked like slow-moving bags of barley. *For two shillings a day*, Fred thought, *they're going to help weld the chains around their fellow blacks.* As everyone waved farewell, only the gods could foresee that the Germans and Soudanese alike were marching to certain death at the hands of the Wahabi slavers.

At Mozambique, the capital of Portugal's East Africa colony, the British soldiers debarked with their silent Sikhs. They would travel overland to Lake Nyassa, board gunboats and resoundingly defeat the Wahabi slavers, though not before Lieutenant Edwards succumbed to the blackwater fever.

Only five-hundred miles to Beira: Fred's excitement mounted. Soon they would begin an overland trek of three hundred miles up the Pungwe River to Fort Salisbury. Fred had their steamer trunks on deck when the ship dropped anchor in the silty mouth of the Pungwe. Portuguese officials abruptly waved them off, ordering the *Reichstag* to leave under penalty of quarantine.

The Pungwe was in flood and for thirty miles the narrow-gauge railroad was under water. There was danger of blackwater fever so no one was allowed to leave the ship. Such were the risks in booking passage to Beira, a notoriously unhealthy, fever-ridden mud-flat.

The *Reichstag's* final port of call was at Port Natal, another thousand miles south. If the Burnhams debarked there, they would be forced to journey overland via Johannesburg, Pretoria and the Transvaal into Mashona Land. It would mean an extra seven hundred miles

51

of land travel, but there was no other choice. At Port Natal, the *Reichstag* would turn back for Naples.

Three days later, the Burnhams walked down the gangway to Durban, the new name for Port Natal. It was Thursday, March 23, and Fred was in a truly splendid mood. They were ten days out of Zanzibar, one month from Naples and eighty-one days from their farewell to family in California.

"So we close out this voyage across two oceans, three seas, six bays, a channel and a sound," he told Blanche. "Our vacation is at an end. Seventeen thousand miles of travel, and as many flags, puts us in a country of gold, diamonds, apes and ivory. After seeing Europe, I am ready to tackle the frontiers again and build a new empire. The active strife will be at full pressure, two thousand pounds to the square inch and every safety valve tied down."

"Fred Burnham," Blanche said after her husband's ebullient soliloquy, "I may never understand you but I'll never regret marrying you."

Durban was a little England. It boasted imposing stores, fashionable shops, green parks, brilliant flower gardens and charming homes. The Burnhams took a room in the Clarendon Hotel and Blanche had a good laugh at the many things she'd bought in London in the belief that trade goods would be scarce in Africa.

The extra fare to Durban had drawn on Fred's remaining cash and the city was enjoying boom times. A gold rush in Johannesburg had increased the demand for food and supplies, and it had drawn away labor. They had to outfit here for the thousand mile trek to Fort Salisbury.

A standard team of eighteen oxen with a covered wagon cost more money than Fred possessed. Everything on wheels was ponderous and built to last a hundred years. The lightest Cape Cart needed six oxen or mules. The smallest up-country trek-wagon required ten.

The papers carried appalling news from America. Congress had repealed the Sherman Silver Purchase Act and the silver mines closed. Money disappeared. Times were bad. Fred cabled a message to Mother Burnham-Clapp, instructing her to withdraw a thousand dollars from the Pasadena National Bank and forward it to him in Durban. He also asked her to forward another thousand for his account in Fort Salisbury. Banks paid high interest in Africa.

While traveling, oxen pastured on grass. Horses and mules needed grain, which was more expensive, but it produced harder muscles and greater endurance. On the other hand, horses and mules were vulnerable to a disease called the *dikkop* sickness. Fred recalled

The Call to Monomotapa

a passage from *Allan Quatermain*. The donkey was immune. If so, let it be the lowly jackass. A day's search in the suburbs produced four burros at fifteen dollars each. Fred named the natural leader among them Doctor, which became Doc. The Kid gave the others their names: Ta-Ra, Ah-Sin and Ty-Wink.

All were speckled grays with assorted brown spots.

Two days of hunting in warehouses called *godowns* turned up the running gears of an American buckboard. Long ago in an attempt to develop new markets, the Clement Studebaker Wagon Company had dispatched them to Natal. Fred would have preferred gears for a freight wagon, which could hold more, but the Studebaker people built sturdy products. So he decided to upgrade the buckboard into a spring wagon. When he expressed an interest in buying the running gears, the merchant set the price at a hundred dollars.

"A complete buckboard in America costs twenty-five dollars," Fred cried. "You're offering just the running gears."

"This is Africa," the merchant replied.

"A heavy-duty freight wagon, equipped with steel brakes and eight coats of enamel over an oak body, costs fifty-five dollars."

"The price is one hundred Yank dollars."

It took much of Fred's remaining money, but he paid. Back at the hotel, he sketched an American buckboard and joined it to a heavier three-spring wagon. It was a compromise of the best American designs and Fred hoped the running gears would meet the challenge. He hired a carpenter to build according to his sketches. The man agreed, muttering to himself the wagon would never get as far as the Limpopo River. There were no burro harnesses in Durban, so Fred bought ox-hide belting and rivets: the makings.

When completed, the outfit brought guffaws from Durbanites who insisted, "That's not the way it's done, you know." After three weeks, the hotel bill mounted, so the Burnhams loaded up. They left during church services on Sunday, April 16, 1893. Behind the seat of the wagon was Blanche's new Singer sewing machine. Flanking her pride and joy were two Charter Oak steamer trunks filled with clothing, bleached cotton and muslin, bull hide shirting and blue denim. Blanche had shopped in the Victoria Street Market. Packed in stout wooden boxes in the rear were tea, salt, pepper, sugar, flour, curry, beans, rice, blackstrap molasses and spices. There were lugs of raisins, dried prunes, apples and figs. Laid in for emergencies were tinned apricots, peaches, pears, corn, tomatoes and peas.

Under the wagon's seat, available for quick use, were Fred's 1892 lever action Winchester .44 repeating carbine, a 12-gauge Remington scattergun, two thousand rounds of bullets, a supply of primed empty shells, hand-loading tools, gunpowder and bullet lead. Piled atop the boxes of foodstuffs were two folding canvas beds, a tent, five gallons of axle grease and a shoe-repair kit with extra leather. An acetylene gas lamp, useful for scaring lions, hung from a peg on the side of the wagon.

A thought crossed Fred's mind. What if the great Cecil Rhodes could find no use for a stray scout from the American West? He confided his fears to Blanche.

"We trek north," she said firmly.

"You'll always be my favorite tiger bait."

Ox-Drawn Trek Wagon

8

Trek North Rapidly

The Transvaal • April 1893

THE JOURNEY of a thousand miles was expected to take about three months. In Pietermaritzburg, Fred reinforced the springs and bought two more burros, which he named Babe and Chub. As the family climbed from the hot, subtropical coastline into the coolness of the rounded Drakensberg Mountains, the burros hardened to the harness. Smoky *veld* fires on the Zulu hills created a yellow haze that reminded Fred of prairie fires in Minnesota. From behind the century plants and eucalyptus trees, called blue gums here, fierce-looking Zulu warriors peered at them.

When they arrived on the *high veld*, it was early in May, at the onset of winter in the Southern Hemisphere. The sun shined brightly, but a brisk wind made the days cold and the nights freezing. Fred celebrated his thirty-second birthday anniversary on Thursday, May 11, with a camp fire dinner on a barren hillside. Fred thought it was the happiest birthday of his life.

The Burnhams were on flatland now, making better time. They were averaging more than ten miles a day. Eleven days later they arrived at Johannesburg, a chilly, mile-high metropolis where they bought sheepskin coats for the three of them. Johannesburg dwarfed Tombstone, which itself was three times the size of Los Angeles. Horse-drawn transit cars linked city center and fashionable suburbs equipped with electric lights. They rode for miles past stamp mills and piles of exposed mine tailings.

Ritornello • an Interlude

London • April 1893

JACK HAMMOND met with Barney Barnato, the English mine owner who lived in southern Africa. Handing an envelope to him, Hammond said, "Here is my resume. Tell me about yourself."

"Five years ago," Barney said, "Alfred Beit, Cecil Rhodes and I combined our holdings into De Beers Consolidated Mines. We now control one of the world's largest corporations. We produce most of the world's diamonds and by rationing we control the prices."

As Barnato spoke, Hammond studied the short, plump and blond man with hair stuck down. A scented dressing wafted from a shiny face as rosy as Cupid.

"You talk diamonds," Hammond said. "Yet you offer me a position to manage your gold holdings. Tell me about your gold."

"I began acquiring gold claims four years ago, using Barnato Consolidated Mines Company," Barney said. "Now I need talent to manage these properties."

Jack could scarcely believe this smiling man with bow-tie, cuffed shirt and tight trousers was known throughout the world for intense business shrewdness.

"I'm told you engineer the market for your stocks," Hammond said. "That's not my kind of engineering. My reputation must not be used to rig the stock market."

"If you did as I told you to, what use would you be to me?" Barnato said. "I will offer you twenty-five thousand dollars a year, the biggest salary any American engineer gets in South Africa."

"I do better than that at home," Hammond said. "Double it."

"That is entirely satisfactory."

"When I am saving you more than that amount, I want a much higher salary."

"I agree perfectly," Barnato said.

Counterpoise • Equilibrium

THE TRANSVAAL • JUNE 1893

FORTY-MILES north of Johannesburg the three Burnhams found themselves in Pretoria, the capital. While sipping tea under the lavender blossoms of a jacaranda tree, Fred and Blanche caught a glimpse of Paul Kruger, the huge, wily and superstitious old bear who was the president of the Boer republic. Fred told Blanche, "Oom Paul believes literally in the Bible and he thinks the world is flat."

In the stores of Pretoria, they saw displays of canned beef, condensed milk, tinned butter, beef and mutton from England and America, and oats and flour milled in India. There were dried tomatoes and apricots, bottles of brandy from Los Angeles, and rock crushers from San Francisco.

They soon departed, hoping to be in Salisbury by late July. The order of march was get up before dawn, eat breakfast, *trek* four hours, rest three and *trek* until dusk. On Sunday, Fred overhauled the har-

The Call to Monomotapa

Oom Paul

nesses, greased the axles and hunted game. Blanche washed and mended clothes, and roasted meat and baked bread with an aluminum reflector while she wrote letters. Rod tended the burros. Monday saw them resume the *trek*. They traveled in desiccated, thornbush country where the sand ran ankle-deep and clouds of gnats bit into anything alive. Everyone walked. The next day a throaty roar said they were in lion country. Fred guessed lions might be fond of burro meat—they looked like zebras—so at night he lighted the Magic Eye acetylene lamps and kept fires going on each side of their camp. By day they rode through herds of zebra and giraffes, while troupes of baboons scampered into the piles of basalt rocks called *kopjes*. The Boers pronounced it as *koppies*.

Early in July, they arrived on the banks of a large river: the great, gray, greasy Limpopo, as Rudyard Kipling had called it. A Boer wagon train was camped about a mile downstream. They had formed their *laager* in a square with the people inside and the animals grazing outside. After the ribbing in Durban, Fred was reluctant to join the locals so he made camp some distance away. After an hour, two horsemen rode over and the taller man spoke.

"What you doin with flop-ears in grass freight country?"

The friendly Western patter was music to Fred's ears.

"These Arizona nightingales will out-trek your ox-wagons any day," Fred replied.

"Bob Bain, here," the tall man said through a soup-strainer mustache. "And this is Pete Ingram from Montana." Ingram was sinewy and as lanky as a young ash sapling.

"The *veld* is no place for a family," Ingram said. Pete was all knees and elbows.

"You better shut your yap or I'll bounce you around until there's nothing left of you but your belt, boots and bonnet." Fred was mad.

"Easy, Pete," Bain cautioned. To Fred he added, "Mr. Burnham, I think you'll do quite well on the *veld*. Truce, gents. We're looking for Yanks. The Fourth is just around the corner."

"Hey, that's right," Fred said, patriotism smothering anger.

"You shoot it, I'll cook it," Blanche called out. She emerged from the tent leading The Kid. At the sight of a pretty woman, the visitors' eyes lighted up.

The men rode onto the *veld* and shot a springbok. While Blanche roasted a haunch over a spit, the men got acquainted. Bain was a Canadian tracker drawn to Africa by the lure of adventure. Ingram, who stood five feet ten and was the shorter of the two, admitted to being one-quarter Blackfeet Indian. He said he'd grown weary of busting broncs in Montana.

"I took the rough out of 'em," was all he said.

Fred remembered that Blackfeet, unlike the friendly Shoshones, had a reputation for slitting their enemies' throats at night. *Better keep an eye on this guy.*

As they ate, Bain spoke. "Join our wagon train," he said. "With the family, you'll benefit from our numbers."

"Maybe," Fred replied. "We'll see." First, he wanted to talk to the Boers.

"You could make a meal for a hungry croc," Ingram said.

"They're called alligators in America," Bain said, "but crocodiles everywhere else."

After dinner, the three men rode over to the *laager*. Bain introduced Fred to Louis Botha, the leader, who told him that Limpopo meant crocodile in Zulu.

"The river is full of em," he warned. "The safest way to cross is in a trek wagon. Put your wife and boy in my wagon and they will be safe."

The trek wagon was larger and heavier than a Conestoga wagon. Too slow for fast overland travel, Fred decided, but he accepted Botha's offer to let Bea and The Kid ride across the river.

By the fire that night, Fred said, "Three hundred miles and we're at Victoria."

Blanche glanced longingly at the Limpopo and said, "Fred, we haven't had a bath since Pretoria."

"Bea, if we bathe in that river, we'll leave a ring."

Since arriving in Africa, Fred had taken to calling Blanche by the nickname Bea. She didn't seem to mind.

"On our wedding anniversary in Naples, I was thinking about the day I married you. I promised to go anywhere with you, but until today I never dreamed that we'd be bedded out half way around the world beside a river full of crocodiles."

"Are you sorry?"

The Call to Monomotapa

"Not while you are here." Blanche wasn't sorry, but she certainly was afraid for the safety of her son.

• • •

THE BOERS, UNLIKE the British in Durban, didn't laugh at the Burnhams' frail-looking spring-wagon. These people reasoned that if the vehicle had made the trip safely to the Limpopo, it would probably last to Mashona Land. Louis Botha, on examining the spring wagon, suggested that Fred move his provisions into one of the bigger wagons while they forded the river.

"You got too much supplies for such a small wagon," Botha said. Fred agreed and offered to supply Botha with meat in exchange. It took three days to get the trek wagons across. Two tipped over and three others were damaged. Botha ordered the train to *laager* on the north bank while repairs were made.

Men who could be spared were assigned to hunt game. The women made *biltong*, the jerky of Africa. During the hunt, Fred used the Bogardus snap-shooting technique he'd learned from Jeff Clark. Riding a borrowed horse and carrying his Winchester carbine, Fred brought down three animals. The springbok were vulnerable when making their long, graceful display leaps, which the Boers called *pronks*. When the hunt was over, Fred had taken more game than anyone else. After they returned from the hunt, Bain and Ingram helped Fred butcher the meat.

After dinner, Louis Botha described the new land they were entering.

"We'll soon begin a long climb to the high *veld*. At Fort Salisbury, we reach a flat ridge. From there the rivers flow south to the Limpopo or north to the Zambesi."

Some of the fellows called it the LimZam Ridgeback.

"What are the people like?" Fred asked.

"The Mashonas are a dirty lot vot eat rats and live in huts of mud," Botha said. "Your wife and child will be safe among the cowardly Mashonas."

"Mineral deposits?" Fred probed.

"Some mines in Mashona Land, but prospecting gets better as you go west," Botha said. "Stay out of Matabele Land. Matabeles are cousins of the Zulus."

Bain said, "I hear their capital is Bulawayo."

"In Zulu, it means the Place of Killing," Botha said. "The men are allowed to marry only after washing their spears in the blood of an enemy. Twice a year at a big *konza* ceremony, Lobengula steps into a

59

large circle of warriors who are seated around him. He whirls his spear and lets it fly. In whatever direction it points when it falls, that is where the Matabele will wage their next war."

"How do you know these things?" Ingram asked.

"From white men living in Bulawayo," Botha said. "Fred Selous lived there as a white hunter for many years. Jimmy Fairbairn and Bill Usher are traders in Bulawayo. Most of my information comes from Johann Colenbrander of the Bechuana Land Exploration Company. He is Lobengula's interpreter."

For some time, Fred had been puzzled by the Matabele. He couldn't put his finger on it. Maybe some palaver would help.

"In Arizona," Burnham said, "the Apaches were pirates. Blood was sweeter than booty and both were as dear as life. Corner him and he's as dangerous as a wounded wolf. But we subdued them. Can't that be done in Matabele Land?"

"What were your odds?" Botha asked.

"Uh, five thousand Apaches against two thousand soldiers and thirty thousand armed, white settlers."

Botha's smile was thin. "Here those odds are reversed. There are a hundred thousand warriors in Matabele Land. In Mashona Land, there are two thousand whites and no army whatsoever. Stay out of Matabele Land. The gold isn't worth your life."

• • •

FRED GROUSED AT the slow pace of the trek wagons. Seven miles was a good day of travel. Well, at least he was learning about African *spooring* and the habits of the wild beasts. He was learning to identify African animals by their dung.

During the noon lager, Fred would borrow a horse, ride ahead to scout the land and choose a campsite for the evening *outspan*. On one foray, he spotted a man astride a speckled mare.

"I'm Hendrik van der Merve," the man said. "I'm scouting for a party of Boers returning to the Transvaal. There is a threat of a native war and we are trekking down country."

"I'll ride back to alert our people," Fred said. "Follow my trail and guide your wagon train to us."

An hour later, Louis Botha had a hot meal waiting. While they ate, Van der Merve spoke.

"About a month ago, the Mashona tribesmen stole some telegraph wire to melt into copper bracelets for their women. Magistrate Vigers hauled the offenders into court and assessed a fine. The Mashonas paid in cattle."

"Cattle?" Botha cried. "The Mashona don't own the cattle. The

The Call to Monomotapa

Matabele do."

"That's true," Van der Merve replied. "The Mashonas get to drink the milk from the cows in payment for caring for the animals."

"Never heard of such a thing," Fred snorted.

"What's important," Botha said, "is the Mashonas had a right to the milk, but not to give away the cattle."

"When Lobengula heard about the Mashonas paying the fine in cattle," Van der Merve said, "he sent an armed war party to punish the offenders."

Botha asked if the warriors attacked any whites?

"No, Lobengula sent Manyao, one of his best *indunas*. When the Shonas saw armed Matabeles coming, they came groveling at our feet. Before we knew what was happening, the Matabele used their *assegais* to slit them open like ripe melons. About two hundred Shonas died. The bodies got to stinking so we let the hyenas eat them.

"Doctor Jameson told Captain Lendy to run Manyao out of Mashona Land. Lendy had only forty men against Manyao's thousand warriors. But there was outrage in Fort Victoria so Lendy poured artillery fire into the black *impi*, killing forty of the royal blood. The others ran into the trees."

Botha gasped. "The young men will demand to wash their spears in blood."

"That's why we trek south," van der Merve said.

Fred was still puzzled.

"Why didn't they attack?" he asked.

"Only the king can make that decision," Van der Merve said. "But royal blood has been shed. At an *indaba* in Bulawayo, the young warriors will demand war. Manyao has threatened to come back and cut off Captain Lendy's ears."

During the afternoon, uncles, aunties, cousins and nephews held powwows. A kaffir war was serious. After dinner that night, Botha called on Burnham.

"The family men will turn south in the morning," he said. "You have your family to think of. Come with us."

Fred agreed to give his reply at dawn. He crept out of the laager and climbed atop a *kopje* to weigh his choices. For days, something had puzzled him. Like a flash, it came to him. The Matabele fought like the Roman Legions, in phalanx style, formed into ranks with shields and spears. It took Attila the Hun, the horse-mounted cavalryman, to defeat the Roman Legions.

"Holy hop-toads," Fred cried out as a curtain of mental fog lifted. Everything that Botha and Van der Merve had said implied the

61

Matabele were horseless. The whites had horses and rifles. With good scouting, it meant the whites enjoyed a clear-cut advantage. And Fred Burnham was a good scout. He hadn't traveled half way around the world to quit now.

If Fred had a tail, it would be wagging.

9

Trapped at Fort Vic

Mashona Land • August 1893

A COMBINED WAGON TRAIN inspanned shortly after dawn. The Boers and the British with women and children turned south. Less than a third of the original ox-wagon train, single men only, would continue north. When Fred said he was northbound, Blanche's face turned the color of an old bruise. She pulled Roderick to her side and looked sharply at her husband.

The terror showed in her eyes.

"Only the roughest elements are going north."

"Bea, we weren't born to be killed by Matabeles." Fred's face wore a look of assurance that had been lacking since they crossed the Limpopo. Bain and Ingram rode up and said they too would continue on to Mashona Land.

"Botha says there's a telegraph relay-station west of here," Bain said. "Let's nip over and get the latest gen."

"Good idea," Fred said. "I'll need a horse."

After a ride of six miles, they found the telegraph line and followed the humming wires to the relay station. The man in charge was a peach-faced youth of nineteen from Dublin named Dennis Dillon. He showed the visitors a sheaf of messages sent by the British administrator in Fort Salisbury, Doctor Leander Starr Jameson, to Cecil Rhodes in Cape Town.

Burnham and Bain read the telegrams.

"We need guns and ammunition." "Send horses from the Transvaal." "Dispatch medical supplies and food."

"It's all Jameson's fault," Dillon blurted out. "Rhodes sent him up here to chop costs. The Chartered Company is draining the old man dry. So Jameson laid off all but forty of the police. When the niggers learnt that, they attacked. There'll be the devil to pay."

63

"How many white men in Mashona Land?" Fred asked. Everyone had a different version of the facts.

"Maybe a thousand. Mostly able-bodied. This is no place for old men," Dillon said looking at Fred.

"Can you send a telegram to Doctor Jameson?" The menacing look on Fred's face got young Dillon's attention.

"Certainly, Sir. Write it out."

Fred composed a message describing their party and requesting instructions. An hour later, the ticker sounded.

"Trek northward rapidly. Form laager at night. When inspanned, throw out scouts. L.S.J." Fred's eyes sparkled when he saw the administrator's initials. *Doctor Jameson needed him. There is no turning back.* His life's dream of scouting for a military expedition would be realized.

Back at the wagon train, Fred gazed on a new arrival, bronzed and wiry, a man about Fred's size wearing a pencil mustache. His neck was thick and corded with muscle and he wore a Stetson hat of beaver fur. Beside him was a Cape cart drawn by a matched pair of gray mules. A holstered six-gun was tied low on his leg. No question, he came from North America.

"Meet Maurice Gifford," Blanche said. "The Right Honorable Maurice Gifford." She pronounced the name as *Jifford*.

"When did you leave the West?" Fred asked.

"Right after you," Gifford said, the stern mask on his round, shiny face breaking into an easy smile of welcome.

Although he was British, he displayed American mannerisms of speech and gesture. While they ate lunch, the two men got acquainted. Gifford had spent eleven years in Canada where he'd fought in Riel's Rebellion. Louis Riel had led the Indians of Manitoba and Saskatchewan in rebellion against the Canadian government. Riel was captured, tried and hanged. Gifford never said which side he fought on, but he did say he was a younger brother of Lord Gifford. His elder brother was the London financier who controlled the Bechuana Land Exploration Company. That was the company, Fred remembered, which employed Johann Colenbrander, King Lobengula's interpreter.

The Call to Monomotapa

"What draws you to Monomotapa?" Gifford asked.

"Mono-what?" Burnham asked, stumbling.

"MO-no-mo-TA-pa. It's the old Portuguese name for Mashona Land. Monomotapa was said to be an ancient empire in central Africa. In the 1650s, Commandant Jan van Riesbeeck of the Cape Colony sent an expedition to find the legendary gold and diamond treasures in Monomotapa. But they returned from Davagul empty handed." Now Fred knew where Rider Haggard got his inspiration for *King Solomon's Mines*.

"I guess you're attracted to Africa by the lure of the Oof bird," Gifford said eagerly smearing a layer of orange marmalade on thick bread toasted over the campfire.

"I came to Africa to work as a scout in the service of Cecil Rhodes," Burnham replied. He had never heard of any Oof bird.

"I too am on the lookout for the elusive Oof bird's feathers," Gifford said. "Of all the strange furred, horned and feathered denizens of Africa, the mysterious Oof bird is the most often sought after and the least often found."

"What is this Oof bird you're talking about?" Blanche finally asked.

"In Africa, there is a firm belief that wherever the Oof bird builds its nest, there will be found the outcropping of a reef of gold or a deposit of the diamond-bearing clay-pipe that makes southern Africa famous," Gifford said. "An Oof bird's eggs are called nuggets. Wherever the Oof bird makes its nest, treasure unlimited is found."

"Sounds like the elusive pot of gold at the end of the rainbow," Burnham said, thinking he might be the butt of a joke. "The faster you pursue it, the quicker it recedes from your grasp."

"The very rarity of the Oof bird explains why the world's great naturalists have been wholly unable to gather a specimen of this curious fowl," Gifford said, slicing off a thick piece of cold boiled springbok.

"I suspect," Burnham said, "the horizons of this bird baffle the imagination."

"From Cairo to Cape Town, the Oof bird calls to the sons of men," Gifford continued. "I still follow the twitter and remain on the lookout for the glint of its feathers."

"Well, you can count me as a dedicated hunter for the Oof bird," Burnham said and the men handed over their dishes to Blanche.

"I must leave for Fort Vic," Gifford said. He pointed to his Stetson and said, "I'm taking one of these hats to Captain Allan Wilson. When you get there, look him up. We'll need men like you." With that, Maurice Gifford hopped into his Cape Cart and was off.

65

Fred said, "I like him, Bea. He rings true." He had no idea their paths would cross many times in the future.

• • •

THE WAGON TRAIN edged slowly northward, entering Mashona Land proper. Fred studied a group of about thirty Mashona who were building a small, circular, windowless pole-and-dagga hut near a *kopje*. To Fred the *kopjes* of Mashona Land looked like California rock piles he had seen near Perris and Temecula and down near the Mexican border east of San Diego. The only difference, Fred decided, was the African kopjes were piled high while those back home had been toppled by earthquakes. Whatever, these *kopjes* were nothing compared to the rugged Sierra Anchas of Arizona.

He continued watching the Shonas work on the hut.

"Looks more like a Navajo hogan than an Apache wickiup," he said to Blanche. He said it as a compliment. An Apache wickiup was little more than a living archeological dig.

Blanche, morose and edgy, said nothing. The weather had grown hot and when Fred asked how she felt, Blanche replied she was quite well, thank you. But she remained closemouthed. Fred wondered if she was upset by the roaring of the lions last night. A family of baboons had frolicked on the trail this morning and a flock of hyenas set up a ruckus after the noon meal. When she had little to say for the next three days, Fred became concerned. Late in the afternoon, he waved to Bain and Ingram.

"We're going on to Salisbury. Care to tag along?"

Bain shook his head. "Our plunder's in that ox wagon; we'll stick with the train."

"Suit yourselves." He cracked the whip and the burros, rested and fat from the leisurely pace, moved smartly ahead. After two days Fred saw they were making twenty miles a day, three times as fast as the Boer wagon train. It was the dry season and the *veld* grass crackled as they moved. The sound of roaring lions warned them of the danger to the burros.

They began traveling by night, carrying the shotgun at full cock and using the acetylene lamp to guide their way. Blanche and The Kid slept in the wagon while Fred drove at night. By day Blanche and Rod stood guard while Fred slept. By traveling twelve hours out of twenty-four, they came to Fort Victoria late Monday night, August 7.

Another week's travel would bring them to Fort Salisbury. But on checking into the Victoria House Hotel, Fred learned they'd never reach their destination. Fort Vic was preparing for war and everyone

The Call to Monomotapa

was quarantined. This was the end of the road.

Lagnappe • a Little Extra

MAJOR STEPHE BADEN-POWELL was back with his regiment, the Thirteenth Hussars, now in Ireland. The tour of duty of his commanding officer, Colonel Russell Baker, was drawing to a close and it was widely expected that he would be appointed as Inspector General of Cavalry, a position that could greatly enhance Sir Russell's ability to nurture Baden-Powell's career.

Stephe's return to the United Kingdom had produced a new financial dilemma: While he was stationed in the British Isles, his expenses were seven hundred pounds a year. His military pay and the modest fees he earned from selling articles and sketches to the London newspapers totaled half that much. Stephe was forced to live on handouts from his mother and brother. He needed to win a combat assignment to bring that promotion.

There was always hope. Little Wars were a superior kind of sport. Stephe had missed one recent Little War in Uganda, a billet that would have proved an open sesame to a combat command. Stephe was lamenting that dismal circumstance when a telegram arrived from Colonel Sir Frederick Carrington in Natal. The message came not a moment too soon. It invited Stephe to join Sir Frederick in Matabele Land as his chief staff officer in the upcoming hostilities with King Lobengula. Major Baden-Powell began to pack immediately. To celebrate the rebirth of his flagging career, he made plans for a farewell party before embarking on a steamship for Africa.

Counterpoise • Equilibrium

AFTER THE LONG journey across the veld, the Burnhams strolled into the dining room of the Victoria House Hotel, reeking of the washtub and looking the very height of well-scrubbed fashion.

Fred and Rod wore matching suits of burnt-chestnut cloth. Blanche was attired in a navy blue skirt and a fluffy white blouse trimmed with lace that she'd bought in Paris. There was a yellow ribbon in her hair and a new sparkle in her eyes. It was the first time Blanche had worn more than one petticoat since they camped at the Limpopo River. During the trek, she always wore Mother Hubbard dresses.

"How do you like the place, Bea?"

"It's great, considering we're in the middle of Africa," she replied. "I think I'll have the steak and kidney pie."

The selection puzzled Fred. Steak and kidney pie wasn't Bea's favorite dish, but if it made her happy, she'd have it. Funny how quickly her good graces returned once they were out of the wilderness and back in civilization.

67

After checking into the hotel, they'd enjoyed their first hot bath and a sleep in a real bed since leaving Durban five months ago. Blanche had slept soundly, but Fred got up about noon to mosey around town.

"What did you learn today?" Blanche asked. She was animated tonight. Fred knew she enjoyed city life. "Whom did you meet?"

"The people here are as worked up over the Matabele threat as the folk in Globe were after the Indian outbreak at Cibicue," Fred answered. "One rumor says Lobengula is camped outside Fort Victoria with ten thousand warriors eager for a washing of the spears. Another says the Shonas will join the Matabele and butcher us all."

"Is there danger?"

"Not here. Everywhere I went, the wagons were drawn so close together the hubs touch. But it's not wise to travel to Fort Salisbury now."

"Did you see Maurice Gifford?"

"Yes, and I met Allan Wilson. He's a big, rangy, square-jawed string bean with a droopy mustache. He's the kind of guy you don't have to look over your shoulder once you pass him on a horse. You can trust him. They also took me over to meet Doctor Jim."

"Oh, it's Doctor Jim already? I understand he's a real doctor, but he got into trouble at the Kimberley diamond digs when he misdiagnosed a smallpox epidemic. What's he like?"

Their meal was served by a Shona waiter wearing a cast-off dinner jacket and baggy black pants.

"He's about forty, a small, round-shouldered man with a heavy neck, thick chest and a large head. He has expressive eyes. He puts you at ease and lets you speak your piece. He ignores everyone but the person he's talking to. He's Cecil Rhodes's right hand man, you know."

"I understand that Oxford's finest son cannot bear to have women fussing around him. How about Doctor Jim? Are they both some kind of—" Her voice trailed off at the thought of using the taboo word *homosexual*.

"I dunno, Bea. I didn't see any distaff members. But women are scarce in Fort Vic."

After Blanche's acerbic mood in the final days of their journey, Fred was happy to know she was feeling better. City life was good for her.

"Any luck finding good horses?"

"The *dikkop* sickness got most of 'em. Salted horses command a king's ransom. Doctor Jim has agents in the Transvaal buying up

The Call to Monomotapa

fresh stock. Until they get here, we'll stay in Fort Victoria."

"Is it really dangerous up north?"

"Probably not. But if war comes, we may as well meet it here."

"Oh you men and your games. I've no love for the Matabele, the brutes. But I don't see the need to go to war over some copper wire stolen by a few Shona natives."

Heads turned in the restaurant. There were grim stares from men and women alike.

"It's no different from General Crook fighting the Apaches. Lobengula is a savage and his people must be pacified for civilization to expand."

"It sounds like a land grab to me."

"That's the same as calling Lincoln the ruthless destroyer of the Old South. Or denouncing President Monroe for subjugating Latin America. If the causing of pain is a sin and an evil, then The Kid should never have been born. Mark my words, Bea, one day the flowers of civilization will bloom here where now only rank weeds of savagery and ignorance grow."

Later, in their hotel room, Fred waited for Blanche to put Rod to bed. He wanted to tell her something.

"I learned some things today, Blanche, things I didn't know before," he said. "What we face is bigger than Lobengula and some ignorant savages. In the scheme of world events, central Africa is in a power vacuum. It's a prize to be carved up, like the great powers that are carving up China. Right now Rhodes is more concerned that Oom Paul Kruger will seize Matabele Land than he's worried that Lobengula killed a few Shona."

"Oom Paul? You mean that crude old man we saw under the jacaranda trees in Pretoria?"

"The same man who thinks the earth's flat. I learned he's close enough to Count Leo von Caprivi in Germany to share the same toothpick. Germany wants Oom Paul to take Matabele Land so he can link German East Africa with South West Africa. That east-west link would block Rhodes' plan for a British railway from the Cape to Cairo. Unless Rhodes gets there first, central Africa could fall to the Germans."

Blanche glanced at Rod, sleeping in a cot. She didn't say anything.

"I happen to believe in what Rhodes is doing," Fred said. "Besides, we're broke. These are shy-money times. Our capital is gone. In the United States, there was a terrible financial panic. Wall Street stumbled in May and the stock market crashed in June. The whole country is in a deep depression. All American is feeling the effects of our defective monetary system. Farm after farm has been foreclosed. The Reading Railroad, Northern Pacific, Union Pacific and Santa Fe have been forced into bankruptcy."

"Omigod," Blanche cried.

"There was a telegraph message waiting for us from Uncle Josiah," Fred continued. "The thousand dollars I cabled for when we were in Durban never arrived. On June 27, just before we crossed the Limpopo River, the whole market went south. Six hundred banks have closed their doors, including the Pasadena National. There's no money to take us back home."

Blanche began to cry and Fred knew he was facing a crisis in his marriage. After a few minutes, she composed herself and wiped her eyes with a handkerchief, then asked, "We have come half way around the world only to go broke in a strange, harsh and remote land of savages. I feel so helpless. What shall we do?"

Fred wasn't exactly sure, but something Maurice Gifford told him buoyed his spirits. In his mind was the iridescent glitter of an elusive bird.

"Nothing will happen for a month," he said to his wife, grinning as he got up to draw back the blankets. "Until then, I think a change of scenery will do all of us some good. We leave here at dawn."

Zimbabwe Ruin

CHEVRON PATTERN.
TEMPLE WALL, ZIMBABWE.

10

Oof Bird at Zimbabwe

ZIMBABWE • SEPTEMBER 1893

ZIMBABWE WAS THE panacea that seemed to relieve Blanche's lingering blues. Seventeen miles from Fort Victoria, the Zimbabwe Ruins were the remains of an ancient collection of large stone structures. The Burnhams arrived at dusk, in time to make camp, build a fire and eat before bedtime. Fred was eager to hunt game and make biltong for iron rations. His family needed a supply of food. After breakfast, they explored Zimbabwe.

The ruins dated so far back in time that the British insisted there were no native legends to account for their presence. Fred entertained the idea that the Shonas might have had their own Ho Ho Kams. The ruins rested on a gentle hill about three hundred feet high that was randomly strewn with boulders. The first of three groups of ruins was a fortress-like acropolis that occupied the summit of a hill. To Fred, it appeared to be some kind of defensive position.

In a valley nearby was an elliptical temple about two hundred feet long with walls twelve feet thick at the base, rising to a height of thirty feet. A band of stone in a chevron pattern decorated the walls. The rocks had been fitted with great care and the walls were thick because no mortar had been used in the construction.

The third landmark was a conical tower, looking like a phallic symbol. Between the elliptical temple and the conical tower were jagged and broken walls that extended for nearly a mile. It looked to Fred like a vale of long-neglected ruins. The Burnhams walked through narrow passages and climbed a rock stairway that opened on the acropolis. They looked out on two large stone towers, each shaped like a Mashona pole-and-dagga hut.

"Sheba's breasts," Fred mumbled.

"Wash your mouth!" Blanche said at his mention of female privates. "In front of young Rod too. You should be ashamed."

"In *King Solomon's Mines*, Sheba's breasts were the landmarks that Allan Quatermain sought in finding the diamond mines."

"Wasn't *King Solomon's Mines* written before this place was discovered?"

"No, Maurice Gifford told me Adam Renders found the ruins in 1867. Haggard wrote *King Solomon's Mines* in 1886, the year Rod was born."

"Will we find buried treasure, Papa?" The Kid asked. Somehow, the idea hadn't occurred to Fred. He looked around. The Shona had knocked down some of the walls and used the stones to make goat kraals. Fred walked over to a crumbled wall and studied the debris. He squatted and began pulling loose rocks from the jumble. At first he saw nothing of interest. He removed some larger rocks and after ten minutes of rummaging, he was rewarded by a discovery.

"Look at this," he said. Fred held a gold figurine of a lion about an inch tall, a remarkable example of primitive art. Blanche and Rod pitched in to help and after half an hour, they had removed several dozen figurines, some depicting humans, others in the shape of animals. Although they searched for another hour, they found no more loot.

Fred walked over to the wagon to get his batea, the gold pan he had packed. He found a little *spruit*—the Afrikaans word for stream—that was almost dried up and began panning for gold. He was well rewarded; in two hours he washed out about a hundred gold beads and ornaments. None was so refined and graceful as the figurines, but there was a substantial take in nuggets. Seemingly without effort, he had snared the tail of the *Oof bird*. Now they weren't broke. Now there would be money for food and lodging.

Blanche and Rod wanted to try their hands at gold panning, so Fred taught them to use the batea. Once they got the hang of it, Fred picked up his carbine and went hunting. He wondered why the other tourists—Boer and British alike—paid no attention to the gold panning. Maybe they didn't know how to do it.

Fred walked around the conical tower and saw two oribi copulating in the brush. When the male completed his duty, Fred popped him. Oribi were the swift gazelles of southern Africa. Wary animals with a keen sense of smell, the oribi was a difficult catch. Fred considered himself lucky to flush one. That evening they enjoyed a meal of pan-fried oribi steak and the next day Blanche set up an aluminum reflector oven to braise a western stew.

An ox-wagon outspanned nearby and a family of British Coloni-

The Call to Monomotapa

als made camp. A girl of about eleven began teaching Rod some words of Shona. She said the native word for Zimbabwe was *Masvingo*. If so, Fred wondered if Zimbabwe was the Portuguese name. When the parents came over, Fred invited them to share a meal: an African version of Arizona's son-of-a-bitch stew—a nourishing range dish of the tongue, liver, heart, kidneys, sweetbreads and brains of a fresh kill. Potatoes, carrots and onions floated in the bubbling gravy.

Fred boasted idly, "We tossed in ever'thin but the hair, horns and holler."

The British husband frowned, unable to comprehend the barmy speech of this dotty Yank. During the meal the wife complimented Blanche on the delicious flavor of the food. Blanche attributed it to the spices she'd brought from Durban. When Fred mentioned the meat was oribi, a look of disbelief spread over the husband's face. Obviously, this was springbok and the tenderness and flavor were imparted by the rare spices.

That afternoon, Fred went bird hunting. With a shotgun, he brought down partridges, plover and pigeons. Switching to a Winchester carbine, he shot a klipspringer, a small, stocky and sure-footed antelope that leaps great distances. In the mid-leap of a pronk, the klipspringer proved to be an easy target. The bristly hair was good for stuffing saddles so Fred salted the hide.

For several days they feasted as Fred brought meat to camp and Blanche dried it into jerky. They still hadn't learned to appreciate the rock-hard biltong, which seemed at its best when shaved and used as a soup base. A few days later, another wagon train of visitors arrived at the Zimbabwe Ruins. Bob Bain and Pete Ingram were among the new arrivals.

"At Fort Victoria, they told us you'd come out here," Bain said. "Tomorrow we're goin to Manica Land down by the Sabi River. There's good grazing and a chance to trade with the natives."

That night there was a powwow among visitors. After a feast of wild game roasted over a spit, the Yanks were pressed with questions about life in America.

"Our family was so rich," Bob Bain boasted, "we had two water wells. We had to tear one down though. There wasn't enough wind to turn both windmills."

"Hey, that's rare as a rooster's egg," Fred said.

Pete Ingram enjoyed being the center of attention among the Colonials. So he demonstrated a cowboy airin of the lungs: a western augurin match.

"It's a talkin contest," Pete said, speaking in rapid-fire tempo. "Two

73

loose-tongued cowboys sit cross-legged, knee to knee and face to face, talkin as fast as they can, to see which one can keep it up the longest without runnin out of wind. There's just a constant flow of words that don't make no sense a-tall, both of 'em talkin at the same time, and each one's got so much to say that it gets in the way. At the start, they talk fast and furious, but after an hour or so they slow down to a trot to be savin of both words and wind. By the time it's over, neither of 'em's got enough vocal power left to bend a smoke ring."

Most of the Britishers were unable to follow Pete's rapid-fire tempo, but they laughed all the same. When it was Fred's turn, he described a blizzard that he had been caught in while herding cattle in the Texas Panhandle. He said that during the height of the storm he'd killed a yearling steer and wrapped himself in its hide to keep from freezing.

"I never saw a place so cold," Fred said. "Why, there was nothin 'tween me and the North Pole 'cept a bob-wire fence. And that was full o knot holes."

Bain and Ingram roared with laughter at Fred's little funny, but the British didn't seem to know the meaning of bob-wire.

The next morning, Fred showed Bain and Ingram the gold he'd found. They decided to let the wagon train go on ahead. This was the midpoint of the dry season, and the spruit had dried up. For pocket prospecting in a dry spruit, the batea could not be used so Fred began carving a horn spoon from an African antelope horn.

"Black horn's best, so you can see the gold," he said. "See, it's a little gold pan. You can use it with the water in your canteen."

Pete watched intently and began carving his horn spoon. Fred told them about the strange *Oof bird* that the Right Honorable Maurice Gifford had described on the trip to Fort Victoria.

"Those who have seen the Oof bird describe it as the most beautiful feathered creature in the world," he said. "The plumage is iridescent, ever-changing. Some say the Oof bird has the power to send its song across vast stretches of country, penetrating closed doors and thick walls. Others declare they have been awakened from a profound sleep by the siren song of this bird."

The Call to Monomotapa

"Yeah and a rooster's got teeth," Pete said, laughing. He knew a spoof when he heard one.

"Sounds to me," Bain added, "like somebody's chasin the pot of gold at the end of the rainbow."

"If you don't believe my husband," Blanche chimed in, "you are perfectly free to drop any nuggets you find in young Rod's croaker sack here. We'll use those Oof bird eggs for his college fund."

Before long the prospectors made a strike in an area of rock-strewn rubble a hundred yards from the stream bed, providing bona fide confirmation of the existence of the Oof bird. Fred moved the wagon close by and all hands fell to the task of panning gold. Blanche earned a one-fifth share for cooking, washing and mending clothes. After a rewarding week, the vein played out so they inspanned and headed toward the Sabi River in lower Manica Land. Fred was happy—the brief visit of the Oof bird guaranteed food and shelter back at Fort Vic.

"Is there enough for passage back home to America?" Blanche asked.

"When we get back to Fort Vic, M'love, things will be at wartime prices."

•••

IT WAS ON August 22, Rod's seventh birthday, that The Kid spotted the grotesque baobob tree. The botanical monarch of Africa was partly obscured by green foliage. At first, Fred thought it wasn't a tree. It looked more like a rogue bull elephant had torn the tree trunk from the ground by the roots. The taproots stuck up in all directions. *Whatever it is, it's a big sucker.*

"There's a legend," Bain said, "that God ripped up the baobob and replanted it upside down."

"Weirdest thing I've seen," Fred said.

They rode up to the tree, an ancient specimen. Fred tested the wood with his hunting knife. It was soft and pulpy. A Cockney colonial said elephants eat the tree—pulp, bark, branches and all—for its water content.

"During a drought," he said, "an entire tree might be scoffed by elephants. But baobobs can fall and crush an elephant too, so all's fair, Guv."

Later in the day, they saw more baobobs. The trunks of some were hollow, providing shelter for countless colorful birds—eagles, parrots, drongles and buffalo weavers—nesting in the cavities. Many species of insects made their homes in this strange, almost leafless tree: sweat bees, thorn moths and the praying mantis. In turn, the red hornbills preyed on the insects. A young Colonial told Rod to beware of the boomslang tree-snake. Though timid, its venom was more poisonous than a rattler's.

Manica Land proved to be a veritable zoo of wild animals. A Britisher showed Fred how the black-throated honey-guide had entered into a symbiotic relationship with the Shonas. The birds would lead the Shonas to a baobob containing a bee-hive. The natives enjoyed eating the honey and the birds coveted the beeswax. The natives would open the nest, remove the honey and leave the wax for the birds to feast on. *The honey-guide must be the source of the Oof bird legend*, Fred decided.

Rod chased the bushbabies that took shelter in the hollow limbs of the baobob, coming out only at night. That was when the baobob flowers blossomed, an hour after sunset, filling the air with a musky odor. Blanche saw an English wife collecting the seed pods of the baobob.

"We get cream of tartar from this tree," she said.

"Wonderful," Blanche said and joined the collecting.

"Keep a sharp lookout," the woman said. "It's called monkey bread. The baboons prize it. They can smell it from a distance. They may attack. Baboons are dangerous, you know."

Blanche froze.

• • •

FOR THE NEXT two weeks, the visitors grazed the stock and traded with the natives of lower Manica Land. The locals were friendly and there was much good-natured haggling as the blacks traded their beans, lentils, fowl and goats for the whites' calico, wire, mirrors, beads and black powder.

As a symbol of their authority, the village elders carried their muzzle-loader guns at full cock. They prized the black powder the white men traded because it allowed them to fire their old guns now and then, to remind lesser natives who was in charge.

The trade goods ran out. Each side believed it had gotten the best of the bargain. That meant there was a fair exchange. The stock was fat and it was time to return to Fort Victoria. Best of all, Blanche seemed much relaxed. *With the unexpected gift from the Oof bird, maybe things would work out for the best,* Fred decided.

Lagnappe • A Little Extra

Cape Town • September 1893

THE LINER *H.M.S. Scot* anchored at dawn in Kaapstad Bay. Jack and Natalie Hammond and their young sons, Harris and Jack Junior, stepped onto the promenade deck for their first glimpse of the Tafel-

The Call to Monomotapa

berg—Cape Town's fabled Table Mountain. It stood out clear and stark in the peach-colored sunrise. The great mesa of yellow stone was slashed by deep ravines which were choked with dense green forest.

"Look," cried Natalie. "The mountain is covered by clouds. It's like a tablecloth."

"Forever a tablecloth," Jack admonished. "That white cloud will never reach the lower slopes. The mist will evaporate as it reaches the heat of the lower elevations."

Natalie Hammond was still learning to cope with the world's greatest ego.

Barney Barnato, an overcoat covering his pyjamas, met them at shipside. After clearing Custom House, they rode in his private carriage to the Queens Hotel on the western tip of Cape Town Harbor. Harris and Jack Junior were fascinated by Barney's green parrot. Barney then took the boys to his office in Cape Town to show off his collection of famous diamonds.

Shortly after 11 a.m., the Hammonds boarded the *Blue Train* for the thousand mile journey to Johannesburg. Already the *Blue Train* was beginning to show the flourish that one day would make it the most luxurious train in the world. At noon, to the boom of the cannon on Signal Hill, the train departed Cape Town at a sedate forty miles an hour. The Hammonds' parlor car comprised a sitting room, three bedroom compartments, a bath, a galley with chef and a black attendant to care for their traveling needs. Jack Hammond fell in love with this most civilized mode of travel.

That day the American family traveled over the fertile plains of the Cape Colony, looking out on broad valleys dotted with conical green peaks. The land looked for all the world like the American West. They passed through the desolate wilderness of the Great Karoo at night, so they missed seeing that drought-stricken sheep land.

They arrived at the mile-high city of Johannesburg just before noon. One day after the Hammond family was settled into the Grand Hotel, Jack looked up an old Freiberg classmate, Edgar Rathbone. During their undergraduate days at the Royal School of Mines in Prussia, Ed Rathbone had gotten involved in a scandal beyond his ability to extricate himself. Jack Hammond, with his Nob Hill checkbook, bailed out Rathbone and had the scandal quietly hushed up. As a result, Rathbone was able to graduate. He was sincerely grateful and quite willing to repay his indebtedness.

That night, Hammond and Rathbone chatted over a champagne dinner at Johannesburg's finest restaurant. Edgar had never worked

77

as a mining engineer. Because of a talent for writing, he became the mining editor for Johannesburg's biggest daily newspaper. He boasted that son, Basil, was following in his footsteps as a writer. Basil Rathbone wrote detective stories.

Over dinner, Jack Hammond invited Ed Rathbone to be his guest in the wedding suite for a week at the Rand Hotel. Jack guaranteed the best hot and cold running entertainment in Joburg. He told Ed the sky was the limit for room service food and champagne. At the end of the most memorable week in Ed Rathbone's life, Ed and Jack sat down to discuss payback.

In three days of intensive skull sessions, Rathbone drew upon his vast collection of knowledge and facts, published and unpublished, that was available to him as a mining editor. Much of this news was insider information, often involving both sides of a dispute, and it was priceless. Ed laid before Jack intimate facts, secret events, in fact the detailed history of Johannesburg mining companies. Here was information that could never be learned elsewhere, secrets that even Barney Barnato was not privy to. The knowledge was so valuable that Hammond was able to conduct his business flawlessly.

Ritornello • An Interlude

LONDON • SEPTEMBER 1893

STEPHE Baden-Powell was devastated. The British Colonial Office had refused to pay the costs of Imperial offices from England to reinforce Cecil Rhodes' Chartered Company in Africa. It meant the Colonials would have to work out their own problems with King Lobengula, without any aid from the homeland. Stephe had missed the Little War in Uganda and now he would be forced to pass up the fracas in Matabele Land as well.

To further compound Stephe's woes, Sir Russell Baker, newly minted to brigadier general, failed to get his expected appointment as Inspector General of Cavalry. Instead he was dispatched to an obscure post in the Northwest District. It meant Sir Russell would have no influence at Whitehall to get his favorites promoted. After all these years, Major Stephe Baden-Powell needed a new mentor to salvage his sagging career. He felt as if his whole life had been a colossal waste of time.

The Matabele War

The 3rd Chronicle

King Lobengula

In 1868, Lobengula (circa 1836-1894) succeeded Moselekatze as king of Matabele Land and Mashona Land, which on his death then became Rhodesia. Lo Ben showed considerable friendship to white hunters and traders. In 1893, while trying to reassert authority over the Mashonas, he came into conflict with the Chartered Company.

11

Marching on Lobengula

MASHONA LAND • OCTOBER 1893

FORT VICTORIA, the frontier post they'd left a month ago, was an armed camp. And hotter than blazes, causing Blanche to complain of a headache. A war fever permeated the town like smoke from an approaching prairie fire. Wagon trains arrived daily bringing food, ammunition and medical supplies. There were horses now, horses salted against the *dikkop* sickness, which the British called blue tongue. Armed men galloped in the streets, yelling like excited schoolboys. The echo of gunfire from a nearby valley lent a sense of authenticity to the atmosphere. It was noisier than Globe during an Indian scare.

The Burnhams had no difficulty securing lodgings. The presence of Blanche and Rod told landlords that here were two Americans who would remain for the duration. The sight of Fred's gold assured them that the bills would be paid. Fred saw to the quartering of his burros and to the storage of his spring wagon and supplies. That's when he encountered Maurice Gifford.

"I've been looking for someone who's half horse and half jackrabbit," Gifford said. "You seem to be that man." Gifford held out his hand.

"I can ride as fast as any Apache," Fred said. "And comin down a mountain, I can beat a jackrabbit."

"Speaking of horses, you'll need a good one. Come with me."

They walked to a corral that flew the Lion Flag of the British South Africa Company, which the locals called the Chartered Company. Fred studied the mounts in the corral.

"See one?" Fred nodded at a high-stepping buckskin with a brown mane and tail, and zebra stripes on its lower legs. The horse had a white patch on its back.

"Good choice. Name's Zebra." Gifford pronounced the word in the British manner, ZEH-bra. A trooper issued Fred a saddle and harness. Burnham saddled Zebra and mounted so quickly that Gifford blinked.

"I dare say, that was remarkable," he said.

"Had a good teacher in Arizona," Fred said, laughing. Moments later they were riding toward a large tent at the edge of town. Fred guessed it was military headquarters. After the long wagon journey with the donkeys, it felt good to be mounted on a horse again—even if the saddle was English.

"Bain tells me you're tougher than anything that could happen to you."

"I wasn't meant to die by a Matabele spear."

"Everyone who serves the Chartered Company will share in the spoils of war," Gifford said. "Six thousand acres of land, twenty mineral claims and a share of Lobengula's cattle."

"The loot alone ought to draw every fifer, tootler and catgut scraper in Africa."

"Most are here already. There's one group from Australia. Quite a few Yanks and Boers came up from the Transvaal."

Gifford veered away and headed toward a dry stream bed.

"Those who don't join the Victoria Column must stay here to defend the women and children." Gifford halted by the dry spruit and reached into his saddle bag. "I hear you're a bang-up shot. Hit this!" Gifford tossed an empty tin can into the air.

Quick as a rattler, Fred unshucked his six-gun and fired, hitting the can. It fell to the ground and bounced. He fired again, hitting it a second time. A look of incredulity came over Gifford's face. Fred fired once more, splitting the can.

"Ruddy good. You'll do."

"What was that all about?" Fred asked.

"Just checking. Bain vouched for you, but some folks have been grumbling about boastful, conceited Yanks."

"Judge me by what I do. Too many gas-bags here."

Gifford spurred his horse toward the tent.

"You do have eyes like a hawk. Maybe you did shoot that oribi."

"Would you like to see a pair of hides?" It dawned on Fred that some visitors to the Zimbabwe Ruins had been spreading dandies. Inside the tent, Gifford introduced Burnham to Captain Harry White, a grim-faced man who was the commander of scouts for the Victoria Column. Fred was delighted that the British had the good sense to

The Matabele War

enlist scouts into the military service. It was certainly superior to hiring Indians.

"We've a need of riders with good reconnoitering abilities," Harry White said. "Gifford says you've seen service in the American West against the red Indians and he avers you're pukka."

"When scouting, I know the enemy is watching, so I avoid trails. I expect the unexpected and don't assume anything. I also make a go-to-hell plan. Beside that, I read sign and find fresh water and grass."

"Sounds tight as the bark on a tree."

"Harry, this Burnham chap is as gritty as fish eggs rolled in sand," Gifford said. "I can assure you he's got gravel in his gizzard. Bob Bain observed him on the veld and says he's an experienced outdoorsman."

"Welcome to the Victoria Scouts." White offered his hand. "I hear you've been mugging up on the Matabele."

"When dealing with the enemy," Burnham said, "it's good to know his customs, traditions and superstitions. Then you can predict what he'll do."

Captain White blinked. There was a grunt of approval from a bearded man working in the back of the tent. He seemed to be in charge of some armaments task.

"Burnham, meet Aubrey Woolls-Sampson," Captain White said. "He's a many-sided fellow." The captain said nothing about Burnham's rank or duties. Fred had secretly entertained hopes of being named chief of scouts, but he was willing to accept the fact that as a newcomer he would first have to prove himself in the ranks.

Gifford and Burnham rode back toward Fort Vic.

"Allan Wilson has been promoted to major. He'll command the Victoria Column."

Fred reached into his shirt-pocket and produced a plaited hatband.

"Give this to him for his new Stetson. Here's one for you too."

Gifford examined the workmanship and nodded in approval. "Captain Charles Lendy of the Royal Artillery has five Maxim guns."

Fred asked what a Maxim gun was.

Gifford said. "It has the firepower of about three of your Civil War Gatling Guns. Let Lendy himself tell you about it."

"It ought to be a great equalizer," Fred said.

"You'll like Captain Lendy," Gifford said. "He's the magistrate. His father was a major, his grandfather a colonel. He studied chemistry and he speaks French and German. He's a noted hunter and works

83

out every day with twenty-pound weights."

Fred decided that Lendy could pull his own weight.

As the pair rode into the rifle-range valley, they saw Captain Lendy supervising the training of gunners on the Maxim guns. Gifford offered Lendy the plaited hatband. While Lendy affixed it to his hat, he said, "Stick around, Yank, and we'll show you some action."

"How are Lobengula's men armed?" Fred asked.

"The usual," Gifford replied. "Assegai spears and bullhide shields. Some rifles too. Four years ago, Rhodes gave King Lobengula a thousand Martini-Henry rifles as payment for the minerals concession in Mashona Land."

"What's a Martini-Henry?" Fred asked.

"For forty years, the Martini-Henry has been the British Army's rifle of choice," Gifford said. "It's a halfway design: a breech-loading metallic cartridge rifle that uses black powder."

"It has a punishing recoil," said Lendy, "but the .45 caliber slug can penetrate two human bodies, inflicting horrific wounds." He said the rifle became obsolete in 1888 when Alfred Nobel invented smokeless powder.

"The Army began replacing the old Martini-Henrys," Gifford said.

Lendy added, "They now issue the .303 Lee-Metford, a five-shot magazine rifle that uses smokeless."

Just then Lendy's five Maxim guns erupted in a stentorian chatter that echoed across the rifle-range valley. Two hundred yards away, the targets shattered into fragments.

"Yank," Lendy said, "you've just seen the Devil's own paint brush in action."

Fred nodded, thinking about what might happen if these guns jammed and they were unhorsed behind enemy lines. On foot, they wouldn't last a week. If the Matabele could shoot like Apaches, Fred thought, they would face certain death. Here they were: a thousand whites riding out to do battle with a hundred thousand black warriors known for sacrificial courage in battle. Even with five Maxims, the odds were in favor of the Matabele impis.

"I'd suggest you say good-bye to your family tonight," Gifford said. "We leave tomorrow."

"Let's hope Captain Lendy here knows how to keep those Maxims working."

• • •

THAT NIGHT, Fred, Blanche and The Kid took dinner in the dining room of the Victoria House. Fred said nothing of the Column's impending departure until they had returned to their room and Rod

The Matabele War

was asleep. During their last hours in each other's arms, neither Fred nor Blanche had any inkling of what lay in store for them. They had no way of knowing that when they saw each other again, Fred's name would be famous from Scotland to Singapore, from Paris to Peking.

What Fred did learn that night was the reason why Blanche had been so irritable in recent weeks. She had missed two monthly periods and a doctor said she was three months pregnant with their second child.

• • •

IN A LAND WHERE the seasons were topsy-turvy, October 4 was a refreshing spring day. At headquarters, the gathered men were as noisy as cowboys in the pay line at the end of a cattle drive. Nearly three hundred eager men had lined up to sign the attestation roll, qualifying each for a farm, mineral claims and cattle. Burnham found the scouts grouped midway in the queue. He was joyous at the idea of being part of an organized scouting group in the military.

Led by Captain Harry White, the scouts signed the roll. Duncan Dollar, a twenty-eight-year-old farmer who spoke fluent Zulu, was named lieutenant of scouts. Burnham signed on line one hundred eighty-nine of the roll. After him came Pete Ingram, who gave his home town as Cottonwood, Iowa, not Montana.

"Look at this," cried Bain. "Pete's real name is Pearl."

There was laughter and Ingram stalked off in a fit of pique.

"Bain's not a Yank at all," said Art Cummings. "He's Canadian."

"By accident of birth," Bain said, looking miffed.

When Major Allan Wilson signed the roll, the bugler played mess call and the men ate their first meal courtesy of the Chartered Company. By mid-afternoon, the Victoria Column was formed up ready to march. Burnham mounted Zebra and Major Allan Wilson, looking like a Texian, rode alongside straining the dregs of a billy can of tea through a droopy walrus mustache.

"If you're as tough as that pony, you'll make some hard rides."

"I can run like a Nueces steer," Burnham said. "I can look right through a wall. And when I wear moccasins, I can't be heard at all."

"For a Yank, you're unusually modest," Wilson said tossing his head back. "I think I'm going to like you."

Burnham found himself drawn to this craggy British likeness of a frontiersman. Wilson was lean and square shouldered, a man with a powerful frame. He was the manager of a mining syndicate in Fort Victoria and had once worked with Johann Colenbrander for the Bechuana Land Exploration Company. People said he had won his commission in the Cape Mounted Rifles. Fred noted two things with satisfaction. Wilson was astride a larger version of Zebra and he was wearing Fred's plaited hatband on his Stetson. Fred decided Wilson was the kind of man who could be trusted.

The Victoria Column marched northwest toward Iron Mine Hill, the meeting point with the Fort Sally lot. They traveled through a wooded countryside dotted with basalt kopjes. A pair of vultures circled lazily in the sky, waiting for something to die. Ahead, a herd of elephants led by a big matriarch lumbered ahead, indifferent to the affairs of mortal man. Pete Ingram and another scout caught up. Though Ingram was four inches taller than Burnham, he followed Fred around like a puppy.

"This here's Bob Vavasseur," Pete said. "He's a friend of Maurice Gifford."

Fred nodded at the stranger.

"What's this bit about right honorable in Gifford's name?" Fred asked.

"That's a courtesy title," Vavasseur said. "His elder brother is an earl, so he gets a courtesy title." Despite a name that suggested French, Vavasseur's British accent proved he was English.

"Why has Gifford disappeared?"

"Called up north to scout for the Salisbury Column," Vavasseur replied. Fred's interest picked up when Bob said he was a friend of Johann Colenbrander. Vavasseur produced from his shirt pocket a hand-drawn map of western Matabele Land.

"I made this sketch after a visit to Bulawayo. I came up through the Mangwe Pass. It doesn't show much about Mashona Land."

"Why did Gifford go to Fort Salisbury?" Fred asked.

"There was trouble up north. Do you know William Brown?"

"I'm new here, Bob. Who's he?"

"He's a naturalist from your Smithsonian Institution."

"Oh? You mean Curio Brown." Fred had heard of Brown, mostly that he was an outdoorsman who had ridden the American plains.

"Brown was pottering around Fort Sally looking for fossils when this business happened, and he volunteered for the scouts. He helped Captain Burnett organize a team of well-mounted scouts, but Jameson and Forbes knocked them down."

"Why, for God's sake?"

"You don't know much about our Good Old Boy Net, do you?" Vavasseur said. "It's a longish sort of tale and awkward to describe, but the British believe that God's greatest creation is the English gentleman mounted on a thoroughbred horse. So they appointed as scouts several gentlemen of Fort Salisbury who weren't willing to

The Matabele War

join the common ranks, but who agreed to have a go at galloping about the hills a bit."

"What? Don't they choose the best qualified men?"

"It seems rather beyond arguing about. It's not the British way, old cock."

"Sufferin Shadrack," Fred said. "What a misbegotten idea."

"In light of events, Burnett was in a bit of an upset. Jameson and Forbes were adamant though, so he went base over apex and resigned. Then Curio Brown refused to join the Sally Scouts, saying those Hyde Park bushmen would get lost ten miles out on the veld. So Gifford had to nip up to Sally to pinch hit."

Fred began to wonder about the Salisbury crowd.

The next day Ingram's horse lost a shoe. Lieutenant Dollar sent Willie Posselt to ride with Fred on the day's scouting. Posselt was thirty-five, one of the few men in the column older than Fred. Major Wilson was thirty-five too, but of course he was the commander. Posselt was a meek game hunter from Natal who wanted to own a farm.

"What do you Yanks think of our war?" Willie asked. Posselt's expression appeared serious.

"To some people," Fred said, "we'll be perceived of as apostles of civilization. To others, we'll be freebooters and land pirates. To the Matabele, we'll be murderers and invaders. To the Mashonas, we'll be what a lion is to a jackal—the giver of offal and stray bones, welcome but not loved. To the historian in later years, we'll be proof of the continuity of evolution. To the young—the adventure-hunters of the world—we'll be considered as lucky to fall on stirring times."

12

The Ridgeback

RIDGEBACK • OCTOBER 1893

A WEEK LATER, a group of stragglers caught up with the Victoria Column. The latecomers signed the attestation roll six days after the main body. When they arrived, Major Wilson ordered a parade and roll call. There was a new scout among the latecomers. John Carruthers was a six-footer, about thirty, a former Cape Colony prospector who spoke Zulu. His eyes were deep set and shadowy, his ears floppy. He was a large man with a pugilist's big biceps. Fred thought the guy moved about with the enthusiasm of a small boy doing his chores. Because of his skill with the Zulu language, Carruthers was named sergeant of scouts under Lieutenant Dollar. Although well mounted, he seemed to know next to nothing of horses.

Fred smarted that night. The British seemed to regard foreign language fluency as the chief qualification for scouting. Fred believed that speaking the enemy's language should be a qualification for the intelligence department, not scouting. For fourteen years he'd trained as a scout, but until now he couldn't point to a single enrolled military campaign he had participated in. By the time he grew up, the West was won. This patrol was his first official military assignment, so he steeled himself to being a good soldier and a credit to family and country.

As planned, the Victoria Column met the Salisbury Column at Iron Mine Hill. The Sally group was in laager and Doctor Jameson was standing in a freight wagon. With him was a man Vavasseur identified as Sir John Willoughby. Vavasseur said "Digby" Willoughby held the rank of general, a courtesy title bestowed by the Queen of Madagascar. Willoughby was debonair, a man of charm attired in a splendid uniform. Burnham was suspicious of British rank and titles. He wondered if Willoughby—being a general and all—would

The Matabele War

be named commander-in-chief of the Combined Column. But that was not to be.

What happened next defied belief.

The tall, rangy and square-jawed Major Allan Wilson stroked his droopy mustache and sized up Major Patrick Forbes, the commander of the Sally group. In America, Allan Wilson would have passed for a Texas cowboy. Forbes looked to be every bit the plump urban English gentleman, cherubic and pink with a dapper mustache and curly brown hair. He appeared to be younger than Wilson.

The two majors, Wilson and Forbes, rode toward one another, circling on their horses, as wary as male lions from opposite prides. They saluted and began quarreling. Each claimed seniority and the command of the Combined Column. When it looked as if there might be a duel, Digby Willoughby whispered to Doctor Jameson, who shouted from the freight wagon. Forbes, an Imperial officer, would command. Wilson, a Colonial officer, would be second in command. Willoughby would serve as military adviser. Doctor Jameson, the administrator, was to be the political leader, the real power.

At roll call, the Combined Column numbered seven hundred whites, four hundred horses, thirty wagons, ten Maxim guns and two Hotchkiss artillery pieces. There were three hundred fifty Mashona camp-followers. If the two majors could overcome their rivalries, the Combined Column might give a good accounting of itself — specially with those ten Maxims.

They began the march west to Bulawayo—the Place of Killing, the kraal of King Lobengula and his numinous *konza* ceremonies. Fred and three other scouts were told to study the land, to spy out ambushes and to find water and grass. That afternoon they reported the land was wooded savanna with outcroppings of kopjes. There were no ambushes and there was ample water and grazing ahead. To Fred this was as much fun as galloping around the hills of Globe and the prairies of Tombstone.

• • •

A FEW DAYS LATER, the Combined Column neared the border of Matabele Land. Captain White told Lieutenant Dollar to ride with the scouts. Burnham, Ingram and Vavasseur were ordered to join him. Lieutenant Dollar and Ingram took the lead.

"What do you think of our little army?" Vavasseur asked.

"What am I supposed to think?" Fred replied. He didn't want to be thought of as a whiner. Then he saw the twinkle in Vavasseur's eyes.

"Our army consists of one commander-in-chief, three other commanders-in-chief, forty-seven major generals, fifty-three leftenant colonels, eighteen captains, twenty-two leftenants and six privates."

"And we are the six privates?"

"Dead right, old cock. By the way, watch out for Sergeant Jack Carruthers."

A dubious look crossed Fred's face.

"Carruthers has many friends. He used influence to become sergeant of scouts. He's the blue-eyed boy at Fort Vic, but he's a bitcher and a back-stabber. Be wary."

"I'll remember that. Thanks, Bob."

Fred wasn't worried about the likes of Carruthers. He could take care of himself in any encounter, regardless of his opponent's size. If Hunkey-Dorey Holmes had taught him the fine points of scouting, it was Dead-Eye Lee who had taught him the vile tricks of personal survival.

"Your pint-size won't you let you whip nobody in a dogfight," Lee had told him back in Wickenburg, Arizona, "so you'd better learn to use your knife and pistola."

Burnham's cheeks had reddened.

"Don't get your bristles up," Lee had warned. "Out West, you reach and fumble and that's a fatal weakness. Once we line our flues, I'll teach you how to use that forty-four. First, open a can o' air-tights."

Sharing a can of peaches was a treat and both men savored the flavor. Then began Fred's training in close-quarter shooting. Lee tossed the empty tin can into the air and yelled, "Shoot."

Fred drew, fired and missed.

"Son, when you go for your hardware, then and there you change from peacetime to wartime," Lee said. "All of a sudden, you find yourself operating against terrific resistance—like runnin in thick muck or swimmin in molasses." Burnham had felt that way when he fled from pursuing Apaches on Pinal Mountain south of Globe.

"You need to learn about the Magic Circle," Lee said. "Gunfights is a curious mixture of two things: the eye and the intellect. Most people have not disentangled these two points." Lee explained that gunfights could be divided into close-range and long-range fights, each conducted in a different way.

"In a short-range fray, the fighters mix it up inside a Magic Circle of about seven yards—call it twenty feet. The requisite here is speed—you don't aim, you jest point. If you're acquainted with your blue lightnin, you blaze away. If you're the fastest, you'll see sunlight tomorrow.

"Beyond that Magic Circle, a different set of rules applies," Lee said. "Outside that circle, aim is important. And good aiming is a mental process. When the fight happens outside the Magic Circle, there are an amazing number of flat misses, even by expert gunfighters. Here it is not the first shot fired that matters. What counts is the first shot that goes home. So you got to learn two kinds o' shootin: close-up snap-shootin and the cold, calculated aim at longer distances."

Burnham had learned his lessons from an expert.

• • •

LOUIS BOTHA had described a long, LimZam Ridgeback that divided the Limpopo and Zambesi watersheds. To their right, all the streams flowed north toward the Zambesi River. To their left, the water flowed south to the Limpopo. According to Vavasseur's map, the ridgeback ran west to Mangwe Pass. If they followed this ridge, they should come to Bulawayo.

According to Fred's wild guess, they were at least a hundred miles from Bulawayo. If they made ten miles a day, that meant two weeks of travel, with time out for battles. Counting the Shonas, there were a thousand men to feed — plus six hundred oxen and four hundred horses. It was obvious they were going to have to use the countryside as their commissary for food.

Ahead, a broad valley spread out before the column. The approach was gentle and it was two hours after noon before the Combined Column entered the valley proper. Fred asked permission from Lieutenant Dollar to ride ahead and study the terrain. Dollar nodded.

Fred rode at an easy pace thinking about what Vavasseur had told him about the Matabele people. Before the Matabele nation was founded, they were Zulus living in Natal. The Zulu king sent his eldest son, T'Chaka, south to the End of the World, where the Great Rock reaches out into deep blue water that thunders. T'Chaka was told to bring back information about the white men in flaming red coats who fought with guns fastened to spears.

T'Chaka studied the soldiers drilling at Cape Town and saw that the principle of cold steel and close contact was the deciding factor in their method of warfare. When T'Chaka returned, his father died. As king, T'Chaka formed his army into companies and made them use the stabbing spear and shield. Cowards were beheaded.

Moselekatze, a Zulu warrior, who had distinguished himself in battle rose to the rank of general. Then he differed with T'Chaka over a war with the Swazilanders, who outnumbered them ten to one. Calling his warriors together, Moselekatze said, "Why return to King T'Chaka to be beheaded? Let us conquer a kingdom for ourselves."

Moselekatze led his followers across the Drakensberg Mountains to what became the Transvaal. They wiped out most of the tribes between the Orange and Limpopo rivers and established an independent kingdom. Contact with the Boers led to a bloody war. The Voortrekkers pushed north and after many battles defeated Moselekatze. The defeated blacks crossed the Limpopo into the land of the Mashonas, whom they easily conquered.

On the death of Moselekatze, eldest son Lobengula took the throne. Every year a huge feast and dance—called the *konza*—was held in his capital at Bulawayo. At the conclusion of the dance, King Lobengula stepped into the center of the *kraal* twirling a spear which he then hurled over his head. In whatever direction the spear pointed when it alighted, there the warriors were to wage war for the coming year.

King Lobengula's *impis* maintained their strength by keeping their spears wet from the blood of their enemies. That how the Matabele provided a splendid example of what brave, determined and organized men can do against a larger population of unorganized and cowardly people. The Mashonas possessed equal natural resources. They matched the physique of the Matabele. The Shonas lived in impregnable hills with kopjes and caves that were well protected by thorn bush. Yet they were enslaved by the *impis* of Lobengula and forced to pay tribute. The Matabele fought with spear and shield, but they had something the Mashonas lacked—courage. In Fred's mind, that made the Matabele formidable.

Burnham was about three miles ahead of the scouts when he spotted longhorn Matabele cattle, scrawny beasts, scarcely more than skin, bones and hide. Fred had heard that the Africans kept a hundred cows on a pasture that would feed fifty. In the Matabele scheme of values, mere numbers of cattle—not their fatness and health—was what determined wealth. So the Matabele overgrazed the veld and ended up with hospital cattle. These animals were being tended by adolescent herdsboys, and that gave Fred an idea. If he could cut a few of those critters out of the herd, the Combined Column could eat red meat tonight instead of second-rate slaughter oxen.

He was about to set the spurs to Zebra when something caught his eye. On the far side of the valley, hidden by a grove of mopane trees, a group of men was resting on the hillside. They were beyond the sight of the Combined Column, but they had a good view of the valley and cattle. Fred climbed a kopje to study the men in his bring-'em-up-close glasses.

One glance convinced him that he was in Matabele Land. These men wore warrior headdresses. Their bodies were striped with white daub. Each warrior held a leaf-shaped shield of bullhide. Behind the shields he saw what looked like assegais—Matabele stabbing spears—and Martini-Henry rifles. The warriors were well-armed and positioned to ambush the Combined Column.

Cecil J. Rhodes & Dr. Leander S. Jameson

Cecil John Rhodes (1853-1902) was Britain's empire builder in Africa. He planned a Cape-to-Cairo railway. He controlled Kimberley's diamonds through the De Beers Consolidated Mines and owned much of Johannesburg's gold. He was the premier of the Cape Colony and administered Rhodesia through the British South Africa Company, which his friend Dr. Leander Starr Jameson (1853-1917) managed.

13

Treachery in High Places

BECHUANA LAND • OCTOBER 1893

ONE HUNDRED FIFTY MILES southwest of Bulawayo, Jimmy Dawson rode into the kraal of a mining concession on the Shashi River. It was Wednesday, October 18, and for the past week, Jimmy and three Matabele envoys had been traveling south from King Lobengula's capital at Bulawayo. Jimmy, sweat-stained and dog tired, reined the mule-drawn Cape cart in front of the Tati Gold Mining Company.

Dawson's mouth was as dry as trail dust and he had an itch for a sundowner. He dismissed the Matabeles to find their own place in the nigger kraal. Or sleep on the hay pile. Dawson didn't care. After all, savages couldn't take rooms at Edwards Tati Hotel.

Anyone who knew his way around Africa could see the Matabeles were *indunas* of high rank. They wore loincloths of spotted leopard skins and on their belts hung monkey tails. Their hair was braided in the dual rings of the *ring kops*. Two of the them, Ingubo and Mantuzi, were generals, impi commanders. The third, Ingubogubo, a brother of King Lobengula, held the rank of ambassador.

Lobengula hired Jimmy Dawson to convey the three envoys to Cape Town to attend a peace parley with the British high commissioner. Sir Henry Loch had invited them to the *indaba*. In a locked strongbox chained to the floor of the Cape cart was a gift of copper trinkets, gold figurines and uncut diamonds—peace offerings from King Lobengula to the Queen's high commissioner. The four men had ridden a hundred fifty miles in six days.

Tati was a concession southwest of the Shashi River that Lobengula had granted to Englishman S.H. Edwards. One reason for Lobengula's generosity was that he didn't own the land. The Shashi River was a disputed border area between Matabele Land and King Kha-

The Matabele War

ma's Bechuana Land. Everyone except Edwards knew the border between Bechuana Land and Matabele Land was the Shashi River, which ran south, then eventually turned east to flow into the Limpopo.

Considering Dawson's leisurely speed, they would arrive at rail's end in Mafeking on November 2. Allowing three days for the train trip to Cape Town, the blacks could expect to arrive at their destination on Sunday, November 5, and meet Sir Henry the next day. Dawson figured that schedule was fine. By then, Doctor Jameson should be camped in Bulawayo with Lobengula in chains.

Dawson bedded down his mules and headed for the pub where a knight of the spigot dispensed white mule. By good fortune, Dawson met his old chum, Fred Selous, the white hunter. Selous was downing a nipperkin and soon they were swapping prattle. Tumblers of neat whisky were repeatedly toasted to Home, Wives and Sweethearts. The thirsty pair tossed off white lightning as if Satan had flung open the door to Hades. Never did it occur to Dawson to tell Selous why he was traveling south. Nor did Selous feel obliged to explain his presence.

Selous was waiting for Commandant Pieter Raaff whose Tuli Rangers would arrive in a day or two to meet Colonel Hamilton Goold-Adams and his Bechuana Border Police. They would join forces for an assault from the south on Bulawayo's soft underbelly.

In time both men were too roostered to exchange any meaningful news. They staggered over to Edwards Tati Hotel to gorge down a meal, then tottered off to their rooms to puke and collapse into oblivion. Dead to the world, neither man heard shots fired that night.

Dawson was up first. He awakened long after dawn with a splitting headache. Downstairs, he sipped hot tea and toyed with eggs poached in hippo lard. Then he repaired to the Tati Mining Company's corral to collect his mules, Cape cart and niggers. The blacks were nowhere in sight. The guards were coarse looking fellows armed with loaded rifles. They identified themselves as members of the Bechuana Border Police.

"Where's my niggers?" Dawson bellowed.

"Jest a minute, Guv," the sentry said, "I'll get the leftenant of guards."

Moments later, a BBP officer arrived. After being questioned, the officer led Dawson to a foul, fly-ridden manure pile behind the barn.

"These yours?" The lieutenant, his eyes as drab as oysters, was unconcerned, but a mangy hound seemed endlessly fascinated. Lying dead on the dung heap was Mantuzi, shot in the small of the back. Blowflies buzzed around, laying maggot eggs in a pool of blood oozing from an ugly Martini-Henry wound. Farther away was Ingubo, face down in straw and muleshit. The back of his head was caved in. The lieutenant kicked at the hound as it lapped blood from Ingubo's wound.

Dawson's body shuddered.

"Where's the other one?" he cried hoarsely.

"In the barn. We got him chained."

Dawson lurched to the gate and puked.

"I must see your commander."

Ten minutes later, Jimmy Dawson was standing in front of Colonel Hamilton Goold-Adams, an imposing figure in his Imperial uniform. As best he could, Dawson explained to the colonel what had happened.

"Call Selous," Goold-Adams barked. "And have the guards remove the manacles from Ingubogubo."

For half an hour Goold-Adams questioned the two men, trying to find out how the king's envoy had been manhandled and two indunas murdered. Next he grilled the guards. To them, it was a simple case of mistaken identity. The Bechuana Border Police had seen three strange niggers. They were dressed up fancy and probably up to no good.

The guards shouted an order to halt, but the niggers ran, so the guards fired. Mantuzi was hit in the back and fell dead. When Ingubo reached for his comrade, a second guard clubbed him with a Martini-Henry, felling him too. Ingubogubo, who witnessed the double tragedy, decided it was hopeless to resist. He submitted to capture and was chained.

"That's the whole story, Colonel."

Goold-Adams was beyond furious. Without doubt, an enquiry would be held. A misadventure of this magnitude could leave a blemish his military record.

"Bring the king's brother to me," Goold-Adams said. An orderly ran outside, returning a few minutes later with the lieutenant of the guards, who snapped to attention.

"Where's Ingubogubo?" Goold-Adams yelled.

"That nigger done run off, Colonel. We untied him like you said, and he nipped off. At the rate he was going, I don't think he'll stop until he gets to Bulawayo."

Dawson remembered the Cape cart. In a flash, he ran out the door. When he got to the stable, it was too late. His worst fear for the treasure box was realized.

The Matabele War

The lock was broken and the strongbox was empty.

Counterpoise • Equilibrium

Matabele Land • October 1893

BURNHAM STOOD on a kopje and waved his bandana to attract Lieutenant Dollar. Moments later he saw the scouts spur their horses. Soon they were at his side.

"What ya see?" Fred asked, offering his field glass.

"Bloody *kaffirs* herding cattle." Dollar said. K*affir*, an Arab word, meant *infidel*, but the British and Boers used it to refer to Bantus, much as Americans used the term nigger, which the British also freely used.

"Look, over by those mopane trees," Fred said. "See the Matabele. They're armed with rifles and stabbing spears. With the shields they're carrying, they won't be able to manage either weapon. Let's steal some beeves."

Dollar seemed wary but the idea of red meat raised a cheer among the scouts. When Dollar nodded, Burnham, Ingram and Vavasseur galloped into the valley. The warriors stood up for a better look. Fred galloped zigzag toward the herd, firing into the air to spook the cattle.

The herdsboys ran for a kopje and the scouts were in control, so Fred dismounted. He studied the Matabele *impi* in his glasses. They still hadn't moved.

"Let's herd 'em back."

"Red meat tonight," Pete shouted.

The cattle were unaccustomed to horses, and they responded slowly. Some of them stampeded, creating a cloud of dust on the veld. While trying to halt the stampede, the scouts lost sight of the warriors on the far side of the valley. The warriors rose en masse and began running in silent pursuit, forming the horned-crescent formation.

Major Wilson had briefed his troopers about the horned-crescent. It was a Zulu tactic that symbolized the head and horns of the Cape buffalo. At the center, representing the bone-hard forehead, were the elder, more experienced warriors. On the flanks, protruding like horns to snag the unwary, were the younger men, fleet runners who circle and trap an enemy so the head can crush it.

A motion on his left caught Fred's eye. The youngest, the most fleet of foot, ran in single file to snare the scouts in a trap. Fred fired to warn the scouts and the Matabele shouted a brittle "jee," the killing cry. A dozen bullets thudded into the rocks and trees around Fred. The scouts abandoned the cattle drive and fled for the cover of

97

two kopjes.

The warriors halted to let the herdsboys round up the cattle. Fred sat on a kopje, watching. Then he heard the sound of galloping hoofbeats. The shooting had attracted more scouts and the whites were back in control.

Moments later Fred counted ten horsemen in his field glasses. They were being led by Captain Campbell of the Salisbury Scouts. The Matabele began a controlled retreat and Fred galloped in pursuit of the beeves. He wanted the critters not merely to feed the Combined Column, but as much to deprive the enemy of its ambling commissary.

"Look out, Fred." Ingram's cry was urgent.

Over his shoulder, Fred saw warriors running toward him from the north, trying to isolate him. He dismounted by an ant heap and ordered Zebra to lie down. Cries of "jee" echoed across the veld.

"They yell to work up their courage," Bob Vavasseur shouted. Fred tried his best imitation of an Apache war cry. At that moment, the Salisbury Scouts began firing. Fred watched the Matabele fire in volley style, just like the British redcoats had done at Yorktown. Long plumes of white smoke spewed from the Martini-Henry rifles. A thrill surged through Fred's veins at the prospect of dancing with death. A Martini-Henry bullet struck the ant heap, tossing dirt into Fred's eyes. He wiped away the dust and saw a broad-shouldered black man six-feet tall running toward him.

A loincloth of yellow cheetah hide, spotted with brown dots, said this guy was a regimental commander. The *induna* cast aside his shield and assegai and raised his Martini-Henry. A puff of smoke from the black man's rifle was followed by a hot sting. Fred touched his left temple and felt a trickle of blood. He dropped to the ground, hoping that the bullet had only grazed him.

"Are you all right?"

Fred didn't recognize the voice. A bullet bounced off the flat of a rock and ricocheted in the air with a thwang. Another bullet thudded into the ant heap, this time too close for comfort. The nearness of the miss induced new respect in this *induna's* marksmanship.

The enemy commander was coming at Fred at a full run. The ice in Fred's blood vessels turned to fire, then back to ice. It was exciting and mind-numbing at the same time. He raised his carbine and fired several Bogardus snapshots. The brittle crack of his 30-30 carbine seemed like pistol shots amid the violent reports of the Martini-Henry rifles. Twice more he fired and his carbine was empty. He reached for his six-gun, but the shouting ceased, soon replaced by wailing.

The Matabele War

The Matabele warriors fell back. Ahead, the body of the *induna* lay sprawled on the ground twenty feet from the ant heap. The death of this regimental commander had taken the taste for blood out of the *impi*. At that moment, the sun disappeared behind a hill and darkness quickly followed. Fred led Zebra out to recover the assegai and shield of his deceased opponent. A thought crossed Fred's mind, something Hunkey-Dorey Holmes had told him. *It was a tactic practiced by Attila the Hun. You kill the enemy leader to demoralize warriors in the ranks.*

"You got five," Pete cried, "but Captain Campbell got killed."

By count, twenty-two Matabele lay dead. While the Salisbury Scouts lifted the body of Captain Campbell onto his horse, Fred, Pete and Bob galloped out and captured two hundred head of enemy cattle.

Ritornello • An Interlude
JOHANNESBURG • OCTOBER 1893

JACK HAMMOND inspected all the mining properties in Johannesburg. Not just Barney Barnato's gold mines, but everyone else's as well. After a trenchant survey of the Witswatersrand's formations, Hammond recommended that Barnato acquire the deep-level claims which were available at low cost.

Barnato was preoccupied with family affairs, social matters and the temptations of the stock market, and he ignored Hammond. A colossal ego was sorely injured. Unless Barnato acted on this advice, Hammond would be unable to earn the bonuses they had agreed on. Jack hadn't come to Africa to be treated like a lackey.

Counterpoise • Equilibrium
MATABELE LAND • OCTOBER 1893

TROOPERS OF THE Combined Column were overjoyed at the sight of the captured cattle. With every meal, the supply of slaughter oxen dwindled and the food ration of ox-meat was limited to even days in the week. The aroma of fresh beef being roasted over an open fire filled the night with cheer. Fred was tired, but he was elated that even in moments of sheer panic he had felt that special thrill at the prospect of danger. *Why is this lure of peril so exciting and titillating?*

When Sergeant Carruthers told Major Forbes that Captain Campbell was dead, Forbes exploded. He gave Major Wilson a severe tongue-lashing, complaining that they'd lost a good man while gaining nothing. Forbes acted like it was Burnham's fault. He punished Fred by restricting him to the wagon train for a week.

The next day Fred learned about the assegai he had captured. He held his war prize by the shaft and examined the sharp steel blade. It was made with excellent craftsmanship and was well balanced.

"T'Chaka himself designed it," Vavasseur said. "It was the Zulu answer to the redcoat bayonet."

"In skilled hands, it looks like a nasty weapon."

"A Matabele will shove one of these blades into your chest. When he pulls it out, the force sucks your life blood right out of your body. It's a horrible way to die."

• • •

FRED ALREADY knew about knives. During his summer outing in 1881 with Dead-Eye Lee, he had practiced throwing his Bowie knife until he could bury the blade in a saguaro cactus.

"Knife throwin is a stunt," Lee said. "Knife fightin is a science, the fastest, bloodiest kind of personal combat. The fatality record exceeds that of firearms. It's blood chillin because of its precision. That's why armies use swords, sabers and bayonets in combat. The sight of a man armed with a knife can send a brave man fleeing in terror."

Fred recalled a bloody fight in a dark livery stable in Prescott where a Finn used a Bowie knife to carve up a cowboy nervously waving his pistol.

"Remember this," Lee said. "The fighter who loses a finger or thumb may get killed for his carelessness."

That afternoon Lee tied one end of a bandana to his left wrist and the other to Fred's. Standing in a marked off circle, they used blunt sticks to have a go in a rough-and-tumble melee. Because of his experience and strength, Lee won the initial rounds. In time Fred got the hang of it, and he used his smaller size and greater speed to outwit his mentor. That night around the campfire, Lee described the tactics of knife fighting.

"Wrap a coat or blanket around your left forearm," he said. "Use it to entangle his blade. If all else fails, take the blade between the bones of your forearm. Twist your arm to hold your enemy's blade while you drive your own steel into his gut. Plunge deep and rip up, always up."

• • •

AFTER A WEEK OF IDLE grazing, Zebra was fat and sassy and Fred was eager for a good gallop. Dollar assigned Burnham and Vavasseur to scout the left flank. The scouts rode quietly, keeping an eye peeled for Matabele.

"What kind of fight will Lobengula put up?"

"Lo Ben doesn't want war. His battalions are ill-equipped and his men poorly trained. They are ravaged by smallpox."

"The Matabele weren't fleeing when we chased their cattle."

"Cattle are their most sacred possession. They'll fight to the end to protect their skinny old cows."

"A cattle cult, eh?" *Good to know the enemy customs.*

"I dare say that Lo Ben knows where we make laager each night. His runners carry the news of our location to Bulawayo."

"How about those reports that Lo Ben was camped at the city limits of Fort Victoria with an impi prepared to attack?"

"The tale has winsomeness in London, but it's utter rot."

"What do you mean?" *Vavasseur sure is a gold mine of information. Better keep pumping him.*

"On your honor not to tell tales out of camp?"

"Yes, but why?"

"Events in the hinterland often must be shrouded in a little confusion. Those reports of Matabele atrocities were products of Harris's imagination."

"Who's Harris?"

"Rutherfoord Harris is the secretary of the Chartered Company. Down in Cape Town, he dug into musty files for twenty-year-old missionary letters on atrocities. He changed the dates and cabled them off to the British press in London to fan indignation against the Matabele. Rhodes needed support for a war the Crown didn't want. With his old letters, Harris was able to generate the public outrage that Rhodes needed."

"You're saying England doesn't want war with the Matabeles, but the British South Africa Company does?"

"When the war became inevitable, public opinion required that Imperial forces step in. That's why we're in such a hurry to get to Bulawayo."

"Hurry, I thought we were just shogging along?"

"We must plant the Lion Flag of Rhodes' Chartered Company on Lobengula's doorstep before Colonel Goold-Adams gets there from Mafeking with the Union Jack. If his Imperial troops arrive first, Matabele Land belongs to the Crown. If we get there first, the treasure belongs to the Chartered Company."

"Can a commercial company own a country?"

"Rhodes has a royal charter. It's rather like those charters granted to your Crown Colonies in America."

Fred suddenly understood what was meant by The Chartered Company. *It really is a land grab.* While riding back to the Combined Column, Vavasseur said, "Watch yourself. Carruthers is in an upset over the death of his friend, Captain Campbell. He's spreading rumors that Campbell sacrificed himself to save your hide.

"That's cock and bull!"

"A bit of a rotter, that Carruthers. He told the troopers that you cut the ears off some of the pickanin herdsboys while you were stealing cattle."

"Bob, you know I never got within fifty yards of those herdsboys. Hey, Jack Carruthers wasn't even with the patrol. He was back at the Combined Column. What does he know?"

"He says it comes from an eyewitness. What's more, some of the chaps believe him."

Fred Burnham never did 'fess up about those two black ears. They came not from the herdsboys, but from the big *induna* in the cheetah skins. While Fred kept the induna's shield and assegai for the Burnham Collection, he presented the dead induna's ears to the commander of artillery, Captain Lendy. It was payback for Manyao's threat to cut off Charley Lendy's ears.

14

Maxims at the Shangani

MATABELE LAND • OCTOBER 1893

JOINING THE SCOUTS on Tuesday, October 24, was a Cape native who spoke English and Zulu. Jan Grootboom was a keen-eyed man six feet tall. Seeing this broad-shouldered, black man astride Contango, a brown bay, made Fred think of Allan Quatermain's faithful Zulu guide. If a living embodiment of Umslopogaas existed, Grootboom was that man. As the scouts followed a baboon trail, Vavasseur rode alongside Fred.

"If this map is accurate, the Shangani River is ahead. Once we cross, we'll be in Matabele Land."

Half an hour later, they saw the Shangani flowing north toward the Zambesi River. During the dry season, it wasn't much of a stream, but ten-foot cut-banks testified to the its ferocity during the rainy season. No ox wagon could cross here.

"Let's ride over where the crocs are stalking those wildebeests," Fred said. "Maybe we'll find a crossing." The scouts turned left toward where the LimZam Ridge crested. Groves of trees and patches of brush blocked their view, but Fred found a route through a meadow, avoiding any spot where the Matabele could lie in ambush.

"That open veld up ahead is a good place to laager," Fred said. "There's a decent river crossing not far away. Let's send Jan back to Major Forbes with a map. Then we can nose around here to see if the Matabele have any tricks planned."

Late in the day, Forbes hadn't arrived. They decided to ride in a semicircle to try to cross the column's wagon tracks. *Hadn't Jan gotten through?* Vavasseur saw smoke rising from a valley to the north.

"Bad business," Bob said. "Forbes has laagered in the mopane trees."

"Lord, spare us." It would never occur to Fred to look for camp in the woods. Brush concealed the columns, but the odds favored the spear over the rifle. As the scouts rode into camp, Fred saw the Victoria and Salisbury Columns had made two laagers. Forbes and Wilson still hadn't come to terms. Forbes had laagered the Salisbury Column in brush. Allan Wilson formed the Victoria Column into a hollow square of wagons in an open meadow south of the Sally lot. Lendy had mounted a Maxim gun at each corner of the two squares with two Maxims in reserve.

The troopers were building fires for the evening meal. The Shonas laid out a *scherm*, a crude fence of thornbush, that connected the laagers. Ordinarily, the Shona would be bedded down with the horses and oxen inside the *scherm*, but tonight they had built campfires outside.

Battle of the Shangani River

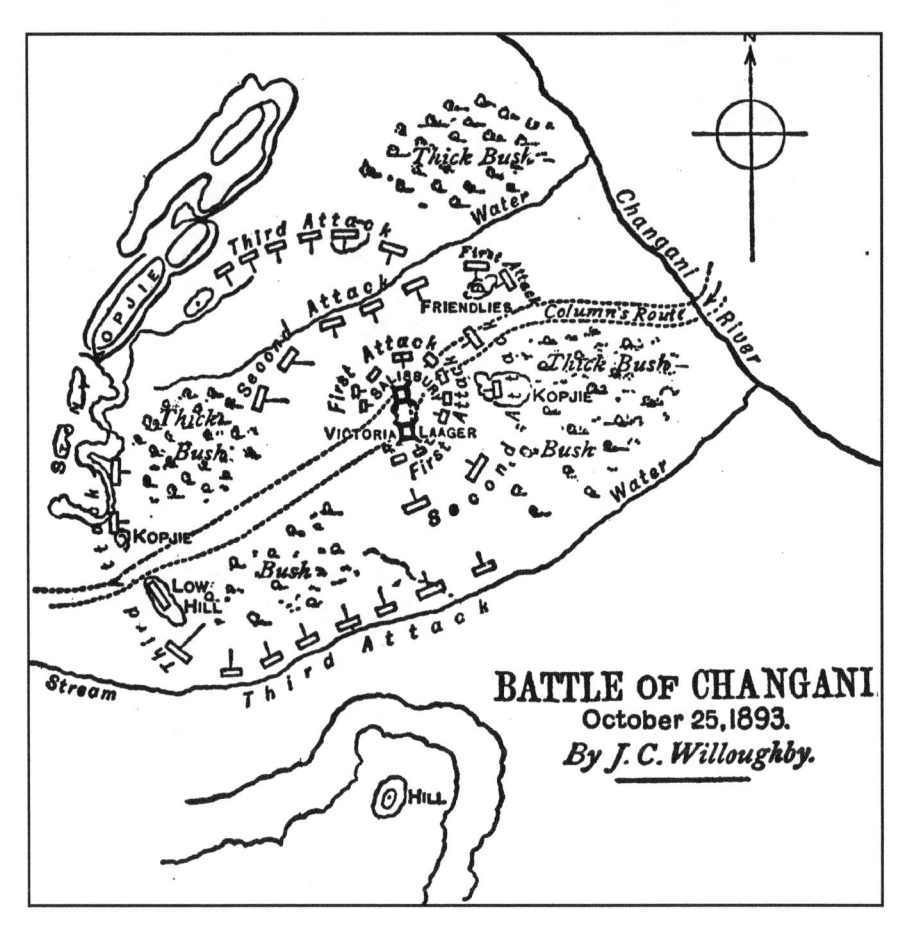

BATTLE OF CHANGANI
October 25, 1893.
By J. C. Willoughby.

The Matabele War

During the day's march and under covering fire from the Combined Column, the Shonas had raided a Matabele village and rescued some of the women and children who'd been captured in the Matabele attack on Fort Vic. The Shonas were holding a celebration outside the scherm, singing and drinking stolen Matabele beer. The cacophony could be heard for a mile.

The singing and dancing made Fred nervous so he rode out of camp to the grassy campsite he'd chosen earlier that day. It was as quiet as a cemetery so he hobbled Zebra, laid down on a blanket and fell asleep.

• • •

FIVE HOURS LATER, a distant cry of mortal agony rent the silence. Rifle shots echoed across the veld, and a bugle sounded a panicky call to arms. Fred saddled Zebra and rode toward the Victoria laager. A thrill surged through his loins and his nerves tingled with expectation. *This is war for real*. When he arrived, the air reeked of gunsmoke and fresh horse piss.

Inside the laager, men took up positions between the spokes of wagon wheels. Other troopers milled around in confusion, their bodies silhouetted by the dim light of campfires. Burnham found a space between the wheels of two wagons. But what to shoot at? The Zulus were not like the Apaches of Arizona who, fearing the loss of their spirits, avoided hostilities after dark. The Matabele were night-fighters. The light of the campfires provided little aid in seeing black men in the ebony darkness. The occasional muzzle flash of a Martini-Henry rifle fired by an overeager Matabele was greeted by return shots from a dozen Victoria riflemen.

Fred looked over his shoulder at the Salisbury laager. Shona fires were burning, quickly rekindled from coals. Fred saw groggy husbands leading wives, children and goats to the *scherm* between the two laagers. By the light of a campfire, Fred saw a lone warrior, his body painted with white stripes, waving an assegai. As he ran toward them, he yelled the killing cry "jee."

He had made his way almost to the cook line when a stentorian burst from Charley Lendy's Maxim gun cut him in half. A trooper standing next to Fred spattered the most awful-smelling puke all over. It was Fred's introduction to the firepower of the Devil's paint brush. It was, in fact, the first time in the world the Maxim had spoken in anger.

Fred forced his mind to reason out what was happening. He decided the Matabele attack was directed at the Mashonas camped in the brush scherm between the two laagers. When the Shonas had collapsed into drunken stupors and their campfires burned down, the Matabele had launched a surprise assegai charge.

In time, the bruised-apricot glow of the false dawn brought reality to the scene. To the north, toward the Salisbury Column, Fred saw a row of blacks charge the cattle kraal, with its captured livestock. The Maxim gun barked, cutting down all but one—a young girl. *Hey, these are friendlies. The Shonas are running into the line of fire and are being shot down as hostiles.* The howls of dying men were replaced by the shrieks of women and children in their death throes. That's when Fred lost his dinner.

The light of dawn soon rendered the panorama in detail. There were no Matabele to be seen. The gunfire played out. The Maxim gunner sprayed a parting burst at the kopjes. Ricocheting bullets made an appalling racket and maimed a few hostiles. A thought struck Fred. *Holed up in the kopjes, the Matabele are safe from rifle and Maxim fire. If they remain there to starve us out, the Combined Column's need for water will become acute. They hold the key to victory.*

As the sun burned off the morning fog, the chief induna ordered his men to launch a daylight attack. The Matabele, armed with assegais and shields, began the brittle "jee" killing cry. *If they had attacked in the fog, when we couldn't see to shoot, they would have prevailed.*

Daylight gave accuracy to the Combined Column's rifles and the chattering Maxim guns cut down the attackers like tin ducks in a shooting gallery. That morning Fred learned two powerful lessons. The Maxim gun really was the Devil's paint brush. The other lesson buttressed his view of the black impis' courage. *Don't ever accuse the Matabele of cowardice.*

For an hour, the impis attacked in wave after wave. They charged the muzzles of the rifles and Maxims. The squander of human life was appalling. Shortly after 7 a.m., the Matabele launched their biggest assault, a thousand men advancing. They came at a run in such numbers that the whites were hard-pressed to repel the charge. A second column followed the first. There were so many attackers there was danger the two laagers might be overwhelmed by sheer numbers alone.

A new sound burst forth, drowning the small-arms fire. A Hotchkiss gun opened up, belching a great plume of white smoke. A charge of grape shot from the seven-pounder hit the front of the ranks, downing a swath of men sixty feet wide and bringing the advance to a halt. Charley Lendy's white bulldog, Ruff, barked and ran back and forth behind the Hotchkiss. He wagged his stub tail furiously. For Ruff, it was like maneuvers at Fort Vic.

The Matabele War

Within a quarter of an hour, the Matabele reformed and launched another assault. This time, they discarded their stabbing assegais, concentrating on Martini-Henrys. A bullet splintered the sideboard of the wagon above Fred'. He ducked and his eyes focused on an incredible sight.

A tall Matabele induna wearing a large headdress, his face painted red and white, was leading an advance of nearly two thousand warriors crying "jee." It was the ultimate horned-crescent charge, aiming to win or die trying. It was awe-inspiring and terrifying, ghastly and exciting all at once. The whites poured a steady hail of rifle fire at the blacks, but only a few fell and the Matabele continued to advance. Fred heard the Maxim operator swear—his gun was jammed. The next Maxim was too far north to be of help. The advance continued. So many men were shouting the killing cry that it sounded to Fred like someone had kicked a nest of angry hornets.

Then Charley Lendy's Hotchkiss gun opened up. The seven-pounder, loaded with a canister of grape-shot, was timed to explode in midair. The new danger of shrapnel raining from above created a wholly unexpected reaction among the Africans. The warriors fired wildly in all directions, as if trying to defend themselves from flying witches.

As more shells exploded, a panic broke out in the enemy ranks. Several of the warriors fired at the duds, which exploded, blowing arms, legs and heads about like popcorn. That ghastly scene aggravated the panic and the warriors stampeded to every point of the compass. The Maxim came alive again, pouring a hail of lead at the retreating enemy and the momentum of the Matabele impi collapsed. The blacks seemed to evaporate.

In time Burnham became aware, with a latent sense of relief, that he hadn't heard a shot fired for more than a minute. Silence told him the battle really was over. The defenders rose to stretch, happy to be alive and suddenly hungry. They'd been under attack for three hours.

Fred stood on the seat of a trek wagon to get a look at the battle scene. If the Matabele were as vengeful as the Apaches, there'd be survivors out there among the dead waiting to kill any unwary whites intent on looting.

Fred's eye caught a movement. An exquisitely attired induna stepped out from between two large boulders and walked up beside a tree. He stood there, holding his rifle, his assegai and his bullhide shield as he surveyed the field of battle. Fred raised his rifle, planning a long shot.

I'll get him before they do. Fred took aim, but behind him a horse reared, throwing its rider who cried in alarm. Fred lost sight of the induna. When he looked back, the man was gone. He scanned the kopjes with his field glasses, searching for the enemy leader, but the man was not to be seen.

A slight movement in a tree caught Fred's eye and he trained his glasses on the lower branches. There was a motion among the leaves. Fred guessed the induna was hiding. *Just pepper a few shots into the branches and that headdress, rifle and shield will become a part of the Burnham Collection.* The induna dropped from the tree, jolting to a stop two feet off the ground. Fred focused his field glasses again and saw the black body hanging from a primitive noose. Biting his lip, Fred leaned on his rifle, like a cane.

That induna might be untutored, but he was no coward.

• • •

AFTER BREAKFAST, the troopers rode out to study the scene of battle, to count the dead and to collect the spoils of war. Blowflies swarmed around the wounds of the dead. Vultures and hyenas arrived from some unknown hell to compete for a ghastly feast. Fred rode out to survey a stack of mean and oozy corpses.

He spent two hours tracing the battle lines and studying the Matabele fighting gear. On returning to the laager, he estimated the death toll at six hundred.

"It'll run higher," Bain said.

"I didn't see any wounded."

"The Matabele carry off their injured, though most will die from a lack of medical attention."

"Bob, Captain Lendy tells me this is the first time the Maxim gun has been used against live infantry," Fred said. "I really think it will change the nature of warfare."

"You mean to say it was a resounding victory for the Maxim and a decisive defeat for the assegai?" Bob asked.

"Even the weapons of the Civil War have become obsolete."

Casualties among the Chartered Company numbered six wounded and two dead. The Shonas fled to Forts Victoria and Salisbury, their thirst for battle slacked.

Back at the laager, a Matabele prisoner revealed that two impis remained in Bulawayo to guard Lobengula. Four impis had confronted the Combined Column. The *induna* who hanged himself was the commander of the Always-Ready Regiment. Fred was dumbfounded at how freely the Matabele responded to questions of great value. No Apache, even if tortured and hideously disfigured, would ever reveal a single scrap of information.

The Matabele War

What astonished Burnham was the news that three impis had marched south from Bulawayo to meet Colonel Goold-Adams. Nobody in the Combined Column seemed alert enough to ask how a mere soldier in the Insukomeni Impi knew that Goold-Adams was coming up from Mafeking. *That knowledge speaks volumes for Lobengula's intelligence apparatus.*

After the noon meal, the scouts learned that several indunas had drowned themselves in the Shangani River rather than return to Bulawayo in disgrace. The surviving warriors had scattered into the trees and kopjes. At an after-battle debriefing, Lieutenant Dollar told the scouts that the Combined Column had been outnumbered five to one.

"Do you know why the Matabele lost?" Fred asked.

"They believe it is cowardly to use rifles in battle," Vavasseur replied. "At first, they used their assegais. Only at the end did they turn to their Martini-Henrys."

"They believe that if they raise the sights, the bullets will travel faster," Lieutenant Dollar said. "So they end up aiming too high."

"The niggers think that the tighter they hold the rifle, the farther it will shoot," Sergeant Jack Carruthers added.

"Those things may be so," Burnham said, "but they lost because they're in transition. If they'd settled on a cold-steel charge in the foggy night, we'd be dead and they'd be dancing over our slit bellies. If they'd learned to use their rifles, they could starve us out. But they tried to balance a nine-pound rifle and a heavy bullhide shield and use an assegai, too. It can't be done."

"Listen to the Apache fighter," Carruthers scoffed.

"If the Matabele had been Apaches, Sergeant, you'd be tied upside down on a wagon wheel with your brains roasting over an ironwood campfire."

109

15

Hotchkiss at the Bembesi

MATABELE LAND • NOVEMBER 1893

THE NEXT DAY, the scouts returned from a recon and found the Combined Column watering the horses and stock at the Bembesi River. Fred described an ambush awaiting ahead. Art Cummings and Andy Main pleaded with Major Forbes to turn south and laager in the meadow that Fred had marked. Forbes nodded slowly and issued the order somewhat reluctantly.

What happened next belongs to the fog of war—what instructors at military academies call the *friction factor*. When the Combined Column turned south, the Matabele scouts mistook the white outflankers on the right for the advance guard of the Combined Column. They waited for the column to enter the mopanes, believing the ox wagons were unwittingly blundering into their ambush. By the time the blacks understood the column had turned south, it was too late. The whites had gained the advantage.

In an hour, the Combined Column outspanned and laagered in one of the finest defensive positions in eastern Matabele Land. All around them was open country. The nearest bushes were a quarter of a mile away, giving the whites a free line of fire and offering no protective cover for the blacks, should they attack. Cape friendlies built a cattle scherm. All the Shona friendlies were gone.

At 1 o'clock, with the sun shining through cotton-ball clouds, Major Forbes ordered mess call. The troopers were forming in line to eat when the bugler sounded the alarm of an enemy attack. The Cape boys abandoned their scherm-building and sought shelter inside the two laagers. From the onset, this battle was a real corpse-and-cartridge occasion. The air was hot and thick with bullets.

Fred heard the blowing of bugles and the shouts of officers yelling orders. White soldiers dashed about, searching for their weapons and running toward battle stations. Burnham took up his post at the rear wheel of a trek wagon. He saw a blaze of flame issue from the regiment's rifles. His view of the enemy was blocked by the Salisbury Column laagered to the north. Major Allan Wilson rode up on his bigger version of Zebra.

"I want volunteers."

A trek wagon was pulled out of line to make an opening for Wilson's volunteers. Fred laid down the Martini-Henry issue rifle and picked up his Winchester carbine. Mounting Zebra, he rode out to catch up with Major Wilson.

"Forbes won't get all the credit this time," Wilson yelled over the din of battle. Burnham could scarcely believe what he was hearing.

Sweating profusely, the commander of the Victoria Column galloped north, leading a small group of men into the thick of the action two hundred yards away. Fred was pondering Wilson's jealousy when he heard a commotion behind him. He looked over his shoulder and his heart skipped a beat. Horses and oxen from the Victoria laager were escaping from the unfinished cattle scherm. If the Matabele were to perfect a stampede—as the Apaches surely would—the whites would be unhorsed in the heart of Matabele Land. *For that mistake, the penalty is death. I'll never see Blanche and Rod, or the unborn baby. I hope the end will be swift.*

Fred spurred Zebra to warn Major Wilson. As he drew alongside, the rattle of Maxim fire drowned out his voice. Ahead, he saw a large induna leading an assault. Suddenly, the hairs on Fred's neck stood out. Running behind their leader, wearing war paint and carrying shields, were more Matabele soldiers than he had ever seen. They were formed into an unwavering line in the deep veld grass, their horned crescent formation spread over the open meadow for nearly a mile. The blacks, screamed "jee" and ran toward the Salisbury laager.

Their charge was answered by a peppering of rifle fire, followed by the heavier, staccato burst of the Maxim guns. Hundreds of blacks fell. Still the horned crescent rolled across the veld like an ocean wave. Seemingly nothing could block it.

"My God!" Wilson cried out. "Thousands of them."

"Major—" Fred tried to warn his commander about the escaping horses, but an explosion from the Salisbury laager cut him off. It was the Hotchkiss. A moment later, a shrapnel charge from Charley Lendy's cannon exploded over the left flank of the horned crescent. A score of Matabele fell, dead or wounded. More Hotchkiss shells exploded. The acrid smell of cordite mingled with the reek of horse manure. The young blacks on the left flank of the horned crescent

111

crumbled, broke ranks and retreated toward the Bembesi River.

The center of the impi—the older, more experienced warriors—continued a stern assault. A shrapnel charge from the Hotchkiss exploded over the right flank, dismembering a dozen attackers. Like the grape-shot cannons of the American Civil War, each shot from the Hotchkiss gun cleared a swath twenty yards wide of all humanity. Survivors fled to the trees to fashion nooses and hang themselves. Fred could scarcely believe his eyes.

That's when Captain Lendy turned his attention to the center of the horned crescent, the symbolic head of the Cape buffalo. In quick succession, the Hotchkiss barked three times. Shrapnel charges exploded over the center of the black impi, and the regiment began coming apart. Panic stricken, the elder warriors ran in circles while others tried to fire at the incoming artillery shells.

Then the Maxims found the range and swept the Matabele down like blades of grass before a farmer's sickle. The sun augured mercilessly on this scene of dismemberment and destruction. Unnatural noise filled the air, a sonic horror. Hyenas and vultures awaited joyfully. As dying men evacuated their bladders and bowels, the combined stench of human piss, shit and death was overwhelming.

Three times more the Matabele regrouped to launch attacks, and thrice more the Hotchkiss broke up the horns of the crescent and then the head. Finally, the Maxims opened up in to mow down the survivors. It was the worst military defeat that Burnham could conceive of, and he was sickened at the frightful squander of human life. Then he recalled the escaping horses.

Burnham looked back at the Victoria Column, blood racing. Two men were chasing the fleeing stock. One was Captain Henry Borrow, the adjutant of the old Pioneer Column, the group that had opened Mashona Land in 1890. Borrow was well mounted and doing a splendid job. It was the other rider who astonished Fred. Digby Willoughby was astride a bay horse and riding as if they were pursued by lions. With pistols in each hand, he drove back a score of running Matabele who tried to capture the galloping horses. He then maneuvered the animals toward the Bembesi River, a resourceful act because after a good gallop thirsty horses will always stop to drink. Fred relaxed knowing the stampede was ended.

• • •

IF THE MATABELE commander planned a fifth assault that day, it never came. The firing died away and in time the troopers rode out to survey the battlefield. Within half an hour, the area had returned

The Matabele War

so much to normal that a herd of zebra began crossing the Bembesi River.

The number of dead was enormous. At least eight hundred bodies lay in the field, some warriors blown apart by artillery and machine gun fire. The wounded appeared to number equally high. The ultimate count was that fifteen hundred blacks died as a result of the forty-five-minute engagement. The officers called roll to assess casualties: four men killed and seven wounded.

This time there weren't enough black survivors to carry away the wounded. Almost all the dead had Martini-Henry rifles and each black soldier was well supplied with ammunition. But it was the assegais, beautifully made and sharp as razors, that the white troops prized. Greedy men soon squabbled over the spoils of war.

In mid-afternoon, the sky clouded over and a thick, opalescent fog settled over the veld. Once again the tactical advantage shifted to the blacks. The white men returned to the protection of the laagers.

A wounded prisoner freely confessed that elements of five regiments had massed for a combined assault. At one time or another, as many as five thousand warriors had taken part in the assaults. Three regiments—the Ingobu, the Imbezu and the Insukomeni—had been defeated with a heavy toll. The Imbezu and the Insukomeni were annihilated. Before all of this was known, Fred penned a note to Blanche:

So insolent and egotistical were the crack regiments of Lobengula that they refused the aid of other regiments and said they would show the white men what true fighting really was. The other part of Lo Ben's army was told to stand by and watch. The Matabele charged in splendid shape and with wonderful pluck. Nothing but death could stop them, but under such fire as we poured in, a bird could not have escaped. In a few moments the crack regiment was no more. Only a handful of them were left.

Major Forbes walked up. "Today's battle confirms my opinion of the Matabele as inferior to the Zulu."

"They were brave men," Burnham said. "You couldn't ask more of any man on the field of battle."

The grim-faced Captain Harry White spoke next.

"If we had walked into that Matabele ambush, Major Forbes, it would have been us who'd gone down in defeat."

Forbes smiled. "That's what I have you chaps for: to warn me."

Turning to White, he said, "Tomorrow I have need for your best men for an important patrol. Have three of them report to me at dawn."

113

Battle of the Bembesi River

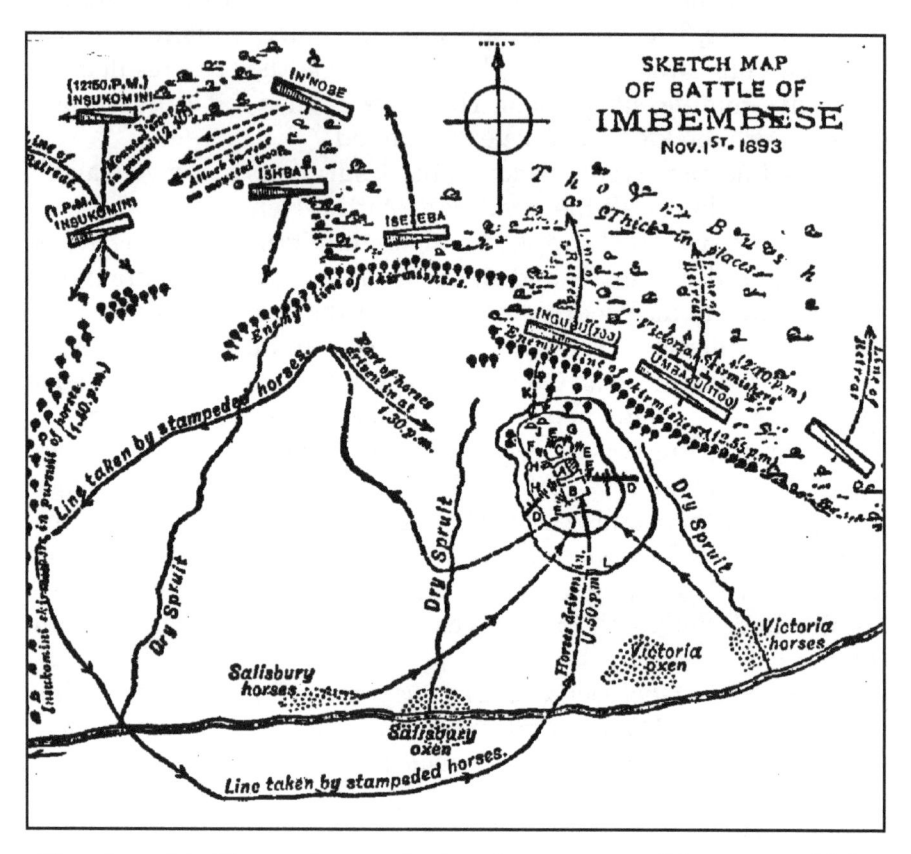

Despite a big Konza dance, the battle was a terrible waste of life.

16

Lo Ben's Konza Kraal Aflame

MATABELE LAND • NOVEMBER 1893

ACROSS THE Bembesi River, it was Texas with trees. But there were no Apaches to harass them. Nearing Bulawayo, the scouts came in for the heavy work of the campaign: creeping into the night, cutting their way through enemy lines, watching and listening, killing those ahead and getting a shower of shot in return. The scouts were told to find Bulawayo—lacking that they were to locate Colonel Hamilton Goold-Adams' spoor as his Imperial Column moved up from Mafeking.

"Look for the Thabas Induna," Bob Bain said.

"The what?" Fred asked.

"The Mountain of the Chiefs. It's the main feature east of Bulawayo." Zebra snorted and a flock of ostriches trotted off to safety. For two hours the scouts rode, but they saw no Thabas Induna.

"Let's catch a kaffir and force some information," Ingram said. "Bob speaks the lingo."

In a kraal ahead of them, elders were tending goats. When the scouts galloped into the scherm, the menfolk scattered, but an old woman balancing a clay jug on her head couldn't run. She was so frightened of the horses that she dropped her water jar. Bain dismounted and squatted in front of her, studying the broken jug. He observed the prelude of silence essential to African decorum, then he began to speak, in the soft, polite Zulu language. He spoke of things he had seen on a visit to Bulawayo. The woman overcame her fear and began talking.

"She has a son," Bain said. "He's a soldier in the Insukomeni Regiment." He switched. "Where's the Thabas Induna?"

"There," she said, pointing.

"What? Burnham knew some Zulu. "That mole hill? It's only

Thabas Induna: the Mountain of the Chiefs

three hundred feet high, a flat mesa."

"The Matabele haven't seen the Rockies," Bain said. Then to the woman: "And that smoky haze is Bulawayo?"

"Yes, the home of King Lobengula."

"Would Auntie advise calling on the king?"

"He has taken his wives and cattle and trekked north. But there's an impi in Bulawayo that would be delighted to feed you to the crocodiles."

Bain handed the woman a gold coin.

• • •

MAJOR FORBES blinked on learning that King Lobengula had abandoned Bulawayo, but he got downright angry and swore when he learned the scouts had made no effort to find Goold-Adams' spoor. Forbes ordered Sergeant Jack Carruthers to lead a search party to hunt for him. Later in the day, Carruthers returned empty handed.

The next morning sounds like distant thunder rolled across the veld. Minutes later, a column of brown smoke rose from the direction of Bulawayo. Was Goold-Adams fighting his way into Lo Ben's kraal? Burnham wondered why Major Forbes didn't lead the Combined Column in an attack on Bulawayo. The major came toward him. *Maybe I should ask.*

"Burnham, take two chaps and ride ahead. See what's going on in Bulawayo. Find Goold-Adams' spoor."

Bain's horse was lame, so Fred asked Willie Posselt to join him. *Willie ain't much for airin his lungs, but that's a favorable trait.* Burnham also took Ingram and Grootboom. As they rode, the column of smoke rising over Bulawayo turned out to be four columns merging into a single column. More explosions were heard.

The scouts were south of the Thabas Induna and Fred could see that the mesa was sharply uplifted, making it easier to identify. *This land looks like southern California, particularly Orange County south of Anaheim. It's wild and savage like that.*

"I think Lobengula's warriors are burning the city," Posselt said.

The Matabele War

Fred wrote a note.

"Jan, take this message to Forbes. He'll be laagered for mess by the Koce River. We'll ride south to look for Colonel Goold-Adams' spoor. Be sure you tell him that."

Grootboom grinned and galloped away—the only black man in Matabele Land mounted on a horse.

The scouts crossed a stream that Willie thought might be the Umguza River. An hour later, they were southwest of Bulawayo. They saw the spoor of Matabele cattle but no wagon tracks from Goold-Adams. They halted to talk.

"We know he hasn't gotten this far," Burnham said. "Let's ride into Bulawayo. The Matabeles won't expect us from the west."

Ahead, flames licked at the roofs of pole-and-dagga huts. Multiple stinks assailed their nostrils. Columns of brown smoke arose from adobe buildings. A muffled black powder explosion erupted from a building, which settled to the ground, enveloping the area in yellow dust.

"Must be Lobengula's powder magazine," Fred said.

"I wish it were the king's hoard of gold, ivory and diamonds."

As they entered the kraal, they smelled fresh manure and the one-of-a-kind rotten potatoes stink of putrefying human flesh. No one paid heed to three white men riding into town. Black men dashed among the buildings that went up in a blaze. Fred started to spur Zebra to a gallop.

"Wait!" Pete cried. He dismounted to raise his rifle.

"What'cha see, partner?"

"A little target practice on top of that building."

Fred trained his glasses on a European-style building.

"Hold your fire, Pete. They're white men."

"Aw, shucks."

The scouts rode at an easy gait toward the building, one of the few structures in town that hadn't been put to the torch. As the scouts rode up, the two white men scrambled down from the tin roof to greet them.

"I'm Jimmy Fairbairn, and this here's Bill Usher. Are you gents from the Imperial Column?" Fairbairn was skinny.

"We're from Jameson's Column," Posselt said.

Fred recalled that Louis Botha had told him Usher and Fairbairn were white traders, bartering calico, trinkets and trade goods for rhino horn, elephant ivory and gold.

"Join us," Fairbairn said. "We have food."

It was cool inside, and the scouts sat down to a leg of mutton, cold boiled potatoes and hot tea.

117

Fred was struck by the irony of their situation. *Here we are eating lamb in the Place of Killing—the great konza kraal of the Matabele King—as it is being consumed by flames. Ebony men dash about, yelling and plundering the treasury, others drinking the king's beer. And we are daubing jam on bread as if we were in a Yorkshire tavern. Soon the great konza place of Lobengula will be no more. What were the words of Allan Quatermain when he entered the capital of the defeated King Twala? Ah, yes.* "The eyes of mankind are blind to the discredited. He who is defenseless and fallen finds few friends and little mercy." *How prophetic.*

The traders pressed the scouts for the latest news. Jimmy Fairbairn was talking to Willie Posselt when Pete Ingram interrupted: "How come Lobengula didn't feed you guys to the crocodiles?"

Bill Usher replied, "The king left Bulawayo seven days ago, when he learned of the defeat of his impis at the Shangani. He took seven thousand cattle, his three hundred wives and two impis of the royal guards. Before the sun sets, I suspect the Matabele will kill us."

After the meal, Fred asked Pete and Willie to carry a message to Forbes. Fairbairn wrote a letter of profound gratitude to Jameson. In the shank of the afternoon, the two scouts rode out of Bulawayo and Burnham laid down to snooze.

It was clear and sunny at nine a.m. when Captain Harry White showed up with the Victoria Scouts. The main force of covered wagons arrived at two p.m. The troopers decorated the trek wagons with gay bunting, and the drum major played the bagpipes as they formed dual laagers by the home of Johann Colenbrander. The king's interpreter was in Palapye visiting his wife, Mollie. Under an acacia tree in the Colenbrander compound, Jameson supervised the raising of the Lion Flag of the Chartered Company. With that act, the occupation of Bulawayo was accomplished.

The look of apprehension that Doctor Jameson had worn for a week was replaced by an expression of relief. Matabele Land, the key to central Africa, now was in the hands of Rhodes' British South Africa Company. It was Saturday, November 4, 1893, one month to the day since they had left Fort Victoria.

• • •

ON SUNDAY, troopers poked through the ashes in search of plunder. Relaxing in front of Fairbairn's Store, Fred was mending a stirrup and feeling lonesome for Blanche when Doctor Jameson rode up.

"Burnham, you're a better man than Gifford told me. You are the greatest tracker I've ever met. You took Bulawayo single handed."

Fred looked up, feeling flattered. "Thank you, Sir."

"I've watched you closely during this campaign," Dr. Jameson

The Matabele War

said. "What a fellow you are. If we'd had ten men like you, we'd have finished this campaign in half the time."

"I'm honored," Fred said, laying down the stirrup and standing.

"I have most vital information to communicate to Mr. Rhodes," Jameson said. "Can you get through Mangwe Pass to Tati? There's a telegraph station there. I must send messages to Mr. Rhodes."

"Give me maps and I'll find Tati."

"If you succeed," Jameson said, "the company will double your land grants and mineral claims."

Fred knew what Doctor Jim needed. The occupation of Bulawayo had been one thing. Now it was important to tell the world, to show everyone that the Chartered Company had defeated the Matabele without the aid of Imperial troops. Fred was being chosen to deliver that message.

"See Willoughby for the maps," Jameson said. "Take Ingram along. He's a hard rider too. Take as many horses as you need. Speed is important."

"We'll leave within the hour." Burnham arose.

"Wait until dawn," Jameson said, remounting.

"By day, an enemy can draw a bead on you from a great distance," Burnham said. "I prefer traveling at night when a rifle is of no value." *Why are Englishmen loath to travel at night?*

"I won't have my reports ready until later," Jameson said. "The land south of here may be occupied by hostiles."

"Have your messages ready by midnight," Fred said.

"Once this campaign is over, we should do well to have a chat," Jameson said and rode away.

While Ingram chose a remuda of horses, Fred called on Sir John Willoughby. On examining the maps, Fred discovered that it was the same distance from Fort Vic to Bulawayo as it was from Bulawayo to Tati. He was being asked to gallop in hours the same distance the Combined Column had spent a month traveling.

"Fig Tree," Willoughby said, "is forty miles southeast of here. Thirty miles later, turn south through Mangwe Pass. Tati is eighty miles south of there. It's just across the Shashi River in Bechuana Land." The trip was a hundred fifty miles over territory Fred had never seen.

Shortly after midnight, Fred picked up the dispatch bag from Doctor Jameson. Fred and Pete galloped out of Bulawayo, trusting to darkness to avoid Matabele guards. Each rider had four horses. They rode southwest down the gentle grade of the LimZam Ridgeback. To the southeast, in the early light of dawn, they saw the outline of kopjes. That would be the Matopo Hills. After passing Fig Tree—which was just that, a large cannibal fig—they rode south through The Nek.

Later in the day, they arrived at Mangwe Pass, a narrow tree-lined swath that cut through the western Matopo Hills. The clearing in the trees was a hundred feet wide and appeared to be a couple of miles long. The scouts halted.

"I don't like it, Pete."

"Me neither, pard. Natural spot for an ambush."

Fred recalled something on Digby Willoughby's map. The Empandeni Mission Road ran west, around Mangwe Pass. The route was longer but through open land. They rode west and penetrated bush country too thick to pasture cattle, trusting it to be devoid of any Matabele. At dusk, they saw a rider on a horse. Pete yelled.

"Who's there?" The voice was British.

"We're from Bulawayo with dispatches from Doctor Jameson. Are you from Colonel Goold-Adams' column?"

"No, I'm Johann Colenbrander. Rhodes sent messages to me in Palapye to be forwarded to Doctor Jameson. Has he arrived in Bulawayo yet?"

"Yes, Sir. Have you seen Colonel Goold-Adams?"

"I passed him yesterday," Colenbrander replied. "His wagons are heavily loaded and moving slow."

As they spoke, Fred sized up the famous Boer hunter. *He's not the jolly, rotund, blond I expected.* Instead, Fred saw a tall and thin man. Colenbrander wore a serious look, and had dark hair growing in a widow's peak like Fred's own hairline. He appeared to be a few years older than Fred.

"Watch about yourself down south," Johann said. "Gambo's impi is mucking around there. On the way up, I hopped the twig and avoided him. Be wary of Gambo. He is Lobengula's best general."

After sharing a cup of tea, Fred and Pete rode on. Differences in hut construction told them they were now out of Matabele Land. All night the rain pattered down.

Toward dawn, they smelled smoke from campfires. It sounded like a wagon train in laager, so Fred and Pete let out cowboy yells to identify themselves. When they entered the laager, Goold-Adams was eager to hear news from Bulawayo. Over a breakfast of Boer meal and bully beef, the scouts summarized their adventures.

Goold-Adams said, "When we crossed the Shashi into Matabele Land, Gambo's impi pinned us down. They gave us a stiff fight, but a thunderstorm ended it. In the attack, Fred Selous was wounded."

Goold-Adams pronounced the name like Sah-LUH. *The great*

Selous? Wounded? It must've been some battle. The rain came down heavier and Goold-Adams offered to let Fred and Pete catch forty winks in a covered wagon.

"Thanks, Colonel, but we must get to Tati," Fred said. "Oh, I've a message for Commandant Raaff. Can you direct me to him? And I need a horse re-shod. Could you manage that?" Goold-Adams called the blacksmith.

Pieter Raaff was tending to Selous' wound. Burnham blinked. *This little guy is Commandant Raaff? The man who led Raaff's Rangers in the Zulu wars?* Before Fred was a man of handsome features, with strong, forceful eyes and a straight, clean nose. He was older than Fred by a dozen years. Though was a Boer, he spoke with a British accent. He had a large bushy beard and he parted his curly-red, shoulder-length hair in the middle. More surprising, he was two inches shorter than Fred and he couldn't weigh more than a hundred pounds. Finally, his boots would fit a Chinese princess whose feet had been bound. Fred decided Raaff was a strange piece of work.

While Raaff read Major Forbes' letter, Fred chatted with Selous. His wound was minor and Fred studied the famous white hunter who'd been the inspiration for Allan Quatermain. Selous was blond and handsome, maybe ten years Fred's senior. He had lived in Matabele Land for twenty years and served as guide for Doctor Jameson's Pioneer Column which Cecil Rhodes had sent to Mashona Land in 1890. Then it was time to leave. The scouts rode south in a steady rain, smelling like wet chicken feathers. The night crawled by like an injured inchworm. Three hours before dawn on Wednesday, they crossed the Shashi River and rode into Tati.

The journey that took Jimmy Dawson six days in a Cape cart took the Americans fifty-one hours. While Pete stabled the horses at the Tati Mining Company corral, Fred checked into Edwards Tati Hotel. The men slept in luxury under real sheets. When daylight arrived, the sky was covered by thick clouds. Before eating, they walked over to the telegraph office.

"Here are important dispatches for Mr. Rhodes," Fred told the telegraph operator, a little man with a happy, wine-fed face.

• • •

BULAWAYO • NOVEMBER 1893

DAVID BOTTOMLY sat in his tent feeling knackered. The sun blazed outside, and the day was perfectly horrid. After the fire last week that leveled the royal kraal, a cloud of dust had settled on man, beast and wagon train alike.

Dave Bottomly pondered the peculiar turn of events that had landed him in this godforsaken place. Dave was no soldier; that was for dang sure. Granted, he was a stunt kind of chap with a curious itch to live it up a bit. But he was no rotter.

If only he could remember that wowser of a night. Even after six weeks, a fog obscured the mystery eve. What he did recall was waking up in the Salisbury Gaol with the world's worst hangover. His mouth tasted like he'd dined in the cat's sandbox. Gor-blimey, it must have been one paralytic evening. Yes sir-ee, bob.

Later that morning, Magistrate Patrick Forbes had charged him with attempted murder. The specifications alleged that during a shooting melee, he had wounded five Shona niggers. Bottomly drew a blank on that count. In any even, it was a tight corner.

After a severe slating, he got a choice of facing stern British justice or enlisting in the Salisbury Column then forming. To Dave Bottomly, the prospect of galloping on the veld and pot-shotting at niggers was preferable to hard labor, or a hangman's noose if those unfortunates died. So he enlisted and now he regretted that clanger, wishing he'd gotten off with three months in Salisbury's Greybar Hotel.

Laying on a packing box in front of him was a diary bound in red silk. When sunset brought relief from the heat of day, Private Bottomly picked up his pen.

Friday, November 10. Oh, the heartlessness of Jameson's camp. No more of the Chartered Company for me. Our rations are tea and Boer meal, no coffee or vegetables. The meal is not enough and we have to live on kaffir corn. There is a lot of discontent in the two laagers. Nothing is known of the Imperial Column, but I believe they have no rations and I don't know what will become of us. A patrol of two hundred mounted men has been warned to go out tomorrow morning, but I don't think it will go. The very idea of two hundred men attacking the Matabele impis in country where it is almost impossible to take a horse — it's absurd! The officers made such a fuss objecting to it that Major Forbes had to give in. He wants to do everything himself before the Imperial Column comes up.

Dave Bottomly fell asleep, little suspecting that so far everything had been cakes and ale. The worst of this campaign was yet to come.

Wilson's Last Stand

The 4th Chronicle

17

Chasing King Lobengula

BULAWAYO • NOVEMBER 1893

RED AND PETE arrived in Bulawayo as weary as shipwrecked sailors. Cecil Rhodes had included in his cabled instructions to Doctor Jameson orders to reward the two messengers who carried those dispatches. But Doctor Jim, as he greeted Burnham, was so elated that he absently laid Rhodes' telegram aside.

"Burnham, old chap, you're like a drop of rain in a desert," the administrator said and told Fred that Colonel Goold-Adams had arrived two days earlier.

"Commandant Raaff got here yesterday," Doctor Jim said. "He joined Major Forbes on a patrol to bring King Lobengula back. Would you and Ingram nip up there to scout for them?"

Fred's face dropped. For once he felt he had earned a rest. He had been in the saddle day and night for a month. Doctor Jameson laid his hand on Fred's shoulder.

"I know you're knackered, but this task is vital. We must fill a power vacuum. If we don't get the king, there are impis that may rise and destroy us."

Burnham nodded. "Guess my feathers got ruffled."

"What a fine fellow you are. Leave in the morning. Meanwhile, you and Trooper Ingram come to my tent right now. I'll give each of you a physical exam." Jameson checked temperature, heartbeat and pulse and declared each of them half biltong and half rawhide.

Forbes had a two-day head start and the scouts faced thirty miles of catchup. It rained all day on Thursday, but Fred and Pete followed them. The trail Lobengula's seven thousand cattle had left was as wide as a boulevard. Shortly after dawn Friday, the scouts caught up with the Shangani Patrol and they reported to Major Forbes.

"Eat breakfast and sleep in a trek wagon," Forbes said. "Raaff is second in command."

"Raaff?" Fred said. *Why not Major Wilson? Why didn't Doctor Jameson sent any of the other scouts? Where are Captain Harry White, Lieutenant Duncan Dollar, Sergeant Carruthers, Bob Vavasseur, Willie Posselt, Art Cummings and Andy Main? Except for Pete and me, the only men in this patrol who have scouting experience are Bob Bain and Johann Colenbrander.*

On the fifth day in the field, the patrol came to the banks of the Bubi River where the trail of King Lobengula played out. A messenger from Doctor Jameson galloped up with an order recalling the patrol to Shiloh for food newly arrived with Colonel Goold-Adams.

The men gleefully turned back, arriving two days later in a driving rainstorm. While the endlessly patient Captain Bill Napier tallied the supplies, the men bolted down a hot meal. There was food for three hundred men for ten days—at three-quarter rations. There was enough Boer meal to feed the blacks while they walked back to Bulawayo.

"At inspection," Forbes said, "we will weed out the sickest men. We'll keep the horses and let the men walk to Bulawayo."

Three more days of marching out of Shiloh, the re-provisioned patrol had advanced a mere seventeen miles. Many of the horses were knocked up. Forbes ordered a hundred thirty of the feeblest men to take the lame horses back to Shiloh with the supply wagons, two of the Maxims and the heavy Hotchkiss cannon. The patrol's food and ammo would be carried on pack horses, with the two remaining Maxims mounted on mule-drawn carriages. The patrol was now slimmed to the ablest one hundred sixty men. During a scouting patrol that day, Burnham discovered spoor, indicating the presence of King Lobengula. He also heard that Gambo's impi had moved up from Mangwe Pass to the Shangani. Bummer.

• • •

BRITAIN'S VERSION of Custer's Last Stand began on Sunday, December 3. Burnham and Colenbrander rode as scouts. Fred was still taking the measure of this noted white hunter and interpreter. He was still trying to unlink his mental picture of a cherubic blond Dutchman who turned out to be tall and slim, with dark hair. So far, Colenbrander seemed to have spizzerinctum.

They were south of the Shangani River, seventy-five miles downstream from last month's battle. This time the odds were incomparably worse. The small patrol had only two Maxim guns to fend off a large enemy force.

125

That afternoon Fred and Pete rode out to torch some Matabele huts, but their adventure was cut short when Zebra threw a shoe. They returned to the patrol.

Clouds had gathered and at 4 o'clock Forbes ordered the men to make camp five hundred feet from the south bank of the Shangani. Forbes' decision violated rainy-season custom, which was to cross a river before making camp, before the river became flooded.

Fred knelt by the water to wash and let Zebra drink. The Shangani was about a foot deep and there was spoor of cloven hoofs, ample evidence of Lobengula's recent presence. The aroma of food being cooked reminded Fred he hadn't eaten since breakfast. Forbes rode up.

"I've been looking for you, Trooper Burnham. Major Wilson's going on patrol. He needs you as scout."

Fred shrugged and stood. Forbes saw that Zebra was favoring the hoof that had thrown a shoe.

"Here, take Omega. While you're away, I'll have your horse reshod." Fred climbed onto Forbes' horse, a coyote dun beige with a flax mane and tail. Omega was a well-fed horse that loved to prance and rear.

"Pete, save some grub for me."

"Okay, pard."

Fred caught up with Major Wilson about six hundred yards away. The squad had splashed across the Shangani.

"You left your coat," Wilson said, "but with Omega you're well mounted."

"I hope so, Sir. Zebra is a tough horse to follow."

Fred felt good to be riding with this big, rough-hewed soldier. He forgot about food, but it suddenly seemed odd that a twenty-man patrol should have eight commissioned officers. Two would be the normal complement.

Fred glanced around. All were from Fort Vic. There were none of the Sally Lot or Raaff's Rangers. Maybe Wilson had chosen men he trusted.

Wilson gave an order to trot. By the time they'd gone two miles it was dark. Flickers of fire around them told Fred they were passing through a Matabele camp. Boys were milking cows, and the women and children were grinding maize for *sadza*, the Matabele ration. *Hey, this isn't an impi. These people are civilians, ordinary people.* The sound of hoofbeats touched off a murmur in the camp, accompanied by scurrying and jousting. Scores of blacks milled around in the trees. Major Wilson urged Bill Napier to quiet the people.

"The war is over. Put down your arms," Napier said in Zulu.

Several blacks slipped behind trees. Fred heard the click of hammers being brought to full cock. How quickly the blacks had come to depend on the Martini-Henry.

"Where's your king?" Napier asked.

A young man stepped forward and pointed ahead.

"Run on. We'll follow."

"If he even scratches himself," Wilson called out to Burnham, "shoot him!"

They rode into the darkness, the young man leading. Soon they saw the fires of another camp. A Cape cart was stuck in the mud.

"Good," Wilson cried. "Only Lobengula is allowed to ride in a royal wagon. We're on to him now."

The cart proved to be empty—one wheel broken.

The patrol rode through three more native camps, each time meeting Matabeles and each time hearing the cocking of rifles in the dark. After three or four miles, the patrol came to an opening in the forest, a grassy meadow. There were no fires.

"The king's scherm is here," the lad murmured and melted into the darkness. Accompanied by Bill Napier, Fred rode ahead. He smelled turpentine from fresh-cut wood and saw a circular fence of thin ironwood mopane poles driven into the ground. The stakes, sharpened to points on top, were six feet high, forming an enclosure fifty feet in diameter.

Inside, the flicker of a campfire revealed two royal carts. This was the king's kraal. Fred and Bill rode back to tell Wilson what they'd seen. There was a powwow. Should they capture Lobengula or wait for Forbes?

"Call the king out," Wilson told Captain Napier. Rain began to splash down in large drops as Bill Napier rode toward the mopane enclosure.

"*Bayete, Lobengula. Bayete, Lobengula;* He of unlimited capacity, He who swallows the rhinoceros with its horns—and the elephant, tusks and all. Lion of the mountain fastness and mainstay of your people, praises unto Thee, Thou Great One."

Napier was using the most grandiloquent form of Zulu speech, addressing the Matabele King with all his titles and honors. He declared the patrol consisted of distinguished messengers sent by the great Doctor Jameson to escort the King to Bulawayo—there to conclude a treaty of peace. He assured Lobengula that all honors would be bestowed on him in retirement.

There was no reply. The rain fell harder, drowning the sound of cocking rifles.

"I think they're about to shoot," Napier said.

"Fall back to the vley," Wilson ordered.

"We can't," Fred said. "They've closed in behind us. Follow me." Burnham held up a white handkerchief.

"Leftenant Hofmeyr," Major Wilson called out, "take Sergeant Bradburn and Corporal Colquhoun to act as rear guard."

Fred led the way into a thick grove of trees. In time the patrol emerged in a large, open meadow where they gathered around an ant heap.

"My orders," Major Wilson said, "are to give the message to the King and if possible to capture him, tie him to a horse and bring him in. If that can't be done, we're to keep an eye on him until Forbes can bring up the main patrol and use the Maxims to force the issue."

Was the patrol supposed to spend the night? If so, why hadn't Forbes told him to wear a jacket? Why hadn't they taken rations? Why didn't they have a Maxim?

The rain began to pour.

"We must get word to Forbes," Wilson said. "Who'll volunteer to backtrack?"

"Use Burnham," Napier said. "He's the best tracker."

"I can't spare him," Wilson said. "Our rear guard is lost. Burnham must find them."

Hofmeyr, Colquhoun and Bradburn were missing.

"While they are lost, this patrol doesn't budge."

Burnham's respect for Wilson instantly doubled.

Lieutenant Hofmeyr was a balding Afrikander from the Cape Colony, the son of a clergyman of the Dutch Reformed Church. Sergeant Cliff Bradburn, twenty-five, was a surly Englishman recently arrived in Mashona Land from the Cape Mounted Rifles. He'd been three years in Africa. Corporal Fred Colquhoun was a sour puss from Edinburgh, twenty-four years old, six of them in Africa. He'd come up with the Pioneer Column three years ago.

Captain Napier suggested sending Bob Bain and Jack Robertson for the Maxims. Wilson nodded, adding, "Captain Napier, I think you'd better go along to impress on Major Forbes that we need those Maxims."

A flash of lightning was followed by the rumble of thunder. Heavy rain continued to fall. If the Matabele attacked in this meadow, the Wilson Patrol would make good targets. Fred pointed to a small stand of young mopane trees and Wilson led the patrol to their protection.

"Wait here. Captain Kirton's in command. Burnham and I will go back to search for the rear guard."

Fred became acutely aware that night of the fierce intensity of an African rain storm. Within the hour, two inches of water covered the low spots, flowing north and gathering in rivulets. The runs collected into dozens of little streams feeding into raging creeks that eventually dumped into the Shangani River.

By 9 p.m. the rains had doused the Matabele fires. The stormwater runoff washed away the spoor of the patrol's retreat. Fred worked on hands and knees in the cold mud to find the hoof prints. After fourteen hours in the saddle, he was so hungry and tired his senses began to fail. His fingers were chilled to the bone. Working in the dark, he traced out the direction and stride of the horses.

Several times he lost the trail in the soft slop, and panic nearly overcame him. By using his hat as a shield and striking a match, he traced the direction of the hoof prints and resumed backtracking. It had taken ten minutes to ride from the king's scherm to the meadow, but it took an hour to backtrack. They came to the mopane enclosure and listened—all they heard was the muffled sound of voices and dogs barking in the distance.

"I think Lieutenant Hofmeyr will decide to wait until morning to look for our trail," Major Wilson said.

"No chance then," Fred replied. "Long before dawn, the rain'll wash out all our spoor." *Damn, Major Forbes will probably be of the same mindset. The British aren't trained to see in the dark. Most likely the city-bred Forbes will sit tight at the Shangani River, considering it poor tactics to move the men and Maxims by night. Should I tell Wilson?*

Allan Wilson threw back his head and let out an Australian *cooee*. Fred echoed it with an American cowboy yell. The noise raised a commotion among the Matabele who likely interpreted it as a signal for the whites to attack. Moments later Wilson and Burnham heard a faint *cooee*. Guided by a few more calls, the lost rear guard, Hofmeyr, Bradburn and Colquhoun, rejoined them.

"You have Burnham to thank for your lives," Wilson told them. "I don't think another man in the whole world could have retraced our spoor in that sea of mud."

The three men were effusive in their thanks to the Yank who had found them in the dark. The rain had stopped but the leaves were dripping, so Fred allowed the horses find their way back to the patrol, trusting to their acute sense of smell.

Wilson posted a guard and told the men to sleep. It was nearly 11 p.m. and after sixteen hours in the saddle—the last six in the rain without a coat—Fred was ready to collapse. Every nerve and muscle in his body cried out in ache. Wilson took off his coat and offered it to Fred who laid down to let sleep overcome his sense of uneasiness. If the Matabele were to attack, it probably wouldn't come until dawn.

Some time later, Fred awakened. Clouds blocked the stars so he had only a vague idea what time it might be. The sounds of chirping insects told him the enemy had not intruded on their solitude. He emptied his canteen and laid it on the ground, using it as an echo sounder. The deep breathing of sleeping men and horses muffled any other sounds.

Burnham sensed, rather than heard, reverberations. He crept out of camp to listen. Now he could hear it, faint but unmistakable. Fred had a perception of human feet moving quietly but in great numbers. He crept back to camp, where he awakened Major Wilson and told him an impi was moving between them and Forbes' camp.

"They seem to be trying to surround us," Fred said.

"Hold up your coat while I strike a match," Wilson replied. It was 4:30 a.m. "Burnham, that relief column was due here half an hour ago. Will you ride out and see if you can guide them back to us? If Forbes doesn't get here with those Maxims before daylight, we've little hope."

Fred arose, reluctant to leave the warmth of the coat.

"Keep it."

Fred mounted Omega and rode into the darkness. The sleep had refreshed his senses. For a long time he heard only the water dropping off the leaves and the yipping of hyenas in the distance. The black sky turned a dull purple, like an old bruise, preparing for a bleak sunrise. After a few minutes, Fred could see the ground ahead. The hoof prints were crossed by footprints. Human footprints.

As it grew lighter, the seeing became better. Fred guessed their galloping around in the night had left them about five miles north of the Shangani River. When he'd ridden about a mile, he heard the faint sound of animals. He dismounted and put his canteen to the ground to listen. It had to be Major Forbes with the Maxims. The Matabele never moved cattle that quietly.

Fred whistled and moments later there was a faint whistle in reply. He mounted and rode toward the sound. From out of the gray morning fog there appeared the figure of a man astride a horse. Reinforcements!

A feeling of immense relief welled up and only then did Fred realize how utterly demoralized he had been. Suddenly, he was supremely happy. He waved his hat and yelled. With those Maxims, they could stand off an attacking impi. A lone figure emerged from the drizzle and the form became familiar.

"Pete?" Fred could scarcely believe his eyes.

"Yeah, pard, it's me."

Fred spurred Omega.

"Hurry, we've got to move those Maxims to Wilson's camp before sunup."

"There are no Maxims."

Burnham looked into the gloom ahead and saw Captain Henry Borrow riding toward him. He was accompanied by several troopers.

"Forbes decided not to move the Maxims until daylight," Captain Borrow said. "He sent me with twenty men as reinforcements."

The look on Borrow's face told the whole story.

"We're forty men to stand off an impi of thousands," Fred cried throwing his hat to the ground. "That idiot. Without those Maxims, we're dead!"

18

Burnham Breaks Out

SHANGANI • DECEMBER 1893

WHILE LEADING Captain Borrow's twenty-man patrol to Wilson's bivouac, Fred thought of Blanche and young Rod at Fort Victoria. *Will I see the new baby? Will it be a boy or girl? This time I'd like a girl. Would Blanche remarry? She'd have to—to support the children. Death isn't always the worst fate for a soldier.* When they arrived, Borrow said Napier and Bain had arrived at Forbes' camp shortly before midnight. Napier told him he should support Wilson with the Maxim guns by 4 a.m. Then Captain Napier collapsed with an attack of blackwater fever.

At 1 a.m. Forbes decided not to move the Maxims until sunrise. Instead he chose to send a patrol of well-armed men, led by Borrow, with Ingram as scout in the place of Bain whose horse had gone lame. He issued each man a hundred rifle cartridges and twenty rounds for their pistols.

Wilson halted the patrol in a clearing between two stands of mopane trees. At roll call, thirty-seven men responded. Wilson asked each man for suggestions.

"There's no best move," Argent Kirton said. He spoke from twenty years' experience in Africa.

"There's only one thing left to do," said Fitzgerald, the police inspector. "We must cut our way out."

"Impossible," Fred said. "Our horses are too weak. To gallop into a horned crescent is foolhardy."

"It's the end for us," said Bill Judd.

Harry Greenfield, a father of two, said nothing.

"We came through a big impi to get here," said Captain Borrow in a voice full of remorse.

"Any idea whose regiment we might be facing?" Wilson asked.

"It could be M'Jaan's," Pete Ingram offered. M'Jaan was King Lobengula's commander in chief.

"True, the Royal Imbezu would be close to the king," Wilson said.

"I'd say Gambo's impi is also out there," Fred added.

"Either way or both, it's a first-rate regiment mucking about out there," Kirton reasoned, puffing on his pipe. "We've drawn a bad hand this time."

A break in the clouds allowed a ray of sunlight to pierce the morning haze, producing a shimmering glow all out of harmony with the circumstances.

Wilson said, "It's rather beyond arguing about. We must ride to Lobengula's camp. If we can't capture him, we have a bash at him and cut down his indunas."

Fred nodded. Before surrendering their lives, they would give a good account of themselves by taking as many of the royal blood as possible. If they died fighting, at least their names would go down in the history books.

Wilson formed his men for the ride to the royal scherm. By the light of day, the long distances of the night seemed to shrink. They rode at a walk through the forest and into the grass, past the burned-out campfires. Along the edge of the meadow, they saw a line of warriors. The Matabele wore headdresses and carried Martini-Henry rifles, but they made no aggressive moves. *We are inside the enemy ring of iron. The blacks have no urgent need to attack.*

Wilson rode toward the king's stockade.

"Captain Kirton," Wilson said, "you know the King. Tell him we've come to accept his surrender."

Argent Kirton spoke at length in the grandiloquent Zulu manner, repeating the same titles and honors that Napier had used the night before. There was no response. Fred rode inside the scherm of mopane poles. The royal wagons were gone, and the camp was empty.

As he left the mopane enclosure, a tall induna leaped from behind a bush. His striped body was attired in a loincloth of leopard skin, the insignia of an important chief. Omega pranced and Fred fought for control as the induna advanced, shouting, "*Bulala umlungu.*"

Fred knew the words well: "Death to the white man."

He spurred the horse and waved his carbine, carrying it like a pistol. The black man fired on the run, a wild shot. The induna tried to reload, but a thong of leopard hide got tangled in the rifle's action. He cast aside the weapon, drew an assegai and ran, screaming "jee."

Fred was galloping when the induna raised his assegai. He fired point-blank and the man crumbled, red blood gushing from a gaping wound. Pinkie-lavender organs burst from the left side of his belly. The Matabele impi suddenly vanished—not one warrior was in sight. The whites wouldn't learn until afterwards that Fred had killed M'Jaan's son, an *induna* regarded as invincible.

The death of the *induna* gave the patrol an hour of relief. Then, from the cover of their trees, the Matabele began peppering the men with Martini-Henry fire. Two horses brayed and fell, their life's blood pumping out of gaping artery wounds. Pete Ingram galloped in to sweep Captain Fitzgerald onto the back of his own horse. The owner of the other wounded animal was Trooper Dennis Dillon, the young telegrapher from the relay station. Captain Kirton held the reins of Dillon's horse while the young trooper drew his pistol and shot the struggling animal. A man whom Fred didn't know was bleeding from the nose and mouth. Half of his jaw was shot away and he was trying to scream. Then his head exploded, shattered by a Martini-Henry slug.

Major Wilson reformed the patrol and they rode at a canter to a grove of mopane trees where they took cover behind the ant hill. While Wilson called for a casualty count, a hundred Matabele rifles cut loose from the trees. Eventually their position became untenable, and Wilson gave an order to retreat.

Burnham led the patrol into the meadow where they had camped the night before. The retreat drew the blacks into the open and the firing continued. More horses fell—dead, dying and maimed. Two of the captains gathered the reins of the wounded animals and began geeing them into a semicircle. Fred and Pete shot the injured horses, their falling bodies forming a breastworks. Riflemen took up positions behind the horses' bodies.

The warriors charged, firing at will. The defenders returned a steady round of pistol and rifle shot, dropping a hundred of the attackers. Sporadic shooting continued for an hour until the indunas called back the attack. Among the defenders, the sole casualty was one horse, wounded. Wilson ordered the ammo redistributed. He climbed onto the body of a dead horse.

"We must find a better position. Everyone save one bullet for himself." Wilson ordered the unmounted men to walk in the center, protected by horse-mounted outriders. Borrow and Ingram brought up the rear, taking potshots at anyone who followed.

For an hour they rode back toward the Shangani, putting distance between themselves and Lobengula's scherm. A faint glimmer of hope began to replace despair. Every step brought them closer to

Wilson's Last Stand

Forbes' camp. Major Wilson rode up alongside Fred. "It seems quiet enough now. Do you think you could ride ahead to meet Forbes?"

"There's an impi between us and the river. Even if Forbes had crossed over, it would be a miracle if he could get here in time."

"You don't think he's crossed?"

"I don't hear the Maxims."

"Will you try getting through? It's our only hope."

Fred mopped his forehead and nodded. At this point, he figured that it mattered little where he died.

• • •

FORT VICTORIA • DECEMBER 1893

BLANCHE WROTE to Mother Blick in Pasadena.

The world looks dark. It is two months tomorrow since Fred went away. There has been no mail since he returned from Tati. Part of the Combined Column followed Lobengula. The others are still in Bulawayo. I feel certain that Fred has gone after Lobengula. I received a telegram from Arthur Cummings, one of the scouts who is a friend of ours. He is at Tuli en route to Fort Vic. He asked where Fred was.

Later that day, Blanche added a post script:

The coach arrived bringing Mr. Cummings and a letter from Fred. He was going with Majors Forbes and Wilson on a patrol after the King. They expect to be gone about six days. When they return, Fred has the promise of a good horse to ride cross-country to Victoria."

• • •

BURNHAM ADJUSTED his Stetson and waited for Major Wilson's final instructions.

"Gooding here is well mounted, " Wilson said. "Let him have a bash at it."

Fred studied the lad. George Gooding was a Hyde Park bushman who didn't shave yet. Fred knew nothing of his abilities.

"Ingram and I have ridden many a mile together," Fred said. "How about Pete instead?"

Wilson nodded and rode away. When Pete arrived, Fred said gently, "Trooper Gooding, you'll be safer here with the patrol."

The two scouts spurred their horses. Ahead lay a long, open vley between two stands of trees. The meadow was arrow-straight almost as if trees had been cleared for the right-of-way of a railway line. The men had ridden less than half a mile when they came to veld grass where an impi lay in wait.

"Horned crescent," Pete said.

Fred glanced ahead. He saw no chance of penetrating the bull's forehead. To the right was a grove of mature mopane trees. The

Matabele could use their assegais to good advantage there. To the left was a stand of young trees growing like a bamboo thicket. It seemed no horse could penetrate that grove—for sure, no man could.

Fred spurred Omega and plunged into the thicket. Forbes' horse dropped to its knees, and Fred spurred the animal harshly. The horse charged into the saplings. Pete's horse reared. Ingram dug his spurs deeply, forcing his horse ahead. Behind them a volley of Matabele rifle shots rang out.

Again and again they spurred their mounts until the animals' flanks were bleeding. The horses used their great strength to force their way through a hundred feet of dense growth, until they emerged into a clearing.

"We might make it," Pete said.

From behind came the sound of something crashing through the mopanes. Fred and Pete saw Trooper George Gooding bashing his way through the trail.

"What you doin' here, pilgrim?" Pete asked harshly. Ingram's tone accused Gooding of desertion. "How come the Matabele didn't stick a spear up your ass?"

"Crikies, Guv, Cap'n Borrow said I could." Gooding's voice cracked.

"Look out ahead," Fred yelled.

From the meadow ahead, two hundred Matabele lads were running toward them. They carried assegais and they were moving fast. *There isn't enough gallop in our horses to outdistance these boys.*

"Pete, we gotta trick 'em."

"Double and cover? Where, for Gawd's sake?"

"This wouldn't work with Indians, but follow me."

Fred led the way, traveling slightly faster than the young blacks could run, but they couldn't stay ahead for long. The wet ground was firm enough to leave hoofprints that the youths could trace.

"Head for those wattle trees," Fred called. "There's rock on that plateau."

They broke into a gallop—behind them the Matabele lads ran crying "jee." As the horsemen entered the timber, the ground became rocky and their trail became difficult to follow.

"Ride in circles through the trees," Fred said. "Put yourselves over as much ground as you can but leave some tracks. We'll rest in that little spruit until they work out our spoor."

The three fugitives enjoyed the luxury of ten minutes' rest for their horses while the runners beat out the trail. Often the lads lost the spoor and spent precious minutes running around in circles to find it again. Pete looked hard-pressed not to howl with glee. Gooding shook his head, seemingly unable to figure out what was happening.

"They'll have it worked out in a minute," Pete said.

"Time to cinch up and ride for it," Fred said.

A cheer rose from the trackers. They raised their assegais and ran toward the spruit where the scouts were hiding.

"Let's get the bloomin 'ell outta here," Gooding cried.

From the direction of the Wilson Patrol came a new sound: continuous rifle fire. The blacks turned, listened and began running toward the shooting.

"We're safe now," Fred said. "Those lads want wives and they see a better chance to get their spears blooded at the Wilson Patrol."

"Hard cheese for those guys," Gooding said.

The three men rode toward the Shangani River. After half a mile, Omega began to limp. They were no longer being pursued so Fred dismounted and trotted alongside. At the river, the foot-deep stream had become a torrent. Snarls of brush, debris and dead game were caught up in the swirling eddies. Ingram looked at Fred and shook his head.

"I know," Fred said. "Forbes is still on the other side. He could never cross in this flood."

The silence was broken by the staccato chop of Maxim gunfire. Forbes' column was under attack At that awful moment, Fred came to realize that both patrols were surrounded.

"From the sound of the Maxim, I'd say they're about a mile upstream."

"Let's cross here," Ingram suggested.

Holding their weapons aloft, they rode into the water. They drifted with the current, allowing themselves to be carried along by its flow, until they came to a spot where they climbed onto solid ground.

On arrival, Fred told Major Forbes, "I think we're the sole survivors of the Wilson party." At that moment, he was depleted of all emotion and intellect.

19

The Shangani Retreat

S<small>HANGANI</small> • D<small>ECEMBER</small> 1893

THE BLACKS concentrated their fire on the horses and mules, killing eighteen. The Matabele meant to unhorse the Shangani Patrol and capture the Maxims, leaving the whites afoot and unarmed.

When the firing died down, Fred felt his tape worm hollering. He trudged over to the mess wagon and bolted down his overdue ration. As he cleaned his mess gear, Raaff began arguing with Forbes.

"Our horses are being shot and our men have no cover," Raaff grumbled. "Let's get this patrol to a better defensive position." Forbes ordered the column to retreat six hundred yards to yesterday's laager. He sent up rocket signals and awaited news from Allan Wilson.

Fred, too exhausted to assimilate what had happened, vomited the food he'd eaten. In the sixty-three days the Combined Column had been in the field, counting his trip to Tati, Burnham had ridden three times as far as the others. At Officers Call, Burnham made a report.

"I think we're surrounded," he blurted out. "I think those natives will come at us until they've killed us all."

Forbes ignored Fred who was barely mindful.

"We'll wait until tomorrow for Wilson and his men to rejoin us. Then we'll march up river

"We'd better send word to Bulawayo about our new route," Johann said. "If Jameson sends a relief patrol along the trail we took, they'll get lost and the kaffirs'll wipe us out for sure."

"It would be suicide to ride through those impis," Fred said.

"Burnham, I think you're knocked up," Forbes said. "Get some sleep." Fred left in search of his bedroll.

"We fight again soon," Johann said. "They're gonna call the horses in."

"Wake me when it starts." Fred said and fell asleep. He didn't awaken until dusk. Pete Ingram shook him.

"Me and Billy Lynch are riding to Bulawayo," Pete said. "We'll carry a dispatch to Doctor Jameson. Want to send a letter?" Fred scrawled a note to Blanche and gave it to Pete.

"Lookit," Ingram cried. On the far side of the river, Matabele warriors high-stepped on the riverbank wearing the uniforms of the Victoria Column. Forbes walked up.

"Ingram, you and Lynch say nothing of this in Bulawayo, lest it stir panic," he said. "That's an order!"

During dinner, a breeze blew up. Within minutes, dark clouds formed and the patrol was laced by sheets of stinging rain, followed by thunder and lightning. A fierce wind bent the smaller mopane trees almost to the ground.

The storm was relentless, with freaky gusting winds. Fred felt like he was between hay and grass after a winter on poor pasture. He laid down inside a trek wagon and slept until reveille at 5:30.

The next day Fred's outlook on life was brighter, and he was able to hold down food. He and Johann scouted a route ahead along the Shangani. They saw hoofprints in the ground left by Ingram and Lynch. Human footprints covered the tracks.

"They're being trailed," Johann said.

"Pete knows some tricks," Fred replied.

That night Fred told Raaff about Ingram's trail being topped.

"Tell no one," Raaff said. "I'll report it to Forbes."

"I don't think men riding tired horses can outrun those young Matabele lads running in relays," Johann said. There was clear worry in his voice.

"We'll see," Fred replied, still affected by the jitters. That night he slept under dry blankets and awakened in the morning fully recuperated from the adversity of the Wilson Patrol.

Forbes ordered Colenbrander to take charge of the prisoners. This task was important because the whites dared not free any blacks to inform their indunas how few horses and how little food the patrol had on hand. After breakfast, Forbes summoned Fred to his tent.

"Trooper Burnham, would you volunteer to swim the river and see if you can find Major Wilson and his men? I'll hold the column here until you return."

Was there a tremor in Forbes' voice?

"I'll go, Major, but I want it as a direct order."

"Lose your nerve there, Trooper?"

Forbes manifested the pallor of a cholera ward.

"It strikes me as strange, Major, that this patrol wouldn't reinforce Major Wilson. After seeing the blacks wearing European military uniforms last night, do you wish to reinforce Major Wilson's patrol with one man?"

"I'm not trying to reinforce Wilson," Forbes snapped. "I'm seeking information."

"If you wanted information, you should have sent me last night," Fred said. "To cross a swollen river on a starving horse in broad daylight and ride through a narrow vley in the face of an armed enemy is suicide. It's not likely that thousands of hostiles will allow a solitary horseman to ride among them in broad daylight. Of all orders I've received, this is the most bizarre."

"Are you refusing?" Anger suffused Forbes' face.

"Persiflage, Major. I fully believe that a scout, if so ordered, must go to his death as a sacrifice of one to save many. And if ordered, I'm prepared to go. But I do not volunteer. Make it an order, Major, because I've never yet disobeyed an order."

After an abnormal silence, Forbes said in a cawing voice, "Forget it."

Trooper Walter Howard walked up.

"I'll volunteer," Howard said. "I'm down on my luck and may as well make a record or die." Before the war, Howard had been robbed of his property by the natives.

"Walt, you're too good a man to throw away for no object," Forbes said dryly.

"Do you consider me a throwaway?" Fred asked. He walked off in a huff. Half an hour later, Forbes called a meeting to plan the retreat back to Bulawayo.

"My horse is knocked up," he said, glaring at Fred. "Napier is ill with blackwater fever and Colenbrander's horse was shot dead today. Commandant Raaff's pony is fit, so I've asked him to take charge of the guards. I'll walk with the main column. Commandant Raaff and Trooper Burnham will serve as advance scouts." *Has Major Forbes abandoned his command?*

As they rode, Burnham studied Raaff.

"I've little hope of help reaching us," Raaff said. "It's up to us to find our own way back." Forbes' plan was to trek fifty miles along the north bank of the Shangani River to the Old Hunters' Trail. There they would turn south and ride back to Bulawayo.

"With the Shangani in flood, we have the river on our left for protection," Fred said. "We still have the Maxims."

"Is that a careful estimate or wishful thinking?"

"The Matabele respect our Maxims. If we can keep them from shooting our horses, we have a chance. Have you seen their spoor? They're driving their cattle away from the river."

"Only to deny us food," Raaff said. "And our gunfire scares away all game animals that could be used as food."

They made good headway that day, more than a tenth of the way to Bulawayo. As they made laager, pistol shots echoed through the camp. Near the quartermaster wagon, two horses lay dead, shot as unfit to travel.

The following week was a series of miseries. The patrol fought three major engagements and several minor skirmishes. Their rations ran out. The horses stampeded and almost escaped. Once, the patrol was trapped in an indefensible position. More downpours produced rivers of mud. But the storms saved their lives because heavy rain prevented the Matabele from attacking.

On Wednesday, December 6, they trekked eight miles. The men made laager, shot two stringy African cows, dug pits and hung the beeves over coals to roast. Torrential rains snuffed out the flames and the meal was a loss. Rain poured all night, and by dawn the men were complaining of rashes and sores.

The next day Raaff led a patrol into the field and returned two hours later with a hundred head of cattle. At 3 p.m., as the patrol inspanned for the afternoon trek, an impi attacked, bent on recovering the cattle. The patrol poured a heavy return fire, cutting down scores of warriors with the Maxims. But the whites failed to post a guard at the rear, and a band of Matabele crept in and stampeded cattle and horses alike. Fred and Johann galloped out to recover the horses.

In the excitement, no one thought to shoot some beef for dinner. Lightning and thunder erupted, breaking off the engagement and forcing the exhausted patrol to make camp on the spot. The patrol's ration that night was boiled Boer meal.

The men were up at dawn on Saturday, December 9, trekking through heavy brush. The rain pattered down and progress was slow because the men had to break trail for the gun carriages. The men's boots were wearing out, and they complained the rocks cut their feet. The rain grew worse and the patrol made laager where it was—trusting that the Matabele wouldn't attack in such bad weather. That night the men came within a thread of revolting.

The lowest point on the Shangani Retreat came on a Sunday, December 10. The grass stood shoulder high and the going was slow.

There was a slow drizzle and the men had been without food for twenty-four hours. Some dug wild leeks to boil, but the rain quenched the fires. Those who ate the leeks raw came down with the collywobbles. Underarm sores broke out. Everyone complained of crotch itch, and they smelled worse than billy goats. Some men lurched around like half-filled bags of barley.

Early in the afternoon, the Matabele attacked in a horned-crescent assault. That created a scare until Charley Lendy got the Maxims into action. His white bulldog, Ruff, pranced in front of the gun, wagging his tail and barking. Fred and Johann scrambled into the kopjes and manned rifles to peck off indunas.

One of the Maxims jammed. Lendy erupted in a stream of violent oaths and Ruff barked happily. The Matabele concentrated their fire on the pack horses and within a few moments eight animals were dead. Zebra was shot in the left front hoof. The other horses milled about in terror. Captain Lendy, sweating and swearing, tried to free the jammed gun. Ruff pranced, wagged his tail and barked defiance. Then Maxim Charley succeeded. The machine gun took the spirit out of the Matabele attack and after ninety minutes the engagement ended.

Forbes reformed the patrol and the men were crossing a brushy valley when the Matabele struck again. Raaff, in charge of skirmishing, made it hot for the attackers until darkness brought an end to the shooting. The men, more than exhausted, sought the protection of some nearby kopjes. The patrol was being followed by well-organized and well-trained Matabele—men who had learned how to shoot and what targets to take out. The patrol's only chance was to move ahead as fast as possible and hope that Ingram and Lynch had gotten through to Bulawayo.

At Officers Call that night, the leadership decided to abandon everything except food and ammunition. The food and medicine were already gone, so that left only gun carriages and pack saddles to dispose of.

Forbes ordered Burnham to survey the terrain. At dusk, Fred slipped outside the camp and returned an hour later with news that impis were massing on three sides. The kopjes on the far side were so rugged the enemy had dismissed them as impractical to cross for horses burdened by gun carriages. Forbes was skeptical, so Fred took Raaff outside for a look. On their return, the commandant convinced Forbes of the gravity of their situation.

"If we stay, we'll be wiped out," Raaff warned.

"Your recommendation?" Forbes asked slowly.

"Evacuate at midnight, going through those kopjes. Burnham showed me a route. When the Matabele strike, we'll be gone."

Forbes' face was gray; his features had gone slack.

"Give it a try," he said with a sigh. "Pass the word to the ranks." Forbes sat down by the fire, shoulders sagging. Raaff climbed onto a gun carriage.

"Chaps, our situation is perilous. There's one chance of escaping but we must carry it out in silence before the enemy grows suspicious. If we're to succeed, I must have your full cooperation. I know you are perished, but keep your peckers up."

The grumbling among the men quieted.

"Get thorn bushes and construct a scherm," Raaff told the men. "Build it like we intend to defend this camp to the last man. Make the brush thick so they can't see inside. Bring firewood and get some mopane poles the same size as Maxim barrels.

"Then each of you build a mound of earth to resemble a sleeping man. Make fires and bank them. Act like you're sleeping. I want total silence. No talking. No smoking. Not even pipes. Kill all the dogs. No shooting."

There were gasps. Raaff nodded at Lendy.

"That goes for Ruff too, Charley," Raaff said grimly. Lendy started to protest but Captain Napier placed an arm on the gunner's shoulder.

The men turned to their tasks. Pickets were posted in the usual manner. When the camouflage was finished, the artillery men took the Maxim guns off their carriages and mounted mopane poles in their places. At length, the camp became silent. Johann was adding wood to a campfire when Charley Lendy crept over to join them.

"I can't kill Ruff," Lendy said. "He's been our mascot since the artillery group was formed at Fort Vic."

Johann looked at Charley and nodded. He arose, picked up a shovel and led the dog into the darkness.

From out of the night came the taunts.

"*Bulala umlungu.*"

When Johann returned, he translated.

"We will assegai you. We will wash our spears in blood. Your life's blood will mingle with the waters of the Shangani. If you run away, we will strangle you. If you surrender, you will be beheaded. You will never live to see the sun rise."

20

Forced Night March

SHANGANI • DECEMBER 1893

ONLY THE heartiest of horses were taken, their hooves covered with cloth cut from old jackets and worn blankets. Fred guided the men along the escape route. Behind him was a Maxim gun on a pack mule, followed by six men carrying ammo. Then came the wounded, strapped to horses. Though each suffered great pain, none uttered a sound. Behind them, sixty men led those horses which had not been slaughtered as lame or dying.

At the rear of the column was the other mule-mounted Maxim gun, with six more men carrying ammo. The last men to leave the camp added fuel to the fires. Raaff was the only unwounded man astride a horse. He saw that the men kept closed up during a night as opaque as India ink.

Progress was slow as men and horses climbed step by step in single file up a rocky kopje. An occasional peal of thunder echoed in the distant veld. Once they had crossed the kopje and gotten down to level land, they put as many miles as possible between the abandoned camp and their new laager. Daybreak found them in open country where they could give a good accounting of themselves.

"We'll let everyone, except the guards, sleep for six hours," Raaff said.

"Shelldrake's missing," Johann said.

"We can't go back," Raaff said gruffly.

Pickets were posted. The men slept until noon and resumed the march. Nine horses went lame and had to be shot. Three of the heartiest animals were spared until the patrol made camp, then butchered as rations. The cooks built fires to boil the horse flesh. The animals were bony and the meat was stringy and tough, with little more than hide and sinew. Fred walked over to the quartermaster.

"Can I have the head?"

"If you're that hungry, take the guts too."

Back at his campfire, Burnham cut out the brain.

"What you doing with the scrag end?" Bain asked.

"Trying to stay alive."

"With that?"

"A well-fed horse is nutritious, but a starving animal is almost worthless as food. The last bit of nourishment is in the brain and the marrow. The cooks kept the bones to boil the marrow and enrich the soup."

Burnham fried the brains like scrambled eggs.

"Mind if I try some?" Bain asked.

"If you've got leeks, we'll share. Stuff needs flavor."

"It's not baron of beef with Yorkshire pudding," Bain said. "But out here what is?"

The other troopers complained the horse flesh was tasteless and full of air bubbles. Fred and Bob decided the scrambled brains and boiled leeks provided a filling if not satisfying meal. Bain vomited only once. Raaff came over.

"We rest until midnight, then march."

"I'm perished," a trooper complained.

"Me boots're worn out," another groused.

"Tear up your blankets to wrap around your feet," Raaff growled. "Come midnight we march till dawn."

The medical officer appeared out of the darkness.

"The men complain of headaches and dizziness," he said. "Some are hallucinating. Captain Finch says he saw a rocket fired by a relief column."

The grumbling was followed by ugly threats.

"—better not turn his flipping back on me or he'll go arse over tit in—"

"—some dark night that rotter Raaff'll wake up—"

"—we get back to Bulawayo, gorblimey, he's a dead man."

Raaff called Fred and Johann to a meeting.

"Pass the word to the men. If we march by day, we will have to make laager at night. The men don't have the strength, so it's best to make night marches—and rest by day when our Maxims have the advantage. If we march in silence, the enemy won't know where we are."

"Depends on the weather," Fred said. "The thorns on these bush-

145

es are as sharp as fish hooks. They're almost as bad as the cholla cactus of Arizona."

"Well," Raaff said, "give my plan a try."

Burnham, out scouting, rode into camp with the news that the Old Hunters Road was ahead. Much heartened, the Shangani Patrol turned south and trekked for ten miles without seeing a Matabele.

By Fred's reckoning it was only forty miles back to Bulawayo, but they were moving too slow. In their failing condition, the patrol would be lucky to survive three days. The men grumbled, but they marched. When they made laager, pistol shots rang out. Horse meat again. The officers stood guard and the troopers slept, most of them without eating. At 3 p.m., the sky cleared up and Raaff ordered the men awakened.

The men shogged along for two hours, covering four miles. As they entered a brushy area near a small river, shots signaled a new attack. It was their sixth engagement since the Shangani Patrol began its retreat. The troopers forgot their weariness and dashed for the river to take shelter in the gullies along the banks.

Enemy rifle fire came from both banks of the river. Captain Lendy mounted the Maxims on an outcrop and aimed one at each side of the river. For three quarters of an hour the shooting continued, but there were no casualties among the troopers.

"Under Raaff," Johann said, "we can use natural cover for defense."

A Matabele bullet bounced off a rock and whirred through the air.

With darkness came heavy rain and the engagement was broken off. Fred emerged from his gully and slogged through the mud in search of Commandant Raaff.

"The men are in poor condition," Fred said. "I don't think they can hold out until we reach Inyati."

"What do you suggest we do?" Raaff cried out. "Call on the Lord?"

"This little stream has to feed into the Bubi River. We're not far from Inyati. Let's send Jan Grootboom ahead for aid. At night, he might slip through the lines."

"Good idea," Raaff said. "By the way, Zebra's hoof is infected. We'll have to shoot him for rations."

That night the patrol trekked from 11 p.m. until sunrise which found them at a tributary of the Shangani River. The men were hungry, tired and in poor spirits. The dawn of Wednesday, December 13, arrived as stealthy as an assassin, with gray clouds threatening more rain. Would the storms never end?

Standing around their campfires, the men grumbled as they ate boiled horse meat and tended to various and sundry itches, blisters and pustules. After an hour's rest, Raaff ordered the men to get moving. Under threatening skies, Burnham and Bob Bain rode ahead in the brush to search for a shallow place to ford the stream.

"Be on the lookout," Fred warned.

"What's up?"

"In brush like this, the assegai has an advantage over the rifle."

They halted by the stream to let their horses drink.

"Sure could use some West End belly timber," Bain groused, referring to good eats in the theater district of London.

"Don't look around, Bob." Fred's voice was guarded. "Mount up, casual like, and follow me." The scouts rode slowly back toward the patrol, pausing occasionally to let their horses nibble on a patch of fresh grass. When they were well away from the stream, Fred dismounted near a grove of mopane trees.

"What was that all about?"

"Matabele ambush," Fred said. "I wanted them to think we hadn't seen 'em."

"A bad place for a fight, eh?"

"You bet." Fred said nodding. "Wait here with the horses. I'll be back soon." Fred disappeared into the brush and was gone for twenty minutes. When returned, they rode back to the patrol, arriving at noon to find the men in laager on open ground near a kopje. Today they were roasting their ration of horse meat, a variation in the menu from boiled horse. Fred told Commandant Raaff of the ambush and outlined a plan to outflank the waiting impi.

"Not good tactics," said Forbes, suddenly recovered from his blue funk. "We should attack directly."

"With this awkward squad?" Fred yelled

"I fancy Burnham's plan," Raaff said. The argument became a quarrel, with Forbes holding out for a frontal attack. When Raaff, Napier, Lendy and Colenbrander lined up behind Fred's plan, Forbes capitulated.

The troopers were red-eyed with fatigue, their clothes in tatters. Wearily they trudged along. The men were concerned only with their personal aches, pains and hunger, unaware and uncaring that a counter-ambush was being deployed. Most of them were beyond a patriotic appeal to duty, so Raaff hurled stinging personal abuses.

"Get on there, you colonial experiencers, or it'll be an unmarked grave for you rotters." Raaff's abusive term referred to the spoiled sons of wealthy Londoners who grand-groused in the colonies on fat expense accounts. The men hurled abuse at Raaff but marched. At length they arrived at the drift.

"Captain Lendy," Raaff said, "pick a squad of men and remain here with the Maxim guns. Give us ninety minutes to get behind that impi. Then start shooting."

Fred's plan meant taking half the men across the tributary, marching upstream, recrossing and closing in behind the impi that was waiting in ambush. The men complained at having to wade through cold water. They were weary, hungry and sore. Their spirits sagged, but Raaff was going to extract one more battle from them.

In the thirty-one days since leaving Bulawayo, the men had trudged through two hundred fifty miles of unmapped brush, fought a dozen major battles and been wet, cold and hungry all the way. They'd lost more than a quarter of their comrades in a campaign that was worse than the war itself. Now it was time to give their all—or quit. Raaff borrowed a phrase from a London music hall song that was in vogue.

"Come on, you boys of the Bulldog Breed, show us the way. This is a schoolgirls giggle. Let's bash away!"

Raaff's challenge had the same effect on the men as the Jingo song. A wild cheer arose, followed by hostile rifle shots. There was a burst of machine-gun fire. Charley Lendy's Maxim opened up. The ambushing Matabele—astonished at being hit from both sides—abandoned the brush. They took cover in the river and dashed for the nearest kopjes. The troopers pot-shotted at the fleeing warriors. In less than ten minutes, it was over, a rout.

The short, sharp fight bolstered the men's spirits and they rested an hour until Maxim Lendy's machine-gun squad caught up. Then it began to rain. The fatigue and hunger pangs set in, and the flush of success died. Piet Raaff kept the men trekking until 5 p.m. when the patrol came to a halt near a kopje—the men were too tired to care if they laagered or died. Fred had scouted ahead for a campsite and he returned with news of a clearing where they could bed down in safety. It took stinging abuse from Raaff to get the men up and marching, even with Fred and Johann lending support.

"Keep going, you bags of bones," Johann scolded.

"Dash it, we're knocked up," one trooper whimpered.

"It's only two miles," Fred chided. "You can do that."

When the patrol arrived at the campsite, the men collapsed on the ground and fell into deep sleep. Fred wondered if Jan had made it to Inyati. Then he laid down to sleep, too tired himself to eat. Heavy rain fell all day on Thursday, December 14, keeping the Matabele at bay. The troopers shot a horse for dinner. Burnham and Bain, after making sure it wasn't Zebra, took their usual ration of bonce.

"It's boot and saddle time," Raaff cried. "Let's move."

The startled men shogged along, dragging their rifles in the mud. By now even the grumbling had stopped. The rain grew more intense, punctuated by loud thunder and bolts of lightning that froze silhouettes of the men in rout step. Two horses went lame and were shot. More men hallucinated. They scratched at sores, real and imaginary. Troopers who'd been close friends for years snapped at each another, their tempers frayed beyond endurance. Some men fell, forcing others to drag them.

Fred and Bob returned from scouting late in the afternoon and saw the ugly mood of the men. Everyone smelled unbelievably foul, a mixture of dirt, decay and pus. The men had run out of everything but hope, vermin and weary feet—and hope was rapidly fading.

"There's a good campsite ahead," Fred said, "but we should laager now. When the men stop complaining, they're at the breaking point. If someone's nerves crack, there may be shooting."

"We'll rest for an hour," Raaff said.

The men collapsed in the mud. By now, the rain was only a minor irritant. No one made any attempt to build a fire, so Fred, Bob and Johann started collecting brush. By the time they had a small fire going, it was dark. Even Raaff's abuse couldn't get the men to move.

There was a soft cooee, and out of the darkness two men emerged, mounted on horses.

"Hold your fire," Johann called out. "It's Selous."

At first there was astonished silence, then loud cheers. Fred Selous and another man rode up and dismounted.

"You chaps look perished," Selous said. "We're from the relief party at Inyati."

Jan Grootboom had gotten through.

"Got any food?" Half a dozen voices asked in unison.

"Lashings."

There were cheers, then expressions of relief. Men who an hour earlier vowed they wouldn't walk another step arose to gather around their rescuers.

"Build bonfires," Selous said. "Our patrol is only two miles back."

An hour later, the men fell on a hot meal, scoffing like trenchermen. Many of them bolted down their food and threw up. While they ate, Captain Heaney's men called out the names of friends and comrades trying to learn who were among the dead and missing.

Among the survivors, the expressions of joy knew no bounds. Some of them pledged to hand over their land and mineral claims to their rescuers. When they finished eating, a sense of complete exhaustion set in. While Captain Heaney's relief patrol stood guard, the survivors fell asleep under the luxury of blankets and canvas. It was their first peaceful night in a month of hunger, fatigue and fighting. They were so tired that no one noticed that the Matabele had suddenly disappeared.

Ritornello • An Interlude

TROOPER DAVE BOTTOMLY, the wheyfaced chap who had seldom been exposed to the ravages of direct sunlight, watched in absolute horror as the survivors of the Shangani Retreat bedded down. Some were in tents; others collapsed in the mud with only a blanket wrapped around them. All were oblivious to the rain.

Their bodies were gaunt and covered with filth and sores. Their clothing was little more than tatters. Scores of wounded were bandaged with odds and ends of clothing and blankets. Many had lost arms and feet. Their wounds had putrefied and the stench of rotting human flesh was beyond belief.

Bottomly listened in awe as the survivors recounted their experiences. Had he not seen them, he would never have believed their tales. Nothing in life had prepared him for the images he looked upon. When he was relieved of picket duty, Bottomly crept into his tent and wrapped himself in an overcoat. Only after he was snug against the damp of the night air did he light a candle and unwrap his red, silk-bound diary.

December 14—Last night we had an alarm. It turned out to be Jan Grootboom coming in with a message from Forbes. At sunrise we all started out for the Shangani River and at 7:30 p.m. we came into Forbes' camp at the Bubi. Never in my life have I seen such a lot of mowed down, miserable men as these poor fellows are. Their tale of woe is simply astonishing. They had to ride their horses, then shoot and eat them. The whole time they expected to be killed at any moment and they never expected to get out alive. One poor fellow was shot and they couldn't see his last moments to bury him. Nearly every horse was shot or assegaied.

Bottomly put down his pen and closed his diary. He picked up his candle to blow it out, then thought better of it. He'd forgotten to mention the fate of Major Allan Wilson and his thirty-three comrades. Bottomly was no intellectual giant, but his emotions ran as deep as the next man's. He knew a tragedy of this magnitude must not go unrecorded. He opened his diary.

Allan Wilson and Captain Borrow, with about thirty-three men, went on ahead. Shortly after, very heavy firing was heard in their direction. It gradually grew less, then ceased. And from that day, not one word has been heard from them. Not one man of us expects to see any of them return. Forbes is in bad odour with everybody, and he deserves it. After the first battle—they had at least six—Forbes gave overall command to Raaff, who has proved himself a salvation of the men. Curses loud and heavy from everyone against Forbes, and nothing but praise for Raaff.

The ill-fated Shangani Patrol

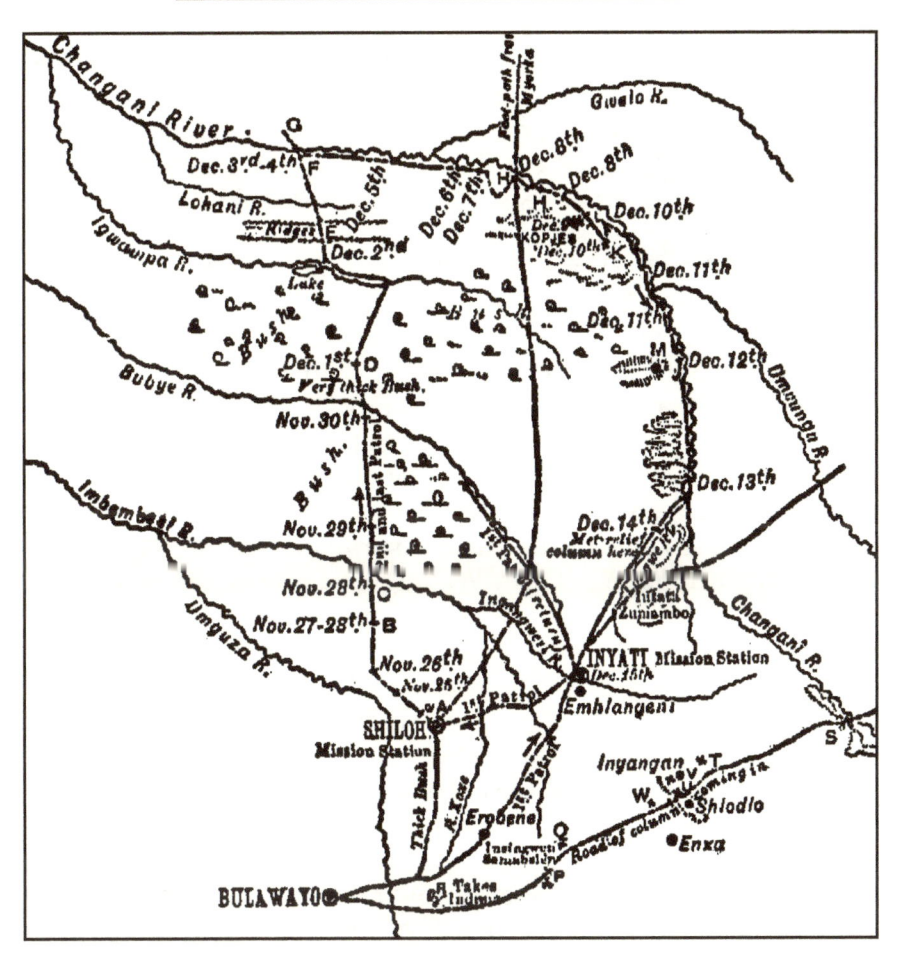

Burnham and Ingram caught up with Major Forbes' Shangani Patrol at Shiloh. They escaped from Wilson's Last Stand on December 4. Fred Selous met the returning patrol December 14 north of Inyati.

21

Burnham Meets Rhodes

BULAWAYO • DECEMBER 1893

THE MEN OF Captain Heaney's relief column gave up their horses to the survivors. Everyone trekked south on the Old Hunters Trail, coming in four hours' time to a camp of many wagons and large fires. Cecil Rhodes and Doctor Jameson presided over a feast of roast mutton, baked potatoes, biscuits and vegetables. As the men ate, there was acrimonious conjecture on the fate of Major Allan Wilson and his thirty-three men.

Major Forbes insisted some had survived, suggesting they were on the Old Hunters Trail en route to Salisbury. Not a man in camp believed him. Many spoke ominously of Wilson's Last Stand.

At 2 o'clock, they inspanned and trekked until sunset brought them to Inyati, where another banquet awaited. Fresh clothing was issued and the men rested for two days while messengers galloped ahead with the news of the patrol's survival. By easy stages they rode to Bulawayo where Digby Willoughby presided over the taking of photos of the survivors. An official campaign ribbon was authorized.

In Bulawayo, Colonel Hamilton Goold-Adams, the senior Imperial officer, held a court of enquiry. It lasted five days, during which the survivors of the Shangani Patrol were questioned about the fate of Major Allan Wilson and the conduct of Major Patrick Forbes. The hearing was concluded on Christmas Day.

The findings were classified and forwarded to Sir Henry Loch, the British high commissioner in Cape Town. The Combined Column was disbanded—eighty-one days after signing on at Forts Victoria and Salisbury. Colonel Goold-Adams and his Imperial Column remained in Bulawayo to occupy the town.

Captain Bill Napier, the second in command to Major Wilson, inherited the duty of mustering out the officers and men of the Victoria Column. He gave each of the men certificates entitling each to six thousand acres of land, twenty mineral claims and a share of King Lobengula's cattle. Similar documents were forwarded to the survivors of deceased campaigners. The certificates were instantly accepted as mediums of exchange—as good as gold. There was a brisk trade in farm rights and minerals claims. Burnham exchanged his double share of farm stands for hundreds of mineral claims.

That night Captain Lendy invited Fred Burnham to dine with him in his tent on roast beef and vegetables.

"I wanted to thank you personally for those ears you gave me back on the veld," Lendy said.

"If it wasn't for your Maxim guns," Burnham said, "neither of us would be here tonight."

"I told you they were the Devil's own paint brush."

"True, at the Battle of the Shanganii, I was impressed with the Maxims," Fred said. "But later at the Battle of the Bembesi, it was those Hotchkiss guns that saved us. For awhile, I became skeptical of the Maxims."

"What made you change your mind?"

"Those Hotchkiss cannons were too heavy to lug along on the Shangani Patrol," Fred said. "But we were able to strip down the Maxims and use them in tough fighting. It was the Maxims that saved our lives. I now join with you in believing the Maxim machine gun will change the essence of warfare."

"That's the message I intend to carry to London."

• • •

ON WEDNESDAY, December 27, every able-bodied man from Salisbury and Fort Victoria rode out of Bulawayo. Most went to get their women, children and possessions and bring them back to Bulawayo to stake out farms and mineral claims in Matabele Land.

Johann Colenbrander, who had been placed in charge of prisoners during the Shangani Retreat, became Chief Native Commissioner. His new position held more police power and judicial authority than any American Indian Agent. The CNC and his staff of Native Commissioners would serve as policeman, judge, jury and executioner for the blacks. Johann began disarming the Matabele warriors, who turned in their rifles and assegais—at least some of them. Colenbrander immediately won the sobriquet Collar and Brand 'em.

By separate routes, Fred Selous and Patrick Forbes left for London. Selous planned to write a book about Africa. Though he had spent two decades in the Dark Continent and earned renown as a white hunter, he had accumulated little more than his wagons, hunting rifles and a few tusks of ivory, which he had to sell to pay his passage back to England. Forbes was escorting his brother, Eustace, who was being sent to London to receive medical treatment for a war wound.

Toward evening that Wednesday, Commandant Piet Raaff collapsed with a sharp pain in his stomach. He was taken to the dispensary and placed under the care of Doctor Leander Starr Jameson, the administrator. Doctor Jim diagnosed Raaff's condition as inflammation of the bowels. Sometime during the night, Commandant Pieter Raaff, the Boer kaffir fighter with the big reputation and little girl feet, drew his last breath and died.

Three weeks later, Captain Charles Lendy arrived at Tati by the Shashi River and checked into Edwards Tati Hotel. That night, after scoffing down three pints of grog and grand-grousing a memorable repast, Maxim Lendy collapsed. He was carried to his hotel room where during the night he died. The medical examiner's diagnosis was bowel inflammation, which touched off rumors that both Raaff and Lendy had died at the hand of Doctor Jameson.

Major Patrick Forbes arrived in London in a state of complete disgrace. While crossing the Umzingwane River where it joined with the Limpopo, Pat Forbes allowed his wounded brother, Eustace, to drown in the rapids. His loss of reputation and prestige was total.

The deaths of Allan Wilson, Pieter Raaff and Charley Lendy and the contempt accorded Patrick Forbes meant that the horrifying capabilities of the Maxim machine gun would remain unrecognized until the Battle of Omdurman in the Anglo-Egyptian Sudan. No foreign observer was in Matabele Land to witness the Devil's Paintbrush in action.

Lagnappe • a Little Extra

Cape Town • December 1893

HIGH COMMISSIONER Sir Henry Loch classified as Secret all documents relating to his peace offering to King Lobengula, including the part about Lo Ben's envoys being murdered at Tati. Then, caught up in the spirit of the victory, Sir Henry announced that six hundred white men had defeated ten thousand hostile savages at the Battle of the Shangani. He let out all stops in describing the Battle of the Bembesi as Britain's greatest struggle in native warfare since Rorke's Drift. Fred came to understand that recalling Rorke's Drift in the British Empire was akin to crying "Remember the Alamo" in the United States. Rorke's Drift was when a hundred thirty British soldiers held out in Natal against four thousand Zulus.

Counterpoise • Equilibrium

Bulawayo • December 1893

BEFORE LEAVING Bulawayo, Cecil Rhodes summoned Burnham to his presence for a private audience. It was Fred's first meeting with his hero and he privately warned himself to mind his Ps and Qs. The great man had come to Africa for his health, but from what Fred could see Britain's most powerful man acted like he was the king of the land.

"I'm pleased to meet a man of your rare courage and exceptional qualities," Rhodes said as they shook hands. A male servant served tea.

Fred wished it was Arbuckles.

Despite a ghastly falsetto voice, Rhodes was accustomed to having his commands instantly obeyed.

"This meeting is my honor," Burnham replied. "I came half way around the world to serve you."

"Really now?"

"I came from California to serve your cause," Fred said.

"Is that a fact?" Rhodes seemed to be all the more impressed because the guy talking to him was such a little fart. Yet his cobalt-blue eyes instantly took in every detail of the room.

"Doctor Jameson tells me if there were ten of you, the war would have been won in half the time."

"Like the devil at a baptizing," Burnham said, "we did a lot of rushing around. At other times, we were stuck in mud up to the buggy hubs."

Rhodes flinched. His life was so filled with intense action that he had little time for ordinary jocularity. Fred decided that give or take a pterodactyl or two, Rhodes was the first child of Adam's breed.

"Did you ever come across any Mormons while you were knocking about in America?" Rhodes asked. "I hear they are first-rank desert farmers."

Fred told of his experiences with Sirrine, the engineer who'd reclaimed the gradients of the Ho-Ho-Kams east of Phoenix. He repeated what Sirrine had described to him of the municipal layout of Salt Lake City.

Rhodes, his interest piqued, invited Fred into an inner sanctum where they talked for several hours. Rhodes' voice broke into a falsetto whenever he became excited.

Fred drew sketches to show how the Mormons built their cities on a pattern of rectangular city blocks with streets so wide a span of eighteen oxen could make a U-turn.

At length, Rhodes said, "You've given me valuable ideas."

Fred rose to take his leave.

"May I ask you a personal question, Mr. Burnham?"

"Certainly." Fred replied.

"You're a many-sided fellow, a jolly mixture of the physical and the intellectual. Why is it that you choose to live out here on the borders of savagery?"

It was widely known that Rhodes spent his time in the splendor of his grand mansion, Groot Shure, on swelldoodle hill — the slope of Table Mountain in Cape Town.

"I thrive in the outdoors, Mr. Rhodes. Take London. The sidewalks are narrow. To walk is to battle your way to your destination. London is miles and miles of narrow, foggy streets and unadorned, plain, back-to-back houses. No desert is so dreary."

Rhodes quivered and his jowls shook like jelly.

"I shall never forget that description, Mr. Burnham," he said, once again scrutinizing Fred carefully. Then at length, he added. "By the way, is there some way the British South Africa Company can repay you for the valuable services you've rendered to the Chartered Company?"

For fifteen seconds, Burnham seemed lost in thought.

"I appreciate the honor of your offer, but I fought to defend the lives of people, not to promote the interests of a commercial enterprise. I cannot accept any reward from the Chartered Company. If permitted, I might say that Matabele Land is as fine a place as it ever has been England's privilege to steal."

Rhodes' jowls shook and his face flushed. He arose, pursed his lips — his version of laughter — and reached across the desk to shake Fred's hand.

"I admire honesty," Rhodes said. "I'll disregard that remark."

Fred, still standing, tipped his hat and walked out. For several minutes, Rhodes sat at his desk in silence. Then he turned to the open doorway.

"Doctor Jameson, please come in here. That Burnham chap, he's quite a remarkable fellow. To see him once is to know him always."

"That's I've been trying to tell you, Mr. Rhodes."

"But he's so American, so ruddy cowboy."

"Give us a year and we'll have him speaking the Queen's English."

Rhodes pulled a badly wrinkled envelope from his jacket pocket. He scribbled on the back of it and handed it to Jameson.

"Maybe he won't accept a reward from the Chartered Company," Rhodes said enigmatically, "but from me? Well, see that this order is carried out."

Jameson studied the note and an expression of pure delight spread over his face. "Yes, Mr. Rhodes. It will be my greatest pleasure."

The next day, Cecil Rhodes left Bulawayo for Cape Town and London. He was accustomed to being the richest man in the world, the man who controlled ninety percent of the world's diamond market. Now he owned a country that was bigger than England or Germany, almost as big as France. Already people were calling it Rhodesia. For Cecil Rhodes, this was his finest hour.

Escape from Wilson's Last Stand

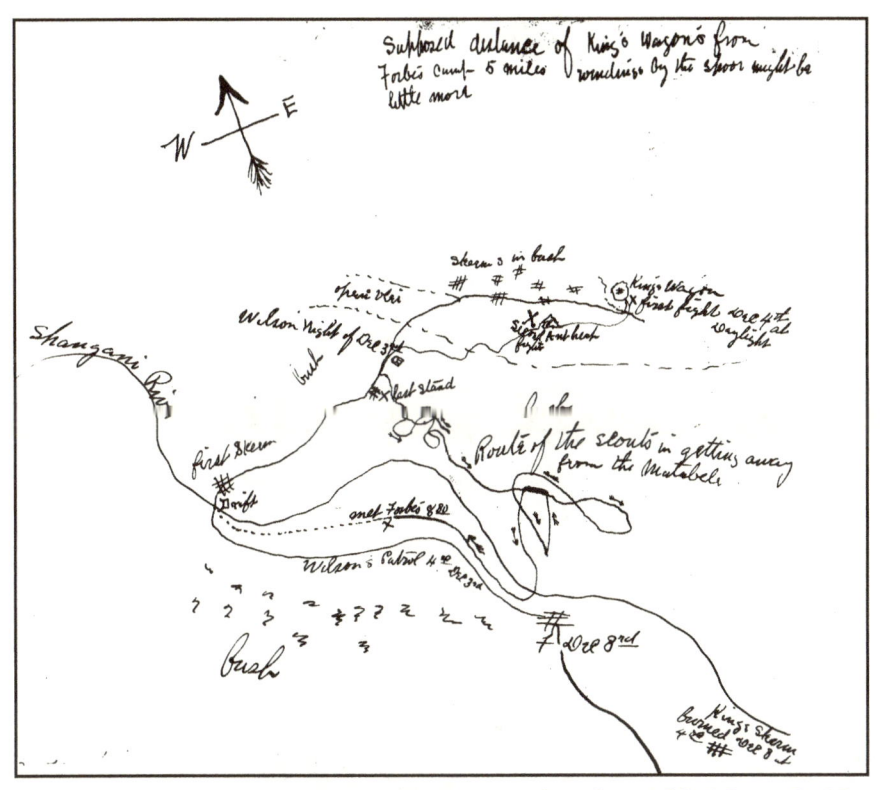

After the patrol's return to Bulawayo, Colonel Goold-Adams held a court of enquiry. Here is the map Burnham drew to describe his and Ingram's escape from the fate suffered by Wilson and his 33 men.

Chasing Rainbows

The 5th Chronicle

22

The Birth of Rhodesia

Fort Victoria • January 1894

IN BULAWAYO, Fred organized the Burnham Syndicate. He exchanged his dual six thousand-acre land grants with farmers and would-be cattle ranchers who had no interest in mineral rights. Several of the scouts turned over their mineral rights to Fred. Within hours, Fred had acquired the rights to file more than five hundred mineral claims. Meanwhile, Pete bought salted horses that were immune to the dikkop sickness—the blue tongue. The next day they mounted up and left Bulawayo.

"This's fine horse flesh, Pete."
"I spent all my life around animals, pard."
"What'd they cost?"
"Salted horses is scarce in Matabele Land."
"It's being called Rhodesia now. How much, Pete?"
"A hundred sterling."
"For both?"
"Each."
"Each? That's five hundred dollars apiece!"
"I said they're scarce."
"Slow down, let's don't run 'em to death."

When they reached the Shangani River, the bones of the slain Matabele warriors lay bleaching on the veld. Hyenas and vultures had devoured the flesh and only the white ants continued to display an interest in the remains. The scouts rode south toward the LimZam Ridgeback, now called the Rhodesian Ridgeback. There, on the patch that Fred had dubbed as Texas with trees, they staked out twenty-seven mineral claims. Pete erected a sign:

Keep Off! Scouts' Reef

At the Gwelo River, midway between Bulawayo and Fort Vic, the Chartered Company had built a wooden hut where Fred filed their claims in the minerals book. In expectation of a gold rush, the Chartered Company had sent to Gwelo a mineral claims book bound in red leather. It was four inches thick and measured an imposing three feet by four. Fred made the original entries, dated January 1, 1894, the day when claims became available for filing.

Burnham and Ingram arrived in Fort Victoria on the afternoon of New Year's Day. They had been away eighty-six days. Seemingly from nowhere, Blanche produced a feast. Afterwards, they talked and laughed away the day. That night, Fred wrote to uncles and aunties in Pasadena.

One year ago today we left San Francisco and without a doubt this has been the most eventful year in my life. The closing months of ninety-three have filled out the measure of my boyhood dreams, a sharp and desperate war, long, hard rides and the pitting of a man's skill and courage against savage cunning and ferocity. Today I'm home from the wars and Ingram, my young American comrade, has ridden back with me for good company. There were four Americans in the Scouts and they were no disgrace to their country.

Victoria is on a picnic with a royal reception and all the trimmings that go with a reunion. It's delightful to have sight of women once more and to hear the laughter of children. There were tables loaded with all the luxuries dear to the heart of a campaigner: real butter and milk, sponge cakes, coffee and sugar, spices and jam—a civilized feed. And only a few days ago, the somber forest was around us, full of savages, and we ourselves were a hungry band, eating our skeleton horses and boiling grass to keep soul and body within hailing distance. Ninety-three is now gone. I make no resolves, no oaths, no promises for ninety-four. What I find to do, I shall do.

The next day Fred sold the burros and the spring wagon. He visited the offices of the Chartered Company where he borrowed a trek wagon and a span of oxen. Pete bought food, ammo and mining tools.

Within ten days they were in Gwelo, where they prospected on the mineral claims they had filed on the Scouts' Reef. They found nothing and abandoned the claims. Within two months, they filed a hundred new claims: ten each on the Scouts' Reef, Burnham's Reef and Bain's Reef. All proved to be bastard quartz—a mere frost of gold along the cleavage. By late March, Fred got the eagers to be in Bulawayo. Blanche's time would come in two months and Fred

Chasing Rainbows

wanted their baby to be born in a house, not an ox-drawn trek wagon.

Ritornello • An Interlude

Johannesburg • March 1894

BECAUSE Barney Barnato repeatedly failed to act on his timely recommendations, Jack Hammond submitted a letter of resignation at the end of a six-month-long honeymoon. Barney begged Jack to reconsider and he agreed to delay the action for ten days.

Barnato forgot about it and sailed with his family for London. Jack dropped off his notice at Barney's office and went home to Natalie. Hammond believed that Barney's neglect of his counsel would damage his professional reputation.

Counterpoise • Equilibrium

Bulawayo • April 1894

IN FOUR MONTHS, the ruins of Bulawayo had become a modern community of six hundred Europeans. Each day ox-drawn wagons lumbered into town from Mafeking carrying settlers, equipment and provisions. Buildings of wood, block and galvanized iron sheeting were being erected in the European manner. The streets were wide. Cecil Rhodes had ordered them built broad enough for a span of oxen to turn a trek wagon. For the time being, Fred and Blanche lived in their trek wagon.

When the rainy season ended, Jimmy Dawson rode north to find out what had happened to King Lobengula. At a kraal near the Shangani River, an induna told Jimmy that the King was dead. While trekking north toward the Zambesi River, Lo Ben had became ill with fever, lapsed into a coma and died. The commander-in-chief, M'Jaan, conducted the burial rites. He declined to reveal the site where his King's remains were interred.

Dawson next searched for the bodies of Major Allan Wilson and his patrol. Five miles from the Shangani River, he found the mortal remains of the thirty-four-man patrol. Hyenas, vultures and white ants had devoured the flesh—only some bones remained. Jimmy dug a large pit and buried what there was left in a common grave. On the trunk of a tree, he carved a memorial:

To Brave Men

On returning to Bulawayo, Dawson forwarded his findings to Cecil Rhodes in Cape Town who released the news to the world. It was accepted as proof of the fate of Lobengula as well as Wilson and his missing patrol.

Not in a generation had any event in British arms more profoundly stirred the public's imagination. The massacre of the patrol went down as Wilson's Last Stand, a symbol of courage. It became an example to hold up before men of arms. And it became the British equivalent of Custer's Last Stand. Each battle produced three scouts who survived to describe all but the final moments. Each had patrols that survived to tell their side of the story, a bit different from the tribal views. Wilson and the Matabele fought with identical rifles. Custer spurned the Gatling gun and faced Indians with modern repeating rifles. After their battle, the Indians rode away in serenity, but the Matabele pursued resolutely. American retribution was severe—the Indian leaders were hunted down and killed. The British took virtually no revenge.

Lagnappe • A Little Extra

LONDON • APRIL 1894

THE NEWS OF THE Chartered Company's victory over the Matabele nation became headlines around the world. The story electrified the public in the British homeland and in the colonies alike. In London, crowds of cheering Britons gathered in Trafalgar Square to celebrate.

Fred's accomplishments were saluted in Singapore and Calcutta. From Ceylon to Glasgow and elsewhere in the far-flung British Empire, Fred Burnham was credited with saving the Shangani Patrol when Forbes had quit. Raaff and Lendy, both dead, were conveniently forgotten.

London stonemasons erected a memorial to the last stand. Poets, songwriters and playwrights weren't to be denied their offerings. A London theater staged the epic drama before packed audiences; the run would last two years. At the climax of each stage show, when Burnham the American Scout rode off to fetch the Maxims, the actors on stage clapped with the audience.

Counterpoise • Equilibrium

BULAWAYO • MAY 1894

THE NEW weekly newspaper reported seven thousand mineral claims had been filed and predicted a gold rush was in the making. Everyone hoped so because potatoes and eggs cost a dollar each. A large sack of onions fetched forty pounds sterling—two hundred Yank dollars.

While elbowing his way through a milling crowd at the mineral claims office, Fred saw a smiling redhead whose face looked familiar.

"When did you leave the Cattle Kingdom?"

Jefferson Clark, his face wearing a puzzled look, studied Fred closely. Then he recognized the sweet pea he had hired a decade ago to hunt wild game in Black Lava Canyon in Arizona.

"You were just a tenderfoot greener," Jeff Clark said, pumping Fred's hand eagerly. "What brought you to these parts?"

"It was on the anvil when President Harrison lowered the gold reserves," Fred replied. "I'm a hard. When soft money started floodin the market, I put on my conjurin cap and left for Africa."

"Not a minute too soon," Clark said. "I got cleaned out."

"There's sufficient here for a man of grit," Fred said glancing at the claims book. "I see you filed on another Tip Top."

"And a lot more." In fact, Jeff was filing claims even faster than Fred, but Burnham didn't care. There was plenty for everybody.

"Come over to my trek wagon for dinner tonight," Fred offered. "My wife is a wonderful cook."

That afternoon, Fred bought a parcel of land in Bulawayo five hundred feet from the market place. He hired Andy Main to build a wood-and-brick house with a corrugated-iron roof. To raise cash to pay for the house, Fred agreed to survey plots south of Bulawayo for Doctor Hans Sauer.

Mousy little Doc Sauer was the medical officer in Kimberley who had discovered the smallpox epidemic that Doctor Jameson had failed to detect. After that Sauer returned to London, read the law, passed the bar exams, then decided not to practice law. Instead he joined forces with Lord Gifford and emerged as Cecil Rhodes' financial manager in Rhodesia.

Fred told Blanche he would be gone about ten days surveying plots for Doc Sauer. Andy Main promised to have the house finished by then. While Fred was away, Blanche lived in the trek wagon and wrote to Mother Blick.

We came out to Arthur Cummings' farm five miles from town. It seems quiet out here. Art was one of our party on the road to Victoria and was a scout with Fred. He and Bob Bain have bought this farm and are running a dairy. They insisted on my coming out here while our house is being built. I was glad because it's too cold—it's equivalent to October—to live in a trek wagon.

Fred knows so many men. He's full of new business. Strange how well-known he's become in such a short time. His deeds of daring in the campaign made him a favorite at headquarters, but you know how most people like him anyway. Already we've received under the canvas awning of our trek wagon Doctor Jameson and Colonel Frank Rhodes, a brother of Cecil Rhodes—he has six brothers. They made a long call and had tea with us.

The next morning came Doctor Sauer, who looks after Cecil Rhodes' moneyed interests here. In the afternoon came Maurice Gifford, a brother of Lord Gifford, and then Captain Heyman, the magistrate of Bulawayo. I'm determined that we shall do well in this, Fred's chosen

163

land, so I've overcome my natural reluctance to society. I've spoken to only one white woman in three months. There are only Mollie Colenbrander and three Dutch wives in Bulawayo, but two English families have just come in. We still have the use of the company wagon and the oxen.

Fred was engaged to peg ten farms for Doctor Sauer at fifty dollars each. He knows where there's vacant land and he'll be gone for awhile. So we have contracted to build the house. Fred is in with the right stamp of men. They let him do practically as he likes. Things may shape themselves so that he'll need John Blick in a year or two. So study hard, Brother John, and devote more time to your math and chemistry. Blanche.

Burnham did not get back from surveying the land parcels until the first week of June. When he did arrive, Andy Main had finished the house and Blanche had delivered a girl child, with Andy, a discomfited bachelor, and Rod, eight, in attendance. Both mother and daughter were healthy and in good spirits. Fred was thrilled beyond description and he couldn't take his eyes off the baby.

"Let's name her Nada," Blanche said, "after the lily in Rider's new book."

"That's a wonderful idea, Bea." While cuddling the baby, Fred made plans for a celebration that night. He'd shoot a springbok for dinner.

The next day Fred went to the Chartered Company offices to see Doctor Sauer. As he strutted inside, he felt a foot taller. While he waited in an outer office, he boasted what a beautiful daughter he had—blonde with fair skin and the bluest eyes in central Africa. The birth of a white girl in Bulawayo would've been news in any event. The fact that her father was Fred Burnham, the American scout, drew a crowd.

In due time, Fred was summoned to Doctor Sauer's office. Burnham laid out plot plans showing where he'd pegged twenty thousand acres of prime land north of the Matopo Hills. Sauer studied the map carefully and asked detailed questions. He wanted to be certain he held clear title to these properties, because he'd be selling them to Cecil Rhodes for fifty thousand pounds, a quarter of a million Yankee dollars. Satisfied at last, he paid Fred one hundred pounds sterling, then added a bonus of ten pounds because the maps were carefully drawn. For an outlay of a hundred pounds, Doc Sauer stood to profit by nearly fifty thousand.

As Fred walked out of Doc Sauer's office, he was summoned to Doctor Jameson's inner sanctum.

"I've been trying to find you, Mr. Burnham."

Fred started to tell him about Nada, but Jameson turned around, opened a drawer of his desk and took out a wrinkled envelope.

"Mr. Rhodes wants you to have this."

Fred took the envelope and read the words scrawled on the back. His eyes began to blur. He shook his head and read it again:

Good ideas are useless without the money to carry them out. Burnham has good ideas. Give Burnham and Ingram the mineral rights to all the ancient ruins in Rhodesia, without royalty payment. Let each peg one hundred square miles of mineral claims in Barotze Land. C.J.R.

"Where's Barotze Land?" Fred asked.

"North of the Zambesi River. After we develop it, we will call it Northern Rhodesia," said Doctor Jameson.

Fred's hands shook so much he almost dropped the envelope. If he'd read this scrap of paper right, he'd better guard it with his life. The writing said the gold riches of all the ruins in Rhodesia were his and Pete Ingram's to do with as they wished.

23

Zimbabwe & Dhlo Dhlo

Gwelo • April 1894

FRED GALLOPED to the Scouts' Reef in Gwelo. The camp was empty so he built a fire and had fresh coffee brewing when Pete returned from the digs.

"How's it going, Pete?"

"Keep findin sign. Nothin worth developin."

They drank their coffee in silence.

"Wish we could get Arbuckles out here." Fred said. He removed the wrinkled envelope from his shirt pocket and handed it to Pete who squatted by the fire to read it.

"Is this for real?"

"Those are Rhodes' initials. Doctor Jim gave it to me."

Fred was shaving a piece of biltong to boil for soup.

"Can we sell 'em? The rights, I mean." Pete asked.

"Suppose so. Why don't we try our luck first?"

"In old ruins? They're picked over for sure."

"I had good luck at Zimbabwe."

"That's back by Fort Vic. Besides, your pal, Sergeant Jack Carruthers, has pegged Zimbabwe as his farm. It's his entitlement for service against the Matabele."

"This piece of paper says if Carruthers picks up a gold pan, he's trespassing. Besides, there's more here than Zimbabwe. Bob Vavasseur told me about some ruins not far from here. They're called Dhlo-Dhlo."

"How's he know?" Ingram asked.

"Before the war, he and Colenbrander had a business. Johann ran across Dhlo-Dhlo a couple of years ago but he never did anything about it."

"I'll bet they're all picked over."

"In the middle of Matabele Land? Come on, Pete. Besides we

don't have to pay royalty. On regular claims, we have to give half of what we find to the Chartered Company."

"You're right, how do we get to this Dhlo-Dhlo?"

Ingram tossed the dregs of his coffee into the fire and took a bowl of biltong soup from Fred.

"Bob Vavasseur said it's fifteen miles south of the Shangani battle site."

They rode back to the Shangani River, turned south and in a few hours found the Dhlo-Dhlo Ruin. It was in open country, among a sprinkling of trees in the veld. The ruins sat on a mound sixty feet high and five hundred feet in diameter. The scouts could see it from a mile away. Save for the warblers singing, there was not a sound.

The ruin was a smaller version of Zimbabwe. The decoration was more elaborate, but the workmanship was inferior. They made camp on an outcropping of basalt and surveyed their prize. Like Zimbabwe, the walls were laid without mortar.

Inch-high gold figures of animals and men were cached in the niches of the rocks. The scouts pried loose as many as they could find, then turned their attention to the veins. Fred traced out how someone had built fires on the ledges and dashed water on the rocks to crack them and expose the quartz. By the end of the week, they had filled two leather bags with gold. Agreeing they had all they could carry, they pegged the ruin with a sign.

Keep Out.
Property of the Ancient Ruins Syndicate

On their return to Bulawayo, Fred and Pete displayed their hoard of nuggets to Blanche, Rod and the baby Nada. The assayer at the mining office said the bags contained six hundred forty ounces of gold: fifty-three pounds. They were rich.

That weekend Burnham asked Selous and Vavasseur to join the Burnhams for a home-cooked Sunday dinner. While dining on one of Blanche's dutch-oven roasts of springbok haunch, they talked about life in the new country now called Rhodesia.

"Immigrants are taking over the place," Selous said.

"Not only those who fought," Vavasseur said, "but also important segments of English society who stayed home during hostilities."

"Rhodes means to give them a stake in the success of his new colony," Selous added. "It helps build his political base in Albion."

"Rhodesia is being flooded with young aristocrats," Vavasseur said, "all imbued with the spirit of making a million and clearing back to Piccadilly."

"Why are Rhodesian mining claims so small?" Fred asked

"They're only a tenth the size of American claims."

"The idea," Selous explained, "is to make trading in Rhodesian gold shares seem active in the Kaffir Circus."

"The what?"

"The Kaffir Circus is the section of the Stock Exchange where Rhodesian gold shares are traded," Selous said.

Fred looked puzzled. Vavasseur explained.

"Selous' dad is the chairman of the London Stock Exchange. Fred knows about these things. If many shares are traded, it gives the appearance that there's plenty of mining activity in Rhodesia."

"How then can anyone clear a million on those tiny claims?" Fred asked.

"By trading shares," Selous said. "Cecil made his bob by dealing in claims, not by digging for diamonds."

"I'll have to conjure about that." *I had better explore some new avenues of enterprise.*

The following day Fred and Pete rode out to the Belingwe mountains, sixty miles southeast of Bulawayo. There they filed one hundred thirty claims for the Burnham Syndicate including June Bug, Mexican, Idaho, Tammany, Spanish, Columbia, Apache and Central Park.

In their own names, the Americans organized the Rhodesia Development & Exploration Syndicate. They filed a hundred sixty claims: Cart Wheel, Buzz Saw, Sabi, July, Bow Bells, Twinkle, Moonbeam, Right Angle, Jingle Bob and Nada. They would need some help to develop these properties so Fred proposed to Blanche that they bring her younger brothers to Africa.

"By all means, if you think the prospects will generate sufficient income, let's ask them to come."

"Did I ever say that you're my favorite tiger bait?"

"Oh, Fred, I forgot. Here's a letter from Howie. He resolved the fire insurance claim on the Alvord Mine in our favor."

"That's great news for Mother Burnham."

"Not only that, Fred, but he is coming to Africa. He has graduated from the Houghton School of Mines, and he has a job working in a Johannesburg gold mine."

"Will wonders never cease? Howie is coming too."

Lagnappe • A Little Extra

CAPE TOWN • MAY 1894

JOHN HAYS Hammond sat on a stone bench in a grove of pine and oak trees in front of the Dutch-gabled mansion called Groot Schure. Rhodes' home had a thatched roof and large windows. It sat on a shoulder of Table Mountain called Devil's Peak. Hammond and Rhodes glanced over Cape Town Harbor, one of the world's glorious seaports.

To fig-nosed Jack Hammond, Rhodes presented a mixed figure. He had a heavy forehead and a strong mouth with a square chin. His curly hair was always tousled. His blue-gray eyes were as cold as ice. His big boned frame seemed to tower over his companions. His hands were blunt and powerful, yet he rarely moved them to gesticulate.

"You are not in Cape Town for your health." Rhodes said with his usual bluntness. The news of Hammond's resignation from Barney Barnato had spread rapidly, and soon there was a telegram from Cape Town suggesting a meeting. Rhodes had recently become the prime minister of the Cape Colony and couldn't get away, so Hammond took the train to Cape Town to visit the great one at Groot Schure.

"Would you take charge of my gold mines in South Africa?" Rhodes asked. "Name your salary."

"Seventy-five thousand dollars a year."

"That will be satisfactory."

"But only if I deal with you directly, not through your board of directors."

Hammond said he had examined Rhodes' holdings in the Witswatersrand and he had a poor opinion of them. "I can acquire new mineral interests to substantially improve your investments."

Rhodes studied Hammond for ten seconds, nodded thoughtfully, picked up a scrap of paper and wrote:

Mr. Hammond is authorized to make any purchases for going ahead and has full authority, provided he informs me of it and gets no protest.

With that scrap, Jack Hammond became consulting engineer for the Consolidated Gold Fields of South Africa and the British South Africa Company in Rhodesia as well.

Ritornello • An Interlude

JOHANNESBURG • JULY 1894

REPORTS BEGAN to reach London that Rhodesia was a mining bust, all bastard quartz. Trading on the Kaffir Circus declined precipitously as the predictions of Lord Randolph Churchill seemed to come true.

Three years earlier, while traveling in Africa, he had visited Mashona Land. There he collected material for a series of articles in the *London Daily Mail*. One article dealt with gold mining and he hired two Americans to examine the Shona mine workings. They condemned Mashona Land on the theory the veins were only gash reefs without persistence in depth. Churchill published this valuation in his book *Men, Mines and Animals in South Africa*. With Lobengula's impis on the prowl, few people had dared to muck about for gold in Mashona Land, to say nothing of Matabele Land.

The arrival of European adventurers in Rhodesia had sparked a new search for the yellow metal. Nearly ten thousand claims had been filed, but save for Zimbabwe and Dhlo-Dhlo, almost no gold had been found. The book had become a serious blow to Rhodes' aspirations for Rhodesia. Without mining, the new colony was a bust.

Rhodes asked Hammond to investigate Rhodesia's minerals deposits—not only the gold reserves but other minerals as well. During August and September 1894, Rhodes and Hammond toured Rhodesia. They were accompanied by Doctor Jameson, Digby Willoughby, Maurice Gifford and Robert Williams, the British geologist who had introduced Hammond to Rhodes. Aside from Hammond, Jefferson Clark was the only other American invited. When the inspection party arrived in Bulawayo, Burnham and Ingram were digging for gold in Belingwe.

The geological survey began in August, at the start of the African spring. For nearly two months, the experts toured the countryside. They sampled mineral deposits, studied the pitch and dip of rock formations, drew maps, analyzed ore samples and made notes. When Hammond told Rhodes that Churchill's people had been mistaken, Rhodes drew a huge sigh of relief.

"The geology is similar to the gold bearing areas of the United States," he told Rhodes. "The gold is chiefly in quartz veins. Some of these veins are many miles wide. Using dynamite and modern recovery methods, there is the potential for considerable amounts of gold to be taken. These fissure veins have persistence in depth."

"I appreciate your attention to detail," Rhodes said.

Each evening after supper the explorers sat around the fire while the talk ranged from trivia to world affairs. One night as Rhodes stirred the campfire, he spoke about Hammond's Witswatersrand Gold scheme. For weeks, Jack had been pursuing a theory that the Johannesburg outcrops were unusually deep. So carefully reasoned were Hammond's arguments that Rhodes became convinced his theory might be valid.

"Would it not be good business to sell our shallow holdings in the Outcrop Companies and use the funds from the sale to buy up all the available deep-level areas?"

"That's what I told Barney," Hammond said. "He was too busy with social matters so I resigned."

"Are you really quite sure your geology on this is sound?" Rhodes persisted.

"I'll stake my reputation on it."

Rhodes asked Doctor Jameson for pencil and paper and he wrote a message to Lord Gifford in London.

Have decided best policy for company would be sell out our holdings in Outcrop Companies. Do this at once. Hammond approves. Rhodes

"Starr, have your fastest runners convey this message to Mafeking for cable to London," Rhodes said.

Three weeks later, the sales of Rhodes outcrop holdings were quietly executed during several days of trading. Witswatersrand stocks on the London Exchange were at the peak of a boom, so several hundred million dollars worth of shares were sold at prime prices.

A month later, Rhodes made the geological report public. Hammond's standing in the mining world was held in such high regard that the news ignited a trading boom in the Kaffir Circus. It was back to full throttle.

Counterpoise • Equilibrium

BULAWAYO • OCTOBER 1894

THE BLICKS arrived from Pasadena while Fred and Pete were in town to buy supplies. Fred had asked for two Blicks—five showed up. The eldest brother-in-law, limber Homer, was thirty-four years old, a sturdy, blue-eyed six-footer with a mobile face and a bony body. He walked and talked in a steady, dependable manner. Fred and Homer had run away together.

Judd was twenty-four, Pete Ingram's age, and he wore a built-in grin. At five feet eight inches, he had the slouching walk and sinewy body of a Texas cowhand, a man well acquainted with hard work. He had a croaky voice that irritated some people, but Fred didn't mind. Judd was keen to become a white hunter and was eager to meet Fred Selous. He fondled Fred's rifles with an acquisitive gleam in his eyes.

John, twenty-one, was a younger version of Judd. He was five feet nine and heavier. He held himself more erect than the cowboy Judd, so he seemed taller, specially in his pinch-back suit. Like Homer, John had a deliberate gait which somehow suggested he was a slow thinker. He was quite thoughtful and by far the best educated of the lot. He'd studied hard at Throop University—the four-year-old Pasadena school about to become Caltech.

The surprise arrivals were Grace Blick, Blanche's younger sister, and that patriarch of the clan, James Blick, a silver haired stringbean of sixty-four years. Grace was a buttercup of twenty-six who favored her elder sister. Blanche showed off Rod, eight, and the baby Nada.

There was a week of feasts as the Blicks listened to tales of Fred's adventures. Nada gurgled and threw up on Grandpa Blick's arm. John and Judd were so smitten with Africa they wrote to chum Kingsley Macomber, inviting him to join them to hunt lions and elephants. King's father was the teetotaling physician who had delivered Rod into the world.

"Up and at 'em, you layabouts," Fred called. "There's work to be done—gold to be found." Fred and Pete outfitted Homer, John and Judd with rifles, horses and mining tools. They rode off for the Belingwe Mountains in search of adventure and treasure. In the next month, Fred filed a hundred twenty claims, including the Kinlock, Big Ben, Montezuma, Chebani, Black Man, Northern Railroad, Franchise, United South Africa, Bulawayo and the Bamba Longa.

All but the Bamba Longa would border on claims held by a Highlander from Scotland's Black Watch Regiment. Tyrie Laing was a bachelor, with an oval face, a bristling mustache and a burr in his voice. One glance convinced Fred that Terry combined the good looks of Major Forbes with the intelligence and integrity of Major Allan Wilson. Terry Laing was a rare man: strong as a Cape buffalo and just as resourceful.

With the Christmas season on them, the prospectors filed thirty more claims: Cloudy Day, Yankee Girl and Twin Nugget. Fred put one of the ten Cloudy Day claims in The Kid's name as a Christmas gift.

When they returned to Bulawayo, Blanche gave Fred a note from Maurice Gifford. After lunch Fred rode over to Gifford's office. His Stetson still bore the ornamental hatband Fred had plaited.

Gifford handed Fred a handwritten note from Cecil Rhodes. It awarded Lord Gifford a hundred square miles of mineral claims in

Barotze Land across the Zambesi.

"Don't you and Pete have similar grants?"

Fred said nothing, not wanting to commit himself.

"My brother is chairman of the Bechuana Exploration Company. He is also responsible for Mr. Rhodes' financial affairs in London."

"I've heard that," Fred said.

Lord Gifford was said to have powerful political ties. He was said to be an intimate of the Rothschilds bankers. They said Rhodes attracted Lord Gifford's support for the Chartered Company by dangling a directorship in De Beers Diamond Mines. In return, Gifford arranged a line of credit from the Rothschilds. That loan allowed Rhodes could buy out his Cockney partner, Barney Barnato, and take over De Beers.

"My brother asks us to come to London," Gifford said. "He wants to finance an expedition to Barotze Land."

If Pete and I get equal billing with Maurice, the deal must be gold-plated.

"When do you propose that we leave?" Fred asked.

"Right after Christmas."

24

Rider Haggard and Lo Ben's Seal

LONDON • FEBRUARY 1895

FIVE WEEKS LATER, Fred and Pete registered at the First Avenue Hotel north of Fleet Street. The walk was less than a mile to Lord Gifford's offices at 19, St. Swithin's Lane, which was only a short hop to the Bank of England, which some people called the Old Lady of Threadneedle Street. From the exterior, Gifford's office looked anything but imposing. St. Swithin's Lane was a narrow, crooked alley scarcely fifteen feet wide. It was flanked by three-story buildings of brick—mossy, old, eroded brick. The ground floor housed offices but the upper level looked more like flats or storage lofts. The walls of the offices were relieved by an archway of pink granite that framed polished mahogany doors. Bricked up windows dated from a window tax imposed to finance a long-forgotten war against Napoleon.

Maurice Gifford made the introductions. While everyone sipped tea, Fred studied the man who would play a major role in his financial future. Lord Gifford was stout—mostly tallow, some of it muscle. His mutton-chop beard created an imposing demeanor. He was several years older than brother Maurice, and he looked like wealth personified. He was attired in finery far more fashionable than Rhodes whose dress tended toward bachelor wrinkle. Gifford wore a Seville Row frock coat and stiff white shirt with a boiled collar. Fred, wearing a store-bought celluloid collar, felt like a dirt farmer on a Sunday visit to the county fair.

The teak-paneled room was well appointed with oil paintings of rich, royal and famous personages, no doubt valued clientele of Lord Gifford. The room served as a reception center for the boards of directors of the various companies that Lord Gifford controlled. Before the day was over, Fred became acutely aware that Lord Gifford organized, bought and sold companies as casually as Pete and he traded in mining shares.

The Rhodesia Development & Exploration Syndicate, which held Fred's and Pete's mining claims at Belingwe, was the first topic raised. Fred wanted shares to trade on the Kaffir Circus. At Lord Gifford's counsel, the syndicate was incorporated and renamed Rhodesia Exploration & Development Company.

At Fred's request, Lord Gifford arranged for them to incorporate the Ancient Ruins Syndicate as the Ancient Ruins Company. He then helped them with its sale to two London financiers, W.G. Neal and R.N. Hall. Fred and Pete received five thousand pounds sterling, the British equivalent of twenty-five thousand American dollars—gold coin not paper.

That night while hosting the two scouts at a West End restaurant, the Rt. Hon. Maurice Gifford taught Burnham and Ingram some of the latest red-brick university slang, expressions that only a few weeks ago had originated at Oxford.

"The suffix *ers* is added to the first syllable of a business name," Gifford said.

Fred and Pete looked at one another, perplexed.

"Here," Gifford said pouring champagne, "take the word champagne. Add *ers* to champ and you get a glass of champers. Members of the Wig Club, a fraternity for solicitors, are called Wiggers. In the Far East, the Hong Kong and Shanghai Bank is known as Honkers and Shankers."

"What's that got to do with us?" Ingram asked.

"Rhodesia Exploration & Development Company, is henceforth known as Rhoders Exers," Gifford said. "The Bechuana Exploration Company, of which my brother is chairman, is called Bechers Exers. Get it?"

"Does that mean we just sold Anchers Ruiners to Neal and Hall?" Fred joshed.

"You have nailed it down precisely."

The next day the business discussion turned to a company called Charterlands Goldfields, or Charters Golders in red-brick jargon. Lord Gifford said that company held title to one hundred square miles of mineral claims in the Barotze Land.

"That's a new egg in the omelet," Fred mumbled.

"Wonder what else is up this old pirate's sleeve?" Ingram responded. If Fred, Pete and Maurice Gifford each had a hundred-square-mile claim and Lord Gifford had a similar grant, that meant Rhodes had parceled out four hundred square miles of mineral rights north of the Zambesi River.

"I wonder if the old croaker has the right to dispose of that much land?" Ingram said.

Lord Gifford cleared his throat for silence.

"I propose that we form the Northern Territories (BSA) Exploration & Development Company."

Fred turned to Maurice. "I know, Northers Terrors."

"It'll scare 'em all," Ingram cried.

"We'll exchange our four Barotze Land claims for common shares of stock in the new company. I nominate Mr. Burnham and Mr. Ingram as salaried co-managers to lead an expedition north of the Zambesi River to survey those four-hundred square miles of Barotze Land claims."

It seemed impossible to lose. The arrangement was approved and the details were worked out. Two of Gifford's financial aides, Major Ricarde-Seaver, clean shaven and hatchet-faced, and the bearded, roly-poly Percy Tarbott, contributed their rights to peg twelve thousand acres of coal seams.

How the two Gifford aides acquired these coal claims at Wankie was a mystery to Fred, but they would be vital to build a railway from Bulawayo to the Zambesi. *It feels good to be in with the right stamp of men. Given time, Northers Terrors is sure to earn a ton of money.*

Solicitors were called in to draw up the boilerplate paperwork. A total of eighty-seven thousand five hundred shares were divided into five blocks. Burnham, Ingram and the two Gifford brothers received blocks of seventeen thousand five hundred shares. In exchange for their coal claims, Ricarde-Seaver and Tarbott split the fifth block.

The next day Fred and Pete took a horse-drawn cab to the Wood Street Smelting Works north of Cheapside. There they sold the gold they had fossicked at the Dhlo-Dhlo Ruins. After retaining the best figurines as family heirlooms, the nuggets and dust assayed at five hundred eighty ounces, which they sold for two thousand eighty-eight pounds sterling. It came to about ten thousand five hundred dollars.

Fred and Pete each had the sterling equivalent of twenty-two thousand five hundred dollars in cash and eighty-seven thousand five hundred dollars in shares of Northers Terrors. They were worth a hundred and ten thousand dollars each. That was striking in an economy where a new suit cost four dollars.

Pete went off to celebrate. Fred stopped to buy a book for Blanche and walk back to his hotel. That's when the thought occurred to him. Northers Terrors probably was organized with a hundred thousand shares, not eighty-seven five. Lord Gifford probably reserved for himself the other twelve thousand five hundred shares as his vigorish.

"Why that old jiggle-billy," Fred said with a smile.

At the First Avenue Hotel, the concierge told Fred he had a visitor, a reporter seeking an interview. Fred wanted publicity for his Zambesi Expedition—it would boost the value of his Northern Territories shares—so he agreed to speak with the man.

In the smoking parlor, a tall, Lincolnesque gent arose from a winged club chair to greet him. *This guy is so long legged he wouldn't know if his feet were cold.*

"I'm from the *African Review*," the man said. "My name is Rider Haggard."

Fred dropped his book on the floor. For ten seconds, he stood there speechless. Then he blurted out the first thing that came to mind.

"You're a world-famous author. Why do you work as a reporter?"

"A good deal of my life I've been accustomed to eating," Haggard replied. "I have to work to eat."

"It's that time," Fred said. "Would you join me?"

"I'm famished, old cock."

"My stomach's sore at me too."

The roast baron of beef with Yorkshire pudding was at its Beefeaters' best. While dining, Fred learned that Haggard was more than a mere reporter. He was the lead feature writer and a part owner of the *African Review*, a weekly that smothered the Dark Continent with news. Its pages carried the gossip of society in London, Cairo, Zanzibar, Durban and Cape Town. It published the passenger lists of ships traveling to and from Africa. There were in-depth reports of wars, politics and business, including notes on the annual meetings of African mining companies that met in London. To promote circulation, Haggard's latest novel was being serialized.

Fred confessed to Haggard that *King Solomon's Mines* had lured him to Africa. He said the embodiment of Umslopogaas had come to life for him in the form of Jan Grootboom. By the time Fred mentioned he'd named his daughter Nada after Haggard's latest novel, the two men were fast forming a lasting friendship. After dessert, Fred invited Haggard to visit his hotel room where he showed off the inch-high gold animal figurines he'd dug out at Zimbabwe and

Dhlo-Dhlo.

"Mr. Burnham, you're a far greater man than Allan Quatermain of *King Solomon's Mines*," Haggard said. "You know, Quatermain was fictional; you're the real thing—a genuine hero on horseback. I've heard of great treasures and seen many men who've hunted them. But you're the only man I ever saw who actually found the lost pot of gold in Monomotapa."

Burnham was beginning to feel as if he had known Rider Haggard half of his life.

Haggard got down to the nitty-gritty of the interview.

"Do describe the single most thrilling event of the Matabele War," he said.

"I will if you'll mention my Zambesi Expedition," Fred said. "Would you like to hear about the hardest ride of the campaign?"

"By all means." Haggard said eagerly, his pen poised.

"That was when Pete Ingram and Billy Lynch rode into a terrible thunderstorm and through thousands of Matabele warriors to get help at Bulawayo. We had almost no rations and there was danger the enemy might force our patrol into laager. That would have meant death by starvation."

"Real hard cheese, you know. Please go on."

Fred described the story of the ride in detail.

"That's exceptional," Haggard said. "I'll write it as you described. By the way, would you be willing to tell me the details of Wilson's Last Stand? I daresay the authentic story has never been made public, you know?"

"It would take too long," Fred said. "While I'm sailing back to Cape Town, I'll write it down and mail it to you."

"Mr. Burnham, may I presume to ask you a sensitive question? If it is too awkward, feel free not to respond."

"Shoot."

"It's rumored that the Chartered Company has no right to be in Rhodesia. Some say the Rudd Concession, which gave Rhodes the authority to send the Pioneer Column into Mashona Land, was a defective document."

"Can't help you there," Fred said. "I know precious little about the Pioneer Column. It came to Mashona Land three years before I got there."

"It's a daft business," Haggard pursued, "but my sources say Lobengula did not exercise sovereignty over the Shonas. They say he didn't even claim suzerainty. If that's true, the Chartered Company had no right to be in Mashona Land."

Chasing Rainbows

Fred smiled and a pleased look spread over his face.

"I can answer that question," he said. He opened his valise and took out a fist-sized object. "Here is Lo Ben's royal elephant seal."

Haggard's mouth fell to a gape as he examined the bronze figurine. It was a detailed reproduction of an African elephant. The animal was depicted in a charging gallop with its tail raised and trunk waving wildly in a trumpeting cry. It looked almost alive.

"I've heard of this seal," Haggard said with awe. "It was designed by Thomas Baines and cast in Paris."

Haggard picked up the bronze elephant seal, turned it and read:

Lo Bengula:
King of Matabele and Mashona Land

"It's true," Haggard cried. "King Lobengula did claim suzerainty over Mashona Land. Where did you get this object? It's absolutely priceless, you know?"

"A friend, Bob Bain, found it in the ashes of Bulawayo after King Lobengula's *konza kraal* burned. When I get to Cape Town, I will give it to Mr. Rhodes."

"With your consent, I shall publish a picture of this elephant seal in the *African Review*," Haggard said.

25

The Northern Coppers

BULAWAYO • MARCH 1895

RED CLIMBED onto a wooden table to address the leaders of his three safaris to the Northern Coppers.

"The key to British control of Central Africa," he said, "is the land from the rift valley of the Zambesi through the flood plain of the Kafukwe River and on to the Katanga Plateau. It is my guess that the legendary Northern Coppers lies hidden somewhere there. When discovered, it will be the index finger to a railway line from one end of Africa to the other."

Everyone knew it was important to show the Union Jack. Burnham said it was important to keep accurate logs of their travels, report on weather, elevation, trees and grass, mineralization, animals, rivers and swamps and the people. Most of all, they must leave physical evidence of their travels by erecting prominent stone markers.

"Pete, you explore the Zambesi River Valley," Fred said. "Look for a place to build a railway bridge across the river. John, take King Macomber out to Wankie and peg those coal seams. Coal will provide the fuel to power a railway. Judd, you and I will cross the Zambesi to Barotze Land to search for the fabled Northern Coppers."

The first group, headed by Ingram, left Bulawayo on April 10 with ox-drawn wagons hauling provisions to Wankie to establish a supply base. Then Pete would push on for the Zambesi Valley to explore the north bank up to the flood plains of the Kafukwe.

The coal-hunting party under paleontologist John Blick and King Macomber left five days later. On May 1, Fred and the cowboy Judd Blick led the main Northern Coppers search party to Wankie. There they met with the others, took on supplies and hired porters. Ingram headed east and crossed the Zambesi sixty miles downstream from Victoria Falls.

Chasing Rainbows

Fred and Judd led the main party above Victoria Falls to where the Chobe River dumped into the Zambesi. For his gun bearers and lead porters, Fred had chosen two veteran warriors from Gambo's regiment. Zimundu was a tall, well-built man who knew how to use a Martini-Henry rifle. Mapibana, just as tall, was strong and resourceful. For a guide, Fred chose one of M'Jaan's top lieutenants, an intelligent fellow who had previously raided in Barotze Land.

Shortly before they left, M'Jaan's man killed a Holi slave. The Native Commissioner for the Mangwe District, Herbert Taylor, put the guilty Matabele in gaol. At the last minute Fred had to settle on a Masarwa tribesman named Sambana, a short, wiry, dun-colored fellow who barely spoke English.

A few days later, Fred and Judd camped beside a solitary palm tree at the fork of the Chobe River where it met the south bank of the Zambesi. Fred studied his map and felt he was part of history in the making. A narrow tongue of land called the Caprivi Strip jutted out from German South-West Africa across the top of Bechuana Land to touch the Zambesi River at Kazungula.

Four years ago, Chancellor Leo von Caprivi had deeded Zanzibar to Britain in exchange for several minor properties, including the Caprivi Strip. The German goal was to use the Caprivi Strip to connect Lake Nyassa and East Africa. If Germany could join these colonies, the east-west corridor could block Cecil Rhodes' plan for a Cape-to-Cairo railway. If Fred showed the Lion Flag of the Chartered Company, he and Judd could help lay claim to a valid north-south connection under British control.

For now, Fred had to get to Kazungula, across the Zambesi River six hundred yards wide and a crocodile lurking at every yard. The lead gnu of a herd of wildebeest got nudged into the river where ferocious crocs awaited. The crocs attacked, severing the Achilles tendon of the wildebeest and dragging him into the water to drown. Another wildebeest made a lucky kick, stunning a croc. A pack of hyenas began devouring the hapless reptile.

The crocodiles and hyenas alerted the Barotzes in Kazungula who spotted the camp near the lone palm tree. They rowed across in wooden dugout canoes to bargain for calico and other trade goods. *Their loincloths are so dirty it's apparent they never wash them. Where in this barren land did these men acquire the timber for dugout canoes?*

The prices demanded to convey the expedition across the Zambesi proved to be monopolistic.

"Judd, dig out the rubber navy."

"Danged right, Fred," Judd rasped. "We'll show these brutes."

181

The canoe owners watched as Zimundu unpacked a pair of yellow, rubber-canvas airbags bought in London. Judd pumped them up with a bellows.

The expansion of the lemon-colored airbags hardly kept pace with the bulging of the Barotze tribesmen's eyes. When inflated, Fred tied several bags together to make a raft and tossed the outfit into the water. To convince the blacks that the white man not only could ride on the wind but also commanded fire from the heavens, Fred shot a couple of rocket bombs across the Zambesi. One bomb set fire to the grass and the Barotze tribesmen decided to strike a deal before losing an opportunity to acquire clean calico.

The next day, the expedition marched north through forested flatlands covered with veld grass full of game. They crossed the Sefula River, climbing a low rise before turning northeast at the Majile River. A few days later, at the headwaters of the Majile, they entered timber land and saw black men carving wooden dugout canoes.

Here's the source of those sturdy Zambesi river boats.

At the headwaters, the river was not navigable, but anyone could see the rainy season produced a Venetian flood plain. At that time, the boat builders drifted their craft down to barren Barotze Land.

Ten days later, the expedition came to the Kafukwe River, at a point where it turned east. Fred and Judd continued on north, following a tributary upstream. They sketched maps of the trails and mountains and used a hypsometer to make elevation readings. The device used atmospheric pressure, as measured by the change in the boiling point of water, to determine land elevations.

The meter said they were thirty-eight hundred feet above sea level. Here in the cool winter days of May, the air was crisp and clear. Fred felt a twinge of gratitude to Jeff Clark. Without his redheaded friend's help, he would never have come to Africa and become an explorer.

On the Kafukwe they entered a wildlife cosmos. In their logbooks, they recorded lions, cheetahs and the solitary leopard. A lone zebra braved the Kafukwe. Two crocs attacked, biting its nose to smother the animal and tear it apart.

The expedition entered a buffer zone between the Barotze and Monguoya tribes. There were no people here. For an entire day there were only wild beasts. Then they saw their first Monguoyas, tall, slender and fine-featured people. The cunning looking men walked around naked. They didn't carry bullhide shields, but they were armed with slender throwing assegais. Mapibana warned Fred that the tips were poisoned.

"One scratch, baas, you die."

Continuing north, they encountered more herds of wild animals, handsome creatures—giraffes, hippos, zebra and hyenas—that didn't know the crack of a modern rifle. By night they heard lions roar. By day baboons scampered across the veld, always in awe of the king of cats. What few guns the local natives possessed were muzzle-loaders and the animals seemed able to gauge the weapons' range.

As the expedition continued northward, they came to a well-watered land of rolling hills. The elevation readings were forty-six hundred feet. Unlike East Africa, this land was free of blackwater fever. The trunks of the trees rose smoothly for forty feet before the first branches sprouted. Fred marked the spot on his map as a source of railway sleepers.

At the Upper Kafukwe River, they met the Ilas. A party of forty men was carrying salt southward for trade in Barotze Land. The most striking feature of these tall, warlike people was their tufted hair, yard-high vertical coifs which looked like a unicorn horn.

The explorers knew they were nearing their goal when they saw salt pans, boiling hot springs and crude mine workings. The Upper Kafukwe River was five hundred yards wide and five feet deep, and infested with hippos, crocs and water snakes. The local tribesmen carried barbed assegais and bows inlaid with native copper. So rich were the deposits the blacks took only the pure native copper. The people seemingly knew nothing of smelting.

The mine workings were rich. No question, this was the legendary Northern Coppers. Fred and Judd began pegging mineral claims. They laid out ten-mile-square blocks of land, naming the claims Silver King, Crystal Jacket and Sable Antelope. They reserved the remaining hundred square mile right for a future claim. If Pete found a rail crossing on the Zambesi and if John and King found coal at Wankie, the shares in Northers Terrors would be worth a lot more than one pound sterling.

There was much to enjoy in this parklike land and both Fred and Pete would have enjoyed spending more time exploring. But the term of service of the natives would expire soon, so they turned back. On coming to a tributary of the Kafukwe, they climbed a mountain. The elevation reading: five thousand feet. It provided a grand view of the watershed between the Kafukwe to the north and the Zambesi to the south. Fred and Judd built a rock pyramid. In a Martini-Henry cartridge, they inserted a paper with the names of each member of the exploration party. Fred proclaimed the peak as Mount Allan Wilson.

26

Chasing Rainbows

Victoria Falls • August 1895

FRED WAS eager to see Victoria Falls, the waterfall made famous by Thomas Baines' paintings. He sent Pete Ingram on ahead and led an excursion into the rift of the Zambesi Valley.

The foliage was lush, green and tropical. Water cascading over rock cliffs bathed the valley in a velvet fog. It created a din that reverberated his very bones. Fred now understood why the Matabele had called it the Smoke that Thunders. One gaze at the cataracts and leaping waters and Fred decided the excursion was worth it. It was like the Grand Canyon and Niagara Falls rolled into one—a scene of such breathtaking beauty that he couldn't behold it all at once.

In the canyon, the heat was unending, the sound deafening. The majesty of the scene held Fred enthralled. Baines' paintings of the Rainbow Falls and Devil's Cataract had been splendid, exciting, powerful. But the brush was unable to convey the impact of sight, sound and feeling evoked by being here.

Burnham began exploring. Within the hour, he found a hole in the mist that revealed two large rock abutments. A daring railway engineer would surely want to build a bridge across this majestic rift river canyon. Siting the foundations of the bridge on these abutments would produce a thrilling view for the passengers, a highlight of the Cape-to-Cairo railway. Fred sketched the scene and marked the locations on his map. He must tell Sir Charles Metcalf in Bulawayo.

Lagnappe • A Little Extra
LONDON • AUGUST 1895

FOR A YEAR, George Baden-Powell had been dropping heavy hints that little brother should marry a rich woman who could foot his bills. Stephe briefly entertained the idea of proposing to the daughter of a wealthy family. He reversed his error in judgment upon learning they were common merchants.

Major Baden-Powell was feeling lower than a lizard's belly when, from out of the blue, there arrived *the letter*. Signed by General Lord Wolseley, the commander-in-chief of the British Army, the order bore the magic words: "You have been selected to proceed on active service to the Ashanti." Like a butterfly Stephe fluttered about the room as if he owned the sky. The Army Staff College was irrelevant now. His career was on a fast track.

Once in the Ashanti, Stephe was directed to shanghai a thousand natives and reopen an abandoned road to Kumasi for the combat troops. Bridge-building was his levy's main task. Stephe was impressed by the tribesmen's mastery of intricate knots which they used to make fishing nets. He put this knot-tying ability to work building bridges over the jungle rivers. Stephe also cordoned off a place in the recesses of his mind for knot-tying.

When Baden-Powell's rope bridge builders arrived in Kumasi, King Prempeh offered to surrender. Stephe spurned the offer and burned the ancient priestly houses. On return to London, Stephe was promoted to lieutenant colonel.

Ritornello • Interlude
CAPE TOWN • SEPTEMBER 1895

JACK HAMMOND and Cecil Rhodes had arrived at a point where they were at ease speaking frankly. As premier of the Cape Colony, Rhodes' duties kept him in Cape Town. So Jack agreed to meet at Groot Schure.

"Mr. Hammond, what is your opinion of the gold in the Witswatersrand? What is the life of my mines?"

"There's no reason why the Rand should not produce for decades. You can carry out gold mining profitably to a depth of several thousand feet."

"What are your obstacles?" Rhodes asked.

"Economic and political," Hammond replied.

"Give me an example," Rhodes said, sipping tea, but suddenly alert.

"President Kruger lines his pockets," Hammond said. "He does it through his dynamite monopoly. South Africa Explosives Company charges twice the going world price for dynamite."

"Are you an expert on explosives too?" Rhodes asked.

"In San Francisco, I was a consultant to the Vigorite Powder Company. I learned all about using explosives," Hammond replied.

"Then I really did hire an expert," Rhodes said with an amused smirk. "Go on, Sir."

"Premature explosions in the mines are too frequent. Because of such poor quality, Kruger is responsible for many unnecessary fatalities."

"I'll have my people look into that matter," Rhodes said. "Anything else?"

"Kruger grants licenses to sell Cape Smoke in your miners' compounds. Some of the natives show up for work so intoxicated they fall out of the elevator cages to their deaths."

"That's a serious accusation," Rhodes said, scribbling a note. "What political obstacles do you encounter?"

"As a newcomer here, it would be presumptuous "

"You have been in Africa for a year, and I am paying you the highest salary in the world," Rhodes barked in a voice as acid as owl shit. "Am I not entitled to my money's worth?"

"You are right. Here is the unvarnished truth."

Rhodes called in a male secretary to take notes.

"Uitlanders outnumber the Boers six to one. These foreigners now own half the land and nine-tenths of the assessable property in Joburg. Yet they have no vote and are forbidden to carry arms."

"Go on."

"The Netherlands Railway to Lorenco Marques has a monopoly," Jack said. "It diverts railway traffic coming up from Cape Town on British Railways."

Rhodes came to attention, his jowls turning rigid.

"Unless changes are made, I think there will be an uprising among the Uitlanders."

"I thought the pot might be close to a boil," Rhodes said, his voice low. "It is interesting that you should notice these things so quickly."

"It's the main topic of dinner table conversation," Hammond said. "Kruger wants to enlarge the Transvaal. He wants Bechuana Land and he wants Rhodesia."

Rhodes arose and shuffled like a sea turtle across the room where he gazed out the French doors at Table Bay. Only after reflecting on Hammond's statements for several minutes did he speak.

"Mr. Hammond, would you take charge of a Reform Committee?"

Hammond put his hands to his forehead and studied the offer. Then he spread his arms and said, "Mr. Rhodes, I would consider it an honor."

Counterpoise • Equilibrium

BULAWAYO • SEPTEMBER 1895

BURNHAM AND the Blick brothers spent three months digging shafts at Belingwe, hoping to uncover a rich vein so they could sell shares in their mine. The work was hard, and they found enough gold to pay for their time and make a profit too. If they'd just strike a fat vein, those Roders Exers shares would become another Oof Bird's nest.

By an evening campfire, Tyrie Laing entertained them with Scottish ditties. One time he made *haggis*, a Scot dish of minced sheep heart, liver, lungs and suet sewn into a sheep's stomach that contained oats, barley and onions, then simmered in mutton stock. Fred insisted *haggis* was Caledonia's response to Arizona's son-of-a-bitch stew. As the kettle simmered, Laing said Billy Lynch had staked several claims north of them. Neither Fred nor Pete asked for seconds, so Laing was able devour his feast of guts.

A few days later, Fred and Pete rode over to Lynch's camp. Billy invited them to join him in a spit-roasted repast of gemsbok.

"I say, Fred, thanks awfully for the nice write-up you inspired in the *African Review*," Lynch said. "It was decent of you, old chap."

"You deserved the recognition," Fred said.

"What's Barotze Land like?" Lynch asked, changing the subject. "Is it dangerous north of the Zambesi?"

"The worst part," Fred replied, "was the lack of water en route back to Bulawayo. The Gwaii was a dry gulch."

"How did you fare up north?"

"Judd and I pegged three copper claims. John Blick pegged coal deposits. After we prove up our gold claims here, we'll make our report in London."

"You're shot full of luck," Lynch said. "I'm taken aback that you didn't run into trouble up north. There's said to be a hotbed of rebellion near the Zambesi. During the war, Lobengula's best impis were quarantined with smallpox. They didn't test their spears against the whites don't consider themselves as being conquered."

"Johann has collared and branded 'em," Pete said.

Billy Lynch lighted a pipe.

"Colenbrander is no longer the CNC. He chucked the job to go prospecting with that friend of yours Jeff Clark. Herb Taylor is now Chief Native Commissioner."

"Who's he?" Ingram asked.

Fred replied, "He's the kaffir wallah who jailed my Matabele guide."

"Herb came up from the Cape Colony to take over the Mangwe District," Lynch said. "When Johann quit, he was named CNC, and I don't rate that as favorable news."

"Why?" Fred asked.

"Not long ago thirty niggers stole some cattle from the Chartered Company at a kraal near Inyati. Taylor sent a squad of police to capture them. The niggers scattered, but the police ran down six of the blighters and brought them before Native Commissioner Graham. At Taylor's behest, Graham sentenced them to twenty lashes each."

"That'll teach 'em to steal," Ingram said.

"Graham had a bash-with-the-lash and some of the blacks are said to have died," Lynch said, speaking low as if in confidence. "It was a real corcus and I hear there's fearful unrest among the niggers."

While riding back to their camp, Fred asked Ingram about the rumors Lynch had mentioned.

"Did you run into any trouble up there?"

"Nothin' but bones. The Matabele are disarmed."

"You know Lynch better than I do. Is he a reliable witness?"

"When I rode with him, he seemed rolled in gold."

"Reckon he's just passing along campfire yarns?"

When they returned to Bulawayo, they were in for a surprise. The town boasted a polo field, cricket grounds and there was talk of an opera house. Money was plentiful and small change was not given. The wolf had been driven from everyone's door. Times were good.

"It's like the days of forty-nine," Fred said. "A mild madness is on all. Money is like water. Pete, what's say we get our fingers wet?"

"Yahoo, pard, I'm all for it."

Ritornello • Interlude

JOHANNESBURG • SEPTEMBER 1895

THE NEW CONCESSIONS, a cover name for the Reform Committee, opened a bank account with three hundred thousand dollars and rented dusty offices on side streets of Johannesburg, Pretoria and Mafeking.

Jack Hammond would lead the Uitlander Revolt and Doctor Jim came to Johannesburg to confer with him. The plan was for Jameson to supervise the rescue effort from Mafeking.

On the agreed date, Jameson would gallop into Joburg to support the Uitlander uprising. The committee bought three thousand rifles in London and had them consigned to Gardner Williams, the American engineer at the De Beers Mines at Kimberley in the Cape Colony. Smuggling arms to Joburg was risky. The penalty was seven years imprisonment. Williams' plan was to modify Standard Oil drums with false bottoms and fill them with rifles.

Doctor Jim recruited volunteers in Bulawayo and sent them to Mafeking. Sir John "Digby" Willoughby ran the volunteers through drill practice for a couple of weeks. By late December, the hot season, the volunteers felt like they were trapped in the middle of nowhere.

Counterpoise • Equilibrium

BULAWAYO • NOVEMBER 1895

BURNHAM, THE BLICKS and King Macomber launched an orgy of speculation. They sold mine shares, traded gold claims, bought and sold farms, cashed in shares and never took their eyes off the glint of gold. In two months, King Macomber amassed a small fortune.

After dinner one evening, everyone drifted outside to cool off from the heat. Fred sat with father-in-law, James Blick, at a table in a tree-lined breezeway. They spoke by the glow of a kerosine lantern.

"Business is a ferocious game, Father Blick."

"How's that, Son?"

"While it goes on, all thoughts of beauty and lasting value are forgotten. Calm resolution and continuity of purpose are laid aside."

"Aren't you doing this to provide for your family?"

"That's my excuse. Look at King. He's another Barney Barnato. At least Rhodes puts his wealth into developing a nation. And what about Pete? He's a financial pirate."

"Better not judge until you talk to Pete," Blick said. "Here he comes now."

Out of the darkness, Pete rode up, dismounted and skipped over to the picnic table, a silly grin on his face.

"What's up, Pete?"

The sappy look said something was up.

"Out with it," Fred demanded.

"Are we goin to London after the holidays?"

"Sure, we'll see Lord Gifford. We'll tell him we have poured salt on the Oof Bird's tail."

"Could we go by way of Paris?"

"Sure. Why?"

"It's romantic. Grace wants to honeymoon in Paris."

"Honeymoon?" Fred blurted out. In the lantern light, the look on Pete's face said Fred would get no answer.

"I think Pete's trying to ask you to be the best man."

"Hey, we'll be brothers in law. Let's leave now." Fred ran into the house. "Bea, pack my suit and claw-hammer coat. We're gonna spend Christmas in Paree."

Ritornello • Interlude

Johannesburg • December 1895

DECEMBER 28 WAS SET for the uprising. During the Christmas holidays, Joburg would be too crowded. And Jack Hammond was overwhelmed by a problem.

Only a thousand rifles had arrived. Hammond wired a poorly worded message to Jameson telling him to sit tight until January 4. He dared not speak clearly for fear the Boers would crack the simple commercial code he was required to use. At Mafeking, the troopers remained unaware of why they had been brought there. They threatened to go back to Bulawayo. Doctor Jameson faced a dilemma: march or lose all his men.

Hammond sent another telegram declaring, "On no account must you move." It was Sunday and the telegraph office was closed, so Jameson ended up launching his invasion two days early.

Digby Willoughby ordered the signalmen to cut the telegraph lines to Johannesburg and Pretoria. The men, on a premature victory drunk, cut the line to Joburg, but missed the line to Pretoria.

Within hours the Boers had prepared an ambush.

27

The Jameson Raid

PARIS • JANUARY 1896

RED AND BLANCHE served as the best man and bridesmaid while Grace Blick became Mrs. Pearl Ingram. The wedding party stayed at the Le Grande Hotel, an oasis in the heart of Paris. In the days that followed they explored the Avenue des Champs-Elysees, the Tuileries Gardens and the Bastille. Evenings were buoyed by snacks in the Café de la Paix and at the market in Les Halles. There was no hurry to resume the active life.

On Monday, January 20, they returned late from a visit to the Louvre when they learned the most appalling news. Two weeks ago, Doctor Jameson and five hundred troopers of the Rhodesia BSA Police had been ambushed and captured while making a raid on the Transvaal.

"Let's go to London," Fred urged. "We'll get details there."

Two days later they were booked into the Horse Shoe Hotel on Tottenham Court Road. It was close to the British Museum, a depository of the empire's booty that Blanche wanted to explore. The next morning Fred and Pete called on Lord Gifford in St. Swithin's Lane. Cables arrived each hour and Fred made notes to take back to the family.

- Thursday, January 2 — Doctor Jim is captured at Doornkop outside Joburg, and taken to Pretoria Gaol. He is to be shot outright, without the benefit of trial.
- Monday, January 6 — Rhodes was implicated in the plot and forced to resign as premier of the Cape Colony. He immediately departs by ship for England.
- Thursday, January 9 — The Boers arrest the Reform Committee leaders and charge them with treason. John Hays Hammond, Digby Willoughby, Frank Rhodes and Aubrey Woolls-Sampson are confined

in Pretoria Gaol while awaiting trial and execution.
- Sunday, January 19 — Doctor Jameson, released from gaol, leaves for London. The Boers agree that he can stand trial in a British court.

The next day more cables from Cape Town put the picture into better perspective. When the word was given, Digby Willoughby was supposed to lead the irregulars on a military strike of Pretoria, removing Oom Paul and the Boers from power.

Details were leaked and President Kruger mobilized a commando of sharpshooters under General Piet Cronje, who ambushed and captured the column, including the five hundred members of Rhodesia's BSA Police.

A political scandal erupted when Oom Paul produced telegrams as evidence of Rhodes' advance knowledge of the raid. Rhodes was compelled to resign as premier, and Doctor Jameson was forced out as administrator of Rhodesia.

In the dining room of the Ivy Tower Restaurant in the West End, the Burnhams, Ingrams and Blicks discussed the situation over a côte de beuf de prime rib. Young Rod toyed with a roast pullet leg.

"Could it mean war?" Father Blick asked.

"Possibly," Fred said. "Being here I feel like a deserter unable to raise a finger to help." It never occurred to Fred why neither Rhodes nor Jameson had summoned him to serve as a scout for the Jameson Raid.

"You had no way of knowing this would happen," James Blick said gently. "Don't blame yourself."

"I think Pete and I should leave for Rhodesia. We'll put you and The Kid on the next ship for New York. Rod needs to start school."

Father Blick, who sorely missed his wife, was only too happy to escort Rod back to Pasadena. Fred's plans to leave for Africa were thwarted when he was summoned to St. Swithin's Lane.

"Mr. Rhodes has arrived in London. Doctor Jameson's ship is due directly," Lord Gifford said. "When Starr gets here, you are to meet with him and Mr. Rhodes. Meanwhile, Ingram and his bride are free to leave on the next ship for Cape Town."

When Fred asked to make his report on the Northern Coppers, Lord Gifford deferred the request, pleading that his first priority was to find a successor to Doctor Jameson as administrator of Rhodesia. Back at the Horse Shoe Hotel, Fred paced the floor as fidgety as a caged leopard with the itch.

"I know the ways of the frontier," he groused. "Had I been there, I might have found a weak point in the lines."

"Instead of imitating a Hyde Park tiger," Bea said, "let's go out for dinner."

When they got back, Blanche showed Fred a news article. Jeff Clark was confined to a West End hospital near Harley Street. The next day, Fred and Blanche visited him and learned he was undergoing treatment for kidney disease. His condition was perilous. After the Burnhams assured him that he would be up and around in no time, Clark took Burnham's hand and became serious.

"Fred, we've ridden many a mile together."

"Yes, and we'll ride many more."

"Don't indulge me, my friend, I'm dying," Clark said, grasping Fred's arm. That afternoon Fred held Jeff's hand while the shadow of death settled.

"He died as a man, steadfast and brave," Fred said.

Two days later, Fred served as a pallbearer for his mentor.

• • •

FRED PACED the floor, eager to return to Rhodesia. A week later, he received a summons to St. Swithin's Lane. Lord Gifford introduced him to Albert Henry George Grey, a former member of Parliament and member of a prominent family. Earl Grey was a short, spare, mild-mannered man, about ten years older than Fred and he had hair the color of an Arctic snow fox.

"I say, Burnham, you're an old African campaigner. What do you make of this Bathing Towel fellow?" Lord Gifford asked, a twinkle in his eye. Fred shook his head.

"Have you read about the Kumasi niggers raiding our colony on the Ashanti Gold Coast?" he asked.

"Oh, sure," Fred said. Now he made the connection. The British Army contingent sent to West Africa to put down an insurrection included a Major Baden-Powell.

"Earl Grey has been telling me about Bathing Towel," Lord Gifford said with a chuckle. "Seems his father was a professor at Oxford. He was the eighth child of his father's third missus. All told, Professor Powell begat fourteen offspring.

"His mum, the third Mrs. Powell, was ambitious for her children," Lord Gifford continued. "Years ago, she changed the family name from Powell to Baden-Powell."

"No doubt, to give the family more social standing," Earl Grey observed.

"Dead right, old cock," Lord Gifford conceded. "She came to be known as Old Missus Hyphen."

"I read where he received a promotion," Fred said.

"Sticky wicket," Lord Gifford replied. "I wonder how he will live down his nancy-boy nickname."

"How's that?" Earl Grey asked, his interest piqued.

"He used to muck about with a baby-faced chap, The Boy McLaren." Gifford said. "The two were known as The Boy and The Bloater."

Fred didn't think it was funny.

"Ahem, I called you here to meet Earl Grey," Gifford said. "He'll succeed Doctor Jim as administrator. Directly he settles his personal affairs, he'll leave for Bulawayo. But now, I want you to brief him on Rhodesia." Fred spent the next three hours telling Earl Grey what he knew about the people, the culture and business affairs in Rhodesia.

"Now if you'll excuse us, we have urgent business," Lord Gifford said. "Major Ricarde-Seaver and Mr. Tarbott will hear your report on the expedition to Barotze Land. You're to have breakfast with Mr. Rhodes tomorrow. After that, you're free to return to Africa."

• • •

THE BREAKFAST in Rhodes' suite at Burlington House Hotel began as a gloomy affair. Not that the food wasn't fit for royalty: smoked salmon from Scotland, roast grouse from the moors, broiled English lamb chops, Cornish pasties, hunters pies—a first class graze.

What produced the glumness was the continuing bad news from Africa. Doctor Jim, looking remorseful, paced the floor. Digby Willoughby, John Hays Hammond, Frank Rhodes and Woolls-Sampson had been condemned to hang. On reflection, President Kruger agreed to commute their sentences to banishment on payment of fines of one hundred twenty-five thousand dollars each. Cecil Rhodes and Barney Barnato agreed to pay the fines.

Rhodes was preoccupied by a stack of telegrams on the table. A waiter served Irish bacon, scones with double cream and marmalade. Jameson sat opposite Rhodes.

"Sorry about that telegram I sent to you in Pretoria Prison," Rhodes said. Rhodes, on learning of Jameson's capture, had sent a coded telegram to Pretoria Gaol asking Jameson to take responsibility for the raid, which would have shielded Rhodes so he could remain as premier of the Cape Colony and head of the Chartered Company.

"How did President Kruger decode those messages?" Fred asked. "Weren't those cables the only evidence of your prior knowledge of the raid?"

Rhodes' face remained a blank. Jameson answered.

"General Cronje captured Major Bob White's dispatch box containing diaries and code books," Jameson said. "It was hidden under the brandy in the supply wagon. It also contained a letter from Hammond asking us to come to the aid of the Reform Committee."

Rhodes' skin was ashen, but his expression remained impassive. "So that's how they implicated Hammond."

"It was Digby Willoughby who got us lost," Jameson blurted out. "He veered away from Hammond's route. Then he got confused at Doornkop."

Fred knew then that had he been summoned, he could have saved the day.

"We must see that Willoughby loses his standing," Rhodes said, his voice rising barely above a whisper. "He is trying to defend himself by suggesting that Joe knew of the Polo Tournament and approved of it."

Rhodes, who was reading a cabled message, nodded abstractly and took a bite of pastry.

"When Joe Chamberlain took up the seals of office," Doctor Jim said, "we believed that the same policy of passiveness would remain in effect. But then Joe had to go pry into everything."

To Fred, the affairs of cabinet ministers were matters of another universe. He was suddenly mesmerized.

"All along, Chamberlain knew we were organizing the Uitlander Revolt," Jameson said, absently spilling eggs on the tablecloth.

"He knew?" Fred blurted out.

"Certainly he knew," Rhodes said irritably, suddenly looking up and laying down the telegrams. "But he was more worried by another matter. What if that damn coup resulted in an Uitlander government under its own flag? What if it had produced a breakaway republic led by Americans mucking about with their democratic ideas?"

The possibility had never occurred to Fred. *So that's why I wasn't called on to scout for the raid.*

"Joe had to keep things under control while publicly not knowing too much," Rhodes continued

"If the plot failed," Doctor Jim added, "he could plead ignorance. If it succeeded, he could share the credit. So he protected Prime Minister Salisbury by keeping him in the dark."

"That tricky jiggle-billy," Fred said, unable to resist a smile. "Just like a courtroom lawyer." The dirty work was becoming interesting. He poured double cream on a scone.

"Joe was being briefed every day," Rhodes piped up in his falsetto voice. "High Commissioner Milner sent cablegrams every day to Chamberlain in London, laying bare the most intimate details of our scheme."

Fred glanced at Jameson, seeking confirmation of this startling news.

"Oh, yes," Doctor Jim conceded. "He knew all about the Polo Tournament. That was our code name for the uprising. We were called the shareholders. Chamberlain sealed away all those secret telegrams in his red boxes. He's covered his trail in the event there's a parliamentary enquiry."

"By the way," Rhodes said, looking up at Jameson, "I learned why he was able to send those cables urging us to hurry things along."

"Tell us," Doctor Jameson urged. "The publication of those telegrams would implicate Joe as a coconspirator."

"When Chamberlain saw war clouds on the horizon," Rhodes said, "he sought foreign support. He prevailed on Lord Salisbury to make cooperation with the Americans a cornerstone of British policy. Only after Salisbury had secured the backing of President Cleveland was Joe able to send the hurry-things-along cables."

"How did he possibly achieve American support?" Jameson asked.

"When Venezuela suspended diplomatic relations with us over some piss-ant gold mine on the Orinoco River," Rhodes said, "President Cleveland invoked the Monroe Doctrine. Prime Minister Salisbury agreed to arbitration on condition the Americans support the British against the Boers."

"How did you possibly learn of these developments?"

"While you were sailing up from Africa," Rhodes said, "I paid a secret visit to Joe at his estate. We struck a deal."

"A deal?" Doctor Jim asked. His face grew ashen and he dropped his lamb chop.

"Starr, I'm afraid it's hard cheese for you," Rhodes said casually. "During your trial, you will remain silent. We'll protect Joe. We'll not produce those telegrams in court. Those hurry-things-along cables could topple the British government. Would you care for more scones, Mr. Burnham?"

"And in return?" Jameson asked, his face now haggard and slack.

"You'll be found guilty as charged and sentenced to serve eighteen months in gaol," Rhodes said matter of factly. Doctor Jim's hands went to his face.

"Don't fret, Starr," Rhodes said, his voice a falsetto chuckle. "It'll be a glorified house arrest. Buck House deems gaol is necessary to satisfy public opinion."

Fred know Rhodes well enough to understand that Buck House meant Buckingham Palace, a personification of Queen Victoria.

"After six months," Rhodes continued, "you will be given a physical examination and paroled on the basis of failing health."

Jameson's face flushed. Fred feared the good doctor might be having a stroke.

"And in return?"

"In return," Rhodes said, jowls shaking like jelly, "Joe won't be able to nullify the charter of the British South Africa Company."

Jameson placed his hands on the table and a look of resignation came over his face. He said, "If even one word of this conspiracy were to—"

Rhodes pursed his lips—his equivalent of a smile. "We've covered that eventuality," he said, his voice tinged with menace. "If word gets out, Joe will offer a junior member of the colonial staff as a scapegoat. He'll say the man had misunderstood his orders. As a result, he failed to inform his superiors of the Polo Tournament."

"What if he—?"

"Fortunately," Rhodes cut in, "this individual recently suffered a fatal stroke, so he cannot deny the allegation."

Silence pervaded the room.

"You've saved the Chartered Company," Jameson said in a monotone.

"Yes and we have old Joe where we want him," Rhodes said with a shrill giggle. "We'll let him perjure himself in open court. Then if he threatens to meddle with the charter, we supply the missing telegrams to Fleet Street. He's our boy now. We've got a lasso around his colonial gonads."

At that moment, Fred knew that Digby Willoughby's career was as good as dead.

Rhodes resumed studying cables, looking as proud as if he had invented the water wheel. Rhodes was sacrificing his longtime friend Doctor Jim and turning personal tragedy into a political triumph. While Fred sipped tea, Doctor Jim slowly regained his composure. He asked about matters in Africa. Rhodes pawed through the mound of cablegrams.

"Mr. Burnham, what do you make of this message?"

The cable was from Chief Native Commissioner Herb Taylor. The contents were unimportant, but a post script caught his eye. There was a drought and the Matabele were restless. The rinderpest plague, which had slowly been migrating south from Russia, was nearing Rhodesia.

"How many Rhodesian Police are left?" Fred asked.

"Fifty," Doctor Jim replied absently.

"Fifty?" Burnham blurted out in a dismayed croak.

"We bally well couldn't take those kaffirs on the raid," Jameson said. "So we left those fifty behind to keep order in Rhodesia."

Quick as a rattler, Billy Lynch's warning came back to haunt Fred. With drought, there'd be hunger. If the white BSA Police were in Pretoria Gaol, there was no one in Rhodesia to protect the settlers.

The Matabele police were armed with Martini-Henry rifles and trained to use them. The circumstances were strikingly close to Minnesota during Fred's childhood in the Civil War. After the menfolk left to fight the Confederates, the Sioux Indians rose in rebellion.

The prospect of a native uprising sent a pang of terror through Fred's heart. His daughter, Nada, too young to travel, had been left in Bulawayo in the care of the Cummings family.

"Mr. Rhodes," Fred said, "you must prepare at once for war."

The Rinderpest

Since antiquity, the cattle plague known as rinderpest had spread over Asia and Africa. It arrived in Uganda in 1890 and reached Bulawayo in March 1896. The plague spread like lightning and in a matter of weeks killed about 4.5 million animals with cloven hooves.

The Matabele Rebellion

The 6th Chronicle

Burnham Scouting with Swinburne

In the 1896 war, artist Melton Prior made this sketch of scouts U.P. Swinburne, in the tree, and Fred Burnham, on the ground, as they stood watch for Matabele warriors that might attack Bulawayo.

28

The Battle for Colenbrander's Farm

CAPE TOWN • MARCH 1896

THE BURNHAMS were met at dockside by the Ingrams and the worst of Fred's fears were confirmed.

"The Matabeles have risen," Pete said, thrusting a sheaf of telegrams and newspapers at Fred. "It started at Insiza. They killed Tom Maddox. Harry Cummings jogged fifty miles to Bulawayo to warn the settlers. The uprising has spread all over Matabele Land."

"How's Nada?" Blanche asked, her face frozen in fear.

"Safe with the Cummingses," Grace said. "Bulawayo is under siege."

"The Blick boys?" Fred asked.

"Rode up to Insiza to fortify Harry's store," Pete said. "They held out until Gifford arrived with reinforcements. Maurice lost an arm. John was wounded. Homer lost three hundred and fifty dollars when the house burned."

Two days later, when the train arrived at rail's end in Mafeking, they learned that only able-bodied men were allowed to go north. Lieutenant Colonel Herbert Plumer, an Imperial officer, was massing eight hundred troopers for the five-hundred mile march to relieve Bulawayo. Mafeking had taken on the worst trappings of a Wild West town so Fred and Pete called on Plumer to lodge a protest against the travel ban.

"Burnham and Ingram, eh, the American Scouts?" Plumer said. "I've heard of you. Wilson's Last Stand, eh? We've a special need men like you up there."

Fred liked Plumer. A compact man with a rooster's neck and elephant ears, he was a spit-and-polish man who brooked no nonsense.

"I've no choice but go north," Fred said. "My little girl is trapped in Bulawayo. But Pete here doesn't have to go."

"You have my word," Plumer said. "Your wives will be safe. At roll call, I'll declare martial law. Any man who harms a white woman will stretch a rope."

Ritornello • Interlude

SOUTHAMPTON • MARCH 1896
A SWARTHY MAN in his twenties whistled a gay tune as he strolled along the promenade deck of the steamship *HMS Scot* departing from England's premier seaport.

Despite his Spanish surname, Frederick Ramon de Bertodano y Lopez was English by birth, a solicitor by profession and a gentleman by Navarrese lineage. Yet his speech was as twangy Australian as a swagman.

Fred Lopez had been hired by a London mining syndicate to hie himself down to Rhodesia and liquidate the syndicate's mining properties before the niggers overran Bulawayo. If he succeeded, Lopez would earn a tidy sum for his efforts and enhance his career as a solicitor. Lopez was sure of his ability to carry off this task so he repaired to the first-class saloon where he bestowed a dazzling smile on the bartender.

Counterpoise • Equilibrium

MAFEKING • MARCH 1896
AMONG THE PASSENGERS on the Zeederberg Brothers stagecoach were Doctor Hans Sauer and Aubrey Woolls-Sampson, who was on parole from Pretoria Gaol. The Boers had paroled the BSA Police to fight the Matabele.

The travelers gasped at the devastation inflicted by the *rinderpest* on the cattle and oxen. Teams of hulking oxen lay dying in their harnesses, froth flying from nostrils, foam billowing from mouths. The drovers abandoned their wagons and hiked back to Mafeking. The stench was putrefying, and the hyenas and vultures were treated to a ghastly banquet.

At Gaberones, the capital of Bechuana Land, a news reporter fleeing from Bulawayo told Fred there was little ammunition and only a few guns. Burnham walked over to Doctor Sauer.

"We're loaded with Her Majesty's mail. What's to gain carrying

The Matabele Rebellion

mail to dead people? Those who live will want bullets more than patent medicine ads."

"Good idea, old cock. Let's chuck the ruddy mail."

At the Post Office, they were met by civil servants steeped in the rigid traditions of colonial India.

"You know, Sir, it can't be done. No orders, Sir."

"You bloody ass," Sauer cried. "People are dying."

"Doc," Fred said, "the total armed force representing Her Majesty here is two soldiers. We number twelve."

"It *can* be done," Ingram said, drawing his pistol.

"Piss off," Woolls-Sampson barked. The guards fled.

An hour later, the mail was languishing in the Royal Post Office at Gaberones and the stage was traveling north with five thousand rounds of Martini-Henry ammunition.

At Tati, Magistrate Vigers, a friend from Fort Victoria days, said, "There's an assortment of hillbillies laagered at Mangwe with the hunter Hans Lee," he said. "See Bonnar Armstrong. He can tell you if it's safe to make a run."

"We'll do that," the stage driver said.

Captain Bonnar Armstrong was a friendly young man with a peaches and cream complexion. He couldn't vote, yet he was the Native Commissioner for Mangwe and a captain in the Bulawayo Field Force. He said the Matabele had left Mangwe Pass open as an escape route hoping the white people would leave.

At Bulawayo, Fred learned that Nada was safe. The *rinderpest*, fatal to all cloven-hoofed animals, had wiped out Art's dairy herd, so they had moved to Bulawayo.

Fred sent a telegram to Blanche, then reported for duty with the Bulawayo Field Force, which had been called up as a Colonial Militia. Bill Napier, second in command of the old Victoria Column, was the colonel.

"Good to see you, Fred. Colenbrander has a hundred Natal friendlies in red capes. Jimmy Dawson has organized Dawson's Scouts and George Grey has formed Grey's Scouts. You'll be a captain. What would you like to do?"

"Seems there're lots of scouts. Who's George Grey?"

"He's a cousin of the new administrator."

"I met Earl Grey in London."

"So I hear. As for scouts, neither Dawson's chaps nor Grey's gents have any scouting duties. They're mounted infantry. George Grey has organized a force of fifty select gentlemen who are willing to have a gallop on the veld. You can scout for George, if you wish."

203

"Spare me. I'd like to work with Aubrey."

"Good. Captain Woolls-Sampson is our engineering officer. He'll build forts between Bulawayo and Mangwe Pass. The *rinderpest* killed the oxen, so we're switching to horses and mules."

That meant grain had to be stored at each stage stop along the five-hundred mile route. Oxen pastured on grass, but horses needed a diet of hay and grain.

"You, Pete and Aubrey ride with Captain Molyneux," Napier said. "Build a fort and telegraph station at Fig Tree. Report back when you're finished."

The natives at Fig Tree were neutral, so Fred called on Bulalima Native Commissioner Bill Thomas to recruit labor. In four days, they erected a breastworks in the kopjes suitable for one hundred fifty troopers. Fred rode back to Bulawayo.

That night Fred and Pete joined the Cummings family for dinner. Fred held Nada on his lap as he read the *Rhodesian Weekly Review*. An editorial suggested someone should kill the M'Limo and bring an end to the rebellion.

"The M'Limo promised to turn the white man's bullets into water," Cummings said. "If the black deity can't change a bullet aimed at him into water, the whole deception will be exposed."

Lagnappe • A Little Extra

MAFEKING • MARCH 1896

IN THE BANTU language, Mafeking meant *the place of stones*. It was a blemish on the desert, the northern end of the railway replete with tin warehouses. Sprawled in the middle of nowhere, it was eight hundred miles north of Cape Town and five hundred miles south of Bulawayo. If the tracks didn't end here, Mafeking wouldn't exist.

Blanche and Grace, on the verandah at the Mafeking Hotel, were appalled by what they were seeing. For the past three hours, locusts had been flying overhead. The air was so thick with insects that they blocked out the sun, creating an eerie beige glow. The locusts ate flowers, plants, insects and other locusts. Moles, rats and frogs enjoyed a banquet. Countless species of birds assembled for a once-in-a-lifetime feeding frenzy.

Dinner produced a different kind of surprise. In the dining room, a traveler from London introduced himself. Hoping for news from the outside world, Grace invited Fred Lopez to join them for dinner. He spent most of the meal complaining because only military passengers were allowed to proceed northward.

"Why don't you volunteer for the Bulawayo Field Force?" Blanche tried to cheer him up by telling him about her husband's adventures in the American West. Among the yarns she related was the story of Fred and Homer meeting Buffalo Bill. During the meal, Blanche noted that Lopez consumed three tumblers of whisky. She thought, *This character has the table manners of a messy child.*

Counterpoise • Equilibrium

BULAWAYO • APRIL 1896

FRED WAS patrolling seven miles east of town on Saturday, April 25, when he met black scouts from an impi camped along the Umguza River. He galloped back to Bulawayo, and told Napier the enemy numbered two thousand men. Napier dispatched Captain MacFarlane with two hundred men to have a go at them. Captain Grey's gentlemen galloped in and opened fire, receiving a hot reply. Horses of Grey's Scouts kicked up dust on the open veld as they galloped, the chargers breaking wind with every leap.

A thousand Matabele soldiers armed with Martini-Henry rifles and bull-hide shields were hiding in the thick brush. They formed a horned crescent for a counterattack. Dawson's Scouts, riding over open ground, came under a galling fire and several men fell.

Fred saw that a second impi of a thousand warriors intended to nip Grey in the rear. He spurred his horse to warn MacFarlane but the fighting became general. In the bush, the Maxims couldn't get a bead on the enemy.

"Burnham, old chap, do something." MacFarlane pleaded. Fred galloped toward the company of a hundred Fingoes. These Colenbrander friendlies from the Cape Colony wore red capes and were armed with assegais.

Fred called out, "Follow me. We're gonna kill some Matabele." He dismounted, grabbed an assegai and ran. The Fingoes followed, flashing their spears and crying "jee." On foot in the brush, they were scarcely visible to the Matabele, who were hindered in the brush by Martini-Henry rifles and bull-hide shields. The black and white stripes of the Matabele made them stand out.

As the two sides closed, Fred counted on the tribal hatred of the Cape blacks to carry the day. A gust of wind fluffed up billowing clouds of dust and Fred bellowed as he charged across the grubby Umguza riverbed leading the Red Capes into the Matabele lines.

The sounds set Fred's adrenaline flowing. His senses stirred. The wild yelling thrilled him. Fred wondered if he was developing an addiction to the sights and sounds of war—to the bedlam of battle.

His assegai found a target and the gurgling scream of a mortally wounded man lured the Fingoes behind him into a shrieking attack. When Fred pulled the assegai from the dying man's chest, blood gushed from the wound. Fred looked at the mortally injured Matabele and his jaw dropped. It was Zimundu. When not encumbered by the bull-hide shield, that Northern Coppers vet was a crack shot.

For the next half hour, Fred cut and slashed at partly seen foes. The Cape friendlies launched a frontal assault and cried "jee." It was a frenzy of hacking and jabbing, slicing cheeks and faces, piercing eyeballs, slitting bellies, carving the calves off legs—hot blood spurting like at hog-killing time. The screams of the dying were shrill and harrowing. The blood of young men trickled down their legs, flowed under the fallen leaves and collected in the soil. The Matabele line wavered and there came the sound of galloping hoofbeats. The relief columns were coming in to mop up. Fred's Red Capes had flushed the Matabele into the open where the Maxims and Hotchkiss made short work of the fight.

That night, Selous said Burnham's attack was the first time a white man had used an assegai in hand-to-hand combat against Matabele. It went down as the main action in the Battle for Colenbrander's Farm. More important to Fred—the food was running low. Because of the *rinderpest*, there was no meat. Would Nada be forced to eat horse flesh? He couldn't bear the thought.

Lagnappe • A Little Extra

BULAWAYO • APRIL 1896

TWO DAYS LATER, Bill Thomas penned a report on the reason for the Matabele Uprising. Thomas was the Native Commissioner for the Bulalima District down by Mangwe Pass. Summoned to Bulawayo, he wrote in response to an order from CNC Herb Taylor, who was smarting from the editorial in the *Rhodesian Weekly Review*. Bill was Taylor's blue-eyed boy, but he was also an astute observer. Before signing the report, he looked it over.

The Matabele felt they were never fully conquered in 1893. The five regiments that attacked the Combined Column did so against King Lobengula's will. The most powerful Matabele impi had been raiding in Barotze Land and took no part in the campaign against the Europeans.

Soon the native commissioners were ordered to round up and send in cattle once a month, causing a fearful amount of discontent. Then came the locusts, the drought and the cattle plague, the last straw. Leaders of the malcontents spread rumors that the M'Limo was saying the white men brought these evils. The natives treated these as rumors, nothing more.

The ringleaders then said the M'Limo would remove the plagues if the blacks would kill the Europeans. Even then the Matabele did not rise, so the ringleaders took the bull by the horns and killed a native policeman. Then they killed Europeans near native kraals, knowing the innocent blacks would be implicated. Suddenly it rained, confirming the faith of the natives in the M'Limo's promises.

At the time, Thomas didn't know that the man who started the rebellion was an induna named Umlugulu who was Fred Selous' neighbor in rural Essexvale. Selous had thoughtlessly spilled the beans to Umlugulu about the Rhodesia BSA Police being captured in the Jameson Raid. Umlugulu, eager to invest a new Matabele king, took advantage of the weakness to incite the rebellion.

When Taylor read the Thomas report, he became so incensed he classified the document and buried it in the files. He wrote his own version of what happened. He singled out a Mashona called Stone Swallower, a priest deputized by the M'Limo. Taylor said that after the Battle for Colenbrander's Farm, Stone Swallower took refuge at Thabas Imamba, a mountain northeast of Bulawayo, an account that proved to be true.

Taylor said the Matabele were fleeing into the Matopo Hills south of Bulawayo. Should they suffer a defeat, Taylor said, they would return to Zulu Land. Taylor said Babiyan's Impi in the Matopos was neutral, taking no part in the rebellion.

• • •

LATER THAT WEEK, Earl Grey arrived to take up duties as administrator. To quell fears in England, he announced that since the Battle for Colenbrander's Farm, Bulawayo was as safe as London. Fred used the statement to prevail on him for a permit allowing Blanche to come up from Mafeking. Grey approved the request and Blanche boarded the Zeederberg stage for Bulawayo.

Shortly after Grey's arrival, Colonel Herbert Plumer's eight hundred irregulars arrived from Mafeking to take over the defense of Bulawayo. Widespread reports said his troopers looted the abandoned ox wagons along the way and drank all the red-eye.

Plumer's arrival freed the Bulawayo Field Force to ride out to the Insiza Hills and join the Salisbury Column. Rhodes' plan was to destroy the Matabele commissary by burning their grain kraals.

Blanche was scheduled to arrive on May 11, Fred's thirty-fifth birthday. That day Napier was scheduled to lead the BFF into the field. Fred had been assigned to scout for that patrol but he was eager for Blanche to arrive so she could care for Nada. The Zeederberg stage was late and when the BFF left, Blanche still hadn't arrived so Fred applied for compassionate leave. Some of the youngsters, Nada among them, had come down with whooping cough.

The next day a telegram from Bonnar Armstrong said the stage had passed through Mangwe. Fred left Nada in the care of Mrs. Cummings and rode to Fig Tree where he met the stage. Fred and Blanche rode back to Bulawayo, arriving on Wednesday afternoon. Nada was so sick that she failed to recognize Blanche, but now she had a mother's love to restore her to good health.

At dawn Thursday, Fred rode out to Pongo Creek fifty miles east of Bulawayo. That night Fred joined with Rhodes and the campaigners for a campfire dinner.

Lagnappe • A Little Extra

IN BULAWAYO, Blanche wrote to Rod in Pasadena:

Dear little Nada has been ill. Bronchitis, the doctors say. Mrs. Cummings, who's quite a doctor, gave Nada a preventive which keeps her from coughing. Baby has had the cough for a week, but the fever for only the last five days. She's been quite ill and grown so very thin. Of course, we can't expect her to be well all at once. Say your prayers. Love, Mama.

29

Scouring the Insizas

Insiza Hills • May 1896

AT SUNRISE IN THE Insiza Hills, Burnham awakened to flashes of lightning, the rumble of thunder and the tingle of cold raindrops. His nose was assailed by the stench of steaming horse dung. He studied the sixteen horse-drawn trek wagons that Cecil Rhodes had brought from Salisbury and appraised the men. Though well dressed, the two hundred fifty Salisbury troops were a queer lot. Half were unmounted and many were ill with fever. On the trip cross country, they had lost six hundred badly needed commissary cattle to the *rinderpest*.

The hundred fifty Gwelo volunteers described what was left of the town as a stink hole of bloated carcasses from three thousand cattle felled by the *rinderpest*. Fred knew Gwelo. After the Matabele War, he had surveyed the townsite and pegged out the residential lots, starting at the Gwelo River.

The Combined Column comprised a thousand men. How would they act when they met the hostiles? Fred wasn't worried about the men from Bulawayo and Gwelo. They'd lost kin and were smarting for revenge, but the Salisbury lot looked like lace-ruffled hooligans.

After breakfast, the column separated into two flying regiments. The Bulawayo group, led by Colonel Napier, rode along the western flank of the Insiza Hills, a low, rolling range that ran south. The Salisbury group, under Colonel Spreckley, patrolled the east flank. Their mission was to sweep the area clear of hostiles and burn the granaries. The columns would rejoin at Belingwe Road at the south end of the mountain range.

• • •

THREE DAYS LATER, on May 19, the sky was still the dull purple of a healing bruise. Light rain had pattered down since Monday. Chaplain Douglas Pelly, a city-bred Anglican serving with the Salisbury Column, was searching for the remains of a family that had been butchered and left to rot in the hills.

Fred Selous led the way through the scrub, guiding the minister to the site of the remains. A hundred yards ahead of them, something rose above the concealment of the veld grass. Pelly had no sooner recognized the figure as human than Selous fired, killing the Matabele instantly.

"That's the quickest shot I've ever seen."

"It goes with the territory, Chaplain."

They walked over to look at the body. It was a woman. Pelly vomited.

"Come with me," Selous said.

After several minutes of walking, a horse-mounted trooper pointed out the remains of seven persons the Matabele had slaughtered and left to rot in the veld grass. Pelly's eyes glazed over when he saw his first direct evidence of the hostilities. Hacked-up bodies were scattered over the land. The odor of putrefying human flesh — like the smell of rotten potatoes — was almost unbearable. Pelly's eyes filled with tears.

While Doug Pelly huddled over human remains, Selous fended off a pack of yipping hyenas. The minister discovered the body of the father on the riverbank, near the upper torso of what had once been his wife. Her breasts had been sliced off with an assegai, and white maggots wiggled like two moons on her chest.

That night a signal man climbed a telegraph pole to tap the wire between Salisbury and Bulawayo. Soon there were cries of excitement. The Imperial Army had been called in to aid the defenders of Rhodesia. Major General Sir Frederick Carrington, the military adviser to the high commissioner in Cape Town, would command the British Army forces. He would arrive in Bulawayo early in June, accompanied by his chief staff officer, Lieutenant Colonel Robert Baden-Powell.

"Excuse me, Chaplain," Selous said. "I happen to know the general. Do you have a pencil and paper?"

Pelly rummaged through his rucksack, producing writing equipment. As Pelly watched, Selous scribbled a note to Colonel Bill Napier. He predicted that Carrington wouldn't cease hostilities until he'd driven the Matabele out of Rhodesia—maybe run them back to Zulu

Land.

"You know, Chaplain," Selous said after dispatching the note by runner, "I can see the handiwork of Sir George Baden-Powell here."

"I cannot say that I know Sir George."

Selous stirred the coals of their campfire.

"When George was raised to the peerage, he became a mentor to Carrington, then a colonel in Natal. At the time, Sir George was the assistant to the high commissioner in Cape Town."

"I see," Pelly said. "The Good Old Boy Network."

"Precisely," Selous said. "Sir George has several times tried to get combat assignments for General Carrington, who agreed to take young Baden-Powell along."

"Like in 1893? When Whitehall squelched the deal?"

"So you heard about that?" Selous lighted his pipe before continuing. "Well, Colonel Plumer carelessly allowed his troops to pillage the abandoned freight wagons. That got him into a bit of a kerfuffle."

"Did the goods owners in Bulawayo complain?"

"The scandal reached London. Sir George suddenly had the implement he had lacked. Using influence, he had General Carrington appointed to command in Rhodesia. Stephe Baden-Powell was named chief staff officer, and Colonel Plumer gets sent out to some remote spot where the Matabele can wear him down."

• • •

BULAWAYO • MAY 1896

FRED LOPEZ arrived on the May 19 Zeederberg stage. Though he had departed Mafeking ahead of Blanche, he'd been detained at Palapye for three weeks until Earl Grey approved a sanction for him to enter the war zone.

The Bulawayo Field Force had rejected his application for a captaincy. Colonel Napier suggested that he enlist as a sergeant, but Lopez declined the offer. It wasn't until cables were dispatched to London and political pressure was applied that Lopez's entry to Rhodesia was finally pushed through. Despite a Navarrese father, Lopez was born in England to a British mother. That counted for something.

By chance, Lopez arrived in Bulawayo on his twenty-fifth birthday anniversary. He regarded that date as an event worthy of celebrating, so he went to the Bulawayo Club. Before retiring, he made an entry in his diary.

"Most men forgather in the Bulawayo Club in the evening to spend their time drinking and passing on information—mostly incorrect—

on the movements of the Matabele impis." Then he collapsed.

• • •

INSIZA HILLS • MAY 1896

THE HAZY DAWN OF Friday, May 22, was a glum prelude to three days of gunfire. The shooting lasted all day, through the night and all Saturday. Late in the afternoon of Sunday, Colonel Napier ordered Grey's Scouts and Van Niekerk's Afrikander Corps to attack the Matabele and join with Spreckley's force near the top of a hill.

"That's Burnham, the scout," Selous said. He and Pelly watched as Fred approached a group of men from Spreckley's force. The men talked for a few minutes and Fred galloped back toward Colonel Napier's line.

"Whatever news he is carrying, it must be important," Pelly said. "That man rides like the wind."

Grey's Scouts galloped in pursuit of a Matabele force that was herding cattle toward Bulawayo. Fred rode toward Major Grey.

"The kaffirs want to supply the impis who are laying siege to Bulawayo," Selous said.

"And Major Grey means to hive them off?"

"I dare say," Selous said.

A group of fleet, young Matabele runners charged out of a hidden ravine, cutting between Burnham and Grey's Scouts. Fred saw them, spurred his horse and galloped around the end of the pincer, rejoining Grey.

"Good heavens," Selous yelled. "I know that impi. Those boys are the Ingobu Regiment, one of the best."

Hundreds of warriors appeared out of crevices and ravines, and in ninety seconds encircled Grey's Scouts.

"Sweet mother of Jesus," Pelly cried. "The Matabele'll massacre all of them."

They watched as Major Grey shouted an order. Grey's men dismounted, kneeled in the grass and began firing at will, but the enemy continued to advance.

"Why fight as infantry?" Selous cried. "Grey's only hope is in a cavalry charge. He must be dotty."

They saw Burnham gallop up, waving his arms and shouting. Selous and Pelly couldn't hear what he was saying, but they saw Major Grey give another order. The fifty select gentlemen mounted their horses and formed a cavalry charge, galloping into the Ingobu Impi with sabers flashing. The black ranks broke just as Cecil Rhodes and Sir Charles Metcalf arrived at the head of reinforcements.

"When its time to put his life on the line," Selous said, "Rhodes is certainly no coward."

Ritornello • Interlude

BULAWAYO • MAY 1896

WHEN THEIR MISSION to burn kraals was done, the Salisbury and Bulawayo columns disengaged. They had destroyed three hundred granaries, killed a thousand Matabele and driven the rest out of the Insiza Hills.

The Bulawayo Column returned home but the Sally Gang continued south on a flying trip to clean up the Filibisi District. They would burn kraals and flush out the surviving blacks who had fled into the ball-granite kopjes of the Matopo Hills.

The BFF arrived in Bulawayo on Sunday, May 31, the troops having spent twenty days in the field. The men were ordered to make camp at Doctor Sauer's farm south of town, but Cecil Rhodes granted leave to the married men to visit their families.

That was splendid news to Fred—it was Nada's birthday. She was two years old today. On the way home, he banged on the door of a mercantile store so noisily that the proprietor opened up. Fred wanted to buy Nada a gift, but the only appropriate toy available was a rag doll. The weather was nippy at the end of May, so he bought a baby blanket too, promising to come back on Monday to pay for the purchases.

The men, yelling and waving their rifles, galloped into town, and the children piled wood on fires while the wives cooked whatever food was available—some wagon trains had begun to arrive. At the Cummings' home, Fred saw that Pete Ingram had come up from Kimberley, probably with a herd of horses and mules. Pete looked grim—*was he still smarting about the commission that had never come through?*

Fred grinned at Pete, waved to Homer and said hello to John and Judd who seemed strangely somber for a family reunion. Then Fred saw Blanche, standing alone.

"Where's the young 'un?" Fred asked. "It seems pure naked around here without our little girl?"

Fred saw the tears in his wife's eyes.

Where's Nada?" Fred demanded, holding the rag doll in his hands.

Blanche was sobbing, unable to speak.

"She's dead," Homer said, his voice breaking. Blanche moaned and ran to Fred. He wrapped his arms around her, hugging both his wife and the rag doll. He sat on a bench holding her tightly. To Fred, it seemed essential to bind the moment to some kind of reality—lest it seem too incredible to be recalled at a later time.

"When?" Fred asked. "WHEN, Homer?"

"On the nineteenth," Homer mumbled.

"Darling lily," Fred cried. Blanche sobbed and began shaking uncontrollably. *The day we rode into the Ingobu Regiment.*

"For three days we couldn't bury her body," Homer gasped. "An impi of Matabele was laagered in the cemetery. We had to get up an armed patrol and shoot our way in."

On hearing the words, Blanche collapsed on the floor. Fred carried her into the bedroom. After eating a hastily prepared dinner, the others found polite excuses to be somewhere else. Fred spent the next three hours talking softly to his mate. He recalled their courtship in Iowa and how Father Blick had declined to allow their marriage until Fred had earned enough money to support her. He told of his days prospecting for gold in the organ pipe cactus country south of Casa Grande.

He recounted his happiness at their reunion in Iowa, their marriage and the wedding trip to Pasadena where they built Burnham Manor. He described his joy at the birth of The Kid and later his happiness when Blanche had agreed to move to Africa.

Sometime during the evening while listening to the soothing resonance of Fred's voice, Blanche fell into a deep and profound sleep, her first since Nada's death. Later that night by the light of a beeswax candle, Fred wrote letters to friends and kin. The first was to The Kid, two months short of being ten years old:

When we parted at Southampton, I little dreamt how much of life's stream of events would pass in so few months. Another war is upon us and a hard one. All the town is forts and cannon, marching men, blowing bugles, the tramp of horses, all the women and children gathered in the big market building in the square, and little Nada among them. But the hardships were too much for her; a cold settled in her lungs and she died.

You are now the only one to bear the name, and you will dwell in our hearts always. I am in hopes your mother and I can come to Pasadena next year. Just now I wish you were here to comfort your mother, but you must do the duties that come to you. With unbounded love for you, I am yours. Papa.

Fred next wrote to Rider Haggard. At their meeting in London a year earlier, they had agreed to collaborate on an article about Wilson's Last Stand. During his voyage to Cape Town, Fred had actually set down many of the facts. But somehow he had never gotten around to finishing the account. Too many treks, too many wars, too many demands on his time. Would it never get finished?

This war was a complete surprise to all and it shows what fanaticism will do in a savage. It came within a hair's breath of being a second Sepoy Mutiny. Each servant in Bulawayo was to kill his master and each in the outlying districts was to kill all whites on a certain hour and day. But some hot-headed ones sprang the trap too soon, else I think it possible to have succeeded.

It does seem this year of '96 was destined to be dark. For African ambitions and reputations, the brightest are burning to ashes. Our Nada died in laager of inflammation of the lungs, caused by the draughty market buildings into which the women and children were huddled during the siege. Mrs. Burnham arrived on the first possible coach and had the consolation of being with her at the last. On the day of her death, I was making a desperate ride through the Ingobu Regiment and I knew nothing of it until my arrival in Bulawayo. You know the tempest that is raging in my soul.

The circumstances of her birth tied her to me in a strange way, and like the Nada of your book, she bound all unto her. Her loss leaves us all in deepest sorrow. I am hit awful hard, but for Africa and the Empire I will fight on. Even the ten plagues of Egypt had an end. And in the aftermath of the Jameson Raid, the political sky in southern Africa is still gloomy.

P.S. Mrs. Burnham has written the dates on the back of this photo of Nada. She was much moved by the way you mentioned Nada in the dedication of your latest book, The Wizard.

That night, as Fred climbed into bed beside his sleeping wife, a rage born of hatred seared his breast. It would burn deeply and change the course of events in Rhodesia.

Fort Marquand

30

Turning Bullets into Water

BULAWAYO • JUNE 1896

BLANCHE'S VOICE WAS crystal-clear, her tone firm, her position unyielding. "Fred Burnham, I know this is your chosen land. I haven't yet complained of living in the most isolated spot I ever laid eyes on. But Nada's death is too much. I want to go back to Pasadena."

Fred knew Bea had no intention of backing down, yet to go back to California now would shatter his scheme for building a nest egg. During his patrol in the Insizas, Fred had worked out his blueprint to develop the Wankie coal seams and the copper prospects north of the Zambesi. Everything they owned was tied up in the Belingwe gold mines and their interests in the Northern Territories. To leave now would be to throw up all he'd worked for in the past three years.

But Blanche was adamant and Fred offered her a compromise. They'd go to Pasadena where she could recuperate. In good time they would come back.

"The regulars will be taking over the fighting," he told her. "The Bulawayo Field Force will be disbanded on the Fourth of July. At that time, we'll leave for America."

"Promise?" Blanche asked. Tears filled her eyes and she grasped one of Nada's tiny dresses in her hands.

That conversation had taken place five days ago. Now Fred was riding with Sir Charles Metcalf to the Umguza River seven miles east of Bulawayo. Colonel Beal's Column had arrived from its flying thrust through the Filibisi District and the men were resting in bivouac.

When Metcalf asked Fred to guide him to the camp, Burnham had readily agreed. Sir Charles was Rhodes' handpicked railroad builder. Fred wanted to tell him of those abutments at Victoria Falls—

outcrops so matchless for a railway bridge across the Zambesi.

The two had met while dining with Rhodes at Pongo Creek, but they hadn't talked. Now they rode in silence and Fred was wondering how to introduce his idea. As the sun dipped to the horizon, a chill wind sprang out of nowhere. By now the stench of rotting flesh from cattle killed by the rinderpest was gone. Hides, guts and flesh had been consumed by the world's fattest hyenas, bloated vultures and largest ant colonies. Fred was about to bring up the railway abutments when a fresh stink caught his attention.

"Hold it, Sir Charles," Fred said. "Those aren't Beal's campfires. I smell Matabeles."

"Hippo shit." Metcalf said.

"The smell is like roosters in the barnyard. *Sadza* is being cooked. There's an impi of hostiles camped across the Umguza River. Now I can see their fires."

"What would kaffirs be doing here?" Metcalf asked.

"Mebbe an ambush. We'd better tell headquarters."

A voice cried out and the night came alive with angry sounds. That convinced Sir Charles, who reined his horse around and spurred it to a gallop. Fred trailed in pursuit.

Lagnappe • A Little Extra

BULAWAYO • JUNE 1896

MAJOR GENERAL SIR Frederick Carrington had arrived in Bulawayo on June 6 to head the Imperial Army force in the defense of Rhodesia. After two days of mugging up on things, Carrington launched a three-pronged offensive.

• Captain MacFarlane would take a column of men to pacify Inyati in the northeast. They would be gone three weeks. Fred was assigned to scout for MacFarlane, but Napier insisted Burnham was needed at headquarters. Bill was sympathetic to Blanche's inconsolable grief.

• Colonel Plumer and his irregulars from Mafeking would clear out the Gwaii district in the northwest. They would be away twenty-one days.

• Tomorrow morning Colonel Spreckley would begin a three-week-long foray to the north in the Shiloh District. Fred Selous would be the scout.

General Carrington's plan meant that for the next three weeks, Colonel Beal's Salisbury Column camped out by the Umguza River would be solely responsible for the defense of Bulawayo.

Fred and Sir Charles galloped into Bulawayo after dark and dismounted in front of military headquarters. Despite the chill winter evening, both men had worked up a sweat. Sir Charles bolted inside with the assurance of a man accustomed to exercising authority. Fred followed.

Seated at a table was a middle-aged man wearing the insignia of a lieutenant colonel. His uniform was directly from Seville Row in London.

"Where's General Carrington?" Sir Charles barked.

"Perhaps I can be of assistance," the uniformed man replied. With precision, he placed a staff report in the drawer of his desk, then arose. "I am Colonel Baden-Powell, the chief of staff. General Carrington cannot be disturbed."

"The kaffirs are massing on the Umguza River," Metcalf growled, annoyed by bureaucratic formality.

"I doubt that," Baden-Powell said. He appeared to be an unusual soldier, like an actor playing a role. "Though it's none of your concern, I am obliged to say that Colonel Beal is camped out there."

"I'm Charles Metcalf and this here is Burnham, the American scout. We saw hostile niggers at the Umguza. All of this is rather beyond arguing about."

"I've heard of you chaps," Baden-Powell said as he sized up his visitors. "The evidence suggests you've made a hard ride. Come with me to the map room and show me where you encountered these alleged hostiles."

Fred pointed to a spot on the map between Johann's farm and the Art Cummings dairy. A pin on the map indicated that it was the site of the Salisbury Column's bivouac.

"That is Beal's camp," Baden-Powell said.

"No, Colonel," Fred replied. "I used to live out there and I know the land. Those are Matabele camped there."

"Burnham's right," Sir Charles said with authority. "It's a warm trap with a piece of cheese in it."

"Your story has a manner of winsomeness," Baden-Powell responded. He was tall and lithe, wearing the assured look of a gentleman sportsman. His sandy hair was balding and, like Fred, he had a cleft chin and a friendly smile. Unlike Fred, his ears stuck out. "How many hostiles?"

"It was dark," Fred replied, "but from the number of campfires I'd estimate about fifteen hundred."

"Thank you, gentlemen," Baden-Powell said. "I shall convey the information to General Carrington directly. You are now free to leave."

• • •

U<small>MGUZA</small> • J<small>UNE</small> 1896

FRED AWAKENED at sunrise, eager to see what the day would bring.

He picked up his Winchester carbine and two six-guns, then rode along a small knoll toward the Welch Harp Hotel, an inn on the road to Salisbury. The hotel overlooked the Umguza River and Fred figured he could watch the action over an *al fresco* breakfast. They served agreeable ham and eggs.

When he saw the hotel, only the skeleton remained. The battens on the walls had been removed, exposing the studs. Fred tied his horse to the stump of a tree near the Umguza River, far enough away to be safe from stray gunfire.

The hostiles were camped in an open field encircled by a scherm of thorn brush. Incredibly, the blacks were making no attempt to conceal themselves from the whites. Even more bizarre, the pickets from Salisbury had failed to detect the impi across the little stream. *How could that be?* At least two thousand blacks were noisily stirring pots of *sadza*—a ration of ground maize mixed with pumpkin and meat. *Were Colonel Beal's men deaf and blind?* Fred studied the scene. With his field glasses, he could see what had happened to the cladding on the Welch Harp Hotel. The Matabele had torn the walls off the building and used the wood as fuel for their campfires.

Shortly after 7 o'clock, Colonel Baden-Powell arrived leading a small patrol of men. Fred rode over to join them. When they came to the Salisbury camp, they saw why no one had detected the impi. The Salisbury men were in Bulawayo on weekend leave. Only eighty troopers were on picket duty. Many of these were ill with veld fever and those few men posted to guard duty were fast asleep. *Truly an awkward squad.*

Colonel Baden-Powell said nothing. The scowl on his face suggested that he expected little from these rascals. He wrote a staff memo and dispatched a galloper to carry the message to Bulawayo.

"I've ordered Colonel Spreckley send a large patrol to assist us," Baden-Powell told his aides.

Spreckley's force arrived shortly after 9 o'clock, with Colonel Beal and his men trailing behind. The Salisbury troops, believing themselves to be on garrison duty, were attired in smart gray uniforms with blue trim and broad-brimmed hats. The Bulawayo boys wore cowboy hats, short-sleeve shirts and corduroy breeches. Bandoleers of ammo were strung across their chests. Their pistols hung low in their holsters. *It's like Arizona in Africa. Smart-ass Sally Boys and raggedy-ass Bully Boys.*

At the sight of Bulawayo's cowboys, Baden-Powell's face took on a look of ill-disguised contempt. To Fred, it was Baden-Powell himself who presented the ludicrous sight. The man that Lord Gifford had described as Bathing Towel was attired in gray woolen breeches trimmed in robin's egg blue piping. He wore a fastidious crimson blazer and a pith helmet, the garrison uniform of the British Army in India. To top it off, a scarlet cummerbund bound his waistline. *He looks like the grand panjandrum at the door of the Ritz Hotel.*

Colonel Baden-Powell led the joint force toward the Umguza River. Fred moved to a sideline to watch. While three baboons scampered into bushes, two hundred white soldiers rode toward what looked like two thousand black warriors. Though the troopers were less than five hundred feet away, the Matabele ignored the advancing horsemen. They sat quietly on the other side of the little stream, calmly eating their rations of *sadza* porridge.

The whites rode at a deliberate pace down the gentle slope toward the river bed, now dry except where water collected in the low spots. The troopers rode at a walk toward the rebel scherm. A dozen troopers dismounted. Using their rifles, they parted the scherm of thorns, then remounted.

At a hand signal from Baden-Powell, the troopers charged. The black warriors didn't budge. In a moment the horsemen were upon them. There followed a wild melee of shooting, shouting and profanity. Rifle shots peppered the blacks who toppled left and right, crying out in anger and mortal anguish.

Then came the resounding chatter of the Maxim gun. Suddenly the black warriors cast aside their porridge pots and rose en masse to flee. Those carrying rifles dropped them. Every man ran in panic. Baden-Powell's troopers fired at will at the howling men who failed to return fire.

The horsemen, hacking with their sabers, galloped into a sea of fleeing, bellowing humanity. Some of the Matabele were trapped by the thorn scherms, pinned there as the horsemen slashed with their sabers. Fred watched this ghastly spectacle, curious about the absence of alarm, followed by abject terror.

The battle ended quickly. The Bulawayo cowboys and the Salisbury chaps pursued the blacks until their horses gave out. As the stragglers returned, Fred rode out to estimate casualties. He saw that at least three hundred, perhaps more, had been slain outright. Another two hundred lay injured, abandoned by their fleeing comrades and destined to die. By noon, the troopers had returned to Colonel Beal's laager. Baden-Powell rode over to relax in the shade of a gray-thorn tree while tea was brewed.

Charles Metcalf arrived in a buggy from Bulawayo. Sir Charles was boasting about Burnham's ability to smell out the Matabele when

The Matabele Rebellion

a shot rang out. The sound was earsplitting close. Everyone including Baden-Powell hit the dirt. Colonel Beal crawled to Stephe's side, searching his crimson blazer for signs of wine-red blood.

A Bulawayo cowboy drew his pistol and fired three times into the upper limbs of the gray-thorn tree. A Matabele wearing a dirty loin cloth fell to the ground with a thud. Even in death, he clutched his Martini-Henry rifle in a fast grip. At this range, the biting smell of black powder was strong.

Two of Beal's troopers helped Baden-Powell to his feet. The colonel was not injured, but his pride was severely bruised. His face was spattered with flecks of gunpowder. Metcalf handed Baden-Powell a handkerchief to wipe away the grime.

"You mustn't wear that red jacket," Fred said. "The Matabele like to kill enemy commanders."

"What a curious fellow you are, Captain Burnham," Baden-Powell said, suddenly smiling. "I merely took things for granted. We should have a talk."

Baden-Powell examined the body of the warrior and he claimed the Martini-Henry rifle as his spoils of war.

"Handsome devil in those painted stripes" Baden-Powell observed. "I rather assume he was a jolly fine chap by his own standards."

Fred looked at the dead man. It was the tall and once-resourceful Mapibana.

"He never was much of a shot," Burnham said to no one in particular.

Only after questioning the Matabele prisoners did the whites begin to put together a story to explain the absurd behavior of the blacks. The enemy force consisted of warriors chosen from the top seven impis. All had been *doctored* by the high priest of the M'Limo, who promised to turn the white man's bullets into water. The priest said the whites were dying of starvation from the drought, the locusts and the rinderpest. He told the indunas that when the horses rode into the Umguza, he would cause the riverbed to open and devour them.

When the white men were dead, the impi could take custody of Bulawayo and hold it for King Lobengula, who would return to life. The yarn, which had been crafted in the manner of African beliefs, traditions and superstitions, was accepted by the warriors. That's why they showed no fear when the white soldiers galloped toward them. When the Umguza failed to swallow the horses, the blacks became suspicious. When the bullets didn't turn to water, their faith in the African deity vanished. They knew they'd been deceived and they fled in confusion and terror.

The *African Review* wrote up the Battle of the Umguza as a major victory. *South Africa* magazine sowed the seeds of long-term dissent that week when it characterized Colonel Plumer's Mafeking Column as a mixed lot of expert marksmen, hunters, tenderfeet, experienced bar loafers, deadbeats and men who'd never shouldered guns. The rancor over bar loafers and deadbeats would color events far into the future.

• • •

BULAWAYO • JUNE 1896

PETE INGRAM was alone, gathering a talkin load at the Bulawayo Club when a swarthy young man bellied up to the bar.

"G'day, mate. Stand you to a round?"

The stranger ordered his whisky neat. Pete was open to exchanging stale news for a free drink, even if this bloke did speak with an Aussie accent. The bartender brought a glass. Pete tossed away the drink and the stranger nodded to the bartender to bring another round.

"Earl Grey got a cable from London today," he told Pete. "Old Cecil's Chartered Company has to cough up all expenses for the Imperial Army troops while they're defending Rhodesia."

"A pile o wampum," Pete allowed. His was studying his glass wondering if it had a hole in the bottom.

"A hundred thousand pounds sterling each month. That's half a million of your Yank dollars."

"Rhodes is rich," Pete said. By now the tonsil varnish was warming him. "Rhodes is a kettle-bellied buggy boss, gone to tallow plumb to the hocks."

"When the rainy season comes," the stranger said, "Carrington means to put his troops into winter quarters. The Chartered Company still has to pay."

"Might cost two million bucks." Ingram belched.

"Rhodes wants to end the war to chop expenses."

"Carrington wants to win medals," Pete said. "He'll drag out the war until he kills the Matabele, jes like the Americans killed the Indians back home."

The stranger ordered another round, looking up at Ingram four inches taller.

"Aw, this war's just a brush hunt," the stranger said. "Melton Prior of the *Illustrated Sunday News* went back to London. Maybe the shootin'll be over by your Fourth of July, Yank."

"Don't call me a Yank," Pete said. "My ancestors met the *Mayflower*."

"Are you a red Indian from America?" the stranger asked. Both men had swarthy skin.

One of Grey's Scouts lurched toward the pair.

"I say, Pete, did 'ja hear Tyrie Laing's gonna nip in from Belingwe? Tell Burnham he'll be here on the first." The tipsy trooper arched his eyebrows and disappeared.

"Say," the stranger asked, "are you the mate of that American scout chap?"

"My brother in law," Pete replied.

"Related to that swagman, eh?" The stranger was favoring his right side.

"Fred's nickel-plated. Throws a long shadow."

"If I may permit myself the remark, cobber, I've heard otherwise."

"I'll ride with him any day. More'n I can say about you, alligator."

"It's a matter of indifference to me," the stranger said. "If you're so good, why aren't you in the BFF?"

"I was too young for a commission, pilgrim."

"You're at least twenty-five."

"Twenty-four," Pete allowed.

"Down at Mangwe, Bonnar Armstrong is nineteen, and he's the major commanding. At least he was, till they sacked him for Commandant Van Rooyen."

"Your cinch is gettin' frayed, sheep man. Why don't you amble out of here while you've still got your health?"

"Cheeky wampus." The stranger with the accent was beginning to slur his speech.

"You courtin a plot on Boot Hill?" Pete asked. There was a growing threat in his voice. "Better shut up or I'll blow out your lamp."

"You're a ravin loony. Have a last dram of tanglefoot on me. It's good enough for Indians."

"Jingle your spurs," Ingram said. "Before I'd drink with you again, I'd get a tin lard pail and peck shit with the barnyard ducks."

The stranger collected his chits and left. The next morning, he had difficulty writing the daily entry in his diary.

"Mouth tastes like I had supper with a hyena. Ill with the dingbats all day."

Scouting with Baden-Powell

The 7th Chronicle

31

Mapping Mineral King

BULAWAYO • JUNE 1896

FRED was writing a letter seeking authority to build a railway to the Wankie Coal Seams when a mounted messenger summoned him to report to the Chief Staff Officer at headquarters. Burnham put down his pen and mounted his horse. At the office, he was escorted to the presence of Colonel Baden-Powell. Gone were the Seville Row garments. The chief staff officer was wearing a plain khaki uniform.

"Burnham, you have a fine reputation as a tracker. I hear the Matabele are massing in the Matopos. What you know about it?"

"Only rumors, Sir. Other than riding twice through Mangwe Pass, pegging farmlands southeast of Bulawayo and digging for gold at Belingwe, I've never been to the Matopo Hills proper."

"Our friendlies are of little use. No reliance can be placed on them. I think they're acting hand in glove with the rebels."

"Why not scout the hills and learn firsthand?"

"Splendid idea. I'll send a patrol of fifty men tomorrow."

"You can't reconnoiter that way, Colonel. It's impossible to maneuver a large body of men in the kopjes without being seen. You send out one or two scouts."

Baden-Powell arose. At first he looked startled, then he smiled.

"How very sensible," he said. "The enemy always has warning of our approach. They disappear and we get no value for our money. I'll go alone. Will you guide me?"

"It would help to have someone who knows the area."

"I'll see to that." Baden-Powell gave the appearance of achieving results with almost no effort. They left on the evening of Friday, June 12, 1896. What the two men learned in the Matopo Hills not only set the stage for the rest of the Matabele campaign, but it also changed Baden-Powell's life forever.

• • •

MATOPOS • JUNE 1896

LIEUTENANT COLONEL Stephe Baden-Powell rode into the Matopo Hills as a dilettante, a wil-o'-the-wisp dandy, a pretender given to light banter and dressing up for lavish social dos. His practical knowledge of frontier life, of scouting, of tracking and trailing was exactly zero. Zip.

Three days later, he rode out of the kopjes a man possessed. Within a month, he'd be inspired to a new purpose in life. In little more than a decade, he'd found the Boy Scouts. And Fred Burnham, the American scout from Pasadena, was his inspiration and constant though silent mentor.

The two men arrived at Fort Marquand in time for an early breakfast. Baden-Powell introduced Fred to the chief native commissioner, Herbert J. Taylor, the hard-liner who had succeeded Johann Colenbrander. Fred wondered how good a scout he was.

Taylor was tall, with dark curly hair. His craggy clothing complemented natural good looks. When talking, he had a habit of looking into the distance through eyes resembling marbles.

"This is Corporal Bradley of the Mounted Police," Taylor said. "John speaks Zulu and knows the Matopos." Taylor rubbed his bristling mustache.

"Good," Baden-Powell said crisply. "We must make maps."

Fred wasn't happy at having two additional chaps on patrol. Bradley seemed to have qualifications for the task, but Taylor seemed like excess baggage. While they were in enemy territory, a thousand eyes would spy on them.

The Matopo Hills served as a barrier between Rhodesia and the Transvaal. The hills rose out of the veld and ran east for sixty miles from Mangwe Pass to Belingwe.

As they entered the kopjes, Fred saw that in no way could the

Matopo Hills be compared to the vertical, monolithic Sierra Anchas of Arizona. The Matopos were foothills. The highest of them rose a couple of hundred feet. Avoid the box canyons and you could ride through the Matopos so fast your horse would scare the baboons off the trail. He saw that herds of elephants did roam at will, as did the white rhino, prides of lions, herds of zebra and countless wildebeests. Fred thought the Matopos would make a fine park.

"I must say this area is rich in caves and defensive positions," Baden-Powell said. "I think the Matabele will retreat into the kopjes and this will become the main theater of war."

"You are probably right, Colonel," Fred said.

Herb Taylor insisted the local natives were neutral.

While riding beside the Maleme River, Burnham explained many tricks of scoutcraft. He described the quick draw, and he gave an exhibition of dry-fire snap-shooting as practiced in the American West. He then introduced some basics of woodcraft, a term that was new to Stephe. It was Baden-Powell's first exposure to honest-to-goodness scouting and he proved to be a fascinated and responsive student.

By noon they were seven miles into the hills and they came to a big camel's hump, too large to be a hill and yet too small to be a mountain.

"I think this is Mount Inugu," Corporal Bradley said. To the west was a grassy glade where two rivers joined. Fred scouted ahead and returned an hour later.

"I saw a large impi in a canyon," he said. "I captured this guy so we could get information."

Bradley questioned the Matabele boy, who said the induna of the impi was Babiyan.

"Babiyan's friendly," Taylor insisted.

"Friendly or not," Fred said, "that impi's armed."

"If the Matabele remain holed up in that box canyon, they're no threat," Stephe said. "Still, I need to make maps of this area. That mountain to the east is a good place."

From Mount Inugu, they rode three miles northeast to a long flat-topped hump of rock that rose six hundred feet above the valley floor. The monolithic mass of coarse granite looked like the back of a giant hippo. At the top, a dozen big boulders the size of houses formed a lesser Stonehenge. The rock was slippery, so Baden-Powell asked Taylor and Bradley to hold the horses at the bottom.

From the circle of boulders, the view of the country was magnificent. They looked on a rolling meadow, with groves of trees.

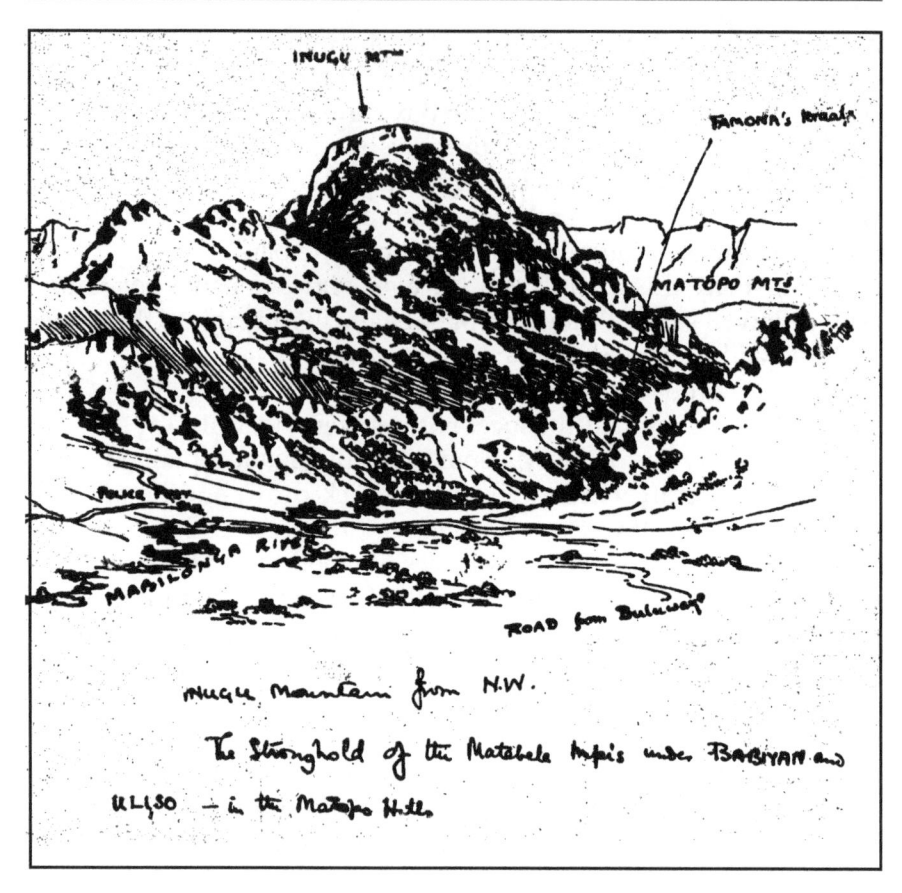

![sketch with handwritten annotations: INUGU MTN, FAMONA'S kraal, MATOPO MTS, POLICE, MABILONJA RIVER, ROAD from Bulawayo]

Inugu Mountain from N.W.
The Stronghold of the Matabele Impi's under BABIYAN and ULISO — in the Matopo Hills

Leaning against a boulder, Baden-Powell sketched the valley. He was able to draw with either hand. With amazing speed, he finished his sketches. When they got back to the horses, Taylor spoke.

"This nigger says the hill is called Malindidzime. It means View of the World."

"Three years ago, several white prospectors explored the Matopos," Corporal Bradley said, as if just recalling the fact. "They called this area Mineral King."

That was strange. There were few outcrops here that would interest a prospector. All the same, Mineral King rolled off the tongue. *Hey, that was the name of the California silver mine in the Sierra Nevada west of Cerro Gordo, the mine run by religious zealots.*

Burnham was impressed with Baden-Powell's map-making skills and he showed him how to trace the spoor of an enemy and how to cover his tracks. He described Indian sign language. He showed B-P how to slash a trail. He described how a crushed leaf found on an empty path could tell the story of a lone rider's passage. Stephe paid attention and little escaped his notice. The scouts crossed two rivers and rode seven miles west, passing a kraal of goats tended by women.

"I want to sketch the location of Babiyan's impi from the west," Baden-Powell said. "Burnham, come up the hill with me. You two, hold our horses."

Fred led the way up the kopje. Once again Baden-Powell delighted Fred with an ability to accurately portray the kopjes, trees and brush. Baden-Powell penciled in Babiyan's impi and a kraal at Famona.

That night under the stars, as Taylor and Bradley slept, Burnham

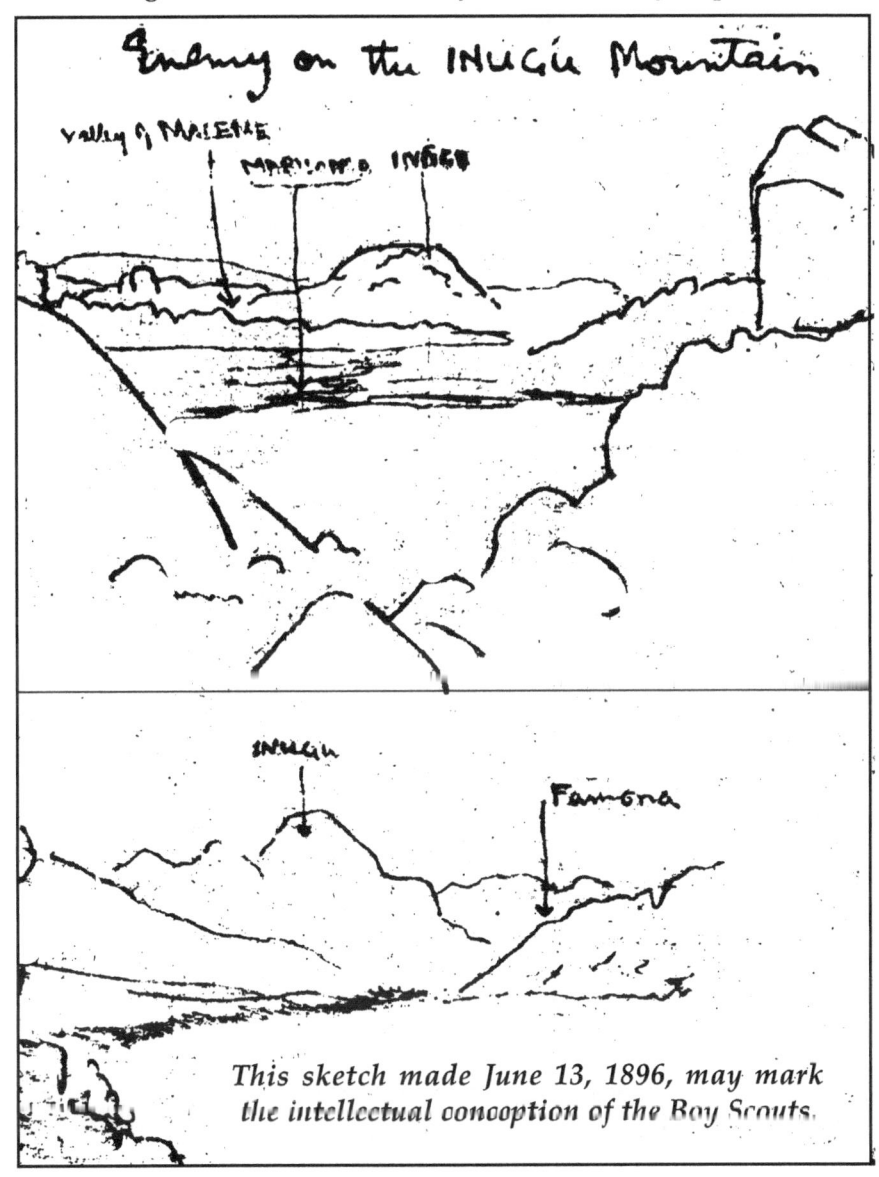

This sketch made June 13, 1896, may mark the intellectual conception of the Boy Scouts.

showed Baden-Powell more of the tricks of woodcraft. "The scout working alone at night can learn more than a squadron of horsemen by day."

"I'm coming to understand that, Sir," Baden-Powell said.

His eyes glistened as Fred described Apache methods of finding water, of observing game and traveling without compass or maps in wild country.

"All my years in India seem to have been a waste of time," Baden-Powell said moodily.

The next day they made a fast-moving survey. Stephe sketched while they rode. Late in the day they left the Matopos and dropped off Taylor and Bradley at Fort Marquand.

Burnham and Baden-Powell rode under the stars, continuing to exchange thoughts. That night they shared their last cups of hot cocoa over a tiny, smokeless fire. For the next hour, under the starlight, Baden-Powell poured out his dreams, misty ideas. Years later, Fred would recognize that his new friend's ultimate goals were only beginning to take shape.

"The time is short," Stephe said. "A war is coming that will make all others seem like a feeble flame. It will come from the Continent, but the Empire is in more danger from within than from without."

Burnham put out the fire and they mounted up.

"When I look at some of the recruits in our army," Baden-Powell said, "it sends a shudder through me. Robin Hood would've had a poor time recruiting longbowmen from modern cities. The blood stock of the English Empire once was a hardy people living close to the soil. A new age has sent farm folk swarming to the cities. Our very body measurements are shrinking. We must get back to nature."

Fred grunted in approval.

"By the way, I owe you a debt of gratitude. I must say I've learned much from you on this patrol."

"This scout," Fred corrected.

"Yes, scouting patrol. You bring new experiences to bear and are most instructive. There's not a thing that escapes your quick-roving eye."

Fred was glad that an important staff officer of the British Army had developed a yen for scouting. Maybe one day soon he could get Baden-Powell to help organize a Scout Corps.

"Jove," Baden-Powell burst out, "The young men of today will be the rulers of tomorrow. Yet England has become a nation of schoolboys in cricket flannels, gone rather slack. Out of our alleys and streets, our youth must be taught to preserve our best virtues, to keep alive in the hearts of men the fires that should not perish."

"Those are powerful ideas, Colonel," Fred replied.

When they arrived at Bulawayo on June 14, the moon was setting. Fred knew he'd never forget this outing. It was more than the beginning of a friendship. Fred sensed that the seed of an idea had germinated in B-P's mind

Ritornello • Interlude

JOHANNESBURG • JUNE 1896

ON JUNE 14 President Oom Paul Kruger commuted the death sentences of the members of the Reform Committee. Jack Hammond, banished from the Transvaal, decided to establish engineering offices in London. He booked passage two weeks hence for his family on the *H.M.S. Drummond Castle*. Then he hired porters to box his engineering records, personal effects and household goods for the thousand-mile journey to Cape Town via a private railway car.

Counterpoise • Equilibrium

BULAWAYO • JUNE 1896

TWO DAYS AFTER Burnham and Baden-Powell returned from their scouting foray, devastating news arrived. A telegram from Salisbury said the Mashonas had rebelled. They attacked white prospectors and miners in the hills, hacking them to death and dashing out their brains.

"Shonas?" Blanche cried. "They would never attack white men."

"Implausible, but true. The telegrams are official."

"Oh, Fred, what's this place coming to? Let's leave for home right now."

"We've booked passage three weeks from today," Fred replied. "The Shonas are too far away to bother us."

Daily reports arrived of similar atrocities elsewhere in Mashona Land. Before the week was over, one hundred twenty white settlers in eastern Rhodesia had been hacked, speared or bludgeoned to death. The *Bulawayo Chronicle* headlined news of a new fright to threaten the lives of the citizens of Bulawayo.

"In the Matopo Hills the Makalaka natives, who have hitherto been loyal, are preparing to revolt," the paper said. If the Makalaka joined the Matabele, Fred reasoned, they could block Mangwe Pass and seal Rhodesia's fate.

All the food and supplies for Bulawayo had to come through that pass—or around it on the old Missionary Trail. A blockade would devastate Fred's dreams for the Barotze Land coppers, the Wankie coal seams and the Belingwe gold mines. At a time when Rhodes was in political peril, it might bankrupt the Chartered Company.

There was a knock at the door. Fred answered the summons and saw Sir Charles Metcalf.

"Just the man I need to see," Burnham said. "I've been wanting to talk to you about a railway to Wankie."

"No time now," Metcalf blurted out. "You're wanted at Earl Grey's office."

While Fred saddled up, Metcalf caught his breath, then said, "I have to nip off to the Cummings place, but first I must warn you about that partner of yours."

"Pete Ingram? He's in Kimberley buying horses."

"Take care," Metcalf said in a confidential tone. "He talks a lot when he's drinking. He has a mean streak."

"I know about Pete's thirst," Fred said irritably. "I can take care of him."

"Hope so," Metcalf said as he rode off.

Soldiers and clerks in Government House scurried around on various duties. Fred was shown into the offices of Earl Grey, who was talking with three men. Fred knew Baden-Powell. He guessed the uniformed giant with pips on his shoulders was Carrington.

"Captain Burnham, this is Major General Carrington," Baden-Powell said. "I believe you know Native Commissioner Bonnar Armstrong from Mangwe."

Fred shook hands with Carrington, who wore glasses, was bowlegged and stooped. Fred knew Carrington had earned his reputation as a kaffir fighter. *He is a stiff-upper-lip bulldog. Not brilliant, but strong and dependable, like an ox pulling a trek wagon.*

"NC Armstrong has put a plan before the General," Earl Grey said. "I want the benefit of your counsel."

Burnham nodded at the young man from Mangwe.

"Armstrong says he has found a native informant who knows where the M'Limo's lair is," Lord Grey said. "He says it may be possible to track the high priest to his cave and kill or capture him. In the light of recent events in Shona Land, capturing or killing this native deity might bring about an early resolution to hostilities."

Fred was alert to every word the administrator said. The words he had just uttered blew the sawdust from his mind. Today was June 19, one month since Nada's death. In his mind, he saw Blanche holding the dying child to her breast. There were no fine points to ponder. This was what he'd waited for.

"I'll go," he said. *Vengeance will be mine.*

"The whole plan might be a trap baited with warm cheese," General Carrington warned. "The Matabele might be trying to capture an American scout as a hostage."

"I'll bear that risk, if Armstrong will," Fred said. "Grass will wave over that black deity before week's end. If he can't turn my bullet into water, I'll have his head to show for it."

"If you go, gentlemen, it's a volunteer effort," the general said. "Capture him if you can. Kill him if you must. But under no circumstances should you allow him to escape."

To Fred, there was no need for that admonition. The thought of Nada buried in Plot 219 at Bulawayo Cemetery made him feel like hell with the hide ripped off—he was feeling as riled as a teased rattler.

"I'll go with you," Baden-Powell suddenly offered.

General Carrington shook his head.

"With the Shona uprising, I can't spare you, Colonel. Good luck, gentlemen and Godspeed.

Burnham turned to Armstrong.

"We leave at midnight. Until then, we've work to do."

At dinner, Fred told Blanche of his mission. She listened in silence, unmoving and tearless beside a packing crate they used for a table. A candle cast a pale glow over the left side of her face, the right side hidden in shadow. Her expression told Fred that she had reasoned the mission through to an end. He and Armstrong would penetrate many miles behind hostile lines, gain access to the native deity in his darkened cave, then try to capture him or carry him away. This black god would be guarded by an impi of warriors that would rush the cathedral at the first sign of danger. The warriors would think nothing of sacrificing their lives to save the high priest so he could continue his deception.

In Blanche's mind, there was not a chance in a million that he could find the M'Limo, capture or slay him and escape with his own life. Blanche neither cried nor asked him to renounced his mission. She sat in her chair, staring at the blank wall. Her breast heaved as Fred wrote a letter to Rod. She knew this would be his last letter to The Kid.

The war news is still coming in, and patrol after patrol is being sent out. I think this war will last all year, as the Shonas are rising. I leave tonight to go into the Matopo Hills. Papa.

It was Fred's first letter to Rod since telling his son a month ago of Nada's death. An inexpressible grief came over him and he got up to go outdoors and walk in the dark.

When he returned, Blanche was in bed. He climbed in beside her and put his arms around her. In two short hours, he and young

Armstrong would set out for their journey to the Matopo Hills. What the future would bring was in the hands of the gods.

Meanwhile, Fred had one hundred precious minutes with the woman he loved. As he leaned over to kiss her, she pulled him to her side. The next hour was a time of physical intensity that could never again be equaled.

Fleet Street's View of the M'Limo

32

Slaying the M'Limo

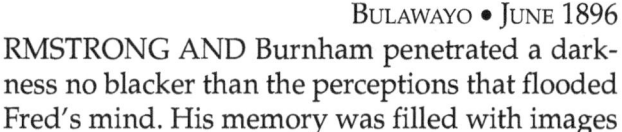

BULAWAYO • JUNE 1896

ARMSTRONG AND Burnham penetrated a darkness no blacker than the perceptions that flooded Fred's mind. His memory was filled with images of the mutilated body of mild old Tom Maddox. Still fresh were accounts of the Ross and Fouris families, whose remains fit into two burlap sacks. But the most painful memory was of his own Nada, who lay cold in the ground, her life extinguished by this black fiend. Now by an ironic turn of fate, Fred was setting out to meet the author of these horrors.

"The M'Limo is a spirit of rain, fertility and harvest," Armstrong told Fred. "He is worshipped by many Bantu tribes in eastern Africa. The Shonas in Salisbury call him Mwari. The Makalakas in the Matopo Hills call him Umlimo. M'Limo is the Matabele name. His presence is accounted for by a deception carried on by subordinate priests called wosana. As I understand, they issue commands from a ledge in front of a cave. The echoes make the commands seem to come from the M'Limo himself inside the cave."

Armstrong's description brought to Fred's mind his visit to the church of Santuario della Madonna del Rosario in Pompeii. There the clergy climbed into the statue of a goddess to speak through her mouth. If the imposture of the bellowing priest had worked with the Italians, it should work here with untutored natives on the veld.

"Does this pope have cardinals and bishops?" Fred asked.

"Several high priests or wosana are scattered about, but mind you only one proper M'Limo. He lives in a mountain recess south of Bulawayo. After the war in 1893, Captain Hook cornered the M'Limo in his lair, but when he scrambled up to the entrance, the blighter nipped out some side exit. If an M'Limo priest gets killed, the next ranking wosana takes over, continuing an illusion of immortality."

"If that's true, why kill him?" Fred asked.

"The idea is to disprove the notion that the M'Limo can turn the white man's bullets into water."

At dawn they arrived at Fort Luck, nine miles north of Fort Mangwe. It was marked on the map as The Nek, a nickname for Manyami Pass.

"We'll stay at the Mtoli Starr Hotel," Armstrong said. "Our informant will meet us tonight in the bush east of here. He's fearful of being seen with white men."

The thought occurred to Fred that it was odd for Armstrong to call on Earl Grey about this mission. Normally, Armstrong would report any findings to CNC Herb Taylor. In turn, Herb would present the case to Earl Grey. A black waiter wearing castoff European attire arrived with a tray of hot tea, burned toast and tinned orange marmalade.

"Why did you report to Earl Grey?" Burnham asked.

"I couldn't report to General Carrington," Armstrong retorted. "I was relieved as major at Mangwe Fort."

Commandant Van Rooyen and Captain Hans Lee were running the military side at Mangwe Fort. Both had lived for twenty years in Mangwe. Fred still wondered why Armstrong had not gone to CNC Taylor.

"Don't you have an itch to know why I was sacked? What happened is that I spoke out against the murder of natives." Bonnar's brittle voice cracked as he spoke.

"You mean shooting hostiles?"

"I mean shooting prisoners of war, native prisoners, men captured by troops serving under my command. These prisoners were Matabele being detained for trial by civil court when I was ordered to try them by court martial and shoot them."

"They always try rebels and shoot 'em," Fred said.

Armstrong tugged at his ear lobe.

"Not since martial law was revoked, mate."

"What?" Fred hadn't heard of any such development.

"When General Carrington arrived in June, the high commissioner in Cape Town rescinded martial law. By due process, prisoners must now be tried in civil courts."

Fred shrugged. *Some fuzzy British legal point?* He was more interested in finding the M'Limo. Fred poured tea

"If I'd complied with the officer commanding, I'd be guilty of willful murder. When I refused, I was deprived of my command. By and by, the prisoners were tried by courts martial and shot."

Fred recalled a warning from Billy Lynch in Belingwe. Some natives had been flogged to death for cattle stealing in the Bubi District. He asked Armstrong if there was any truth to the rumor.

"Do horses piss?" Armstrong snapped. "Let me tell you some dark, bedrock facts. High officials in the Chartered Company are covering up the facts. The BSA Company is bloody well corrupt."

Fred was surprised by the bitterness in Armstrong. He himself had scant respect for Herb Taylor who seemed to have a knack of calling all the shots wrong. But if Bonnar kept talking like that, he might lose his job. Fred mentioned that possibility.

"Let them try," he said nervously tugging at his ear lobe. "My appointment is revocable only at the sanction of the secretary of state for colonies, Joseph Chamberlain."

"True," Fred conceded, recalling the noose around Joe's nuts. "But Herb Taylor can transfer you to some land infested with *tsetse* flies where you'll contract blackwater fever or die of sleeping sickness."

"Frightful," Armstrong said. "Thanks awfully, mate."

The two men went to their rooms and slept until the shank of the afternoon. As they saddled up, Fred wondered why Armstrong was so reluctant to kill prisoners of war, yet willing to assassinate a religious figure.

From the Mtoli Starr Hotel, they rode southeast along a dry stream bed until it joined the Shashani River on its way from Fig Tree to the Limpopo. At the Shashani, they struck out east, traveling four miles until coming to a large hill. Armstrong said it was Mount Fumugwe. The brushy veld ahead was broken by kopjes. Many of the trails were in daily use and Fred saw the recent spoor of goats. The few natives he saw looked different from the Matabele.

"They're Makalaka," Armstrong said. "They are a non warrior tribe who lived in the Matopo Hills before the Matabele came up from Zulu Land. By day, you'll see their skin is a rust-colored hue. They don't wear the marriage rings in their hair like the Ring Kops."

Armstrong said his informant had agreed to meet them after dark at Mount Fumugwe. They waited until well after midnight, but when the man failed to appear they rode back to Fort Luck.

The next day they made a daylight foray into the Matopo Hills and Fred got an opportunity to learn more about the land. About ten miles east of Fumugwe, they saw in the distance a solitary domed monolith, like half a watermelon lying face down. The mound appeared to be three hundred feet high.

"That might be it," Fred said. The monolith was smaller than Malindidzime, the View of the World that he and Baden-Powell had explored the Mineral King area.

Several youngsters could be overheard tending goats along the trails. The two white men were unable to get closer to the monolith without being observed and they rode back to Fort Luck to eat. After dinner, they talked.

"Do you have a map of the Matopo Hills?"

"Upstairs, in my room," Armstrong replied.

The map revealed intimate detail around Mangwe Fort, Bonnar's area of operations. North of Fort Mangwe, there were penciled in the six forts recently built along the Old Missionary Trail: Forts Luck, Halstad, Molyneaux, Marquand, Selous and Dawson. The Matopo Hills east of Mount Fumugwe was a blank area.

"Got a pencil?" Fred asked.

"In that drawer over there."

Burnham laid the map on the table. Fifteen miles south of Bulawayo he marked an X for Mount Inugu and View of the World in Mineral King.

"I scouted this area ten days ago with Colonel Baden-Powell," he said. "Babiyan's impi is holed up in a box canyon at Inugu. Maybe he's guarding the north entrance to the M'Limo's cave. That big rock we saw today seems to be due south of Mount Inugu—about here."

Fred marked another X on the map, at the spot where they found the watermelon earlier in the day. The map now showed three Xs along a north-south axis: Bulawayo, Inugu and the M'Limo's lair.

"Let's assume that bald mound we saw today is the M'Limo's church," Burnham said. "We'll be coming from the west. We could ride past Fumugwe and continue on to his place."

"Like we did today?" Armstrong asked.

"Yes, the thick brush and scattered kopjes are fine for sneaking up on the M'Limo. But brush and kopjes are bad places to be if an impi of hostiles is chasing you."

"Oh," Armstrong said. "You're referring to what happens after we do the deed. Sticky wicket. Then the Matabele will be on to us."

Fred drew a line from Mangwe Pass due east.

"South of that line, would we be out of the Matopo Hills?"

"Yes," Armstrong replied, leaning over the map. "It's veld and brush for sixty miles down to the Shashi River."

"So it'd be clear sailing," Fred theorized. "When we finish our chore, if we ride south, we can get clear of the brush. In open land, our horses will have the advantage. We can outrun the fleetest pursuer on foot. Then we canter back to Mangwe at our leisure."

"Jolly fine idea. Glad I'm with you on this do."

That night they rode back to Mount Fumugwe for another try. This time Armstrong's informant appeared, but only after being passed by a series of go-betweens that sorely tried Burnham's patience. Armstrong seemed to display the forbearance of a saint.

When he saw the man, Fred could scarcely make out what the guy looked like. He'd disguised his face with mud. Armstrong spoke at length in Zulu. Bonnar seemed to be a master of the language. He might be moody, but he had nerves of steel.

"He says the mountain we saw is the M'Limo's own cave," Armstrong said. "He says it is called Njelele."

Bonnar pronounced it as Ahn-Juh-LAY-Lee.

"He says that in two days an impi will be doctored to make them immune to the white man's bullets."

"After the Battle of the Umguza?" Fred asked. "I thought none of them would be duped again."

"It takes time for the word to get around," Armstrong said. "There will be a smaller ceremony tomorrow for the elders. But the main body gets doctored the next day."

"We must do the deed tomorrow," Fred said.

• • •

FORT LUCK • JUNE 1896

TUESDAY, JUNE 23, was the longest and most trying day in Fred Burnham's life. Before the first light of dawn, he and Armstrong were riding out of Fort Luck, carrying the loaves of the biltong bread Fred had baked in Bulawayo. They shared a calabash of water.

The weather was crisp and clear, the equivalent of a fine December day in southern California. After crossing a tributary of the Shashani River, they sometimes saw groups of women carrying clay pots on their heads. Armstrong said the pots probably contained the sweet smelling beer used in the M'Limo's doctoring ceremony. The presence of the women hindered their progress, forcing the horsemen to take cover whenever they heard voices.

"Hell, Bonnar, let's ride south of these Matopo Hills," Fred said. "We'll never make it to Njelele with these beer-women gallivanting all over the place." Bonnar nodded and they rode south of the line Fred had marked on the map last night. It took them out of the kopjes, coming at length to a rolling veld where they could make good time.

"Our spy told me the M'Limo's cave is part of an amphitheater high on that big rock," Armstrong said. "It's not really a cave, but rather a cleft in the monolith, providing an open gallery to the sky. Sheer walls rise a hundred feet"

"Where's the entrance?" Fred asked.

239

"There are two or three, but the main one seems to be on the south side between two pointed rocks that look like a Gothic arch."

About 10 o'clock Burnham and Armstrong rode through a vley that led out of wild animal land toward bushy hill country. To the north they saw their goal. Not a tree or blade of grass grew atop that solitary monument. Fred sensed a parklike quality about the area. It looked more like California than Africa—kaffirs weren't noted for keeping neat yards. The grass here was close cropped, probably by the goats. Trees and shrubs grew in small clusters that dotted meadows of grass an acre in size. No birds sang here. Even the insects had deserted the place. Except for the occasional voices of women speaking in hushed tones, there was silence.

When they got within a mile of the Njelele monolith, there were more sounds of people moving about. The white intruders dismounted and moved with caution. The sun burned down strongly now. While Fred worked out a route for their next advance, Bonnar held the horses in a clump of bushes.

Fred spotted a trio of kopjes that formed a natural box canyon. The entrance was shrouded by young trees, a good place for concealing horses. Fred watched for half an hour to make sure no natives came by. He was thirsty but Bonnar had the calabash.

At length, Fred returned to Armstrong's hiding spot. After a swallow of water, he put down the calabash and they unsheathed their rifles. With care they crawled a hundred yards. Using a branch, Fred scratched out any tracks left as they crossed a path. Fred glanced at the sun and reckoned it was noon.

"Look on ahead beside that kopje," Fred whispered. "Isn't that an impi camped inside the scherm?"

Bonnar gasped as he saw several hundred Matabeles. They were reclining inside a fence of thorn bushes.

"Hard cheese," Armstrong said. "I thought the impi wouldn't be doctored until tomorrow."

"We'll have to try the entrance on the east side," Fred said. "Going in, we don't dare alarm that impi. When the deed is done, it won't matter how much noise we make."

They slithered back to the boxed kopjes, mounted and rode east until the bald, half-melon hill was over their left shoulders. Then they turned north, riding in grassy, red-earth country through young trees and leafy green bushes. Fred wished they'd find a stream so they could water the horses. This detour already had cost them more than an hour's lost time.

The two men studied the lay of the land. They seemed to be in the clear. Fred found a thick cluster of trees where they could hobble the horses. Where the foliage was sparse, they crawled on hands and knees across flat ground, taking care to hide in what shadows the bushes offered.

"The trickiest part's ahead," Fred whispered. "Rub this charcoal over your face and clothes. Then stuff some grass and branches in your collar, belt and shirt pockets. It'll help to disguise you. If you see anyone, don't move a muscle. If you even twitch, they'll see you." Fred ran his index finger across his throat.

After disguising their faces, they worked their way past small boulders, clumps of brush and tufts of grass. At length they saw the east entrance to the Njelele cave. The only safe route would take them north of the east entrance. About 2 p.m. they arrived at the side of the monolith. The walls rose at a sixty degree angle. The entrance was forty yards south of them and there wasn't a bush in sight to provide concealment. They were in open view of the goat herds, who were passing to and fro. On hearing any sound, the two men would freeze.

Burnham and Armstrong had crept to within twenty yards of the entrance when six women carrying clay pots walked into view and sat down to rest. Fred and Bonnar lay still for half an hour while the women took their ease, squatting to urinate and chatter among themselves. A flock of hungry vultures circled in the sky looking for something to die. Sweat trickled over Fred's forehead and the salt stung his eyes. Not six feet away, Bonnar lay, his face in shadow. Not a sound came from either man as the sun edged slowly westward, casting them in the solace of the afternoon shadows.

One woman glanced in their direction, studying the scene intently for fifteen seconds. She arose and began to walk toward them and Fred experienced extreme bladder urge. As he reached for his pistol, the faint sound of male voices chanting in the distance captured the women's attention. *The men of Babiyan's impi must be thirsty.*

The women lifted the beer pots to their heads and began walking dutifully toward the impi. Fred's pulse rate dropped forty points. Motivated by impulse and abandon, the two men slowly crawled the remaining sixty feet to the cleft in the wall. Like a flash, they scrambled up the entrance and into the amphitheater.

As Armstrong had said, it was a natural gallery with walls rising a hundred feet. They weren't vertical like the Sierra Anchas, but they were steep basalt. Over time, wind and rain had carved a pathway into the exfoliating slabs.

They were in the enemy's lair and soon they'd learn if they'd been duped. As eyes adjusted to murky light, Fred saw the amphitheater was empty. The shadows suggested it must be after 3 o'clock.

The quiet of the interior gallery imbued Fred with a degree of confidence he hadn't felt outside. No Bantu would dare enter this cavern. Only the M'Limo or his high priest, a wosana, would dare step inside. Signaling with his thumb, Fred suggested to Bonnar that they climb to a higher point. Armstrong nodded.

They crawled to a narrow ledge where they could sit in the shade. In the distance, beyond the Gothic southern cleft, the men from Babiyan's impi squatted in a scherm, no doubt practicing for the doctoring ceremony.

From the corner of his eye, Fred detected a motion. He heard no sound, but he saw a lone man walking slowly up a curving path that led to the cavern's south entrance. The black spirit strode purposefully toward the gallery entrance.

There in full view of the impi, he began a ritual dance, waving his hands and feet and swaying his head. Then he sat down and clapped his hands, chanting in a remarkably forceful baritone voice. Inside the cavern the sound wasn't loud, but the actions of the warriors outside suggested they were hearing echoes that were magnified and carried down to them. *This is as fascinating as a Hopi rain dance in Arizona.*

The black priest completed his chant and strolled purposefully toward his inner lair. As he drew closer, Fred could make out the man's features. He was close to sixty years old, with large bones, a broad forehead and wide-set eyes. He had a white goatee about two inches long that gave his head the hatchet-faced look of an eagle. His skin wasn't black—it was mahogany. There were no bones or monkey-skin ornaments of the ordinary witch doctor. The man carried himself erect, with dignity. *As a young man, he must have cut an admirable figure.*

Though Bonnar was only four feet away, Fred dared not whisper. No telling how any sound might reverberate in this echo chamber. Using sign language, Fred asked Bonnar if this was the M'Limo. Armstrong shrugged, unable to understand the hand-signing of red Indians. With his finger, Fred spelled out on the palm of his hand ZULU. Bonnar understood and shook his head. This man wasn't Zulu. With his lips, Bonnar formed the syllables of Em-LEE-Mow. Fred understood. This man *was* the fiend they were entrusted to eliminate.

A sound behind Fred's back — an echo like the church of Santuario

The M'Limo's cave at Njelele, south of Inugu in the Matopo Hills.

della Madonna del Rosario in Pompeii — alerted the black spirit. Bonnar had knocked his hat off the ledge. As he dove to retrieve it, a look of amazement crossed the eagle-face of the high priest. It was quickly replaced by a glare of outright contempt for any mortal who would dare to enter his sacred cavern.

The M'Limo stopped, but he neither turned nor ran. He simply stared with a cruel gaze into the deep shadows. That look told Fred all he needed to know. The black spirit's eyes hadn't yet adjusted to the dim interior light.

Fred's heart pounded like a bass drum and his vision became fuzzy as he raised his Lee-Metford rifle. *Here's the author of your woes. Because of this fiend, your little daughter lies dead and the bones of hundreds of brave men and women lay scattered across the veld.*

Then he recalled the voice of General Carrington: "Capture him if you can. Kill him if you must. Under no circumstances should he be allowed to escape." With eyes glazed over, Fred raised the rifle, barely seeing the target. At this range, he couldn't miss.

"Turn this bullet into water," he cried out. The priest turned to face Burnham who slowly squeezed the trigger. There was a short, sharp recoil and a pop as the shot echoed inside the amphitheater. The Lee-Metford .303 bullet caught the black priest below the heart.

The M'Limo never knew what hit him.

Frank Dadd's drawing of Burnham shooting the M'Limo from outside Njelele may have given rise to Frank Sykes' claim that Fred shot an unresisting old Negro after asking the man to walk into the cavern.

33

At War with Fleet Street

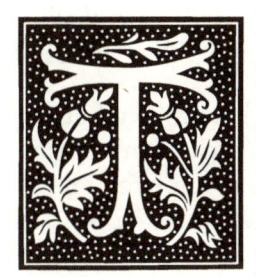

NJELELE • JUNE 1896

THERE WAS no need for haste, but Burnham and Armstrong wasted little time getting out of Njelele cavern. The sound of Burnham's rifle shot echoed in the amphitheater and trumpeted into the meadow like an apocalyptic explosion. The sound so startled the beer-besotted warriors that they jumped up and fled en masse, none looking back. Fred remembered his bladder urge and relieved himself on the slab of basalt next to the body of the M'Limo.

"What you doin' there, Mr. Burnham?" cried Bonnar. "Let's get outta here."

"Got any matches?" Fred asked, buttoning up.

"I do, in fact. Why, mate?"

"Go down there and set fire to those thatched huts. I'll bring the horses in five minutes. You'll be perfectly safe."

Armstrong shrugged, pulled down his hat and slung his rifle over his shoulder. Then he scooted down the path used by the late-departed M'Limo. Fred scrambled down the east entrance of the cavern and ran smack into the women. Two pistol shots scattered them to the winds and Fred dashed to the clump of trees where their horses were grazing.

Leading Armstrong's horse, Fred spurred his own to a gallop. It was odd how those long distances so painfully gained while crawling in the hot sun melted away on a horse. Fred saw smoke ahead from the thatched huts. He spurred his horse in the direction of Armstrong.

"Push on your reins," Fred called.

"You bet."

They rode at a canter through the trees, bushes and grass, dodging people who ran around in confusion and alarm. Fred looked back.

245

Warriors with assegais were chasing them.

"Use your gut lancers," Fred called out, spurring his own horse to a full gallop. For a hundred yards it was a race, but they outdistanced the running soldiers. They galloped until at length they arrived in the open veld south of the Matopo Hills. Nada and the others had been avenged. Fred felt no emotion whatsoever.

Ritornello • An Interlude

MANGWE • JUNE 1896

CHARLIE FRIPP SAT at a hand-hewn picnic table in the open air, listening to a symphony of yipping hyenas. The dapper artist for the London *Daily Graphic* felt sorry for himself. It was hard cheese getting chucked off the stage and being left isolated in this outpost of hillbillies. He wondered what prompted this conglomeration of wantwits to gather in a no-man's-land, living in sod houses dug into the hillsides. A nappy lot.

At dusk, Fripp was about to go inside to take his drops when two men rode up. One of the men, a short, muscular chap in his early thirties, looked like a Yank. He had fiery steel-blue eyes and he seemed to command the respect of the other, who was taller but a bit young to be riding on the veld during hostilities. Charlie Fripp asked one of the locals who these men were.

"The taller chap is Native Commissioner Armstrong," the rustic said. "Dashed if I know the other, but some say he's Burnham the American scout. There's a rum story goin about says they rode into the Matopo Hills to kill the black god M'Limo. If it's true, that's good news. It'd mean the end the rebellion."

"Burnham the American scout? Of Wilson's Last Stand?"

"So they say, Gov."

Fripp suddenly was beside himself with joy. Getting kicked off that Zeederberg Brothers stage turned out to be good luck. Instinct told him he'd stumbled onto the Big Story. And with the main actors here, Fripp had them to himself. No need to share this scoop with any reporters in Bulawayo. He introduced himself to the two newcomers and invited them to join him for dinner.

"I'm ready to take on the dough wrangler," Fred said.

"I'm could scoff the leavins of a hyena," Bonnar added.

The food was cooked with crude indifference, but after the day's turbulent adventures, the two men were hungry as pigs and they ate like horses. After their risky mission, both men were happy simply to be alive, and boisterous to the point of silliness.

"Stone the crows and bring on lashings of belly timber," Bonnar cried out.

"This is real throat-ticklin grub," Fred added in his own good spirits. "Almost as choice as the sowbelly and fartleberries back in Arizony."

Despite the revelry, they revealed nothing about the day's activities, which irked Fripp. He smiled helplessly.

After dinner, Fripp asked a question, but Fred made a big affair of ordering coffee. The waiter took Fred's teapot back to the kitchen and scurried around for a few minutes, returning in time with a pot of coffee.

"Thanks for the nacket," Bonnar said, nodding.

"Gotta go now," Fred said, rising.

While they went to the telegraph office to compose a message for General Carrington, Charlie Fripp did some serious thinking. An hour later, the two adventurers were back from the postal office, looking for a place to sleep.

"Chaps, I have an offer to propose," Fripp said. "This is a big story. Out here, things are bound to get a bit foggy, probably distorted. I can make one promise. Tell me what happened and I'll record your story accurately. If there's ever any question, your version of the story will be on the record. It will be the first news story written after the deed was done."

Fred had planned to give his story to Rider Haggard, as he'd promised to do with the article on Wilson's Last Stand. After all, in a month, he'd be back in England, almost as fast as Fripp could get his article and sketches mailed off to London. But Fred knew enough about news reporting from working for Uncle Josiah to recognize one thing. It is important to get an accurate story into the record and do it quickly.

Late that night, while Burnham and Armstrong slept, Fripp wrote his news dispatch. His account was based on an interview done at Mangwe Fort scant hours after the M'Limo's death. Because Fripp was fresh from London, his knowledge of the M'Limo cult was nil. He was forced to depend on what Fred and Bonnar told him, plus some background pried out of Commandant Van Rooyen and Captain Hans Lee. For that reason, his article reflects the statements and opinions of others.

MANGWE, June 23—Not 24 hours after my arrival, an event occurred which—at an early period of the Matabele outbreak—might have been attended by a speedy suppression of the rebellion. The event to which I refer is the slaying of the M'Limo in his cave by the Messrs. Burnham and Armstrong. Credit for the plan may be ascribed to Mr. Armstrong, and credit for the execution to Mr. Burnham.

247

Burnham: King of Scouts

  A cave in the hills about twelve miles east of Fort Luck, in The Nek of Mangwe Pass, was known in 1893, but when Sergeant Hook went to see the M'Limo, the attempt was made too openly and he failed to find anything.
  Armstrong proved to his satisfaction the identity of the head priest or, as he is now called, the M'Limo. They waited thirty seconds before shooting—a space of time which seemed endless to those watching him. Then Burnham went for the horses while Armstrong fired the huts. They evaded pursuit after galloping five or six miles, and returned to Mangwe at 5:30 p.m.

Artist Fripp read over his dispatch and made a sketch for the article. It showed Burnham and Armstrong riding away from Njelele. The monolith was partly obscured by smoke from the burning huts that Armstrong had fired. Fripp had the two white men riding over veld grass on flat terrain, pursued by about a hundred angry young black warriors brandishing assegais.

Ritornello • Interlude

BULAWAYO • JUNE 1896

COLONEL BADEN-POWELL recorded in the staff diary a telegram from Mangwe. He sent an orderly to tell Blanche that her husband had succeeded in his mission and was safe at Mangwe. Baden-Powell then roughed out a sketch for the *Illustrated Sunday News* that depicted Burnham and Armstrong riding from Njelele.

Melton Prior, before leaving Rhodesia, had hired Baden-Powell to mail in illustrations. Baden-Powell's sketch drew on his knowledge of the Matopo Hills acquired during the scouting patrol with Burnham. With skill, he sketched the two horsemen in the foreground, waving their rifles in gestures of victory. Their emaciated horses struggled over boulders typical of the Matopo kopjes. In the background about a hundred Matabele warriors waved assegais in pursuit. The sketch was quite different from Fripp's version. For one thing, Stephe's Njelele looked like Mount Inugu, the big, half-dome he had explored with Burnham.

Baden-Powell studied his creation, frowned and tossed it into a waste basket. The second drawing had Fred astride a healthy horse galloping over boulders. Fred, himself, was riding tall in the saddle and waving his rifle victoriously. This time Njelele was closer, a jagged peak right out of the Swiss Alps. The Matabele warriors were close, enhancing the drama.

There was keen competition for space in the *Illustrated Sunday News*. If he was to earn a fee, he'd better make this drawing good. A staff report already had informed him that Charlie Fripp of the *London Daily Graphic* was coming up from Cape Town. Baden-Powell posted his sketch by Zeederberg stage. It would be the first picture to arrive in England to depict the killing of the M'Limo.

Digby Willoughby learned of Burnham's success at Njelele. As a correspondent for the *London Times*, he sent a cable to England. He beat Baden-Powell and Fripp by a month:

BULAWAYO, June 23—Burnham the American scout reports he has killed the native god M'Limo in a cave in the Matopo Hills fifteen miles distant from Mangwe. It wasn't possible, he said, to capture the prophet alive, as there were too many kaffirs about.

The news of the M'Limo's death electrified the British Empire. Englishmen believed that the Matabele Uprising would quickly end. Willoughby's brief cable dispatch was amplified by rewrite men in London. It trumpeted Fred's achievement as the courageous action of a distinguished war hero. All of those factory managers, cherubic clerks and grimy mechanics who'd thrilled to news of Wilson's Last Stand were thrilled to hear their favorite American scout had killed a god.

Lagnappe • A Little Extra

MANGWE • JUNE 1896

BONNAR ARMSTRONG spoke to Alf Taylor, a longtime resident of

Matabele Land who had once farmed a stand of cropland near Njelele.

"This man's a prisoner," Bonnar said. "He has a kraal near Njelele. Will you talk to him?"

Taylor disregarded the Zulu prelude of silence.

"I see you. What're you called?"

"Banko."

"What's the news?"

"The white men have killed the M'Limo."

"Are you sure? Was it the proper M'Limo? The M'Limo that Lobengula used to send cattle to, asking for rain?"

"Yes, Nkosi."

"Was this the head M'Limo, the one who told the kaffirs they were to fight the white men and that our bullets would be turned to water?"

"I ought to know," Banko said. "He was my own brother—the same father, but a different mother."

Counterpoise • Equilibrium

BULAWAYO • JUNE 1896

THREE DAYS LATER in Bulawayo, Fred learned that the grapevine was active. A dozen tales told contradictory versions of what had taken place in the Matopo Hills. Lord Grey summoned Fred to Government House.

"There are too many rumors," Grey said. "While the details are fresh in your mind, I want you to make a full report on what happened. Use the reading room next to my office."

I have the honor to report that upon the information obtained by Native Commissioner Armstrong and laid before me here, we believed it possible to get into the Matopos and get M'Limo in his cave. It was found that there was to be a big indaba about the full of the moon, and almost with certainty he would be there some time previous. After several attempts that were failures, on the 23rd of the month we succeeded in catching the M'Limo in the act of going through his incantations in the cave.

Our orders from General Carrington were to capture him if possible, but on no account to allow him to escape us. We were surrounded by kaffirs in all directions. The ground is very rough with huge granite kopjes and boulders and dongas. We hid our horses as near the cave as was possible. With great difficulty we got ourselves into the cave. The M'Limo was going through a preparatory indaba this day, and the women and old men were carrying beer and utensils for the big indaba to come off the following day. The impi was behind the big granite hill. Just as the M'Limo had finished his dances in the smaller crevices and pathway leading to the main entrance and was starting into the main cavern, I shot him with a Lee-Metford rifle, killing him instantly.

We left his body at the entrance to the cave. He was a man sixty years old, with short-cropped hair. He was not dressed with any snake skins, charms or any of the ordinary equipment of the witch doctor; neither had he any articles of white manufacture of any kind. He is not a Ring Kop; he is a Makalaka. His features are rather aquiline for a Negro, wide between the eyes. His skin is more red than black.

Immediately after killing him, we rushed down the side of the mountain. Just at the foot there is a large kraal of over a hundred huts built of woven grass, no dagga (adobe) being near it. The huts are conical with low doors and were used as temporary resting places by the people coming to hold indabas with M'Limo. We fired these huts. The winds blowing strongly against the kopje carried a huge sheet of flames and volumes of smoke over the top.

The kaffirs saw us and shouted and shrieked as we got to our horses. For two hours we were hotly pursued and were nearly exhausted. Fortunately, the kaffirs abandoned the chase after we crossed the Shashani River. We arrived at Mangwe at 5:30 p.m.

Fred read his report, feeling he had earned the right to the embellishment of being hotly pursued for two hours. He wondered if he should mention that the Makalakas were working hand-in-glove with the Matabeles. He decided that information was military intelligence, as was the chain of signal fires he saw in the vicinity of Fort Luck. He would pass the word on these intelligence activities in a separate report directly to Colonel Baden-Powell. Then it occurred to him that if this was a purely political report, he needed to better identify the M'Limo. With all the rumors going around, someone was likely to challenge the assertion that the principal deity had been assassinated:

I would say that all the trails leading to this cave have been worn and beaten down several inches in depth by constant travel this year. The dust on all the trails is an inch or more in depth, showing that this was the great konza place for the whole country.

The kaffir information by which Mr. Armstrong was enabled to discover the movements of the M'Limo was obtained under strict bond of secrecy never to betray their names to the white government or anyone, as it would mean absolute and certain death to all of them. I do not even know any names myself, but as I heard the ceremonies with my own ears and saw the preparations of the M'Limo myself, I am convinced the information given was absolutely correct and that

this was the principal M'Limo of the nation. We have information of two minor priests whom we may be able yet to capture, but they are of slight importance compared with the head priest, who always practiced in this particular cave. I have the honor to be, Sir, your obedient servant.
F.R. Burnham

Fred left the report with Lord Grey's aide and went home. Blanche was writing to Rod, to tell him the family would return soon to Pasadena. Fred added a note: "You will see by the papers that I have been doing all in my power to crush this rebellion and have succeeded in killing the great M'Limo in his big cave in the Matopo Mountains. It will be a tale I can tell you when I come home to Pasadena."

In the days that followed, conflicting reports continued to fly over the Rhodesian grapevine. So much so that once again Lord Grey called Fred to Government House and asked him to give an interview to the *African Review* magazine, which had widespread circulation in Africa and England. He agreed.

"There seems to be a great deal of misunderstanding about the so-called M'Limo," the reporter said. "Give me your information."

Fred studied the man. Probably just out of school with no knowledge of Africa to clutter up his reporting.

"The M'Limo is the supreme power of religious belief. He is represented on earth by a sort of pope who has a few minor ecclesiastics under him. They all belong to one Makalaka family. On the death of the high priest, the next one in seniority succeeds to the chief dignitary."

"Do the Matabele worship the M'Limo?"

"Church and state pull together. The M'Limo retains his office, despite the change in kings."

"What was the M'Limo's object in inciting the natives to rebellion?"

"The M'Limo was not responsible. Probably the war was incited by Umlugulu, the late chief of the Onkandeni Kraal in the Matopo Hills. He hoped to reestablish the dynasty of M'Silikatze and regain his lost position."

"Is the M'Limo under the influence of the chiefs?"

"To a certain extent, yes. He endeavors to work with those in power. His principal shrine is in the heart of the western Matopo Hills, in a cave. The mountain containing his retreat is situated about fifteen miles east of that portion of Mangwe Pass known as The Nek. This granite kopje can be seen from Mangwe, and from the western portion of the Filibisi District. Minor M'Limos reside at Thabas Imambo, north of Inyati, and in the district south of Belingwe Peak."

"Do you really think it was the M'Limo that you shot?"

"I do that, and what's more Van Rooyen corroborates it. He's known the cave for the last twenty years as the spot where they hold their yearly festivals. Selous knows it too, and all the old hunters, as the haunt of the M'Limo. You can bet it was the right man."

"What effect will the M'Limo's death have on the rebels?"

"My opinion is that when the news of this shooting gets around, they'll hold an indaba amongst themselves. Some will say it's nothing and they'll have another M'Limo. Others will think it's terrible and will want to break up the war. Inside of fifteen days we'll have offers from various chiefs and little tribes to come in and make terms on which they can surrender and close the war. But the old fighting stock, now being committed to the war and knowing that their indunas and leaders must be killed, will fight to the end and clear away up north."

"Thank you, Sir," the reporter said. "Do you have a photograph?"

Blanche rummaged through a steamer trunk and found a photo made after the Ingrams' wedding in Paris. In the picture, Fred was wearing a dress suit with necktie and stickpin.

"That'll do," Burnham grunted. After the reporter left, Fred was satisfied. But he had overlooked one important point. The request for the photograph should have alerted him to the fact the writer wasn't going to cable his story to London for publication the next Saturday. He was going to post the article and picture by Royal Mail. The date was June 29, six days after the death of the M'Limo. The article wouldn't reach London for three or four weeks. And it wouldn't get back to Bulawayo until August. Only the gods knew that in such time, a lot of damage would be done.

Ritornello • Interlude

CAPE TOWN • JUNE 1896

ON JUNE 24, John Hays Hammond, his wife, Natalie, and their two boys, Harris and John Junior, left Cape Town by ship for England. Their private railway car had arrived a week earlier from Johannesburg. But in Cape Town, police arrested Hammond at dockside as the *Drummond Castle* was preparing to sail. The Cape Colony Parliament subpoenaed Hammond for questions on Rhodes' advance knowledge of the Reform Committee's plans.

Hammond hired a barrister and the Cape Colony Parliament accepted his defense that they had no jurisdiction over his activities in Johannesburg. He was released, but the *Drummond Castle* had sailed and the family was obliged to book passage on the next ship.

34

The Metamorphosis of Baden-Powell

BULAWAYO • JULY 1896

IN THREE DAYS the corps of colonial irregulars that had defended Bulawayo since March would be disbanded. Before he and Blanche left for Pasadena, Fred wanted to apply for official authorization to build a railway to the Wankie coal seams. He addressed his letter to Earl Grey.

On behalf of the Northern Territories (BSA) Exploration & Development Company Limited, I submit to you the following proposition: Being owners of certain coal fields and mining claims south of the Zambesi River and of large mining interests in the copper and gold fields north of the river, we are desirous of making these available and profitable by building a light railway from Bulawayo to the coal fields, and the privilege of extending to the northern interests at a later date.

We are prepared to build this road with all possible dispatch and economy, providing the BSA Company are willing to give us some assistance as regards timber privilege for railway purposes, and agree to purchase from us coal required to operate the BSA railways to various points, i.e. to the amount of one thousand tons per month at a cost not to exceed $11 per ton at Bulawayo.

I would call your attention to some of the advantages to be gained by the BSA Company and the country in general by the construction of the road. It will tap the most available timber forests and coal fields and enable the mining companies to be supplied with a durable and ant-proof timber, and also coal at reasonable rates. If we, in good faith, open up the coal fields, we ask the following privileges: To extend the line to the northern mining fields via Victoria Falls or by the most practicable route. For each hundred miles north of the Zambesi River, we ask for a land grant of every alternate block of ten square miles on either side, and the right to build telegraph lines along the railway.

Scouting with Baden-Powell

When Fred showed it to Blanche, her face grew ashen.

"I thought we're going to Pasadena."

"We are, Bea. We can't begin construction until the route from Mafeking to Bulawayo is completed. That will take a year. In the meantime, we can enjoy ourselves in California. When permission is granted, we'll get Sir Charles Metcalf to build our rail line." The explanation seemed to satisfy Blanche. Fred sealed the letter and rode into town to deliver it to Government House.

• • •

BULAWAYO • JULY 1896

THE CITY WAS a blaze of color on the Fourth. The BFF staged a colorful parade in front of the Bulawayo Club. Colonel Bill Napier addressed the men, lauding them and handing out campaign ribbons before he dismissed them amid cheers. This time there were no land grants.

Cecil Rhodes shuffled onto the rostrum and made a speech saying it would take six months to quell the Shona uprising. He asked for volunteers for a relief force, but almost none of the war-weary veterans of the Matabele Rebellion responded. Fred thought Rhodes had aged since they shared breakfast in London.

While riding home, Fred saw his likeness in blue ink on the cover of the weekly *Bulawayo Sketch*. A week earlier, the paper had promised to publish details on the death of the M'Limo. Fred bought six copies to take back to Pasadena. At the house, he unfolded the paper and saw a full-page drawing of himself on the front cover; on page two there was a sketch of him in a cave shooting the M'Limo. He looked for the story, but there was none. Instead, the pages were devoted to an account of the *Drummond Castle* disaster.

The *Drummond Castle*, on its Southampton run, had piled up on a reef off the coast of France, ripped out its keel and sank in five minutes. The accident occurred while the ship was traveling at full speed at night in a fog. There was an appalling loss of life. Only three of the two hundred fifty persons aboard survived. Suddenly Fred was glad he had given that interview to Charlie Fripp down at Mangwe.

Counterpoise • Equilibrium

BULAWAYO • JULY 1896

SIX DAYS before the Burnhams were scheduled to leave, a messenger summoned Fred to Government House for a meeting with Earl Grey. Because of questions raised over the fate of the M'Limo, Sir Richard Martin was planning an enquiry. Whistling Dick Martin was the representative of the crown. He served as a stand-in high

255

commissioner for Rhodesia, a personal representative of Queen Victoria. Fred returned to Mangwe Fort on July 6 to reexamine the scene, delaying his departure a few days.

"In your second report," Earl Grey said, "include the military details you left out of your original report."

"But Sir, that's secret—"

"I'm aware of that fact," Lord Grey said mildly. "This report is for Sir Richard's Court of Enquiry, not for the newspapers."

Further to my report of the 26th June, I can say that I am now familiar with the district from which Mr. Armstrong has captured the nephew of the M'Limo and others belonging to the family of priests.

The cave is east of the Shashani River and in the Gwanda District, which is hostile. Between this cave and Mangwe live most of the family of the M'Limo.

I went into this district believing these kaffirs to be loyal, knowing they took no visible part in the first war. I found them mixing with the Umvaan and women of a hostile impi. This impi Colonel Baden-Powell, Chief Native Commissioner Taylor and myself all know by a previous reconnaissance to be in this range of hills. On the day we were at the cave, we crossed the fresh spoor and other positive signs well known to military men of the close proximity of an impi near to this cave.

The heavy, well-worn trails leading to this cave come from the Matopo Hills, as well as from this district, but they are traveled over by much greater numbers of men. Around the cave are many camps and shelters and at the foot, a solidly built mass of huts, described in my first report, showing beyond all doubt that this is the great meeting place of the kaffirs.

I know now that these friendlies mix up and are in daily contact with the hostiles. I am quite sure that every move of the whites is constantly conveyed to the hostiles. I saw few young men among the friendlies. I believe they are away with the impis or acting as messengers for the priests.

Fred enclosed a letter from Alf Taylor summarizing the interview he had with Banko at Mangwe on June 27. "That ought to settle this hash," Fred said. "Now for Pasadena."

Ritornello • Interlude

BULAWAYO • JULY 1896

STEPHE Baden-Powell sat at the desk in his office at military headquarters pasting newspaper cuttings in his scrapbook. He studied the news dispatch he was holding. A month old, it had just arrived from London via Cape Town and Mafeking.

BULAWAYO, June 14 (Reuters)—Colonel Baden-Powell and

Scouting with Baden-Powell

scout Burnham have returned from two days' reconnaissance in the Matopo Hills. They discovered two thousand of the Babiyan Regiment occupying caves in the Inugu Mountain near the Maleme-Famona Valley. The enemy's position is a strong one, but sketches have been made, and the details have been carefully noted. This impi is a most important one and its defeat would be a severe blow to the Matabele.

With a warm glow, Stephe recalled that patrol one month ago when they had discovered Babiyan's impi. It was Stephe's own introduction to scouting. He'd been in Rhodesia only ten days then, and so much had happened since—the Shona Rebellion and the shooting of the M'Limo. He'd little time to think about the outing.

The men were whooping it up next door at the Bulawayo Club. It occurred to Stephe that now—three days after Burnham's departure, while the details were fresh—it might be a good time to put on paper some of the insights he had gained from the American scout.

Stephe removed his diary from a lower drawer in the desk. Since he'd begun his military career two decades ago, he'd kept a daily journal of his activities. The entries for the Matabele Rebellion followed a familiar pattern. The initial entry told of his boarding the steamer *Tantallion Castle* at Southampton. There was a report of the railway ride from Cape Town to Mafeking, the stagecoach journey through Bechuana Land with comments on the *rinderpest* scourge and his arrival in Bulawayo.

At the end of a daily entry, it was Stephe's custom to discuss one aspect of the campaign. There were sections titled The Origin of the Rebellion, Organization of Supply & Transport, and The Invisible God M'Limo & His Three Priests. Baden-Powell hoped the diary might provide the basis for a published history of the Matabele Campaign when he returned to Great Britain.

Suddenly Baden-Powell chortled. The last entry in his diary was made three weeks earlier, June 23, the day that Burnham had shot the M'Limo. Stephe thought about his first scouting patrol in the Matopo Hills from June 12 to 14. A tingle of excitement surged through his body as he recalled the valuable lore on scouting that Burnham had passed on. He dipped his pen:

July 14—A bit of a break in the diary. We've been pretty busy and I've been repeating my experiences of June: I've been back in the Matopo Hills, frequently by day and often by night, locating the enemy's positions. I sometimes go with one or two whites, sometimes with two or three black companions. It's in the very smallness of the party that the elements of success and safety lie.

Stephe wrote swiftly, calling on his experience in drafting military staff reports. In the paragraphs that followed, he laid no claim to a knowledge of scouting. Indeed, he admitted ignorance of tracking, trailing and reading sign. He said he couldn't follow a spoor. He even confessed to such blunders as returning to Bulawayo by the same route that he took into the Matopo Hills, deploring that action as an invitation to ambush.

One well-trained, capable scout can see and report on an object as well as fifty ordinary men of a patrol looking for the same thing. Peacetime training of such men is important. With no training, a man cannot have confidence in himself as a scout, and without confidence in himself, it's not of the slightest use for a man to think of going out to scout.

It's almost impossible to describe all the little signs that go to make up information for one when scouting. It's like reading the page of a book. In scouting, the tiniest indications, such as a few grains of displaced sand here, some bent blades of grass there, a leaf foreign to this bit of country, a buck startled from a distant thicket, the impress of a raindrop on a spoor, a single flash on a mountain side, a far-off yelp of a dog—all are letters in the page of information you're reading. If you're a practiced reader, you can grasp the sequence and aggregate meaning all at once, without considering them as separate letters and spelling them out. That's what goes to make scouting the interesting, the absorbing game it is.

Baden-Powell, a lively student of this newfound learning, reviewed what he had written. He nodded, picked up his pen and wrote the title *Scouting* at the beginning of the day's entry. Though he had no way of knowing it, these paragraphs were destined to become famous, to be quoted as his original thinking in establishing the Boy Scout movement. At that moment, what Stephe was thinking was that he might as well continue writing. Because of all that racket from the party at the Bulawayo Club, he couldn't sleep.

So long as you're clothed in non-conspicuous colors, you can escape detection, but you must not move about. Directly you move, they see you! If clothed in things that match the rocks, you can boldly sit out in front of a rock with little risk of detection, so long as you remain motionless. Apart from the fun of besting the enemy, the art of scouting is as interesting as any detective work.

Since sitting down to write, Stephe had made progress. At first, he had called scouting a game. Now that he had some time to consider it, scouting was an art. Gone were the military tactics of earlier diaries, the logistics problems associated with the campaign, or the table of organization of a new battalion. He was espousing a new cause, scouting, and he saw it with the passion of a born-again religious convert.

In future expeditions of this kind, it may be useful to jot down what kit I've found best for the work.

Hat — *A cowboy, broad-brimmed felt hat with ventilating holes punched in the crown and a brown silk puggaree. The hat is better than a helmet because it shades the whole of the face and so prevents that awful affliction, veld sores on the face.*

Handkerchief — *A grey kerchief loosely tied around the neck prevents sunburn and can be used at night as a comforter.*

Shirt — *Brown or light grey flannel.*

Cummerbund — *Grey or brown flannel. Don't wear any bright colors about you. I noticed that, after I had been on the sick list and resumed duty, the enemy caught sight of me much more quickly than they used to, though I took just as much care and remained just as motionless. I then came to the conclusion that this was due to the fact that I had, in accordance with the doctor's advice, taken to wearing a flannel cummerbund wound round my waist. The only flannel at the time procurable was of a crimson red and that was what caught their eye.*

Spurs — *The spur should be very short so as not to trip you when on foot.*

Revolver — *Service with an open cowboy holster, with cord lanyard around your neck.*

Almost all he'd written bore the stamp of Fred Burnham. It seemed as if the colonel had made a flying trip to Arizona. In the years to come, he would draw heavily on this diary entry to expand his writings on scouting. These entries, published two years later as *Diary of the Matabele Campaign*, became the written acorn seed of the Boy scout movement.

Counterpoise • Equilibrium

LONDON • JULY 1896

AFTER A SEVENTEEN DAY voyage from Cape Town, the Union liner *Tartar* sailed past the Isle of Wight and up a well-protected estuary to a berth at Southampton. The Burnhams debarked 7 a.m. on Sunday, August 16, three months after Nada's passing and two months after the death of the M'Limo. Fred led Blanche, Homer and Judd off the ship. Homer boarded another steamer for New York, eager to return to Pasadena to marry his sweetheart.

Pete and Grace Ingram, John Blick and King Macomber had remained in Cape Town. At the last minute they decided to go trophy hunting and would come home later.

In London, the Burnhams and Blicks took rooms at the Hotel Metropole in the West End.

Fred sent Judd out to buy newspapers so they could catch up with what had happened. Doctor Jameson had been sentenced to serve fifteen months in prison. In Rhodesia, Colonel Plumer's column had cleaned out the rebel stronghold north of Inyati. In the Matopo Hills south of Bulawayo, General Sir Frederick Carrington attacked Babiyan's Impi at Mount Inugu. The assault was nearly a disaster for Tyrie Laing's Belingwe Field Force.

Major Laing, acting on the advice of Herb Taylor, camped in a box canyon near Mount Inugu. His men were eating breakfast when Babiyan's impi made a surprise attack. Boxed in, Tyrie Laing's men suffered heavy casualties. The Matabele had all but scored a victory when Baden-Powell arrived with a seven pounder, which settled the matter. Though Terry escaped with his life, Inugu Valley was now being called Laing's Graveyard.

As for the M'Limo, the facts in London were more garbled than they had ever been in Rhodesia. Some reporters were using the foolish quotes from those harebrained wantwits at Mangwe as if they were verified facts. The *Westminster Gazette* reported the M'Limo was alive and at the head of the very impi that Colonel Plumer had just defeated.

The *Bulawayo Chronicle* credited Burnham and Armstrong with averting an uprising in southwestern Matabele Land by shooting the M'Limo. Another story in the same paper told of a second M'Limo gathering a large impi in the southern Matopo Hills. No one seemed to understand that the M'Limo was a religious figure and not a military leader.

Charlie Fripp's original story and picture, based on the interview at Mangwe Fort on the day of the shooting, was published one day before the Burnhams arrived in Southampton. The June 29 interview with the *African Review* still hadn't seen the light of day.

At a dinner party celebrating Fred Selous' completion of the manuscript for his book *Sunshine and Storm in Rhodesia*, Burnham invited Selous to join him in the Rocky Mountains for some bighorn sheep hunting. The next week, Lord Gifford invited the Burnhams to visit Scotland and hunt grouse at his country estate. It was after Fred and Blanche returned from this weekend in Scotland that good news arrived from Africa. First off, the *African Review* set the record straight. Fred's long-delayed interview of June 29, in which he accurately traced the cave to Njelele and described the M'Limo cult, saw the light of day after fifty-four days. Moreover, an *African Review* sub-editor in London apologized for questioning the M'Limo story in the previous week's issue.

The biggest news of the day, Saturday, August 22, was a cabled report announcing that organized fighting in Rhodesia had ended. "The Matabeles have sued for peace." "Hostilities are suspended in the Matopo Hills." "Cecil Rhodes, Johann Colenbrander, Doctor Hans Sauer and the Fingoe scout Jan Grootboom are holding a peace indaba with the Matabele indunas in the Matopo Hills."

News of the cessation of hostilities came on the same day that Burnham's M'Limo article appeared in the *African Review*. That coincidence gave birth to an enduring legend that shooting the M'Limo had ended the Matabele Rebellion. In the minds of the public, the two events were irrevocably linked together.

After writing to Rider Haggard thanking him for dedicating his new novel, *The Wizard*, to the memory of Nada, a messenger summoned Fred to St. Swithin's Lane. On arrival, Fred was greeted like a conquering hero and invited to give an account of his exploits to the board of directors. As the keynote speaker at a catered lunch, Fred read his report on the M'Limo episode. When he concluded his remarks, there were cheers and clapping. Lord Gifford joined him at the lectern.

"For his valuable services in disposing of the M'Limo, I have the honor of presenting to Mr. Burnham this engraved gold watch on behalf of the board of directors of the British South Africa Company."

"Hear, hear." More clapping and cheering.

"In closing," Lord Gifford said, "you have the permission of the board to make public your report to Earl Grey. Don't mention the second report."

Fred nodded, examining the engraved gold watch. Before Fred could ask about the expedition to Barotze Land, he was artfully dismissed—the board had weighty matters to deliberate. Fred didn't press the Northern Coppers matter because he was busy wondering what, if anything, was being done about a gold watch for Bonnar Armstrong.

The next day, as Fred and Blanche walked up the gangway to board a ship for Boston, a newsboy handed Fred a copy of the *London Daily Telegraph*.

In the story of the Rhodesian War, there is no more dramatic incident than the shooting by Mr. F.R. Burnham, the famous American scout, on June 23rd last, of the witch doctor who impersonated the M'Limo. Mr. Burnham, who has been several days in London, was found at a West End hotel by our representative to whom he was prepared to speak freely on every subject except his own exploits. It is hardly necessary to recall the fact that the shooting of the M'Limo is his latest, but by no means his most notable feat. Only thirty-five years of age, he has been engaged in seven campaigns. His name is best known in connection with the heroic last stand of the Shangani Patrol.

Of this and his other personal performances, Mr. Burnham has nothing to say. He has the modesty which seems characteristic of men who are accustomed to carry their lives in their hands. As to the M'Limo incident, he has endeavored to transfer all credit and honor to Mr. Armstrong, who accompanied him.

Fred's first report to Earl Grey was quoted in full.

As they boarded the ship for America, Blanche reached into her purse and withdrew a cablegram. It was from Pete Ingram in Cape Town. A contract had been signed to extend the railway from Mafeking to Bulawayo. Completion was scheduled for the fall of 1897. It meant that in one year, the Northers Terrors could begin building its railway to the Wankie Coal Seams and the Zambesi River.

Fred Burnham was on top of the world.

35

Walk Softly & Carry a Big Stick

NEW YORK • AUGUST 1896

BURNHAM'S NAME was as much a household word in the United States as it was in Europe. As an authentic war hero, Fred was invited to take lunch at the Boone & Crockett Club with the president of the New York Board of Police Commissioners. In front of police headquarters at 300 Mulberry Street, Fred paced the sidewalk for ten minutes before working up the courage to meet his host. He'd heard the man was a cop's cop.

One glance and Fred knew it was true. The police commissioner had a thick neck, close-cropped hair and ears so flat his head looked like a bullet. A shaggy mustache divided his face. The upper half was framed by steel-rimmed pince-nez the size of quarters. Below the mustache was a row of gleaming incisors. At first glance, Fred judged the man to be twenty-four karat.

"How do you do, Mr. Roosevelt."

"Call me Teddy." The cop had a piping voice, not quite a Cecil Rhodes falsetto. "Shall we take lunch? I keep a table at the Boone & Crockett Club."

Fred could scarcely believe Roosevelt's attire. He wore a black cape and slouch hat, pink shirt and a silk sash. People said Roosevelt was rooting out corruption in a police force where a patrolman's job cost three hundred dollars. Teddy was hiring and promoting on merit.

At lunch, Roosevelt was a living, walking question mark.

"Burnham, I've read of your earlier exploits in Africa. But tell me about the M'Limo episode."

"Tell you what," Fred replied. "I'll do better than that. When we get back to the hotel, I'll give you a copy of my report to Earl Gray. It tells everything."

"Do you know the hunter Fred Selous?"

"We've scouted together on many an outing. He just finished a book on the Matabele Rebellion. It's called *Sunshine and Storm in Rhodesia*. I'll send you a copy."

"From what I've heard and read, I think I would be greatly attracted to the man."

"Selous will not disappoint you. If you should meet him, camp out with him. He's a hunter, not a killer. He's lent his voice to a small band of naturalists who're laying plans for the conservation of African wildlife."

"Bully, let's invite him to the United States. We'll make him a member of the Boone & Crockett Club. With some friends, I founded this club to protect the wildlife."

"Selous would be flattered. I understand membership is limited to one hundred frontiersmen."

"You are invited to join too," Roosevelt said.

During dessert, the conversation turned to politics.

"What do you think of Mr. McKinley's chances of winning the presidency?" Teddy asked.

"Politics seem to be the same everywhere," Fred said. "Let me tell you an African proverb. It's a Zulu saying and it might apply to American politics as well."

"What's that?"

"When the elephants fight, the ants tremble."

"Bully. But it would never sell with American voters. Know any more lively Zulu epigrams?"

"Sure. Walk softly and carry a big stick."

"If you don't mind, I'd like to use that one."

"Be my guest or the Zulus'. As for McKinley, he's a sound money man. I admire his stand. I was driven from this country by a flood of worthless paper."

"William Jennings Bryan is a dynamic orator with a large following."

"You should sell prosperity with the gold standard."

"The party talks about a full dinner pail, a chicken in every pot," Roosevelt said.

"By now, people should vote for hard money. I'll do my bit in California."

At dessert, Roosevelt asked Burnham his opinion on the possibility of a war with the Boers.

"Rhodes may find a way to prevent the shooting."

"My own feeling is that war is inevitable."

"If so, it will be a stern contest. The Boers will give a good account of themselves."

"Think so? Bully."

"I once thought that the Boers were model patriots and their republic was destined for a great future."

Roosevelt's pince-nez sparkled like the chandelier at Diamond Jim Brady's Restaurant. They hailed a horse-drawn cab.

"That was before I went to Africa," Fred said. "Then I saw the Boers as they really are."

The celebrated incisors vanished, replaced by tightly pursed lips. Sparks of fire flashed in Teddy's eyes.

"The Boers believe they are right on every question and the rest of the world wrong," Fred said. "But they're destined to be left behind in the march of civilization. They hate knowledge and oppose it with all their might. They're not in sympathy with this century. And they seem to have skipped that step toward godliness that is allied to culture, for they have an aversion to cleanliness."

"Here now," Teddy gasped, "My family comes from Huguenot stock."

"I'm sorry if I offend you, but my opinion stands. After two hundred fifty years in Africa, the Boer is no longer a Huguenot. He insists the world is flat and he believes the Bible commands him to keep slaves. He bears no resemblance to his former kin in Europe or America. You will have to take my word on that."

"Bully. I appreciate honesty. We must be friends!"

Ritornello • An Interlude

RHODESIA • OCTOBER 1896

THE HIGH COMMISSIONER, Lord Rosemead, would have preferred to try Colonel Baden-Powell in a civil court, where Stephe would almost certainly be found guilty of murder. But Baden-Powell was a soldier and he had a right to be tried by courts martial. So Rosemead did the next best thing. He directed General Carrington to arrest Baden-Powell and try him in a military court.

In a telegram, Lord Rosemead said, "The courts of the country are still in existence and martial law is not in effect. The execution of the induna Uwini, a Mashona prisoner of war, appears prima facie illegal and I must therefore request that, without prejudice to military operations, you place Colonel Baden-Powell under arrest and order a court of enquiry."

The events leading up to Baden-Powell's arrest began on a Sunday, September 13, ten days after the Burnhams arrived in New York. General Carrington had dispatched Baden-Powell to the Samabula Forest, a hundred miles northeast of Bulawayo. There he was to relieve Major H.M. Ridley and take command of the Seventh Hussars, a force of three hundred fifty men fighting the Mashonas.

During an attack on Thabas Imambo, the Shona induna Uwini was wounded and captured. No sooner had the doctor bandaged Uwini's shoulder than the surly chief ripped off the dressing, glaring at Stephe with loathing.

Baden-Powell demanded that Uwini order his people to surrender. Uwini refused. Baden-Powell ordered Uwini to be court martialed. He named Ridley to be president of the court. The smarting Ridley reminded Baden-Powell that General Carrington had issued a written order that forbade shooting prisoners of war. POWs were to be turned over to a native commissioner for trial in the civil courts. Major Ridley then told Baden-Powell that if he had remained in command of the hussars, he would have sent Uwini to Bulawayo for civil trial.

Despite Ridley's opposition, Baden-Powell convened a court martial. The court found Uwini guilty and ordered him shot at sunset. The matter might have passed without reaction except for the fact that Stephe ordered the Shona indunas to watch the execution. That action touched off an uproar of protest among the Mashona, a complaint that reached all the way to Cape Town. At that point, Lord Rosemead, was forced to intercede.

Carrington, concluding that Stephe's confinement to gaol would be prejudicial to military operations, allowed him to remain in the field until hostilities ended. By early October, Stephe was leading a column of a hundred fifty men on a sweep to clear the holdouts in Belingwe, an action that brought Matabele hostilities to an end.

Baden-Powell returned to Bulawayo and three days later faced a formal court of enquiry. As Lord Rosemead feared from the outset, the Good Old Boy Network was at work. Lieutenant Colonel H. Paget, a man whom Stephe outranked, was ordered to preside over the court. Like any good soldier, Paget knew which side of the toast had the jam. Native Commissioner N.D. Fynn gave testimony endorsing Baden-Powell's actions. He cited a deposition from Native Commissioner Val Gielgud of Bubi in support of Uwini's execution. Stephe then testified: "In vindication of my action, I would cite the result of the execution of this rebel chief. It caused the collapse of the rebellion in these parts without any bloodshed."

Paget's court exonerated Baden-Powell, asserting that the execution of Uwini yielded practical results. At dawn, General Carrington and Colonel Baden-Powell removed their headquarters from Bulawayo to Salisbury to pursue the Mashona hostiles. By the time the record of the court of enquiry reached Cape Town, the

Mashona Rebellion was history and Stephe was sailing back to England.

Counterpoise • Equilibrium

PASADENA • OCTOBER 1896

FRED AND BLANCHE had been away three years, nine months and seventeen days. The reunion with Mother Burnham-Clapp, the Russells, the Blicks and young Rod prompted feasts, frolic and festivities. The *San Francisco Chronicle* was quick to discover that Fred Burnham was a genuine, circulation-building war hero from Africa. In its first report, the Chronicle trumpeted in headline:

SCOUT BURNHAM AT PASADENA
The Slayer of the Matabele Priest

A lengthy article quoted Fred as saying the M'Limo was not an individual but the titular head of a sacred family. In subsequent articles, the newspaper reporters ignored these fine points of religious ritual.

The change of scenery and the exposure to family life was beneficial to Blanche. She spent countless hours playing with Rod, now her only child, spoiling him while Fred discovered the cerebral experience of politics.

True to Teddy's word, the McKinley ticket promoted the gold standard with a full dinner pail. Fred capitalized on his war-hero fame by making political speeches in California. The Burnhams, Blicks and Russells were good nineteenth century liberals. *The fewer laws on the books, the less likely anyone was to break any of them.*

Two days before the balloting took place, Fred wrote to Rider Haggard at Ditchingham.

In the mail forwarded from Bulawayo was the splendid letter from you, written after Nada's death. I shall keep it always and it will form one of the furnishings of a temple in my inner world, which seems more real than the world without. I send you a San Francisco Chronicle *with a review of your last novel,* The Wizard. *I believe by the present copyright laws you'll get some return in this country for your labor and genius. I'm gathering the seeds of American trees to take back to Bulawayo. I believe some of them will grow, as the climate there is similar.*

The book review that Fred enclosed was unusual by any standard. Rider Haggard had dedicated his book, *The Wizard*, to the memory of Nada Burnham. The editors of the Chronicle purchased the North American rights to publish the novel in serial form and they pulled out all stops to promote it. To garner publicity for the upcoming series, they published an eight-column banner headline on the second front page.

THE TRAGIC DEATH OF NADA BURNHAM

A lily-bedecked grave in the heart of darkest Africa is the cradle of a little child whose name has been made famous by Rider Haggard, the novelist. The lonely tomb is that of Nada Burnham, who bound all to her, and while her father cut his way through the Ingobu Regiment, she perished of the hardships of war at Bulawayo. Nada Burnham was the infant daughter of Fred Burnham, the Californian who achieved great distinction as a scout during the recent wars with the Matabele and other savage tribes of south Africa, and as the slayer of the Matabele prophet M'Limo, whose death settled the fate of that rebellion.

Mr. Burnham and family soon after this sad event returned to their old home at Pasadena, Los Angeles County, the long journey being undertaken partly with the hope that the change of scene would benefit Mrs. Burnham who is heart-broken over her little daughter's tragic death. The family expects to return to south Africa next January. The Burnhams were in Matabele Land, the country described in Haggard's novel Nada the Lily, *when that book appeared. Mrs. Burnham, on reading the story, was so impressed with the beauty of the name that she named the baby after the heroine in Haggard's novel. Little Nada, being a winsome baby, became a favorite in the settlement and "bound all to her," as Mr. Haggard remarked in the book dedicated to her.*

When the natives rose in rebellion, Mr. Burnham at once took to the saddle and assisted the white settlers in repelling the attack. Practically all supplies were cut off. It was hard on the children. Exposed to the cold winds which swept through the market building where the women and children huddled, pneumonia added its terrors to the other hardships. Baby Nada, two years old and the idol of the camp, succumbed to the disease.

Mrs. Burnham succeeded in reaching Bulawayo under armed escort five days before her baby's death. The little one was already too far gone to recognize its mother. Strong men wept at the parting hour and the death scene was most pathetic. The tears and prayers of the people and all of a mother's tender care and love could not revive Nada, the fading lily, and so the fairest flower in the Dark Continent perished. The black foe still lurked in the vicinity, and it was only with the aid of a heavy escort of soldiers that the little body could be taken outside of the laager to be consigned to the earth.

To make the affair still more pathetic, the father of the child was, at that hour, engaged in deadly conflict with the savage foe some fifty miles distant. That accounts for his absence at the time of her death and burial. After the hostiles were subdued, Mr. and Mrs. Burnham started on their return to America, via England, where they renewed their acquaintance with Haggard. The novelist was deeply affected at the news of their daughter's death, to whom he felt as a godfather. And he dedicated his latest novel to this fair but short-lived flower of darkest Africa.

That article helped to solidify a legend in America that the shooting of the M'Limo had ended the Matabele Rebellion. In truth, it was only after a lengthy indaba between Cecil Rhodes and the indunas at Malindidzime—View of the World in Mineral King—that the Matabele chiefs agreed to a peace treaty.

When *The Wizard* was serialized in the Chronicle, other American newspapers began to credit Burnham with ending the war with a single shot to the M'Limo's heart. That fairy tale helped to sell papers—fulfilling the goal of a newspaper publisher to turn green trees into green dollars. As for Fred, he rode off to Mexico in search of new treasures.

36

Baden-Powell, the Scout

DUBLIN • MARCH 1897

INSIDE THE Officers Mess at Marlborough Barracks on Wednesday, March 17, there was enough good cheer to overcome the misty rain outside. Colonel Baden-Powell of the Thirteenth Hussars, attired in dress uniform, studied the audience of fellow officers from India. It was jolly good to be back with his outfit once again and delightful to see his old chums, specially The Boy McLaren. Stephe was ill at ease over his recent promotion to full colonel—he now outranked his own commanding officer.

He'd solved that problem by engineering an appointment to command the Fifth Dragoon Guards in India. But he would not depart for another two weeks. It would be fun getting back to garrison duty with weekends of playing polo again.

Stephe's other problem was that General Roberts, not General Wolseley, was presiding over this affair tonight. After the banquet, Lord Bobs was scheduled to introduce Stephe as the featured speaker. What he had prepared had originally been intended for the ears of General Wolseley. On the other hand, Stephe also had long ties with the India Ring, of which Lord Bobs of Kandahar was the leader. And Baden-Powell was scheduled to return to India soon.

On the whole, Stephe felt buoyant because his African memoirs, *Diary of the Matabele Campaign*, would be published as a military history. Now, only weeks before its release, he would address the Military Society of Ireland. After years of service in India, his combat record came during two tours of duty in Africa—a brief stint in the Ashanti, then the rebellion in Rhodesia.

Stephe had a rare opportunity to appraise the latest developments in hardware and tactics. But he'd have to avoid giving offense to certain senior officers. After all, he was a only a field-grade officer—below flag rank—so he would not be expected to offer suggestions to general officers on how to organize and equip the British Army for future hostilities.

The echo of Lord Bobs hammering for silence brought Stephe back to the present. The sound of the gavel carried to the far corners of the noisy room and a hush slowly fell over the Officers Mess. Lord Roberts made several routine announcements and got down to the business at hand.

"Gentlemen, the leading newspapers, including *The Times*, have published Major General Sir Frederick Carrington's official dispatches to the high commissioner of South Africa on the campaign in Rhodesia." There was clapping, punctuated by cheers and whistling. Members of the Africa Ring were getting in a gen for Sir Frederick, one of their own.

"Those dispatches contain a list of officers, non-commissioned officers and men of the ranks who have distinguished themselves." Another round of clapping and cheers, this time louder. It was the highest hope of British soldiers from private to general to be mentioned in dispatches.

"In introducing you to tonight's lecturer, Colonel Baden-Powell, who was chief staff officer to Sir Frederick, it is unnecessary for me to say more than that his name was given a prominent position in the official dispatches list." Lord Roberts nodded toward Colonel Baden-Powell, touching off a loud burst of applause accompanied by cheers from the India Ring. Stephe was being recognized by his own kind.

Baden-Powell opened his lecture with a review of operations in Rhodesia, beginning with his arrival in June. He ignored the Bulawayo Field Force and its defense of Rhodesia for ninety days until the Imperial forces arrived. Stephe even obliquely criticized the colonials for their inability to import rations during the rinderpest plague.

When he came to his first scouting patrol in the Matopo Hills, Stephe figuratively covered himself with glory. Not once did he mention he'd learned the basic knowledge of scouting from an American named Fred Burnham. He did give credit to Burnham and Armstrong for shooting the M'Limo, but his reasons for that action were not altruistic. He wanted to create a mental climate to accept an execution as a necessity of war. Although Stephe had beaten a murder charge, he was concerned lest it cast a cloud over his record. He wanted to create a precedent for shooting the Shona induna Uwini.

271

It was in the context of establishing such a precedent that Stephe cited Burnham's role in the slaying of the M'Limo—an assassination necessitated by the demands of war.

At length, he came to the second part of his lecture:

Lessons Learned in the Campaign—Scouting!

"The best lesson that I personally learnt was the art of scouting," he said. "I could spend a week telling you all about it, as it is the most interesting work that one could possibly be engaged in." Baden-Powell warned his audience that scouting couldn't be learned in a week. Then he proceeded to lecture everyone including his superiors on how to become proficient in scouting.

"If you go across country with a trained scout, his eye will be everywhere. He'll find the tiny signs on the ground at his feet, or other signs in the far distance. He'll notice details that you can hardly see yourself, and he'll read them out in a moment and tell you what they mean. The scout sees such small signs as four broken twigs or a bent blade of grass and he'll put several of these signs together to give him full information." What followed would become famous as the Blade of Grass anecdote, a quote in the growing Baden-Powell lexicon of outdoors lore.

"I was out scouting with my native boy in the neighborhood of the Matopo Hills," he said. "Presently we noticed some grass blades freshly trodden down. This led us to find some footprints on a patch of sand. They were those of women or boys, because they were small. They were on the march, because they wore sandals. They were still fresh, because the sharp edge of the footprints were well defined. And they were hostile, because they were heading into the Matopo Hills. My native tracker found a leaf that belonged to a tree that didn't grow in the vicinity. The leaf was damp and it smelt of kaffir beer."

It was almost as Burnham had originally told it.

"They'd passed this spot about 4 o'clock, because at that hour there'd been a strong wind blowing, such as would carry the leaf some yards off the track. They'd probably take another hour to reach the Matopo Hills, and the men for whom they were bringing the refreshments would probably start work on it at once, while the beer was yet fresh. If we now went on following this spoor up to the stronghold, we should probably find the men in too sleepy a state to take much notice of us, and we could do our reconnaissance in comparative safety. So you see there's a good deal of information to be picked up from a crushed blade of grass and a single leaf, then reasoning out the meaning."

As he spoke, Stephe sensed that the senior officers in the audience didn't seem enthusiastic about a lecture on the fundamentals of scouting—tactics ordinarily left to junior officers and senior non-coms. He turned to other topics, discussing the typical subjects of military men: transport and supply, the establishment of forts and outposts and tables of organization.

But he couldn't resist expounding on his newly gained lore of the outdoors. In the section on mistakes and recommendations, he suggested the British Army might conduct night marches. He pointed out that most successful battles against the Matabele impis had taken place at dawn following a forced night march.

It got such a good response that he was impelled to switch the subject to military uniforms. He endorsed battle dress of khaki instead of red coats, and he came out in support of the American cowboy hat in place of the regulation pith helmet. While the senior supply officer glowered, Stephe launched into a spirited argument for the Montana-peak Stetson headgear, which eventually became the Boy Scout hat.

"In that country," he said, "a broad-brimmed cowboy hat is the best thing you can wear. The pith helmet is useful for warding off a blow, but I don't think it's good for anything else out there. The helmet allows the men to become blistered by the sun. But a hat protects the lower part of the head and neck from the sun. It protects you in going through thorn bush. You can sleep on it. It doesn't get damaged from getting trodden on as a helmet does."

He closed his remarks by endorsing rigid military discipline. He attributed this superiority to a tradition of teaching men to play by the rules. The officers began clapping and soon the men rose in an ovation. Even the supply officer forgave Baden-Powell's indiscretions.

Lagnappe • A Little Extra

Sonora • January 1897

BURNHAM WENT to Mexico to look for gold. Instead he found a Bonanza Farm in need of irrigation. As he rode south, his mind drifted back to the days of his youth in the hills of Sonora when he had delivered messages for Slats McLeod of Tombstone. For several weeks, Fred poked through the foothills of the Sierra Madre Occidental and prospected whenever the urge struck him.

In time, he found himself three hundred miles south of Tombstone in the Yaqui River Valley—inland from the port of Guaymas. While seeking shelter one night at a rude cabin, he met an elderly American who was bedridden, perhaps as much from heartbreak as from illness. While Fred fed him chicken and egg soup, the old man introduced himself as Earl A. Nettleton. In the days that followed, Nettleton recovered enough to sit up. That's when he began babbling a disjointed tale, speaking at a rate of two hundred words a minute.

"Lissen, I'm dyin and there's no one else in this Godforsaken corner of the world to pass this information on to," Nettleton said. "As a civil engineer, my life's work here lies unfinished. It began shortly after the Civil War. A Southern gentleman of uncommon vision named Charles Conant was so enraged by what happened during Sherman's march that he turned his back on his native land. He came here to the Sierra Madre in Sonora, married, sank roots and changed his name to Don Carlos Conant."

Burnham offered Nettleton a leg of roast chicken.

"Don Carlos befriended a Mexican soldier named Porfirio Diaz. He fought at Diaz' side in the war to throw off the French occupation of Mexico. When Diaz became president, he rewarded Don Carlos' loyalty by awarding him the irrigation rights to the Yaqui River Valley."

Fred rocked back at the idea of such a lofty prize. Nettleton began coughing and he dozed off. Two hours later, he awakened, once more alert.

"Don Carlos sought financial backing for his venture. He went to New York where investors formed a syndicate to finance his plan to farm the Yaqui River Delta. Don Carlos hired me to make a civil survey.

"It didn't take long to discover that Don Carlos had the perfect site for a Bonanza Farm. The Yaqui River flowed southward through a flat alluvial plain of great fertility. At one point, ribs of rock jutted out in a perfect damsite. I returned to New York with detailed drawings. The syndicate proceeded to seek financing.

"By the next year, I had cut an arch through the rock and diverted the river into a canal seventy feet wide. Then I designed lateral canals that would bring water to the parched fields. Just as the project was giving promise of success, the Yaqui Indians went on the warpath. They burned our dredge. The syndicate decided to cut short its losses."

"That's quite a story," Fred said gravely.

"Oh, there's more," Nettleton said. "President Diaz came to Don Carlos' aid by putting down the Yaqui uprising. He relocated the rebels to the Yucatan Peninsula. By the grapevine, word got back that the Yaquis were dying like flies. More Yaquis rebelled. Once again, Diaz moved in to quell the uprising. In time, nearly all the Yaquis were moved to the Yucatan.

"That gave us hope," Nettleton continued. "Don Carlos went to New York seeking funds to get on with his work. But elections were coming and investors were reluctant to risk money in foreign ventures. Unbroken in spirit, Don Carlos went prospecting and with great good luck discovered a rich vein of silver at what is now the Esperanza Mine near here. For years he poured all the profits of this mine into his irrigation venture. He worked day and night but in time his health failed and he died.

"I tried to carry on, but there was no money. Now my health too has broken and Don Carlos' vision remains unfulfilled. On my deathbed, I beg you to take over this project and complete it."

Burnham had listened to Nettleton with interest. His surveying work with the Mormon engineer Sirrine at the Mesa Water company had taught him about gradients and canals. Burnham rode out for an examination of the delta. The old weir was sanding up and the fields were returning to scrub for lack of flowing water. The ore deposit in the Esperanza Mine looked promising, but it had been abandoned for several years and needed re-timbering. Bringing this scheme to fruition would take money, far more than Burnham had. Fred returned to Nettleton's bedside.

"My capital is tied up in Africa," he said. "I have a partly developed gold mine in the Belingwe Mountains. I have interests in a large undeveloped coal deposit at Wankie. And there are hundreds of square miles of claims in the Northern Coppers. So far none of these projects has brought in any money."

Nettleton fixed him with an accusing stare, as if youth, passion and good health could solve any problem.

"A Mexican gold or silver mine is one thing," Fred continued. "I don't have the capital or wherewithal. I must decline your kind offer. Ask me anything else."

"Mr. Burnham, I will then pass on to a dear friend, Davis Richardson, the land, mine and the irrigation rights of the Yaqui River Delta. Deliver it with these deeds to Davis. Promise?"

"It's as good as done," Fred vowed.

In a shaky hand that afternoon, Earl Nettleton penned a will leaving the Yaqui River Delta irrigation scheme to Davis Richardson of Los Angeles.

That night the old man died.

The Call of the Klondike

The 8th Chronicle

37

Ploughed by the Good Old Boy Net

Cape Town • May 1897

THE BURNHAM FAMILY celebrated Fred's thirty-sixth birthday anniversary at the captain's table on the *R.M.S. Scot*. Fred told fellow diners how Teddy Roosevelt, now Assistant Secretary of the Navy, was hoping to camp under the African stars with Fred Selous. Everyone at the table agreed that was a splendid idea. The next day the ship dropped anchor in the magnificent Table Bay Harbor—with its huge ship repair dry-docks. The Burnhams took a handsome cab to Green Point below Signal Hill to board a train for Kimberley where they would visit with Cecil Rhodes.

After a railway journey of six hundred miles, they arrived in Kimberley, the world's diamond mining capital. Rhodes escorted the couple through a barbed-wire fence of unspeakable barbarity to inspect the Big Hole, the pit from which the diamond riches of De Beers gushed forth.

It was the largest hole ever dug by man—the model used by Rider Haggard for his book *King Solomon's Mines*. But where Haggard had written of a pit of blue clay three hundred feet deep, the hole at Kimberley had grown in the decade since into an excavation a thousand feet deep. The Big Hole was now fifteen hundred feet across at the surface. It had a crater like a funnel, then it cut straight down for a thousand feet. The ore trapped in the vertical pipe was a an eerie blue-gray hue, metallic in texture.

"Diamonds are found in the vertical pipes of extinct volcanoes," Rhodes explained.

"How much ore must you mine for one diamond?" Blanche asked.

"We've excavated twenty million tons of rock," Rhodes said. "We have recovered ten million carats of diamonds."

Burnham: King of Scouts

The Big Hole Diamond Pit at Kimberley

The Call to the Klondike

All on the backs of black labor. Africans have removed two tons of rock for every carat recovered. Fred winced.

Next the visitors visited De Beers Diamond Museum where sepia photographs told the history of Kimberley and the diamond mines. Kimberley had been a remote backwash in the north backblocks of Cape Colony until the pretty stones made it a magnet for adventurers. It was only a few miles from the border with the Orange Free State and its flowering capital at Bloemfontein.

As they walked through the Diamond Museum, Fred and Blanche watched the story of diamond mining unfold in sepia brown pictures. At first, miners were allotted claims ten feet square. In the search, the Colesberg Kopje was dug away and before anyone knew it the hill had became a hole — a checkerboard of square pits.

"So rich were the claims," Rhodes said, "they were measured to the fraction of an inch. In the scramble, some men dug faster than others, and it soon became impossible to walk from ground level to a given claim. The miners developed a wire-line trolly system."

"When did you come to Kimberley?" Blanche asked.

"Seven years after the diamonds were discovered," Rhodes said. But he quickly made up for lost time. He traded claims and shares and organized De Beers Consolidated Mines.

"My long-term goal was to combine the Kimberley, Bulfontein and Dutoitspan mines into De Beers," Rhodes said. "Difficult task."

"What stood in your way?" Fred asked.

"That knockabout clown, Barney Barnato," Rhodes groused. "He's a piano-player-turned-diamond buyer, but he proved to be one tough nut to crack."

As they entered the Kimberley Club for lunch, Rhodes said, "I took that little Cockney Jew through this door just like we're doing now and said to him, 'Give me what I want and I'll make you a member of this club.'"

Barnato jumped at the opportunity and De Beers grew to be the most powerful company on earth.

"Soon after that," Rhodes continued, "gold was found on the Witwatersrand." Once financial success was assured, the profits of Rhodes' gold and diamond properties were directed to the creation of Rhodesia and its governing body, the Chartered Company.

To Fred, consolidation sounded like a good idea for Rhodesia. While dining that night, Fred told Rhodes how the various Rhodesian companies were now competing. He suggested integrating all holdings north of the Zambesi River into Northers Terrors.

"In a few months, the railway from Mafeking to Bulawayo will be

279

completed," Fred said. "If we agree to consolidate, we can work together, not at cross purposes."

"I'll have Alfred Beit look into it," Rhodes said. "Dessert, Mrs. Burnham?"

Blanche nodded demurely. In her mind, she was composing a letter to her mother describing the Kimberley Club and dining with the world's richest man. It was a social feat that no other woman in Pasadena could hope to equal.

• • •

BELINGWE • JUNE 1897

PETE, JOHN, Judd and King had piled up a sizable hoard of gold. That was splendid, because they'd need plenty of capital to finance the railway to Wankie and the Zambesi River.

A few weeks later, W.L.G. Gooding arrived for a visit. George was the lad who had escaped with Fred and Pete from Wilson's Last Stand. Judd shot a springbok and while they roasted a haunch over an open fire, Gooding produced a copy of the *St. James's Gazette* from London. It contained a review of a newly published book titled *With Plumer in Matabele Land*. Gooding seemed reluctant to hand over the newspaper to Fred.

"It's critical of you and Armstrong," Gooding said.

"How's that?" Fred asked.

"Frank Sykes describes accounts of the shooting of the M'Limo as Fenimore Cooper fiction," Gooding said. "He says the newspaper reports were sensationalized to suit the palates of the masses in London."

"True, many of the accounts were lurid," Fred admitted. He had never heard of the author, Frank Sykes. He would never have placed Sykes as the young trooper standing guard when Colonel Plumer placed Mafeking under martial law—to protect Blanche and Grace.

"I know that wildcats could take lessons from you in fightin," Gooding said, "but Sykes said you and Mr. Armstrong rode up to a native who was mending his fence. He says Armstrong led the guy to a cave and you shot him dead."

"If that were true, I'd be guilty of the cold-blooded murder of an innocent old Negro."

"T-that's what t-the *St. James's Gazette* concluded."

"Fred," Ingram protested, "you were acting under direct orders of General Carrington."

Burnham drew his revolver, fired twice at the dead springbok's head, severing both horns. "Who is this Mafeking popinjay?"

"Sykes fancies himself as a historian," Gooding said.

"Hey," Fred said, suddenly remembering. "When I shot the M'Limo, Colonel Plumer and his gang were sixty miles away on the Gwaii. This Sykes guy is talking rubbish."

Counterpoise • Equilibrium

BULAWAYO • JULY 1897

THE BELINGWE PROSPECTORS rode into Bulawayo to celebrate the Fourth of July with a barbecue dinner. While waiting, Fred wrote to Haggard, now a shareholder in the Northers Terrors.

The railway from Mafeking to Bulawayo will be completed soon and the day is not far distant when the grants and concessions given our companies will become quite valuable. At Kimberley I stopped to meet with Rhodes about consolidating all the Barotze Land companies.

The Germans are making a move, and as soon as the Belgians end their native troubles, we'll find them coming down from the Katanga Plateau in the north. We must act before they do. There will have to be several towns in that country and one successful sale of stands will repay all our expenses. The country has coal, copper, gold, timber and possibly rubies. If you can drop a word into the ears of our directors, I'm sure it will be to the benefit of every shareholder.

"Bea, I'm gettin' narrow at the equator," Fred called out. "When's dinner gonna be ready?"

Pete burst through the door, waving a newspaper and shouting incoherently.

"What's up, partner? Have some Arbuckles." Pete tossed the paper on the table, spilling Fred's coffee.

"The Klondike!" His eyes were as big as fried eggs.

"What's a Klondike?" Fred asked.

"At Dawson!" Pete said in a harsh, cawing voice. He waved his arms wildly. As Blanche wiped up the spilled coffee, Fred read the headline, a size ordinarily reserved for the outbreak of war:

GOLD! GOLD! GOLD!

The article was from Seattle, Washington. Sixty-eight grizzled miners from the Yukon Territory of Canada had arrived unexpectedly in Seattle on the steamer *Portland*. To the surprise of the world, they were carrying a ton of gold.

In the summer of 1896, they had unearthed rich—fantastically rich—gold deposits in Bonanza Creek that fed the Klondike River. But because of the early freeze-up, they were forced to spend the winter at Dawson City. Not until the thaw in June of this year were they able to catch a steamer down to the United States. The original discovery had been made on August 16, 1896.

"Why, Bea, that's the day we landed at Southampton, after I killed the M'Limo," Fred said.

"Come on, pard, jingle your spurs," Pete cried. "Let's hit the trail for the Klondike." He was so excited the hairs on his neck stood out. Pete began talking excitedly about catching the next stagecoach. Fred's pulse also had been pounding like a jungle drum. Then reality dawned. This was July.

"It's too late," Fred said. "We couldn't get to Seattle until September. By then the Yukon River will be frozen solid. If we left today, we couldn't reach the Klondike until next year."

"Oh, Fred," Blanche said, "I wish you'd get Klondike fever instead of Zambesi fever. Then I could go home."

• • •

NOVEMBER 4, 1897, was the fourth annual Occupation Day, and it was set aside for dedicating the new railway line linking Bulawayo with Mafeking and Cape Town. It would now be possible to travel by rail from wharf-side at Table Bay in Cape Town to Bulawayo.

At noon the festivities got under way. Bulawayo was crowded with more people than flies on an outhouse. The Burnhams, Blicks and Ingrams, wearing their Sunday-go-to-meeting clothes, exchanged formal nods with Cecil Rhodes and Earl Grey on the reviewing stand.

It was like the Fourth of July in Phoenix, even to the presence of gaudily attired aborigines. The Matabele indunas wore the regalia of their regiments—kilts of animal tails, cloaks of fur, headdress of feathers and colorfully painted rhino-hide shields. In the spirit of British ritual, each impi now had its own regimental colors. While the photographers touched off puffs of flash powder, Cecil Rhodes and Earl Grey shook hands with Babiyan and Gambo. Any hound dog would be utterly fascinated by this diverse gathering.

The sound of coronets announced the beginning of ceremonies. It was a warm, cloudless, spring day so the speeches by Cecil Rhodes, Earl Grey and lesser dignitaries continued in excess of two hours. At length, a steam locomotive chuffed up to the station and released an immense, cloudy hiss of steam that startled the Matabele indunas. Rhodes cut a ribbon to inaugurate railway service between Cape Town and Bulawayo. While more flash powder exploded, cannons fired their own smoke, and the band played "God Save the Queen." Then it was over and the people repaired to the watering holes of Bulawayo to get jass-eyed on white mule. With the arrival of the iron horse, everyone felt glad to be alive.

While riding home, Fred ran into Bill Driver, the native commissioner from Gwelo.

"Well, slay the dragon, if it ain't Fred Burnham," Driver said in his reedy voice. He wore an ibex-horn mustache, waxed to spear-points. His eyes missed little.

"Hello yourself. Haven't seen you in three years."

"I dare say, it's been a dashed longish time. By the way, have you seen that chap Bonnar Armstrong lately?"

"Six months ago, we came through Mangwe and I said hello," Fred said.

Driver became coquettish, reluctant to talk.

"I think he's unhinged," he said in a low register. "He's been flogging his niggers and firing 'em. Then he got into a big kerfuffle with Van Rooyen."

Fred studied Driver. The troubled look on his face said the man was clearly worried. Driver glanced over his shoulder, then spoke.

"He's in an upset with the Chartered Company. It's a roguish sort of tale, but a few months ago he tried a case involving a border dispute. Herb Taylor's blue-eyed boy, Art Lawli, passed the word down the grapevine that the Chartered Company would be pleased if Armstrong ruled against the chief."

"That must have tossed the fat in the fire."

"Dead right. Bonnar didn't like it, but stiff upper lip and all. Herb Taylor made a big do of congratulating him on his judicial wisdom."

"So then what unhinged him?"

"Mr. Rhodes did. When he came up for the railway dedication. The chief appealed Armstrong's decision. And Rhodes upset the judgment, giving Bonnar a slating. Now Bonnar's ass over tit for revenge."

"Always was moody," Fred said. "Told me one time the Chartered Company was covering up the murder of natives."

Driver stroked his ibex mustache.

"Better not mention that around Government House."

"Look, Bill, next time I get a chance, I'll ride out and have a talk with Bonnar. Right now I'm busy scratching out some gold so I can build a railway to Wankie."

A dotty look came over Driver's face.

"Did you say a railway to Wankie?"

"That's right, Bill."

Driver laid his big, beefy paw on Fred's shoulder.

"You seem to be havin no more luck than a duck sittin on a doorknob."

"What are you talking about, Bill?"

"Roger the King's daughter, Mr. Burnham, you got plowed by the Good Old Boy Net. You're not gonna build that railway. George Pauling is." The words were spoken gently, but their meaning struck

Fred like a runaway locomotive.

"Calf-slobber, Bill. George Pauling is the commissioner of public works. He's a government official. He can't build a railway. That would be a conflict of interest."

"Lor forgive me, I'm not here to chaw blubber," Driver said. "This is a clanger on my part. It's supposed to be a state secret, but I thought you knew."

"Knew what?" Alarm crept into Fred's voice.

"As sure as the old baboon barks, you've been buggered, Fred. George Pauling has got you by the short and curlies. Not a week after you left for home last year, Pauling wrote to Lord Grey suggesting that permission be denied for you to build the railway. A deal was struck. Pauling agreed to remain as public works commissioner until the railway from Mafeking arrived at Bulawayo. Now he's gonna resign and build that railway to Wankie himself."

A sudden rush of heat flooded Fred's neck and shoulders. He tore off his hat and threw it on the ground. Almost everything he had worked for since coming to Africa was coming apart.

"Damn," he swore. "I might expect that of Pauling but I didn't believe Earl Grey would stoop that low."

Bill Driver, looking sheepish, dismounted to pick up Fred's hat and hand it to him. Then, with the shake of his head, he mounted and silently rode off. Suddenly a lot of loose ends came together for Fred Burnham. As he rode home, he was consumed by a primitive desire for that basest of human motives: revenge.

38

Race for the Riches

SEATTLE • MARCH 1898

THE TRAIN TO Seattle was jam-packed, yet at every station would-be Klondike prospectors clawed their way aboard. The last two hundred miles from Portland was a delirium as frenzied men grappled for space. When Puget Sound came into view, Fred, John and Judd laid eyes on a grotesque flotilla of ships, both steam and sail: freighters, tankers, whalers and coalers.

Seattle was a lunatic asylum. Streets were jammed with yahoos in rough garb. The seventy-five dollar posted price of for a steamship ticket to Skagway was a myth. The actual cost was five hundred dollars. Scalpers bought all the tickets and sold them for up to a thousand dollars. Merchants dusted off old stoves and camp kits that for years had gathered dust on the shelves. Adorned with shiny Klondike labels, they sold for premium prices.

Fred oversaw the outfitting of supplies for four, then led the way to a lumber mill to buy sawn cedar boards. Whipsawing logs by hand in the arctic, Fred knew, would be just about the hardest work in the world. During their brief stay in Seattle, they spent money like confetti. One of Thomas Edison's paper-movie camera crews was on hand to document the adventure.

A week later the Rhodesians sailed into the Lynn Canal, a ninety-mile-long fjord that knifed through the chilly Alaska mountains. They were dumped off on the reeking mud flats of Skagway, Alaska.

"Hurry," the purser cried, the vapor of his voice condensing in the freezing air. "There's a thirty-foot tide. The ship must depart before tidefall."

Pete Ingram, who had gone ahead, appeared with sled and horses. They spent two hours sweating as they lifted five tons of supplies: lumber, tents, food, medical kits, mosquito netting, gold pans,

285

Burnham: King of Scouts

hammers, shovels, picks, axes, saws, nails, tallow, oakum, augers, planes, oars, canvas, hooks and poles.

If Seattle was a madhouse, Skagway was demented, depraved beyond description. It was as though Satan had thrown open the doors of Hades. The row of storefront tents and buildings seemed out of place in the eerie half-light of winter. Hard-nosed men wore six-guns in low-slung holsters. The streets were rivers of icy mud, clogged with mired wagons, frenzied horses and cursing men airin their lungs. In the background, honky-tonk music rent the air.

Ahead the road was blocked by a gaggle of men clustering around a building. A sign identified the place as the Bureau of Information. Fred ambled over and a crowd of men jostled him toward the door. He found himself thrust inside, where an eye peered balefully at him through a peep-hole. Fred's hand went for his lead chucker.

"Light a shuck, or six of you are dead," he growled, drawing and cocking. As the mob melted, a white-haired man in a black frock coat ambled up.

"I'm Doctor Ira Moore," he said, shaking Fred's hand. He had a strong, handsome face, floppy ears and a friendly smile. His long white hair floated in the breeze.

"Fred Burnham here."

"Congratulations, Mr. Burnham. I've heard of you, and I've been waiting for someone like you to arrive in Skagway. You've just sent some of Soapy Smith's gang scooting."

"Who's Soapy Smith?"

"He's a bearded cutthroat from Denver," Moore said. "His real name is Jefferson Smith. Up here he runs Jeff's Oyster Palace as a front for his illegal schemes and shell games. Come to my clinic."

"Can we cache our supplies in your yard?"

"I like your stamp," Moore said. "Sleep in the barn. The hotels are bursting with men sleeping in shifts. Hot sheeting. Guard your dunnage. Nothing's safe here."

Doctor Moore's home was a wood frame building painted white; one wing served as his medical clinic. The yard was fenced and the Rhodesians unloaded their sled. Moore invited them to dinner.

"There is no law here," Doctor Moore said. "Alaska isn't even a territory. It's a district left to its own devices. The laws of Oregon prevail, but there are no police, no courts, no judges, no city or county government. Without doubt, Skagway is the toughest place on earth."

"What's a cheechako?" John asked.

"Many early arrivals to the Klondike came here from Chicago and the way the Chilkoot Indians spit the word out, it sounded like Cheechako. It has come to mean a newcomer."

"What's the best way to get over to Lake Bennett?"

"Chilkoot Pass up over Mount Ridgel used to be the golden route. Until last month, it was the only known gap in the armored underbelly of Alaska. Chilkoot is steep, with tiny steps hacked out of the ice. The grade is forty-five degrees, the winter snows pile up seventy feet deep but you can carry fifty pounds each trip. To cross you must use the Chilkoot Lockstep. It'll take you twenty trips to ferry your dunnage to Lake Bennett. It's called the Devil's Portage."

"The other way?"

"It's longer. They're building a railroad over White Pass. If you've got horses or oxen, you are free to use the right-of-way."

"We're horsemen," Fred said. "We'll use White Pass."

"Be careful. The route is narrow and treacherous. The saw-tooth mountains look like the skeletal spines of those dinosaurs in the museums. One misstep and you'll fall a thousand feet into the fjord."

"Can we rent horses?"

"Cheaper to buy 'em. When you're done, sell them to someone else at a profit. Up in White Pass, men take leave of their senses. There are bottomless pits of snow and muck up there where horses can get mired. Crazed gold-seekers strip the packs from the raw and bleeding animals and carry them by hand, abandoning the critters to the elements. Some men have the mercy to shoot the crippled animals, but others simply leave them to starve. If you shoot a stranded horse, one of Soapy Smith's henchmen will show up to demand compensation."

"We'll keep our blue-lightnin loaded," Pete said.

"You can't carry arms in Canada," Moore warned. "It's against the law. Wear them while ferrying your dunnage to the border, then check them with the Mounties.

"From the Canadian border to Dawson City, five-hundred miles to the north, you will find nothing made by man: no road, no village, no store, nothing. When you come to Moosehide Slide, where the hillside has slid away, you have found Dawson. During the Ice Age, it was a glacier-free zone, which explains why the nuggets were left in place instead of scattered."

Counterpoise • Equilibrium

THE YUKON • APRIL 1898

AT THE CANADIAN border, Fred, Pete, John and Judd watched packers with mules carrying crates of turkeys. Sheep were being herded to Dawson. Fred went on ahead to survey a route and find a site for their camp. The others built a wooden sled to haul supplies on the forty-mile overland journey to Lake Bennett.

Because they had lumber, Fred was able to choose a campsite near the lake. Most of the prospectors had to pitch tents in the woods three miles away where they could fell trees and handsaw the logs into planks. Those rude, hand-planked boats would be slow and leaky. Half would sink before completing the ride down the Yukon.

Fred saw another campsite about a hundred yards away where a broad-shouldered man looked familiar. Fred walked over and spotted Tyrie Laing of Belingwe.

"Well, look who just blowed in with the doodlesack, the lucky Caledonian," Fred grasped Laing in a bear hug.

"Aye, laddie, is it really ye?"

Fred saw that Laing had boards of light cedar too.

"Wha took ye from your gold mine in Belingwe?" Laing asked.

"Three things," Fred said. "First, I got ploughed on my plan to build the railway to the Zambesi. Second, the board of directors of Northers Terrors decided to play kick the can. They declined to send a second expedition to Barotze Land. When Blanche became pregnant with our third child, I took her home and came north."

"How aboot a race to Dawson?" Laing challenged. "Tis ordained, I'll beat ye to tha placers."

"All four of us'll best you."

"Be ye all Rhodesians?"

"I'm with John, Judd and Pete."

Laing's merry eyes squinted into glacial slits.

"Be ye still chummin wi'that Blackfoot?"

"Careful, Pete's my brother-in-law."

"Some kin," Laing said, scratching at his red woolen underwear. "Dotty muckibus had a go at ye too long."

"Ride over that trail again?"

"Hoot mon, all thet grandgrousing at the Bulawayo Club, I thought ye be ken to him. With those liars fillin him with swill, t'was like a symphony uv hyenas."

"I've never been in the Bulawayo Club."

"When Pete gets his throat wet, he tells tall tales."

"What kind of stories?"

"Like how ye shot some harmless old kaffir oot Mangwe way." Laing's words were spoken in a casual manner, but his voice was carefully modulated. Fred's face went slack and his shoulders slumped.

"Sorry, laddie, that I have t'be the one t'tell ye."

Fred felt as weak as a tubercular girl. He sat down on a bushel bag of pinto beans and a doleful expression crossed his face. For several minutes, he didn't move.

"Thanks," he said. "I didn't know." He rose and shuffled back to camp, his mind black with rage. The next day Ingram was gone.

• • •

LAKE BENNETT • APRIL 1898

THE CEDAR board hulls took shape over a three-week span. They lapped the boards, caulked them with oakum, then sealed the seams with rosin. There was no need for a fourth boat, so they used the remaining wood to build storage, firewood bins and sand boxes for cooking-fires. They christened the boats *Doctor Jim*, *Rhodesia* and *Zambesi*.

In the days that followed, avalanches roared in the mountains and the ice on Lake Bennett creaked, threatening to break up at any time. At John's suggestion, they took in three partners, men of clear grit, so they could travel around the clock en route to Dawson.

George Coffey was a six-foot American with the muscles of a polar bear. Charlie Anderson was a Swede, all knobby knees and bony elbows, with a toothy smile and unruly hair. He had been to Rhodesia. George Burke was a wide-shouldered prospector from Montana who had spent five years prospecting in the Klondike. His neck was thick and corded with muscle and sinew.

By the last week of May, daylight lasted nineteen hours and Lake Bennett presented an amazing site unlike anything on earth. The cutbank shores twenty-feet high formed a forty-five degree angle of repose. Thirty thousand men were bedded out along the shores of Lakes Lindeman, Bennett and Tagish while they put the final touches on seven thousand boats. Along the perimeter of the three lakes, the prospectors had built the biggest tent city Fred had ever seen.

On Saturday night, May 29, the tent city flickered with campfires. Men sat around lubricating their spirits and singing in the gloaming. After dinner, Fred, John and Judd walked around to inspect the other camps. There were boats and scows of every classification, and they carried cargoes that beggared description.

Two entrepreneurs had loaded twenty scows with eggs. Other boats contained cargoes of books, magazines and newspapers. There were watercraft loaded to the gunwales with cows, grain, milk and canned food. One vessel's cargo was men's boots. There were mud-scows filled with condensed milk, whisky, live chickens and dynamite. One Arctic veteran loaded his boat with fine-mesh mosquito netting—destined to sell for its weight in gold. One Californian loaded his craft with five tons of fruit packed in sawdust.

Fred, John and Judd wandered over to Tyrie Laing's camp. Fred heard the faint sound of ice cracking.

"Wha da ye ken, laddies?"

"Use your judgment," Fred joshed. "Depart at your peril."

"If you start too soon," John added, "you'll be caught in an ice jam and be wrecked for sure."

"Maybe you'll drown," Judd added mirthfully.

"Laddies, when ye reach the riverbank at Dawson City verra tired from your journey, I'll be there t greet ye." Laing's face wore a grin.

Their conversation was interrupted when a silver-haired sourdough with a pot gut shuffled into camp hoping to cage a drink.

"You should go back to your wives and children," he said with a sneer. "Every claim on Bonanza and Eldorado creeks is taken up."

"Aw shucks," Judd boasted, "we'll find heaps o' gold."

"Tain't worth it," the sourdough said. "First, you'll spend two weeks getting from Lake Bennett to Dawson City. If you do find gold, you got to pay location tax. Then you move a hundred tons of ice. Below that you find twenty feet of frozen muck. You gotta thaw it out and throw it away. Near the bedrock, you'll see gravel. There may be gold or maybe not. So you pile up the gravel and in the summer you wash it out. You can't do that sooner 'cause the water'll be ice. Them's the frozen facts. And if they ain't sufficiently cold, you pilgrims will be when the mercury gets down to sixty below."

After sensing this was a dry camp, old silver hair vanished like a wisp of smoke. Each man sat in silence, wrapped up in his private thoughts. Had they traveled half way to nowhere on a wild goose chase?

A sound alerted Fred and he picked up a billycan can to use as a sounder. The ice was cracking. Fred, John and Judd ran to their tents to strike camp. Coffey, Anderson and Burke pitched in. In the drab predawn, they worked feverishly launching the boats and loading them with supplies. Within two hours they were ready and the six adventurers climbed aboard. The race for the riches was on.

39

Oof Bird on the Klondike

LAKE BENNETT • MAY 1898

IN THE ARCTIC twilight, the men folded the tent city and jammed into man-made boats. Eight hundred craft left the first day, the Rhodesians among the leaders. After a mile they hit slush ice.

"By yiminy, dig out dem vooden poles," George Burke cried. Burke, orphaned during infancy in Montana, had been reared by Scandinavian immigrants.

"What say let's rig up some tarps and set sails," John suggested. Others who had no tarps hung up blankets. Cheers arose when two women stretched their petticoats between a pair of oars. For twelve hours the wind kept them going.

By day's end, they had cleared Lake Bennett and entered Lake Tagish. In their light craft, the Rhodesians quickly passed through Whitehorse Rapids. They bobbed out, drenched but safe, in a quiet pool. Boats with holes in their hulls lined the riverbank. Fred saw Tyrie Laing and his partner, Elmer Ferguson, mending a hole in the hull of their cedar boat.

"See you in Dawson, you haggis-eater," Fred cried out. Laing tossed a rock at them, but the Rhodesians were already out of range. Now came the easy part, the long, leisurely float down the Yukon River to Dawson City.

They passed through forests of spruce, cedar, birch and cottonwoods. Moose, caribou, bears, bighorn sheep, white goats and timber wolves roamed at will. Along the river banks, Fred saw muskrat, wolverine, mink, otter, rabbits and birds. Trout and salmon leaped in the water. Fred would come to cherish memories of this abundance of wildlife. With two men aboard each boat, they sailed all day and through the twilight of night, outdistancing the others.

Fred told Burke about the London Syndicate. He'd met with Lord

The Call to the Klondike

Gifford to ask why the second Barotze Land expedition was canceled. Gifford said developing copper mines in central Africa was a risky undertaking with little chance for a payout in less than twenty years. The outlook would improve after the railway was completed. Against his better feelings, Fred was forced to agree with the board's assessment. It was like the copper discoveries in Arizona—no railway, no market for ore.

When Fred said he would search for gold in the Klondike, Gifford asked if he could organize a private syndicate to back the venture. Fred agreed but only after a guarantee of a salary, expenses and a cut of the profits. And so the London Syndicate was born.

"Would you like to be a partner?" Fred asked.

"I'll shake on dat, Mr. Burnham."

It was on the morning of Monday, June 6, that they came to the Klondike River. It appeared out of nowhere on their right, abruptly spilling into the Yukon River.

Dominating the scene was a rounded mountain with a scoured-out hillside, Moosehide Slide. At river's edge, a crowd of men welcomed the new season's cheechakos.

"Yahoo," Burnham cried. "We beat everyone."

Eager hands pulled the boats to land. The newcomers were besieged for news. Fred rummaged around the boat and found an old copy of the *Seattle Post Intelligencer* in the woodbin. He gave it to a sourdough to read aloud.

During the winter, the suffering in Dawson had been appalling. Those who were frozen-in during the winter might dig gold worth ten thousand dollars in the morning, yet be forced to eat their dogs for dinner.

There remained only days—perhaps hours—to secure claims. The most valuable gold deposits were at a place called Grand Forks, where Eldorado Creek joined with Bonanza Creek. At Burke's urging, they headed fourteen miles south to Grand Forks.

In two days, Fred secured options on three claims on Eldorado Creek fourteen miles south of Dawson City. The claims were two miles south of the discovery claim of Cariboo Billy Dietering on Bonanza Creek. Cariboo Billy's Cheechako Hill discovery was west of Bonanza Creek.

For months, veterans of the Yukon had been trying to puzzle out the riddle of the Klondike. Most of them believed that a lost channel ran through the Klondike Hills. It probably followed a winding route that paralleled Eldorado and Bonanza Creeks, eventually feeding into the Klondike River at Lousetown across from Dawson City.

"I vonder how good Cariboo Billy's claim is?" Burke asked. "Da sourdoughs call it Cheechako Hill. Dere's talk of Billy having salted his claim so he could sell it."

"Billy is a German immigrant," Fred said. "I don't make him out to be a con-man. He's too innocent."

Burke looked skeptical.

"Billy showed me how he found gold," Fred said. "I retraced his trail and I agree. He told me the miners were taking out fortunes up to a certain point, then the gold played out."

"Everyvun knows dat," Burke snorted.

Fred thanked the fates for his prospecting experience in Arizona.

"When Billy reached the French Bench, he worked his way up to the rimrock where he found an ancient creek bed that was cutting its way downward. There he dug and discovered bedrock gold. He found gravel so white it looked bleached. Three pans yielded eleven ounces of fine nuggets."

Burke shook his shaggy head, still skeptical.

"This is the original gold," Fred said, "left in place by nature. The White Channel has the biggest nuggets. Come and I'll show you."

Burke followed Fred up the hill. An hour later, Burke confessed, "By yiminy, you've got somet'ing. But vhy did Billy go two miles nort to file on Cheechako Hill?"

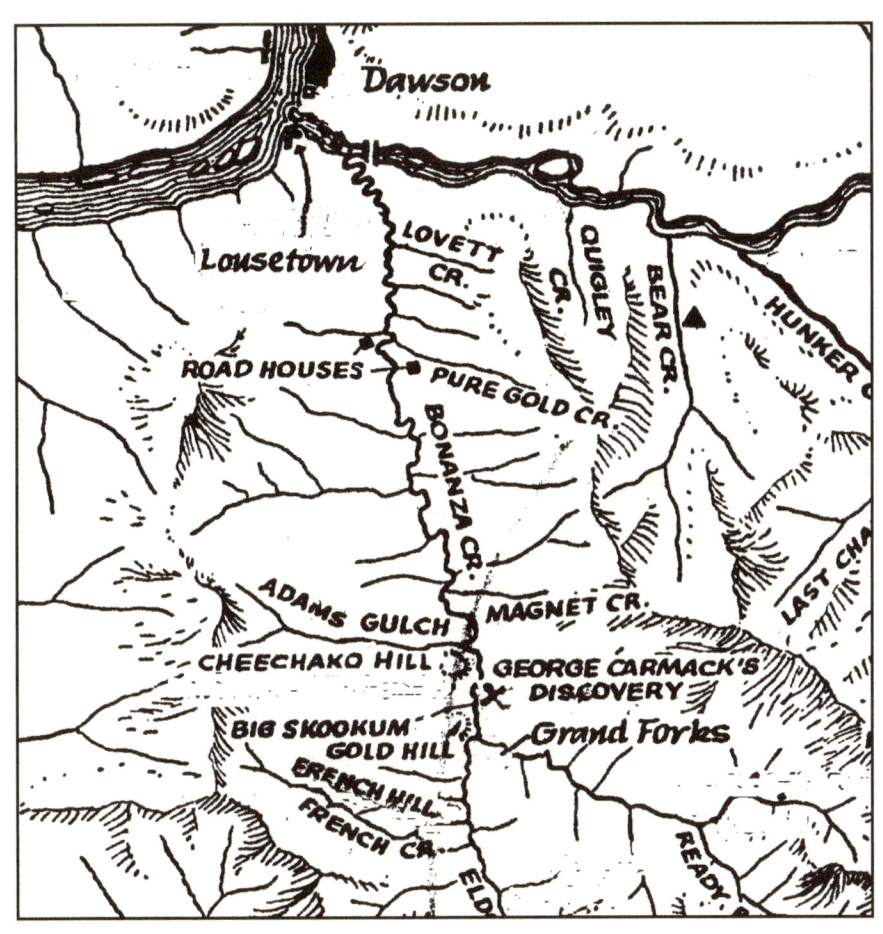

"Because he rediscovered the White Channel over there and took out even bigger nuggets."

"Let's try our luck on da French Bench," Burke said.

Before the sun dipped below the Ogilvie Mountains that day, they'd bought several claims, including one at French Hill from J.A. Gerrow of Seattle, Washington.

"The price is fifty-one thousand dollars and that's a flat-out bargain."

"Sold," Fred cried. Fred and George had just shot their wad and all the cash of the London Syndicate too.

Ritornello • An Interlude

BULAWAYO • JUNE 1898

CHIEF NATIVE Commissioner Herb Taylor was worried right down to his toenails. Seated at his wooden desk in Government House, he tried to recall how often Bonnar had been a thorn in his side. Offhand, he could think of half a dozen times when Armstrong had made scurrilous charges that embarrassed the Chartered Company.

Now the lad wanted to blow the whistle on a certain regrettable incident which had resulted in the death of some unfortunate natives. That information could be a sticky wicket for Herb. Unless an end was put to Bonnar's rantings, Herb's chances to become Sir Herbert were slim indeed. Worse still, if these charges were investigated, Taylor might end his career in gaol.

"Let's see," he muttered, prompting an orderly to peek inside his office—Taylor waved the lad away. While Bonnar was trying the Radlitladi case, Art Lawli had passed down the word that Mr. Rhodes would be pleased if Bonnar ruled against the chief. Actually, Herb himself was responsible for that bit of spinach. Rhodes knew nothing of the case. When Rhodes finally came up for the dedication of the railway, he'd overturned the ruling. Bonnar had protested, but Herb managed to quash the report before it got to Cape Town. At Herb's urging, the administrator summoned Bonnar for a slating.

Next Bonnar wrote to the board of directors seeking an audience with the secretary of state for colonies. He sought vindication by charging maladministration by the Chartered Company. Herb had a tough time convincing Earl Grey to quash that memo. He'd heard through the grapevine that Bonnar planned to tell all he knew about the Graham Incident, a well-guarded secret in the CNC Department where six cattle thieves had died. Herb had ordered the affair hushed up. During the 1896 Rebellion, Graham was killed in action, so at least there were no witnesses who could testify.

How had Bonnar learned? Had Bill Driver spilled the beans? He'd better keep a sharp eye on Driver up there in Gwelo. Herb had no choice. If Bonnar were to make public those allegations, Taylor would have to answer to charges of conspiracy to cover up multiple murders. Herb had placed Bonnar on sick leave and sent him off to Natal to contemplate the future of his career.

Two months later came the Nkolomana Episode, and it was a heaven-sent opportunity. This time Bonnar was vulnerable. Herb learned that Armstrong had diverted the Nkolomana's salary as head induna of Mangwe to another native. He called Bonnar to his office and told him if he didn't resign immediately, he would formally charge him with misappropriation of government funds. Bonnar resigned and Herb put it down as the end of a tawdry series of events.

Counterpoise • Equilibrium

FRENCH BENCH • JULY 1898

THE RHODESIANS dug a shaft three feet square and twelve feet deep, working for two weeks. To thaw the frozen muck, they used hot coals from a campfire. Two of them felled trees to keep the flames alive. At the bedrock, they dug laterals. In this permafrost, there was no need for shoring.

After weeks of labor, an accumulation of white gravel graced the surface and the men turned to constructing a dam and sluice box. They ran water for twenty minutes, let it settle and ran it again—the custom in the Klondike. At the end of the day they'd pick out the gold. At the cleanup, they happily measured out thirteen hundred ounces — a hundred and eight pounds of gold nuggets — plus a large bag of town dust for living expenses.

"Better'n Dhlo-Dhlo," Fred said. "And there's more here for the taking."

Indeed, they'd only scratched the surface. That night in his tent, Fred refined a plan suggested by George Burke. John and Judd would remain in the Klondike to build cabins and work the claims. He and George would go to London and lay out a bold scheme for capturing the bulk of the Klondike's riches.

The next day they bagged their nuggets. Fred asked Judd to help lug the gold to Dawson. In the six weeks they had been in the gold fields, that ragged collection of tents called Dawson had blossomed into the Paris of the North.

Dawson had wooden buildings, running water, steam heat, electricity and city telephone service. They saw banks, newspapers, churches, hospitals and countless bars. Saloons changed hands with the luck of the dice. Edison movie crews documented the action.

Prices exceeded the mere outlandish. Boiled beans, stewed apple, bread and coffee cost five dollars. An egg fetched fifteen dollars. Milk commanded thirty dollars a quart, champagne sixty bucks a bottle—four ounces of town dust. Drunken men lurched out of saloons to puke on the sidewalks. Women cavorted in the nude for incredible sums. In the better establishments, men wore tailcoats, dined on pate de fois gras and drank vintage wine. Restaurants boasted string ensembles.

An enterprising syndicate, the British and Yukon Navigation Company, established paddlewheel service up the Yukon River to Whitehorse Rapids. Fred and George booked passage. After saying farewell to Judd, Fred and George enjoyed five days of idle relaxation. From Whitehorse Rapids, the miners hired mules and formed a tight band while hiking to the Alaskan border to retrieve their shootin irons. At White Pass they boarded the new White Pass Railroad for the short ride to Skagway where they learned that Soapy Smith had been shot dead. It was Saturday, July 23, 1898, seven weeks and four

Burnham: King of Scouts

Placer Mining in the Klondike

days since the Rhodesians launched their cedar boats at Lake Bennett. The Skagway *Alaskan* headlined:

ANOTHER BIG LOAD OF DAWSON DUST

Gold in hand satchels, rolled up in blankets, carried in canvas bags and in old tin boxes. There was excitement when a party of Klondikers arrived at the Brannick Hotel laden with heavy packages. One man had an old tin box so full of dust it took two men to lift it. He is J.A. Gerrow who worked a claim on French Gulch, struck paydirt and set the odd price of fifty-one thousand dollars on it. For sixty days he averaged a thousand dollars a day on the diggings until Fred Burnham snapped it up. Burnham, a scout in the Matabele War, has been in Dawson for a London syndicate, and he leaves here on the next steamer with options on several valuable claims.

A point of great interest was the immense nugget brought by George Burke. He was showing it in town this morning and it was declared to be the largest and handsomest ever seen in Skagway. Burke found the nugget on his claim above the discovery on French Gulch. He is now on his way to London.

The nugget, which was reproduced in the paper with gold ink, was shaped like a tiny loaf of bread with a pointed lump on one end. It weighed twelve ounces and it was the main topic of conversation that night in the bars and saloons of Skagway.

To those newly arrived from the Klondike, the news was not gold—that was commonplace. The miners were startled to learn that Spain had sued for peace. They didn't know the Spanish American War had begun, much less ended. And the hero of the war was none other than Colonel Teddy Roosevelt.

Doctor Ira Moore told Fred that Teddy had resigned as Assistant Secretary of Navy, and with Sheriff Buckey O'Neill of Prescott, Arizona, organized a regiment of western Rough Riders. O'Neill was killed while Roosevelt led a charge up Kettle Hill. Now the name Teddy was on the lips of everyone in America.

Ten days later, Fred arrived in Pasadena where he learned he was the father of a six-week-old son, Bruce. Mother and child were healthy.

• • •

London • September 1898

FRED BURNHAM and George Burke carried their satchel of elk leather containing one hundred and eight pounds of gold into the Chartered Company's offices. Theirs was the first Klondike gold to arrive

299

in England and visitors flocked to the offices to see the strange metal. George untied the oversized poke and lifted out several sturdy coffee tins containing the nuggets. At the sight of the wealth, the eyes of stock clerks, brokers and newspaper reporters bulged like saucers.

"It's red," Lord Gifford cried in alarm. "Are you sure these nuggets aren't alloyed with copper?"

"They are too soft and too heavy to contain copper," Fred said. "It's typical of Klondike gold."

"I do say, your nuggets are rather granular," Major Ricarde-Seaver said.

"We think da granular look comes from rippling over da rocks," Burke said. "That and the red color may be impossible to duplicate."

After the reporters were ushered out, Burnham and Burke sprang their scheme for the London Syndicate.

"I propose that we send six Hindi Giants to the Klondike and clean up the gold-bearing creeks of the Klondike," Fred said.

"What could six WOGs from Calcutta do for us?" Lord Gifford said with a snort.

"I'm talking about buying six hydraulic water cannons from the Hindi Iron Works in San Francisco," Burnham explained. "These hydraulic monitors use water power to dredge the placers."

"Are you talking about naval cannons?" Gifford wanted to know.

"Not really," Fred replied, "though a ten-inch diameter Hindi Giant looks like one."

"And probably costs as much," Gifford said.

"Using water from the Yukon River, one ten-inch Hindi Giant can pump a million gallons an hour of water at a pressure of two hundred pounds," Burnham explained. "It can throw this spray a quarter of a mile."

"How will you get this Hindoo cannon to the Klondike?" Gifford asked.

"That's the easy part," Fred replied. "We ship them from the plant in San Francisco to Nome, transfer them to a paddlewheel steamer for the ride up the Yukon River to Dawson. We'll clean up millions."

Lord Gifford and his partners pursed their lips greedily. But for such a venture, they would have to call on the Rothschilds bankers for financial support.

The next day Gifford, Burnham and Burke walked across St. Swithin's Lane to the granite-walled offices of the Rothschilds. There they entered a spacious room fitted with a hundred year old grandfather clock. Fred noticed a number of portraits in oils hanging on the walls.

"They are monarchs for whom the Rothschilds made loans," said

Lord Gifford. He explained that as Mayer Rothschild's money-changing business in Germany grew, he made his sons bank managers in Frankfurt, Vienna, Naples, Paris and London.

"During the war with Napoleon, the Bank of England was tapped out," Lord Gifford said. "Son Nathan raised a hundred million pounds to finance the British victory at Waterloo. Now the Rothschilds rule all of Europe's finance."

A door opened and from the inner sanctum Fred heard the gabble of voices: "Mocatta, sixty bars." "Sharps, forty." "Montague, thirty."

"They're fixing the price of gold through bids," Lord Gifford said.

George Burke was unwrapping the elkskin poke on the table when Sir Nathan Rothschild walked into the room, stroking his muttonchop beard.

"That's a heavy load," Sir Nathan said.

"More than a hundredweight," Lord Gifford replied with a proud smile.

Burnham outlined the scheme for the Hindi Giants, explaining that much gold was lost because of the strong head of water used in sluicing.

"They don't save nuggets finer than wheat grains," he said. "And while this twelve ounce nugget may be awe-inspiring, it doesn't take long to sluice up twelve ounces of gold in grain-sized nuggets."

Sir Nathan said he would ask his engineers to study the proposal, and if it looked promising he would lay the plan before the board of directors.

The next day, the *African Review* published an article on Fred's adventures in the Klondike. It said he looked none the worse for his arctic travels and quoted him as saying the trip was an ordinary experience for an active man.

On Tuesday following, Fred was summoned to St. Swithin's Lane. The countenance on Lord Gifford's face was as dour as wet chicken droppings.

"The Rothschilds decided not to finance our scheme to use Hindi Giants for hydraulic mining in the Klondike."

"Did Sir Nathan say why?" Burnham asked.

"He said the risk is too high — from a legal point of view. The hydraulic claims do not dispossess those of the placer miners."

Fred dropped Burke's lopsided gold nugget. It rolled to the edge of the table and fell to the floor with a clatter. Lord Gifford picked it up.

"There's no need to displace the claims of the placer miners," Burnham said. "The Klondike miners are high-grading — taking only the big nuggets — ignoring the color. When you see Sir Nathan, tell him he has made the worst financial mistake of his life."

While walking back to the Chartered Company offices, Burke pulled Fred aside.

"From now on I paddle my own canoe. I take my share of the gold, go back to Montana and marry my sveetheart."

40

Teddy Roosevelt

NEW YORK • OCTOBER 1898

COLONEL ROOSEVELT invited Burnham to lunch at the Boone & Crockett Club. Fred was eager to hear firsthand Teddy's account of the war. In London, the British — still implacable foes of the Spanish — boisterously referred to the fracas as the Yanko-Spanko War. The two men had no sooner shaken hands than Fred knew he was talking to a new Teddy, a man destined for greater things. His manner of speaking and his inflection of words suggested he was different. He was primitive. Yet he had a gift of charm and generosity that could command absolute loyalty.

Roosevelt was running for governor of New York. The newspapers predicted he'd win by a huge margin. During the meal, Roosevelt described his adventure.

"We landed near Santiago," Roosevelt said. "It's between Guantanamo Bay and the village of Daiquiri. By the way we discovered a bully rum drink at Daiquiri."

"Sounds tropical and exotic," Fred replied.

"It was Friday, the first of July," Teddy continued. "Already our regiment was horseless. The Spanish held Kettle Hill, blocking the road to San Juan Heights. What happened next was—nobody gave an order. Entirely on their own, the men began charging up San Juan Heights. The shooting was a hand-to-hand fire-fight. We ran into a miasma of Mauser bullets. During that day I learned to respect the courage of Captain "Black Jack" Pershing's soldiers on our left flank. Their assault on that blockhouse was bully. It saved our souls."

"You mean the Buffalo Soldiers?" Fred asked.

"Yes, the Tenth Cavalry. One of four regiments that Congress established after the Civil War. Without those blockhousers, I wouldn't be here today. Men dropped all around me and yet—only God knows why—I was barely nicked. Half way up Kettle Hill, a Spanish soldier charged at me with a bayonet. I raised my pistol and fired a snapshot, killing him instantly. It was pure reflex on my part. The opposition faltered and the next thing we crested the hill. By Jove."

"Was that when Buckey O'Neill got it?" Fred asked.

"He died like a man."

"I rode for him as a deputy in 1882 when he was sheriff."

"Then you know that a good man died that day," Roosevelt said. "The Spanish lost half their force."

"Sounds like you earned your pay that day."

"Like the Matabele War," Roosevelt said, "the worst came afterward. We were sapped by the sun and soaked by rain. Malaria struck, then yellow fever, along with the black vomits. The men ran out of food. For two days, the Spanish put up a spirited fight, but we held that hill."

Fred knew what happened. Four hundred years of Spanish Empire—dating from Columbus—disappeared from the face of the earth. Overnight America became a world power with colonies reaching all the way to the Philippines. And Teddy was the hero.

Counterpoise • Equilibrium

PASADENA • NOVEMBER 1899

AT HOME, a letter from John and Judd said things were in good shape on the French Bench. The boys continued to pile up a hoard of gold so Fred indulged in the luxury of Christmas and New Year's with Blanche, Rod and the infant Bruce. They watched participants in the tenth annual Tournament of Roses decorate carriages and hitch up horses on Maylin Street, the road named after Fred's late sister which began life as the Burnhams' driveway.

A few days later, Fred left for the North. At Skagway, he powwowed with Doctor Ira Moore and bought two St. Bernard dogs, a light sled, fur robes, a tent made of silk and a large supply of dried food. He sewed leather moccasins for the dogs' feet. Then in the dead of winter he set off in this light rig for Dawson City.

Each day about an hour before noon, the sun peeped over the horizon for a couple of hours before dipping again. The temperature was below zero, and it dropped once to fifty-five below. Even the Perry Davis Painkiller, that noble thermometer of the Arctic, froze solid. *Quicksilver, whisky, kerosine and Perry Davis Painkiller froze in that order.*

After twenty-four days of arctic travel, Fred mushed into Dawson. It was Monday, February 20, 1899, and it was thirty-five degrees below zero. He tarried in Dawson long enough to sample one of Irish

Nellie Cashman's moose steaks and buy two sides of frozen caribou carcass. Then he struck out to join his brothers-in-law and dig for gold.

At the diggings, game animals and firewood were scarce—the miners denuded the countryside of trees and game. Everyone had to haul wood from longer distances. The sled dogs came in handy.

The prospectors settled into a routine that Fred came to cherish. The stillness of the north proved to be vastly different from the scorching deserts. While hauling wood, he saw thin lines of blue smoke from campfires rise as vertical as plumb lines until they faded at the zenith. In the still air, he carried a kerosine lamp from cabin to mine without a flicker. The snow was so dry that it piled inches high on twigs and branches, though the slightest jolt would send it tumbling down. Through the valleys, the singing of sled runners and the tinkling of sled-dog bells floated in the clear winter air for incredible distances.

The work was difficult and they hired miners from Dawson at wages of fifteen dollars a day—an ounce of town dust. They melted gravel that had been frozen for thousands of years, sometimes disturbing the icy tombs of ancient monsters whose ivory tusks were still white and solid. Without giving thought, the mastodons had hidden their graves more successfully than the pharaohs of Egypt, but in the search for gold, their remains were destroyed. That fact greatly disturbed John Blick, the paleontologist.

The cold spring of 1899 surrendered to a delicate summer where wildflowers bloomed in profusion. Birds appeared from the south. As the snows melted, the water flowed with a strong head and the trio of Rhodesians sluiced white gravel.

The cleanup was rewarding. A coffee can of gold dust was too heavy to lift without placing it in an elkskin bag. There was ample dust to pay the financing of the London Syndicate, to cover all expenses and to pay dividends to all. Fred wrote a letter to Lord Gifford, asking how he'd like the funds to be delivered — in gold or by bank transfer. He decided John and Judd deserved some time off to make merry. The brothers hiked into sin city to dine on Nellie Cashman's tough steak and mail the letter to London.

It was now a small matter to have a hundredweight of gold. After a few months' toil, many Argonauts amassed two hundred—even three hundred—pounds of gold onto sleds and trudged off for Dawson. But only a lucky four hundred hit gold in any big way.

Ritornello • An Interlude

BULAWAYO • APRIL 1899

ONE THING FOR SURE, Armstrong was a resilient chap. On March 15, he appealed to Sir Alfred Milner, the new high commissioner in Cape Town. In a letter of eight legal-size pages, he charged the Chartered Company with maladministration of justice, with shooting innocent natives, and with interfering with his duties as native commissioner. He demanded to be reinstated with back pay.

But Bonnar's mistake was in sending the letter through channels. As a civilian, Armstrong was free to write to the high commissioner in Cape Town. But he thoughtlessly addressed it to Government House in Bulawayo and the letter landed on Earl Grey's desk. Herb couldn't recall another day quite like that one. Lord Grey administered a severe slating and it was only after Herb read the entire letter twice that he figured out how to hop the twig.

Herb had the sole copy of the document. That was the clanger on Armstrong's part. It gave Herb a chance to construct a defense against each of Armstrong's charges. The whole lot could be combined into one packet and forwarded to Sir Alfred in Cape Town. Herb could defuse the charges and bugger Armstrong to boot.

With misgivings, Lord Grey granted Herb's request to prepare a rebuttal, allowing him one week. That had been on April 6. Now it was April 25 and in those nineteen days Herb turned the Native Commission Department upside down.

Twice he'd secured extensions. Twice he'd ordered Bill Thomas to prepare documents to discredit Bonnar. In his first report, Thomas had weasel-worded, failing to nail the lad. When Herb explained the gravity of the situation, Thomas—always the good soldier—was inspired to deliver the goods. Fabricating depositions, he made up enough evidence to put Bonnar in the loony bin.

For hours, Herb weighed plausible explanations for each of the charges. The best evidence was Thomas' latest batch of depositions that cleared Herb of those conspiracy charges including the deaths of those flogged niggers up by Gwelo.

Herb completed his report at 7 o'clock and decided to take dinner at the Bulawayo Club. He joined friends for sundowners and tarried for two hours before eating. When he got back to his office, he re-read his rebuttal. The report contained mention of the M'Limo affair, which had taken place three years ago. At that time, Sir Alfred had been stationed in Egypt. Taylor reasoned that the new high commissioner might appreciate being filled in on the M'Limo matter.

Herb was struck by a startling thought. Sir Alfred might never lay eyes on this report. The HiCom was said to be busy preparing for the Bloemfontein Conference, which would begin in thirty days. The outcome of that meeting between British and Boer leaders could determine if there was to be war in southern Africa. Sir Alfred would be too busy with the affairs of state to read a rambling dissertation by some half-baked native commissioner in a godforsaken corner of Rhodesia.

In all likelihood, the report would be reviewed by a civil servant who would sign it off on behalf of the high commissioner. The bureaucrat would endorse Earl Grey's recommendation. And the mild-mannered Lord Grey, his tour of duty expiring soon, was already packing to leave Rhodesia. He might sign anything that Herb put on paper.

Taylor conceived a plan. Two years ago, a young trooper named Frank Sykes had published a book titled *With Plumer in Matabele Land*. It contained a misleading account, based on bar talk, of the M'Limo's shooting. Aside from Armstrong, there was only one person at this time who could challenge Sykes' version of what really happened. And that someone was Fred Burnham, now half way around the world in the Klondike. It meant Taylor was free to cast the M'Limo episode in such a manner that Bonnar Armstrong would be the villain. Herb picked up a pen.

The Shooting of Jobane, a Friendly Native, the Supposed M'Limo

It is my duty to bring to light certain facts that have been revealed to me lately in connection with the shooting of this native.

In June 1896, during the height of the Rebellion, I received a telegram from Armstrong at Mangwe requesting to be allowed to come to Bulawayo on urgent private affairs. I could not spare Armstrong from this district just then and replied to that effect. Two days later I received instructions to muster Gambo's friendlies and proceed with them to the Gwaii River for the purpose of pacifying that district.

A few days afterwards, I returned from the Gwaii. I was informed by Earl Grey that Armstrong and Burnham had killed the M'Limo. I was also requested by Earl Grey and General Carrington to allow him as much rope as possible, in fact, to give him a free hand while discharging his duties at Mangwe.

It was growing late and Herb was tired from the stress of the past three weeks. The grog hadn't helped either, but he continued:

It appears that Armstrong had heard there was a certain cave near Banko's kraal, close to the Shashi River, within about thirty miles of the Matopo Hills, where the Makalakas used to offer up their sacrifices

307

to the M'Limo. He concocted a story with reference to this cave so as to completely deceive both Earl Grey and General Carrington, and put it in such a light that they were convinced that Armstrong knew the whereabouts of the true M'Limo who had influenced the natives of this province to openly rebel against the Government of the country.

Taylor made two mistakes in that paragraph. Banko's kraal was not in the hostile Gwanda District south of Bulawayo, where Njelele was situated. Banko's kraal mentioned in Taylor's post script was west of the Matopo Hills in Bill Thomas' peaceful Bulalima District.

More significant, Taylor had written Shashi River instead of Shashani River. The Shashi River wasn't even in Rhodesia. It originates in Bechuana Land and flows south serving as a border between Rhodesia and Bechuana Land. South of Tati, it turns east and serves as the border between Rhodesia and the Transvaal until it joins the Limpopo.

The Shashani River begins southwest of Bulawayo between Fig Tree and The Nek, the site of the Mtoli Starr Hotel. It flows past Njelele, eventually joining the Shashi River far to the south. Anyone reading Herb Taylor's report might erroneously conclude the M'Limo's cave was somewhere out in the Kalahari Desert — in Bechuana Land. Herb then borrowed from Sykes' flawed version of the M'Limo episode.

General Carrington deemed it in the interest of peace to remove the M'Limo, and the well-known American scout, Burnham, was sent with Armstrong to put this plan into execution. They proceeded to Mangwe and left for this place in the company of a native called Kutji, who has since died. On arriving at the cave, Kutji pointed out Jobane in the fields. Jobane was sent for by Armstrong, who told him to walk toward the cave. When at the mouth of the cave, he was deliberately shot from behind.

Then they returned to Mangwe and Mr. Armstrong called together all the principal natives of the district and informed them that he had killed the M'Limo and they were all told to spread the news throughout the country. When the rebels began to surrender, it was ascertained that the true M'Limo was still at large, convincing proof having been brought to the Government of this fact. The real native who represented the M'Limo was Mkwati.

Herb had a long track record for sloppy reporting. It dated to when he denied the native unrest on the eve of the 1896 Rebellion. This time he picked the wrong person as the M'Limo. Mkwati was a Mashona rainbringer who claimed to have inherited the mantle of the recently departed M'Limo. But the Mashonas wouldn't accept his claim. They harpooned him with assegais, then drawed and quartered him, reasoning that if he was sent by the M'Limo, they had better make sure he could not come back and cause more trouble.

The rebels denied all knowledge of Jobane. In fact, he was not even known by them. When Armstrong heard this, he began to fear that the deception he had so cleverly carried out would be exposed. In order to defeat this, he requested the Government to cause an official enquiry into the killing of Jobane. Judge Watermeyer presided, and Armstrong by threats and bribes—see enclosed affidavits—caused certain natives to perjure themselves. I make this report on the M'Limo Episode believing it to be true.

After the shooting of Jobane, a complete change came over Armstrong and at times he behaved in a most extraordinary manner. I thought this would gradually wear off, but such was not the case, and I can only surmise that the killing of the unfortunate Jobane had unhinged Armstrong's mind.

The next day the document entered official channels. The process of British justice was meted out. Bonnar's career with the Chartered Company was ruined and he left Rhodesia. As for Herb's report, based on the fiction of Frank Sykes and Herb's own geographic errors, it was filed in the Chartered Company's archives where it was classified as Secret. For seventy-five years, the file would repose in isolation—stored not in the CNC's outgoing files where it belonged, but safely hidden in the incoming files. And Taylor went on to become Sir Herbert.

Counterpoise • Equilibrium
FRENCH BENCH • AUGUST 1899

IT HAPPENED on a long, hot summer day. As if by an arrangement with the gods, the Klondike gold ran out. Word of the bust spread like a Nebraska prairie fire. Everyone began to pack up to leave because in two weeks Bonanza and Eldorado Creeks and the French Bench would belong to the arctic foxes.

Fred, John and Judd crammed nuggets and gold dust into any receptacle they could find and dragged them into Dawson. Shipping containers sold at a premium. Hoards of the yellow metal were stored in twenty-gallon wooden barrels marked Salted Fish. John saw a man and his mule dragging a heavy sled containing thirteen hundred pounds of gold, worth a third of a million dollars. It looked to be twice the size of the Rhodesians' treasure, which had to be divided with the London Syndicate.

Burnham: King of Scouts

No matter, the Burnham party members were still rich. Fred figured that after expenses, he'd have fifty thousand dollars. Considering that in Pasadena a suit of clothes cost four dollars and a four-course dinner went for twenty-five cents, fifty thousand was a fortune.

The postmaster in Skagway learned of the exodus, so he held up the mail, waiting for the miners to pick up their letters en route back to the Lower Forty-Four. Fred opened a letter from Lord Gifford instructing him to make payment by bank transfer: Shipping gold half way around the world was expensive and risky. Gifford told Fred to withdraw twenty-five thousand dollars from the London Syndicate and credit that amount to his own account. Fred's heart leaped with joy at the thought of such a generous bonus.

The explanation that followed brought anger and rage. Lord Gifford said the Northern Territories (BSA) Exploration & Development—the Northers Terrors—had been sold in June. The twenty-five thousand dollars represented Fred's share of the proceeds. The shares of stock, when originally issued, were worth nearly ninety thousand dollars. Now they brought thirty cents on the dollar. Fred was so angry he tore up the letter—an act he was later to regret.

While they sailed down the inland sea to Puget Sound, Burnham skulked and paced the deck. On arrival in Seattle, he deposited the gold in a bank and settled accounts with the London Syndicate. The Blick brothers bought tickets for Pasadena, urging Fred to hurry up and buy one as well .

"To hell with Africa," Fred said tartly. "To hell with England." Fred hawked a goober into a brass spittoon and said, "When you get home, tell Blanche and the boys to join me in Skagway. I'm going into business with Doctor Ira C. Moore."

"Business," John cried. "What kind of business?"

Fred bowed, doffed his hat, waved it to one side like a circus impresario and announced, "We are going to generate and sell electric power in the city of Skagway."

The Boer War

The 9th Chronicle

41

Summoned to Africa

BLOEMFONTEIN • JUNE 1899

JANNIE SMUTS swore under his breath. The Peace Conference had degenerated into a disaster and he couldn't do a thing about it. As the state attorney for the Transvaal, Jannie sensed that Sir Alfred Milner wanted to wreck the negotiations. Lord Milner wanted to seize the Transvaal so that tub of lard, Cecil Rhodes, could control the Witswatersrand's gold riches.

Each time the high commissioner spoke, Smuts felt the man's fiery eyes fix on him with an accusing stare. Smuts regarded this lean Britisher with his piano-player's fingers as a ruthless imperialist. The Peace Conference in Bloemfontein was being held under the eyes of Oom Paul Kruger of the Transvaal and Martinus Steyn, the newly elected president of the Orange Free State. Steyn was a man of great political acumen. He was as sophisticated as Oom Paul was ignorant.

Sir Alfred made demands that were unacceptable to Kruger. The wily old Boer led his delegation — including Jannie — out of the conference, leaving Steyn holding the bag. Oom Paul then disappeared. Soon after that, the Uitlanders began an exodus.

Ritornello • Interlude

CAPE TOWN • JULY 1899

ALTHOUGH SIR ALFRED had done his best to provoke war, the high commissioner lacked the full support of Whitehall. London was reticent because the British had only ten thousand troops to defend the Cape Colony and Natal. The Boers had fifty thousand frontiersmen of military age in the Orange Free State and the Transvaal. Several thousand others were living in the Cape Colony and Natal and could be expected to come to the aid of the two republics.

The Boer War

Even worse, the British general commanding, Sir William Butler, was sympathetic to the Boers. General Wolseley was forced to sack Butler. But when he asked for reinforcements, the penny-pinching war secretary, Lord Lansdowne, declined to dispatch troops. That's why Wolseley's war plan had to be fashioned out of chicken feathers and horse manure.

It began in Bulawayo with a backhanded assist from Sir Alfred. On his own, one Colonel Jack Nicholson, the dapper commandant of the British South Africa Police, hatched a daring plan. When war with the Boers came, he proposed that the British replicate the Jameson Raid by launching surprise attacks on Pretoria and Johannesburg. Like the Jameson Raid, the attacks would originate from Mafeking. Even if unsuccessful, the scheme could save Natal from invasion until reinforcements could be brought over by troopship from India.

In Cape Town, High Commissioner Milner eagerly endorsed Nicholson's Plan. He forwarded it to London for approval by the military high command. Sir Alfred assumed that when the scheme was endorsed, Jack Nicholson would be appointed to carry out the scheme.

Lagnappe • A Little Extra

LONDON • AUGUST 1899

NICHOLSON'S PLAN reached London two months after the Bloemfontein Talks collapsed. To carry out the plan, Lord Wolseley wanted one of his own Garnet Ring officer, not that oaf out in Rhodesia. Wolseley saw Nicholson's plan as little short of romantic balderdash.

But if such an idea was properly leaked, it could pin down five thousand Boers, keeping them out in the backblocks for a month or more. During that span, Wolseley would have time to dispatch troops from England to the Cape Colony and from India to Natal. All he needed was a sacrificial lamb to head up the operation.

Lord Wolseley told his aide-de-camp to send a cable to Colonel Baden-Powell at the Fifth Dragoon Guards in India, summoning him back to England. The aide sent a cable, then went to the Naval and Military Club for tiffin.

While enjoying the view of Green Park and Buckingham Palace, the aide spotted Baden-Powell seated at a table across the staff officers dining room. It was pure coincidence that Stephe happened to be in London. A year earlier, while hunting in the Kashmir, he began outlining his next book, *Cavalry Aids to Scouting*. It was based on his 1896 outing with Fred Burnham in Rhodesia.

313

On returning to his base, Stephe expanded his notes and dictated them to the regimental shorthand clerk. His primary reason for taking leave to London was to seek a publisher. He was feeling good now, having signed a contract with Gale and Polten of Aldershot, a firm that specialized in publishing books for Sandhurst students. That's when Wolseley's aide walked over and told Stephe to report to the commander-in-chief after lunch.

"Come in, Colonel," General Wolseley said to Baden-Powell. "Good to learn you're in town this week."

Stephe stood at attention. It was his first meeting with the commanding general.

"I am relieving you as commanding officer of the Fifth Dragoon Guards," General Wolseley said shuffling through a stack of papers on his desk as though searching for something.

Stephe's heart almost failed. This was dreadful news. Worse than the end of the earth. What had he done to deserve such punishment? Wolseley's aide entered the room and handed the general a sheet of paper.

"Were you looking for this, Sir?"

"Yes, thank you, Major." Turning to Stephe, Wolseley said, "I'm constituting a new organization, the North West Frontier Force, to be posted in Mafeking. I'm naming you as commanding officer. No orders will be published in the gazette as this is to be a Very Secret operation."

When Stephe learned he was being sent to that rock-strewn backwash called Mafeking, he almost fainted with relief. Though neither of them knew it then, this highly unusual operation was destined to generate as much ballyhoo as Queen Victoria's Diamond Jubilee. It would, in fact, become one of the most bizarre episodes in British history. Though it would come to sound like comic opera, it began in the dead earnest planning for hostilities.

"You will recruit two regiments," the general said, "one from Bechuana Land and one from Rhodesia. In the event of war, you are to obstruct the Boers at Mafeking and keep their forces occupied. If necessary, you are to sacrifice your command. You must block the Boers from advancing on Rhodesia's southern border. And be sure to keep the niggers from siding with them."

Counterpoise • Equilibrium

Skagway • August 1899

DURING THE summer, while awaiting the arrival of equipment for the electric power plant, Fred and Rod explored the rugged coast of southeastern Alaska. They camped on the John Muir Glacier. It was the first time in five years The Dad and The Kid, now thirteen, had bedded out under the stars.

Fred thought Alaska was a fine country. The sea was populated with Chinook salmon and halibut. The streams abounded in trout and dolly varden. The forests were inhabited by deer and bear and the lakes were rich in waterfowl. Wild berries grew on the hillsides. The mosquitoes were so large that Alaskans boasted they could carry off a wildcat.

Fred rented a little steamer and explored a score of islands with veins no less than twenty feet thick. He acquired interests in ten claims in the Athin District, one of them a huge vein that for years could feed a stamp mill of three thousand tons a day capacity. In a letter to Rider Haggard, he invited his friend to visit them in Alaska during the trip he planned to the United States in the summer of 1900.

Lagnappe • A Little Extra

LONDON • SEPTEMBER 1899

THE HAMMONDS' sons were nearing college age, and Jack and Natalie wanted the boys to be schooled in America. Jack sent a cable to Cecil Rhodes informing him of his intention to resign. Rhodes caught the next ship from Cape Town to London.

"I have made a great deal of money listening to your advice," Rhodes said. "I greatly value your counsel and I am prepared to make a generous offer."

"I'm open to ideas," Hammond said.

"I will create a position as manager of all my interests in south Africa," he said. "You can name your salary."

"Mr. Rhodes, these six years have been the most productive and rewarding of my life," Hammond replied. "But I must decline your offer on the grounds that you no longer need an engineer. You need an administrator. You need someone who can chop costs. I am a developer, not a bean-counter. I need worlds to conquer."

It would be their last meeting.

When Hammond reopened his engineering office in New York, his first act was to build an electric power plant in Mexico for Darius Ogden Mills. With Alfred Beit of South Africa, he purchased the horse tramway in Mexico City and transformed it into an electric streetcar system. They repeated that successful scheme in Geneva.

With younger brother, Bill Hammond of Visalia, California, Jack became interested in irrigation. Bill had been working with Ben Maddox of the *Visalia Times* to irrigate desiccated Tulare County farms. Ben reported that a farmer in rural Lindsay hooked a six horse-

Burnham: King of Scouts

power engine to a pump. Pumping from wells a hundred feet deep, the farmer was raising oranges, lemons, olives, grapes and vegetables.

Bill tried to interest San Francisco financiers in building a dam on the Kaweah River. He planned to bring electricity by overhead line to the San Joaquin Valley to power irrigation pumps. The Bay Area money men rejected his views, so Bill turned to elder brother Jack.

Jack Hammond and Darius Ogden Mills put up the capital and the Mount Whitney Power Company came into being. Soon a village called Hammond appeared near the south entrance to Sequoia Park. Here a Westinghouse generator began to hum and electric-powered irrigation soon changed central California. In time, thousands of acres of idle land were put to the pump. Farmers who had never earned fifteen dollars an acre from their crops began taking out profits of a thousand dollars an acre.

Ritornello • An Interlude

CAPE TOWN • SEPTEMBER 1899

COLONEL BADEN-POWELL called on the HiCom. When Stephe explained his mission, Sir Alfred exploded, terminated the interview and dismissed him. But not before he forbade Stephe from recruiting troops in Natal or the Cape Colony. Sir Alfred feared that any operation by a senior Imperial officer could be construed by the Boers as a warlike act. Worse still, it might forestall war altogether.

Stephe took a train to Bulawayo to recruit volunteers. He left his deputy, Major Edward Cecil, behind in Cape Town to muster war supplies. Lord Cecil, with slouch shoulders and soup-strainer mustache, was a martinet of profound ego. After all, he was the son-in-law of the prime minister.

Major Cecil signed notes for half a million pounds at the Ben Weil Mercantile Company to ship grain, fodder, foodstuffs and war matériel to Mafeking. Merchant Weil was delighted. To beat an inventory tax scheduled to go into effect, he had already stashed much of this merchandise in Mafeking for shipment to Rhodesia. Now he would be handsomely rewarded.

In Bulawayo, Colonel Jack Nicholson resented Stephe and bad-mouthed the colonel at the Bulawayo Club. Baden-Powell ignored him and dispatched Rhodesian officers to Natal and the Cape Colony to secretly recruit a military force *sub rosa*. He gave the command of the Rhodesia Regiment to Colonel Herbert Plumer, who had headed the jass-eyed Mafeking Relief Force.

Stephe established headquarters in Mafeking, where he organized a system of fortified emplacements. The train loads of supplies sent to the Weil warehouse in Mafeking tipped off the enemy. The Boer high command ordered General Piet Cronje—the Boer leader who had ambushed the Jameson Raiders in 1896—to surround Mafeking with five thousand Boers.

Baden-Powell boasted seven Maxim machine guns and two thousand men: eight hundred of them blacks. His force was outnumbered three to one, so Stephe resorted to some ruses and tricks learned during the Matabele campaign. During training, he ordered *mines*—in reality, black boxes filled with sand—buried along the outskirts of town. At a test intended to occupy the attention of the Boers, Stephe blew up about fifty sticks of buried dynamite. The stunt was so effective that General Cronje dispatched a rider under a white flag with a memo to Colonel Baden-Powell. He reminded the British commander that land mines were a contravention of the Geneva Convention.

Counterpoise • Equilibrium
SKAGWAY • OCTOBER 1899

ON OCTOBER 12, newspaper headlines announced that eighty thousand armed Boers from the Transvaal and the Orange Free State had attacked twenty-five thousand British soldiers in southern Africa. The Boers invaded Natal in the south and laid siege to Mafeking in the west.

Fred began feeling the giddy Lure of Peril.

"Perhaps your blood is rising to be in the Transvaal now," Burnham wrote to Rider Haggard. "I acknowledge that mine is, and at least six hours each day I see in my mind the roads, trails and streams leading from Kimberley to Pretoria. I pick out the exact and proper spots to camp and where to watch for ambush, where to stage and rest the stock, obtain fuel and make laager."

Fred paced the floor as fidgety as a badger. In six weeks, General Redvers Buller blundered so badly he almost lost southern Africa.

317

Burnham: King of Scouts

The Boers laid siege first to Ladysmith and then to Kimberley, trapping Cecil Rhodes in a ring of fire at the diamond mines. General Gatacre, one of Buller's three field commanders, blundered into a night ambush at Stormberg and suffered seven hundred casualties. His troopers nicknamed him Back Acher.

Five days later, Redvers Buller attacked Colenso, but he was outmaneuvered by General Louis Botha. Buller retreated with a thousand casualties and earned the nickname Sir Reverse Buller.

Time after time the British forces went down in defeat, and always for the same reason: poor intelligence. British public opinion demanded action. When General Buller cabled the War Office to suggest that the British surrender Ladysmith, Wolseley was forced to replace him.

In a turnabout, the cabinet selected the leader of the India Ring to become the commander of British forces in Africa. Field Marshal Lord Roberts—Bobs to his men—believed in winning battles, not sacrificing men for empty battlefield glory. Fred's pacing grew more urgent. He had no idea that a chance encounter half way around the world would change his life.

Lagnappe • A Little Extra

MAFEKING • NOVEMBER 1899

IN THE PLACE OF STONES, five thousand Boers ringed Baden-Powell's two thousand defenders. Boers imperiled Colonel Plumer's Rhodesia Regiment, camped at Pitsani to the north. That diversion was exactly what Lord Wolseley had in mind—keep the Boers occupied on a sacrificial mission until the British Army could transport a dozen shiploads of troops to Cape Town and Durban.

At first, the Boers were content to fire artillery shells at Mafeking. Then they launched an infantry attack. Baden-Powell repulsed the strike so well that the Boers did not repeat that tactic for six months.

Yet, the Boers did nothing to sever communications. They failed to halt mail or telegraph service between Mafeking and the outside world. Stephe mailed the corrected proofs of the manuscript for *Cavalry Aids to Scouting*. Every day Stephe sent off telegraph dispatches.

"Four hours' bombardment," he reported. "One dog killed. All is well" After so many setbacks, the British were starving for reassurance, and the public took these literal truths as stiff-upper-lip understatements. The more casual, gay and offhand that Baden-Powell's dispatches became, the more the British came to believe that Mafeking was suffering hideously.

Ritornello • Interlude
SOUTHAMPTON • DECEMBER 1899

AS HE BOARDED the *Dunotter Castle* for Cape Town, Lord Roberts was thinking that two days before Christmas was a dreadful time to leave a man's wife at home, specially when their only son was at the front.

As the ship steamed down the Southampton estuary, General Lord Roberts conducted Officers Call. Well-known subordinates came to pay their respects and unknowns came to get acquainted. One officer, a colonial who was returning to Rhodesia, caught Lord Roberts' attention. He was the grim-faced Captain Harry White of the Victoria Scouts. When the failures of British intelligence in the field came up, Harry White jumped from his chair and began waving his arms. He spoke excitedly of the American who had scouted for the Chartered Company in 1893.

"Burnham was the finest scout in the Combined Column," he declared. "Jameson said if there were ten Burnhams we would have won the war in half the time."

Roberts ignored Captain White's outburst, a mild violation of military decorum.

"Burnham survived Wilson's Last Stand," White said. "In 1896, he saved Bulawayo with an assegai attack at the Battle of Colenbrander's Farm. And for good measure, he shot the M'Limo, ending the Rebellion."

"If this Burnham chap is so good," Roberts said, "why don't we get him?"

Seven days hence the ship would anchor at Madeira off Morocco. While coaling, they would pick up General Sir Herbert Kitchener of Egypt, who was to be Lord Bobs' second in command.

"When we stop at Madeira, I'll send a cable." White said.

"Permission granted, Captain. I hope this man lives up to your expectations."

"On that, Sir, I will stake my very reputation."

"You just did, Captain."

42

Richard Harding Davis

SKAGWAY • JANUARY 1900

FRED'S SUMMONS came on Thursday, January 4. The *City of Seattle* anchored on the tidal flats south of Skagway. Young Rod Burnham was there to meet the ship and pick up his bundle of newspapers from the *Seattle Post-Intelligencer*, which he delivered to neighboring homes. The ship's purser spotted The Kid and called out.

"There's a cablegram for your papa. Tell him he can pick it up at the Post Office." Rod dropped his papers and ran home to tell The Dad. Burnham jumped up from the breakfast table and ran to the Post Office. The cablegram, from Madeira via London, New York and Seattle, had been addressed to Skagway, British Columbia, Canada. After it dead-ended, a Western Union official rerouted it via ship to Skagway, District of Alaska, USA. Fred's hands trembled as he opened the envelope.

Lord Roberts appoints you to his personal staff, all expenses paid. If you accept, start shortest way to Cape Town and report yourself to him. Captain Harry White.

The *City of Seattle* was scheduled to depart Skagway before the tide fell that day, less than four hours away. By that time, Fred had sold or given away everything he owned in Skagway, save his mineral claims. He sold his interest in the electric power plant to Doctor Ira White, allowing his friend to make payments from future earnings. When the ship left for Seattle, Fred, Blanche, Rod and Bruce were aboard. Fred Burnham was going to be the chief of scouts for Lord Roberts. He had worked all his life for this opportunity and he wasn't going to let anything stop him now. He didn't know it yet, but his day was just dawning. Tomorrow was the beginning of his life.

The Boer War

•••
SOUTHAMPTON • JANUARY 1900

The sun didn't shine and the skies were the color of wet concrete at dawn on Saturday the 27th. It had been like that for several days since the Burnhams arrived at England's premier seaport from America. Southampton, eighty miles southeast of London, was at the north end of a well protected estuary. It was a port of call for ships traveling world wide and a terminal for ferries cruising to the Isle of Wight, the site of Queen Victoria's favorite palace, Osborne House. It was said that since the Queen had been named Empress of India a quarter of a century ago, she had spent a fortune decorating the Durbo Room with memorabilia from India.

At five minutes to seven, the foghorn on the *H.M.S. Scot* tooted a blast of steam and the purser strode the decks calling, "All ashore who're goin ashore."

Fred hugged the boys and kissed Blanche. As she and the boys debarked for a wartime stay in London, Blanche handed Fred a packet of newspaper cuttings. The mooring lines were cast off and the ship slipped into the estuary.

Two hours later, the vessel was slipping through the water with the grace of an otter, making eighteen knots. Fred sat down in a wicker deck chair and covered himself with a tan woolen blanket. He began to read.

WILL SCOUT FOR BOBS
Burnham on His Way to Africa;
The Pasadena Adventurer Has an Opportunity
To Make a Name for Himself in the War

SEATTLE, Jan. 10 — A man and a woman are speeding across the American continent to New York, there to catch the steamship Lucania *for Europe. Within hours of the time the summons reached him in Skagway, Fred Burnham was aboard the steamer* City of Seattle. *He and Mrs. Burnham came to this city a week ago, remaining here two days visiting friends and preparing for the journey, starting east today on the Great Northern Railroad.*

When Fred finished, he dozed. An hour later, he was awakened by Maurice Gifford, whose left sleeve was pinned to the side of his jacket. Gifford introduced Fred to his deck companions, Dick and Margaret.

Fred recognized the husband as Richard Harding Davis, the American war correspondent, a writer with an enormous following. The debonair and handsome Davis dressed the part of upper class New York society. He wore a tailored khaki safari jacket, breeches,

321

knee-length leather boots, a white shirt, tie and striped cap. The only things missing were a walking stick and boutonniere. Davis was reporting for Hearst's *Journal* and for *Harper's Monthly.*

"I read *Soldiers of Fortune* in the Klondike," Fred said.

"You should be part of it," Davis said, "but alas, 'tis only fiction."

"Mrs. Davis is an artist," Gifford said, explaining her reason for traveling to the war zone.

"I'd like to sketch you, Mr. Burnham," she said. Fred saw a woman of striking beauty who looked like she had stepped out of a Fifth Avenue boutique.

"How about the ship's library?" Fred suggested. "I'm reading Lord Roberts' *Forty-one Years in India.*"

"What's the book you are holding now?" she asked.

"*The Nile Campaign* by Winston Churchill."

"Did you hear? Churchill has escaped from Pretoria Prison," Davis said. "Plucky devil." Fred saw Davis as a husky man, with big hands, a large head, powerful jaw and a deeply cleft chin. His image was that of power, the equal of any general or admiral.

Fred had the impression that Margaret was trying to be a man. *She imitates her husband's weaknesses, and looses her feminine charms. If she were content to be a woman, she'd be a queen. As it is now, she is not a wife. She is a competitor, an affront to the institution of marriage.*

The Spanish-American War had proved beyond any doubt that wars build newspaper circulation. A demand for news from the front was making the occupation of war correspondent well-paid. Publishers vied to hire famous names to cover the war, and the luminaries of the writing craft were headed for south Africa. At a time when men were happy to earn two dollars a day, the London *Morning Post* was paying Winston Churchill twelve hundred dollars a month plus expenses. Newsmen covering the Boer War were the cream of the profession.

Among the famous reporters that attracted Fred's eye was one Teddy had mentioned, a man who had covered the Rough Riders in the war with Spain. Stephen Crane's story and picture appeared on the back of one of Burnham's news clips. With his elephant ears and hair parted in the middle, Crane looked like he'd be more at home in a little red schoolhouse.

Victorian newsmen sensed the mood of the home front at a time when Englishmen were the most patriotic people in the world. The vogue in London was, "It's good to be an Englishman." Writers peppered articles with phrases like "the common man of empire" and "the fundamental grit of the breed."

• • •

FRED'S FAME from Wilson's Last Stand and the shooting of the M'Limo, plus his new appointment to Lord Robert's staff, made him a celebrity. For the next seventeen days, officers probed his knowledge of African affairs. During encounters on deck, at impromptu meetings during lunch, and at evening sessions in the smoking lounge, Fred was quizzed by veterans who asked probing questions.

Davis witnessed these encounters. As he looked on, men who had held command in India or The Sudan fired questions at Fred. His answers provided fresh insights for men about to assume assignments in Africa.

"Many years of veld life have honed the Boers into a tall, big-boned people, fine horsemen, good rifle shots, a race blessed with tenacity," he said. "On the veld they are self-reliant. With tools so scanty a European mechanic would throw up his hands in despair, the Boer farmer will repair his ox wagon—or build a new one outright from wood hewn out of the forest."

As Fred spoke, Davis took notes. Maggie sketched.

"Burnham," Davis later wrote, "is as unlike the scout of fiction and the Wild West show as it is possible to be. He possesses no flowing locks. His talk is not of greasers, grizzly b'ars or pesky redskins. He is slight, muscular, bronzed, with a finely formed square jaw, and remarkable blue eyes. Those eyes apparently never leave yours, but in reality they see everything behind you, about you, and below you. In manner he is quiet and courteous, talking slowly but well and he seems extremely modest."

In the privacy of his stateroom, Fred was beginning to understand what others meant when they said the British Army was divided into the India Ring and the Africa Clique. In London, the secretary of state for war, Lord Lansdowne, a former viceroy of India, had nominated Lord Roberts, the former commanding general in India, to head the British Army in southern Africa. And Roberts had taken his India veterans along on his personal staff. Wherever Fred went, he heard the jargon of colonial India. An Englishman was an *Angrezi*. White people were *sahiblog* who gathered at noon for *tiffin*. A *sepoy* was a soldier. The Sepoy Mutiny was a rebellion of common Indian soldiers.

Another night, another crowd. Colonel Sir Charles Hunter asked, "What's the difference between an Afrikander and a Boer?"

"None," Fred replied, "but I like to make this distinction. The Afrikanders live in the cities and generally have come to terms with the British. Many of them have learned to speak English. The Boers are rustic farmers who live on the veld. Let me put it this way. If the Englishman is now entering the 20th century, the Afrikander is still in the 19th century and the Boer remains firmly rooted in the 18th century."

Fred was delighted to hear a voice from the rear call out, "Bayete, Nkosi." It was the Matabele salute to the king, coming from the Africa Clique.

"Is it really possible," asked a British officer, "that one hundred Boers are a match for five hundred European soldiers?" Winston Churchill had recently made headlines with that statement.

"The Boer is a more accurate marksman than his British counterpart," Fred conceded. "But he's not as fast. The Boer is taught to conserve his ammunition, to make careful estimates of the sun and wind. He has an advantage over the soldier who has never fired a shot other than at a black spot in a white ring."

In his stateroom that evening, Davis summarized his notes in a journal. "It is interesting," he wrote, "to see a fellow countryman, one praised so highly, so completely make good. It is not as though he had a credulous audience of tourists. The questions each man asks are the outcome of their own experiences or observations. They want to know what difference there is in a column of dust raised by cavalry and by trek wagons, how to tell whether a horse that passed was going at a trot or a gallop, the way to throw a diamond hitch, or to make fire without becoming a target yourself—why, what and how?

"Not for a single evening could a faker submit to the examinations through which they are putting Burnham and not expose his ignorance. Within two nights, he has us so absolutely at his mercy that we would follow him anywhere. What makes us admire him most is that when he does not know, he says so at once."

At another quiz, Burnham said, "Boers on commando duty wear rough garb, usually shirts and trousers of coarse linsey-woolsey, with wide-brimmed hats to ward off the heat and the glare of the sun," he said. "They are a sullen, unsmiling lot who never bathe in the field. Each man carries his own rifle, and he wears a belt of cartridges around his waist and a bandoleer flung over his shoulder. These people are fond of their rifles and proud of their marksmanship.

"The Boer army is unlike any other in the world," Fred continued. "The men are not paid. No medals are awarded. The officers are elected. Apart from senior commanders and the field artillery, they are barely trained in the military sciences. Their units are organized into commandos, and many of the burghers take their wives and children along into battle. They are tough and they know bush warfare from fighting the Zulu."

There was a stir and murmuring. An officer in his cups cried out, "You sound sympathetic to the enemy."

A flush crept over Fred's face.

"Until now, I've confined my remarks to facts," Fred said. "If you want my opinion, I'll tell you. The Boers are expert riders, crack shots and masters of terrain, but they are destined to lose this war. They'll lose because they're not disciplined. Anyone who goes home to plant seeds or harvest crops will lose a war against a disciplined army."

There was a burst of applause and the talk continued.

"Asking a scout on an ocean liner to prove his ability," Davis wrote that night, "is certainly placing him under a severe handicap. One British officer told me, 'It's about as fair as though we planted the captain of this ship in the Sahara Desert and asked him to prove that he could run a ten thousand ton ocean liner.'"

That evening, Davis made a daily journal entry that was to became the basis for a book titled *Real Soldiers of Fortune*.

Burnham has taught himself to use a gun in either hand," he wrote, *"and to shoot Indian fashion, hanging by one leg from his horse and using the animal as cover. He can turn in the saddle and shoot behind him. Tonight I asked if he really could shoot to the rear from a galloping horse and hit a man.*

"Maybe not good enough to hit him," he replied, "but I can come close enough to convince him my pony's so much faster than his pony that it isn't really worth his while to follow me."

Davis closed his journal. Margaret was asleep, lulled by the surge of water gliding past the riveted steel hull. Davis wasn't sleepy so he decided on a nightcap. While strolling to the lounge, he met Burnham who was walking on deck and eating an apple.

"A penny for your thoughts," Davis said, falling in step and lighting a Cuban cigar.

"I'm suffering from a mild case of the anxieties."

"From your dissertations, I got the impression you are in command of affairs."

"Don't worry about me. It's those British officers."

"Weren't you brought in to improve the scouting?"

Davis tipped his hat in salute to a young couple strolling on deck.

"I've been reading Lord Roberts' book *Forty-one Years in India*," Burnham said. "From his writings and after talking with the British officers, I am convinced they have a false impression of the enemy."

325

"The Boers fight for independence against frightful odds," Davis replied. "In my opinion, their motives are as pure as the American Minute Man called from his farm in 1775. But explain your views. Mine don't count."

"For half a century," Fred said, "the British have been fighting bush wars against tribesmen in India and Africa. Their staff officers have no concept of maneuvering in the field like we developed in the War Between the States."

"Interesting," Davis said. "Go on."

"British generals see their duty as getting men and equipment to the battlefield. They leave the tactics to the field commanders. Assembling the men for a campaign can take several months, but the battle is expected to be over in a few hours. Directed against the Boers, Mr. Davis, that strategy will fail."

"You may have uncovered the major flaw of our British colleagues. But why are they blind?"

"It's easy enough to see," Fred said, tossing his apple core overboard. "British maneuvers are played on the field at Sandhurst. These one-day affairs always end in time for high tea. The Boers will fight around the clock."

"So the British play at war and the Boers work at it," Davis said tossing his cigar into the briny. "You have just sharpened my eyes. This war will be no brush hunt."

43

Scouting for Kitchener

CAPE TOWN • FEBRUARY 1900

HOWIE BRIBED a Boer guard in Johannesburg for a pass to cross the lines to the British side. When Fred debarked in Cape Town, Howie was at dockside to greet him.

"Where'd you get that soup strainer, Fred?"

"During the voyage, the sea air fertilized the hair under my nose."

"I've booked rooms at the Mount Nelson Hotel," Howard said. "It's as lovely as The Shephards in Cairo. Our carriage is waiting."

To Fred, peg-leg little brother seemed as healthy as ever.

In their hotel room, Howard ordered tea for Fred and beer for himself. Howie removed his wooden leg and rested the stump on a footstool.

"You're famous, Fred," he said. "The Boers predict they will have you behind bars in three weeks. Two Boer scouts, Danny Theron and Fritz Duquesne, are publicly vying for the honor of splitting your skull with a Mauser bullet."

"I wasn't born to be killed by any Boer," Fred snapped. "If either of those pilgrims shows himself, he'll go out strapped to his saddle, toes down."

"Hold on, old hoss," Howard said. "That was the Boers talking, not me. Hey, I see your old pal Bathing-Towel is trapped at Spooksdorp."

"Spooksdorp?"

"That's what the Boers call Mafeking."

"I thought Colonel Hamilton Goold-Adams ran the show up there."

"Guess he had the good sense to clear out before the Boers arrived.

327

Do you think it'll be a short war, Fred?"

"I don't know. I feel like I'm waking up after a long, lazy sleep. The blood stirs in my veins."

"Let's put on the nose bag," Howard suggested. "It might be the last civilized feed you get for awhile."

• • •

FRED WAS ONE OF three civilians—he had not yet been sworn in—issued a pass that day to board the military train for the front. It left at 9 p.m. and Fred stretched out on the green leather cushions to sleep. That day he watched the hills of the Great Karroo pass by. *They are flat-topped like the mesas of Arizona. Most of the refugees walking south are black.*

At De Aar, the central rail junction for south Africa, the land was as flat as a billiard table. As the train took on coal and water, he got out to stretch his legs and think. Huge stores of munitions confirmed that De Aar was the main supply base for Lord Roberts' Army.

The following night, at a desolate hour during a rainstorm, the train deposited Fred at Watervaal Drift on the Riet River south of Kimberley. He tried to refresh his memory of the landscape from three years past when visiting Rhodes and the Big Hole. Though the rainy season was supposedly over, the gods this year were angry. Water poured down as if the bung of the ocean had been yanked. How could an army hunt the wily Boer when the drifts were impassable, the spruits were sloshing with water and the vleys were sloppy gumbo?

Headquarters was a wilderness of mud: tents, men, horses, oxen and mules scattered on the veld—transport wagons were mired in mud up to the hubs. Fred slogged to the headquarters tent where he reported to the adjutant, the man who issued uniforms and gear.

"Can you tolerate being lodged with a haggis-eater?" he asked. It was an implausible coincidence and Fred had time only to shake hands with Major Terry Laing before he was summoned to meet the commander in chief.

"This is real African campaigning," Fred said on being presented to Lord Roberts. "You bivouac in what you're standing in."

Roberts laughed heartily.

"Come sit down, Captain Burnham."

Roberts was shorter than Fred, with broad shoulders and a straight back. He was a look-you-in-the-eye kind of leader dressed in a khaki uniform and cavalry boots. A black armband said Roberts was in mourning for a son who had died in combat. Fred heard the lad had earned the Victoria Cross. And this silver-haired man of seventy had, himself, won his spurs fifty years ago when he pacified Afghanistan by leading a force into Kandahar.

"They tell me you're the best spoor wallah in Africa," Roberts said. "Would you care for tea?"

"I hope my services are up to your expectations."

"My expectations are high, specially since your endorsement comes from Captain Harry White."

As Roberts stirred his tea, Fred became aware that Bobs was blind in one eye.

An orderly stepped inside the tent to say General Kitchener had arrived.

Fred rose to leave.

"Stay, I want you to meet him."

General Herbert Lord Kitchener, called Kitchener of Khartoum, was all that his reputation suggested. Twenty years younger than Roberts, he stood ramrod straight, smelling of brass and leather. Kitchener's skin was burned mahogany from the Sudan Campaign where two years ago his Maxims had inflicted thirty thousand casualties on the whirling dervishes. It soon became apparent to Fred that Kitchener regarded the Boers as savages with only a veneer of civilization. *I can see why that, behind his back, the troops call him the Stinking Egyptian.*

• • •

FRED LEFT AT dawn for Paardeberg, twenty-two miles to the east to scout the opposition ahead. Lord Roberts was directing his main force against General Piet Cronje, the commandant of the Western Front. Defeating Cronje, who three years ago had trapped the Jameson Raiders, would provide a boost to British morale.

Meanwhile, General Jack French, a storybook soldier with dark hair, a straight nose and tea-straining mustache, was leading a cavalry column of nine thousand men to rescue Cecil Rhodes who was trapped at Kimberley.

It was a dismal, overcast Sunday as Fred rode well ahead of the main force to the brow of a small hill. Ahead was a meadow several miles wide. The Modder River wriggled like a brown serpent, flanked on each side by green cottonwood trees. *Paardeberg Kopje looks like a mesa back in Arizona, even to the purple haze.*

Burnham: King of Scouts

The Boer general Cronje's column, in laager, was strung out for half a mile. Children played in the field while wives kindled breakfast fires. Little white puff balls appeared in the sky, followed by the pop of bursting artillery. The shots hadn't come from Roberts' column or Fred would have heard the moaning of the lyddite shells overhead. Was it General French? Had he relieved Kimberley and galloped to the other side of Cronje to lock him in a ring of fire?

Children were being blown to bits, tiny arms and legs flying about the air like popcorn. Mothers abandoned the fires. In an incredibly short time, Cronje's sprawling laager inspanned and made a dash for the Modder River. In ten minutes, the Boer leader had hidden his entire force—four thousand men, women and children—in the banks of that crooked river. For such a large force, it was an incredibly fast maneuver.

Fred estimated the banks of the Modder to be eroded to a depth of ten feet. With the flat plain stretching out for a mile, Cronje's Mauser rifles would have the advantage. The only chance of defeating him lay in starving him out. Another Boer general, Christian De Wet, reputed to be in the area, might ride in to break up a British siege. Fred galloped back to Jacobsdal to tell Lord Roberts.

On arriving, he learned that Lord Roberts had been stricken with typhoid fever. General Kitchener, who had assumed command, ordered Fred to escort him to Paardeberg Kopje.

From the summit Fred saw British troopers digging in, forming a long arc a mile back from Cronje's riverine fortress. Kitchener operated from his horse without the aid of staff officers. The commanders in the field seemed unsure and Kitchener refused to issue written orders, counting on verbal commands. *This man wears a general's uniform but he has a captain's mind.*

Somewhere to the south, De Wet was probably riding to Cronje's aid. Fred fully expected that Lord Kitchener would send him to scout the veld for General De Wet's whereabouts. If the Boers were heading for General French's rear, the British would be obliged to cut them off. At 4 p.m., Burnham was summoned to Kitchener's presence. He was prepared for a hard ride.

"Barnum, I want you to nip into Cronje's camp and report back to me on the disposition of his forces."

"Yes, Sir," Fred said, saluting. He was so taken aback by the unexpected order that he failed to protest. Scouting Cronje's fortress was a pure waste of time. Everyone had seen there were four thousand people dug in and ready to shoot.

Fred found a Cape native and asked him to locate a large wooden

The Boer War

box and to skin a dead ox. Next he requisitioned a mule and cart. Half an hour later he found the native by the corral skinning the dead animal. The stench of decaying flesh suggested the animal had been deceased for some time.

"That the freshest hide you could find?"

"Yas, baas. Quartermaster, he issue all fresh oxes as rations."

Fred placed the box on the mule cart, covered it with the wet oxhide, and with his sheath knife cut peep holes in the four sides. He geed the mule toward the river about a mile upstream from Cronje's camp. There he backed the cart into the water. The square outline was a dead giveaway so he had no choice but to wait for nightfall.

"I t'ink dem Boers shoot you sure, baas," the native said cheerfully.

"Hyena milk. Take the cart back to the Quartermaster or I'll shoot you."

It began to rain which washed away only a bit of the stink. As darkness settled, he slithered into the water and came up inside the box. The water was cold and the stench was beyond putrefying. Fred wished he had some mint drops.

He drifted down the river, irritated because the flow was so slow. His foot touched a sandbar that felt like quicksand. His progress was hindered by the limbs of submerged trees that had toppled when their roots became eroded away. Several times he had to swim outside to free the box from branches or roots. He thought of The Kid, who was being tutored by an Oxford scholar, and of Bruce, who was cutting teeth. *We'll have such good times after the war.*

Ahead twinkled the light of a kerosine lantern and Fred entered the Boer camp. The Modder was narrow here and the current picked up speed. He shot through Cronje's nest too fast to accurately estimate the disposition of the forces. In moments, the last of the lamps disappeared and once again it was dark along the river. Had he not known that Cronje had

Burnham: King of Scouts

four thousand people dug in, he'd estimate the force at more like four hundred.

Fred had been two hours in the water. He was numb and nauseated, but he was now far enough from the Boer camp that he could chuck the box and swim to shore.

Then both ankles became tangled. While coasting with the current, he was dragged underwater as the hide and box sailed on down river. He gulped muddy water. He needed air. Stars flashed. With a desperate heave, he pulled himself down to find what gripped his ankles so tightly. He felt a wagon wheel and knew his feet were caught in the converging spokes. Two kicks released the grip. Lungs bursting and arms flailing, he suddenly was free.

Moments later he thrashed to the surface and sucked in huge gulps of cool, fresh air. He lay on the bank for twenty minutes, vomiting and catching his breath.

Half an hour later, he got up and staggered back to British lines where he made a brief report. General Kitchener wasn't impressed.

"Heavens, get yourself a bath, man. You smell worse than a dead ox."

Ritornello • An Interlude

ALDERSHOT • FEBRUARY 1900

WHEN COLONEL Baden-Powell's corrected proofs for *Cavalry Aids to Scouting* arrived from Mafeking, publishers Gale and Polten were scarcely able to believe their good fortune. They had been granted a license to print money. Stephe's telegrams from Mafeking relayed by cable to London had made him famous. His celebrity status turned an obscure military tome into an instant best-seller. In a matter of weeks, Gale and Polten sold a hundred thousand copies of the book.

Counterpoise • Equilibrium

PAARDEBERG KOPJE • FEBRUARY 1900

MISTY RAIN with freaky blowing gusts and rumbles of thunder marred Sunday the 18th. Soldiers were huddled in raincoats around smoky fires. As they sipped tea, word was passed that the First Welch and Scottish Highlanders, Terry Laing's regiment, would make the initial assault.

Kitchener had ordered volley fire.

At 6 a.m., the tranquillity of Paardeberg Kopje was broken by the moan of shells from twenty lyddite guns belching flame and smoke. As the shells cut through the air, they sounded like the tearing of linen. Directed against Cronje's dug-in troops, the guns had little effect other than to smash some ox wagons and kill a few horses. General Kitchener studied his watch and turned to a staff officer.

"It's now 7 o'clock," he declared. "We shall be in their laager by half past 10."

From the ranks came a cockney voice, "Gorblimey, mates, this barmey'll have us dead by then."

"Stiff upper lip, men," Kitchener urged. "Before the day is over, you'll have something to tell your grandchildren." *His mustache masks a cruel mouth that reveals itself only when he speaks.*

At the sound of the bugle, the First Welch and the Highlanders began their assault. As soon as they marched onto the veld and lined up for volley fire, the riverbank came to life. *Kitchener cares little for the butcher's bill. He chooses colonials—Gurkhas, Egyptians, Welsh, Irish and Scots—before calling in the English soldiers.*

The sharp crack of the Mauser rifles was followed by the whir made by the steel-jacketed bullets, sounding like a flight of locusts. A flash of lightning froze the scene, followed by a clap of thunder. A harsh African rainstorm had erupted.

Accurate Boer rifle fire halted the British assault. On the brow of the hill, Kitchener swore under his breath as he rode his horse to and fro. Scores of men toppled, dead or wounded. The general ordered the lines reformed for a new attack. The men regrouped and continued their volley fire, with alternate advances, but they were cut down by the numbers. *This guy is another Major Forbes.*

As the day passed, Fred came to realize that he was watching the birth of a new kind of land warfare. While the British stood in open volley fire, the Boers fired from trenches, with a no-man's-land between. *Can't Kitchener see that troopers standing exposed on the field are on the losing side of this battle?*

Stretcher bearers carried away the bodies of men slain in battle. At the rear, Cape natives dug open pits for the dead, their bodies wrapped in blankets and piled like cordwood. As lightning and thunder crashed across the veld, Fred listened in sadness to the mournful notes of the Black Watch bagpipers skirling for their departed.

Two hours after noon, Lord Kitchener ordered the mounted infantry to join the battle. An unexpected sound of bugles alerted everyone to a new threat. To the south, General De Wet's army was firing on French's cavalry. Kitchener was forced to cancel the assault and order the men to dig in. The tempest of conflicting orders that day gave rise to the nickname Kitchener of Chaos.

● ● ●

ON MONDAY, Lord Bobs, now recovered, inspected the scene of battle. When he learned of the death toll, he ordered that Cronje's force be starved out. For nine days the British bivouacked in a great arc along the Modder River.

The stench of rotting horses, mules and oxen slain in battle grew unendurable. The troopers dragged the rotted, bloated carcasses to the river and let them float down to Cronje's camp. They wanted to pollute the water, creating dysentery—British troopers called it the Modders—and force the Boer general to surrender. Until Cronje's force was dislodged, the British Army could not advance on Bloemfontein, the next target on Lord Roberts' line of march. It was now midsummer and Roberts had set a goal of reaching Pretoria before the winter rains set in.

General Cronje finally surrendered on Tuesday, the 27th. That happened to be Majuba Day, the anniversary of the Boer victory over the British in the first Boer War. As the sun peeped through fluffy clouds, Cronje and his army, trapped in a stinkfontein of maimed women and starving children, raised a white flag.

As dogs barked and children cried, General Cronje, tall, bearded and wearing an overcoat and slouch hat, climbed out of the riverbed at the head of a collection of rumpled people. Lord Roberts, wearing starched khakis and polished boots, accepted the surrender.

A British photographer on the scene recorded the event. The picture, called *The Giant Surrendering to the Midget*, was published in newspapers around the world.

44

Ambush at Koorn Spruit

MODDER RIVER • FEBRUARY 1900

FRED WORKED alone in the Boer War. Cecil Rhodes, formerly trapped at Kimberley, had now returned to Groot Shure in Cape Town. Doctor Jameson, paroled from prison, was ill in London. Fred Selous was hunting elk in the American Rockies. In Rhodesia, Johann Colenbrander debated over which side to join. General Carrington was in England seeking volunteers for a Rhodesian battalion. Baden-Powell was besieged at Mafeking. Fred's only chum was Tyrie Laing, always off on some mission in the backblocks.

As chief scout to Lord Roberts, Burnham worked alone in the field. When the army was fighting, he watched. It was in the lengthy periods between the battles that he saw action. Typically, a mile of veld separated the British and the Boer forces. Fred's task was to cross this no-man's-land and penetrate enemy lines. If he made it, he would spy out the enemy and bring back information to aid in the next attack.

This war was different. The Boer was no spear-carrying black man dashing about on the veld. He was a superb horseman, able to move incredible distances by night. He was fighting on his own turf and he knew every inch of it. This war was being fought on high prairie not unlike the American West. Rolling hills limited the use of the Maxim gun. The land was semiarid, crossed by dry gulches and dotted with cactus like the prickly pear of the American Southwest. Fred felt right at home.

• • •

AFTER CRONJE'S surrender, Lord Roberts sent Burnham to scout Petrusberg, the only settlement on the railway route between Kimberley and Bloemfontein. While riding to Petrusberg Fred felt like

The Boer War

he was near Florence, in Pinal County west of Globe.

Thought it was only twenty miles away and despite several tries, Fred failed to reach Petrusberg. He was foiled by barbed wire so he returned to camp. From the Quartermaster, he requisitioned a set of wire cutters—his problem with barbed wire was solved.

On his second try, he left before sunset, traveling alone. He'd chance a crossing of no-man's-land at dusk, trusting that during the dinner hour the Boers might let down their guard. Some time after passing through the neutral zone, Fred became aware that he was being stalked by a lone horseman. The stranger was a skilled rider, well mounted and drawing closer. At a distance of eight hundred yards, the Boer began to study him through field glasses. Then the man unslung his rifle. Fred wondered if he'd try a shot at that extreme distance.

Burnham geed his horse along a zigzag route. A shot echoed across the veld, followed by a second. Fred knew there was little chance of being hit at that distance, but he worried the noise might attract Boers. The man began riding toward him at a full gallop. Fred hid behind an ant heap, but the pursuing horseman dismounted and moments later bullets began thudding into the ground around him. That's when Fred guessed the Boer's plan. The ant heap provided protection for himself, but not for his horse. His pursuer meant to shoot his horse and run him down. The rider was only four hundred yards away when Fred dismounted, took aim and on his second shot, the Boer pony fell. The power of his pursuer to chase him was ended. Fred mounted and rode into the darkness.

Hours later, as dawn loomed, Fred found himself far behind enemy lines, still less than half way to Petrusburg. He decided to hide out for the day and use his position as a jumping-off point that night. He found a tree-lined vley to hide in.

Half a mile away, a Boer farmhouse on a gentle slope overlooked the gully, but a thicket of trees and bushes minimized any chance of being detected. Fred hobbled his horse and crept fifty yards to a bushy spruit. He slept most of the day and rode along the spruit until he was out of sight.

Toward dusk he saw three horsemen a hundred yards ahead. Two were natives, Boer friendlies. The third was a white man dressed like Fred's pursuer of last night. Fred spurred his horse along a route that would avoid the strangers, an act regarded as not hospitable. The Boer dispatched a native to follow him. Fred spurred his horse, but the native was well mounted and after a good gallop caught up—though not before Fred put some trees between himself and the pursuing Boer. As the black man approached, Fred drew his revolver and ordered the man to ride alongside. The native pulled back on the reins as if to flee.

"If you even blink, I'll shoot you dead," Fred warned.

Only after he cocked his pistol did the man seem to understand.

"You better not kill me, Nkosi," the black man said. "My baas, he be Danny Theron. He now get better horse. He shoot you head off."

"Is his horse fresh?" Fred asked.

"Yas, new. Old horse dead. Danny Theron mad."

Questioning revealed that Theron commanded the scouting patrol. That's why he hadn't been able to get through the pickets last night. Theron's Scouts were the best on the veld. Danny Theron's presence meant General De Wet would be nearby—that news was vital information. Fred dismissed the scout and returned to Paardeberg to report the presence of Theron's Scouts to Lord Roberts. The next day the British Army circled around Petrusburg. On Tuesday, March 13, they rode into Bloemfontein without firing a shot.

Ritornello • Interlude

KROONSTAD • MARCH 1900

STATE ATTORNEY Jannie Smuts served as the recording secretary at a council of war. Presidents Kruger and Steyn made impassioned speeches to their followers. Kruger spoke in Biblical terms, but Steyn was down to earth.

To Smuts, the most important act of the meeting was to appoint General Christiaan de Wet as commandant general of Boer defenses in the Orange Free State. De Wet was a man of medium height, stocky, with a well-trimmed beard and mustache. Wearing a civilian coat, vest and watch chain, he looked like any middle class businessman.

General de Wet issued orders that changed the nature of the Boer War. He gave the commandos ten days leave to visit their farms, after which the ablest men would return refreshed. All the men in poor health would remain behind.

In switching to guerrilla warfare, the trek wagons that had hampered General Cronje at Paardeberg were abandoned. The women and children would remain at home. From now on the Boers would hunt and pick their targets. De Wet sent a column to seize Sannah's Post.

Counterpoise • Equilibrium

BLOEMFONTEIN • MARCH 1900

WHEN THE BRITISH occupied Bloemfontein, it seemed like the war was over. There wasn't a Boer anywhere. The British captured all the enemy military supplies, horses, homes, buildings, meal and warehouses. The Boers failed to practice scorched earth.

Bloemfontein had no sewer system—its water supply was polluted and the town proved to be the most disease-ridden city in southern Africa. Lord Roberts' advance was halted as soldiers were struck down with typhoid fever, a form of dysentery. Roberts himself had been an early victim. Although the disease ran its course in five to ten days, its victims remained weak for a month. A quarter of the troops were laid up in hospital tents and each day about fifty troopers died. Suddenly, the waterworks at Sannah's Post became a prize to be protected at all costs.

For those who avoided veld fever, Bloemfontein was a good bivouac. Lord Roberts' staff was billeted in the mansion of the foreign secretary of the Orange Free State. While dining on roast goose, Fred and Terry sat at a carved table talking to Laing's new friend, the editor of the Army newspaper, *The Friend*.

Rudyard Kipling was famous for having captured the very odors of empire. He looked more like a bank clerk than a famous writer and poet. His steel-rim glasses seemed undersized for his shaggy eyebrows and mustache.

"If Mafeking were to fall, Laddie, it would be seen in London as a dreadful blow ta the war effort," Laing said.

"Out there in the far fringes of nowhere?" Fred asked. "Come on, Terry."

"You fail understand to British mind," Kipling piped in. "War, Sir, is a marvelous game, the greatest sport of all."

To Fred, it seemed that Kipling was trying to explain the mysteries of life itself.

"You've seen those messages Baden-Powell sends oot on the wire. 'One or two field guns shelling the town. Nobody cares.'"

"Why should they care?" Fred asked.

"That's characteristic of nonchalant British courage," Kipling offered. "Those gay messages printed around the world—insisting that all is well—are seen by the British as an indication of just how desperate matters really are."

"Dinna ya see? It tells them to keep a stiff upper lip."

"I'm not sure that I understand," Fred said shaking his head.

"Perhaps you don't, for aw that," said Kipling. "It would be a nuisance to go through it all again. It's a rather intricate story, you know." Having finished his goose leg, the writer-poet-turned-editor put on his straw hat and slouched out of the dining room to meet a deadline.

Fred turned to Terry.

"After Paardeberg, I think that Stinking Egyptian deserves the burial of a jackass," Fred said, "on a refuse heap."

"Aye, Laddie, that may be true. But Kitchener dinna know whether General De Wet would attack him here or exploit the railway breach at De Aar."

"Breach?" Fred didn't believe what he'd just heard.

"Ya n'er heard, Laddie? De Wet cut the line aboot a month ago. It was on February 15. After that, the Boers kept attacking our repair parties."

"Horse feathers. I came up on the train February 15 and it was running fine."

"Yours was the last train ta get through, Laddie. It's a secret, but I thought ye knew, bein on Lord Roberts' staff and all. At the Modder River, De Wet sent a small patrol against General French, just enough ta scare the British."

"I guess Lord Bobs keeps secrets from me too," Fred said toying with a wing bone.

"That breached railway line has dictated Roberts' thinking for the past month. Our supply wagons are all strung oot. Until we repair the railway to De Aar, there'll be no attack on Kroonstad."

"I thought De Wet was at Petrusburg, protected by Theron's Scouts," Fred said. "Theron's presence must have been a bluff."

"Aye, Laddie. Now I must hop down ta De Aar ta have a bash at De Wet so the railway can be repaired."

• • •

DURING THE LULL between battles, Fred was called to Lord Roberts' headquarters office.

"A couple of days ago, I sent General Broadwood out to distribute political posters at Thaba Nchu in the hill country," he said. He pronounced the name as Ta-BAN-Chu. "I'm offering amnesty to the burghers who surrender their arms. I've also instructed Broadwood to secure the countryside around Sannah's Post to prevent the Boers from capturing the waterworks."

Fred nodded. *Good idea.*

"I want you to scout the countryside as far as Thaba Nchu. Learn where that Boer general Oliver is deployed and what he is up to," Roberts ordered. "Then report your findings to General Broadwood. Stay with him until he secures the water supply at Sannah's Post."

• • •

THE REMOUNT Department was short of healthy, grain-fed animals and for this mission Fred was allotted two sorry nags that should've been sent to the glue factory. He saddled the weaker of the two, keeping the stronger in reserve for an emergency.

The ride to Thaba Nchu was forty miles. Fred left at sundown and traveled east down a gentle meadow. It was grassland like the open range around Tombstone. After five hours, Fred was feeling satisfied with himself when a pair of white oxen loomed out of the darkness. It spooked his good horse and the animal galloped into the darkness. To be poorly mounted behind enemy lines was like trying to fight a duel with a broken sword, so Fred hunted up the stray animal. It took four hours of searching. He found the horse grazing in a grove of wattle trees.

It was 3 a.m. and Fred was close to the main road so he took to the highway, trusting to luck instead of cutting fences and riding cross-country. An hour later, he was nearing the waterworks when the outline of a building loomed on his right. On his left was an outbuilding, a barn enclosed by a stone kraal. It was risky to ride between a farmhouse and a barn, so he dismounted and tied his horses to a tree. A door slammed and he saw the outline of a small earth dam ahead. From a map he had studied at headquarters, Fred decided this must be the Pretorius farm.

He must get across Koorn Spruit to join Broadwood's army and warn him that enemy forces were maneuvering in the vicinity of Sannah's Post. He crept back to the horses and switched his saddle to the stronger mount. It would be daylight in thirty minutes. He abandoned the weaker horse and rode to Koorn Spruit, looking for a place to gallop across the stream to friendly lines.

Suddenly a tiny shaft of sunlight stabbed through the clouds. The scene brightened enough to reveal a spruit full of armed Boers—about four hundred—waiting to ambush Broadwood when he arrived at the stream.

Fred cast about for a place where he could cross this trifling creek and warn Broadwood. Giving a wide berth to the patrol, he rode back to the kraal. In a few minutes, the sun cleared the mountains and the whole view was etched in frightful detail.

General Oliver had designed an ambush to trap Broadwood. Far to the east in the hills at Thaba Nchu, De Wet had launched a diversionary attack. Broadwood, believing that Oliver's main force was still in the mountains, was retreating west toward what he thought were friendly lines at Sannah's Post.

Broadwood made two blunders. He had bivouacked for the night, confident that he was outpacing the Boer general Oliver. His delay allowed Oliver's men time to gallop around the British and capture Koorn Spruit. Broadwood, believing the Boers were behind him, had

Burnham: King of Scouts

failed to post scouts. Now he was backing his army—in textbook retreat fashion—into an ambush.

Fred untied his neckerchief and began waving it, hoping to attract the attention of someone in the British column. But Broadwood had not posted scouts to probe his rear.

"*Hants oop!*" The Boer voice came from behind.

Fred knew enough Afrikaans to understood that he had been captured by nervous scouts who were wary of a counter-ambush.

"Who are you?" a Boer voice called out.

"I'm an Englishman out making maps," Fred replied, doing his best to fake a British accent. He was trapped and couldn't ride a hundred feet before being riddled with bullets. He had to surrender, but he wasn't going to let it be known that he was Burnham the American scout.

"You are our prisoner," said a tall Boer. "Dismount and lay down your rifle."

Fred did as ordered, taking a moment to stuff his neckerchief into his pants pocket. Half a mile away, Broadwood's retreating army was drawing near. First came eighty transport wagons, followed by ten mess wagons, wounded in the Cape carts, then Q and U Batteries of the Royal Horse Artillery.

Roberts' Horse was fighting a splendid rear-guard action against a thousand Boers advancing on them. By the books, every step of Broadwood's retreat was bringing him closer to a relief column riding out from Bushman's Kop to reinforce him at Koorn Spruit. But this war wasn't being fought by the books used at Sandhurst.

By 7 a.m., the Boer ambush had grown to a thousand men. As the strung-out British rode over the bank and into the drift, they were silently disarmed and taken prisoner. Without a shot being fired, Broadwood's column seemed to be slipping into the Boer trap. Fred's teeth gnashed in fury. He recalled Winston Churchill's headline-making statement that one Boer was equal to five Englishmen. Fred hadn't been so distraught since Nada's death.

In minutes, the transport and mess wagons were in Boer hands. A sudden commotion erupted. Some British officer refused to surrender and another fired a pistol. That was followed by rapid rifle fire. The retreating column halted and a handful of British cavalry officers rode ahead to see what the fuss was about. There was a burst of Mauser fire, followed by the locust-like whir of steel-jacketed bullets. The noise alerted Roberts' Horse and the officers galloped ahead. The commander of the British cavalry recognized the ambush and cried, "Files about. Gallop."

There was a tumult of yells, followed by fusillade of rifle fire. The cavalry leader and his horse were riddled with Mauser bullets. The retreating horses and wagons hadn't gotten turned around when the shooting reached a crescendo. The noise of the gunfire stampeded the horses and a rout was in the making. There was a mass of rearing animals and falling men, punctuated by faint screams, yells and oaths from the distant field.

The Boers turned their rifles on British wagons that stretched across the veld. Terrified horses and oxen fled in all directions, trampling officers, troopers and blacks alike. Then Q Battery of the Royal Horse Artillery, protected by a row of overturned wagons, wheeled about toward Koorn Spruit. The gunners were met with a fresh hail of Boer rifle fire.

Men dropped at every step, writhing in death throes, but some survived. Gut-shot horses, flanks shiny with spurting blood, fell in their tracks as the troopers strained to cut them from their harnesses. When Q Battery was a thousand feet from Koorn Spruit, a Boer artillery shell thumped into one of the horses, tossing it into a somersault and exploding the animal's belly in a shower of bloody froth and gyrating ropes of entrails.

The men of Q Battery wheeled their cannon around to face the enemy, but the gun jammed. For long seconds, Fred's eyes were riveted on the gun-carriage while the three surviving horses struggled to free themselves from the remains of their dead stable mate.

The other guns of Q Battery fired on the Boers with grape shot. There were no officers to be seen and Fred wondered who'd ordered that deed of sacrifice. Did the men, seeing one gun carriage turn, assume that an order had been given? Whatever, it saved the day for the British.

In short order, five guns of Q Battery had opened fire, scoring well and forcing the Boers to take cover. The grape shot prevented the Boers from riding out to capture the British, and it gave Broadwood vital moments to reform his column and send the rest of Roberts' Horse into action with their sabers. If there was one thing the Boers feared, it was the sabers, and it saved the bulk of General Broadwood's command from death or capture.

The British organized into a defensive perimeter, and Fred's captors turned their Mausers on Q Battery. As the Boers sought the range, their bullets kicked up tiny puffs of dust. So accurate was their shooting that Q Battery began firing back at them. In minutes, the British artillery peppered the Boer kraal with four dozen shrapnel charges but the only casualty was Fred's horse.

The Boer sharpshooters ignored Fred while he walked over to the dead animal to retrieve his field kit. He dipped his neckerchief into the dead beast's wound to saturate it with blood, then tucked the rag inside his shirt.

Although taking fire from three sides, the gunners of Q Battery never betrayed the least alarm. They went through their routines as coolly and calmly as if on drill practice at Salisbury Plain.

By 8 a.m., five thousand Boers were lined up in Koorn Spruit. The odds lay with De Wet's man, General Oliver. Q Battery ran low on ammunition and the fire slackened, then ceased. Just as the Boers were about to mount for a cleanup assault, a gunnery sergeant dragged himself to the cannon and sent another shell bursting over the drift. That action drew a concentrated blast of Mauser fire and soon the sergeant's body lay still. The horse artillery had saved Broadwood's day, but those men had paid the supreme sacrifice. Like an angry swarm of white ants, General Oliver's commandos boiled out of Koorn Spruit to round up the stragglers of Broadwood's broken army.

The Boers had vowed to take Burnham prisoner in sixty days. Now, less than a month in the field, he was in their hands. The question was: Would they recognize they had captured the American Scout?

45

Captured by the Boers

SANNAH'S POST • MARCH 1900

FROM THE START, members of the Boer patrol that had captured Fred were eager for some *rooinek* pot-shotting, so they turned their pint-sized prisoner over to relief guards. The new guards wanted to shoot him outright, so they too could go *rooinek* hunting, but the officer saw that this prisoner was wounded. In the confusion during the change of guards, Fred had removed the bloody neckerchief from his shirt and tied it around his knee. His limp duped the officer and he was taken to a trek wagon to ride with the other wounded prisoners.

At 10 o'clock, the wagon inspanned and the Boers began a slow trek to Winburg. Once there, the prisoners would be put on a train and taken to Pretoria Prison. They traveled until late afternoon, rested two hours, inspanned at dusk and journeyed northward again. Any attempt to escape, Fred knew, would have to be made at night. He decided to slip over the tail of the wagon, roll into a ditch and wait until the wagon train had passed, then make his way back to British lines.

At dusk, an odd apprehension came over him and it wasn't long before he learned why. A Hottentot bushman was lurking behind his wagon. The beady-eyed, leather-gray Totty was keeping a sharp eye on him, leaving no way to escape without arousing the attention of this little human bloodhound. Eventually, Burnham gave up for the night and fell asleep.

During the noon laager on Sunday, while the Boers held prayer service, an intelligence officer singled out Fred for questioning. Had some British soldier let his name slip? Then he remembered the Totty—all along, the Boers had been suspicious of him.

The officer carried an index card that listed his physical features: medium sized, wiry, square set, with blue-gray eyes. The interpreter nodded and pursed his lips each time a fact tallied. From the questions put to him, Fred decided the characteristics attributed to him were little more than wild guesses. He was said to have been born in the Wild West, was familiar with Indian warfare and his practice of scalping was an indication of his ferocity. He was uncouth and deficient in education.

With those tips, Fred launched into a discussion of the exploration of Africa by Speke and Burton. To that he added a little poetry, which seemed to convince the intelligence officer that he was a sure-as-shootin British highbrow. Nevertheless, the beady-eyed Totty remained lurking, just in case.

After prayer service, the Boers resumed the trek and Fred fell asleep. He awakened at night still feeling uneasy. In Boer fashion, the wagons were now moving quickly and it occurred to Fred that they must be close to Winburg. *Once there they would board a train and any chance of escape was nil. The distance inside enemy territory would be too great to hike back to friendly lines. If there was to be any chance of escape, it had to be tonight.*

Then Fred saw his opportunity. The Totty, probably believing Fred was asleep, walked on ahead to talk to the foreloper, who was leading the oxen in the dark. That was all Fred needed. Without a sound, he slipped over the tailgate and dropped to the ground, rolling into the ditch to avoid the wagons that followed. He had no idea what time it was.

Ritornello • Interlude

Mafeking • March 1900

STEPHE BADEN-POWELL was devastated. Word had arrived from behind Boer lines that Kenneth "The Boy" McLaren, had been slain in battle. Stephe organized a burial party and sought permission to cross Boer lines under a flag of truce.

At that moment, news arrived that McLaren was not dead but was wounded and being held as a prisoner of war. On hearing that information, Stephe tried to dash through enemy lines to save his pal, but was restrained by his staff officers. In a panic, he sent gifts to The Boy: cocoa, wine, a mattress, hairbrushes, books, mosquito netting, soup, lemonade, stamps, stationery and eau de cologne.

Counterpoise • Equilibrium

The Veld • March 1900

WHEN THE Boer POW wagon had traveled a hundred yards beyond him, Fred slipped through a barbed-wire fence and jogged until he came to a kraal. In exchange for a gold coin, the black owner promised Fred he would fetch a horse.

After the man disappeared, Fred thought the better of it. What if he returned with a Boer patrol? Burnham ran into the field and found himself in a newly plowed patch of ground. The night sky took on the almond-pink cast of dawn and the black man returned, sure enough, leading a Boer patrol. Fred laid down in a fresh furrow.

The soldiers assumed the escaped prisoner had sufficient intelligence to hide in the nearby kopjes. They searched everywhere except the plowed field. In the hours that followed, the patrol became only a minor irritant compared with the hot sun that blazed down, parching skin and soil alike. For twelve hours, Fred lay in the furrows, yearning for food and water, forced to wet his britches. For sure, that Totty in the wagon train had by now given the alarm. There would be a reward for his capture, dead or alive.

Lagnappe • A Little Extra
LONDON • MARCH 1900

BEFORE LEAVING for New York to re-establish his engineering office there, John Hays Hammond accepted an assignment as consulting engineer to the English owners of the El Oro Mining Company of Mexico.

After reopening the New York office, Hammond made arrangements to visit the El Oro Mine ninety miles northwest of Mexico City. First, he went to Washington, D.C., where he called on his friend, Secretary of State John Hay, who provided him with a letter of introduction to President Porfirio Diaz.

Two weeks later in Mexico City, Jack Hammond was presented to President Diaz, an erect and soldierly man of seventy. Diaz had a swarthy complexion and white hair, white mustache and bushy white eyebrows. High cheekbones and dark eyes half covered by drooping lids accented his Indian bloodline. Like Rhodes and Kruger, Diaz had a massive frame.

"What can I do for you?" the president asked.

"Allow me to examine the El Oro Mine," Hammond replied. "Other than that, not a thing."

"That's quite unusual," Diaz said. "If you change your mind, I shall be of service." In an undertone he added, "If you try a revolution here, you'll not get off so easily as you did in South Africa."

Counterpoise • Equilibrium
THE VELD • MARCH 1900

AFTER A DOZEN eternities, the sun dipped below the western hills, allowing Fred to get up. He was dehydrated and needed water quickly to avoid a case of the fatals. A row of trees told him that a stream lay ahead. He drank his fill and ate the only food he had: a biscuit and a mealie cob. His belly growled for beef and potatoes, but the water would keep him alive until he got back to British lines.

He crept through the fence and jogged toward Koorn Spruit, keeping on the grass at the edge of the road. From time to time, he stopped and put his ear to the ground to listen for the sounds of horses or wagons. There was no one—friend or foe—along the road.

At dawn on Tuesday, Fred estimated he'd covered fifteen miles. He hid in a kopje, sleeping until an hour before dark, then scrambled to the top for a careful look around. The land seemed deserted. There was no activity anywhere. The burghers must have retreated toward Brandford and Winburg.

Why hadn't a patrol ridden back to look for him? Maybe he was in no-man's-land. He abandoned the road and struck out cross-country in what he thought was the direction of Bloemfontein. If he could skirt the village of Verkeerdevle, he should be safe. He traveled at a cautious jog and made good time that night.

Wednesday was a repeat of Tuesday: hide by day and jog by night. Fred's stomach grumbled for food, but the demands were answered only with tepid water. The sky clouded up and twice he lost his directions, wandering in large circles until a break in the cloud cover revealed stars and restored his bearings.

An hour before dawn on Thursday, he saw pickets ahead. Fred knew the British guards would spook easily and shoot without warning, so he took care to elude them and reported himself to the commander of guards.

"Who are you and where are we?" Fred asked.

"This is the Twelfth Lancers," the captain replied. "The Boers still hold the waterworks at Sannah's Post."

Behind Enemy Lines

The 10th Chronicle

46

Aylmer Hunter-Weston

BLOEMFONTEIN • MARCH 1900

FRED RODE in a Yankee Spider to Bloemfontein and on arriving at British Army headquarters, he reported to Lord Roberts. He apologized for being captured at Sannah's Post.

"It might not have happened," he said ruefully, "if I'd had a better horse." Roberts nodded, questioned him about enemy morale and told him to eat, rest up and report back in a couple of days. At Bobs' request, the Reuters News Agency had withheld reports of Burnham's capture until after his escape and return. Richard Harding Davis had begun writing about the Boer side of the war. In time, that act had gotten him expelled from his London club and, still later, provoked his recall to America.

Another newsman, Bennett Burleigh, of the *London Daily Telegraph* was interested in scoops. He had been known to arrive at a government reception posing as an American senator. He discovered Burnham and thought the diminutive American scout might have a good story. Burleigh wanted to know about the British ambush at Korn Spruit, about Fred's capture, how he had escaped and more. After Bennett completed his interview, Fred ate breakfast and slept.

Five thousand British troops at Bloemfontein were stricken with typhoid fever. The British offensive was stalled until the illness could be checked by cooler weather or until the British captured the sanitary waterworks. Tyrie Laing and his Highlanders restored the railway line to De Aar and in good time supplies began arriving. Major General Sir Frederick Carrington took a troop train down from Bulawayo carrying a force of Rhodesians to defend the Western Transvaal at Mafeking and protect the De Aar railway junction.

For three days, Fred bivouacked in splendor at the foreign secretary's mansion, feasting on good food and writing letters to Blanche in London and Rider Haggard in Ditchingham. To Mother Burnham in Pasadena, he said brother Howard was trapped in Cape Town. Fred asked her to cable funds to him from the bank in Pasadena.

I'd be a major general in this war if I had the education. I have a natural instinct for battle on a large scale. I can size up a fighting front twenty-five miles long and grasp it all, something many British commanders cannot do. In my field of scouting, I'm still far ahead of any living man. I don't write this to anyone but you—not even to my own wife—so destroy this letter at once.

Lagnappe • A Little Extra

MAFEKING • MARCH 1900

DURING THE SIEGE, Stephe used his acting talents to bolster morale. He organized cricket games on Sunday, which scandalized the devout Boers across the lines. He directed sports carnivals, judged a baby show, captained a polo team, acted in stage sketches, recited inspiring poems, sang peppy songs, sponsored a billiards tournament and dressed up as a circus ringmaster for which he wielded a thirty-foot whip.

Stephe carried this make-believe world into military operations. Through a megaphone, he shouted orders to nonexistent troops about mythical attacks on the enemy lines. Squads of men were ordered to stalk around the perimeter of Mafeking, pretending to wriggle through imaginary barbed-wire fences. He marked out nonexistence mine fields and ordered his men to parade with homemade lances carried against the skyline to make the Boers think that reinforcements had arrived.

From morning to night, he kept up his own morale by whistling operatic airs and jingoistic music-hall ditties. Stephe's second in command, Lord Cecil, organized and drilled the lads of Mafeking so they could act as orderlies and messengers. Only the indifference of the besieging Boer force prevented Mafeking from being overrun.

Counterpoise • Equilibrium

BLOEMFONTEIN • APRIL 1900

WHEN FRED reported to headquarters two days later, Lord Roberts had a surprise for him. Bobs stood beside a small but supple horse with smooth brown hair that shined like satin.

"This is Steenbok," he said. "He's half Arabian and half Basuto. Although he's small, he's got bottle. He's as tough as his horseshoes. And he is yours as a gesture of my appreciation."

"I don't know what to say, Sir, except thank you."

"Take him for a ride. That's the acid test."

"Yes, Sir." Fred mounted and was off at a gallop.

An hour later, he returned with the horse hardly drawing a breath. What a horse. Steenbok soon became an extension of Burnham's body. Fred knew that one source of the Boers' mystical powers lay with their sturdy little Basuto ponies. These Cape horses had legendary stamina. Their origins dated to a handful of 17th century animals imported from Java by the Dutch East India Company.

Crossbreeding with American and English horses resulted in exactly the kind of animal needed by the early settlers in their treks inland from the Cape. After an hour on the march, Basuto ponies were allowed to roll and graze for ten minutes. If they didn't roll, it was a sign they were too tired to continue. When the reins were left on the ground, Basuto ponies stood unattended. It was a system of ground hitching that added to the Boers' firepower, because it released the one man in four needed for horse holding.

Steenbok, like his namesake, the south African stone buck, was small and handsome with white under parts. The horse could stand so still that he blended with the landscape, making him virtually invisible. Steenbok was destined to become Fred's favorite mount, an extension of body and mind. But in less than ninety days the pretty little animal would almost kill him.

Burnham's first outing with Steenbok was an eight-day rampage with Major General Reggie Pole-Carew, a handsome and debonair man with curly hair and a large tea-strainer mustache. He was the dashing commander of the Ninth Brigade. With a twenty-five man force, Pole-Carew raided the countryside, captured two thousand sheep, forty horses and several loads of grain—without losing a man. Burnham enjoyed the outing while he tested Steenbok's mettle.

The newspapers arrived from London with stirring accounts of Fred's escape from the Boers. Bennett Burleigh's main article in the *Daily Telegraph* measured a remarkable seventy-five column inches, of which sixty percent was devoted to Fred's capture and escape.

• • •

BY THE END OF April, the British had mustered seventy-five thousand men and two hundred guns. The autumn weather had grown chilly and the invasion of the Transvaal was set to begin Thursday, May 3. Pretoria was three hundred miles away, with Kroonstad and Johannesburg along the route of march.

As a cold, cloudy dawn unfurled, a bugler sounded assembly and four columns of mounted men formed up under the leadership of Lord Roberts and General French. The main goal was the capture of Johannesburg, two hundred fifty miles ahead. Then they would march on Pretoria, the capital, which lay another thirty-five miles beyond.

The midpoint on the route was Kroonstad, now the capital of the Orange Free State after Bloemfontein was abandoned.

As they rode through farms bordered by sunflowers, the invasion force took on the trappings of a cakewalk. On the second day, they covered twenty-seven miles without meeting so much as one Boer. They captured Brandford and by Sunday, Lord Roberts' rear elements had recaptured Sannah's Post and Thaba Nchu, assuring Bloemfontein of clean water.

By week's end, the British had advanced eighty-five miles and crossed the Zand River, the Afrikaans name for the Sand River. They were only thirty-five miles from Kroonstad. That's when Lord Roberts called Burnham into his tent and changed the nature of his duties.

"Colonel Mackenzie has developed a collection of capable scouting wallahs in our Intelligence Department," he said. *Am I being relieved?*

"It means I can spare you for more important work," Roberts said. "We are now three hundred miles ahead of our supply base at De Aar and eight hundred miles from Cape Town. There are places where Boer commandos can interdict our rail lines. We can minimize that danger and speed our advance if we can capture food and supplies from the Boers on the route ahead to Joburg."

Fred's face brightened.

"Your mission is penetrate enemy lines and blow up the Boer railways. You must destroy the tracks before the Boers can evacuate their rolling stock. Don't destroy the supplies—isolate the trains. We must capture those rolling commissaries for our army. Report at once to Colonel Mackenzie to mug up on maps."

"Yes, Sir." Fred was elated.

For his first outing, he would blow the Boer railway north of Kroonstad. Two Cape natives would accompany him, each of them carrying twenty pounds of guncotton, a cotton waste saturated with nitroglycerin. The trio crossed no-man's-land undetected. A few hours later Fred smelled sunflowers.

"Dat be Henneman, Nkosi," the larger native said.

"Let's avoid pickets. We'll detour around the town," Fred replied.

They encountered the Boschrand, leaving the veld and entering an area of brown glades fringed with green scrub. The sharp ridges were covered by mimosa trees.

This area is ideal for defense. When pressed, what more could the Boer want than ridge after ridge to fall back on?

But there were no Boers!

Morning found Fred west of Kroonstad, at a drift on the Valsch River near Smalldeel. In the early light, the trio took cover in a mealie field to wait out the day, sleeping by turns while one man stood watch. In the afternoon, Fred was awakened by the sound of horses. General French rode up leading two thousand cavalrymen.

• • •

MAJOR GENERAL John Denton Pinkstone French, eight years Fred's senior, was Britain's blue-eyed boy of cavalry, the great white hope in southern Africa. He looked every inch the horse soldier: bowed legs and a heavy, jowled face resting on a bulldog neck. It was Fred's first face-to-face meeting with the man who'd chased the Boers out of Kimberley and freed Cecil Rhodes.

French ordered his cavalrymen to make camp.

"Lord Roberts told me you were pottering around up here," he said. "Report to the Royal Engineer for a special patrol tonight."

Major Aylmer Hunter-Weston was a short, sturdy man with a droopy gray mustache and a ready smile. He invited Fred to join his mess and urged him to eat a substantial meal. At dusk, they rode out of the bivouac. Sixty horsemen had been chosen for courage and coolness under fire. Fifty were heavily armed cavalry of the Inskilling Dragoons and ten were Royal Engineers, horse-mounted sappers equipped with lethal explosives.

"Our orders are to penetrate enemy lines and blow the rails to isolate the supply waggons at America Siding," Hunter-Weston said.

"That's where I was headed when you got here," Burnham said. America Siding was the railway supply depot north of Kroonstad.

"We've had no opposition and moved faster than expected," Hunter-Weston said. "Lord Roberts decided you could use some help. He expects stiff resistance at Kroonstad where the Boers have stashed thousands of tons of food and munitions."

"Shhh, hold up," Fred called out in a low voice. "Boer commando ahead."

"Captain Yardley," Hunter-Weston grunted. "Lead a saber charge."

In an aside to Fred, he said, "It's bayonets for infantry, but sabers for cavalry." The glint of flashing sabers in the moonlight was a terrifying sight to behold. The swiftness of the silent onslaught paralyzed the Boers. The battle lasted only seconds and the Dragoons rounded up a large group of prisoners which they sent back to General French.

Taking eight sappers, Burnham and Hunter-Weston rode ahead. There were Boers scattered over the veld so Fred led the men on a zigzag route, but they were always met by patrols. At 4 a.m., they were fifteen miles north of Kroonstad.

"I'd estimate we're half a mile from America Siding," Fred said.

"This'll be the most difficult part," Hunter-Weston replied.

Ahead was a fenced pasture that served as a corral for the Boer horses. Beside the wooden fence, a road ran next to an old railway track. Streams of mounted men and ox wagons were traveling north, but other men patrolled the road. Off-duty Boers sprawled beside the road, sleeping. The enemy regarded this rear area as secure.

"I'll crawl around to see if I can find a route through this grass," Fred said. Ten minutes later, he reappeared.

"Any luck?"

"There's a commando camped in the tall grass. We can detour around them. Have your men dismount and lead their horses."

Hunter-Weston led the patrol on a detour.

"We should trim our numbers," Fred said.

"You six, remain behind and stand guard," Hunter-Weston said. "Leftenant Childs, choose your best sapper and come with Burnham and me."

In the graying light before the dawn, the four men led their horses into the pasture. Fred sensed a party of Boers riding in their direction.

"Lie down. Hold the bridles," Burnham whispered. "Let them think the horses are strays out grazing."

The Boer leader halted his column to study the four animals grazing in the pasture. The commandant was suspicious, but his men swore impatiently at the delay, so he shrugged and moved on.

"The horses hinder us," Fred said.

"Childs, take them back to the sappers and rejoin us."

Soon the three men were off on foot to America Siding. Lieutenant Childs stumbled and muffled a whoop. He'd tripped on one of a trio of Boers sleeping on the ground. Hunter-Weston and Childs pointed their pistols at two of the enemy and Fred held his hunting knife to the throat of the third man. They gagged the prisoners, tied their hands behind their backs and led them back to the sappers. On their third try, Hunter-Weston trimmed the raiding party to two men.

"Leftenant, if you hear shooting, forget us and cut your way back to General French."

"There's a special reason why today's mission must succeed," Fred said. In the noise, nobody seemed to hear him. He shrugged.

Burnham and Hunter-Weston crawled through the deep grass, careful to avoid sleeping Boers. At length they came to a pair of spur lines leading to America Siding. Several trainloads of goods waggons reposed with only a few guards. Fred examined one of the carriages and found it sealed. They scraped away the gravel on one of the two railway spur lines.

They inserted dual charges of guncotton at three places. Fred removed his hat to shield the flame while Hunter-Weston lighted the fuses. They crept to the deep grass and jogged at a crouch to get as far away as possible. They were half way to the fence when the sky lighted up and six loud explosions echoed across the veld, shaking the ground and awakening everybody within miles.

Moments later the two men rejoined the sappers and mounted for the gallop back to British lines. The predawn arrived as they crossed a low ridge, and they galloped into an enemy patrol. The sappers surrounded six Boers and disarmed them without firing a shot. Childs ordered his men to break the Mausers against the rocks. They took four Boer prisoners, tying, gagging and leaving behind two men whose horses were lame.

The sun rose, revealing another Boer patrol, which chased them for two miles. One of their pursuers was well mounted and began closing in, firing his rifle from the saddle. In two quick shots, he killed a British horse and wounded one of the sappers. Hunter-Weston halted and dismounted. The Boer did the same, but the Royal Engineer was faster. Before the Boer could draw a bead with his Mauser, Major Hunter-Weston's Lee-Metford popped and the man fell dead. The distance was three hundred yards.

The raiding party galloped south toward British lines. About 9 a.m. they crossed the Valsch River a few miles from French's camp and were greeted by cheers. They'd been fifteen hours in the saddle, had ridden fifty-six miles through enemy territory, had captured scores of prisoners and had isolated three Boer trains loaded with military supplies. As they dismounted, Fred turned to Hunter-Weston, "Remember that I said there was a special reason why we should succeed?"

"Why do you say that, old chap?"

"First, we didn't encounter any sticker fences."

"What's a sticker—?" Hunter-Weston asked.

"We also know bob wire as thorny hedges," Burnham said. "For cattle, it's the finest fence in the world. Lighter'n air, stronger'n whiskey and cheaper'n dirt. The critter ain't been born that can get through it."

"I'm glad we didn't find any of your sticker hedges," Hunter-Weston said.

"Besides that," Burnham said, "today's May 11th, my birthday. I'm thirty-nine years old."

It was also the birth of a close-knit, lifelong friendship.

47

Kempton Park Attack

KROONSTAD • MAY 1900

AFTER THE ASSAULT on America Siding, the Boers abandoned Kroonstad. At dawn the next day, Lord Roberts—with General Kitchener at his side and the headquarters staff behind them—rode into the wartime capital of the Orange Free State. Major Tyrie Laing led the Guards Brigade. To Burnham, Kroonstad looked like any small Western town from Colorado or Texas—except that many newly dug trenches had been abandoned unused.

The Boers had learned the tactic of scorched earth. On the eve of their departure, the enemy burned the food and supplies captured from General Broadwood and dragged up from Sannah's Post. General French had recovered the supplies from the three Boer trains that Fred and Hunter-Weston had isolated.

"Hello, Burnham." The voice was female. "Welcome to Kroonstad. I'm American too."

Fred watched as a bit of fluff ran up the Union Jack in front of a modest home. The woman looked a bit like Blanche, and Fred felt a pang of homesickness. Seeing this likeness of his spouse set his heart aflutter. Then they were past the house and she was history. Lord Roberts and the staff took up stations opposite the National Bank and the troopers paraded in review as the Scots Guards played the fifes, drums and bagpipes.

"Aye," Laing said. "Listen to the happy doodlesacks."

"Thanks to you for restoring our railway route."

"And to you for isolatin the enemy's supplies."

In London, the *Daily Telegraph* headlined the taking of Kroonstad as a gallant adventure. Fred's foray to America Siding got one third of Bennett Burleigh's fifty-inch-long article. Soon the public in London—Blanche included—came to expect a new weekly Burnham

Burnham: King of Scouts

adventure in print. Since Fred's arrival in southern Africa, he'd produced a seemingly endless supply of adventure stories and his newspaper coverage exceeded that of everyone including Lord Roberts. But the publicity was destined to end.

A week after Fred's birthday, Colonel Herbert Plumer led a relief column toward Mafeking. With Digby Willoughby in support, Plumer was planning to launch a column of mounted men to rescue Baden-Powell, who'd been under siege for eight months.

Adding an element of drama in London was the fact that the second in command at Mafeking was Major Lord Edward Cecil, the prime minister's son in law. When Burleigh learned about Lord Cecil, he galloped off to Mafeking for a story. A week after the occupation of Kroonstad, Lord Roberts called Fred to his headquarters.

"We'll launch our attack on Johannesburg in about a week," he said. "I want you to penetrate enemy lines and sever the Boer railway tracks between Johannesburg and Pretoria."

"Like a steer, I can always try."

Roberts smiled indulgently.

"Our spy mavens say the railway traffic is heavy," Bobs said. "The Boers are hauling out gold and bringing in German war materiél. I want to capture as much of the rolling stock as possible. If you can sever the rail line between Johannesburg and Pretoria and keep it severed, General French can capture the switching yards before the Boers destroy the locomotives and railway waggons."

Fred felt the blood tingle in his veins.

"The sound of our artillery will signal the advance," Roberts said. "I hope to see you safe in Johannesburg. May the good Lord travel at your side."

Fred visited the Intelligence Department which supplied him with detailed maps showing the curves, grades, bridges, farms, spruits and rivers along the railway route. For this mission, he'd leave Steenbok behind and travel on foot. He'd take Joshua, a Cape native who spoke English and Afrikaans. Joshua was tall and supple, with the strength of an ox and the emotional fortitude of a rhino. They wore backpacks stuffed with guncotton, blasting caps, fuses, food tablets, first-aid kits and canteens for water. Fred hid his maps in the guncotton, planning to blow up any evidence of spying if threatened with capture. Shortly after sundown, they left Smalldeel—west of Kroonstad—traveling by night and hiding by day. The terrain ranged from open veld to gently rolling hills with large trees and bushes. This was the heartland of the Boers. By avoiding roads and enemy camps, they penetrated twenty miles into enemy territory before sunrise.

Behind Enemy Lines

Ritornello • Interlude
Mafeking • May 1900

LIEUTENANT COLONEL Herbert Plumer stood looking like a gawky adolescent with a brush mustache. His eyes bulged and his ears wagged like an angry elephant. His nose stuck out like an Indian arrowhead. General Sir Richard Carrington had sent him to relieve Mafeking, but his force of mounted infantry was repeatedly turned back with heavy losses. The next day, to his great surprise, there was no opposition. What Plumer wouldn't learn until much later was that General Koos de la Rey, who commanded the Western Transvaal, had been relieved and sent up to join General "Boot" Botha in defending Johannesburg. General de la Rey was the finest Boer military commander, a regular Stonewall Jackson.

Counterpoise • Equilibrium
Johannesburg • May 1900

ON HIS FIFTH NIGHT in enemy territory, Fred saw the twinkling lights of Johannesburg. If Joburg had been a great mining camp when he saw it seven years ago, it was now the gold capital of the world. The town had doubled in size and was guarded by a huge commando of armed Boers. Looking down from atop a hill, Fred saw miles of quartz stamp mills.

Joburg was a mile-high city and it was as cold as a November night in Denver. The Drakensberg Mountains were capped by snow and the night temperature on the veld was freezing. For five days, they'd eaten nothing but food tablets and were ravenous. Fred marveled at being so close to civilization and yet so far. Except for those Boers, he was free to enter town and eat his fill of food.

"Take this money," he said, handing a coin to Joshua, "Buy food at a nearby kraal. See if you can get a chicken and some eggs."

When Joshua returned, Fred had a small fire going. The glitter of the gold piece had induced a native to part with an ancient hen and twenty eggs of dubious vintage. Joshua wolfed down a dozen eggs.

"Dis good, eh baas?" he asked.

"The omelet's okay if you're not picky about what you eat."

He cut up the hen and simmered it until nearly dawn, when he had to snuff out the fire for fear it might attract Boers. Despite lengthy stewing, the old bird was as tough as a parrot and every bit as edible. Even so, the portions seemed small. They went to sleep, concealed by thick bushes.

At dusk they awakened and Fred planned for the night ahead. They made a careful trek around Joburg. Many roads converged on

361

the city and all were heavily traveled, making the crossing of any road risky. By 4 a.m., Fred felt like they'd walked to Diamond Hill, which was up by Pretoria.

The spot they chose for camp that morning was near Zuurfontein, about ten miles north of Johannesburg. They heard a train toot its steam whistle and a few seconds later came the soft chuff-chuff of the locomotive. They'd hide out for the day and wait for the sound of Lord Roberts' artillery. Ahead was a gentle mound of earth with trees for cover. The sound of galloping horses forced them to hide.

Fred saw three aardvark holes in a vley and ran to them.

"Hide the guncotton in that hole and we'll take cover in the other two," he told Joshua. The pig-like aardvark is an animal of nocturnal habits that feeds on ants and termites, a first cousin to the anteater. Its lair is like a wolf den, including the foul stink.

The nest offers a refuge for anyone who doesn't mind sleeping in the barnyard, but it's an annoying trap for horsemen. Many a horse had stepped in an ant-bear hole, broken a leg and had to be shot. The Boers knew all about these holes and could be depended on to avoid them. Fred and Joshua slept in stinky peace all day.

On awakening that night, the odor of wet horses and fresh manure told them they were still surrounded by Boers. Their main body was about three hundred feet away. Fred and Joshua were well inside the perimeter of guards. They'd have to out-wait the enemy.

It was Saturday, their seventh day in the field. At any day now, Lord Roberts should be launching his assault on Joburg. When it was dark, Fred and Joshua awakened to find the Boers gone. They climbed out of their holes to stretch cramped muscles, regain circulation and build up body heat. They drank at the spruit and raided the garbage dump of the abandoned Boer camp for something to eat. While they searched for edible food, the sound of distant artillery suggested that Roberts' advance had begun.

Returning to the aardvark holes, they got a charge of guncotton and hiked eastward to the railway tracks. They walked over open prairie destined to become a runway at Jan Smuts International Airport in Kempton Park. Soon they reached the huge Modderfontein Dynamite Factory, the world's largest. It was Oom Paul's supplier of explosives to the Joburg gold mines. Next to the factory was the main railway line from Johannesburg to Pretoria.

Fred chose a curve between two culverts half a mile north of the railway station and dynamite factory. He buried guncotton in several places along the tracks and lighted the fuses, then ran behind a large gravel pile where Joshua waited. The explosions shattered the silence, sending flashes of fire and smoke skyward and twisting the steel rails at grotesque angles. A dozen armed Boers streamed out of the station house to give chase, but they were night blinded from the floodlights around the building. Fred and Joshua had no difficulty eluding them and returning to their gamy hideaway.

Between naps on Sunday, Fred watched the repair crews shout and curse as they replaced the twisted rails. At dusk, he and Joshua picked over the remaining Boer garbage, then went back to blow up the railway line again. The Boers had posted no guards. Apparently they thought a British patrol had ridden to the railway, blown the tracks and scampered back to safety.

"Come along, Joshua. This'll be easy."

"My *madhlozi* say mebbe not easy, baas."

They planted several charges and skipped back to the protection of their old gravel pile. Once again a series of explosions was a signal for the Boers to storm out of the station house, this time intent on hunting down the culprits. But by the time the Boers got to the gravel pile, Fred and Joshua were safely back in their stinkpot nests.

The repairs on Monday took longer; Fred guessed the Boers were running short of rails, spikes and sleepers. The sound of artillery was still far distant, suggesting that Roberts had not yet taken Johannesburg. That night the wail of a locomotive whistle in the distance suggested a train was leaving Joburg.

"All right, Joshua, it's time to try again."

Joshua seemed reluctant.

"Dem Boers, dey be plenty mad, baas."

For some reason, the Boers still hadn't assigned men to guard the tracks. More than a third of the guncotton remained, so Fred decided to blow the rails in three places. He placed his charges to good advantage and for the third night, the resulting series of blasts brought a horde of angry Boers stampeding out of the station house.

This time, Fred knew, the enemy wouldn't give up until prisoners were taken. They were out of guncotton and it was time to abandon the area. They retreated through the vleys, jogging when they had cover, crawling when they were in the open. At last they came to a grove of blue gum trees. There was no food, but they saw a spruit that offered drinking water.

The sound of approaching hoofbeats told them to take shelter in the nearest tall grass. Out of nowhere, a Boer commando arrived and made laager in the grove, the men scrounging dry grass and dead limbs to build fires. Once again Fred and Joshua were trapped. They spent Tuesday hiding in the grass, unable to creep out for a drink.

Then at dusk the commando inspanned and galloped away. Fred couldn't remember when a sunset had been more welcome. They'd been ten days and nights behind enemy lines and both men were starved and exhausted. Fred's gums were sore from chewing on mealie cobs, and Joshua had acted strangely all day. The distant rumble of horse-drawn artillery caissons told Fred the British Army was close to Johannesburg.

"Let's go," he said. "We'll make it back to our lines before the moon comes up."

"No, baas," Joshua said, his hands trembling. "I have prayed to my *madhlozi*, the spirits that govern my fate. I have asked for more strength, but the *madhlozi* have not granted me strength."

"We're not far," Fred urged. "We can go slow."

"No, baas," Joshua said. "If captured, Boer *mijnheer* shoot me too."

"We'll go back by separate routes," Fred said.

Joshua smiled, looking much relieved. In an instant, he faded into the night like a wisp of smoke. His *madhlozi* must have granted him additional strength because he ran with exceptional speed.

Fred began what would be an all-night trek, circling around Johannesburg, through no-man's-land and back to British lines. Shortly before dawn on Wednesday, May 30, near what would become Alberton, he saw the fires of the British Army glowing in a grove of mimosa trees. In the distant north, he heard the sound of locomotives in the switching yards.

Strangely missing were the sounds of artillery. On entering friendly lines, Fred was greeted by Lord Airlie's Twelfth Lancers who offered him a breakfast of tea, toast and jam and banger sausages. After eating, Fred borrowed a horse to ride to headquarters. There he cleaned up and reported himself to Lord Roberts.

"Splendid work, Burnham," Bobs said. "Today we have annexed the Orange Free State as a British colony. You're in time for us to ride into Joburg tomorrow."

"It's so quiet and peaceful; it doesn't seem like there's a war," Fred said.

"We have an armistice," Bobs said. "The Boers have three days to evacuate."

"Armistice?" Fred blurted. "You mean I spent eleven days behind enemy lines for nothing?"

"On the contrary," Roberts protested. "No doubt your severing the railway lines influenced the Boer decision in our favor. At a ceasefire meeting, Judge Koch warned us that the Boers were threatening to blow up the gold mines."

Fred guessed Bobs was trying to put a good face on the matter, but this was disaster. Roberts had a perfect opportunity to surround the Boers and end the war in one swift move, but now the enemy was being allowed to slip away. Traveling by ox wagon, it would take the Boer Army three days to reach Pretoria. During that time, the British were forbidden to fire except in self-defense.

"Report in dress uniform early tomorrow," Bobs said crisply. "We enter Johannesburg at 10 o'clock sharp."

48

Winston Churchill

JOHANNESBURG • MAY 1900

THE QUARTERMASTER assigned a billet to Fred. When he got there, a new bicycle was parked by the entrance.

"Aha, the blue-eyed boy from Auld Reekie."

"Nay, laddie," Tyrie Laing replied. "The land of cakes n ale. Welcome back. We tho't ye took a bullet behind enemy lines." They walked inside the billet where a young man was standing.

"Meet me newspaper chum, Winnie Churchill," Terry said. The tousle-headed young blond extended his hand. *He looks like a lean campaigner, but his grip is as soft as a schoolgirl's.*

"In the last hundr'd days," Terry said, "this Yank has been behind enemy lines a hundr'd times."

"Heavens," Churchill said. "Are you the American chap who was captured by the Boers and escaped?"

"I understand that you escaped Pretoria Prison," Fred replied. "No one else has done that."

"Ye must tell us aboot your adventure, Winnie," Laing said.

"It's an intricate story." Churchill was perplexed because his escape from prison had been engineered by a man named Burnham.

Fred turned to Laing.

"Terry, this truce is the worst clanger of the war, if not of Lord Roberts' career."

"You dinna understand Bobs' velvet-glove strategy, laddie," Laing said. "He wants to bring hostilities to a speedy and humane conclusion."

"Roberts wants to save those ruddy gold mines for Rhodes," Churchill groused.

"The war's nearly over," Laing argued. "Why waste good lives fighting now?"

"Directly I plan to nip down to Joburg Prison to chat with the prisoners," Churchill said. "Anyone care to join me?"

Both said no. Fred was hungry and tired. He ate some of Terry's fruit and slept. When he awakened in the afternoon, Laing and Churchill were gone, but the bicycle was still there. Fred rummaged through the closet for some civilian clothes. He left a note saying he'd borrowed the bicycle, then rode into Johannesburg.

From a hillside he watched General Boot Botha's army slowly trudging out of the city. The ox wagons carrying the heavy field guns created a cloud of dust as they lumbered toward Pretoria thirty-five miles away. Fred sighed. *If Bobs ever had victory in his hands, it was now.* He watched for an hour, then mounted the bicycle and coasted down the hill to camp. Laing and Churchill were still gone, so he changed into uniform and went over to the officers mess for dinner.

When he returned, the bicycle was gone. Fred was still bushed from the patrol behind enemy lines, so he hit the sack. After a restful night, he was up before dawn, feeling much refreshed. When he returned from breakfast, he saw that Terry hadn't slept in his bed. That was curious because he was assigned to lead the Guards Brigade into Joburg this morning. *Terry must have had night duty*. Fred bathed, shaved and put on a dress uniform. Then he saddled Steenbok and rode to headquarters.

An hour later Lord Roberts, resplendent in his field marshal's crimson dress uniform, led the victory parade into Johannesburg. Commandant Doktor Krause, the Boer official left in charge of Johannesburg, sat next to him. Behind them, General Kitchener and the staff rode slowly as the victory parade proceeded along the Rand Ridge. The Seventh and Eleventh Divisions occupied the place of honor behind the generals.

A swarm of people—Americans, Australians, Bantus, Boers, British and Dutch—was on hand to watch as the conquering army assumed control. Some of the blacks had burned their passes and now walked on the sidewalk, acts forbidden under Boer rule. Troopers of Lord Kerry's Military Police ordered the kaffirs back into the street. Ironically, the British enforced the Afrikaans race laws with better discipline than the Boers.

At the Law Court, Lord Roberts and Commandant Krause walked inside to sign the papers that transferred control from Boer government to British. That simple act, like everything today, Fred thought, seemed to take an eternity. Afterward, Lord Roberts marched smartly out of the Law Court building. A British sergeant-major pulled down the Boer Vierkleur and ran up the Union Jack.

A roll of the drums announced the arrival of the Guards Brigade, but Terry wasn't in the lead. Was he ill? Fred decided that after the ceremony he would check with the medical officer. There was cheering, saluting and calls of "God Save the Queen." Then it was over, the troops were dismissed and the bars were declared open for business. Fred mounted Steenbok for the ride back to headquarters. Along the way, he spotted a bicycle rider ahead and spurred Steenbok to a trot to join Churchill.

"Why don't you ride a horse like a man?" Fred asked.

"I would much prefer a horse," the young man retorted hotly. "But Kitchener is still in an upset over an article I wrote slating his leadership at the Battle of The Sudan. Yesterday he had the Quartermaster deny me a horse."

It was common knowledge that Kitchener detested Churchill for pulling strings to be attached to the British Army in The Sudan campaign.

"He puts on a brave image, but he is betrayed by his braying," Burnham said."

"One day I shall have my vengeance on that jackass," Churchill growled, his youthful voice taking on a deeper timber. Something in the way Churchill spoke made Fred believe that one day this young man truly would have his revenge.

"By the way," Churchill said, "yesterday, I interviewed Colonel Baden-Powell."

"Oh, is he in town?" Fred asked. "I must look him up." Fred was behind enemy lines when Colonel Plumer relieved Baden-Powell at Mafeking. From what he'd heard, London had celebrated with quite a fandango.

"Say, have you seen Tyrie Laing?"

"Haven't heard?" Churchill's face turned ashen.

"I thought he might be ill with typhoid fever."

"Major Laing is dead," Churchill said softly. "He went on patrol last night and took a bullet in the heart."

"Terry? Dead? It can't be!"

"Sorry, old cock, it's true. Perhaps I've let out more than I should."

Terry? That broad-chested Highlander? Gold miner from Belingwe? Pal from the Klondike? Hero of De Aar? Gone to the misty beyond?

"Some armistice!" Fred cried angrily, spitting on the ground and stamping on it. "The loser shoots the victor." A chill passed over him and he felt a premonition of disaster. Only the gods knew, but in five days the war would end for Fred Burnham too.

Lagnappe • A Little Extra

PRETORIA • MAY 1900

IT WAS THE very worst day in Jannie Smuts' life. General Louis Botha's army was streaming into the capital in shame and confusion. The city was given over to looting. Jannie feared a collapse of the rank and file of his people.

"I'm convinced of the hopelessness of continuing the struggle," said "Boot" Botha. He sat warming himself by a coal stove near the telegraph ticker. Three days earlier, Oom Paul Kruger had given way to anguish and despair. He bade farewell to his invalid wife of fifty-eight years and with senior members of the Transvaal Government had fled Pretoria. Kruger and staff took a train east to Machadodorp, half way to the border of Mozambique. When that news came to be known, a spasm of misery had overtaken the Transvaal populace.

Looking out the window, Jannie watched the horses, men, wagons and oxen shamble into town in a mass of confusion. After a conference with General Botha, he had agreed to co-sign a telegram to Presidents Kruger and Steyn— a message suggesting the surrender of both Boer republics. Even as Smuts waited for a reply, he wondered if that message had been a mistake. Each time the Morse Code sounder echoed, Smuts' eyes focused on the telegrapher, who shook his head.

The Boers had told Commandant Doktor Krause to keep Lord Roberts occupied with details of the surrender of Johannesburg. All that talk about blowing up the gold mines had been so much hocus-pocus to intimidate the British. The Boers knew that destroying the mines would antagonize important stockholders in England, Germany and America — the Boers had no intention of doing that.

In return for sparing the mines, Roberts had agreed to a three-day cease-fire that would allow the Boers time to evacuate Joburg. Smuts half expected Roberts to order flying columns to ambush the retreating armies. Jannie fell asleep entertaining the hope that Roberts really was a gentleman.

On Saturday, Jannie was awakened by a timid orderly who thrust a sheaf of telegrams into his hand. One was from Oom Paul, a message of despair. The other was from President Steyn. His telegram accused the Transvaalers of cowardice. Steyn argued that the strength of the Boers lay in the veld, not in the cities. He said the surrender of Bloemfontein and Kroonstad had given his commandos time to organize into guerrilla units. General de Wet was still very much in command of his men. It ended, "We shall never surrender."

Steyn's message hit Smuts like a pail of ice water. Jannie knew guerrilla warfare—he had led a raid on Cape Town, nearly a thousand miles away. He showed the telegram to Boot Botha, who convened a meeting of Boer officers. Captain Danny Theron of the Scouts Corps took to the floor and delivered an impassioned speech in favor of the war.

"I must be growing old," Botha confided to Smuts. "The younger men haven't suffered our loss of faith."

Jannie nodded with relief. "Thank the Lord for Steyn's telegram. It may be the most vital message of the war." Then, emboldened by Theron's enthusiasm, Jannie strode to the front. He told the men that a new phase of the war was beginning. All talk of surrender must be forgotten. The Boers would organize into guerrilla units and fight on the veld as General de Wet was doing in the Orange Free State. Boot Botha would organize a new Transvaal Army. Cheers followed. Clearly the ranks were infused with a new spirit of hope.

"As we did at Joburg," Smuts said, "we'll abandon Pretoria without firing a shot."

"Yes," Botha said. "Under a flag of truce, I'll send my secretary through the British lines. He'll propose peace talks with Roberts. Like Krause, my man will keep the British occupied until we can organize our forces."

"I'll send telegrams to notify Kruger and Steyn," Smuts said. "Shall we pray?"

Counterpoise • Equilibrium

JOHANNESBURG • MAY 1900

FOR HIS HEADQUARTERS, Lord Roberts requisitioned the finest suites in the world's premiere gold city. That act should have suggested that the seventy-year-old Bobs might not be eager to abandon Joburg for a mildewed canvas tent in the field.

Early the next day, Burnham received a summons to headquarters. Only the gods knew this was to be the last time he would stand before his commander to receive orders. Fred was awed by the splendor of the luxurious suite of offices. His mind briefly strayed.

"...importance of destroying the Delagoa Bay Railway Line cannot be overestimated," Roberts was saying. "The Boers are holding three thousand British prisoners of war in Pretoria."

Fred knew that the Delagoa Bay Line linked Pretoria with the Indian Ocean port of Lorenco Marques in Mozambique. If the Boers moved these prisoners to the coast, they could hold them as hostages for bargaining at the peace table. In the humid tropical coast, the men would die by the hundreds.

"You will go with Major Hunter-Weston and a force of two hundred picked men," Roberts said. "They have agreed to make a hard ride without hesitating to sacrifice themselves if need be."

Scarcely forty-eight hours earlier, Fred had returned from his rail-blasting assault at Zuurfontein. He still hadn't regained the strength that had been sapped by that eleven-day outing. But there was nothing on earth that could hold Fred Burnham back from this mission. In his shirt pocket, unknown to anyone else, was a telegram from Howard Burnham. Written in code, it said Howie had accepted a daring spy assignment. He was en route by ship to Lorenco Marques. From there he would travel to the border town of Komatipoort. He planned to blow up the railway bridge at Komatipoort, severing the sole railway route between the Boers in the Transvaal and the Portuguese in Mozambique.

In the Elands Valley between Machadodorp and the Portuguese border, the Delagoa Bay Railway clawed its way through fifty miles of jungle. General Boot Botha had deployed six thousand Boers to protect Oom Paul Kruger, who was hunkered in his railway carriage somewhere short of the Portuguese colonial border.

If Fred could destroy the line between Pretoria and Machadodorp—as Lord Roberts was asking him to do—the two brothers could isolate Oom Paul's train. Then Roberts could send in a flying column and capture the leader of the Boers. It would be the biggest news of the war, and it would make the Burnham brothers famous. So there was nothing on God's green earth that could stop Fred from doing his best to carry out his part of this crucial mission.

Later that day, Fred was riding at the rear of Major Aylmer Hunter-Weston's engineer patrol, eating a cold beef sandwich. Up ahead, the scouts blundered into a superior enemy force—Boers infused with a new fighting spirit. The heavy Mauser fire suggested at least a thousand of the enemy faced them. Outnumbered by five to one, Hunter-Weston gave the order to withdraw.

"We have to run for it or they will surround us," he told Fred. "Ride back to find reinforcements."

Fred spurred Steenbok. The satin-shiny horse zigzagged at a gallop, eluding bullets and outrunning any ordinary mounted pursuer. Fred had grown to truly love this sure-footed horse. After a ninety-minute ride, he found General Dickson, who dispatched a relief force to aid Hunter-Weston's engineers. Dickson told Burnham to wait, then he sent a galloper to advise General French of the stiff new fighting spirit in the Boer Army. Soon thereafter, French appeared at General Dickson's bivouac for a council of war.

"Dickson," French snapped, "tell Hunter-Weston to take his men west and draw off the Boers. Burnham, you seem to be at your best working alone. Study these maps. When you've memorized your target, our sappers will issue you twenty-five pounds of guncotton. Above all, Roberts wants that railway line cut and you seem to be the only man capable of doing it."

Burnham left before sunset, riding over rolling hills covered by grass and occasional blue gum and mimosa trees. He saw no Boers but he did encounter a patrol, a small cavalry unit that General Gordon had sent out to inspect the railway station at Irene south of Pretoria.

"I have no scout," the young captain pleaded. "We're traveling in the same direction. Will you scout for me?" Fred hesitated but he could find no valid reason to refuse. In the light of a half moon, he saw the veld was giving way to rolling hills. That meant they were near Pretoria.

That night Fred helped the captain evade three Boer patrols. At two hours past midnight, with the moon about to set, they came to a hill covered by veld grass. It was the kind of place where Boers loved to hide in ambush.

Fred signaled the captain to halt while he rode ahead. Instinct told him to dismount, leave the guncotton behind and survey the hill on foot. But he was imbued with a sense of high urgency to see this mission through, and much precious time had been lost. They hadn't seen a sign of the enemy in hours and the moon would set shortly, so he decided it was worth a chance.

Fred rode slowly up the hill, leaning over his saddle horn to minimize his outline. When he was within twenty yards of the summit, he decided to dismount and continue his survey on foot to avoid making a silhouette against the skyline.

"*Hants oop*, you."

"*Frints*," Fred cried in his best Afrikaans.

For an instant the startled Boer actually lowered his Mauser. Fred flung himself over Steenbok's side, Apache style, and galloped downhill, quartering to the east to draw fire away from the British cavalry patrol. The whirring of Mauser bullets was answered by the pop of the Lee-Metfords. Fred saw a patch of fire-blackened ground ahead. If he could get over there, the Boers couldn't see him. His foot slipped from the stirrup and he almost fell, but he hung on to Steenbok's mane. What a wonderful pony this equine antelope was. Burnham dropped his rifle—no matter; he simply had to hide in that dark patch of burned-over ground. By the time he'd covered a hundred yards, the enemy fire slackened. While Steenbok continued to gallop, it was impossible to right himself. Fred's entire body was being hammered—in another twenty yards he'd be safe.

Then he was there: the black, fire-burned earth. He hauled on the reins to halt. Steenbok dug in his heels. In the background, Fred heard the faint whir of a Mauser bullet. For one long second he held his breath. Nothing happened. Then the moon and stars began spinning. Steenbok was sailing through the air above him, legs splayed upward. The horse brayed in mortal agony and Fred fell to the ground. In slow motion, Steenbok's body descended. The intense, crushing pain was followed by blackness.

373

49

Delagoa Bay Railway

THE VELD • JUNE 1900

RED WAS FREEZING. Waves of pain stabbed through his gut. His eyes wouldn't focus. *No, it's dark. This silence is total. Ah, I'm entombed in the snows of the Klondike. No, the weight of a pine tree is pinning me to a cliff on the Mogollon Rim. I'm thirsty, trapped in the sandy Harquehala Desert. I'm eating boiled horse on the banks of the Shangani.* Hazy forms began to take shape. The starry sky. Tree tops. No moon. It had set. Lying on the veld, he felt a pain in the gut. He was hurt something cruel. A heavy weight pressed on his legs. Consciousness began to slip away.

Am I going to my glory?

Some time later, he came to and tried to collect his wits. There had been a Boer ambush on a hill, near Irene. He was riding downhill toward a burned-out pasture, galloping like lions were chasing him. That's when he'd been shot in the gut.

No, it wasn't him—it was Steenbok, his wonderful pony. The horse was dead and it fell on him. He couldn't move—his back was broken. No, there was no pain in his back. He looked down. Steenbok's body covered his legs. He pulled his right leg and with effort it slid out. This ground was soft. It wasn't a burned-out pasture at all—it was newly plowed land. The newly tilled soil, and then a rainshower, had absorbed the shock and kept his legs from being broken.

A moist chill rippled over his skin. He trembled. Where was that guncotton? His knapsack was gone. He pulled his other leg free and rose to his knees. About twenty feet away, the knapsack was lying on the ground, its khaki color standing out against the black soil. He lay sprawled on the ground, suffering and wondering at his predicament.

Where was the cavalry patrol? Had they abandoned him? Seeing him fall, had they assumed he was dead? Being hard-pressed, had they retreated under fire? The moon was gone and Fred felt wholly exhausted. He succumbed to an all-encompassing need for healing sleep. Later, he awakened, astonished that he'd been able to sleep at all. The pain in his gut was raging. No, he hadn't really slept. He had passed out.

Damn, but it's cold. Save yourself. Shout for help. Light a fire. Call the Boers. You're helpless now. Even the enemy will provide medical care. You have done your best. His brain concentrated on thoughts of the physical self. His body was now numb. With an easing of the pain, new voices counseled him. *Will I fail Lord Roberts? Can I look Cecil Rhodes in the eye?* The pain eased and he rose to his knees. Immediately a new stab of pain knifed through his gut, then it eased. By crossing his hands over his belly and hugging himself, he could walk. His mind kept speaking: *Cut that railway. Help your brother. Howie is depending on you. Help him.*

The thought of his younger brother brought Fred to his senses. He picked up the guncotton, staggering along toward the northeast. For three hours he shogged along with no idea of where he was. The rolling hills south of Pretoria gave way to the open veld east of the Boer capital. He found a tree-lined road and trudged along the grassy verge. He no longer worried about capture. He simply plodded along, his hands holding his belly.

Was this the kind of pain Blanche felt when giving birth to their children?

It was the mid-morning of a drab, gray day. The road looped back toward Pretoria, so Fred struck out across the open ground in an easterly direction. As he entered a narrow vley that opened onto a meadow, he saw two farm houses made of stone. Horses were tethered outside. Tents dotted the landscape. Beyond was a swamp. The road forked at the farm houses and he found a goat kraal made of stone. It was no more than twenty feet across and it smelled like an aardvark hole, a real stinkpot. But it had a stone shed. He could rest and warm himself without attracting attention.

Once again he slept. He awakened several hours later when new pangs of pain pierced his insides. He peeped over the stone wall at the farmhouses. *It would be so easy to walk over, surrender and get medical aid.* A wave of nausea came over him. He vomited, choking out mouths of brown, coagulated blood. *Am I beyond help?* When the nausea eased, he took out a pencil and paper to write a farewell note to Blanche, but he never finished. His vision blurred and blackness came once more.

Some time later, he was awakened by the sound of men in heavy boots marching on gravel. The Boers were only yards away, going to the farmhouses and probably planning an attack on the British. Fred passed out again and didn't awaken until dusk. By then his gut was numb.

Once again he peeped over the stone wall. There were four houses. *No, two—I'm seeing double.* From the farm houses he could hear singing—religious hymns—it was Saturday night. It must be June 3, forty-eight hours since leaving British lines. The Boers had posted pickets and he was trapped inside their perimeter. But there were no guards at the swamp. They believed the cold water would prevent enemy activity in that quarter.

When darkness came, Fred climbed out of the kraal and shuffled down to the swamp. The water was icy cold, numbing cold. He tried to drink, but the water was so putrid he couldn't swallow it. So he waded across the swamp to the other shore. His legs were so cold he had to roll on the ground to restore circulation. Clouds obscured the moon.

Fred walked northeast, holding his belly in his arms. He was thirsty so he put a pebble in his mouth to make the saliva flow. He shuffled along in the darkness, unsure of where he was. About 2 a.m., the cloud cover broke and the veld was bathed in weak moonlight.

Ahead was a row of trees growing alongside a spruit. Beyond were dim lights. Fred figured he had walked half way to hell. He stopped at a small creek for a drink, but the sound of gruntling pigs told him the water was polluted. Feeling revulsion, he waded through the stream that flowed into the Piensaars River.

When he climbed the bank on the other side, he saw the lights of the brandy distillery, a large building of soot-stained brick. It was Eerste Fabrieke—the Boer name for First Factory. In the distance he heard the clear sound of a steam whistle, a railroad locomotive.

Slowly Fred shook off the lethargy that had dulled his senses for so many hours. Here was his goal. This was the Delagoa Bay Railway Line. There wasn't a moment to lose. That train might be carrying British prisoners. The distillery was still a mile away and the railroad track was just beyond it, on the Pretoria side.

A new sense of urgent purpose filled his mind. Gone were thoughts of surrender and medical aid. The distillery was fenced, so he walked east, figuring the enemy would be less likely to send a patrol to the far side.

First, he must find a place to hide. Then he must work out a route to avoid leaving a trail when he ran for cover. Wisps of steam rising from the distillery told him that inside there was clean, sterile drinking water. How thirsty he was. A feeling of shame came over him.

Why concern yourself with a minor matter like thirst when there is an important task to perform? Of the two hundred men sent on this mission, only you have succeeded in finding your way to the Delagoa Bay Line.

Now you must sever that line, not beg water like some common bum. You owe that much to Howie who wants to cut the other end of this railway.

The crunch of gravel told Fred he had reached the grade. A dark shadow suggested a galvanized iron shed that housed railway maintenance workers. He crept over and listened. Inside he heard snoring. He tried the door and it opened. He felt around and grabbed a blanket from an empty cot. It was his key to survival. He recalled the desert sickness on the Harquehala Plain in Arizona. With a blanket to hold body heat, he had a chance of survival. As he closed the door, someone snorted. In mere seconds Fred melted into the night.

He hiked east along the railway for a mile. The gray light of the predawn revealed a spruit ahead. The railway line followed a gentle curve before coming to a bridge. Across the spruit was a grove of blue gum trees with a hiding place.

Fred took off his knapsack and carefully removed the guncotton, blasting caps and fuses. A steam whistle in the distance suggested the train was fifteen minutes away. His task was completed in less than ten. When the fuse was lighted, he walked through the spruit and hid in the grove of eucalyptus trees.

The explosion came as Fred was rolling himself in the safety of the blanket. He imagined a Boer commando erupting from the Eerste Fabrieke Distillery to search for the British sappers who blew the rails. The train would screech to a halt in front of the distillery, confusing the soldiers and slowing the search. In time, the repair crew would begin work on the twisted rails.

It was too dangerous to chance sleeping while Boer patrols searched, but that night they failed to beat the grass in the grove. Fred decided they must be green-peas from the city with no outdoors experience. Fred slept most of the day.

At dusk he emerged to examine the state of repairs. The Boers had plenty of rails, sleepers and spikes because they'd mended the line in yeoman fashion. At any time, the train might resume its journey.

Fred decided he'd have to sever the line a second time—and do it quickly. He crept along the spruit until he was past the drift where the gruntlings had fouled the water. When he saw the bridge, he smiled. It wasn't much of a span. The stream was only about fifty feet wide. If he placed charges at the truss girders on the far side

Burnham: King of Scouts

where they rested on the concrete foundations, the Boers would be unable to dispatch a maintenance train to make repairs. Using mules and oxen, they'd have to haul the rails through the creek bed. It would take a couple of days to carry out that task.

Even at this stage of the war, the discipline of the Boers remained incredibly lax. Fred divided his guncotton and attached the dual charges to the pair of footings supporting the trusses. With any luck, the span would fall into the creek. He lighted the fuses and limped back along the spruit to the grove of blue gums. He was half way there when the two explosions went off almost as one. There was not a moment to lose. This time he must clear out and make his way back to friendly lines.

The dual explosions told the Boers that a dangerous enemy was lurking in the vicinity. They made it a point of honor to smoke out this intruder. They galloped into the blue gums, forcing Fred to climb a tree. This time he was being pursued by rural Boers, resolute men of the veld who were accomplished hunters. They beat the bush so fast that Fred felt like a fox before the hounds. These were men who'd shoot on sight and not take prisoners. Fred's high resolve and willingness to die, inspired a few hours earlier, deserted him.

When the Boers failed to catch him on the first round, they set fire to the grass to burn him out. By a process of elimination, they narrowed the search to the spot where Fred was hiding. He climbed high in the tree and wrapped himself around the trunk, trusting to the darkness for protection.

The Boer commandant, on a horse twenty feet away, shouted an oath. The men galloped through the grove shooting into the treetops. Nothing alive could survive that hail of Mauser slugs, but in deference to their boss, the men held back their fire when they rode past him.

The Boer leader ordered the men to sweep the grove again. Fred held on, frozen, all thoughts of pain ignored. This time the troopers dismounted to examine each tree. In the dim light of the burning grass, Fred saw a zealous Boer approach him. The soldier fired into a tree and was nearing Fred's hiding spot when there came a welcome sound Burnham wouldn't forget in years.

From far away came the rumble of horse-drawn artillery thundering in high retreat. The members of the Boer patrol, ignoring their commander's orders, joined the fleeing artillery. Once again, Burnham drew a breath without mortal fear.

The peril was over, but Fred was still isolated miles behind enemy lines. He was so thirsty he would gladly drink estuary mud. The abrupt departure of the Boers left him confused. He climbed out of the tree and rolled up in his blanket. The night passed slowly and he drowsed fitfully. If he could hang on until the British arrived and occupied the grove, he might survive. He dozed again.

Some time in the netherworld between sleep and consciousness, a thought occurred to him. Lord Roberts was quartered in that splendid suite in Johannesburg. Maybe he was in no hurry to leave those opulent digs.

Roberts had halted his army's advance before occupying Bloemfontein and Kroonstad. It had happened again at Johannesburg. Bobs might halt his advance before Pretoria too. If he did, Fred would die of hunger and thirst before help arrived.

In that moment, Fred came to the understanding that, if there was to be any chance of survival, he must get back to safety on his own—on hands and knees if need be. He began walking.

Shortly after dawn, the linen-ripping sound of British artillery shells in the distance restored Fred's confidence. He came to his senses, no longer concerned with hunger or thirst. The numbness in his gut now masked the pain. He shogged along toward the sounds of the artillery. After a couple of hours, his knees buckled.

Crawl. Ahead fifty yards is a tree. Crawl to that tree. It's your only chance. When you get there, you can rest. Now, see that bush ahead? Crawl there. Keep moving. Help is ahead. See that rock? Crawl to it. Don't pass out.

The day wore on in spasms of sleep, walk and crawl. He felt numb all over now and scarcely cared whether he lived or died. Sometimes he walked. When his knees gave out, he crawled. He sucked on a pebble to ease his thirst.

"Picket number nine, where are you?" At first, the words didn't register. Then the meaning got through. A guard was calling out in English.

"Help," Fred cried. The word emerged as a croak. He swallowed twice and some saliva moistened his tongue.

"Help." This time it sounded like the yip of a frightened puppy.

"I'm hurt." The words trailed off in despair.

50

Promoted to Major

PRETORIA • JUNE 1900

FRED HEARD VOICES, but couldn't make out the words. He blinked. Suspended from the ceiling by a two-strand twisted wire, an electric light bulb twinkled. Hanging next to the light, a roll of fly paper collected insects. Fred's eyes focused on the figure of a man standing beside him. It was Aylmer Hunter-Weston, the Royal Engineer.

"By the great golden gazanias, Burnham, you're indestructible." Hunter-Weston's face was split by a wide grin. "Everyone thought you were a goner, but I fancied you'd make it back."

Major Hunter-Weston looked like the happiest man alive.

"Where am I?" Fred felt weak and was disoriented.

"Pretoria Hospital. You've had surgery and been in a coma for a day and a half."

"I'm hungry."

"The doctor says you can have liquids, but you're lucky you didn't eat when you were in the field."

"How did I get here?" Fred tried to sit up but sharp pains told him to lie back down.

"One of General Dixon's pickets found you in the dirt five miles east of Pretoria," Hunter-Weston said. "On peeling off an agglomeration of mud and grass, they discovered it was you—barking like an old baboon."

"Oh," he said. His mind remained fuzzy.

"We brought you to Pretoria in a bullock cart. You were rather fogged, but still worth saving. Kept calling for food. The guards offered some hardtack, but you couldn't get it down." Hunter-Weston explained that in his fall, Fred had torn a stomach muscle and ruptured a blood vessel.

"Doc Edwards says your life was saved only because you didn't eat or drink before surgery." The doctor estimated that Fred had hemorrhaged internally for twenty-four hours.

Fred felt deflated. A bullet wound was a badge of honor, a scar to display with pride. But a wrenched gut muscle was mortifying. It took extensive questioning for Hunter-Weston to piece together the facts and pass them on to Field Marshal Lord Roberts. Fred had stumbled cross-country a distance of eighteen miles to blow up the rail lines. Before collapsing, he crawled half way back. It was an exceptional feat for an injured soldier.

"Well, Captain, the war's over for you," Hunter-Weston declared. "They're hiving you off to London for surgery."

Fred digested the news. London—that meant Blanche and the boys.

"You have visitors. Are you up to talking?"

"Only to friends, no reporters yet."

Hunter-Weston opened the door and Stephe Baden-Powell came in, accompanied by Winston Churchill. Fred looked at the defender of Mafeking, and was puzzled to see that Stephe wasn't wearing his colonel's uniform. He was wearing the insignia of—good Lord—a major general. Something else seemed different, but Fred couldn't put his finger on it. He blamed his grogginess on the surgery.

After inquiring about Fred's condition, Baden-Powell chatted about the old days in 1896—the Matopo Hills and the scouting patrol to View of the World and Inugu in Mineral King. Stephe then lauded Churchill's newspaper article, based on an interview in Joburg.

"Reading this Churchill fellow is like listening to a phonograph machine," Baden-Powell said. "He got every word of it."

"If I'd had more time, I could have made it shorter," Churchill added with a chortle.

Fred was eager to learn how Baden-Powell's military career had advanced so dramatically, but Doc Edwards told the visitors to leave so the patient could rest.

Two days later, on Saturday, June 9, Burnham relaxed under an overcast sky in a chaise longue, recuperating with the wounded. He skimmed news articles. *South Africa* for May 19 carried a piece telling how Fred and Aylmer wrecked the Boer railway at America Siding. The *London Daily Telegraph* carried a major article by Bennett Burleigh on "The Defender of Mafeking." The Baden-Powell story ran for eighty-three column inches. Amazing.

When Fred read the article, he was astonished at what had taken place. In the days preceding Mafeking's relief, Reuters reported that

Colonel Plumer was closing in on Mafeking. War bulletins from Lorenco Marques, Pretoria and Cape Town told of raging battles. One report spoke of hand-to-hand fighting saying the defenders had died in the streets. The truth was considerably different.

Ritornello • Interlude

LONDON • MAY 1900

AT DUSK ON Friday, May 18, the lamp lighters were making their evening rounds when the news of Mafeking's relief was flashed by Reuters News Agency. Colonel Plumer's soldiers had ridden into Mafeking wholly unopposed. Yet the relief of Mafeking hit London like a bombshell. The news touched off major merrymaking during warm spring weather. From the start, the level of jubilation was clearly extravagant.

- Within minutes of the report at 9:30 p.m., a crowd appeared. A great swell of shouting arose. People sang "Rule Britannia," and then "God Save the Queen," followed by "Soldiers of the Queen." By 10 o'clock, the downtown streets swarmed with revelers.
- Huge crowds appeared at Charing Cross, Piccadilly Circus and

Trafalgar Square. Cockneys streamed out of pubs swinging their pints. Young men, happy to know they wouldn't be called up to serve, dived into public pools. Daring girls lifted their skirts above their ankles.

• People waved the Union Jack. Cannons were fired. Skyrockets pierced the clouds. Such an outburst had never occurred. By midnight, the people of London seemed to be dotty. They showed no sign of dispersal. Officials became concerned at the lack of public order. The massing in the streets far exceeded the crowds that had gathered for Queen Victoria's Diamond Jubilee.

• An upsurge of joy, patriotism and national pride controlled everyone's' emotions. Newsboys hawked their ha' penny extras for twopence, selling out in minutes.

• Trains chuffing through the midlands blew their steam whistles. Church bells rang. In New York, newspaper extras hit the streets in time to catch people leaving work at the end of the day.

• From Brighton to Glasgow, processions of joyous people took to the streets. The folk rejoiced in Dublin, Montreal, Brisbane, Wellington and Melbourne. Singapore declared a public holiday.

• Friday became Mafeking Day, a hint of things to come. The assemblage was destined to last six days and nights.

• On Saturday, Bennett Burleigh's eighty-three-inch news article on Baden-Powell was published in the *London Daily Telegraph* and the crowds went wild. Baden-Powell became the most popular war hero since Admiral Horatio Nelson defeated the Spanish Fleet at Trafalgar, north of Gibraltar. Mother Henrietta Baden-Powell, waving from a box seat at the Alhambra Theater, accepted the applause of a grateful and cheering audience.

• On Sunday, while people sang and danced in the streets, Queen Victoria sent a cablegram to Colonel Baden-Powell:

I and my whole Empire greatly rejoice at the relief of Mafeking after the splendid defence made by you through all these months. I heartily congratulate you and all under you, military and civil, British and native, for the heroism and devotion you have shown.

—Victoria Regina et Imperatrix

• On Monday came a cablegram grudgingly sent by Sir Alfred Milner with official confirmation that Mafeking had been relieved. The British Army, even less ebullient, didn't get around to posting the news until later in the day. But the public was not to be denied its springtime romp, and that night saw the spread of festivities to the villages in the moors.

• On Tuesday, the people refused to settle down. Pub owners were

Behind Enemy Lines

buoyed by the knowledge that they could settle stale accounts and pay off arrears in mortgages.

• Wednesday, the Queen's birthday, brought victory parades and celebrations. Traffic in London was held to a standstill and crowds showed no inclination to disperse.

• It wasn't until Thursday, after six days of celebrating, that there was a general return to work. The week was a mad rampage that introduced a new word to the British language: *maffick*—to give way to excessive displays of jubilance during national rejoicing.

• • •

Pretoria • June 1900

SO GREAT WAS the public acclaim, the newspapers said, that at her Birthday Honors List, Queen Victoria was inspired to promote Colonel Baden-Powell to major general, ahead of two hundred senior officers. At the age of forty-three, Stephe was the youngest general officer in the British Army.

Now Fred understood why his friend had talked about the Matopos; Baden-Powell's promotion was something of an embarrassment. Stephe knew that during the week of revelry, Fred had been behind enemy lines blowing up the railway east of Pretoria.

Colonel Plumer, the urn-eared infantryman who'd rescued Stephe, was rewarded with a two-inch mention in *South Africa*. Fred puzzled over another article in *South Africa* magazine. Cecil Rhodes had sailed from England to look at a copper discovery in Barotze Land. What did that mean?

The June 9 issue of the *African Review* arrived the next day. Fred learned of Lord Gifford's latest perfidy. The Northern Coppers (BSA) Exploration Company had emerged in the place of the Northern Territories (BSA) Exploration & Development Company. The Northern Coppers Company had dispatched F.R. Lewis to Barotze Land to explore five hundred square miles of copper concessions.

If that wasn't enough of an insult, Lord Gifford had hived off the Wankie Coal Farms to something called the Mashonaland Agency. For one of the few times in his life, Burnham spent the better part of a minute cursing the ground that Lord Gifford walked on. Fred vowed never again to have business dealings with the man.

His eyes landed on a letter from London in Rod's handwriting. The Kid would be fourteen in two months and Fred—sure as shootin—would be there for the party.

I found a boy here who likes playing camping and scouting on the heath. We built a bungalow in their garden and toasted bread and sausages over the campfire. I lead my classes into school every day and they call me Burnham, the American Scout. Now the whole class is called Burnham's Scouts. I like math, but not Latin. Beastly stuff. Your faithful son. Roderick Burnham

Fred's reflections were interrupted by a visitor.

"Am I glad to see you alive!"

"Well, Howie, I thought you were making mischief at Komatipoort."

"I got captured by the Boers," he confided, "but their discipline was lax. I escaped and reached Johannesburg. When I heard about your injury, I got a pass to ride on the railroad."

"Here come the members of the press," Fred said.

"Say nothing of my mission," Howard pleaded. "It would be humiliating."

Fred nodded. He knew Bennett Burleigh of the *Daily Telegraph*. The other visitor was new. Lord Cecil Manners wrote for *South Africa* magazine. The pair spent the next hour asking Fred detailed questions about blowing up the Delagoa Bay Railway.

"In Mafeking," Burleigh said, "I met a Captain de Montmorency who had been with Colonel Plumer."

"Don't know the man," Fred said.

"Curious, he told me nine civilians were killed during the eight months of the siege. If what I hear is right, Baden-Powell spent his time eating crumpets and marching half-grown children around the dusty little compound."

Burnham shrugged. "Doesn't sound like an all-hands-and-the-cook-too sort of fracas, does it Howie?"

Fred's younger brother laughed and shifted his stump to a new resting place.

"In Baden-Powell's report he wrote of an absence of luxuries," Burleigh said. "Captain de Montmorency gave me this menu from Reisle's Mafeking Hotel."

It was dated Christmas 1899. Fred studied the bill of fare: anchovies, croutons, olives, consommé Windsor, oyster patties, smoked calves tongues, giblet pie, tournedos Parisienne, York ham and madeira sauce, fricassee of veal, roast fowl and bread sauce, boiled fowl and bacon. That was for starters. The meal also boasted baron of beef and Yorkshire pudding, veal and ham, roast side of lamb and green peas, suckling pig and apple sauce, roast saddle of mutton, boiled mutton and capers, boiled bacon, corned beef, tongue and ham. If not sated by then, there was roasted marrow, baked and boiled potatoes, pudding, mincemeat pies, Sandringham jellies, Victoria sandwiches, desert and café noir.

"Well," Fred said, "at least he had the good sense to choose Reisle's Hotel. The food at Dixon's is weird."

"Captain de Montmorency said, 'To me the whole affair of the siege has been an enigma. What in the world was the use of defending that wretched railway siding and those tin shanties? To burrow underground at the first shot being fired seems to me the strangest role ever played by a military commander. Had mobility been preserved, as Colonel Plumer's force was, they might have raided in the Transvaal and harassed the enemy.'" Among those who knew—including senior officers in the army—the newly minted Major General Baden-Powell wore a crown of pansies.

Lagnappe • A Little Extra

Cape Town • July 1900

THE BURNHAM BROTHERS planned to celebrate the Fourth of July by taking lunch at the Mount Nelson Hotel with Howard's fiancée, Connie Newton. Howie joined Fred aboard the steamer *Dunotter Castle* in Table Bay. Fred held a letter from Blanche.

"It's dated June 1," he told Howard, "the day I left to blow up the Boer railway line. Bea says Nada would've been six years old. She wishes I was in Bulawayo to cover her resting place with flowers."

"She's still grieving over Nada. Poor Blanche. What news from the boys?"

"They're fine."

"Do you think the fighting will be over soon?"

"The war will turn into a guerrilla action. The British will have to win this land from the Boers the same way we took the West from the Indians."

"Can you take solid food?"

"In moderation. I'm a glutton for chicken soup."

They debarked and hailed a cab to the Mount Nelson Hotel. Fred looked smart in his new uniform. The three diamond pips on the shoulder boards had been replaced by a single crown. When Connie Newton met them in the lobby, she was carrying a copy of the *Los Angeles Herald*.

"Don't be angry at reading this," she said.

Fred saw the headline: "The Story of Frank Burnham, the Kit Carson of Africa."

"In the story, the reporter identifies you properly as Fred," Connie said. "Apparently the makeup editor made a mistake when he wrote the headline."

"That's melodramatic stuff," Fred said after reading the article. "It says I ended the Matabele War with a single shot."

"Well, you know Uncle Josiah," Howie said, grinning. "He's your advertising manager in Los Angeles."

"Back in Iowa, he was a pretty hard-nosed editor at the *Clinton Herald*, a real stickler for facts. It's one reason why I ran away from home."

"When speaking of Africa, the deeds grow in daring for each league of distance," Howie said with glee.

An article on Baden-Powell in *South Africa* magazine gave full credit to Burnham, the American Scout, as his mentor. It quoted Stephe's soon-to-be-famous anecdote on the broken leaf and the blade of grass. The article said *Aids to Scouting* was a best seller.

"Let's order tiffin," Connie suggested.

While they were waiting to be served, Fred asked the newlyweds about their plans for the honeymoon. The waiter arrived then with a creamy potage, serving Connie first. As the waiter leaned over to serve Fred, Connie studied the man who would become her brother in law. Something caught her eye.

"Oh, Fred! What a surprise you are. You're wearing a major's insignia. Do tell me about your promotion."

While they ate, he explained what had happened.

"When I was discharged from the hospital," he said, "an orderly instructed me to report to Lord Roberts. When I arrived, he asked me details of blowing up the Delagoa Bay Railway Line. I told him everything I could remember up to the time I returned to British lines.

"Bobs nodded and sat there in silence for the longest time. Then he withdrew a sheet of stationery and wrote this note." Fred handed her an envelope.

"As I was saying farewell, he handed me these shoulder boards, saying, 'Wear them now. The order will be published later this week.' That was all. We shook hands, saluted and he handed me orders transferring me to London for medical treatment."

Connie Newton, British born, read the letter carefully and a look of awe spread over her face. "Treasure this always!" she said. "I'll be proud to be your sister in law."

• • •

AT 7 P.M., the *Dunotter Castle* set sail for Southampton. While Connie and Howard waved good-bye from the wharf, the ship sailed past Mouille Point and the sun quenched its fiery inferno in the Atlantic.

An hour later the vessel had picked up speed and the dinner chimes sounded. Fred's messmates gathered on the promenade deck and a lively lot they proved to be. Sir Bryan Leighton was a handsome man with a dashing flair, an upturned hat and a mustache.

Fred was delighted to see Sir Abe Bailey, still youthful looking, with close-cropped hair. He stood a head taller than Fred and seemed ever-so-young to be a partner of Rhodes in Joburg gold. Fred knew Abe from his service during the assignment to the staff of General Reggie Pole-Carew.

Lord Brooke wore a black suit and a dark mariner's hat with a white stripe. About thirty, he was the most dashing figure aboard ship. He would be a natural for the stage.

Major Joe Laycock wore a visionary look, as through dreaming of somewhere far away. Maurice Gifford, still touchy about his missing arm, walked with his body turned to emphasize the remaining limb. Fred didn't fault him for the jiggle-billy acts of his elder brother.

As he made his way to the mess, Fred saw the two scouting majors, Bobby and Harry White, old campaigners from Rhodesia days. Harry, the former captain of scouts for the Victoria Column, looked as dour as ever. He was embarrassed when Fred thanked him in public for the nomination as chief scout to Lord Roberts. They had not met since the 1896 Matabele Rebellion.

Fred knew the newsmen: Winston Churchill and Lord Downe. Churchill was the youngest man in the group and the only person in the mess with a valet. During the get-acquainted banter, Churchill vied with the lords to become the center of attention. *He's an arrogant young man.*

Sir Henry Colvile, the ranking officer, arrived as soup was being served. General Colvile, though the senior officer in the mess, was attired in civilian clothing. Even in mufti, he commanded the respect of all as he took his chair at the head of the table. The ocean air had given everyone good appetites and the meal, sea bream from Table Bay, was a treat for fish lovers.

"Major Burnham," Churchill said, "I understand you have a letter from Lord Roberts. May the members of this distinguished mess be honored by seeing it?"

"Go ahead," said Major Harry White. "But make that young pup read it aloud."

Burnham handed the letter to Churchill, who walked to the head of the table, where he stood beside General Colvile. In a stentorian voice that one day would make him famous, Churchill read:

Army Headquarters, 25th of June 1900

Dear Major Burnham:

I take this opportunity to thank you for the valuable services you have performed since you joined my headquarters at Paardeberg. I doubt if any other man in the force could have carried out the perilous enterprises on which you have engaged, demanding as they did the training of a lifetime, combined with exceptional courage, caution and powers of endurance.

I was sorry to hear of the serious accident you met with on your last successful attempt on the enemy's line of railway, and look forward to hear that you are quite well again. Believe me, yours sincerely,

— ROBERTS

Churchill sat down and not a sound was heard over the gentle throb of the propellers and the sea water gliding past the hull. General Colvile rose and spoke.

"By Jove, Burnham, that's remarkable. In thirty years, I've never known of Lord Roberts to write a letter like that. Guard it with your life. It's more valuable than the Victoria Cross."

Behind Enemy Lines

MESSMATES — Standing: Byron Layton, Claud Grenfel, Major Burnham, Gordon Forbes, Abe Bailey, unknown, unknown, Lord Brook. Seated: Bobby White, Lord Downe, General Colvile, Major Harry White, Joe Laycock, Winston Churchill, Charles Bentinck. On floor: unknown, Maurice Gifford, still sensitive about his missing arm.

King of Scouts

The 11th Chronicle

51

The Baden-Powell Letters

DUNOTTER CASTLE • JULY 1900

IF FRED BURNHAM planted the seeds of the Boy Scout movement at the time of the 1896 Rebellion, he fertilized their roots during the Boer War. On his fifth day at sea, Fred wrote a letter to Major General Baden-Powell.

I hope and believe you will be home in a month or two. We'll all shout ourselves hoarse when you come! And after it's all over, I want to talk to you about scouting. Briefly, my hope is this: That you'll still look on it as formerly, an important and vital branch of the service and one that is sadly in need of organization. That in spite of your promotion and honors, you'll take it up at the War Office and make it the special hobby horse to ride up and down the corridors of the War Office until the big officials come to see what all the fuss is about.

My ambition is to become your galloper and aide-de-camp. I feel up to the job and I believe you could carry the plan easily and organize a small corps of the most valuable men who ever fought for the Queen and Empire. During the war, I saw things every day that would make an angel weep. I saw whole troops of men calling themselves scouts who didn't know enough to pound sand in a rat hole. And yet they provided the only intelligence the commander-in-chief could get. So much needless worry could have been spared him if properly trained men could have come in to him every hour or so with the items of news of the enemy—and of our own columns too. I believe the finest kind of material is going to waste in the Army: keen, plucky athletic fellows but no training.

It is in time of peace that a small band of young officers should take up this work. And when a sudden war is sprung on us again, every brigade would have at least one A-1 First Class Scout and several

Second Class. Many of the officers are keen on the work. They should be put through a severe test physically and tried mentally to see if they could stand all night in a drizzling storm, watching a path to catch an enemy dispatch, and do this night after night on half rations. Some fellows are keen for adventure but shy from drudgery performed in obscurity. Their enthusiasm dies as the sun goes down.

After being well tested, it would be a good investment for the government to school them as First Class Scouts and send them to every part of the earth. It is no stretch of the imagination to think the Empire might be challenged sometime by a power that would call for every man from eighteen to sixty-five to do his duty. Where now are the trained scouts to do the work and save regiments and brigades from ambushes, mad charges, hopeless night attacks or wild stampedes?

In this war, fortunately, when we lost a crack regiment, we simply sent out two new ones. But blundering through by force of numbers will not do in the future. It will all depend on the man behind the gun. He will need brains, the cunning of a fox, and courage—the latter all Britons have.

Such a reorganization could be effected without adding much to present expenditures. It would only change their channels a little. I hope you will write me a short note telling me I may see you and where. Yours very truly, F.R. Burnham

This was the first in a lively swap of letters that would last four decades. During those years, Stephe would press Fred for additional advice on scouting. He would probe for details of American frontier lore, of tracking and trailing, of sign language, of what kit and gear to carry. Baden-Powell had an abounding thirst for knowledge of the outdoors. Fred wanted an elite cadre of military scouts, a corps of the most unusual and valuable men who ever fought. He suggested they be Army officers with rank based on merit and accomplishment, not birthright.

Lagnappe • A Little Extra

PRETORIA • JUNE 1900

A WEEK AFTER Fred wrote his letter, Lord Roberts relieved General Baden-Powell, turned his command over to Colonel Plumer and suggested that Stephe take leave of absence—an unheard of chastisement during hostilities.

It happened this way.

Roberts had devised a plan to trap the Boer General Christiaan de Wet and possibly President Steyn as well. Instead of attacking as Bobs ordered, Baden-Powell made camp and allowed De Wet to escape. To absolve himself, he shifted the blame to a subordinate. At

King of Scouts

that point, the hero of Mafeking came into bad odor among his peers. His career was salvaged only through chance.

For weeks, Sir Alfred Milner had been pressing the War Office to establish a mounted force that could police the territories captured from the Boers. When Sir Alfred once again put forward his view, Lord Roberts asked the high commissioner if General Baden-Powell would be a suitable candidate to lead such a police force.

At first, Milner was enraged at the idea of Baden-Powell getting the nod. He had been hoping to nominate his own man, Colonel Jack Nicholson. When it became apparent that Lord Roberts' sole candidate was Baden-Powell, Milner decided to accept Stephe, providing Jack Nicholson was brought down from Rhodesia and assigned as chief of staff. Lord Roberts, who had never heard of the colonial, Jack Nicholson, agreed. Milner smiled. He had just put one over on Lord Roberts.

Within hours of Milner's assent, Baden-Powell was on the train to Cape Town. On arrival, he was carried away on the shoulders of cheering men. It was the onset of a new life for Stephe—the public never forgot their gratitude. Yet as far as the British military was concerned, Baden-Powell was the recipient of glory he didn't earn. The general officers corps would keep him in Africa until that ruddy Mafeking do was history.

Ritornello • An Interlude

BLUE TRAIN • SEPTEMBER 1900

THE HIGH COMMISSIONER dispatched Stephe back to Pretoria to organize the South African Constabulary. While riding the train, he replied to Fred's letter.

On the train en route to Pretoria
10 September 1900

I want to thank you truly for your kind and most interesting letter. I heartily endorse every word you say. I only wish I had the power to put it as forcibly as you do. I shall endeavor to follow in your lead when I represent my views to the War Office. And I should like, trusting you have no objection, to show your letter to Lord Roberts. He will soon be in charge of things at the War Office and your ideas will go a long way with him. He has already asked me to suggest any points I can for consideration regarding the future training of the Army, and I have not forgotten to put scouting in a permanent place in the education of the young officers and soldiers.

To make some practical start in that direction, I should like to get a man like yourself to undertake the instruction of young officers in the art of scouting at Sandhurst. Its full application can be learned

395

only by practical experience in the field after the officer has had his scouting instincts roused and his keenness stirred.

I don't know whether you saw a little book for self-instruction that I brought out for my men. Just an attempt to start them with an elementary idea of scouting. I'm glad to see the inspector general of cavalry in India has recommended that all cavalry officers out there make use of it. If only started, a better system of instruction will no doubt be evolved.

I fear I shall not be able to come home for some time as they have put in my hands the organization of the military police for the new Orange River Colony and the Transvaal. It will be some few months before I shall be free to take any leave. I'm not altogether sorry as England would be too much of a good thing until the exuberance of Mafeking has died down a bit. I found that exultation still much too lively in Cape Town. I hope to see England perhaps next spring.

In the meantime, you may be sure I shall do all I can to get the question of effective scouting recognized as a vitally important point for consideration in the reforms which will be introduced into the training of the Army.

I shall be glad if you will, at any time, write to me any further ideas that may strike you on the subject. It's not that I propose to suck your brains and use your ideas, but that we may act in unison and get this thing through. Now good-bye for the present. Please give my kindest regards to Mrs. Burnham and Believe me, yours truly. R.S. Baden-Powell

One of Stephe's first tasks in organizing the South African Constabulary was to design its uniform. It was a jolly affair, with green and yellow piping and Montana peak Stetson hats imported from America. The hats had feather plumes that were dyed green. The commander himself would wear a strikingly splendid uniform—it borrowed garb from the uniforms of a French constable, a Spanish general and an Italian admiral.

• • •

PRETORIA • OCTOBER 1900

LORD ROBERTS HAD no sooner transferred Baden-Powell to the high commissioner's staff than another idea occurred to him. Why not unload some of this guerrilla warfare on Baden-Powell and let him mire in his own ineptitude? Lord Roberts suggested to Sir Alfred a plan to double the size of the South African Constabulary to ten thousand men. Roberts' idea was to use constabulary officers to replace army troops whose terms of service were expiring. When

Bobs offered to cover the salaries of the additional troops, Milner was quick to spot a bargain.

In response, Sir Alfred suggested that the commander of the new force should report to the army instead of the high commissioner. Roberts agreed. He had publicly declared the war to be practically over, and he already had orders transferring him back to England. That meant he would leave Baden-Powell to the tender mercies of Lord Kitchener.

Under Kitchener, the mission of the South African Constabulary would be to round up the wives and children of the Boer guerrillas who had been raiding on the veld. Kitchener borrowed an idea from the Union Army in the Civil War. The Boer dependents—wives and children—would be placed in fenced camps. That way they couldn't plant seeds, harvest crops or cook meals for their menfolk. The irony of Baden-Powell's new job was this: The man who would found the Boy Scout movement would first organize concentration camps.

52

Queen Victoria

LONDON • AUGUST 1900

FRED'S ARRIVAL in England touched off a minor national celebration just short of the *mafficking* gala staged in absentia for General Baden-Powell. Because Stephe was still confined to southern Africa, the British chose his mentor — the celebrated American Scout — as a surrogate conquering hero. For Stephe, the *mafficking* lasted six days. For Burnham, it began on the wharf at Southampton, with a big reception, and it continued on a grand but quieter scale throughout England for six months.

The day after Fred's arrival, *South Africa* magazine published an article by Lord Cecil Manners on "Burnham's Bravery." A week later, the magazine did a piece on the tactics used in the Boer War, which ended with Fred's forecast of "The Scout of the Future." It was quoted throughout the Empire.

He will need more than keen sight and acuteness of hearing. He must be an engineer as well, and have knowledge of electricity and all the latest scientific inventions. The future scout should be able to judge the facilities for entrenchments and the positions for guns, to distinguish between the various calibers of the enemy's artillery and to estimate the disposition and range of each cannon. In order to acquire the habit of seeing in the dark, men and boys should be encouraged to play games at night. It was not uncommon in the West for men to go hunting by moonlight.

To celebrate The Kid's birthday on August 22, the family had a picnic at Burnham Beeches thirty miles west of London. Once the property of Burnham Abbey, it had passed into the ownership of the city of London and was used for public recreation. Hundreds of acres of oak, birch and beech trees had evolved into strange shapes because people hacked off the lower limbs for use as firewood. There were no restaurants, but picnickers could spread out a blanket anywhere. The Burnhams had a grand time—after the rigors of war it proved to be a wonderful place for Fred to hold a family get-together.

Because of Fred's celebrated status, the Burnhams came to know the brighter side of London: the upper-middle-class Kensington district, the raffish, avant-garde flats of Chelsea, the fashionable embassy row section of Belgravia and that hub of London, Piccadilly Circus, the central meeting place of the city. For Fred, there was also visits to surgeon's row in Harley Street at Marylebone.

The British peerage interpreted Lord Roberts' letter of appreciation to Fred as an imperative social introduction. To them it involved almost an Imperial obligation to the American Scout who had done his bit for the Old Country. In the weeks that followed, the doors of British society were quietly opened to Fred and Blanche. They came to know the charm of English country life by experience instead of by hearsay.

In the Midlands north of London, they were received by lords and ladies and fancy nobles. They visited the moors—tracts of wasteland—and the valleys. They toured Harrogate, where acres of floral gardens produced vibrant color. They rode carriages through the Yorkshire dales, stopping to inspect English villages and view emerald fields divided by stone walls that dated to the Roman Era.

In the afternoons, Blanche and Fred were hosted by lairds and ladies to high tea, dining on fresh scones, strawberry jam and clotted cream. It was a delightful change from the wilds of Africa and it gave the American family new meaning to English countryside living.

Once Blanche learned the rules of the British nobility, she wrote to Mother Blick and warned her not to breathe a word of their social activities to the Pasadena or Los Angeles newspapers. Publicity was regarded as crass and uncouth. It was guaranteed to remove the Burnhams' name from invitation lists. Blanche wrote:

> Lady Jelicoe invited us to meet Princess Christian, the daughter of Queen Victoria, and her daughter, Princess Alberta, the one who visited the United States last summer. We were there two days and enjoyed it. We heard the Queen talked about, and the stories of life with her were like any ordinary dear old mother and her grandchildren. Lady Dorothy Neville was there. Also Sir Herbert Spencer. We are now visiting the Earl and Countess of Portsmouth.
>
> Everyone is anxious to show Fred honors and attention. Of course, we like to tell our relatives what is happening, but it must not get into

the newspapers. Fred wants to stress that you must never say anything in public about our visits to royalty.

The warning was aimed at Uncle Josiah Russell, the newspaper editor from Clinton, Iowa, who had served for seven years as Fred's local publicist. At the drop of a newspaper clipping or letter from London, Uncle Josiah would visit the Los Angeles Press Club, buy a round of drinks and pass on the word. As a result of Blanche's warning, the Burnham name disappeared from California newspapers for six years.

Toward the end of the muggy English summer, Fred and Blanche needed privacy and rest. They'd just returned from grouse hunting in Scotland and someone suggested a weekend on the coast at Bournemouth. Thirty miles from Southampton, Bournemouth was the premier holiday resort in England.

"We'll stay at Ramleh House in Westcliff Gardens," Fred said. "It overlooks the channel. Nobody will know where we are."

Fred was wrong. Curtis Brown of *Pearson's* magazine tracked him down and published an article that began a long association with the Pearson organization:

You might figure him a lean, long, swashbuckler with revolvers in his belt and vast oaths on his lips. In that case, you'd pass without noticing the quiet, low-voiced, modestly dressed little man who strolls the fashionable Bournemouth cliffs. It is not really honest to call him a little man. Although he's not much over five feet, his shoulders are broad and square, and there is something about his appearance that suggests immense strength. His hardest training has been in the matter of sleep. He can get along for two nights and part of a third without a wink of sleep. He's cosmopolitan in the matter of residence. He owns a house in Bulawayo, and another in the Klondike. His home is Pasadena and he lives in London.

Writer Hugh Sutherland followed up with a Sunday supplement feature article titled "A Unique Hero in the Boer War."

Not a great deal of fame has been won in the South African War by those fighting for Great Britain. The world seems to have conferred nearly all the garlands to the other side. But there is no one to dispute the fame of Fred R. Burnham.

His achievements were not only startling, but also unique. Lord Roberts himself declared that no man had done more for the success of the British than this sturdy, keen-witted, tireless American.

From New York came a report by Richard Harding Davis.

King of Scouts

TRACKING THE WILY BOER
An American Is the Favorite Scout of Lord Roberts

In the force that Lord Roberts gathered before Pretoria, there mingled a quiet, keen-visaged man whose dress and demeanor were not those of a soldier. Yet every soldier, high or low, singled him out for respectful attention. "That's Burnham," the word passed along. "That's Burnham, the American Scout." Officers of high rank treated him with great distinction. Privates stared at him and recounted his exploits. They told each other that this Burnham was a magician of his craft, that he was admired by Baden-Powell, that he had killed the Matabele god, that he was the optic nerve of the British Army.

The eyes of the man were what most impressed beholders. They were the all-seeing eyes of a hunter, the eyes that let not the quiver of a twig escape them. They were clear and bright, trained to gather swift impressions for the reasoning brain behind them, familiar with all the aspects of nature, cunning and alert as a wild animal's. As a member of Lord Roberts' staff, he was a personage of importance in the army, although the secret nature of his services prevented him from coming in contact with the main body.

The barrage of feature articles continued until the newspapers and magazines of London conferred on Fred the accolade: King of Scouts. That nickname prompted another round of invitations. When the letter from Oxford arrived, Fred was terrified. He was sensitive to his lack of schooling: one year of high school in Clinton, Iowa.

Fred would have turned down the invitation to speak at Oxford had Blanche not insisted that he accept. When the big day arrived, the Oxford dons proved to be more interested in Fred's military accomplishments than his schooling.

There wasn't an embarrassing moment.

Next came the invitation from Osborne House—a royal command to dine with Queen Victoria and stay the night. Blanche was more thrilled than she could possibly express. It was a social achievement that no woman from Pasadena could possibly hope to duplicate.

And she couldn't breath a word of it to anyone.

• • •

THEY TRAVELED by train to the Royal Navy base at Portsmouth where they boarded an admiral's gig for the voyage to the Isle of Wight in the English Channel. While sailing down the estuary, Fred went over the plan he had been working on. He wanted the Queen's help in getting an appointment with the War Secretary so he could present this plan for a Scout Corps in the British Army.

When they debarked, a royal carriage transported them to Osborne House, which wasn't a palace or castle in the ordinary sense because it was a wooden building. It was almost hidden by high hedges and spacious lawns.

Everything was green.

"It seems to be a modest place," Fred said. As they entered the gate, he saw how imposing the mansion actually was. The building was four stories high—a turret-like rotunda rose to the third floor level. On the left side was a glassed-in tower, which provided a view of the lawn, the flower gardens and the English Channel.

"It's bigger than I thought," he admitted.

"The Queen built Osborne House for Prince Albert between 1845 and 1851," Blanche said. "He died in 1861, the year you were born. During their marriage she bore him nine children."

Before their visit, Blanche had mugged up on things.

"When the Queen was named Empress of India, she renovated the Durbo Room. She now employs Hindu servants."

At four o'clock, the royal carriage deposited Fred and Blanche under the porte cochere. They were escorted upstairs to guest quarters to rest and freshen up. Fred spread-eagled himself on an oversized bed of goose down.

"Ain't this livin, Bea?" he crowed. "A butler at the door and porters to carry your luggage. Maids and waiters to attend your every wish."

"Act grown up, Fred, and don't say ain't. Oh, what shall I wear?"

Fred knew what she would wear: the expensive dress she'd bought in London last week for this occasion. Fred took a leisurely bath: He wanted to say he had bathed in a royal castle.

At five o'clock, they heard a gentle scratching of fingernails on the door—the Queen forbade knocking—and an attendant escorted them downstairs to meet Her Highness. Fred was introduced by name, title and a list of his campaigns and decorations. Blanche had practiced her curtsies and performed flawlessly. Fred, spotless in formal uniform, bowed deeply.

The Queen was pudgy, jowly and moon-faced, with a big body and gap teeth. She wore a dress of wool, and she carried herself upright to compensate for the overhang of a bathycolpian bosom. Her eyes bulged and her mouth was turned down, except when she smiled, a delightful greeting which revealed too much gum. That and the gap teeth explained why there were no photographs of Queen Victoria smiling.

The Queen presented an image of the world's grandmother: serene, timeless and powerful. She was by far the richest person on

King of Scouts

earth. She had a delightful silvery voice, with a slight German accent. Fred was speechless, but she was accustomed to ordinary mortals being struck dumb by her presence.

"We believe a tour of our home might please you."

Fred could only nod dumbly.

Her hand touched a button and a distant bell rang. Osborne House was wired for electricity. The queen led the way, flanked by Indian court chamberlains.

"This is the Durbo Room," she said. "It was designed by the senior Mr. Kipling. While you were in the Orange Free State, Major Burnham, did you come upon young Rudyard? He is my favorite poet."

"We shared quarters in Bloemfontein," Fred replied.

His eyes widened at the breathtaking scene before them. The open, two-story room of granite was decorated with pictures and other memorabilia. A vast collection of valuable gems—crowns, tiaras and baubles—was on display in a room of lavish furnishings. One wall was covered with portraits of soldiers from India. The queen knew the name, occupation, age and biography of each person. Because of their similarity of style, Fred guessed the oil paintings were specially commissioned.

The tour of Osborne House continued for two hours. In one room was a collection of photographs, road signs and markers proclaiming Victoria Station, Victoria Falls and cities named Victoria in colonies from Canada to Hong Kong. Fred saw one that was marked Fort Victoria, Mashona Land.

In another room, he examined cabinets displaying rifles. He saw jeweled swords and scabbards, brass vases from India and Egypt. The British Empire was represented in jeweled miniature. Then a sound of distant chimes announced the arrival of the dinner hour.

"There are so many things we wish you could see," she said. "Perhaps another time. You might be amused by movies of my Diamond Jubilee."

The long walk to the banquet room emphasized the distance they had traveled.

"We are having a small group for dinner tonight. In this manner, each of them shall come to know you better."

A dozen lords and ladies entered the mahogany banquet hall where two cabinet ministers were talking. The introductions came so quickly that Fred barely caught their names. One was Joseph Chamberlain, secretary of state for colonies, the man Cecil Rhodes had hold of. Chamberlain was a lean man with dark hair and black

403

brows. Joe wore a monocle in his right eye. His long, hatchet-face and pointed chin made him resemble a lurking eagle. His heavy earlobes looked like fishing sinkers. Fred muffled a grin when he imagined Rhodes snuggling a lasso around Joe's testicles.

The guests sat and the queen rang a crystal bell.

"We are pleased to say that this meal duplicates to one served by Her Majesty, Queen Elizabeth, on Monday, the first of September, in the year of Our Lord 1578."

"By Jove, we're honored," one of the lords intoned.

The bibacious noble had been belting the grape.

Fred looked at the menu, dated 15 December 1900.

Smoked Sturgeon, Peace Potage, Mussels with Sweet Herbs
Roasted Cygnets, Quails, Snipes, Oysters, Bacon, Pullets
Mutton with Cucumbers, Tongue Roasted with Rhenish Wine
Venison Pastie, Boiled Beef with Sauce Robert
French Puffs with Green Hearbes, Salad
Peris in Syrippe, Mince Pie, Apple Cream
Clouted Cream, Syllabub
Mulled Cider, Mead

Fred was puzzled. He wondered what syllabub was.

"Major Burnham," Joe Chamberlain said, "Sir Alfred Milner has written to me of your achievements. Did you come across him much in Africa?"

"Every time he visited the front," Fred replied. His retort was met with laughter. High Commissioners never left Cape Town.

"Will you be returning to Africa to help finish that business?" Chamberlain asked.

"Only after your renown surgeon, Dr. McNaughton Jones, straightens out some kinks in my equator."

Blanche fixed Fred with a reproachful stare. He winked. He knew better than to talk about body functions at the dinner table, but his head was tangled by this lofty gathering. The tipsy lord made conversation.

"I say, Major, what is your opinion of President Oom Paul's arrival in Holland on the cruiser *Gelderland*?"

"My criticism is personal," Fred replied. "The man abandoned his invalid wife of fifty-eight years."

Blanche smiled and the Queen beamed.

"Do you think it will hasten an end to the war?" Chamberlain asked.

"I doubt the Boers will miss him that much."

"We fervently hope for peace," said the Queen. "With hostilities in southern Africa and that dreadful Boxer Rebellion in Peking, we are due for some tranquillity."

Fred kept his eye peeled for the syllabub.

"Major Burnham," said the Queen. "You may be happy to know that Lord Roberts shall be awarded an earldom when he succeeds General Wolseley as the new commander-in-chief."

Fred reached for his wine glass to propose a toast, but his move was interrupted when a Hindu servant arrived carrying a silver tray. Joe Chamberlain signaled for the letter, glanced at the message and a pallor came over his face. The tipsy lord was talking about the recent American election.

"Do I understand that you are acquainted with the vice president?"

"Prince Christian?" Queen Victoria's voice cried out with a touch of fear in her voice. Chamberlain nodded and returned the message to the tray.

"Where were we?" the Queen asked, returning her attention to the guests. "Did I hear correctly that you know the vice president-elect?"

"I have that honor, Your Grace. We dined after his return from Cuba. He wishes to tour Africa with Fred Selous guiding him on a big game hunt."

"Selous?" the Queen said, irritation creeping into her voice. "He remained in America during the Boer War, did he not?" She looked at Chamberlain.

"Yes, Your Grace."

It occurred to Fred that they had finished the meal and he still didn't know which dish was syllabub.

The party retired to an adjoining library, where the evening continued with music provided by a string ensemble. The Queen chatted with each of her guests. She asked Fred questions about his adventures in Africa. The detailed nature of her queries indicated she was quite familiar with events at the front. The subject of British history came up and Fred told her of the Burnham Genealogy dating to William the Conqueror.

She squeezed his arm and winked conspiratorially.

"Why Major Burnham, you are one of us." She smiled at him.

"Your Grace, I wonder if I might speak to you at a later time on a matter of some urgency."

"Certainly, see my appointments secretary for a date."

Then she turned to the others in the room.

"The affairs of state are many and demanding. We have enjoyed this evening's festivities and it shall remain a part of our cherished memories forever. Major and Mrs. Burnham, we will be seeing you again quite soon. Now we must bid you good night."

The men bowed and the ladies curtsied as the Queen swept serenely from the room. Fred and Blanche began walking toward the stairway to their bedchamber.

"What's syllabub, Bea?"

"It's a drink, silly. It's made of cream frothed with wine. You thoroughly enjoyed it."

Joe Chamberlain joined them.

"I must beg Her Highness's forgiveness," he said in confidence. "Her early departure tonight was occasioned by a cable from Africa. It contained the news that her favorite nephew, Prince Christian Victor, died today in Pretoria. She is grief-stricken and leaves tomorrow for Balmoral Castle to go into mourning."

"I'm dreadfully sorry to learn that," Blanche said.

The Burnhams' second visit to Osborne House—to talk about Fred's plan for scouting in the British Army—never came. Five weeks later, on January 22, 1901, in the third week of the twentieth century, Queen Victoria died in her sleep. It ended a reign of sixty-four years.

53

Distinguished Service Order

LONDON • 1901

THE INTERIOR of St. James' Palace, on The Mall a block from Buckingham Palace, was as ornately embellished as Fred had imagined it might ought to be. He wore a dress uniform with a sword sheathed at his side. His left breast was festooned with campaign medals—gongs from the Boer War and two Matabele campaigns. He was attending an investiture ceremony where the names and deeds of military heroes were being called aloud. Fred felt himself come under the strict gaze of stern veterans of the Sepoy Mutiny and other distinguished campaigns in British history. He was awestruck by the pomp and ritual. The voice of an army general calling the roll of heroes sounded faint and distant. *So many miles—so many adventures—since those days in Globe.*

Months earlier, when he learned that Queen Victoria had selected him to receive the Distinguished Service Order for his actions in the Boer War, Fred had strutted and glowed with exaltation. He, Major Frederick Russell Burnham of California and Arizona, would wear the little enameled band and have the right to use D.S.O. after his name—a military decoration second only to the Victoria Cross.

Later, he'd hoped that only Blanche had witnessed the depth and duration of his lapse into savagery. The presentation of the D.S.O. was delayed by the Queen's death. The Prince of Wales ascended to the throne as Edward VII. Before the investiture ceremony could be held, an offer of outstanding import came from the British West Africa Syndicate.

Fred almost rejected the bid to go to the Ashanti. He had received invitations to head expeditions to Tibet, to Patagonia, to Martinique. These offers sought to capitalize on his fame. The invitation to lead

407

an expedition into the Ashanti sounded at first too much like another Barotze Land fiasco. But the West Africa Syndicate was reputable and it came at the dawn of the twentieth century. Fred had recovered from his injury and was eager to be back in the saddle. All expenses would be borne by the syndicate. He and John Blick would receive substantial salaries and receive a finder's bonus for pegging valid mineral claims on the Gold Coast of Africa.

As much as he mistrusted solicitors, Fred hired a law wallah to examine the contract. When the jurisprudence dog placed his seal of approval on the deal, Fred and John sailed for the Ashanti. It was February 1901 and they were destined for the same West African jungle where Baden-Powell had rescued his flagging military career from oblivion.

As the tramp steamer dropped anchor in Sekondi Harbor, near Cape Three Points, they were surrounded by ebony men in dugout canoes. The Gold Coast people were a shouting, jabbering, quarreling lot.

"Washee washee."

"Go shootee-shootee."

"Me find leopard, monkey—bush full."

Fred and John called on Governor Nathan to obtain prospecting licenses. Nathan was a middle-class British civil servant doing his bit out in the colonies while waiting for a complacent retirement back in Kent. His white, linen suit-jacket was sweat-stained under the armpits. The Ashanti was at five degrees north latitude and the coastal belt was hot, wet and tropical. The humidity usually exceeded the temperature.

"I daresay you may have visited worse places, but not many," Governor Nathan said. "There are no mining laws in the Ashanti. Still, your papers are in order so you have my permission to prospect in the name of the British West Africa Syndicate. Let me warn you there are only a dozen Englishmen in the interior to keep order."

"There were none at all in Barotze Land," Fred responded. His own clothing was also stained with sweat. He had been here only hours and already he regarded the Gold Coast Colony—destined to become Ghana—as the hell-hole of the world.

"Kumasi is the white man's grave," the governor warned. "Avoid it. It's about as inviting as a water well during a cholera epidemic. The place is ridden with fever. Oh, let me warn you about the black mamba."

"We have mambas in southern Africa," John said.

"Your little green mamba grows to only about six feet long," Nathan said. "The black mamba here grows to twelve feet. It's venom is the worst in Africa. Death takes place within a few minutes of a strike."

"Thanks for the good news," Fred said.

"If you survive, pop by for lunch. If I may say so, you'll come to abhor the throbbing of the drums."

To men afflicted by gold fever, the warning of these dangers was a minor irritation. Fred and John returned to the building of mud and wattle that served as the local hotel. There they bought supplies and hired askaries for the journey to the interior.

The next morning, Fred and John began a slow-going journey into the jungle. The porters had to cut through rainforest that was thick with underbrush and tangled with clinging vines. They chopped away at the slithering tendrils, disturbing birds that squawked in protest. At the rivers, crocs snapped at anything that came near the water for a drink. And the tom-toms throbbed—day and night the drums echoed in the jungle.

Two weeks later, they arrived in Kumasi, where the natives proved to be altogether peaceful. When Fred and John saw the fetish grove, they got another impression. Although the cauldron of blood was now dry, they saw a pile of bashed-in human skulls and broken bones, the remains of hundreds of human victims strewn under the trees of the grove.

Burnham and Blick, like other white men, thought the bones were from victims of cannibalism when they actually were the remains of criminals who had been brought to Kumasi for execution. On the Gold Coast, the white man's ignorance was awesome.

"If what a man eats affects his passions and deeds," Fred said, "these people should be mild-mannered. They eat only yams, bananas and tropical fruits. Yet it is evident their passion for blood surpasses even that of Lobengula."

John grunted in support of Fred's vivid perception.

"Let's keep going," he said. "No need to tempt the locals by staying overnight."

From Sekondi, they had traveled two hundred miles to Kumasi. Their destination at Wa was marked on the maps as being four hundred miles inland, so they were half way. In the days that followed, the explorers gained in elevation, and the jungle grudgingly gave way to open plains. The interior climate, animal life and plant growth were similar to those on the high veld of Barotze Land.

After another hundred miles, they came to the Volta River. At water's edge, they watched a pregnant hippo, birds perched on her back, giving birth to a two hundred pound infant. With the newborn still trailing its umbilical cord, the mother nudged her offspring into the safety of the water just as a herd of elephants galloped into the river to splash and bathe. The tuskers were indifferent to trampling a baby hippo.

The preliminary prospecting site was at Bowie. After pegging gold claims there, they moved on to Wa where they established a camp. Thousands of people inhabited the area and, unlike the Ashantis, these people were eager to work for cash money.

Wild animals worked for subsistence as well. Jackals dug up croc eggs. Baboons descended on the acacia trees, searching for the sweet summer flowers—they deftly avoided the inch-long thorns. Elephants knocked down trees to dine on the leaves.

For two months, Fred and John prospected the basalt and granite landscape. The topography was undulating and, while John surveyed a route for a road, Fred examined deposits of gold-bearing quartz and pegged the lands. Their first claim was at Waspi, a two hundred square mile area. Fred traced the outcrops of reefs for more than twelve miles.

The next claim, at Banda, was fifty square miles. The quartz reefs ran half a mile in length. The final claim was, in Fred's opinion, the best. This was the main Wa claim, which lay between the Volta and Wa rivers. He pegged off two hundred square miles—a total of four hundred fifty square miles for all three claims.

"The presence of ironstone and slate," Fred told John, "suggests this area is an extension of the Lobi Gold Field from over the border in French territory."

Blick nodded and reported, "I found a lot of boulders in the main channel of the Volta River, but most of the rocks can be blasted out. At the falls, I surveyed a two-mile route for a tramline. With the Volta River opened to navigation, machinery can be landed at the mines after a trip upriver."

Their task completed, the men prepared to break camp.

"This is good country," Fred said. "I hate the idea of trekking back into that miserable rainforest along the Gold Coast."

"We're well ahead of schedule," John said. "What say we take some time off to visit Timbuctoo?"

"Yeah, how many people can say they've been to Timbuctoo? How far is it?"

Both men welcomed the diversion of a trip to the Niger River country—until the map told them it was six hundred miles to the fabled interior city.

"It would take too long," Fred said. "We'd miss our ship on the return stop."

"Maybe next time," John replied. "We can always say we did it—nobody will know."

So they packed up and turned south, heading back toward Sekondi. While crossing the Wa River, Fred and John watched as hungry lions stalked a baby hippo in a sinkhole of mud. But the lions were afraid to test their prowess against the giant teeth of the mother hippo. Hyenas gathered patiently waiting for a feast that never came. Fred noticed that lions didn't hunt game on moonlit nights.

In due time they began the final leg of their journey through the thick Ashanti jungles to the Gold Coast. The further they traveled in the coastal rainforest, the touchier Fred became. The incessant tom-tom drums upset him to no end. He didn't like the humid, sticky weather.

He was anxious to be up before dawn and moving, so they marched all day and camped at sundown. One night in the flickering light of a paraffin lantern, Fred became riled. He picked up his tin plate and threw it into the jungle with all his might.

"If jungle drums ever go on trial," he yelled, "I want a seat on the jury. We eat, we march and we sleep to the never-ceasing throb of those endless damnable drums."

"For the first time in your life," John said, "I think something's got the best of you."

John spoke too soon. Suddenly Fred jumped, waving his arms. In an instant, John was at his side. Fred's hands jerked in spasms. He pointed toward his right leg. In the flickering lantern light, John saw a large black snake. He grabbed his machete and with a fast swath lopped off the serpent's head.

"Bit bad?" John asked. "It's a black mamba."

There was no doctor within a hundred miles.

"Leg hurts," Fred said grimacing. His face grew pale. "It's getting numb."

John raised the lantern for a better look. He ran the blade of his hunting knife through the open flame of the lantern, then ripped open Fred's trouser leg to lance the wound. He leaned over, sucked at it and spit a mouthful of blood and venom at the dead snake's head. The serpent's body was about ten feet long.

411

"The snake's jaws are open," John cried. He leaned over holding up the lantern to examine the head. "Fred, you won't believe it, but this mamba's got a frog in its mouth. Maybe your bite isn't deep."

All that night John nursed his brother-in-law and at dawn he rigged a sling and hammock. Fred was conscious but pale, saying little. John ordered the porters to carry Fred to Kumasi. The natives, motivated more by the offer of a cash bonus than any concern for human life, moved swiftly through the jungle. They marched day and night, arriving at Kumasi shortly after dawn.

The native commissioner in Kumasi was the only person with any medical training—before coming ashore for this assignment, he'd been a medical orderly in the Royal Navy. While Fred submitted to the primitive medications of the native commissioner, John returned to the jungle to supervise the removal of the equipment and supplies they had abandoned in their haste.

Fred was laid up for ten days. His survival was ascribed to the frog in the snake's mouth, which prevented the mamba from inflicting a fatal wound. Burnham no sooner recovered from the mamba bite than he was struck down by jungle fever. This time he was laid up for two weeks, his resilience sapped by the toxin and by the heat and humidity. For days John feared Fred might die. He remained at his brother-in-law's side, feeding him soup made from the scraps of flyspecked monkey meat procured in the town's open-air market.

Five weeks later when the two men arrived by ship at Southampton, Blanche gasped at the sight of her husband of seventeen years. Fred had lost twenty pounds. His cinnamon-brown hair was dappled with gray. He refused to talk about his trip to the Gold Coast—ever.

• • •

St. James' Palace • 1901

AFTER THE RIGORS of the Ashanti, Major Burnham stood nervously in court—at the very heart of the British Empire—and listened to a dignified general call his name and recite his acts of heroism. Gone were the primitive exaltations he had experienced on learning he would wear the D.S.O. That vainglorious mood had long since passed.

The steps leading to King Edward's throne seemed high and forbidding. The court ritual was lengthy and formal, but in due time Fred was commanded to present himself before the King. As he climbed the steps, his knees grew weak.

With solemn dignity, Edward VII pinned the medal over his heart. At that moment Fred came to realize why Australians, Canadians,

Rhodesians and Scots hurried in response to England's call to arms. He had no desire to boast and strut. He bowed and kissed the King's hand. At that moment, he felt no more important than a grain of sand on the shore of a mighty ocean.

The rest of the day left Fred in a daze. There was a banquet, a fiesta and fandango combined, but the events were foggy. He drank some champagne which left his head fuzzy, but it was the pomp and ceremony more than the drink that affected him.

What seemed most important that day was that King Edward allowed him to hold his rank as major in the British Army without asking him to renounce his American citizenship. Sometime during that jamboree, it was suggested that had Fred agreed to give up his birthright, King Edward might have knighted him.

54

Kenia Colony

NAIROBI • JANUARY 1902

FLYPAPER hung like brown ropes from the roof of the mildewed shed. A female lion crept along the lake front, stalking an impala into the water—when it came to an impala feast, Kenia lions were not fretful of getting their paws wet. Fred hopped onto a table. He judged that the twenty men he had recruited were up to the task. They included Englishmen, Irish, Canadians, Australians, Scots and a few Americans. Each had been chosen for a specific talent.

"In the coming weeks," Fred said, "we'll survey an area larger than England and France. We will carry out a plan that Sir Harry Hamilton-Johnson has been devising since John Speke explored this place thirty years ago."

The men knew what Speke had done.

"One group will plant coffee, tea, cocoa, maize and rubber," Fred said. "Another will explore for mineral resources."

Before resuming, Fred glanced at the men. He thought of Jeff Clark many years ago over a campfire at the Tip Top Mine when Jeff had described the Lewis & Clark Expedition.

"Now," he said, "I'll ask each of you to come up on and speak on your specialty. The first will be Addison Brown, who will describe the topography of East Africa."

Brown, an American mining engineer, was tall and clear-eyed, plainly an outdoorsman. His clothing was a mass of wrinkles.

"The most notable feature of Kenia," Brown said, "is the Great Rift Valley. It begins at the Sea of Galilee, passes through the Red Sea and Abyssinia to Kenia and finally to Mozambique. This rift cuts a swath across one-seventh of the earth's surface, and we haven't the faintest idea what caused this immense gulch."

At the close of Brown's speech, Fred introduced E.J. Briddlebank, a world-traveled Englishman with a pencil mustache who had explored many areas of Africa and was fluent in Bantu.

"Out in the bush, chaps, you'll meet two tribes of note: the Kikuyu and Masai. The most populous are the Kikuyus, whose million members account for most of the people here. They cultivate the land, growing maize, squash, yams, melons and sweet potatoes. The Kikuyus seldom hunt. They sometimes kill an elephant, using poisoned spears, to sell the ivory."

Briddlebank introduced C.E. Howitt, an Englishman whose mouth extended half way to his ears. His body looked like it had been hewn from a giant beech tree.

"Forget the Kikuyu," he said. "The most interesting people are the Masai. They are tall, slender nomads who display the same discipline, courage and tenacity as their Matabele cousins to the south. The Masai number no more than twenty thousand, but they're the Zulus of East Africa—members of an African cattle cult. When you see a Masai, remember that string bean can settle your hash with an assegai."

Fred studied the other chaps. J.H. Brooke was a six-foot two-inch Britisher. Mostly elbows and knees, he could wrestle a rhino. He had a strong jaw and a pleasing smile. Next to him was Ronald Harris, a Canadian educated in the United States. He was a competent mining engineer and a man of rare courage.

Walker Dunn was a New Zealander, a specialist in animal husbandry who had climbed many of the Andes Mountains. At the end of the bench were Henry Harrison and Charlie Barchard, a pair of English adventurers who contributed experience as ivory hunters and geologists.

Fred didn't know much about Duncan and Welch, the Australians. They were of medium height, lean and wiry, good prospectors. They looked like educated connoisseurs of Brisbane's saloons. They seemed willing to have a go at absolutely anything.

Laton Cowper-Cowles, a man of chiseled features and compelling eyes, would teach the men Swahili, the *lingua franca* of eastern Africa.

"Swahili combines words from English, Arabic and Bantu," he said, flashing a smile. "*Tinni-kata* means can-opener. *Boma* is a thorn enclosure, like the *scherm* of the Zulus. *Bwana*, as you might guess, is a white master and *memsaab* is a lady bwana. A *safari* is a walking journey, and if your rifle isn't loaded you should beware of *simba*, the lion."

Burnham: King of Scouts

Fred tabbed Cowper-Cowles as a man with gravel in his gizzard. His neck was corded with muscle, a man who would stick to his post. Fred chose him to lead a safari to the Kavirondo Gulf of Lake Victoria.

That night Fred's shoulder ached from firing practice. The .303 Krag offered no trouble, but a couple of dozen shots sighting in the two-barrel .450 Holland & Holland Express almost did him in. The kick from the elephant gun caused almost as much damage to his shoulder as it did to the target. He rubbed himself with horse liniment, the best medicine for sore muscles.

There was a letter from General Baden-Powell in Johannesburg. A few months earlier, while Fred was in London, a question was brought up in Parliament whether Major Burnham's services as chief scout for Lord Roberts had been properly recognized by the British government. A member of parliament asked why the major had not been put in charge on the instruction of scouts at the Royal Military Academy in Aldershot. London newsmen had rushed to interview Fred, who said, "I have never thought myself competent to teach Britons how to fight, or to act as an instructor with officers who have fought in every corner of the world."

Baden-Powell wrote on March 25, one day before Cecil Rhodes died of Tb in Cape Town at the age of forty-nine years.

I have spoored you to your lair by your announcement in the papers disclaiming the idea of 'teaching Britons to fight.' You've made a heap of friends by that little phrase. Sorry I did not get a glimpse of you while I was at home. I wish in spite of your disclaimer that they would get you to teach them a bit at Aldershot. All's well here, but I don't know what I shall do when the war is over. Everybody is keen and daring. With best regards. R. Baden-Powell.

Lagnappe • A Little Extra

NEW YORK • MARCH 1902

ON MARCH 26, John Hays Hammond and Earl Grey took lunch at Delmonico's Restaurant. During the meal, Lord Grey showed Hammond a cablegram from Cape Town. Cecil Rhodes, perilously ill, would not survive the night.

A week later, the body of Rhodes was laid to rest in Mineral King at Malindidzime—the View of the World. It was the very spot where Burnham and Baden-Powell had stood six years ago to sketch Mount Inugu during their initial scouting patrol into the Matopo Hills.

Matabele warriors gathered for a tribute. They danced the ritual Burial Ceremony over the grave of the Great Lhodsi. Later, the remains of Major Allan Wilson and his thirty-three men were moved to Malindidzime to be interred in a circle around Rhodes' grave. This was the very birthplace of the Boy Scouts.

Counterpoise • Equilibrium

NAIROBI • MARCH 1902

IN THE MORNING the Kenia explorers and two hundred porters imported from Zanzibar loaded their dunnage onto the Uganda Railway — the Lunatic Express — to begin the journey to Uganda.

By jerk and lurch they rose out of the Great Rift Valley and jolted their way to the rim rock at Kisumu, more than two hundred miles away. Here at the railway's western terminal on the Kavirondo Gulf of Lake Victoria, Fred left Cowper-Cowles in charge of natives to dig shafts in a search for precious metals.

Fred and the remaining men boarded a little iron steamer—dismantled at Mombassa and shipped inland on the Lunatic Express—for the voyage of a hundred miles across Lake Victoria to Entebbe. At the Ugandan capital, he dispatched an expedition he would have given his eye teeth to lead.

Briddlebank, the linguist, would take Howitt and Brooke on a cross-country safari of several hundred miles. They'd map the Lake Edward area and explore the fabled Mountains of the Moon, then move down through Lake Albert to follow the Victoria Nile to Murchison Falls.

Fred, meanwhile, led a party of askaries into the iron-capped country around Mengo to explore for minerals. Several weeks of prospecting turned up nothing of value, so they returned to Entebbe, where Fred took a day off to visit King Mtessa's tomb. While he studied the intricate craftsmanship of the native building, a voice loomed from out of the past.

"Burnham, good to see you." It was Fred Selous.

"What trail did you ride to get here?" The last that Burnham knew, Fred Selous was in the Rocky Mountains.

The wails from a nearby mosque notified the faithful that it was time to pray. The blacks here were Muslims and they took out their prayer rugs to kneel, facing Mecca. Burnham and Selous found shelter in an alcove where they could talk without disturbing the faithful.

"King Mtessa's tomb here is the handsomest native building I've ever seen," Burnham said.

"Young girls were buried alive to comfort him on his journey into the hereafter."

"That so?"

"Also tons of ivory and hundreds of bales of cloth so he can pay any needed ransom."

"We're standing next to a treasure?"

"It would cost our lives to try for it."

That evening they talked over old times in Rhodesia, and the wailing music again emerged from the mosque.

"I find myself mesmerized by that strange Islamic call," Fred confided. "It drives away all sleep. I am both attracted and repelled. I class it along with the throbbing of the Ashanti drums and the thwang of an Apache bow. It reaches a corner of my heart untouched by the finest music."

"Coming from you, chum, that's quite a confession," Selous said. "By the way, what *are* you doing in Uganda?"

"Tomorrow, I will hire natives to paddle us around to the north end of Lake Victoria. There we'll look for gold. After that, it's back to Pasadena to get my family."

"Good on you. Tomorrow I'm off for Lake Alberta for some big game hunting."

"Are you still available as a white hunter?"

"Who's the party?"

"I've a friend in America who wants to meet you. He's a former Westerner, an outdoorsman of clear grit who loves the chase. He's a founder of the Boone & Crockett Club and he proposes to make you a member."

"Sounds interesting."

"His home is out on Long Island at Oyster Bay. But right now he's living down in Washington, D.C."

"Are you talking about — about President Roosevelt?"

"I've told Teddy a lot about you. He wants to hunt with you in Africa. A real expedition."

"Do you know him well enough to call him Teddy?"

"Known him for years. I'll see him in New York when I go home to pick up Blanche."

Ritornello • An Interlude

LONDON • SPRING 1903

IN THE SPRING OF 1903, Stephe was transferred to England as Inspector General of cavalry. His assignment was complicated by the fact that the very existence of cavalry was being called into question. The Maxim gun had rendered the cavalry obsolete, but Major General Sir John French was the new commandant at Sandhurst and that made a difference.

General French, the blue-eyed boy of the Boer War, was a cavalryman through and through. And his chief ally, Major General Douglas Haig, the director of military training, was the most influential tactician in U.K. cavalry circles. Without cavalry and polo, these generals could find no compelling reason to serve in the Army.

Baden-Powell's most important act as Inspector General was to establish the British Cavalry School at Netheravon House on Salisbury Plain. There the cavalry could gallop around the meadows of Stonehenge. Generals Haig and French loved it.

When Stephe arrived in London, Mother Henrietta Grace made it clear that he was to live with her and his siblings, Agnes, Warington and Baden, at the family home at Prince's Gate in South Kensington. The Baden-Powells coveted Stephe's salary of three thousand pounds a year. It was payback time.

As Inspector General, Baden-Powell served on the hush-hush Committee on Physical Decline. A medical report said that during the Boer War, sixty percent of the recruits had failed their physical exams. He concluded that the urban, working-class youths who furnish most of the army's recruits were smaller and sicklier than their middle- or upper-class counterparts. Life in the city was unhealthy: physically, spiritually and emotionally. Better food, health care and vigorous exercise would improve public health. Baden-Powell was repulsed by physical deterioration and moral degeneracy.

No political party dared court disaster with the voters by endorsing compulsory military training, so Lord Bobs organized the National Service League. Its purpose was to teach boys to shoot a rifle. He ordered Baden-Powell to inspect the various Cadet Corps as part of his work. In a lecture on military affairs at Eton College, Stephe suggested that boys should be taught to shoot, judge distance, scout, drill, skirmish and take cover.

General Haig at Sandhurst told Stephe that future recruitment of officers might be improved if the Boys Brigades would expand their membership. Admiral of the Fleet Sir John Fisher, the cherubic father of the dreadnaught battleship and the submarine destroyer, suggested the Army should adopt the Navy's practice of recruiting midshipmen. Baden-Powell nodded and looked into the Boys Brigade. It had been founded in Scotland in 1883 by William Smith, and the youth cadets had expanded throughout England. Stephe inspected seven thousand members of the Boys Brigade in Glasgow. The boys displayed great *esprit de corps* and were proud of their uniforms. The event had a profound effect on Stephe.

Later, Stephe was invited to review the Boys Brigade at Albert Hall. By this time, Baden-Powell and Sir William Smith had become friends. Stephe accepted an invitation to become a vice president of the Boys Brigades.

419

Lagnappe • A Little Extra

NEW YORK • 1902

WHEN JACK Hammond arrived from London, he resumed his position as consulting engineer to the Southern Pacific Railroad. Owner Edward Harriman had just swallowed the Union Pacific Railroad. With a railway pass signed by Harriman, Jack could hook his Pullman parlor car onto any UP or SP railroad in the United States, Canada or Mexico. Hammond was told to evaluate mining claims and endorse the construction of spur lines to profitable ore bodies.

Jack and his brother Bill owned the Mount Whitney Electric Company near Visalia, California. Electric irrigation had turned dry land into gold mines of farm production. Hammond suggested that Harriman build a line from Visalia to Lemon Cove near Three Rivers. This spur would transport citrus fruits to Visalia for transfer to the Southern Pacific railway line. Harriman approved the project, then it slipped his mind when he went abroad. Using personal funds, Hammond exercised options for the right-of-way. He held these properties until Harriman's return, and his reward for that action grew all out of proportion to the investment.

Counterpoise • Equilibrium

UGANDA • APRIL 1902

FOR FRED, the next month was one disaster after another. The explorers found no mineral deposits that were worth developing in the Bugosa country, so Fred headed his men back to Kisumu to catch the Lunatic Express. They trekked along the edge of Lake Victoria.

At the end of a week's journey, they were an easy day's march from Kisumu. During the afternoon, they encountered local blacks wandering about in confusion, babbling incoherently. Members of Fred's safari laid down their packs and abandoned their jobs.

"Baas, it be de sleeping sickness," Ali Mohammed cried. "We no go Kisumu."

"Ali," he called out. "Tell the men the entire payroll will be divided among the survivors."

For those who lived, it was a year's pay. At first, half a dozen men accepted, shuffling greedily. Another four porters joined the group, then two more, bringing the total to a dozen. Fred arranged netting over his hat.

"Tell the men to do like me and the tsetse fly can't bite them," he said to Mohammed. "We'll move fast."

An odor of putrefying decay assailed them. The stench, like rotten potatoes, told Fred that disaster had befallen. Bodies of men lay on the ground, scattered at random. The stricken had died so fast that the living had no time to bury the dead. The vultures, hyenas and jackals enjoyed the banquet of a century.

"We go, baas," Mohammed cried in alarm.

"We must find Cowper-Cowles first." Fred ran to the main tent. It took several seconds before he recognized the body on the ground. So much of the flesh was eaten away it was difficult to tell who it was. Fred turned the remains over with a stick. The compelling eyes and finely chiseled features were gone. Only the thickly corded muscles of the neck betrayed its identify. It was Cowper-Cowles.

"Dig a hole," Fred ordered. "This man will have a decent burial."

• • •

A century later, Mohammed Ali's diagnosis was found to be wrong. It was not tsetse flies that killed the explorers. They died from methane gases that erupted from the volcanic lake. Even in the twentieth century, some people found it difficult to believe the geologists when they announced these findings.

55

Oof Bird at Magadi

NAIROBI • NOVEMBER 1903

FRED SAT ON the verandah of his bungalow trying to concentrate on his report. He was distracted by a flock of pigeons that flitted about in the two wild fig trees above him. He had thatched the galvanized-iron roof to deaden the rattle of the figs that showered down on his bedroom. The rainbow-colored pigeons seemed to be the only creatures able to digest the hard, sour fruit of the strangler fig. It was a warm, lazy day and Fred found it easy to let his thoughts stray from the task at hand.

What began as a six-week trip to Pasadena turned out to last nine months. He'd arrived in London in September 1902, and did not return to Nairobi until the following June. On returning to Pasadena, Fred was surprised by The Kid's unexpected arrival from England. Rod had completed prep school and Major Aylmer Hunter-Weston had sponsored him at Sandhurst. He even coached the boy on the exams, but Roderick had failed the orals.

"Tell me about it, Son."

"I can get a football scholarship at Berkeley."

"Can you pass the entrance exams?"

"The British schools are beastly hard, and I didn't get plowed too badly by the Sandhurst exams."

Fred was hurt that Rod had flunked, but he decided not to be hard on the boy. After all, The Kid hadn't stepped inside a classroom until he was nine-years old.

"So be it, lad, Berkeley and football."

"Gee, thanks, Dad."

"You're going to college is to study. Hit the books."

"I promise."

"A few months ago," he said, "I turned down a job that offered a high salary. Do you know why?"

"No, Sir."

"That position required a degree as a mining engineer. Almost everyone thinks that Major Burnham is a mining engineer. But I'm not, Son. I had only one year of high school. I'm a scout and prospector, no more. I turned down the offer and said I was going home for personal reasons. Remember that when the studying gets hard."

Rod's cheeks flushed.

"Say, how'd you like to go to Mexico? I've some business to take care of for Rider Haggard."

"Can we camp out with Uncle Howie?"

"I think so."

After his marriage to Connie, Howie left the mines in South Africa to work for the El Oro Mining Company in Mexico.

After Christmas, Fred and Rod traveled into Mexico where they camped out with Howard and Connie Burnham in Sonora. Fred then left Rod in the care of Howie and went prospecting alone along the misty border of Guatemala. Returning four months later, Fred took Rod to California and picked up Blanche and Bruce to take them to Kenia. Their youngest son was proving to be a spirited water sprite.

Ritornello • Interlude

Nairobi • 1903

THE DEVELOPMENT of agricultural resources had been doing well. Under the leadership of New Zealand animal specialist Walker Dunn, the syndicate had crossbred cattle and sheep that could tolerate the climate of the Rift Valley. Because of its combination of equatorial latitude and mountain elevation, Kenia lay on a climatic battle-line between jungle and frost.

There was a market for beef and wool. Experiments in planting coffee were successful, and immigrants arrived from India and Ceylon to take up stands for coffee and tea plantations. A land office was opened to allocate tracts to farmers from the Empire. All things considered, the British East Africa Company's ventures held the promise of success. Fred was summarizing these achievements in his report when an askary jogged into camp. Fred knew him as the chief porter on Addison Brown's safari.

"Bwana, hippo come rivah. Mastah, he be hurt."

A hippo attack in the river was serious business. Fred yelled to Walker Dunn to make ready for a relief safari. He offered the man water and let him catch his breath.

"Mastah, he help portah who fall into rivah. Hippo, he take blue

423

in boat. Mastah, he hurt."

Brown, a clear-eyed engineer, was a skilled boatman. The relief party left within the hour. Marching all day and night and part of the next, they reached Brown's camp.

"Dunn, didn't you work for a vet in New Zealand?"

"I'm no medic."

"You're all we got," Burnham said. "Fix him up."

Brown's left leg was fractured and the calf was badly lacerated. Walker Dunn stitched up the cut and set the leg in a splint. Brown also had an ugly bruise on the left side of his gut. Suspecting internal injury, Dunn administered laudenum (opium) to kill the pain.

"We'll have to carry him out in a hammock," Dunn said. "If he survives, he'll be invalided home."

"We'll flag down the Lunatic Express," Fred grunted.

Two days later, Brown was admitted to the medical clinic in Nairobi. After having him evacuated to London, Fred returned to writing his report. The document had sections devoted to agriculture, soils, topography, tree planting, minerals prospecting, timber, estimates of the wild game population, transportation and administration. Fred hated the drudgery but recalled that Lewis & Clark had done exactly the same thing.

When the report was complete, Fred made plans to do a little hunting. He would take Blanche and Bruce to the crater of an extinct volcano near Lake Naivasha. Already the lad could swim and fish. Fred was packing guns and gear when two men straggled onto the parade ground heading toward his bungalow, a braying burro in tow.

It was the two Aussies, Jack Welch and the redhead Bluie Duncan. Fred had sent them south to track down rumors of a trail the Hindoos used to the mysterious Magadi. They'd been in the field for ten days and their appearance suggested they were bushed.

"G'daye, Major," Welch called out.

"Did you find the snow that never melts?"

"Square dinkum, isn't he?" said Duncan.

"Greedy bloke," Welch replied. "We're tuckered out from the march and he doesn't offer us a noggin of ale."

Both men wore broad smiles.

"Bea, have the nanny break out some bully beef."

Fred sensed they'd found the Magadi. Blanche came out carrying two bottles of beer.

"Cheers," said Duncan.

"You're a many-sided fellow," Welch added.

Both men fell to consuming the tinned beef and beer. During the meal, they said a ten-year old goat-herd had tipped them to the big lake of snow. They asked which way to the Magadi and the lad pointed south. They studied the trail, and their search was rewarded by the discovery of crystals of white powder. When they came to a fork in the trail, they studied the ground with their bring-'em-up-close glass. After two days, the Australians came to a water hole where they saw tiny splotches of the powder. No doubt someone had paused here to drink and laid down a satchel containing the white stuff. It tasted alkali, probably soda. They lost the spoor and regained it. Then the spoor led them up a large caldera—the crater of an enormous, extinct volcano.

When they reached the rim, they gazed in awe at a lake of snowy alkali reposing in the crater. By then it was so hot they would have traded their souls for a glass of water. So they bagged samples and backtracked to the water hole. Once refreshed, they drew a map, filled their calabashes and trekked back to Nairobi, covering the last thirty miles without sleeping.

"It's quite a sight, mate," said Welch. "Here's a sketch-map."

"You earned your dop call today," Fred said.

"We're gonna catch a shut-eye," Duncan called out.

Welch and Duncan slept through sundowners, not awakening until breakfast. By then Fred was well on his way to the Lost Magadi. After being euchred out of the Northern Coppers and Wankie Coal, Fred wasn't going to let this prize slip through his fingers. This time, he would salt the tail of the Oof Bird for sure.

Lagnappe • A Little Extra

NEW YORK • 1903

AT THE TURN of the century, Meyer Guggenheim began relinquishing control of the family fortune to his seven sons. In no time at all, they changed the nature of the company. Meyer sent eldest son Ben to Colorado to take charge of the family copper mines. The lad was unhappy with the custom smelter that was rendering their ore. Ben bought an interest in a local smelter and out of this developed the American Smelting and Refining Company: Asarco.

After that, Guggenheim Exploration Company was used only to assure a steady supply of ore for their smelters. Seeking ore bodies and developing mines soon became incidental to their goals. From that point on, the Guggenheims concentrated their activities on copper smelting.

Daniel Guggenheim—Mister Dan—emerged as head of the family fortune. With J. Pierpont Morgan and Andrew Mellon, Daniel organized the Anaconda Corporation around his Montana copper deposits and Kennecott Copper for his Alaskan ore bodies.

The sons left copper exploration to Guggenheim Ex, which Bill Whitney managed. Whitney was an important stockholder in Guggenheim Exploration Company. In fact, he was the tail of the rooster. To succeed him in retirement, Whitney decided that Jack Hammond should be the next general manager of Guggenheim Ex. Though he was a minority stockholder, Whitney had influence with Meyer and he wanted his own man in charge. That way Bill would have a secret vote when it counted. Jack Hammond's meeting with Papa Meyer and Mr. Dan came off splendidly.

"Mr. Hammond is a consulting engineer for the El Oro Mining Company," Whitney said.

"Its principal property is a silver mine about a hundred miles northwest of Mexico City," Jack said.

"I know El Oro," Mr. Dan snapped. "Tell me about that gold in Johannesburg. I have no knowledge of that deposit."

Mr. Dan, Bill Whitney and Jack Hammond spent the next three hours in animated conversation. Then the clock struck twelve.

"It's time to eat. We'll continue over lunch at the Midday Club."

By the time they'd finished their meal, John Hays Hammond had a five-year contract as general manager of Guggenheim Ex.

"I'll take the position on one condition," he said.

"What's that?" Daniel asked dryly.

"That I name my own man as manager of exploration and both of us have a seat on the board."

"I would expect that," Mr. Dan said. Having the chief geologist added competence to the board.

"Who is he?" Whitney asked.

"Howard Burnham," Hammond said. "He was with me in Johannesburg. He's a big fellow with a wooden leg, but he's about the best minerals geologist you'll find."

"Get him," Daniel said. "Send a telegram today."

Counterpoise • Equilibrium

RIFT VALLEY • NOVEMBER 1903

BY TRAVELING early in the day and late in the afternoon, Fred and Ali Mohammed avoided the worst of the heat. Five days later, they reached the water hole Duncan and Welch had marked on the map. Another day and night of travel found them on the crest of a basalt ridge that rose two thousand feet above ground level.

A three-quarter moon allowed Fred to peer into the shimmering Magadi. It was a sight he would not soon forget. But by dawn, the setting came into splendiferous view. Inside the caldera, more than two miles across, there was an immense lake of sparkling white carbonate of soda. It was so brilliant the splendor of the scene held him fascinated. He was indifferent to heat, thirst or fatigue. Here, cupped in Africa's black palm, was a white treasure more valuable than the largest gold reef. From Howie, he recalled this stuff was considered to be the pig iron of the chemical industry.

Fred's thoughts raced. The lake in the Rift Valley was fifty miles southwest of Nairobi and twenty miles north of German East Africa. There would be no disputing this ownership. This treasure was unmistakably in British territory. He sent Ali Mohammed and two porters back to the water hole to refill the calabashes—there was thirsty work ahead. Burnham spent six days on a hike around the rim of the lake. It ran about fifteen miles north and south and was a couple of miles wide. This huge lake was fed by dozens of copious hot springs. Fred bagged samples to take back to Nairobi for analysis. He also drove stakes and erected signs:

Keep Out
Property of the British East Africa Company

"I'm rich beyond belief," he said to no one in particular. "Unlike gold, this wealth continues in the making. Even if all else fails in Kenia, the Lost Magadi will vastly repay our efforts and enrich the coffers of the East Africa Company."

Fred's mind was abuzz. They'd have to build a spur line of the Lunatic Express to get this stuff to market. What was the going price for a ton of carbonate of soda?

Once back at Nairobi, Fred felt better. With great care, he filed a mineral claim on the Lost Magadi in the name of the East Africa Company. When John Blick arrived, Fred described his find.

"It seems to be a natural evaporation pan," he said. "As far as I can guess, the lake creates a hundred thousand tons of soda every year."

Blick took surveying tools and assaying apparatus, established a camp and examined the lake. He estimated the size of the find at forty-nine square miles. He tried probing but was unable to find the bottom. He took samples from more than forty million tons of soda, and that was only a small portion of the deposit. When he returned to Nairobi, John predicted that soda would one day be the leading mineral export of Kenia.

The Return to America

The 12th Chronicle

56

The Strangler Fig

OYSTER BAY • DECEMBER 1903

FRED RODE the trolley from Manhattan to Queens where he boarded the Long Island Railroad for the trip to Nassau County, getting off at suburban Oyster Bay. The weather was good so he walked. The names on the mailboxes were household words. Behind the railroad station was the mansion of J.D. Maxwell, the manufacturer of autos that would one day be called Chrysler. Along Main Street toward Cove Neck Peninsula was the home of Louis Comfort Tiffany, the renown stained glass artist.

At Cove Neck Road, Fred turned north for Sagamore Hill. There was the residence of Frank W. Woolworth. The best-known resident was Theodore Roosevelt. For the past two years his three-story home atop Sagamore Hill had served as the summer White House. The place was a large, wooden twenty-room structure with a verandah around three sides. It resembled a hunting lodge, and it reflected Victorian attention to detail. Fred knocked.

"Welcome, Major. You should have called ahead. I'd have sent a carriage."

"I like to walk," Fred said, glancing north over Long Island Sound to the Connecticut coastline.

"That's Old Greenwich. Stamford is on the right. It's an hour before lunch. Shall we walk? We have time for some high spots." Seeing Teddy prompted Fred to think of a close-cropped brontosaurus.

The men strode briskly back to Oyster Bay. Everyone knew Roosevelt took a ten-mile hike before breakfast. When he walked, his barrel chest seemed to precede him. Roosevelt pointed out highlights. At Main and South, he said, "That's Raynham Hall. During the Revolutionary War, it was British Army headquarters."

429

"When you speak of war, I am reminded that many of my ancestors fought for this nation. My main regret in life is that I have never served under the American flag. Out west I volunteered, but was turned down because I looked like a tenderfoot."

"That's right. During the Spanish-American War, you were in the Klondike." The two hikers stopped to drink fresh water at a spring and wipe away the sweat. Teddy set a good pace. Fred admired the trees and vegetation.

"When I was a youngster in Iowa," he said, "the land along the banks of the Mississippi was covered with trees. Clinton was a scruffy little sawmill town. The people were religious zealots motivated by commercial greed. As a result, the forested land is bare today."

"In my State of the Union address, I said forests and water are the two vital problems of the United States. We must plan to develop our forest reserves. The question is: how do we do it?"

"I'm not sure." Fred wondered if his friend would understand what he was trying to say.

"It seems sad. Those of us who love the wilds are destroying them by opening the land to civilization."

"Something must be done before it's too late," Fred replied

"If you were president, what action might you take?"

They turned and began walking back.

"Why don't you authorize Gifford Pinchot to convert portions of the federal domain into national parks?" Roosevelt nodded thoughtfully. Pinchot was the chief forester, a former Yale forestry professor. President Grant had created Yellowstone Park in 1872.

"You must do something to protect the Grand Canyon from private developers," Fred said suddenly.

"There is a law that would allow it," Roosevelt said. It occurred to Fred that Teddy had a mediocre reputation for getting bills adopted by Congress.

"We must maintain some of our lands as wilderness."

"There'll be the very devil to pay in Congress. The cattle ranchers will curse me for it."

"And a hundred other vested interests," Fred added.

"I talk about the presidency being a bully pulpit," Roosevelt said, "but it's a bully pulpit only in dealing with Congress. In matters dealing with the public, it's quite different." Roosevelt swatted at a fly with sufficient force to slay a baboon.

"Really?" Fred said.

"When I asked Booker T. Washington of the Tuskogee Institute to dine at the White House," Roosevelt said, "outraged whites took reprisals against southern blacks. To avoid lynchings, I must backpedal on race relations."

They arrived at Sagamore Hill where they took turns washing in the single lavatory of the thirteen-bedroom mansion. Teddy escorted Fred to a spacious dining room where there was a table of cold roast beef, raw carrots, celery sticks and potato salad. Fred guessed that many of his English friends would regard this meal as barely palatable.

Roosevelt munched on his food all the while looking like he had just brought the Ten Commandments down from Mount Sinai.

"The thing that will destroy America is prosperity at any price," he said, sounding like a gladiator.

"Will you campaign on that platform?"

"We must also guard against multiculturalism," he continued in a solemn vein. "In this country, there can be no fifty-fifty Americans. Any immigrant who comes here should be required to learn English within five years or leave the country. There is room here only for those who are one hundred percent Americans."

"Now I say bully," Burnham replied. "But that stand won't buy you a lot of votes on the Lower East Side."

Roosevelt's face took on a serious look. His jaw grew rigid and he grunted, "They don't vote."

Ritornello • An Interlude

MONTEREY • DECEMBER 1903

JACK AND NATALIE Hammond chose the presidential suite at Del Monte Lodge for their autumn stay because of its prestige and, of course, for family ties.

Jack's father, Major Richard Pindell Hammond, had named the resort. In 1879 he and Jack had accompanied Governor Leland Stanford on a trip to Monterey to inspect the Southern Pacific Railroad terminal there. Stanford, the president of the Southern Pacific, and "Cholly" Crocker, the vice president, built a posh resort at Monterey to lure rich Nob Hill weekenders away from San Francisco. When they asked Major Hammond to suggest a name, Dick had suggested Del Monte.

Jack's elder brother, Dick Junior, built the posh and ultra private Seventeen Mile Drive around the Monterey Peninsula. With the addition of Pebble Beach Golf Course, Monterey became the western homesite of choice for eastern Robber Barons.

To close the season, Jack and Natalie hosted a banquet at Del

Monte Lodge. Lending literary glitter to the affair was the popular British author Rider Haggard. After New Years, when the Hammonds returned to New York, Sir Rider accompanied them in *Kya Yami*, Jack's railway parlor car. In Denver, Harris Hammond and Sol Guggenheim joined the party for the trip to New York.

Counterpoise • Equilibrium

Oyster Bay • December 1904

"BY THE WAY, Major, have you talked with Selous?"

"He's ready when you are."

"Tell me about the Dark Continent. After your many years there, what is your opinion of Africa?"

"When I arrived on the veld, my first impression was of its vast silence, a silence you could almost hear."

"Just like the West. You never find silence in the city."

"My second impression was that central and south Africa's velds are similar to our Great Plains. It's a natural place for the wild beasts. Only in the river valleys and along the coasts do you encounter vines, jungle and fever. Avoid the lowlands and you thrive."

"Well put, Major, tell me about the animals. Are they really more dangerous than our prairie bison?"

"Far more dangerous," Burnham replied. "The perils of our expedition into Kenia were numerous. Within a few days of our start, one of my colleagues was attacked by a hippo. One of my askaries was killed by a lion and partly eaten. Another was fatally bitten by a snake. The dangers are all too real."

"And the people? How do you rate them?"

"When I first arrived in the Dark Continent, I was imbued with a thirst to bring civilization to the savages of Africa. In the past decade, I've gotten to know them: the Zulu, Matabele, Mashona, Fingoe, Hottentot, Ashanti, Fulani, Kikuyu, Masai and others. What I now know is that the American Negro has more in common with his pre-Civil War master here than he has with his tribal brother in Africa."

"Really now? It's a point I must contemplate in greater detail."

The kitchen maid, Mary Sweeney, brought in hot cinnamon-apple pie topped with slices of Wisconsin cheddar.

"I came to know many tribes of black men and I came to respect them for their strengths and, I hope, to forgive their weaknesses," Fred said. "In their own ways and in their own domains, these people are far more sensible than we give them credit for."

The president removed his pince-nez to polish them. As Fred continued, Mrs. Sweeney poured hot coffee.

The Return to America

"When the American newspapers describe my travels in Africa, they speak of my penetrating unknown and trackless jungles. But the black men know their country as well as we know the streets of New York and Washington. They're well aware of the locations of mineral deposits. The Masai in Kenia, for instance, refused to cooperate with me in the search for mineral deposits. To the Masai, a concession to develop the Lost Magadi was nothing more than the legalized theft of their lands."

Before continuing, Burnham walked over to a French door and gazed out at the president's acres of lawns and gardens.

"It matters not to the blacks that they have no earthly use for the minerals," Fred said at length. "They object because the white man brings immigrants, forced labor and land confiscation. Their people are nomads, hunters and farmers who want no more. The white man comes with his railroads, his hut tax and the next thing he forbids the Masai to make raids on their neighbors."

"Unless we enforce laws," Roosevelt objected, "they murder one another like savages."

"Think about our own Indians," Fred said. "Once the white man came and changed the rules, the young bucks no longer had a reason to maintain their discipline, their purity of blood. They become shiftless, lazy and their society went down in a cataclysm."

Roosevelt walked over to join Fred.

"Major, that is a perceptive viewpoint. After you have gone I shall consider it at length. But are you trying to tell me your ten years in Africa were a mistake?"

Before replying, Fred pondered at length.

"Mr. President, the primary reason for my return to America is because the British government has canceled my soda concession in Kenia. Just as our work at the Lost Magadi was coming along toward success, the authorities dispossessed us on the grounds that the lake had been discovered years earlier by a German explorer, Gustav Fischer. But that's beside the point. On the greater stage, I think the direction that colonialism is taking is wrong."

"Major, please explain," Teddy replied suddenly upset. "What do you see as the white man's future?"

"It's hard to predict because some new *-ology* may prolong the day of reckoning. But it's inevitable that one day the white man must set the black man free so he can seek his own destiny."

"Humph. Have you a reason to support that view?"

"Do you see that knoll over there, the one with the trees?"

"I planted those trees."

"My home in Nairobi was built on a knoll a little bigger than that. The bungalow was small but snug. Like so many European buildings in Africa, the roof was built of galvanized iron, which I had my staff cover with a thick layer of thatch."

Teddy nodded. Fred studied the trees.

"The reason I had my roof thatched was to deaden the rattle of African figs dropping down and keeping us awake. Have you heard of the strangler fig of Africa?"

"I cannot say that I have, but please continue. What you say fascinates me."

"In Kenia, the strangler fig became one of my pet peeves and my botanist taught me something about it."

"Go on," Roosevelt said polishing his pince-nez, his eyes gleaming like diamond stickpins.

"This strangler fig is a botanical cannibal. It encloses its host. In the case of my bungalow in Nairobi, the struggle between the host cedar and the fig is protracted, but the outcome is inevitable. In the first stages, tendrils climb up and slither down to surround the trunk of the cedars. Below, fleecy tendrils trace out the host tree's roots."

"You don't say."

"At the surface, fig tendril joins vine. Where stem touches branch, they unite to form lacework. It gradually encloses the host cedars in a living cocoon. Other creepers slither out to swallow the trunk. Limb by limb, this process continues, rising at last to envelop the crown. Below ground, fig root smothers cedar root. The cedar, being caught in an unyielding embrace, is no longer able to sustain life."

The president's brilliant blue macaw, Eli, perched on its stand, echoed a throaty "Arrwk."

"In time, only the little green tips remain at the crown, waving farewell in the breeze. The figs—no longer vines—have climbed as high as the cedars will lift them. They have conquered their hosts, but their fruits are bitter. In time, the host cedar rots, leaving only the trunk of the fig which is hollow and worthless. Mr. President, the fate of that fig tree is the white man's destiny in Africa."

57

Haggard & Hammond

PASADENA • APRIL 1904

THE BURNHAMS LEASED a house on Orange Grove Boulevard five blocks south of the old Burnham Manor, and they vowed to stick close to home. But eight months later, Fred was drawn south of the border by the lure of the Lost Montezuma Treasure. Two years ago, while Fred passed through London, Rider Haggard gave him a document describing the Lost Montezuma Treasure. A romantic in Paris named Gordon Carmichael had written to Haggard describing a mystery city in a remote valley along the border between Mexico and Guatemala. Carmichael spoke of a hidden City of Treasures that Montezuma had concealed from the Spanish explorer Hernando Cortez.

Carmichael's writings were erratic, but he left one clue, an Enchanted Land in tropical lowlands that could be entered safely only after October. A search of the Mexican atlas in the Pasadena Library suggested the state of Chiapas bordering on Guatemala. It was one hundred miles northwest of Guatemala City. There were only two tropical lowland areas: one along the coast and one in Rio Chiapas Laguna, a river valley about a hundred miles inland and north of the fifteen thousand foot Tacana Volcano.

When Fred took Rod into Mexico to camp out with Howard and Connie in 1902, he had visited the lowlands and eliminated the coastal choice, leaving Rio Chiapas Laguna. But time ran out and he had to return to Kenia.

A cold December in Pasadena, with Mount Wilson blanketed by snow, was the perfect time for another visit to Mexico. Chiapas was two thousand five hundred miles south, so Fred took a steamer which dropped him at tiny Puerto Madero in far southern Mexico.

He searched the tropical lowlands of Rio Chiapis Laguna up to the shoulders of the mountains. Like almost all lost mine schemes, the Lost Montezuma Treasure proved to be nonexistent. On his return trip, Fred got off the steamer at Guaymas to visit Davis Richardson in the Yaqui River Delta.

Don Davee had continued to work on Earl Nettleton's plan to dam the river and irrigate the delta. While spit-roasting a leg of wild goat over an open fire, Fred told Davee about his search for the treasure. They had a good laugh over the fruitless quest. The next day, Richardson offered Fred an option to purchase the Yaqui River Delta irrigation project. Fred said he would think about it.

• • •

Pasadena • February 1905

BLANCHE SPENT the afternoon at the dining room table pasting newspaper clippings in her scrapbook—clippings that might one day amuse their grandchildren.

Later, when Blanche called Fred for dinner, he laid a letter on the coffee table. He would finish it after the meal.

"Who's the letter from?" Blanche asked as she carried a roast pheasant from the kitchen.

"Rider Haggard. He's coming to America."

"Here? To Los Angeles?"

"No, to Monterey. He'll stay at Del Monte Lodge."

"What's he doing in this country?"

"He wants to study how the Salvation Army deals with poverty."

"At Monterey? That's for millionaires. If he wants to see poor people, we have scads of poor people here."

Lagnappe • A Little Extra

Oroville • Summer 1905

JACK HAMMOND examined the alluvial gravels of the Yuba River below Oroville. His studies showed that hydraulic mining of old California Gold Rush claims would return a profit at seven cents a cubic yard dredged. His calculations revealed he could recover twelve cents a cubic yard. It would be highly profitable.

Hammond organized Oroville Dredging Company, and began recovering gold from the gravels worked fifty years ago by the Argonauts. The dredging operation was a success. Recovery operations continued for thirty years and earned profits of thirty-eight million dollars—it was the same plan Fred Burnham had proposed to the Rothschilds for the Klondike.

The Return to America

Counterpoise • Equilibrium

PASADENA • MARCH 1905

ON MARCH 24, Sir Rider Haggard came to Los Angeles to study the slums, and he stayed with the Burnhams in Pasadena. The *Los Angeles Times* knew there was an adventure jasper in Pasadena named Fred Burnham. But Pasadena was not in the *Los Angeles Times* circulation area, so the editors chose to ignore the outta-town adventurer.

When word got around that the famous British author Sir Rider Haggard was a house guest, the city editor sent a reporter for an interview. Fred and Sir Rider got their jollies spoofing the journalistic chawbacon.

Julian Hawthorne arrived shortly after dinner. He noted that Haggard was tall, thin and Lincolnesque. The author was relaxed, his booted legs crossed as he leaned back in his chair.

Hawthorne was chosen because he had read *King Solomon's Mines*. To open the interview, he said, "Your books have sold by the millions in this country."

"It hasn't done any good, you know," Sir Rider said. "Before your copyright law went into effect, American publishers pirated my works and sold them for a dime, paying me no royalties." He lighted his briar pipe.

Hawthorne silently cursed, then tried flattery.

"I always liked your books because they are straight-out romance: the most beautiful women, the strongest, bravest men, the most striking events."

Haggard puffed on his pipe and winked at Fred.

"*King Solomon's Mines* turned out to be prophetic, you know. They've since found the ruins of Zimbabwe in the place I indicated. Gold too."

Fred saw the sly twinkle in Haggard's eyes and he knew the author was pulling the reporter's leg. *So what? It wouldn't hurt anyone.*

"Yes," Fred added. "I found gold there. And more at Dhlo-Dhlo. Six hundred ounces."

"Are Sheba's Breasts there?" Hawthorne asked, to prove he really had read the book.

"There are lots of hills like that in the region."

"And Umslopogaas?" Hawthorne persisted.

Fred thought of Jan Grootboom.

"I knew him well. Splendid fellow. Superb figure."

After Fred and Rider bade farewell to Hawthorne, they had a

laugh. It was good, clean fun and, besides, it might promote the sale of some copyrighted books.

Fred told Sir Rider how the Montezuma Treasure had come to a dead end, but the search had led him to a new interest in the Yaqui River Delta irrigation scheme and a plan to take it over.

"Isn't your brother, Howard, in Mexico?"

"Yes, he's tending to mines for the Guggenheims," Fred replied. Haggard digested that fact for a moment.

"Jack Hammond is the manager of Guggenheim Ex."

"That's my understanding," Fred replied.

"Why don't you get Hammond to finance your Yaqui irrigation scheme?" Haggard asked. "I don't know a more honest and dedicated man."

"Hammond and I have ridden many a parallel trail," Fred said. "We started our careers in Arizona. We went to Africa in 1893 to work for Cecil Rhodes. We returned to America about the time of his death. Yet in all those years, I've never met Mr. Hammond."

"You've never met?" Rider asked, stroking his beard while digesting that startling bit of information. "Then you must come with me to London. I will introduce you, for truly, I have never known two men more admirably suited to one another."

Ritornello • Interlude

SALISBURY PLAIN • MARCH 1905

WHEN STEPHE learned that Burnham was coming to London on business, he immediately wrote a letter.

Do you think you could give me a helping hand by coming one day to the British Cavalry School for officers and NCOs, which I recently started, to give the students a lecture on scouting? I can assure you it would be highly appreciated and would do a full deal of good. I shall be thankful if it does not entail too much on you. I shall myself be going to visit the school. I would gladly take you with me if you care to come. Even if you don't want to lecture, it might interest you to see what we try to teach.

The instruction in leadership and training, as well as that in scouting, would no doubt interest you. I would love to get you interested in my Cavalry School and then perhaps get you to take an appointment as instructor in scouting here. I am bringing out a Cavalry Journal *and I'd be more than grateful if you would send us a few words on scouting. Any practical ideas or experience. The journal is intended to educate all ranks—NCO as well as officers—in cavalry work. Robert Baden-Powell.*

The Return to America

Counterpoise • Equilibrium
LONDON • APRIL 1905

AFTER THE desiccated Arroyo Grande in Pasadena, Bruce fell in love with the liquidity of the dung-brown Thames River. He spent his afternoons fishing with a line and hook. *How he loves to fish.*

It turned out that the Burnhams had arrived early. Hammond was in Scotland on business for the Arizona Mining Company. So for two weeks Fred, Blanche and Bruce visited with Rider and Angie Haggard at Ditchingham. General Baden-Powell was away inspecting the Cardiff Boys Brigade, where he urged the lads to do a good turn each day.

Fred assured Blanche they would remain in Europe only to meet with John Hays Hammond and get backing for the Yaqui Delta irrigation scheme. Suddenly, Fred began having second thoughts and he developed a case of the anxieties.

"Compared with Hammond," he confided to Blanche, "I'm a prospector with only a year of schooling."

"Tsh, Fred, you're the most famous prospector in the world. You belong on a pedestal every bit as high as him. Mining engineers need prospectors to find ore deposits. His task is to develop mines, not to find ore bodies."

"I guess I should know that."

A week later Hammond turned up in London to line up financing for the mining equipment he was buying for Mexico. Haggard introduced the two men and they hit it off. Hammond was a lithe man with a fig-shaped nose which he tried to conceal with a silvery mustache. His eyes were partly hidden under shaggy black brows, giving him the faraway look of a dreamer. He had the hands of a piano player. He also had a colossal ego, but Fred got a grip on himself and managed to overlook Hammond's human frailty.

There was great contrast in the two — opposites that attracted — like ham and eggs, apple pie and ice cream. Hammond was tall, austere, intellectual. Burnham was short, emotional, physical. Burnham was a student of the western school of hard knocks. So was Hammond, but he also was Nob Hill, Ivy League and Eastern Establishment. He had friends in high places, presidents, judges, cabinet ministers.

Hammond was the drab thinker — Burnham was the colorful doer. Both men had worked for Rhodes and both seemed to instantly sense how they complemented one another. For a week, the two men spent their evenings dining at West End clubs and comparing

439

notes about their early day adventures in Arizona and Africa.

One night after dinner, Fred returned to his hotel feeling poorly.

"What's wrong?" Blanche asked.

"My stomach hurts."

"Something you ate," Blanche suggested, but Fred isolated the hurt as coming from the stomach tissues themselves. The pain persisted and Fred made an appointment with Dr. MacNaughton Jones. His condition was diagnosed as a stomach abscess, a flare-up of his Boer War injury, and it required surgery. It would take several months to heal and Fred would have to remain in London during the recovery period. Hammond was about to leave for Germany on business.

"Could you delay the surgery for a week?" he asked. "We could get to know each another better while we travel to Germany."

After a visit to Doctor Jones, Fred learned he could not delay the surgery, so Hammond left for the Continent and returned to the United States. Fred's operation was successful but the healing was slow, his recovery was prolonged and he had to spend five months in London recuperating.

By October, Fred was making plans to return to Pasadena. Then he learned Hammond was going to Germany again. Fred made arrangements to join him. It was while traveling through France by parlor car that Fred made his pitch.

"Mr. Hammond, I've a business prospect that may interest you. It is a proposal to build the world's largest private irrigation scheme. I hold an option from my friend Davis Richardson of Los Angeles on the water rights to the Yaqui River Delta and the irrigation rights to three hundred thousand acres of land in Sonora. The topsoil is fifty feet deep and there's not a pebble in it. Once the valley is irrigated, it'll be the garden spot of the world."

Fred explained how he had twice been on the verge of financial success, how he'd been organized out of the Northern Coppers and how the Lake Magadi discovery was lost. Success in either of these ventures would have provided the capital to put across the Sonoran irrigation scheme.

Hammond asked Fred if he had any experience in developing large agricultural projects. Fred told how he had introduced agricultural crops to the Kenia Colony.

Hammond nodded. "Major Burnham, your brother has told me a lot about you. And the most profound thing he has confided to me is your goal to train others in the field of scouting. If that is true, why do you suddenly want to run a Mexican Bonanza Farm?"

"For the first forty years of my life, scouting was my primary goal," Fred said. "I wanted to work in the Scouting Department in the American or British Army and train others in a calling that I had spent a decade mastering."

Hammond looked up sharply and asked, "Well, what happened?"

"When I returned to Kenia in 1903," Fred said. "I learned that just before Christmas, two bicycle mechanics from Ohio killed my horse."

"What nonsense are you talking about?" Hammond snapped.

"The Wright Brothers flew an aeroplane at Kitty Hawk, South Carolina, and killed horse-mounted scouting for all time," Fred said.

"Are you saying the aeroplane killed scouting?"

"No," Fred replied. "Scouts will always be needed. But tomorrow's scout must fly an aeroplane. He must be an engineer and understand ballistics. He must have new skills that I know nothing about. I'm as obsolete as the cavalry, even though the armies of the world don't yet acknowledge that."

A smile crossed Hammond's face. "I'll be in Tucson in April. Let's meet there and we can visit your river." It was the beginning of a friendship that would last for thirty years.

• • •

LONDON • AUTUMN 1905

THE BURNHAMS stayed at Bridge Bungalow in Bowfell Road, off Fulham Palace Road in Hammersmith. It was only a hop, skip and jump from The Thames River, bustling with an endless procession of barges and bum-boats where the air reeked of turpentine and canvas — and green cattle hides. Bruce, the water sprite, spent his play time dipping a line. Fred wrote to Rod:

We thought of returning via Peking, but that plan has gone by the wayside. Bruce has caught several fish about six inches long in the river. When we get home, you must tell me about your hunt with Judd. I hope you got your deer this year."

Before Dr. MacNaughton Jones released Fred for travel, the lease on Bridge Bungalow expired so the Burnhams moved into a hotel. That's when Fred got around to responding to Stephe's request to "write a few words on scouting" for the *Cavalry Journal*.

Fred was clearly delighted that Baden-Powell had organized the Cavalry School. There were still six months until Fred's meeting with Hammond in Arizona — leaving plenty of time for a couple of semesters of instruction. The more he thought about it, the better the idea sounded. Fred decided to ask Blanche to take Bruce back to Pasadena while he remained behind to teach at the Cavalry School. There were still many things he could show the young British officers, things that had nothing to do with flying. He had ideas that were worthy of any scout: horse mounted or airborne.

Fred still had mixed feelings about England. For the most part, the Old Country had been good to him. He'd won a world-class reputation in the service of Imperial Britain, and that was better than money any day. But he also had been swindled out of two fortunes. On the other hand, Baden-Powell had been honest and forthright. Their friendship dated nine years to that Matopos outing of 1896.

Fred decided he would bring up his plan to Blanche and see how she felt about his spending a few months teaching scouting at Aldershot. Having made that decision, he began to feel much better—at last, he could fulfill his oft-deferred ambition to teach scouting to the Army. The matter decided, Fred concluded it was a splendid October day — despite billowing clouds of sulfurous smoke that belched from chimneys, casting their pall of gloom..

"Where's Bruce?" Blanche asked.

"Fishing," Fred replied. "I'll go down to The Thames and fetch him." Fred picked up an umbrella and began whistling as he walked down the stairway. He got as far as the foot of the staircase when the hotel manager met him. He was flanked by two London bobbies.

"Major Burnham," the manager said gravely. "I'm obliged to report these gentlemen have bad news."

"Oh?" Fred stiffened.

"It's your son, Master Bruce Burnham. His body has been found," said the elder policemen. "Dreadfully sorry to tell you, Sir. He drown in The Thames while fishing."

58

Water for the Yaqui Delta

PASADENA • NOVEMBER 1905

BLANCHE WAS inconsolably grieved by the loss of her youngest son—the second of her three children to go to an untimely death. She declared that she would never again set foot in England. The Burnhams' only comfort was The Kid, twenty, now playing football at Berkeley. Shortly before the Burnhams left London, Stephe wrote:

I am sorry you are going because I would love to get you interested in my Cavalry School and then get you to take an appointment as instructor in scouting. I am bringing out in December a Cavalry Journal and I'd be grateful if you would send us a few words on scouting. Any practical ideas or experiences. I was so sorry to miss you at the office. Yours, R. Baden-Powell

In Pasadena, Fred was too grief-stricken to finish the article, much less think about the appointment. He stayed home consoling Blanche.

Ritornello • Interlude

SAN FRANCISCO • JANUARY 1906

LATE IN 1905, the Hammonds came west from Gloucester, Massachusetts, using The City as a base while Jack examined mining projects from his parlor car, *Kya Yami*. Guggenheim Ex underwrote a bond issue to establish the Utah Copper Company. Hammond went to Garfield, Utah, to organize the removal of two hundred million cubic yards of overburden — two-thirds as much earth as would be dug from the Panama Canal. With the coming of the railroads, copper became more profitable than gold. As president of the American Institute of Mining Engineers — the AIME — Hammond was called on to suggest revisions to the nation's mining laws. He delivered that report to President Roosevelt on March 24, then boarded *Kya Yami* for Tucson and a meeting with Major Burnham.

•••

YAQUI DELTA • APRIL 1906

"THOUGH THE SOIL is dry, the option controls access to water sufficient to irrigate half a million acres," Fred told Hammond. "The topsoil ranges from twenty to sixty feet deep. About a foot of rain falls each summer, but the water runs off. With irrigation, the growing season could last all year. This a mining area, employing thousands of men, so there's plenty of demand for food."

Hammond listened with outward care, but his mind seemed to be miles away. When he asked questions, they appeared to be irrelevant.

"What's our location compared to California?"

"East of California. Due south of Salt Lake City."

"How far south?"

"Same latitude as Corpus Christi, Texas."

"What month can you get your first crop harvested?"

"Umm, tomatoes in January, onions come February and strawberries in March."

Hammond's eyes sparkled.

"This looks promising," he said. "I'll send two of my men down here. Please give them your cooperation."

The tour ended in harmony on Tuesday, April 17, and they shared a spit-roasted barbacoa lamb dinner. Shortly after dawn, a runner brought Hammond the worst of all possible news. An earthquake had struck the Bay Area. San Francisco was burning. The richest, most powerful city in the West had ceased to exist.

"Burnham," Hammond cried in panic, "I must leave immediately. My wife and daughter live on Rincon Hill." Within an hour, *Kya Yami* was traveling at high speed, pulled by a chartered locomotive.

•••

YAQUI DELTA • MAY 1906

CIVIL ENGINEER A.P. Davis arrived to examine Fred's Bonanza Farm. "The first thing we must do is build a dam," Fred told him. "During spring when the mountain snows melt, this river flows hundreds of feet wide. But it shrinks to a trickle during summer. If the water could be impounded in storage, it could be released gradually for irrigation."

"That's what I'm here to determine," said Davis, who was as tall, acetic and thin as an antelope horn. The next day he disappeared. On his return three weeks later, he said they should abandon Nettleton's damsite.

"There's a better place a hundred miles north of your concession," Davis said. "It'll form a lake sixty miles wide and a hundred miles long. The dam will furnish power to electrify the area. We can develop the lake as a resort for tourists from California."

"But it's outside our concession!"

"I'm an engineer, not a real estate agent," Davis snapped. "Mr. Hammond instructed me to find the best damsite."

Fred got along better with Frank Olmstead, an easygoing soils scientist who ran test borings and confirmed the depth and fertility of the soil. Then he surveyed the gradients. Beyond Davis's new damsite, the bed of the river would serve as a canal.

"At that point," Olmstead said, "we can use the old dam to check the flow and send it to the diversion canal."

Fred nodded, happy to see that Olmstead agreed.

"Then Hammond will be calling on Bill Whitney for financing?"

"Haven't you heard? Bill Whitney died. We'll call on Harry Payne Whitney. The son is now in charge of the family investments."

Fred thought he'd better come along to help argue the case.

• • •

NEW YORK • JULY 1906

AT HAMMOND'S nod, Fred made the main presentation. Then Hammond took center stage. That's when Fred learned how John Hays Hammond approached a new venture.

"We'll buy nine hundred thousand acres north of the concession," Hammond said. "That'll give us access to the new damsite. All of these lands come within the water grant held by the Sonora-Sinaloa Irrigation Company."

Hammond turned to plans for marketing. "The freight rates from Cuidad Obregon to New York are identical to those from California. Our crops will come on the market six weeks before the produce matures in the Imperial Valley of California," he said.

"Ed Harriman is extending the Southern Pacific to Mexico City," he continued. "The new rail line will pass a few miles from our headquarters in Esperanza. The railroad will transport our fruit and vegetable products to Mexico City and as far east as New York, Philadelphia and Boston.

Harry Whitney asked about the land title.

"It's signed by President Diaz," Fred boasted.

"I've known Porfirio Diaz for five years," Hammond said. "He assured me that any investment we make south of the border will be safe from expropriation."

445

Fred blinked. All along, Hammond had been miles ahead of him.

An agreement was struck. A series of organization meetings followed. Richardson Construction Company spun off a new subsidiary called the Yaqui Land & Water Company, which in turn came to own the Sonora-Sinaloa Irrigation Company.

Yaqui Land was capitalized at ten million dollars with Davis Richardson as president. Hammond was first vice president, Whitney second vice president and Burnham was chairman of the executive committee. All were directors—only Fred and Davis drew salaries.

Capital from Hammond and Whitney brought the holdings to an area the size of Delaware. Fred began to appreciate the scope of Hammond's vision, another Cecil Rhodes, and he was thrilled to be associated with this man.

Soon Yaqui Land drew to its cause specialists from the United States and a new era dawned. The U.S. Department of Agriculture lent soil scientists. Engineers were borrowed from the Reclamation Service to help with dams and irrigation. Masters of power plants were called in to electrify the valley. Drillers tested the sediments for drinking water.

From the University of California came W.W. Mackie, an authority on desert farming. Mackie established an agricultural experiment station where he tested oranges, grapefruit, cotton, rice, alfalfa and garbanzo beans. He planted forty-five kinds of wheat, sixty-five of rice and almost every species of fruit known. Plants were adapted to the locality until out of all these tests, seeds or cuttings from the best two of each variety was adopted. When the Panama Canal opened, the sky would be the limit."

• • •

Los Angeles • 1906

ONCE THE LAND WAS developed, there arose a need for colonists to take up the farms. The Yaqui Land & Water Company organized a Real Estate Department.

Brochures were released praising the valley as a farmers' paradise. Ads appeared in the Los Angeles newspapers, followed by editorials praising Sonora as a prosperous outpost for the Los Angeles empire. The ads proclaimed the Yaqui River Delta as the finest land on earth, available for only twenty-five dollars an acre, with a down payment of one fifth and the balance in four annual payments with six percent interest.

"There is no crop that will not net you at least twice the price you pay for the land," one ad said. "A perpetual water right goes with the land, free of charge." The right was free, but not the water.

Burnham was riding on top of the world. The Oof Bird—its tail well salted—was in his pocket. After this buildup, the Southern Pacific let it be known that it was shipping California farm products into food-deficient Mexico. At that point, all resistance vanished and the farmers, waving their cash and savings, began to sign up.

The deeds of sale gave Sonora-Sinaloa Irrigation Company a perpetual right to charge fifty cents an acre-foot for all water furnished for irrigation. Each farm required at least five acre-feet of water annually, so that clause assured the Sonora-Sinaloa Irrigation a profit of three million dollars a year. Water sales would go on forever.

• • •

LOS ANGELES • SPRING 1906

SHORTLY AFTER Fred turned forty-five, he became famous in America. For the first time since Blanche's self-imposed censorship, Fred's name was thrust into the news.

Richard Harding Davis published *Real Soldiers of Fortune*, a nonfiction book that profiled six worthies of the world. Four of the adventurers were unknowns, men like Captain Philo McGriffin who at the age of thirty-two headed the Chinese Naval College. Only two of the six were popular personalities of the day. Winston Churchill was making a name as a member of parliament.

The sixth and most-famous was Major Fred Burnham, D.S.O., who was engaged with the eminent John Hays Hammond in developing the Yaqui River Delta of Mexico. The publication of *Real Soldiers of Fortune* gave millions of Americans their first in-depth look at Fred. In the past there were newspaper accounts—some quite vivid—of his exploits, but the British reporters had always been vague about Fred's heritage.

Now Fred's name and deeds were recounted by an immensely popular American author. That fact plus Fred's relationship with Hammond helped to open many new doors. Suddenly, there were invitations to all sorts of events. One day he received this telegram:

Am scheduled as speaker at Pasadena Humane Society Wednesday, September 19 stop Unavoidably detained stop Will you substitute for me? Regards stop Gifford

Gifford Pinchot, a lean six-footer with a craggy face and fiery eyes, was Teddy Roosevelt's environmentalist. Both Teddy and Gifford came from well-to-do families. Both were conservationists, nature lovers, crusaders. Both camped out with John Muir. Both were physical fitness fans.

Pinchot occupied a highly unusual position in the Roosevelt Administration. Nominally, he was chief forester, a minor position in the Agriculture Department, but in fact he dealt directly with the president—being a member of Teddy's tennis cabinet.

Burnham delivered a speech that night, but it was Fred's speech, not one of Pinchot's conservation talks. He told an audience of animal lovers of a plan that he had developed himself. He described a talk with President Roosevelt of their concern for the loss of the bison on the Great Plains. Pinchot wanted to buy up the buffaloes to protect them until the herds grew large again. But there was powerful opposition from the cattle ranchers.

"I want to suggest a variation of that plan," Fred said. "I have made a list of African animals that could populate the spaces of this nation. I'm thinking of game animals, such as the Thompson's gazelle and the impala. I have Mr. Roosevelt's permission to say that he is in favor of the idea and Mr. Pinchot endorses it as well."

The scheme was so arcane that nothing happened.

Counterpoise • Equilibrium

THREE RIVERS • MAY 1908

ON MAY 11, Fred turned forty-seven, and he suddenly got ranch fever. He called the Burnhams, Blicks and Russells into conference. Thirty members of the White Tribe agreed a ranch was needed and they fanned out over California in search of suitable cattle land.

It was Jack Hammond who came up with the idea for the snug canyon near Three Rivers. From Sequoia Park, three forks of the Kaweah River drained the shoulders of Mount Whitney, the tallest mountain in the USA. The south fork of the Kaweah River offered promise for a cattle ranch.

Hammond told Fred about the Mount Whitney Power Company, which used water from the north fork of the Kaweah to electrify the irrigation of fruit and nut farms in Tulare County. The generator was at the hamlet of Hammond, between Three Rivers and Sequoia Park.

"It's named after my brother," Jack said.

There was one problem. The Kaweah River dried up in summer, leaving no grass for the cattle to pasture on. Fred and Judd Blick rode up into the Sierra Nevada to explore Hockett Meadows at the eight thousand foot level.

At four thousand feet, they came upon the Sequoia trees. These majestic botanicals rose arrow-like for four hundred feet. It didn't take a genius to figure out these were the largest living things on earth. The lowest branches — a hundred feet up — were as big as ordinary tree trunks.

The Return to America

A giant Sequoia will inspire nearly anyone to be a conservationist.

At Hockett Meadows, Fred gazed on grass, streams and a big lake. Here was the glade to fatten his beeves. Six miles north was a wilderness named Mineral King. In Cerro Gordo days, it had been the site of a silver mine run by religious zealots. The View of the World in the Matopo Hills, where Rhodes and Wilson were buried, was also called Mineral King. This place was a good choice.

Fred leased twenty thousand acres of alpine pasture.

The White Tribe called the farm at Three Rivers *La Cuesta*—the Home Ranch. They planted fruit and nut trees and stocked the yard with deer shipped up from Sonora. They built three adobe houses, for the Burnhams, the Blicks and the Russells. And there was a tribal trophy room to house the Burnham Collection.

For the next three decades while camping at Hockett Meadows, Burnham would gain fame for regaling notables with campfire yarns of his adventures. During one summer outing, Fred taught young Roland Harriman to shoot a rifle, stalk a bear and dress the hide.

Lagnappe • A Little Extra

Washington • May 1908

PRESIDENT ROOSEVELT called a Governors Conference in support of Conservation. He named Gifford Pinchot to head the National Conservation Commission. Roosevelt signed an executive order creating the Grand Canyon National Monument.

On an almost daily basis, Gifford Pinchot began to withdraw federal lands as forest preserves. Soon the newspapers were filled with discussions of forest fires, soil exhaustion, reforestation and the importance of guarding against forest fires and food shortages. Fred decided to relaunch his plan to import African antelope. A few days later, an article appeared in the *Los Angeles Times*.

With the endorsement of the president of the United States and the approval of the Los Angeles Chamber of Commerce, one of the most interesting moves ever made by a public-spirited man in the Southwest is soon to be started.

It is for the transplanting of thirty species of African game animals to our preserves. Congress will be asked to set apart portions of the forest reserves as a perpetual U.S. sanctuary, and when this is done the importation will commence.

"Most concerned are Major Fred R. Burnham of Pasadena and the eminent South African engineer John Hays Hammond. Major Burnham does not propose to bring over lions, tigers or other beasts of prey, but rather creatures which by their hardihood and beauty will greatly increase the picturesqueness of our mountains and valleys.

> *Both Hammond and Major Burnham are thoroughly familiar with the game conditions in South Africa. The backing of Mr. Roosevelt brightens the project. The president is a longtime friend of Major Burnham and recently gave him a lengthy audience in the White House in discussion of this project."*

Ritornello • Interlude

NEW YORK • SUMMER 1907

JACK HAMMOND resigned from Guggenheim, retired from mining engineering. He devoted the rest of his life to developing major projects. Jack was attracted to politics partly because of a dimly recalled event at Yale when he had taught a classmate to play poker.

That brief association was renewed in 1902 during a lunch at the University Club. Five years later, in February 1907, while calling on President Roosevelt, Hammond once again met Will Taft. Now serving as Teddy's Secretary of War, Taft questioned Hammond because of his knowledge and expertise as president of the American Institute of Mining Engineers—AIME.

"Should the Army develop the Panama Canal or should private industry be allowed to build it?"

"The Corps of Engineers might not be as technically proficient," Hammond replied, "but there certainly will be less graft if the Army runs the show."

"Integrity is more important than efficiency," Taft said, "Colonel George Goethals will dig Teddy's Big Ditch."

• • •

CHICAGO • JUNE 1908

DURING THE campaign, Hammond drew Burnham into national politics. At the Republican National Convention in Chicago, outgoing President Roosevelt engineered the nomination of Secretary of War William Howard Taft as the Republican candidate for president.

As Secretary for War, Taft was popular for having chosen George Goethals to build the Panama Canal. Taft was soft-spoken, intellectual, a thoroughly nice man with a rollicking sense of humor. Though he weighed three hundred pounds, he was not sensitive about if. One of the favored quips of the day was, "Taft gave up his seat in the streetcar—to three women." In spite of his size, Will projected an air of dignity.

During the speech-making, Roosevelt advised Taft, "Quit citing your old court decisions, Will. Get out and give 'em hell."

Taft had a weapon in his favor. A jovial man with a smile, he was celebrated for his friendly chuckle, which won him countless votes.

Hammond and Taft Go Golfing

"Bill's laughter is a form of physical enjoyment," Hammond said. "He impels large audiences into spasms of delighted laughter."

Hammond and Burnham campaigned to help assure Will Taft's election. Hammond reorganized the National League of Republican Clubs to enlist young, first-time voters. It was a surprise to no one that on November 3, Bill Taft deftly handed William Jennings Bryan a sound defeat of landslide proportions.

After the election, the Tafts and Hammonds took the *Kya Yami* to Augusta, Georgia, for a couple of months of golf and planning.

59

The Birth of the Boy Scouts

LONDON • 1908

IF BURNHAM HAD gone to England — instead of entering politics with Hammond — he might have learned why Stephe Baden-Powell suddenly stopped asking him to teach scouting at the Cavalry School. What happened is that Stephe got into the losing end of a kerfuffle with Major General Douglas Haig, the director of military training at Sandhurst and the chief theoretician in the British cavalry. Baden-Powell had organized the Cavalry School with a position of instructor of scouting in the organization. Stephe intended to make scouting a required subject, but when Haig learned of Stephe's proposal, he stepped in, delivered a stinging rebuke and modified the plan. Haig thrived on the display of raw power.

The position of instructor in scouting was abolished. As a sop, Haig allowed Stephe to institute three months of dismounted training for cavalry officers. But from that moment on, if Fred Burnham harbored any lingering hope to teach scouting at the Cavalry School, Haig had truncated the plan.

Baden-Powell, smarting from the censure, scooted off to inspect cavalry units from Cairo to Cape Town. When he returned, he directed his efforts toward founding a scouting movement outside of British Army circles.

For two years, there had been a war scare in Europe. Field Marshal Lord Roberts publicly declared the need for an army large enough to render any German invasion out of the question. In one of his final acts as commander in chief, Roberts put out a call for rifle drill for boys. Once retired, Bobs advocated universal male conscription, but military officers on active duty were unable to endorse that cause. General Baden-Powell lent quiet support to a

453

scheme to create additional small-bore rifle ranges in England.

On his return from Africa, Stephe began to revise his 1899 book *Aids to Scouting*. In revising that work, Baden-Powell declared that boys should learn the points of the compass by using the sun, moon and stars. They should learn to read spoor, build fires, estimate distances, render first aid, swim, compose reports and know the British colonies. He suggested tests for memory, tracking, making fire and camp cooking.

When a first draft was completed, Stephe asked for comments from Sir William Smith of the Boys Brigade. He also sent review copies to Lord Roberts, Lord Strathcona, Earl Grey, Lord Rodney of Rodney's Boys and H.A. Gwynne, the editor of the *Evening Standard*. Gwynne forwarded Stephe's manuscript to his boss, publisher Arthur Pearson. In addition to the *Evening Standard*, Pearson owned the *London Daily Express* and *Pearson's* magazine.

In 1900 *Pearson's* magazine had proclaimed Burnham as the King of Scouts. On reading the manuscript, Pearson invited Stephe to be his house guest at Fresham in Surrey. Baden-Powell was flattered when Pearson said he would publish the book in serial form. Meanwhile, hurry and finish the book.

A month later, while inspecting Lord Rodney's Boys on the Isle of Wight, the superviser of the cadet brigades told Stephe the lads needed to be roughened up a bit—away from the powder-puff influence of mamas and aunties.

For the next three months, Baden-Powell became a zealous writer. On receiving suggestions and comments from the lords, Stephe refashioned *Aids to Scouting* into *Scouting for Boys*. He intended the book to be used by existing youth groups, so he did not incorporate close-order drill or rifle practice in his manuscript. That was already being done.

An American emigrant from Scotland named Ernest Thompson Seton sent Baden-Powell a book called *The Birch-Bark Roll of the Woodcraft Indians*. Seton suggested that Baden-Powell might wish to use some ideas from America. Seton said boys between the ages of eight and fifteen were being inspired to identify with natural man, the American Indian. Each tribe of Boy Indians in America would be guided by an adult Medicine Man.

Baden-Powell read *The Birch-Bark Roll*, and he was appalled by Seton's grotesque ideas. In *Scouting for Boys*, Stephe was creating a culture alien to the Woodcraft Indians. From his talks with Burnham, Stephe knew that the Apache, Comanche, Sioux, Cheyenne and Yaqui

The Return to America

gloried in war. The culture of the American Indians was housed in hatred, vengeance and killing. Apaches hated Navajos as much as they hated Mexicans. Apaches disfigured other Apaches as eagerly as they sliced up white folks. American Indians lacked any notion of chivalry, charity and compassion.

Stephe wanted nothing to do with Seton's point of view. He set a goal of doing a good turn each day, with an emphasis on chivalry and patriotism. He adopted positive ideas that would interest any normal young boy: amusing games ranging from knights in armor to map-making. In addition to military scouts, Baden-Powell wrote of peace scouts—pioneers, trappers and prospectors—as heroes for the lads to emulate. He put Birch Bark behind him.

Still, Baden-Powell faced a major stumbling block. He had seriously misjudged the complexity of the task he had undertaken. There was a wealth of information available, but a task that Stephe had counted on to take six weeks was expanding into six months. Arthur Pearson urged Baden-Powell to hurry things along.

• • •

ON MAY 6, 1907, General Baden-Powell's four-year term as Inspector General of cavalry expired. He was promoted to lieutenant general and when no three-star billets became available, he was placed on leave of absence at half pay. This allowed Stephe to spend full time on writing *Scouting for Boys*. What he lacked was a unifying theme that would coalesce his thoughts and make this work come to life.

Help came from an unlikely quarter. While on a fishing trip in Ireland, Stephe met a wealthy stockbroker. Charles van Raalte owned Brownsea Island in Pool Harbor a few miles west of Bournemouth. Van Raalte offered Baden-Powell the use of his island during the summer as a camp for adolescent boys.

On July 29, Baden-Powell and The Boy McLaren set up a scout camp on Brownsea Island. They took twenty-two lads between the ages of thirteen and sixteen to bed down under the stars. They organized the lads into patrols, each with a boy leader. The lads had the rare privilege of saluting the very Union Jack that flew over Mafeking.

The boys regarded it as good fortune to be invited to an outing with the country's most famous military hero. Their days were filled with a variety of outdoor games. After dinner, Stephe spun yarns around the campfire. Wholly American terms like jamboree, powwow, posse, palaver and yarn became part of the Brownsea lexicon. Stephe regaled in telling tales about being pursued by

455

Matabele warriors in the Matopo Hills of Africa. The boys learned to sing Zulu war chants. Then, on August 11, the summer camp ended.

The experience proved to be a powerful force in coalescing Baden-Powell's ideas for *Scouting for Boys*. It provided him with practical experience in which to sift good ideas from the half-baked. From that point on, Stephe devoted full time to his manuscript. The book's new theme continued to promote outdoors life: mapping, tracking, hiking, signaling, first-aid and other skills used in the out of doors.

During his outing with the city-bred lads, Baden-Powell discovered an appalling social convention that one day would be called peer pressure. The term didn't exist, but Stephe recognized its existence by its symptoms and denounced it as a cancer on society. He gave it the name that made the best sense to him: the herding instinct. Baden-Powell saw it as an external force that impelled people living close together to seek group approval, with no regard for common sense.

Stephe recognized that city life was responsible for the herding instinct. It was a product of the rotten core of the inner-city. Stephe regarded it as a destructive blow to human dignity and sanity. The herding instinct reduced an intelligent human being to the intellectual level of a common wildebeest. So serious did Baden-Powell regard this cancer that he reviewed his manuscript stripping out any reference that might sanction the herding instinct.

From that point on, scouting took on a decidedly anti-school and anti-authority streak. Stephe accused both institutions of supporting the reviled herding instinct. This redirection to addressing big-city problems explains why rural youth in Great Britain was never much attracted to scouting. Nor would scouting appeal to the upper classes in England. Scouting would always be popular primarily among the lower classes—the masses in the big cities. Scouting was conceived to be a powerful defense against the wildebeest instinct.

Stephe's new vigor still didn't produce a finished manuscript fast enough for Arthur Pearson, who by now had established a schedule to serialize *Scouting for Boys* in his fortnightly *Pearson's* magazine. To Pearson, *Scouting for Boys* was merely a tool to promote the circulation of his magazine—nothing more—and he urged Baden-Powell to hurry up. Pearson also wanted to use the series of articles to create advance demand for the book itself when it came out in the spring of 1908.

At long last, Stephe completed the manuscript and delivered it to Pearson. By October 1907, the advance publicity and promotion of

The Return to America

Scouting for Boys had created a pent-up demand. To everyone's astonishment, there was an instant cry to establish Scout troops.

It was quickly apparent that *Scouting for Boys* was not a supplementary text for existing youth groups—something entirely new had been born. Late in October, Pearson responded to public demand by setting up a Scouting office in London to take advance orders for *Scouting for Boys*. On November 12, The Boy McLaren became the first manager of the Scouting office.

Baden-Powell wanted to call the new organization the Imperial Scouts, but Pearson, who held the purse strings, held out for Boy Scouts. Stephe accepted the choice and took to the field.

In four months he gave fifty lectures on scouting, talks that helped to promote the Scouting movement. With relish, Stephe set about designing an official uniform. It was a composite of his own reconnaissance outfit in the Matopo Hills and the gaudy uniform of the South African Constabulary, down to the short pants, shirt, neckerchief and a Montana-peak cowboy hat by Stetson.

When on January 15, 1908, *Scouting for Boys* began to appear in serial form in *Pearson's* magazine, tens of thousands of English lads began buying the publication. The Scouting office was overwhelmed by the volume of requests for enrollment forms, hats, flags, badges and neckerchiefs. By January 24, after an interval of only nine days, the first Boy Scout troop was established. Stephe had hit the hot button of lower-class city boys in England.

Baden-Powell hastily came up with plans for lads aged eleven to fifteen to organize into groups of six or seven under a boy patrol leader. He wrote a Scout Law, a code of chivalrous behavior, combined with an emphasis on outdoor activities. He introduced the left handshake, the fleur-de-lis badge and the Be Prepared motto, drawn from the South African Constabulary—they were B-P's own initials.

There were all the trappings of military courtesy: the Scout salute, the Scout motto, a Scout sign, a Scout handclasp, plus badges, medals and insignia. There was an elaborate rite devoted to the wearing of the uniform. Stephe ranked the beginner Scout as a Tenderfoot, an acknowledgment of Scouting's roots in America

From Burnham, Baden-Powell adopted the ranks Second Class Scout and First Class Scout. The highest rank was recognized by a special badge: Queen's Scout in England and later Eagle Scout in the United States.

A system of merit badges was introduced. Badges were awarded for angling, archery, astronomy, basketry, bird study, blacksmithing,

457

botany, bugling, camping, canoeing, conservation, cooking, cycling, first aid, forestry, gardening, hiking, horsemanship, pathfinding, reptile study, rocks, minerals, rowing, safety, signaling, stalking, surveying, weather, woodcarving and zoology. Special attention was given to knot-tying, a skill that Baden-Powell had discovered in the Gold Coast while clearing a trail to the Ashanti.

In March 1908, there were fears of a war with Germany, and Baden-Powell was unexpectedly recalled to active duty and placed in command of the Northumbrian Division, out in the backblocks.

Things at the Scouting office had gotten off to a good start when suddenly The Boy McLaren got into a kerfuffle with the Pearson organization. In a huff he stalked out, leaving a power vacuum in the management structure. At that point, Pearson stepped in to take over management of the Boy Scouts Association.

Two months later, *Scouting for Boys* came out in book form, and it was instantly denounced by the middle class as a radical book. *Scouting for Boys* debunked the caste system so beloved of middle class society. It also criticized social snobbery. It advocated clothing that was identical for members of all of the social and economic classes.

The British middle classes were appalled by this democratic tome. Complaints also poured in from farmers about Scouts trampling crops, leaving gates open and allowing the livestock to escape. But the lads loved *Scouting for Boys* and it sold like griddlecakes—each press run ran into the tens of thousands.

In August, there was a great deal of hoopla and national publicity when General Baden-Powell took leave to preside over a general Boy Scout campout organized by Pearson. Baden-Powell deplored Pearson's promotions, but there was nothing he could do about it. The suspicion was all but universal that Baden-Powell and Pearson were running the Boy Scouts as a profit-seeking venture.

Lagnappe • A Little Extra

WASHINGTON • MARCH 1909

ON TUESDAY, MARCH 2, Will Taft was sworn in as the twenty-seventh president of the United States. Teddy Roosevelt became the

The Return to America

last American president to ride in a horse-drawn carriage. Will Taft was the first to ride in an automobile—a White Steamer being his vehicle of choice.

Three weeks later, Teddy collected his Nobel Peace Prize and set sail for Africa to embark with Fred Selous on a grand safari. Teddy and son Kermit, nineteen, the official photographer of the expedition, were surrounded by a shouting, pushing mass of people as they boarded the steamship *Hamburg* in Hoboken, New Jersey. Roosevelt was wearing an olive drab military coat with his Rough Riders military rank on the sleeves. Teddy was about to introduce the Dark Continent to America.

Five weeks later, the Roosevelts — carrying an arsenal of weaponry — entered Africa at Mombassa. Teddy cried, "By Godfrey, that's a wonderful sight." His safari included two hundred porters and a canvas bathtub. Teddy's expedition dwarfed Burnham's exploration party.

How greatly Kenia, now Kenya, had changed in five years. The Hotel Norfolk was by all standards the finest resort in Africa. The main dining room seated a hundred patrons with fifty waiters to attend to their desires. It was known locally as the House of Lords.

With the United States' frontier gone, Teddy's visit transformed Kenya into the California of Africa. The colony was the richest hunting ground in the world and Roosevelt's great safari, led by Fred Selous, became the grand adventure of the century. The *New York Times* published weekly stories of the Roosevelt Adventure.

• • •

WASHINGTON • SPRING 1909

WILL TAFT CALLED on Yale classmate Jack Hammond to fulfill a pre-election pledge. Before agreeing to run for office, Will had extracted from Jack a promise to provide advice and counsel to the new administration.

With Jack Hammond coaching from the wings, Will Taft surprised the nation with a flurry of new legislative proposals: a federal budget, a Department of Labor, Parcel Post, an income tax amendment, a national banking system, Postal Savings and many other innovations. Most of these proposals were designed to relieve the grinding depression that had gripped the nation for the past two years. Taft's proposals were considered so radical that Congress rejected most of them out of hand—it remained for his successor, Woodrow Wilson, to take the credit.

Fred enjoyed his new unofficial role in Washington. As an officer in the British Army, he had the confidence of the Ambassador,

Viscount James Bryce. The Burnham name was added to the mailing list for British Embassy socials. Given his status, it was only natural that Fred learned a great deal of privileged information. Although he tried not to betray confidences, the counsel that he gave to Hammond and Taft reflected his understanding of intimate knowledge.

At one British Embassy function, an American Navy official boasted about President Roosevelt's Great White Fleet of sixteen U.S. battleships that had sailed around the world on a goodwill cruise. After the American tottered off, the British attaché boasted to Fred of the Royal Navy's recent accomplishments.

He told Fred how the cherubic Admiral Sir John Fisher had invented the dreadnaught, which the Americans renamed the battleship, and developed the submarine destroyer, which the Americans shortened to destroyer. Then he described Britain's latest naval maneuvers.

"All of His Majesty's ships that could be spared took part in the training exercises, half of which constituted the Enemy Fleet and the other half the British Fleet," the attaché said. "The Enemy Fleet gained a complete victory over the British Fleet and took possession of the English Channel."

"How'd they do that?"

"They were fueled with oil, not coal. The oil-burning ships had greater range. They didn't have to stop for bunkering."

"So oil will become the fuel of the Royal Navy?"

"Not yet," the attaché said. "We've plenty of coal in England, but no one has discovered oil in the British Empire. We must stay with an assured supply of fuel."

After the party, Fred mentioned to Hammond the idea of fueling railroad locomotives and steamships with oil instead of coal. Hammond thought that was a good idea, specially in the West where distances were so great.

Fred's primary interest in Washington was to promote his scheme to import African animals. Before leaving for Africa, Teddy advised Fred to see Gifford Pinchot about getting some action. Fred soon learned that simple things were not done in Washington. There had to be a bill offered to Congress and there were a multitude of details to attend to. Receptions had to be sponsored to win support for the cause. To press his case, Burnham was required to attend social functions. Ribbons of red tape tangled his cause, but assistance came from an unexpected quarter.

61st CONGRESS, 2d SESSION.

H. R. 23261.

IN THE HOUSE OF REPRESENTATIVES.

MARCH 21, 1910.

Mr. BROUSSARD introduced the following bill; which was referred to the Committee on Agriculture and ordered to be printed.

A BILL

To import wild and domestic animals into the United States.

1 *Be it enacted by the Senate and House of Representa-*
2 *tives of the United States of America in Congress assembled,*
3 That the Secretary of Agriculture be, and he is hereby,
4 directed to investigate and import into the United States wild
5 and domestic animals whose habitat is similar to government
6 reservations and lands at present unoccupied and unused:
7 *Provided,* That, in his judgment, said animals will thrive and
8 propagate and prove useful either as food or as beasts of
9 burden; and that two hundred and fifty thousand dollars, or
10 as much thereof as may be necessary, is hereby appropriated,
11 out of any moneys in the Treasury not otherwise appropri-
12 ated, for this purpose.

"I'll introduce you to a man who knows quite a lot about African animals," Pinchot said. "His name is Fritz Duquesne."

"I know all about Duquesne," Fred replied.

Duquesne had a trim, lank body, suggesting a man of abundant energy. His head was nearly rectangular, set off by a square jaw, flat at the bottom. His ears, which hugged close to his head, were almost concealed by thick brown hair. His lips were thin, complemented by a pencil-thin mustache. He would have been handsome but for a high forehead and a crooked nose, the result of a youthful brawl. Duquesne had a brilliant mind and he was an entertaining and convincing speaker.

"Bob Brossard of Louisiana has introduced House Resolution 23261," Duquesne said. "The bill has been referred to the Committee on Agriculture. It meets Thursday and we're to testify on behalf of passage."

"Getting a congressman from Louisiana to sponsor the bill sounds like good politics," Fred said. "He has no vested interest, either for or against."

Duquesne explained Washington politics to Fred.

"Water hyacinths are clogging the bayous," he said "Congressman Broussard wants hippos to eat the plants."

"If that news gets out, the bill is dead."

At the hearings on March 24, Brossard outlined the essentials. The next speaker was Dr. Arthur Farmington of the Department of Agriculture. No one opposed the measure and the testimony of Burnham and Duquesne completed the hearings.

Afterward, Brossard invited Burnham and Duquesne to visit his home in Louisiana. Congressman Brossard hosted a Cajun barbecue and Fred was introduced to spicy rice and seafood of French-speaking Louisiana: shrimp gumbo, ham jambalaya and crawfish pie. While eating, recognition suddenly dawned that gumbo came from the Ashanti. *Gombo* was the word for rice on the Gold Coast.

Then it was back to Washington to lobby for H.R. 23261. The bill was not acted on for several months and during that time, Duquesne kept the pot boiling with a series of sensational articles distributed nationwide by the Metro Newspaper Syndicate. All looked favorable.

The vote had to be unanimous. A congressman from the state of Washington expressed the fear that public preserves, if stocked with wild game, might be used by millionaires as hunting grounds. Such joy could not be tolerated. He voted nay and the African animal scheme died.

60

Came Scouting to America

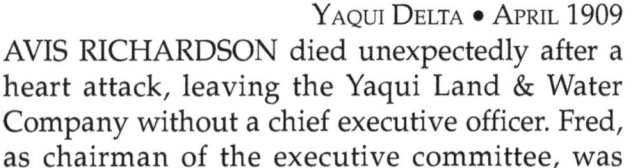

YAQUI DELTA • APRIL 1909

DAVIS RICHARDSON died unexpectedly after a heart attack, leaving the Yaqui Land & Water Company without a chief executive officer. Fred, as chairman of the executive committee, was called upon to step in as acting president and CEO, a position he was destined to hold for eight years. En route to the Yaqui Delta, Fred wrote to Sir Rider Haggard at Ditchingham House.

I am delayed in El Paso, waiting for my wife to arrive from Los Angeles, and I shall give you a short resume of what is happening in this part of the world. The American people have taken to heart your idea of back-to-the-land. Our lecturers and magazines are full of the theory you advanced that a strong race cannot be perpetuated in piles of brick and mortar.

Because of the lingering depression, more than half a million of our farmers have migrated to Canada, and now the tide of emigration has set strongly into Mexico. The enclosed clipping and flyers will explain my interests in Sonora, and the connection of our mutual friend, John Hays Hammond.

We hold a vast tract of land for agricultural purposes, a great delta on the Yaqui River, as rich as the Nile, that would furnish land for fully three-hundred thousand settlers.

The death of the president of the company, Davis Richardson, places me in a peculiar position. It looks as if for the next few years I shall have to devote almost all my energy to the colonization efforts.

I hope that the charming English country life is still as it was in the past years when I was a frequent guest at Ditchingham House. Please give my best wishes to all who remember me. I am yours sincerely, F.R. Burnham

Ritornello • An Interlude

LONDON • SEPTEMBER 1909

DESPITE misgivings over Pearson's materialism, Baden-Powell was inspired by the hothouse growth of Scouting that his organization engendered. The Scouting movement spread through the British Commonwealth: South Africa, Canada, India, Australia and New Zealand. Late in 1909, several Rhodesian boys formed the First Bulawayo Boy Scout Troop. The growth of Scouting was so rapid that Stephe left the army so he could devote full time to the Boy Scouts. The movement made so much news that Fred wrote to Baden-Powell from the Yaqui Delta of Mexico.

It seems incredible that three years have passed since I wrote to you in answer to your kind invitation to pen a few notes on Scouting. From time to time, I have noticed in the papers the wonderful tenacity with which Lord Roberts has clung to the idea of preparing England in times of peace for the inevitable struggle which every great nation is called upon at times to face, or lose all. My brother, Howard, brought from England with him a number of your books which have been issued to the Boy Scouts. They are extremely interesting and make me almost wish I again was a boy to become a leader in one of your contingents, with which I now understand you have dotted almost every county in England. Many of the mysteries of woodcraft have been made public since the days that you and I rode together over the African veld. Much of the literature I have read. Some of it is certainly very truthful and exact. In fact, I don't think there is much more to be written on the subject of Scouting.

Now my dear general, if you will favor me with the literature of your latest work, Organization of Scouting, *I shall consider it a personal favor—as in this odd corner of the world I get fragmentary accounts at best. It may be that now my work in Mexico is not so strenuous and I may see you again before a great many moons. F.R. Burnham.*

A month later, King Edward VII knighted Baden-Powell for organizing the Boy Scout Association. Shortly after that, Sir Robert responded to Fred's letter.

I am indeed delighted to hear from you again and hope that I may keep in touch with you for the future. The Scouting for Boys, *about which I wrote you when you left England, has been developed into a very big affair. We have more than two hundred thousand members now in England, and many more in the different colonies and foreign countries.*

Our newspaper, The Scout, *has a big circulation and I should*

The Return to America

indeed be grateful if some day you could write us one or two true stories on Scouting, with a few hints or morals tacked on for the special benefit of the lads. I shall certainly quote some of the very instructive and suggestive remarks which you made in your letter. If you should ever visit England, do not forget to let me know, and if there is anything I can do for you here during your absence, please command me. Believe me. Yours truly. R. Baden Powell.

• • •

Baden-Powell's tour of duty in Northumberland convinced him the most important work of the Scouting movement was to recruit vast numbers of slum boys from the great industrial centers of the Midlands. And because of Baden-Powell's direction, Scouting in Great Britain remained chiefly a lower-middle- and lower-class affair.

For Sir Robert, a highlight of 1910 came when King George inspected the Boy Scouts at Windsor Castle. More than thirty thousand Scouts wearing Stetson's Montana peak cowboy hats drew up in a Zulu horned crescent formation and pledged to live by chivalrous ideals. In one organization, Baden-Powell had managed to combine the ideals of medieval knighthood, the skirmishing of African tribal wars and the dress of the western plainsmen. It was a splendid achievement for a graying polo player from India.

• • •

PAWHUSKA, OKLAHOMA • MAY 1909

SIX MONTHS before the 1910 jamboree, Scouting came to America, but in a way quite unlike what you may have been led to believe. The official version, authorized by the Boy Scouts *of* America, goes something like this. William D. Boyce, a Chicago publisher, was on a visit to England. In London he was having a difficult time finding a certain address. He was standing looking puzzled when a youth walked up to him.

"May I be of service to you, Gov?"

Boyce told the lad where he wanted to go. The boy smiled and saluted.

"Come with me, Sir," he said and led him to the place. Boyce offered the lad a shilling.

"Oh," the young man replied, "I'm a Boy Scout, and Scouts don't accept chits for courtesies."

"What was that you said?" Boyce asked.

"Don't you know about the Scouts?"

"Tell me about them."

The lad did.

"Interesting," Boyce replied. "I'd like to know more."

"Their office is close by, Gov," he added. "We can nip over in a jiff."

First, Boyce had to complete his errand, but the youth agreed to wait and later led him to the office of the Boy Scout Association, where information was freely given. Boyce was so impressed that on his return to the United States, he headed a committee to establish

The Return to America

a Scouting organization in America.

That's a stimulating tale, and it does tell how the Boy Scouts *of* America was organized, but it does not tell about the first Boy Scouts *in* America.

The first Boy Scout troop in America had been organized almost a year earlier. It happened in May 1909, at Pawhuska, Oklahoma. The troop was affiliated with the Boy Scout Association of mother England it was British, not American. In April of 1909, the Episcopal Church in England dispatched the Rev. John F. Mitchell to serve as rector of the St. Thomas Episcopal Mission in Pawhuska.

The Reverend Mitchell had been active in the Boy Scout Association in England, and he took with him to America samples of the Boy Scout Association handbooks, badges and insignia. On taking office as minister of the church, Mitchell organized the first Boy Scout Association troop *in* America. It had twenty charter members. W.E. McGuire was recruited to serve as assistant scoutmaster.

Early in 1910, Troop One of the Boy Scout Association made its first cross-country excursion, a horse-and-wagon journey to Bartlesville, Oklahoma. All but two members of the troop participated. They left on Friday, March 1, and returned Monday, March 4. Half of the boys rode horses and the other half rode in a wagon owned by John Long, who hauled food and supplies for the excursion.

The people of Bartlesville staged a parade and the lads organized a Boy Scout troop. Assistant Scoutmaster McGuire and Lieutenant Colonel Clarence Tinker of the U.S. Army Signal Corps officiated at the installation service. On Sunday after attending services, the Scouts began their trip back to Pawhuska. When the Cherokee Area Council of the Boy Scouts *of* America was organized later in Bartlesville, the Pawhuska troop was admitted as Troop 33, but its roots go back to the original British Boy Scout Association troop *in* America.

The Boy Scouts *of* America Inc. was incorporated February 8, 1910. Officers were elected: President William Howard Taft was honorary president. Teddy Roosevelt was appointed honorary vice president and chief scout citizen. Ernest Thompson Seton, the author of *The Birch-Bark Roll of Woodcraft Indians*, had muscled himself into the organization as chief scout. Dan Beard, author and artist, was the national scout commissioner, and James E. West was named chief scout executive — the seat of real power. Scout troops sprang up overnight. It seemed that all boys wanted to get Boy Scout training.

• • •

NEW YORK • 1910

SIR ROBERT Baden-Powell did almost nothing to promote Scouting in America. Stephe's unofficial break with the Boy Scouts of America dated almost from its inception. Two months after King George inspected the British Boy Scouts at Windsor Castle, Baden-Powell visited the United States. Stephe was shocked to learn that the power broker behind the Boy Scouts of America was another magazine publisher, William D. Boyce.

He spoke with Edgar M. Robinson of the Young Men's Christian Association, imploring him to take over the American Boy Scout organization. Robinson gave all appearances of being sympathetic to Baden-Powell's plea, so Stephe signed over to him the American rights to *Scouting for Boys* and agreed to let the American lads use the uniforms and badges without paying royalty to the Boy Scout Association. In a turncoat action never suitably explained, Robinson transferred the rights to James E. West's Boy Scouts of America.

Another reason for Baden-Powell's antagonism for the Boy Scouts of America was the American chief scout, Ernest Thompson Seton, who was trying to divert the Scouts toward his ferocious Woodcraft Indian scheme. The third reason—this one paramount—was James E. West, the chief scout executive. At one glance, Stephe saw that West was no outdoorsman. He was a corporate lawyer, a bureaucrat obsessed with dominance. In a later age, he would have been called a control freak.

West was directing the Boy Scouts of America away from the altruistic spirit of a volunteer movement in which devotees of amateur sports gave of their spare time to the community. West organized the Boy Scouts of America along the lines of a profit-seeking corporate endeavor. He hired teams of high-pressure fund-raisers. These salesmen were too sophisticated to be called boiler-room operators.

For their big-bucks shakedowns, the organization came to prey on big business at the CEO level. Typically, they would stage fund-raising banquets on a state or regional basis: Scouting's Banker of the Year, Scouting's Oil Man of the Year, Scouting's Car Maker of the Year. To West, success of the Boy Scouts depended on a constant influx of cash to pay the salaries of bureaucrats and staff.

West shackled American Boy Scouts with a profusion of regulations. He issued rules on how much equipment was to be taken to camp. The ratio of adult supervision was spelled out in detail. When Stephe learned the extent of the bureaucracy, he dismissed

The Return to America

West's organization as Parlour Scouting, and he broke with the American branch of Scouting. After that, when Stephe visited the United States, he directed his activities to the Girl Scouts.

While Baden-Powell was returning to England by ship, Kenneth "The Boy" McLaren committed the unspeakable act of marrying Miss Ethyl Wilson. The Boy and the Bloater never spoke again.

On a similar trip to the United States on Boy Scout business, Stephe, fifty-four, met his bride-to-be. Twenty-two-year-old Olave Soames was a lass of considerable prowess who disdained feminine clothing. The daughter of a brewer, she was reared in England, France and Italy as a multilingual athlete. She rode to the hounds, swam, bicycled, skated, played hockey and squash and played ten sets of tennis before noon. She complemented Stephe's image as Chief Scout.

Baden-Powell recognized the need for programs for other young folk. In *The Headquarters Gazette*, he published his *Scheme for Girl Guides*, a separate organization from the Boy Scouts. His goal was to attract the Cockney girl from the slum without making a tomboy of the cultured, middle-class girl. There were proficiency tests for stalking, cyclist, electrician, clerk, telegraphist, swimmer, pioneer, sailor and signaler—all identical to the merit badge tests for boys. There were badges for musicians, artists, tailors, cooks and florists. A counterpart called Girl Scouts sprang up on west side of the Atlantic.

Based on Rudyard Kipling's *Jungle Books*, Baden-Powell organized the Wolf Cubs which crossed the big drink as the Cub Scouts. The Scouting needs of older boys were served by Rover Scouts in Britain, Raider Scouts in France and Explorer Scouts in the United States. Scouting activities were extended to the world of swimming, sailing and canoeing and the Sea Scouts were born. There were Scouting troops for the deaf, dumb and blind.

By then Scouting had spread to Argentina, Austria, Chile, France, Germany, Greece, Holland, Italy, Japan, Mexico, Norway, Poland, Portugal, Russia, Sweden, Switzerland, South Africa, South America and Trinidad. It looked like Scouting might never stop growing.

Baden-Powell established a Scout Farm School, hoping to educate potential colonists. For lads who took Scouting's message to heart and aspired to live as frontiersmen, the logical destiny of the Farm School Scout was emigration to the colonies to expand the Empire.

Over in America, there developed a special Scouting movement for rural boys. William Boyce, the Chicago publisher, came up with a sure-fire plan to sell magazines. He founded the Lone Scouts of

469

America. Incorporated in 1915, memberships in Lone Scouts produced a bond among half a million boys, brought together through the pages of a magazine. To join, a boy could become a sales agent for one of Boyce's magazines or he could buy five copies of the *Lone Scout* magazine and clip the coupons.

The Lone Scouts were loosely modeled on some aspects of Ernest Thompson Seton's Woodcraft Indian code. The Lone Scouts existed without a troop or patrol leader, relying solely on the honor system. The Lone Scouts went out alone during the full moon. Extending one arm toward the sky, each boy took the Lone Scout pledge: "Do a useful thing each day." Ten years later, the Lone Scouts were folded into the American Boy Scouts.

Lagnappe • A Little Extra

LONDON • 1910

SIR ROBERT Baden-Powell dedicated the rest of his life to the Boy Scout movement, and he enjoyed it as much as any boy. He became the hero of virtually every slum and lower-class lad in the British Empire. He traveled and worked ceaselessly for the movement, and never took a penny of salary. He attended huge gatherings where thousands of boys greeted him as a hero.

Despite the popularity of Scouting among boys, there were problems in dealing with the adults. Coincident with a war scare in 1910, all boys on reaching age fourteen in Australia, Canada and South Africa were required to serve as cadets, a lightly disguised form of military conscription. Inevitably, there was a call in the British Empire to militarize all youth movements. In a fit of patriotic zeal, the Scouts in Melbourne were separated into Military Scouts and Peace Scouts. When Baden-Powell inspected only the Peace Scouts, the Australian press vilified him.

In Sydney, Stephe discovered that the chairman of the New South Wales Scout Council, T.R. Roydhouse, was the publisher of the *Sydney Sunday Times*. Roydhouse was giving the notion that Scouting was a circulation-building device. Stephe exploded. He demanded that Roydhouse resign and he held the line until the publisher was forced to do so. Stephe won that battle, but he lost plenty of others.

When Baden-Powell arrived in Trinidad for an inspection of Boy Scouts in the Caribbean, he discovered there were separate troops for blacks and whites. That upset him. During a visit to India, Baden-Powell said he was in favor of Indian boys becoming Boy Scouts. The Viceroy of India, Lord Chelmsford, vetoed the idea and Stephe was forced to accept the ban.

Over the years, Baden-Powell made many trips to India and Africa trying to sort out the problems of racial discrimination in the Scouting movements. When Scout troops were integrated, the white parents removed their sons. In Rhodesia, the Scouting commissioner told Baden-Powell that mixed-blood Coloureds were keen to join the Scouts precisely because it was a white organization.

In Natal, Stephe was forced to endorse a plan for separate branches for whites, blacks and Coloureds. It was a case of accept a compromise or lose everything. Sir Robert was able to win only two concessions: all would be called Boy Scouts and all wore identical uniforms.

Not so in America. In the northern states, Boy Scout troops were racially segregated like those in South Africa. In the South, there simply were no black Scouts. James West's expert on race relations declared that southern whites would not join Boy Scout troops if blacks were allowed to join—even if they were racially segregated. In a move that further caused Sir Robert to eschew the American Scouts, the Boy Scouts of America rejected out of hand a movement by blacks to organize as the Young American Patriots.

In visits to America, Stephe became depressed by gangster movies and crime novels. He deplored cocktails, high heels, lipstick and nail polish. He denounced these as the culture of pimps and prostitutes. He told anyone who would listen that these were dangerous crazes that spelled an end to a civilized, cultured society — meaning a society where a code of ethics could be handed down to the next generation and find acceptance.

• • •

LONDON • AUGUST 1914

WHEN THE GREAT WAR broke out in 1914, Baden-Powell was appalled to learn that only one in three men of military age was fit and healthy—poor nutrition and bad habits were at fault.

Lord Kitchener brusquely declined Stephe's request to be recalled to active duty. Burnham's son, Roderick, fought with the American forces in France. Brother Howie served France as a civilian. Baden-Powell kept in touch with Fred by mail.

I got your address from General Aylmer Hunter-Weston, and I am very eager to know how you are getting on, not having heard from you for so long. You must be having exciting times in Mexico, and if I know anything of you at all I expect you are in the thick of it. I suppose that the war in Europe will probably bring a stormy petrel like yourself over here to have a hand in it. If you should come, I sincerely hope you will let me know. Having retired from the Army myself, I am afraid I am altogether out of the fun, but am able to do a little work behind the scenes, specially in the matter of training the Boy Scouts.

Because of the war, the Boy Scout Association had to postpone a World Jamboree scheduled for 1918 when it would observe Scouting's first decade. But two years later, with peace restored, Scouting held its inaugural world meeting. Three hundred American Scouts were among the five thousand lads who came to London to attend the inaugural Boy Scout World Jamboree. Boys from thirty countries spent eight days and nights camping out on the open moors. It was called a *jamboree*—a name that was borrowed from the annual fur rendezvous celebrations of the mountain men of Wyoming's Teton Mountains.

As founder of the Scouting movement, Sir Robert was acclaimed as Chief Scout. The meeting made a profound impression on everyone there. Participants agreed to hold a jamboree every four years. Scoutmasters would get together at their own encampments called *indabas*. The American and African roots of Scouting ran deep.

Wealth & Honors

The 13th Chronicle

61

The Dominguez Air Show

LOS ANGELES • JANUARY 1910

THE UNITED STATES Air Show occupied the attention of Los Angeles and the world of flying from January 10 to 20. It was the first time any aeroplane had flown west of the Mississippi. The aerial regatta was staged on a gentle rise at Dominguez Mesa, twenty miles south of Los Angeles. On opening day, the attraction drew twenty-five thousand people. By closing day, the crowd would swell to forty thousand.

The seats held observers from Paris, officials from Whitehall, associates of Count von Zeppelin and one gentleman identified as customs commandant at Shanghai. There was also a ten-year-old lad named Jimmy Doolittle who earned a pass by wiping down the planes. The Burnhams and the Arthur Bents attended the air show and Fred saw each of the pilots as scouts of the future.

Festivities got off to a rousing start when Army Lieutenant Paul Beck dropped bags of sand onto outlines chalked on the ground depicting warships. The audience cheered with gusto and foreign observers scrawled ominous memos.

The starring attraction was Louis Paulhan, billed as the world's greatest flier. Paulhan, with his French Farman plane, had won fifty thousand dollars for flying from London to Manchester, a hundred fifty miles. He had demanded appearance money of fifty thousand dollars from the promoter, William Randolph Hearst's *Los Angeles Examiner*.

American Glenn Curtis, flying a plane whose design duplicated one from the Wright Brothers, challenged Paulhan to a contest of speed. Curtis wanted to better Paulhan's world speed record of fifty miles an hour. On Sunday the 16th, Curtis and Paulhan fired up their aircraft for the spirited contest. At first the race was close, but midway through the course the French Farman began to falter and it proved to be no match for Curtis's Wright Brothers knockoff aeroplane. During the race, the American flier attained an air speed of sixty miles an hour and lapped Paulhan's hapless Farman.

Even so, the community of Eagle Rock, which separates Los Angeles from Pasadena, duly christened a new street opposite Occidental College as Paulhan Street. The people would later say the air show brought aviation to America's attention. In two decades, Los Angeles would evolve into the nation's leading aviation center.

The Dominguez Air Show reminded Fred of two words: *brea* and *pickanin*. He hadn't thought of these words in thirty-five years. They had been spoken to him in 1875 by Art Bent.

Ritornello • An Interlude

Yaqui Delta • 1910

FRED WAS AT Cuidad Obregon bringing supplies to the Yaqui Land & Water Company when he met a half-naked Chinaman staggering along the road.

"Me store lobbed," the Chinaman cried. "Me clelk killee by Yaqui bandits. They blakee me alm."

Such incidents were not unusual in Mexico. Fred took the man to Esperanza and placed him in the care of his number one houseboy, Cholly Wong, who splinted the fractured arm. The next day the Chinaman was gone.

Later, Wong approached Fred for a favor.

"You go Pasadena next week?"

"Yes, Cholly."

Wong produced a small leather pouch.

"You takee money Pasadena? Give my cousin, Woo Chow. He come you house."

Burnham nodded and carried out the errand. After that, Wong occasionally gave Fred small sums of cash to forward to his cousin. When Charlie learned there had been no squeeze, he began entrusting his employer with larger sums. Several weeks later, Wong confided that the merchant Fred had rescued near Cuidad Obregon was "velly big man. He help Sunyatsen findee Homalea."

"What's a Homalea?"

"Homalea big genelal in China Army."

"Where is this Homer Lea?"

Wong looked over his shoulder.

"You go Eagle Lock. Homalea tlain China Army."

Eagle Rock was a sleepy residential community in a bowl-shaped valley between Pasadena and Los Angeles. It wasn't more than two miles from Fred's home. When he next returned to Pasadena, Fred rode over to Eagle Rock.

What he saw amazed him. There north of Paulhan Street—on a flat plain of the little suburban valley— were several hundred men marching in military formation. They carried old broom handles, but they went through their drill with precision. It seemed to Fred that every chop-suey cook and laundry boy in Los Angeles was there.

The man conducting the drill was Homer Lea. At first, Fred didn't see that Lea was a hunchback dwarf. A tailored uniform with a blue cape disguised nature's cruel trick. The impression Fred got was of the head of a child perched on the body of a small man. Lea's brown hair, parted at the middle, flowed down to ears that lacked lobes, producing an elfin appearance. This little elf wore the three-star insignia of a lieutenant general in the Army of the Republic of China.

"For God's sake, what's the Republic of China?"

"Doctor Sun Yat-sen organized the republic to defeat the Manchu Empress and free the people of China."

"I don't believe any of this. I must be dreaming."

Lea smiled, a bittersweet mixture of boy and gnome, not yet thirty years old. He told Fred the U.S. Army had spurned his services so he went to China in 1900 and got caught up in the Boxer Rebellion.

"The empress dowager ordered foreign devils killed," he said. "The Boxers began slaughtering the whites, but the western powers put down the uprising." Fred recalled that Queen Victoria had mentioned the Boxer Rebellion.

After the rebellion, Homer Lea fled to Hong Kong where he met Sun Yat-sen. Doctor Sun recognized that in Lea's misshapen body resided a genius. He invited Lea to Japan and later to California where they raised funds to finance a revolution.

Before returning to Hong Kong, Sun appointed Lea as Army chief of staff with instructions to train the chop-suey cooks in the shadows of the tall Washingtonia palms of Eagle Rock. To help support himself, Lea had written *The Valor of Ignorance*. It was about his visit to Japan, and it was a shocking book that told Americans things they didn't want to know. Only a decade earlier, America had fought the Spanish-American War. The United States had acquired the Philippines and Guam. To protect those properties, the U.S. military seized the Sandwich Islands and began fortifying them as Hawaii. Almost overnight, the United States had acquired a Pacific Empire.

Homer Lea's book told how the Japanese military, after winning the Russo-Japanese War, had become ambitious, how Japan would launch a war against the United States and how Hawaii would play a key role in that war. Soon the newspapers began to headline the threat of a Yellow Peril. Editorials warned that America would be invaded by the sons of the Rising Sun.

Counterpoise • Equilibrium

LOS ANGELES • MAY 1911

TWO WEEKS AFTER Fred's fiftieth birthday anniversary, sensational news was headlined in the papers. Porfirio Diaz, the dictator of Mexico—the man who had given personal guarantees to Jack Hammond—was overthrown and forced to flee his homeland.

Diaz was succeeded by Francisco Madero, the thirty-eight-year old son of a wealthy landowner who had become imbued with the spirit of democracy while studying in the United States. Arrested as a militant on the eve of the 1910 elections, Madero escaped to San Antonio, Texas. There he wrote a political tract calling for a revolt. Much to everyone's surprise, most of all his own, a ground-swell erupted in Mexico. Young Madero galloped south of the border and led the revolution to victory.

President Taft dispatched twenty thousand troops to protect the U.S. border. To the directors of Yaqui Land & Water Company, the news of Madero's assumption of power was calamitous. The revolution had succeeded with the backing of the Yaqui Indians whom President Diaz had banished to the Yucatan Peninsula. Now they were back, demanding vengeance. From the news, it was evident that President Madero intended to reward the Yaquis. Telegrams poured into Los Angeles and New York from the Yaqui Land & Water Company.

YAQUIS WANT OUR LAND, KILLING CATTLE, STEALING MULES.

RUMORED MADERO ORDERING WHITES OFF THE LAND.

INDIANS NOT WAITING FOR A LEGAL DIVISION, DRIVING OFF COLONISTS.

YAQUIS CARTING OFF PROVISIONS STOP SEND HELP!

At an emergency meeting of the board of directors, Jack Hammond outlined what must be done.

"Drastic measures are needed if we are to protect our investment," he said. "Unfortunately, I must leave for the coronation of King George."

"Not now," cried Harry Whitney. "This is terrible."

"The colonists want to remain neutral," Fred said.

"They are unarmed," Hammond said. "We cannot let them down."

"We've a fifteen million dollar investment to protect," Whitney complained.

Harris Hammond, Jack's eldest son, spoke up.

"I can get rifles and ammo if Major Burnham can smuggle them into Mexico."

"I'll handle that end," Fred said. "But you must buy a shipment of junk guns and deteriorated ammo."

"What for?" Whitney asked. He hated to spend money.

"Decoy shipment," Burnham said. "Mexican Customs will be suspicious of anything we send to Esperanza."

"Good thinking," Harris said. "How'll you get the real shipment through?"

"You don't want to know," Fred said. "Now I have to see an undertaker."

Under Harris, a decoy shipment was successfully seized by Mexican Customs. Then Fred shipped several coffins containing deceased Mexican nationals.

• • •

Los Angeles • June 1911

A MONTH LATER, Burnham received a telegram from Ottawa. Earl Grey, the former administrator of Rhodesia, was now governor general of Canada. Fred had not seen Grey in fifteen years.

MEET ME AT WALDORF, NEW YORK, 7 A.M. WEDNESDAY, THE 23RD STOP EARL GREY

At the appointed hour, Fred was on hand at Earl Grey's suite in the Waldorf Towers. While Grey finished shaving, Fred told room service to send up breakfast.

"The reason I sent for you is to learn more about Japan," Lord Grey said. "In a letter to General Aylmer Hunter-Weston, you described a book called *The Valor of Ignorance*. I'm interested in what this Homer Lea has to say."

Before speaking, Fred composed his reply.

"He's not a graduate of West Point or Sandhurst. He's handicapped by a frail body. He is impatient of anyone who thinks the Great Wall of China divides India from Arabia. But if you know your geography and history, he will explain his ideas, plans and goals."

"What are his plans?" Earl Grey asked.

"The downfall of the Manchu Empire and seating Dr. Sun Yat-sen as president of a new Republic of China."

"What did you say?" Earl Grey reacted as if struck by a sledge. England, one of the Big Five Powers, held an immense stake in China. For six decades, the British had taken big profits from China, through the legal sale of opium. Anything that upset that balance of power could have drastic effects on the British trade.

"What, pray tell, are this little gnome's chances?"

"Probably good. In spite of physical deficiencies, Lea is a brilliant strategist like Stonewall Jackson or Napoleon. He has wide support of the Chinese, both on the mainland and overseas. I first heard of him in Mexico."

Earl Grey seemed bewildered. The hair on his turkey-skin neck stood out.

"That's not at all what I expected," Grey said. "In his book, the term Yellow Peril is never associated with a revolution in China."

"The China Revolution is not in his book," Burnham replied. "I doubt if a hundred Americans know what's happening with those Chinamen in Eagle Rock."

"I must convey this information to Whitehall," Earl Grey said, wiping his brow.

That night, after they suffered through the rituals of a formal consular banquet, Earl Grey invited Fred to his suite.

"I sent a hundred copies of *The Valor of Ignorance* to Lord Roberts," Grey said. "That book shall be required reading for every intelligence officer in the British Army. I also conveyed your message about the China revolution."

"I wish every American knew, as well."

Earl Grey rose and put his arm on Fred's shoulder.

"Major Burnham," he said, "the real reason I asked you to come to New York is to talk about oil."

President Taft and the Supreme Court had just broken up the Standard Oil trust. *What prompts Earl Grey's interest in oil?*

"Petroleum has been discovered in Burma," he said. "It's the first oil to be found in the British Empire. A group of Scotsmen has organized Burmah Oil Company to exploit that resource."

"That's good news for England."

"As you know, Winston Churchill is now first lord of the admiralty. Based on that discovery in far-off Burma, Winnie has decided the Royal Navy should convert its ships of the line to use oil as fuel."

"And Admiral Sir John Fisher is not exactly ardent about oil?" Fred asked.

"He has no choice but to follow orders," Grey said. "So the Royal Navy needs a supply of fuel in the Pacific. Shell's reserves in Sumatra and Borneo are partly under Dutch control. If Holland were to side with the Hun, an oil-fired Royal Navy couldn't defend Australia, Singapore and Hong Kong. Can you keep your eyes open?"

"I'm no oil expert."

"Not many people are," Earl Grey said. "Lord Roberts predicts a world conflagration is coming. Before then, we must have an assured supply of fuel. Whoever sails with oil-fired ships will rule the seas."

Fred grew tense, feeling uneasy.

"If you learn anything, get in touch with one of these men." Grey said. He produced business cards for Andrew Weir and Tilden Smith of San Francisco. "They are my representatives."

62

Howard Burnham

FRANCE • 1914

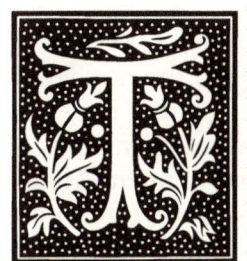

THE KILLING AND MAIMING of fifty million people began in Sarajevo on June 28. A Bosnian student shot Archduke Franz Ferdinand and his wife as they rode in a 1912 Graf und Stift motorcar. Ferdinand was the heir apparent to the Austro-Hungarian throne, Europe's second largest empire. Within the month, war flames spread over Europe. The cause of war was Kaiser Bill's demand for an empire consistent with Germany's new industrial status. Kaiser Bill's mother was Queen Victoria's eldest daughter, the one who had become an Empress when she was married in 1876.

France still resented Germany's victory in the Franco-Prussian War of 1871. The French were eager to kick the bejesus out of Germany for swiping the Alsace-Lorraine District. Hostilities began one week before Teddy's Panama Canal opened.

While staving off revolution in Mexico, Fred kept abreast of the war news in Europe through the mail from colleagues like General Aylmer Hunter-Weston, commander of the VIII Corps. Fred knew all the major actors on the British side. .

Winston Churchill, first lord of the admiralty, was in charge of the Royal Navy. Lord Kitchener, the secretary of state for war, had dispatched Field Marshal Sir John French, the master of foxhounds, to France as head of the British Army Expeditionary Force.

The aloof General Douglas Haig headed the I Corps in the south, while it expanded into the First Army. Haig was joined on the north by General Herbert Plumer in charge of the Second Army. Others included the former Boer foes, Jan Smuts and General Louis "Boot" Botha, now teamed with the Allies. As Britain's minister for air, Jannie Smuts was making plans to establish the Royal Air Force.

481

The rat-a-tat-tat-tat of Maxim guns prompted General French to dug trenches along his thirty-five-mile-long salient. Soon, men were forced to peer through periscopes. Mortars splattered blood, mangled bodies and bent steel. Doughboys shaved in tin pot helmets. The Hun wore a picklehaub with a spike on top. Before battle, troops on both sides swilled wine and afterward sang with relief, having survived one more encounter. In the skies, Sopwith Camels, Fokkers, Nieuports and Spads sputtered around the fluffy clouds. The pilots who got shot down were just as mangled as the doughboys in the trenches. Men everywhere came to know arms and legs blown off or amputated. Life centered on fear, fatigue and the loss of hope.

• • •

FRANCE • 1915

THE MAIN THEATERS of war were Russia and France. Maxim guns that first saw combat in Matabele Land now trapped the first white soldiers, and the Western Front became an unending line of trenches.

When approaching Paris, the Germans met two classical lines of defense dating to Roman days. The first was at Verdun on the Meuse River, and sixty miles behind it was the ancient Roman city of Rheims. Here in France's champagne country the Marne and Somme Rivers jointly formed the second line of defense.

In 1915, the fighting shifted to the Eastern Front. Germany set out to bleed Russia dry, and it inflicted nine million casualties. For miles, the piles of Russian corpses accumulated six feet deep. The bodies served as a ghastly breastworks. Then Kitchener and Churchill concocted a plan to ease the pressure. They dispatched half a million men to invade the Gallipoli Peninsula of southwest Turkey. The idea was to open the Dardanelles, giving Russia an outlet from the Black Sea to the Mediterranean. What possible good that would do is still open to question.

Gallopoli's narrow beaches and high cliffs made it an ideal place to defend. The Turks lacked weapons, so they stood on the beaches waving bayonets as they soaked up Allied bullets. But the British never got beyond that narrow strip of sand. By December, with a quarter of a million casualties, the British withdrew. Soon after that, Kitchener was drowned when the ship he was aboard struck a mine and sank in Scappa Flow.

• • •

FRANCE • 1916

THE FIGHTING shifted back to the Western Front. The peppery Field Marshal Jack French, sapped by the attrition of his old sweats from Boer War days, came down with battle fatigue. The enigmatic

Wealth & Honors

Douglas Haig, by this time a field marshal, wielded the dagger that stabbed Field Marshal French in the back. Haig used the ties of marriage and his friendship with King George V to seize command of the British Expeditionary Force from the hapless French.

General von Falkenhayn, in command of the Fifth German Army, launched a battle of attrition for Verdun. Since the days of Julius Caesar, Verdun had been famous for its defenses. It was no surprise that the French were prepared to fight to the end. Verdun became known for the stentorian rattle of the Maxim and the thunderous blast of Big Bertha artillery. Wet and weary men were harassed by cooties, lice and fleas. Battle-shattered corpses, splattered blood and liquor polluted the land as a million French and German soldiers fell as the casualties of war.

Meanwhile, Germany's initial rush to the sea in 1914 had become this year's retreat from the Marne River to the bend of the Somme. To draw off German pressure on Verdun and to regain the Allied offensive, Haig launched the Battle of the Somme. Haig amassed eighteen divisions. The French Army added fourteen of their own. The Allies preceded the assault with a week-long artillery barrage of a hundred thousand shells a day. Even the rats panicked.

"You won't need rifles," Haig boasted to the men. He assigned the soldiers a goal of winning ten miles on the first day. Instead, a mutiny spread through sixteen French Army corps.

• • •

Sonora, Mexico • 1917

IN A LETTER TO Fred, General Aylmer Hunter-Weston confessed that he should have listened more closely during the Boer War when Fred complained about barbed wire. At the Battle of the Somme, Fred's sticky hedge became the prime obstacle to progress. "That barbed wire stops our men cold, but artillery shells fly right through," Aylmer complained. To cope with the Maxim gun and loosely coiled barbed wire, the British introduced the tank, which terrified the rifle-carrying Hun.

In Mexico, Fred yarned around the evening campfire, telling war stories. "Doug Haig was the blue-eyed boy of cavalry. He has been a Kitchener man since the days of Khartoum," he groused. "Haig is the cavalry boss who vetoed Baden-Powell's plans for scouting. It was Haig who declared that Maxim guns are of no consequence in battle. In a recent letter, Aylmer Hunter-Weston told me, 'Lest the sight of dead bodies cloud his judgment, General Haig has never visited the front.'"

Despite the introduction of the tank, the Somme assault went into the record book as the worst disaster in British military history.

• • •

FRANCE • 1917

GENERAL VON FALKENHAYN ended his attack on Verdun in Lorraine, and the Allies wondered if the Germans might attack down south in Alsace. A point was reached where any advantage might sway the outcome of the war.

The Germans operated an active deception program to confuse the Allies by planting rumors. What better plan could Germany contrive than to make France believe the Germans were planning to make an end run through Swiss territory? Suddenly, in the catacombs of French military intelligence, there developed the notion that Germany might launch an attack against Alsace, using neutral Switzerland as a launching point.

That meant France would have to withdraw forces from Verdun in the Lorraine District to shore up Alsace in the south. The most logical attack route would be south from Stuttgart and across the Rhine River to Basel in Switzerland, then past Belfort or Mulhouse in the Alsace. That prospect produced a dilemma in French intelligence as enigmatic as the smile on the Mona Lisa.

By now, the French Army was in open mutiny and rumors filtered into intelligence from many sources that Germany would reinforce the roads from Stuttgart to the Black Forest and Friburg and on to the Swiss border. The French needed an engineer as a spy who could determine if a railway was capable of transporting a Big Bertha, the cannon from big Bertha Krupp's munitions works. Before an invasion, Germany would have to upgrade bridges and reinforce culverts over which the great guns would pass.

Using a French engineer was impractical. The Germans had extensive files on their enemies. Captain La Due, an eccentric officer in French intelligence, sought help from an American friend, King Macomber. Could he suggest an American engineer who could go into Germany to gather information?

Since becoming a millionaire, King had developed a great admiration for one of France's sons, François de Grasse. It was Admiral de Grasse who in 1781 sailed up from the Caribbean to blockade Chesapeake Bay. It was Admiral de Grasse's ships that trapped Lord Cornwallis at Yorktown, forcing the British Army to surrender to General George Washington, ending the Revolutionary War. And so King Macomber had erected a mausoleum of stunning magnificence honoring Admiral de Grasse.

Wealth & Honors

King Macomber knew that Howie Burnham was suffering a relapse of his tuberculosis. America had not yet entered the war, so Howie could conceivably visit Germany on a plea of ill health.

Howard agreed. He applied for a visitor's permit and told German authorities he thought he might find relief in a visit to the Black Forest, famous for the treatment of consumption. German immigration records revealed that Howard had periodically visited Saxony to buy mining equipment. The Germans decided that a sickly American could create little mischief. They refused to allow him to take along any engineering instruments, binoculars or sketch books.

Howard's secretary was a widowed contessa of great Teutonic efficiency. She saw to it that no word, scrap of paper or letter was sent—even to his Swiss bankers—other than through her. On the other hand, the contessa possessed a mystic power that allowed Howie to float on a magic carpet over most wartime obstacles.

Howard asked if they might visit Baden-Baden, Germany's premiere spa with mineral baths and saunas, which dated to the days of Julius Caesar. The contessa arranged the visit. For more than a month they traveled hither and yon, from spa to resort to mineral spring. In time, Howard concluded that Germany was making no preparation to move heavy artillery south to the area. On April 1, a week before America entered the war, Howard bade farewell to the contessa and crossed the border into neutral Switzerland.

There he stopped for lunch at a popular resort chateau. He had just seated himself when there erupted from his throat a devastating hemorrhage of blood. He collapsed in a coma. Later, he regained consciousness in a Swiss hospital. The French evacuated Howard to the south coast of France. There he told officials that the Western Front need not be stripped of troops.

Down in the catacombs, Captain Le Duc didn't care. The Germans had recently fed him a double-agent, the Mata-Hari, and he was pursuing her. On Thursday, May 10, 1917, Howard Burnham died of the same consumption that had taken his father's life .

Fred, trapped by a new revolution in Mexico, was unable to attend Howie's funeral. He was also unable to get away to attend the funerals of others who died or were killed in 1917: Richard Harding Davis, Fred Selous, Doctor Leander Starr Jameson and Earl Grey.

In Paris, King Macomber interred the remains of Howard in an elegant crypt next to the stately mausoleum of Admiral de Grasse. That's how an American spy for France and a French hero of the Revolutionary War came to sleep side by side for eternity.

63

Burnham Ex

VERACRUZ • 1910

HARRIS HAMMOND introduced his father to the petroleum business. While Harris vacationed at Tampico in eastern Mexico, he met Ricardo Mestres, an oil consultant. Mestres offered Harris an option covering four square miles of oil leases between the Panuco and the Tuxpan rivers. Harris took the offer to his father. As a hedge for the future, Hammond Senior purchased the leases, appointing Ricardo as manager. Three years later Edward Doheny, who in 1890 had struck big oil in Los Angeles, made a stunning series of discoveries at Potrero del Lano near Tampico.

At the time, Harris Hammond was managing the Mount Whitney Electric Power Company in Visalia. He urged his father to get moving in Mexico. Hammond Senior sold Mount Whitney Power to Southern California Edison Corporation, formed Mexican Seaboard Oil and put Harris in charge.

"Go down there, Son, and make us some money."

Counterpoise • Equilibrium

ESPERANZA • 1913

THE YAQUI DELTA was an active scene of battle in a falling-dominos series of revolutions. Victoranio Huerta had deposed Francisco Madero and the new government aggravated the Yaqui unrest. The Gringo settlers held out as long as they could. Fred Burnham spent much of his time in the next four years at Esperanza.

By the time the United States entered the Great War in April 1917, matters in Mexico became grave. Fred hurried down to Sonora to supervise the defense of the settlers. Trapped by Yaqui Indians at Guaymas, he appealed by telegram to The Kid to bring down ammo, rockets, a wireless and a generator. The supplies never arrived because Rod never got the message.

Wealth & Honors

When the United States declared war on Germany, Rod joined the Army, and he was gone before The Dad's telegram arrived. When the news reached Fred that Howie had died, Fred was trapped and unable to get away.

An end to the fighting in Sonora came on December 16, 1918, thirty-five days after the Armistice in Europe. A band of Yaquis attacked Esperanza and burned the headquarters building. During the battle all of the valuable plant seeds and cuttings and the detailed records of their crossbreeding went up in flames. Agriculturally, the Yaqui Valley was catapulted back into the Stone Age — a technology blow from which it would never recover. Thirty colonists who had braved everything to hold their land were captured and tied to wagon-wheels. The Yaquis built fires under them and roasted their brains.

The final blow came when Venustiano Caranza, who had succeeded Victoriano Huerta, signed the Agrarian Reform Law. It prohibited foreigners from buying land. The Yaqui Land & Water Company could continue to hold land but could sell only to Mexicans. The company carried the properties on its books for several years, then sold most of its holdings to the government for three cents on the dollar. Once again, the Oof Bird had flown the coop.

Ritornello • An Interlude

VERACRUZ • 1916

CERRO AZUL NOMBRE Quatro was the fourth oil well Harris Hammond drilled in the fabled Faja de Oro. The Golden Lane eventually would extend two hundred miles along the Gulf of Mexico from Tampico to Veracruz.

Blue Hill Number Four was a real oil bonanza. It was destined to make fabulous profits for its developers and owners, the Seaboard Oil Company. But not right away. The drilling crew consisted of unskilled locals who hit a high-pressure zone and let the well get away from them. By dawn, water, oil and sand gushed out of the hole. By mid-afternoon, a column of oil and gas spewed a hundred feet, drenching the area with crude oil. The flow grew stronger, hollowing out a crater so wide the derrick and drilling equipment were blown away. In the first twenty-four hours, Blue Hill Four spewed out a hundred and fifty thousand barrels of oil. Then it got its second wind and the next day it blew a quarter of a million barrels. The noise was beyond belief.

"We've cut an artery down there," cried Ed McKenna, the chief geologist for Seaboard Oil. McKenna put out a call for help and hundreds of laborers showed up. They worked with shovels to build an earthen dam around the well. The gusher continued to roar. On the third day, the padres led excursions to the site, exhorting the masses to pray that the oil might not bring destruction to the world.

Then Blue Hill Four quit as abruptly as it began.

Counterpoise • Equilibrium

Los Angeles • 1916

WORD OF Seaboard's gusher reached Los Angeles three days later. It touched off a south-of-the-border Argonaut rush for black gold. A couple of weeks later, Major Fred Burnham showed up at Cerro Azul Nombre Quatro.

Fred introduced himself to Ed McKenna, identifying himself as an associate of Jack Hammond. Fred's background in minerals prospecting prompted him to ask a flood of questions of McKenna.

"What happens if you find gold down there?"

McKenna, an earthy man with unruly hair, a plaid shirt and lace-up boots, had been studying rock cuttings with a magnifying glass.

"What did you say?" he asked, puzzled by the witless question. Then he caught himself. He shouldn't insult an associate of the boss.

"Major Burnham? I've heard of you."

"What if you find gold down in the well?"

"If I found gold, I'd look for a new job."

"Why?"

"'Cause if I was dumb enough to drill for oil in igneous rock, Mr. Hammond or Pat Longhan would fire my good-for-nothing ass." McKenna tossed a piece of flat sandstone on the table. It shattered.

"Gold occurs in igneous rock, the kind of stone that comes from volcanoes," McKenna said. "Oil occurs in sedimentary rocks. We call these layered rocks sandstone."

Fred scratched his head, puzzled but interested.

"Oil is found in tiny holes in sediments that were laid down on the bottom of ancient seas," McKenna said. "Oil comes from decayed organic material in these deposits."

"Is that why oilmen call them oil sands?"

"You got it, Major."

"If the oil forms at the bottom of an old marine sea," Fred asked, "why do you drill on a hill?"

"Ever dig a water well?" McKenna asked.

"Sure, everyone has."

"Then you *do* know there's water down there."

"Everybody knows that."

"Oil floats." McKenna said emphatically. "As the sediments build up, water forces the oil to rise toward the surface. When it hits a layer of solid rock, it migrates horizontally until it gets trapped."

McKenna pointed to a map of the underground. It depicted a rock structure that looked to Fred like an inverted soup bowl.

"It's called a caprock," McKenna said. "The oil gets trapped in that inverted dome under the hill."

That made sense. "If you're supposed to look for a hill, why do you drill on flat land here in Veracruz?"

"In hilly areas, surface and underground structures match," McKenna said. "You can see the hill rising over the underground dome. Here and in Texas, where the land is flat, there is no surface expression. During the ice ages, glaciers scraped the land flat."

While listening to McKenna, Fred recalled how in 1904 his car had labored while driving over Dominguez Mesa en route to San Pedro. That mesa might contain a low-relief dome.

In Los Angeles, John Blick, his paleontologist brother in law, told him about the new crop of "bug men" who specialized in micropaleontology. Columbia University and Stanford had graduated their first classes in the new science of measuring the age of fossil rocks.

"Paleontologists have charts showing when each species of dinosaurs lived and died," John said. "They use it as a calendar to determine the age of fossils."

"You mean like the Jurassic, Devonian and Permian ages?" Fred asked. John nodded.

"Micropaleontologists build their geological calendar on the life-cycles of one-celled animals with shells called foraminifera," Blick said. "Oil men call them forams."

"Easier to say," Fred agreed.

"Dinosaur bones are rare," John said, "but every cubic inch of sedimentary rock contains tens of thousands of forams. From the well cuttings, forams are isolated and examined under a microscope. The micropaleontologist can tell when the drill bit comes close to sediments that might contain oil."

Though the lingo differed from minerals prospecting, Fred decided the ideas were similar. After listening to the bug men for a few weeks, Fred told Blanche he felt like a first cousin to a foram.

• • •

FRED'S THIRD lesson in oil — the leasing of mineral rights — came from his son. While serving in France during the war, Rod had met some engineers on military leave from Union Oil of California. When they learned he had a mining degree from the University of California at Berkeley, they suggested that he should apply for a job at The Union.

After the Armistice, Roderick made application to Union Oil and was rewarded by being named as manager of lands, an important position in the Exploration Department. One day, The Kid introduced The Dad to the oil industry's Producers Form 88, a standard lease form used by wildcatters and major oil companies alike.

"An oil lease is a valuable document," Rod said.

"You trying to tell me you've got an important job?"

"A real estate deed might convey title to your home," Rod said. "An oil lease conveys title to minerals that might be worth a hundred million dollars. A lease man cannot afford to make mistakes. In California, we search all land titles to the original Mexican land grants or to a signature by Abraham Lincoln when he was Secretary of the Interior. It would be a financial disaster to spend a million dollars to develop an oil field only to discover you didn't hold legal title to it."

"I know about that," Fred said. "That's how I lost title to the Magadi, my soda lake in Kenia."

Since 1884, Fred had been trading in minerals claims so he felt confident. Now, armed with a pad of Form 88 leases, he began buying, selling and trading oil leases. One time, when negotiations took him to New York, Harris Hammond invited him to spend the weekend at his home in Bordentown, New Jersey.

Harris met Fred at the railroad station in Trenton, and they motored six miles south to young Hammond's farm. After dinner, he invited Fred to join him in the library for brandy and cigars.

Burnham joined him, but declined the offer of stimulants.

"Did you know that your friend Earl Grey almost took a big bite out of The Union?" Harris asked.

"What?" *Rod has never mentioned that.*

"Before the Great War, a couple of front men for Earl Grey dangled fifteen million dollars in front of Lyman Stewart, Union's board chairman. The lure was too much. Stewart needed the money and signed an option allowing them to buy a hundred and fifty thousand shares of treasury stock."

"Who were these men?" Fred asked suspiciously.

"Andrew Weir and Tilden Smith."

Fred recalled the meeting with Earl Grey at the Waldorf Towers. He had forgotten the names, but the mention jogged dim memories.

"The Grey Syndicate made an initial payment on the purchase of the stock," Harris said. "The second payment was due in 1914, but the war broke out."

The picture began to fit. Winston Churchill had given orders to the Royal Navy to convert to oil as fuel. But the admirals had dragged their feet. Came the war and there was no time. Conversion was postponed. Then Earl Grey died. Alarms began to ring.

"What became of Earl Grey's holdings?"

"Now in the hands of Commonwealth Petroleum."

"Don't know the outfit."

"It's a syndicate controlled by Percy Rockefeller."

"John D's nephew?" Burnham's eyes grew wide. "They don't know the meaning of failure."

Harris laid down his brandy and lighted a cigar.

"The shares Percy got from Grey amounted to two percent of Union Oil's shares," Harris said. "Then Percy went out on the open market and bought another twenty-three percent of the shares."

"Are you saying the Rockefellers own one-fourth of The Union?"

"My informants have yet to be wrong," Harris said. "Would you care for some coffee or tea?"

"Coffee is fine."

"You know, Major, there's money to be made in oil."

"I'm spending full time trading in leases."

"I'm talking about exploration—drilling."

"I'm no expert in exploration."

"You know far more about geology than I do, Major. Let me show you how the financial side works. Once you get started, you hire professionals in each field."

Hammond took pencil and paper from his desk. He began sketching a financial structure, so many shares of preferred stock, so many shares of common.

"I don't know how to create a corporation."

"That's what lawyers are for," Harris said.

Fred thought of Lord Gifford and nodded. *Harris is right.*

"Now, here's how you do it without putting up your own money," Harris said. Unlike Lord Gifford, Harris took the time to explain the purpose of each step. He spoke of leases and options, of common shares and preferred shares, of drawdowns, farmouts, payouts and concepts Fred had never imagined.

The clock struck midnight but they continued. By dawn, Fred had signed his name to several documents. With a flourish, he scooped up Hammond's brandy snifter and took a big swallow. Major Frederick Russell Burnham, D.S.O. was now the chairman of Burnham Exploration Company. Fred's pride knew no bounds.

64

Courtin the Union

Los Angeles • February 1921

ACCORDING TO HARRIS'S plan, Burnham Ex would issue a million shares in three kinds of securities: The preferred stock would be the only shares put on sale. For each share of preferred, a buyer would receive a bonus share of common. Fred and Rod would draw down a compensating share of organizers' common.

"When it comes to dividends," Fred said, "preferred shares have first priority. But only the common shares can be voted. If Hammond buys a hundred shares of preferred, he gets a hundred shares of common as a bonus. And as our organizers bonus, we get to draw down a hundred shares of common."

"Our backers will own two-thirds," Rod protested.

"Only until we strike oil. If we hit a gusher and the money flows in, we have an option to buy the preferred shares at a ten percent premium plus interest."

"So if we buy up the outstanding preferred, we end up fifty-fifty owners with our backers," Rod said.

"Pretty good deal," Fred said, "considering that we don't have to put up any cash. That was Harris's idea."

"First you have to sell the preferred stock, Dad."

"I've sold a hundred and fifty thousand shares," Fred boasted. "Whitney took seventy-five thousand shares and Ogden Mills bought an equal amount."

"Mills? Where do I know that name?"

"Grandson of Darius Ogden Mills. The old man made it big on Comstock Lode silver, then became a financier."

"Again, you come up with the haystack needle."

"Burnham Ex won't be an operating company. We'll deal in options and leases and farm out the drilling."

"That'll cost you half your production," Rod warned.

"Half of a million is better than all of nothing."

Dealing in options, Burnham Ex lost fifty thousand dollars on Mexican and Texas oil ventures. Fred returned to California to buy and sell leases in Bakersfield, Ventura and Los Angeles. Big strikes were being made in the Golden State.

• • •

SHORTLY AFTER THAT, Fred's boyhood pal, Art Bent, invited the Burnhams to dinner. Art owned a construction firm that was working on a joint venture to be called Six Companies that one day would build Hoover Dam.

During the meal Art and Fred talked about their childhood days in Los Angeles during the 1870s. They recalled swimming in the sankey ditches that served as open sewers, riding as mounted messengers for the Western Union and hunting ducks in the slough at Dominguez Mesa.

"Remember when you fell in the water and came out dripping with tar?" Art joshed. Because of the tar, Art had called Fred a *picaninny*.

"Well cover me with Namaqua daisies," Fred cried. Like a flash, it all came back. Though it happened forty-five years ago, Fred could see the sticky black stuff like it was yesterday. Art's father had called it *brea*, the Spanish word for rock oil. Judge Bent told Fred to clean it off with kerosine.

Brea? Rock oil? Hey, that means petroleum.

The next day Fred began tracking down the landowners at Dominguez Mesa. Dominguez wasn't a very high mesa, but like Santa Fe Springs it was more than a mile across. It might hold a million barrels of oil. Fred thought of the Thabas Induna.

By March, Fred had acquired mineral leases on nine hundred acres of land and royalty rights on an additional five hundred acres. Burnham Ex's holdings were in the center of Dominguez Mesa.

Now he had to find an operating company willing to drill a farmout well on a fifty-fifty basis. He wrote to Standard Oil of California in San Francisco. Several weeks later, the reply came back: no interest.

"They're all blockheads," Rod said. "Try Standard of Company of New York." Socony's reply was negative too. Fred tried other companies and elicited no interest.

"Ask The Union," Fred suggested.

"I'll talk to the geologists."

493

A week later, Rod had his answer. Half a dozen oil companies had drilled at Dominguez Mesa. None had found oil. That's why the leases came so cheap. The big strikes were being made at Signal Hill to the south and Santa Fe Springs to the north. Dominguez Mesa was cow pasture.

"There's oil at Dominguez," Fred said. "I know it. As a boy, I got tarred in it. I'm going to write to the president of Union Oil. What's his name?"

"Bill Stewart," Rod replied. "But it wont do any good. He'll send your letter downstairs to Rolfe McCollom, the manager of exploration. Rolfe will prepare a so-sorry letter for Bill's signature."

It didn't work out that way.

Ritornello • Interlude

LOS ANGELES • MAY 1921

BILL STEWART USUALLY arrived early at his office in the Petroleum Building at Sixth and Spring streets. He was a tall, athletic guy who liked to get away from his desk by noon. As usual, his secretary had placed his incoming mail in three stacks, sorted according to priority.

Stewart, square-jawed and deeply tanned, worked his way through the Immediate Attention pile and dictated letters of reply. He turned to the mail marked for delegation. He picked up a letter: Burnham Ex. The signature meant nothing to him. Sounded British. He glanced at the letter, a proposal to earn an interest in a lease at Dominguez Mesa in return for drilling a deep test well.

Bill had a vague feeling that somebody—maybe even The Union—had drilled a dry hole at Dominguez. He marked the letter for the attention of Rolfe McCollom. The manager of exploration was paid to know these things.

"Compose a reply," he wrote.

The sportsman in young Stewart was urging him to set sail for Catalina Island after lunch in his yacht *Chubasco*. As he put the letter in the out-basket, something caught his eye. The letterhead carried the names of the board of directors and an imposing list it was. They were a blue chip cast of characters, better than Union Oil's own homegrown board. Stewart amended his note to Rolfe to say, "Considering the composition of the board, compose the reply for my signature."

• • •

TWO DOORS DOWN the hall sat Lyman Stewart, the chairman and founder of Union Oil. Unlike his brawny son, Lyman was small-boned with a Prince Albert beard and pince-nez. He had the demeanor of a church deacon.

Thirty years ago, Lyman Stewart had merged three small oil firms into The Union. Since then he had devoted his energies to charity. For years he had endowed the Bible Institute of Los Angeles, known as BIOLA. Lyman had been on the telephone most of the morning with his stockbroker. He was forced to sell Union Oil stock to help BIOLA cope with a cash crunch. Lyman looked at his watch. He had an appointment for lunch with Brick Elliott at the Los Angeles Petroleum Club.

Lagnappe • A Little Extra

Los Angeles • May 1921

STANFORD-TRAINED geologist John "Brick" Elliott had quit Shell Oil to establish Elliott Petroleum. Brick was pioneering the development of a coring tool that made it possible for drillers to retrieve core samples from the bottom of the well bore. Core samples were now a valuable tool to recover the forams so vital to finding oil.

The Union was one of four companies that had given Elliott a contract with up-front money for coring services. Lyman suspected that Brick had invited him to lunch to ask for more money. Well, technology had put California ahead of Texas in oil production, so maybe the expense was worth it.

After ordering, Elliott said, "I think you know that I no longer owe any allegiance to The Shell."

"Not after van Pellekaan tried to destroy your reputation."

"Then I'm not breaking any confidence to tell you that next month Shell Oil plan a hostile takeover of The Union. It will happen at your stockholders meeting."

"Have you been drinking?" Stewart blurted out.

"It's true. They hold one quarter of your outstanding shares, purchased from Percy Rockefeller."

Stewart almost puked. He knew the Rockefellers bought those shares, but the Shell grab was news to him.

"I have to protect my best interests," Elliott said. "If The Shell takes you over, my company goes under."

• • •

BACK AT HIS OFFICE, Lyman Stewart collapsed into his chair, still shaking, as he called his secretary. The assistant was a pious young man who carried a notepad everywhere.

"Tell my son to come here," Stewart said.

"What is it, Dad?" Bill asked.

"At lunch, Brick Elliott told me Percy Rockefeller sold his shares to The Shell. They plan a hostile takeover."

For years, young Stewart had privately blamed his father for caving in to the financial demands of BIOLA. The family now owned only eight percent of The Union.

"We might lose the company," Lyman stammered.

"That's terrible," Bill said. *Would he lose Chubasco?*

"Son, we will fight. I don't know how, but we'll win." The elder man's voice grew brittle. "We're on God's side. We must seek help from Wall Street."

"Wall Street?" The mention of Cash Alley touched Bill Stewart's hot button.

"Get Rolfe McCollom up here now," Bill barked to his father's secretary. "Tell him to bring that letter."

"What letter?"

"Some wildcatter wants a farmout at Dominguez Meadows. Hurry."

"What's going on?" Lyman asked.

"You need help from Wall Street? I can get you all the help you want. All we have to do is drill one well down at Dominguez Meadows."

"Dominguez Mesa, Son. There's no oil down there."

Minutes later, McCollom, imposing with a shock of silver hair, stormed into the office prepared to do battle. If the Stewarts had plans to drill in that cow pasture—

"Mr. McCollom, would you please show that letter to my father?" Bill's face gleamed.

Lyman Stewart, a gentle man, bade the chief geologist be seated. He studied the letter with care. A beatific smile spread over his face.

"John Hays Hammond?" he said. "Cecil Rhodes' right hand man? Struck it big down at Veracruz. Harry Payne Whitney—married to Corny Vanderbilt's daughter? Ogden Mills? His grandpa's money from the Comstock Lode helped finance the Civil War."

"MilHam Ex," McCollom said, "stands for Mills and Hammond. Oil strikes at Kettleman Hills and Coalinga up north of Bakersfield."

Burnham Ex's directors represented big money with lots of slam-bang on Wall Street and Lombard Street too. Political clout in Washington and London to boot.

"Son, you're a genius." Lyman said "Mr. McCollom, we're going to drill that well at Dominguez. Were going to be extra nice to these people at Burnham Ex. During this fight, we're going to have the Hammonds, the Whitneys and the Mills in our pockets."

Chubasco remained at anchor that day.

Counterpoise • Equilibrium
Hockett Meadows • June 1921

ALL DAY LONG, Blanche pondered her choices. After forty years of marriage, she was the practical, hardheaded business side of the family. Fred was sixty-one and their savings were gone.

The Yaqui Delta project had collapsed. The Land Act forbade the sale of property to foreigners. Fred had wasted what remained of their savings on mineral leases at Dominguez Hill.

Blanche had a feeling—she called it intuition—that things weren't going smoothly at The Union. There'd been no response to Fred's letter. Fred was the incurable romantic, chasing rainbows, looking for that pot of gold, pursuing the Oof Bird. *Would her lovable rascal ever learn?*

The cattle at Hockett Meadows and the orchards at La Cuesta covered living expenses. But there was no capital appreciation. They'd have to build a nest-egg for their retirement. There was only one way that she knew. Twenty years ago, Arthur Pearson had offered Fred two thousand pounds—ten thousand dollars—to dictate his adventures in Arizona, Africa and the Klondike. If Fred wrote his autobiography, the royalty income would provide security for their retirement years. As she washed the dinner dishes, Blanche saw Fred seated by the camp fire, lost in thought. Her heart swelled as she walked toward him.

"Hi, Major," she said. "May I join your fire?" At this elevation, the evening skies were a blaze of blue turning to purple at the zenith.

"There's something comforting to watch the glowing of coals," he said. "I think the words camp fire, rest and peace were synonymous to our ancestors. I believe a little of that heritage comes down to us now."

For several moments, Blanche said nothing. *He's given to philosophy while tending a fire. Now get busy. Hardened your heart for the task ahead.*

"A penny for your thoughts." Her voice was low. "Who was the best scout?"

"The best what?" Fred seemed puzzled.

"Who was the best scout to roam the woods and plains? Will Cody?"

"When Homer and I—"

"I know all about you and Homer meeting Buffalo Bill back in Clinton," she said. "The fact is his fame rests on a fictional account by Ned Buntline who glamorized the slaughter of buffalo."

"His Wild West Show taught people that an Indian was a human being and not some kind of wild animal."

Fred isn't cooperating. I must make him see his niche in the world of scouting.

"How about John Fremont?"

"The Pathfinder?"

"How do you rate him as a scout?"

"He pioneered the West."

"With help from Kit Carson to show him which end of the horse was front." Blanche said. "During the winter, he led his party on an ill-advised journey over the Sierra Nevada and they almost died."

Fred stirred the coals.

"He helped win California from Mexico."

"Got court martialed for mutiny. How about Kit Carson?"

"He pacified the Navajo."

"By laying waste to their orchards and corn fields, by slaughtering their cattle and sheep."

"No man in New Mexico was more respected."

Blanche stirred the coals angrily.

"How about Fred Selous?"

"Selous was famous from the Cape to Cairo."

"Yes and he got himself killed when he walked into a German Army ambush in Kenya. How about Colenbrander?"

"Johann served bravely in the Shangani Patrol. And he put his life on the line at the peace indaba."

"He went bankrupt as an auctioneer. He was unsuccessful at big game hunting and farming. In America and went broke again. He had to prevail on friends to lend him money for passage to England."

"Guess a man shouldn't squat when he's wearin spurs."

"Oh, Fred, what I'm trying to do is make you see that you're probably the greatest scout who ever lived. If the West hadn't been won by the time you grew up, you would be the most famous name in scouting."

"I guess I know that as well as anyone."

The fire had burned low and he had made no effort to revive the coals. Blanche had to strike swiftly.

"When we get back to La Cuesta, you're going to start writing the book."

"What book?" In twenty years he hadn't thought of Pearson's offer. Since then a new generation had grown up who'd never heard of him.

"What book?" Blanche mocked. "The story of your life. You'll begin it right away."

"All right, Bea," he said, putting his arm around her. "I'll begin as soon as my oil well comes in."

Blanche rose, tears in her eyes, fire in her voice.

"You must tell the truth about Wilson's Last Stand."

"That was thirty years ago."

"You must tell the real story of the shooting of the M'Limo. The facts are so garbled."

Blanche knew that even after twenty-five years, the mention of that African deity caused him anguish — by indirectly producing Nada's death.

"You must describe how you inspired Baden-Powell's interest in scouting," Blanche said. "When he founded the scouting movement, he hadn't been within five thousand miles of a real Indian. He knew nothing of tracking and reading sign until you taught them to him."

"We must not make light of the peerage."

"When he met you, he was nothing but an entertainer nicknamed Bathing-Towel. He carried on with that Boy McLaren fellow and—"

"Baden-Powell's married now and has children."

"He didn't get married until it was a social necessity for the reputation of the scouting movement. Besides, the McLaren boy had more charm than that female athlete he took to the altar."

"It was Baden-Powell who founded the Boy Scouts, not me. He deserves the full credit."

"Fred Burnham, you're too modest," Blanche cried. "If it hadn't been for you, there would have been no Boy Scout movement. At least not as we know it. Besides, you must tell about being Chief of Scouts in the British Army during the South African War."

"For a workhouse kid, I didn't do too bad."

"Set the record straight," Blanche cried. "Art Pearson proclaimed you as King of Scouts." Fred slipped his arm around her waist and hugged her tightly.

"All right, Bea," he said. "I'll start on the book as soon as we get back to La Cuesta."

Little did either of them know that Fred's promise would be delayed by events over which they had no control.

65

The Shell Game

HOCKETT MEADOWS • SUMMER 1922

RED AND BLANCHE had enjoyed one month of alpine summer fun when John Blick showed up on one of his occasional visits. Most of the time these days, John was in Abyssinia with Charles Frick of U.S. Steel searching for fossils for New York's American Museum of Natural History.

"How are things with the Frick and Blick show?" Fred asked. Since retiring as president of U.S. Steel, Cholly Frick had been directing his fortune to funding the Museum.

"Some bones; no valuable finds," John replied.

Blick brought along the mail from Three Rivers. Everyone grabbed for the newspapers.

"The *Times* says President Harding has nominated Will Taft as Chief Justice of the United States."

"Bully," Fred said. "The job was made for him."

John munched on a sandwich. Blanche, reading, said, "Teddy Junior is Assistant Secretary of the Navy."

"More bully."

"Say, Fred," John said, "here's a telegram for you. I didn't see it before."

"Open it," Fred cried.

John tore open the envelope and read the message.

Back from Colorado digs. Big news. Come to Los Angeles. Rod

Fred rose, "Boys, you'll have to do the chores today."

Blanche was packed within the hour. At Three Rivers, they caught the Sequoia Park commuter bus to Exeter where they boarded the Southern Pacific train for Los Angeles. They arrived at 7 o'clock the following morning.

"Mother, Dad, here I am." Roderick called.

"You've lost weight, Rod." Blanche scolded.

"Been hiking like a billy goat," he boasted. "I pegged out twenty thousand acres of the richest oil shale lands in the world. Some day it'll be worth millions."

"What's the big news, Son?"

"We're having breakfast with Pat Longhan."

When it came to oil, Pat Longhan was Hammond's right-hand man. Pat was a senior officer of Seaboard Oil, MilHam Ex and Burnham Ex. Pat was a regular limber Jim with protruding ears, a pronounced Adams apple and a ready grin. He was fun to be with.

At the Biltmore Hotel, a reserved table awaited them. While the waiter poured coffee, Rod broke the news.

"Dad, you're gonna get your well at Dominguez. Pat has signed a contract with The Union. After breakfast, we'll go over and introduce you to Lyman Stewart."

Fred nodded as if he had expected it all the time.

"Do you know why you got your well?" Pat asked.

"Don't keep me in suspense," Fred implored.

Pat told about Royal/Dutch Shell launching a hostile proxy battle to take control of The Union.

"Sounds like the British," Fred snorted. "Twelve years ago, Earl Grey tried to put me up to a deal like that. But if The Shell's taking over The Union, why do we meet with Lyman Stewart? Why not Ben van der Linden?"

"The Union beat The Shell grab," Rod said.

"What?" Fred asked. "David conquered Goliath?"

"Burnham Ex was the key to victory," Longhan said.

"I know nothing of this," Fred protested.

While the waiter served bacon and eggs, Pat told how Shell's open-market purchase of Union Oil shares drove the price of the common stock to more than two hundred dollars a share. Lyman Stewart was forced to postpone the annual meeting. The newspapers had a field day.

"Stewart saw Dominguez as just a dry hole," Pat said, "but he saw something more important. For the cost of drilling one well, The Union could ally itself with the wealth and prestige of Burnham Ex."

"You trying to fluff my feathers? We don't have one barrel of oil reserves."

"The greatest asset of Burnham Ex," Pat said, "is its board of directors. With their prestige and wealth, they're a powerful influence here and in Europe."

501

Fred recalled the company letterhead. At the urging of Harris, he had agreed to list the names and affiliations of the board members on the company stationery.

"Yes," Fred said, "but they don't command the sums of a Royal/Dutch Shell. That outfit has strings right into the British and Dutch thrones."

Pat laid his hand on Fred's shoulder.

"Major oil companies are operated by managers, the ownership scattered over shareowners, pension funds and other holdings. The managers are nameless, faceless men. Other than John D. Rockefeller, I doubt if many Americans could name one oilman."

"Hmm, probably true," Fred said.

"You seem to overlook your own reputation," Pat said. "In England, you were Rhodes' Yankee Scout. It was Burnham who staked out the copper and coal deposits for Rhodes and introduced coffee to Kenya."

Fred flushed, but said nothing.

"You brought the first Klondike gold to London. You are friends with Teddy. You and Mr. Hammond helped to put Will Taft in the White House."

"Don't you see, Dad," Rod asked. "How do you think the financial gnomes in London reacted when Lyman Stewart leaked word that men like Jack Hammond, Ogden Mills, Harry Whitney and Major Burnham were allied with Union Oil?"

"Few people over there ever heard of The Union," Longhan added, "but they all knew Burnham, Hammond, Mills and Whitney, whose brother-in-law is the Ambassador to the Court of St. James."

The waiter poured coffee.

"When that news got out, the tide of public sentiment rose to a fever pitch." Longhan placed a copy of the *Los Angeles Times* on the table. On the day of the fateful shareholders meeting, Union Oil had placed a full-page advertisement:

This is the last day of the battle, the last day you can throw the influence of your shares into the balance, which must determine whether or not Union Oil shall remain an American institution. Will it become a mere subsidiary of Royal/Dutch Shell, a pawn resident in Holland but recently moved from London? Tonight at midnight, the books will close.

"You should have been at that meeting," Pat said. "It lasted all day and night. The counting of proxy votes began under glitter of arc lights. People stayed to watch. Officials from The Shell and The Union challenged any irregularity. There were recounts, so the results weren't known until dawn. When it was over, Lyman Stewart let out a sigh of relief. By a margin of twenty-five thousand proxies, the shareholders had voted in favor of Union Oil. The Shell grab was upset."

"And," Pat said, "the alliance with Burnham Ex helped supply the thin margin of victory." The waiter brought the check and Pat paid the bill.

"There's one question," Rod said, puzzled.

"What's that?" Pat Longhan asked.

"When I got back from Colorado, the geologists at The Union were hotter'n a pistol to take farmouts at Dominguez. But so were the geologists at Shell Oil. If Union and Shell were at it tooth and nail in a takeover battle, why were the exploration departments at both companies fighting for a piece of the action?"

"Yes, The Shell did get five hundred acres," Pat said.

Rod, the manager of lands at Union Oil, looked at Longhan with a puzzled expression. Then, with a look of amazement, he turned to his father.

"Dad, you didn't?"

"Yes, I sold those five hundred acres to The Shell," he said with a sly grin. "We have a one-eighth royalty. We get one barrel in eight and The Shell pays all expenses."

Rod broke out in a sappy grin.

"Dad, you're as clever as an old bitch fox."

As they left the Biltmore Hotel, Blanche felt proud. Even if they didn't find oil, she was married to the most wonderful man alive. And while neither of them knew it then, a whole new world awaited them.

66

Union-Callendar No. 1

Los Angeles • November 1922

WHEN SHELL OIL made its bid to grab The Union, Lyman Stewart fought with every weapon he had. Once he had staved off the takeover and the pressure abated, the old man relaxed. Stewart had to honor his commitment but with the battle won, nothing in the contract said he had to assign top priority to probing that godforsaken cow pasture. Nor did Stewart feel compelled to use the latest equipment and technology. When a tired old rig became available, he ordered it hauled down to Dominguez Mesa.

Drilling on Union-Callendar No. One commenced on November 1. Oil wells, Fred learned, were named for the company doing the drilling and for the landowner, followed by the well number. The leaseholder was not mentioned. Drilling the well was expected to take several months so Fred retreated to La Cuesta Ranch to spend the winter. At a depth of eighteen hundred feet, the drill bit got stuck and the hole had to be abandoned. Fred wasn't worried. His contract called for a clean hole to seven thousand feet. The Union had no choice but to skid the rig over fifty feet and commence another well.

Weeks went by without further news. On most days nothing happened because the drilling crews had been called to Santa Fe Springs or Signal Hell to work on a new discovery. The solitary Callendar rig stood on the mesa, a squat reminder of earlier failures on the accursed dome. When a drilling crew wasn't busy at Signal Hill or Santa Fe Springs, The Union directed a crew over to Dominguez Mesa and make a few feet of hole. That action was necessary to satisfy the "diligent efforts" clause which, at Harris Hammond's suggestion, had been inserted into the contract. It was necessary on Union Oil's weekly drilling report to show that some hole had been made.

Lagnappe • A Little Extra
GRAND CANYON • MAY 1923

SIR ROBERT Baden-Powell, on a rare visit to the western United States, planned to call on the Burnhams when he got to Los Angeles. Stephe hadn't had a letter from them in some time so he wasn't aware that the Burnhams spent most of their time at La Cuesta Ranch near Three Rivers or at the eight-thousand-foot-level at Hockett Meadows south of Sequoia Park. As it turned out, Stephe's always-tight schedule got knocked awry when his hosts took control over his itinerary. Stephe dashed off a last-minute apology to Fred:

Grand Canyon, Arizona

You will have forgotten me long ago—but here I am alive and kicking—only so very sorry that my intended visit to Los Angeles had to be abandoned. I have to be in Boston for a public meeting and Scout Rally on the twelfth, and kind friends took me in their motor car from San Francisco to the Yosemite and the Grand Canyon.

Two weeks later, Fred wrote back.

I deeply regret not having found your spoor in the East, but had I struck it, I would have followed it with zest and pleasure. It so happened that when you wrote I was in New York and Washington, D.C.

The Blick boys who served under you in that fight on the Umguza River are still with me in California. We have a cattle ranch in the mountains south of the Yosemite Valley. Our summer camp is located right next to Sequoia Park, eight-thousand feet elevation just south of a place called Mineral King.

We would have been more than pleased to take you up there, where we could have a real yarn of the days gone by as well as catch a few trout and spit roast a haunch of venison. Please promise me that the next time you come to America you will cable or write me in advance. Among mutual friends, I have heard from General Sir Aylmer Hunter-Weston and from Sir Rider Haggard. I see the results of your great work in the various organizations of the Boy Scouts, which seems to be getting stronger all the time.

Counterpoise • Equilibrium
LOS ANGELES • SEPTEMBER 1923

FRED AND ROD bolted down a hurried lunch of cold fried chicken and potato salad prepared by Rod's wife, Isabella Harrah Burnham. They were so eager to be off that neither noticed the headline in the *Los Angeles Times*: "Earthquake Shatters Tokyo; Hundred Thousand Perish." The date was September 1.

Moments later, Rod and Fred were racing toward Dominguez Mesa. While they were still a mile from the rig, they saw a flurry of activity ahead. Cars and trucks converged from all directions. Men on horseback galloped alongside their car. Fred saw a thin, vertical, black plume.

"What's that, Rod?"

"Dad, you've hit oil." Rod applied the brakes and they came to a stop a quarter of a mile from the wooden derrick. All cars had to stop lest a stray spark ignite the crude oil. The Pacific Electric Redcars were being pulled by teams of horses past the zone of volatile gases. Fred and Rod ran the remaining distance. The oil spewed straight into the sky, creating a plume two hundred feet high. Fred spotted geologist McKenna.

"What's happening, Ed?"

"The drill bit punched through the caprock, a layer of impervious shale," McKenna cried. "I think it's cut into the very Mother Lode. It's blowing like Blue Hill Number Four in the Faja de Oro."

Fred threw his arms around Rod.

"I knew it, Rod! I knew it! Fifty years ago I hunted ducks here with Art Bent. We got tar all over us." Fred was beside himself with joy. Then, turning to McKenna, he yelled, "Can't you stop it, Ed? That oil's worth money."

A young curly haired man about Fred's size emerged from the crowd of strangers that was milling around to gawk. He carried a sample of oil in a small vial. Fred saw Army leggings and guessed he was a geologist.

"Mister Hill, I'd rate this as thirty gravity," he said. The man was short, handsome and friendly.

"Major Burnham," the production manager, Frank Hill, said, "meet Cy Rubel. Cy, this is Fred Burnham of Burnham Ex."

The two men shook hands and the young geologist called Cy assumed an air of respect for the co-owner of this important discovery.

"Cy's The Union's geologist assigned to this well."

"Thirty gravity?" Fred asked of Cy.

"That's my guess, Major," Rubel said. "If it is, she'll bring a premium over twenty-six gravity marker crude."

"Son, what's the posting of marker crude?"

"Dollar and a half. Reckon this stuff will bring a buck six-bits a barrel."

The higher the gravity, the more gasoline the crude contained, hence the higher price. Fred stood clenching his fists and shaking his head. *Is this a dream? Will it last? Will it plug up and stop flowing? Or will someone come along and steal this treasure, as the others were stolen? It seems too good to be true. Have I finally salted the tail of the Oof Bird?*

• • •

WORD OF THE strike spread quickly. Whenever oil was discovered, it meant big money would be spent on labor, supplies, transport, food. Everybody shared. Within an hour a thousand men swarmed around the derrick to behold the marvel. Frank Hill walked back five hundred feet and studied the geyser through a weir box.

"Blowing two thousand barrels a day," he ventured. "Rod, hire all the farmers you can and have them plow a berm around this well. We'll trap as much of the crude as possible." Hill ordered the driller, Iron Mike O'Grady, to hie himself over to Signal Hill and buy tankage, line pipe and a christmas tree.

Everyone was so certain that Dominguez Mesa would be a duster that no one had bothered to stock the drill site with well-completion equipment. As O'Grady drove off, the noise of the oil and gas escaping from the hole increased. Men fell back at the air-tearing sound. The spout of oil rose another hundred feet.

"It's dislodged an obstruction in the well bore," Cy Rubel said.

The roar from the gusher continued. Fifty teams of horses and five hundred men labored to erect a dam that would trap the flow. Fred and Rod ran hither and yon, urging spectators not to smoke lest the volatile oil catch fire. At dusk, farm wives appeared in wagons laden with kettles and washtubs of meat, potatoes, corn, bread, hot coffee and apple pie. Hill signed the meal chits on Union Oil's credit.

That night, Fred and Rod slept on the ground. To Fred it was like a feather bed; nothing could disturb the heady feeling he was experiencing. He awakened twice during the night and heard the roar of the gusher and the farmers geeing and hawing their teams. Then he fell back into a profound sleep.

At dawn, Fred was awakened by two Best steam-tractors chuffing up from Signal Hill pulling loads of oil field tubulars: large-diameter pipe, valves, elbows and flanges, along with sheets of galvanized steel, nuts and bolts. Within the hour, the drilling crew fashioned an assemblage of flanges, valves and elbows that resembled a christmas tree. A crew of roustabouts bolted steel plates to fashion a small storage tank. Another crew cobbled together a pipeline running over the ground to the tank.

Fred was amazed at how fast an oil field could take shape. Using two telephone poles fashioned into an A-frame, with horses pulling on a block and tackle, the crew lifted the heavy steel christmas tree over the well bore and bolted it into place. The oil flowed through the tree, spewing a geyser even-higher than before.

Iron Mike began turning two oversized wheel valves. One valve diverted the crude into the pipeline. The other closed the opening on top of the christmas tree. The oil flowed through the pipeline and into the storage tank. After nearly twenty-four hours of ear-splitting noise, the silence was deafening.

"Let's break for vittles," Hill said. Farm wives were waiting with wagon-loads of ham and eggs, hotcakes, toast and hot coffee. The drilling crew pushed Fred and Rod to the head of the chow line. Both took generous portions of food and sat on the ground to eat.

"Rod, these pancakes taste like they used crude oil for syrup," Fred said, his eyes sparkling.

"The gusher blew a mist of oil everywhere," Rod said.

"Well enjoy. It's our oil."

For the rest of that day Frank Hill was busier than a bob-tailed cow in fly season. With the oil now flowing into a tank of known volume, he could accurately measure the output of Union-Calendar Number One. After four hours, the five hundred barrel tank was half full.

"It's flowing three thousand barrels a day," Hill said. "It'll fill six tanks a day. We'll need five days to build a pipeline to the refinery, so that means two dozen tanks. Until the pipeline's finished, we'll haul the oil to the refinery in mule-drawn tank wagons. Let's get that pipeline started."

A dozen wagons appeared on the scene to haul the oil five miles to The Union's refinery at Wilmington.

"Hey, Dad, look at this." Fred turned to see twenty trucks, Federals, Whites, Brockways, Macks, plus teams of horses and mules, groaning up the incline of Dominguez Mesa, laden with steam boilers, drawworks, lumber, drill pipe and sacks of mud. The trucks bore the familiar red, white and blue federal shield of The Union.

"Look over here," Fred cried. Lumbering up the other side of the hill were a dozen oilfield trucks laden with oil tools. They bore the yellow scallop of Shell Oil Company.

"I must send a telegram to Bea." Fred found a table and composed a message:

> *Come quickly. The acreage we hold here is nothing like the hundred square miles of the Northern Coppers. It is a twenty-fifth the size of the Lost Magadi. Yet this time we've salted the Oof Bird's tail. There are three rigs drilling. More are coming.*

• • •

BLANCHE ARRIVED at Dominguez two days later to see a maze of warehouses, tanks and tents where before only hay had waved in the summer breezes.

"What's that noise?" Blanche cried. There was fear in her voice.

"Shell-Carson Number One just blew in," Fred cried. "It's gonna be twice as big as the Callendar discovery."

Blanche had never been so afraid in her life, even in Africa, but her man was in his element, so she decided she might survive this ordeal.

Mud began boiling out of the casing of another rig. The driller shouted a warning. The derrickman started down the ladder. When he was about thirty feet from the ground, a column of mud and sand cuttings shot out of the hole, rising to the top of the derrick. The derrickman jumped, splashing into a mud pit which saved his life. Steel drill pipe shot out of the well bore like a rocket. Then the hole cratered, swallowing up the drilling rig, boiler and steam engine. By sunset, the drillsite was a cauldron of swirling mud and debris.

In the history of the petroleum industry, almost no one had discovered oil only five miles from a refinery. It meant the cash flow to Burnham Ex would start within the week. Fred saw Ed McKenna running toward him.

"Major Burnham. This well's doing four thousand barrels a day."

Fred looked up at the plume. It rose three hundred feet in the air.

"Don't stand there," Fred hollered. "Get it capped."

McKenna ran off in search of Shell's field manager and soon was lost in the crowd of workers.

Fred hugged his wife and said. "Tomorrow we're going to Los Angeles and buy you the best dress in California."

And he did just that.

Once the secret of Dominguez Mesa was unlocked, discovery followed discovery until it seemed as if the riches of the earth were gushing from the dome. Shell hit it big at Reyes Number One. The well spouted oil and gas for four days before sanding up.

On the day the Reyes well quit gassing, a valve failed on Union-Callendar Number Two and broke away from the drilling crew. The well turned into a gasser, drawing more Redcar spectators from Los Angeles to witness the scene. For two days as the crew wrestled to control it, the well spewed gas at a rate of thirty million cubic feet a day—a spectacle every bit as grand as the Dominguez Air Show. More farmers were hired to plow a new trench for an even larger pipeline.

67

Hollywood Land

Los Angeles • 1924

FOR YEARS, Dominguez Field produced a series of spectacular discoveries. So many rigs were making hole that on calm days, steam from the boilers shrouded Dominguez Mesa in a blanket of fog.

"It's our own Table Mountain," Fred boasted. Daily crude oil production was thirty-seven thousand barrels a day, with ten thousand barrels a day as Burnham Exploration Company's share. That produced an income of seventeen thousand dollars a day for a company with a payroll of five employees.

The most stunning discovery of all was that Dominguez Field was really a series of horizontally stacked oil depositions. Under the guidance of geologist Cy Rubel, drillers kept probing, isolating one producing zone after another, each about a hundred feet deeper. In time they found nine oil-bearing zones with eight of the zones being good oil producers.

What a wonderful two square miles, two miles deep.

The common shares of Burnham Ex, issued at one dollar par value, appreciated to seventy-five dollars each. With a flood of dividends, Fred and Rod purchased the preferred shares at a hundred ten percent of value plus seven percent interest. With the preferred shares retired, Fred and Rod held half ownership in Burnham Ex.

When drilling ended, Dominguez Mesa would boast one hundred fifty oil wells. The field was destined to produce half a billion barrels of crude oil. It became one of the top ten oil fields in California and one of the top fifty in the United States. When the field was depleted after fifty years, the land would became the site of California State University, Dominguez. But right now, Fred had a quarter of a century to enjoy life.

Wealth & Honors

After sixty-two years of wild adventures, with major discoveries and crushing losses, Fred Burnham was rich. And for the rest of his life, his most pressing problem was what to do with the never-ending supply of money that kept flowing in.

• • •

HOLLYWOOD LAND • 1925

WITH CASH flowing into the Burnham coffers at a rate of twenty thousand dollars a day, Fred made plans to live in a manner befitting his new means. From *Los Angeles Times* publisher Norman Chandler, he bought a substantial tract of land in the Hollywood Hills overlooking Los Angeles. Chandler intended the hilltop location to be Los Angeles' most exclusive real estate development.

To promote sales, workmen erected a huge sign on the hillside: HOLLYWOOD LAND. Later, when the LAND portion of the sign fell down, the HOLLYWOOD was reinforced to serve as an icon for the nation's film capital.

Fred hired his stay-at-home brother-in-law, architect Joe Blick, to design two grand mansions: one for Fred and another for Rod. Each was designed in Blick's Spanish-Italianate style that was so fashionable in the civic, metropolitan and business buildings of Pasadena. Access to the hilltop homes was by elevator.

The Burnhams embarked on the Dollar Line steamship *President Pierce* for an ocean voyage around the world. In Pekin, they bought Oriental rugs and ornate red-and-black lacquerware cabinets to display the many gold figurines they had dug at Zimbabwe. While in China, they visited the Forbidden City and the Great Wall. They saw the Temple of Heaven, the Ming Tombs and the Summer Palace. At Shanghai—that great whore of Asia—they rode in a rickshaw from Old Town with its winding alleys to the Bund and on to Nanking Road. In Hong Kong, they dined at a posh eatery atop Old Peak.

Then it was off to India, where they hunted tigers and elephants. Next they visited the pyramids in Egypt where they joined the Hammonds. The two families visited the Valley of the Kings, the tomb of King Tut and made a trip to Luxor where it rained for the first time in decades.

The Burnham and Hammond party continued their vacation, visiting Greece, Turkey, Palestine, Algiers, Costa del Sol and Spain, ending up in Gibraltar. From there, the Burnhams sailed for New York.

"I must visit Paris about the sale of my Kalorama Street home in Washington," Hammond said. "The French want it as their embassy."

511

When the Burnham mansion was completed, Sunday supplement writers vied to produce the most breathless reports on the mansions. Mildred Woodruff of the *Hollywood News* wrote:

Major Burnham helped me out of my car and together we went up his elevator. Never shall I forget the sight as we stepped into an arcade and crossed over to the lawn. The effect of the view on me was so beautiful that it hurt. Lake Hollywood appeared more exquisite than ever before and the surrounding hills greener and more charming. It was almost too wonderful to be real.

With pride, he pointed out Catalina Island and various other places of interest. The whole glorious world seemed stretched at our feet. I was surprised to find the wide, level expanse of lawn, green and velvety. We walked along rose-bordered paths until we came to an extensive putting green. We looked over the wall, down the terraced garden, and he explained the trees and shrubs and flowers.

We went into the house and wandered into the library, which is full of trophies of their travels, not only in Africa but also in China and Alaska. Immense ivory elephant tusks and heads of different wild animals and many of the weapons used were hanging on the walls.

The major pointed out a rug that he designed and had made in China. A likeness of the Oof Bird—the money bird of Africa—was woven into it. As he stood there among the autographed photos of the greatest men of his age the world over, I realized more than ever how great a man he is.

The old adobe house at La Cuesta—the Home Ranch near Three Rivers—was being replaced by a large stone-and-log chateau where Fred displayed his larger African and Alaskan game trophies in museum-like splendor. For the Blicks, Russells and visitors to La Cuesta, there were substantial bungalows. The Burnhams made plans for a world journey to buy more furniture for the new homes.

• • •

Los Angeles • Winter 1925

BLANCHE WAS seated at the dining room table, her eyes red. The look on her face told Fred that she'd been crying.

"Sir Rider's dead," she said.

"Rider Haggard?"

Fred sat down, saying nothing, but deeply shaken. Rider's books had inspired Fred to travel to Africa. He had dedicated a book to Nada. It was Haggard who had introduced Fred to Jack Hammond.

"It's here in a newspaper story from England," she said. "A dozen years ago, he wrote an autobiography and sealed it in a bank vault,

Wealth & Honors

Burnham Mansion at Hollywood Land

Burnham mansion overlooks Los Angeles and Catalina Island.

Burnham: King of Scouts

The Elevator and Lake Hollywood

This is Fred's trophy room at La Cuesta Ranch in Three Rivers. The ranch had 5,000 acres and there were 20,000 acres of summer pasture at Hockett Meadows. The Burnhams lived here nearly thirty years.

to be opened upon his death. He mentioned you in it. Why don't you read it?"

Fred picked up the newspaper. His eyes were misty and it was hard to see the words.

> *You ought to know him. In personal appearance, Fred Burnham is small, quiet mannered, with steady blue-grey eyes that have the faraway look such as those acquire whose occupation has caused them to watch continually at sea or the Great Plains. Like old Allan Quatermain, he is an extremely polished and thoughtful person, and one with a wide outlook on affairs. He is not at all communicative.*
>
> *In real life, Burnham is far more interesting than any of my heroes of romance. When he dies, I fear the record of all his extraordinary adventures, of which he has experienced more than Quatermain in fiction, may perish with him. In their adventurous aspect, they have no equal.*

Fred laid down the paper and for the first time since Bruce's funeral, tears came to his eyes. For two hours, he sat at the table. He had never made good on his promise to Rider for a report on Wilson's Last Stand.

"Better get dressed," Blanche said. "The Everetts are coming for dinner."

Fred was glad Mary and Torrey Everett would join them tonight. It would help to forget. They had met the Everetts ten years ago. Mary Everett came from Council Bluffs, Iowa, and she was delighted to know that Fred and Blanche hailed from the same home state. When she learned the Burnhams were friends of the Roosevelts and the Pinchots and they'd labored in the Conservation Movement, her joy knew no bounds.

After dinner, the talk turned to Sir Rider.

"Weren't you friends?" Mary Nixon Everett asked.

"Nada was named after one of his books," Blanche said. She explained that *nada* was the Zulu word for lily, and the Burnhams had thought their Africa-born daughter was the lily of the Dark Continent.

"Sir Rider dedicated one of his books to Nada's memory," Fred said, his thoughts seemingly lost in time. Mary was fascinated with Sir Rider's reference to Fred.

"Major Burnham," Mary said, "don't you think it's time to make good on your promise to Bea? I think Mr. Haggard's plea is eloquent and I believe you should write the story of your life. It's important for the world to know."

"Perhaps," Fred said wistfully, turning to Blanche. "But I'm not a writer and I've never looked forward to this moment."

"In Iowa, you were apprenticed to Uncle Josiah at the Clinton *Herald*," Blanche said. "Writing is not altogether foreign to you."

Mary Everett's eyes sparkled. "Major Burnham, I think you have a marvelous way with words. I was once an English teacher. Why don't we work together? I'll guide you and you can put the words on paper. Then I'll edit the manuscript and type it up for the publisher."

The look on Blanche's face implored Fred to accept the offer.

"If it's not too much trouble," he said.

"I'd be honored."

"Things at Burnham Ex are in good shape," he said.

"Good," Blanche said and got up to pour coffee. She believed in sealing any important agreement with food and drink. "Tomorrow I'll dig out the scrapbooks."

"What?" Mary Everett asked.

"Bea's a packrat," Fred said. "She's saved newspaper and magazine cuttings. There's a heap of them."

Smiling, Blanche walked in carrying hot apple pie.

"We also have the Burnham Genealogy, the picture albums and Fred's letters from people around the world."

"This is wonderful," Mary said. "I'll be here early."

Mary Everett arrived carrying pads of ruled, yellow paper and a box of sharp pencils. While Blanche poured coffee, Mary marveled at the treasury of papers, newsclips and scrapbooks lying on the table.

"I've forgotten dates and the spellings," Fred said.

"No you don't," Mary scolded. "You can't back out now. Write it out and I'll check the names and dates in these scrapbooks. Now get busy."

Fred picked up a pencil and while the women drank coffee and nibbled butter cookies, he began doodling on a yellow legal pad. He wrote: *Scouting on Two Continents*.

Mary Everett proved to be a taskmaster and Fred approached the writing of his memoirs with all the energy at his disposal. For months he sat at home writing in longhand on yellow pads. Mary prodded him.

"Tell about this," she cajoled. "Write about that."

With a patient sigh, Fred handed over the pages to Mrs. Everett for editing and typing. When news clips were missing, Fred wrote from memory. He made little effort to check the spelling of names and places. The Shangani River came out spelled in the nineteenth century version: Changani River. Jan Grootboom was recalled as John Grootbaum. Tujunga Wash north of Los Angeles came out Tejunga. Fred got confused by Earl A. Brininstool's new book, *Fighting Red Cloud's Warriors*. Little Crow of the 1862 Sioux Uprising in Minnesota got renamed Red Cloud.

After a decade of listening to Fred's adventure tales told and retold around the campfire at Hockett Meadows, Mary was afflicted with a case of hero worship. When Fred handed over a chapter, she complained, "You've failed to put in the best part." Some of the fireside tales had been enhanced in the telling and Mary was enamored of the campfire versions.

In the summer of 1925, he completed the manuscript. Jack Hammond wrote the foreword. Lord Baden-Powell sent his drawing of Fred and Bonnar Armstrong fleeing Njelele cave after shooting the M'Limo. He also sent an ink sketch of Fred astride a pony.

Doubleday agreed to publish *Scouting* and Fred sat down to begin the long wait for the book to appear.

68

Scouting on Two Continents

GLOUCESTER • AUTUMN 1925

WHILE WAITING for *Scouting* to appear, the Burnhams toured the United States. At Gloucester, Massachusetts, they called on Jack and Natalie Hammond at Lookout Hill overlooking the site of *the Wreck of the Hesperus*. The Burnhams were introduced to the other house guests: Baron Rosen, the former Russian ambassador, and his wife; Calvin and Grace Coolidge and Finley Peter Dunne, the Chicago editor who had created the popular Irish saloonkeeper, Mr. Dooley. Rounding out the party was the Hammonds' youngest son, John Junior.

For lunch, the party boarded the Hammonds' yacht, *Natalie*. The captain cast off from Western Harbor and sailed south past Black Bess Rocks and dropped anchor at the beach where a new road led to Hesperus Street. John Junior led them to a picnic table under an elm tree. There he presided over an al fresco lunch of smoked China pheasant from Oregon, vichyssoise soup, sliced peaches and tomatoes and champagne. After lunch he led his guests to a green pavilion-style tent on the beach.

"Look up there." Jack pointed up to what was already being called Castle Hill Road above Hesperus Avenue. "My new home will be on that hilltop," he said. "Inside this tent is an architect's model."

Everyone gasped in wonder. What young Hammond unveiled was far from being a mere run-of-the-mill mansion. It was a castle. It would cost five million dollars, and it was destined to become one of America's palaces, a home befitting the Vanderbilts, Rockefellers or du Ponts.

"It's magnificent," Blanche cried. "I'm struck dumb."

"Can you afford it, Son?" Hammond Senior gasped.

"He has been selling his remote control devices for torpedoes to the Navy," President Coolidge said. "He can well afford it."

From outside the canvas pavilion came the putt-pop sounds of cars. Junior looked at his watch. It was 2:30 p.m.

"That'll be the reporters and newsreel cameras."

As the Hammonds, Coolidges, Rosens, Burnhams and Dunne stepped outside, they encountered a dozen news reporters and cameramen getting out of four cars.

"What's this all about?" Hammond Senior asked. He was being protective of the president's privacy and his youngest son was using Coolidge's presence to gain publicity for his new home.

• • •

JACK JUNIOR'S ATTEMPT to garner publicity for his new home backfired. One of the newsmen mentioned that Fred had written his autobiography. Did the Major have any comments?

After so many months of work writing, Fred was weary of reciting his adventures. Miffed by what his son had done, Hammond Senior sent the newsmen packing.

To flesh out their stories, the reporters dug into their libraries where old clippings repose. That's how the *Boston Sunday Post* came out with an amazing story. A sensational feature article was topped by an eight-column banner headline that read:

Cecil Rhodes Yankee Scout Visits President Coolidge

The article recounted Burnham activities of thirty years ago. It fixed on the death of Nada Burnham during the Matabele Uprising of 1896. It said Burnham's revenge-shooting of the M'Limo broke the back of the Matabele Rebellion. "Rhodes walked boldly into the indaba and laid down the peace terms," it said. The Post said *Scouting on Two Continents* would be published in two volumes.

• • •

Los Angeles • Spring 1926

ON THEIR RETURN home, the Burnhams caught up on an accumulation of mail.

April 11, 1926
Boy Scout Headquarters, London
Dear Burnham,
I should much like to get you down to Gillwell Park in Epping Forest, our permanent training school for officers of the Scout movement, if it were possible, particularly as the president of the Boy Scouts of America is so anxious to get a similar school of woodcraft established for the Boy Scout officers in the United States. Indeed that is one cause of my present visit. I am certain it would interest you to see

how we can turn city men into scouts.

While in Washington, I will certainly look up your friend John Hays Hammond. If you have to put off your sailing for America, why not defer it to the Homeric *on the 21st and go over with us? It would be a joy to talk over old times and revive reminiscences of Rhodesia. Back at that time, I published my diary, though possibly you may not have seen it, under the title* The Matabele Campaign, *in which I had sketches of you as well as notes of our working together. I expect that the book is now out of print. I return herewith the photograph, signed as requested. Yours sincerely, Robert Baden-Powell*

Also this letter:

June 17, 1926
Boy Scout Headquarters, London
Dear Burnham,

I was delighted to meet your friends, Mr. and Mrs. Torrey Everett, though unfortunately I did so only a day or so before they sailed for America, owing to their having written to me at a home in London which I left ten years ago. Mrs. Everett showed me some of the proofs of the forthcoming book, and I can cordially congratulate you on it. It should be a tremendous success, and I sincerely hope it will be. Yours sincerely, Robert Baden-Powell

Mary Everett showed Fred the galley proofs of *Scouting*. In many places, it was scarcely the same book he had written. Doubleday had decided against a two-volume version and in Fred's absence Mary had edited it—cutting with a heavy hand. She had removed entire chapters on the early West, the Klondike, the Northern Coppers, the Yaqui River Delta. In the process, she had failed to write the transitional paragraphs needed to span lengthy breaks in time. After going over it, Fred felt glum.

"After all that work, those chapters are gone."

"Cheer up," Mrs. Everett said. "Baden-Powell read proofs of quite a few chapters and he complimented you on its merits."

"Before the editing?" Fred asked.

"Naturally. I wasn't told about the decision to shorten the manuscript until we returned to the United States."

• • •

LOS ANGELES • 1926

WHEN *Scouting on Two Continents* was published in the summer of 1926 and it became something of an accent of the literary season. Again, Fred became hot copy for the newspapers. His oil wealth had brought a new round of fame.

Scouting was reviewed in the *Los Angeles Times*, the *San Francisco Chronicle*, the *Pekin Leader*, the *Aberdeen Press-Journal*, the *Manchester Guardian, East Africa* magazine and others. The *Bulawayo Chronicle* predicted the Burnhams would return one day to reclaim Nada's remains.

The *Boston Post* headlined "The Shot That Brought Peace to Africa." *South Africa* magazine declared that in Africa no man is held in higher esteem. *Punch* in London said the 1896 Matabele Rebellion had fizzled after Fred shot the M'Limo. *Zodiac* in Sydney said Burnham had finished the rebellion by a single act of almost incredible daring. The *Pasadena Star-News* said Fred was a stranger in his own home town. The *New York Times* said *Scouting* was a thrilling book. The *Saturday Review of Literature* said his adventures were almost incredible.

A flood of mail arrived. There were letters from General Aylmer Hunter-Weston, Bill Crocker, Winston Churchill, Teddy Roosevelt Jr., King Macomber, author and poet Earl Brininstool and western author Charlie Lummis and from lesser known family and friends.

February 13, 1927
Port Elizabeth, South Africa
My dear Burnham,
I have delayed in answering your kind letter because I had been waiting to receive the book which you said you were sending me. It was a real joy to hear from you, specially as I got your letter when I was back in our old haunts in Rhodesia. I am longing to see your book and am proud to have been used at all in the making of it. Your kind offer of presenting some copies to the Scouts is most heartily appreciated, and I am certain it will bring joy and good influence to the lads who are fortunate enough to possess the book. Yours truly, Robert Baden-Powell

Fred cherished the personal notes of friends too. Neighbor Tom Chatten of Visalia, California, chided him for his modesty. "You might have told a lot more," he said. Irving Kinney, formerly of Clinton, Iowa, groused that *Scouting* "hits only a comparatively few high points in your career." Samuel F.B. Morse of Del Monte Properties in Monterey wrote, "I felt it would be nothing short of a crime to leave your story unwritten." W.W. Cummings of Orange, California, declared, "You have raised scouting to a profession. I think Daniel Boone, Davy Crockett, Kit Carson and all owe you a debt of thanks." General Aylmer Hunter-Weston said Wilson's Last Stand had never been properly and authentically told before. Cowboy-poet Earl Brininstool called Fred's book "the greatest adventure story I have ever come across." Western author Charlie Lummis added, "A great book, Burnham, a noble book."

Baden-Powell wrote on Fred's sixty-sixth birthday.

THE BOY SCOUTS ASSOCIATION
Buckingham Palace Road, London
May 11, 1927
Dear Burnham:

I returned from South Africa to find your book awaiting me, and the extra copies of it for presentation to the Boy Scouts. Let me thank you for your kindness and generosity in sending these. They will be of immense value in encouraging the right ideas among boys. It brings back old times with a fresh force, which is all the stronger seeing that I have just been back to Matabele Land and over much of the ground that we covered in those days. You ought to see the country for yourself and see how things have gone ahead in the way of civilization and industry on the foundations which you and others laid there. There is a beautiful motor road now through the Matopo Hills which gives visitors an idea of the wonderful country in which we had to fight. It takes them to Rhodes's grave on the World's View.

We found our Boy Scouts and Girl Guides established all over the country, even in places like Gwelo, Fort Victoria, Umtali, Mazoe, Salisbury, Bulawayo and such. The astonishing thing was the rally at the Victoria Falls, to which Boy Scouts and Girl Guides came from Broken Hill and Bwana Malumba, seven hundred miles to the north. So you see, civilization is spreading. I hope you have big success with your book and that it will be widely read. I had an enthusiastic letter about it from a man who strongly urged that your chapter on "How to Become a Scout" should be published as a pamphlet for all boys to read. You can be sure that we will make the book as widely known as we can among the boys through the medium of our papers. I hope that before long you'll pay us another visit and have a chat over old times. Yours sincerely, Robert Baden-Powell

Scouting did become a widely read best seller. Soon the translation were made into Dutch, German, Spanish, eventually eleven languages plus Braille. The American scouting movement, meanwhile, had thrived for seventeen years without suspecting the existence of the American who had inspired Baden-Powell to his life's purpose.

• • •

NEW YORK • 1927

WITH THE PUBLICATION of *Scouting*, the Boy Scouts of America discovered Fred Burnham. The American Scout establishment took steps to rectify its oversight. At its seventeenth annual meeting in 1927, the Boy Scouts created an Order of Honorary Scouts. Membership was granted to "men of adventure and exceptional character, men who had captured the imaginations of boys."

Fred was elected as one of the seventeen Honorary Scouts: one person for each year of the BSA's existence. Among the others honored were aviation pioneer Orville Wright, explorers Admiral Richard E. Byrd and Roy Chapman Andrews who had explored the Gobi Desert in search of dinosaur bones.

Chief Scouting Executive James E. West wrote:

Burnham has proved in many lands that the American scout is still as keen on the trail as he was in the great days of Carson and Crockett, Boone and Wetzel. Sir Robert Baden-Powell felt like a tenderfoot before this American scout.

Two months later, West solicited from Fred a series of articles for *Boys Life* magazine, which he edited. "The American Boy Scouts," he wrote, "have developed little literature on tracking and trailing, most having come from Baden-Powell." West enclosed a copy of *Scouting for Boys* to inspire Fred to write similar features "that you above all are qualified to render."

It would be five years before Burnham got around to responding. At the time, Fred was busy. He had joined Charlie Lummis's Archaeological Society and they were absorbed in founding the Southwest Museum in Highland Park, a suburb between Los Angeles and Pasadena. Under the direction of Dr. Frederick Hodge, the Southwest Museum grew into the première repository of American Indian lore. Dr. Hodge authored the landmark *Handbook of the American Indian*. The museum, perched atop a mesa, was entered through an elevator that rose from street level. It was uncannily similar to the one at Burnham Manor in Hollywood Land.

Fred remained faithful to the memory of President Teddy Roosevelt and to Governor Gifford Pinchot of Pennsylvania. He was active in the American Committee for International Wildlife Protection, the British Society for the Preservation of Fauna, and the Boone & Crockett Club. He helped organize the Save the Redwoods League, which set aside a three thousand acre park in Northern California to be called the Avenue of the Giants. Situated a few miles from the Pacific Ocean between Eureka and Fort Bragg, the Avenue of the Giants included fifty thousand acres of scenic redwoods along a thirty mile stretch of the Pacific Coast Highway. The road came to be called the Redwood Highway. John D. Rockefeller quietly underwrote the conservation project.

The Governor of California appointed Major Burnham to the newly created California State Parks Commission, along with San Francisco attorney William Colby, president of the Sierra Club; Los Angeles attorney Henry O'Melveny of the O'Melveny & Meyers law firm, State Senator Wilbur Chandler and Dr. Ray Lyman Wilbur, president of Stanford University.

As their first action, the five commissioners sponsored Proposition Four, the State Parks Bond Act, on the November ballot. It authorized the sale of six million dollars in bonds to buy three hundred private beach and park sites and convert them to state parks. Burnham suggested that the public put up matching donations, bringing the total available for conservation purposes to twelve million dollars.

There was simply too much to do to write a series of articles for *Boy's Life*.

Trail Dust

The 14th Chronicle

69

The Return to Africa

LOS ANGELES • MAY 1929

THE BURNHAMS BOARDED the *S.S. Makura* on the first leg of an eight-month long, around-the-world journey to promote the conservation movement. For maximum press exposure, Fred organized the cruise as an expedition, which he financed himself. Rod resigned from Union Oil Company to join his parents. They purchased five new DuPont Vita-Color motion picture cameras to record African wildlife.

The traveling party also included Blanche, Rod's wife, Isabella, and granddaughter, Marta. In Nairobi, they would meet John Blick, who was in Abyssinia—now Ethiopia—searching for fossils for the American Museum of Natural History.

The Burnham party left San Francisco on May 15, amid great press hoopla. They sailed leisurely along a popular route, touching at Hawaii and proceeding south between Samoa and Tahiti to the Cook Islands, stopping at Rarotonga. Next they visited New Zealand, Tasmania and Australia.

At each port they were met by Boy Scout honor guards or by conservation officials. In New Zealand they were reunited with old Kenia hand Walker Dunn, the animal expert. The popularity of *Scouting on Two Continents* assured Fred of a reception from reporters at every port of call. He willingly posed with old cronies—colonels, generals, admirals and lords—as long as he could make his pitch for conservation.

On June 24, the party boarded the *S.S. Themistocles* in Perth, Australia, bound for Cape Town. In South Africa, Rod chartered a touring car and a truck for an overland expedition. They retraced old Boer War haunts from Kimberley and Paardeberg through Bloemfontein and on to Kroonstad, Johannesburg and Pretoria.

From there they crossed the border to Rhodesia, where they followed the route they had trekked thirty-six years ago. They visited Willie and Harry Posselt who lived on a farm between Fort Victoria and Gwelo. All over Rhodesia, the settlers had planted trees and preserved the game that everyone had so relentlessly hunted as youths.

Fred sat on the verandah of the Posselt home and his eyes wandered across the tawny veld. Back of the house was an orchard of oranges as glossy as those in California, but grown without the need for irrigation. The Posselts had planted flowering vines at the bases of the trees. The vines slithered up the trunks and produced a profusion of blossoms that produced a whole new spectrum of color to the trees.

"I cannot but salute the great strides that the Rhodesians have made compared with how little has been accomplished in the American Southwest," Fred said.

"But you have so much more territory to develop," Willie gently responded.

At Bulawayo, the party made a pilgrimage to the cemetery to visit Nada's grave. Flowers and trees were now growing luxuriantly, and all around Nada were the graves of the Old Pioneers. After talking things over, the Burnhams decided Nada should belong to Africa forever. There followed a journey to World's View at Mineral King to visit Cecil Rhodes' and Major Allan Wilson's graves.

So happy had Fred been to see Rhodesia and talk with old friends like the Posselts that it wasn't until he was preparing to leave the country that a thought struck him: Except for the *Bulawayo Chronicle*, no newspaper reporters had interviewed him. No invitation came to call on the governor, Sir Cecil Hunter Rodwell. Fred shrugged it off. He'd been away thirty years. Most of today's people weren't born when he was making history.

They boarded a train for Beira. There they'd catch a steamer for Mombassa to join John Blick for a movie safari in Kenya. King Macomber would come down from Paris. He promised to bring along a young writer friend named Ernest Hemingway who had written *The Sun Also Rises* and was working on a new book called *A Farewell to Arms*.

• • •

BEIRA • SUMMER 1929

IN THREE DECADES, Beira had certainly changed. When they passed through in 1895 en route to Paris for the wedding of Pete and Grace Ingram, there had been only a corrugated iron hotel, a few godown warehouses and some native huts.

Beira was now a tidy, up-to-date town with paved streets, modern buildings, smart shops and ships in the harbor. The three-story Savoy Hotel stood in contrast to the old galvanized iron shanty.

"Burnham, I say there, Fred Burnham."

It was a voice from the past.

"Art Lawli," Fred cried. "Or is it Sir Arthur now?"

"To you, it'll always be Art," said the man who'd been assistant to Chief Native Commissioner Herb Taylor. Lawli was nearly bald, with only a fringe of silver hair around his ears. He was dressed in a safari suit and wore his mustache pencil thin. Art invited the visitors to dinner at the Savoy Hotel.

"What have you been doing since I left?" Fred asked.

"After leaving the BSA Company, I worked with Sir Charles Metcalf to build railways. We built your bridge over the Zambesi River in 1904."

After dinner, Blanche asked the waiter to compliment the chef on the excellent cuisine.

"Mendoza will appreciate that," Lawli said.

"Do you know the chef?" she asked.

"I own the Savoy."

While Roderick took the women on a stroll of the beach, Art and Fred retired to the lounge for an after-dinner chat. Fred was about to decline, but something in Art's voice prompted him to accept.

"I daresay the people of Rhodesia ignored you."

"How's that?" Fred asked, puzzled.

"It's stale news in High Street, let alone the bazaars, so I may as well pass it along."

"What are you talking about, Art?"

"The Rhodesians have defamed your good name." Lawli's face looked pained. "You're considered in bad odor. They say you shot an unresisting old Negro while he was mending his kraal. The record is classified, but everybody in Rhodesia seems to know."

"What?" Fred asked. *Killing an unresisting old Negro? That's what Frank Sykes had said in his absurd book* With Plumber in Rhodesia. *Sykes had been sixty miles away at the Gwaii River. How could that malarkey continue to be passed around?*

To Fred, the light in the lounge began to dim. Vaguely Fred recalled the tasteless report in the *African Review* about Colonel Plumer's men looting the supply wagons and drinking their way to Bulawayo. The Review had spoken of bar loafers and deadbeats, men who had never shouldered a gun. Sykes' men did have grounds for anger.

Trail Dust

"Can you tell me about it?" Fred asked.

"While you were in London making headlines with that big Klondike nugget, CNC Herb Taylor forced Bonnar Armstrong to resign as native commissioner. Six months later, Armstrong wrote an appeal to the hi-com in Cape Town. He charged the Chartered Company with corruption, maladministration, shooting native prisoners and interfering with his duties."

"Armstrong always was moody," Fred said.

"Taylor then wrote a rebuttal and attached it to Bonner's letter. It was a character assassination, designed to forestall any court of enquiry."

"What's all of that stuff got to do with me?"

"To discredit Armstrong, Taylor had to punch holes in the M'Limo story. So he wrote a new M'Limo report. He classified it as most secret, but I made notes."

Lawli laid several sheets of paper on the table. Fred read: "It appears that Armstrong had heard there was a certain cave near Banko's Kraal, close to the Shashi River, and within about thirty

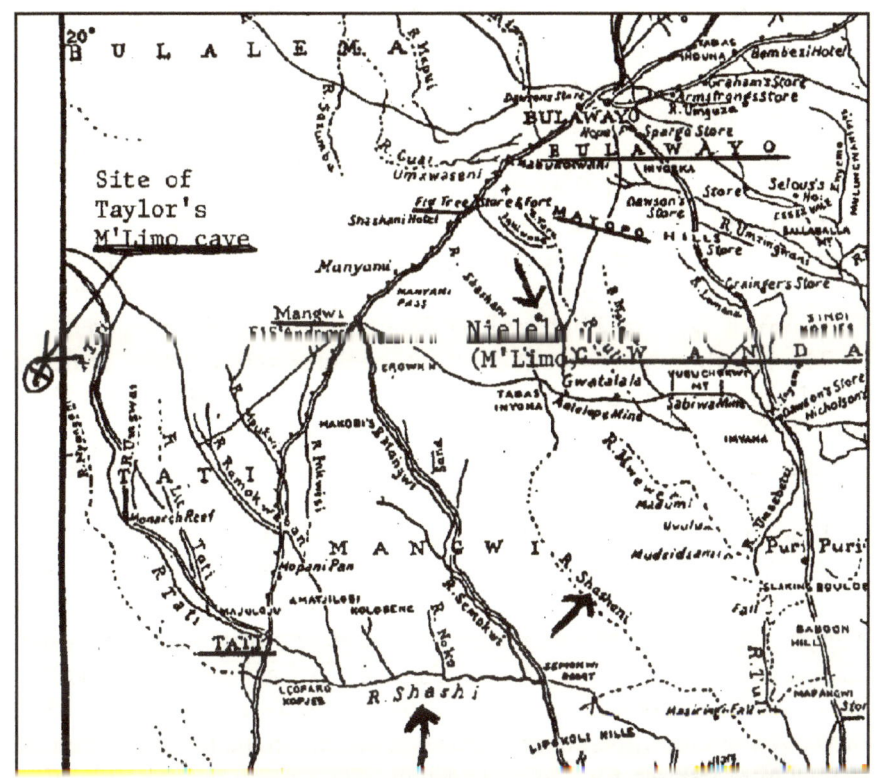

Njelele is in Gwanda. Taylor's cave is in the Bulalima District.

529

miles of the Matopo Hills, where the Makalakas used to offer up their sacrifices to the M'Limo. He concocted a story—."

"Wait a minute," Fred said. "This report is nonsense. Did you see this? Banko's Kraal? Close to the Shashi River? Thirty miles from the Matopo Hills?"

"So? What of it?"

"The Shashi is on the border of Bechuana Land," Fred said. "Armstrong and I crossed the Shashani River, not the Shashi. The Shashani River begins at The Nek near Fig Tree. The Shashi is out in Bill Thomas's Bulalima District. Taylor is full of calf slobber." Fred's eyes bristled.

"Jove, Herb's description is base over apex. If word ever got out, Sir Herbert would be doing time in gaol."

"He should be," Fred said. "Taylor is lying."

"How perfectly bloody," Lawli replied. "You know, that report is still classified as most secret."

• • •

NAIROBI • OCTOBER 1929

COUNTLESS SAFARIS had followed in the aftermath of Teddy Roosevelt's 1910 expedition to East Africa. The most spectacular was the George Eastman safari which continued for six months — with trucks, pavilion tents, bone china, goose liver pate, bourbon and mineral water.

When the Burnhams arrived, John Blick had both good and bad news. He told Fred that during an outing in Ethiopia, he had encountered what appeared to be stone cutting tools—a possible sign of early man. But the funds for his explorations had dried up. Since the death of Henry C. Frick, support from the American Museum of Natural History had declined and finally ceased.

The Burnham party went south to the Serengeti on a film-making safari, then returned to Nairobi late in the month. After that they planned week-long visits into the bush to make movies of wild animals under the gray-thorn trees. On weekends they would return to the Norfolk Hotel in Nairobi to get away from the "savage life" and take refuge in the comfort of the House of Lords.

As Fred and Rod were unpacking their five DuPont Vita-Color cameras, popular film-makers Martin and Osa Johnson arrived in Kenya. Their safari boasted ten trucks and two hundred fifty crates of equipment, requiring an equal number of askaries to transport the gear into the bush. John learned the Johnsons were being funded by the American Museum of Natural History. On the Johnsons' return to the United States, they released *Congorilla* to wide acclaim, followed by *Baboona*. Fred decided that he and Rod had invested in the world's most expensive home movie outfit.

In his suite at the Norfolk, Fred completed a letter to General Baden-Powell on the state of the world scouting movement.

Written in Nairobi on October 4, 1929

Dear Baden-Powell,

For many months, the news of the world has been laden with items of the great jamboree. We heard of it Down Under. It came to us out of the air on Van Diemen's restless Tasmanian sea, from the backblocks and bush of Australia and the never-never land of New Zealand, it was clicked to the world over their solitary wire: The Scouts are coming. From a beautiful island in the South Seas, Rarotonga, one of your original twenty Scouts on the little island was going strong, leading a troop and sending a contingent. He won the sobriquet of the Irish Devil, but is known to the world as Captain T.O. Campbell.

One could ramble on for pages telling of this rising tide of interest in the inspiring movement that calls the youth of the world from the Himalayan deodar cedars to the tundras, and from beyond the Rockies to the Pampas. It leaps national boundaries as if they were chalk marks on the pavement. The mighty stone walls of ancient churches cannot hold it. It even penetrates racial antagonism, the greatest barrier of all.

It so happens that while you were marshaling the Scouts at Birkenhead, I was on a long trek in Africa over the camps, trails and battlefields of our youth. Finally, after a pilgrimage to Mineral King and Umzingwane—World's View—to visit the tomb of the mighty Rhodes, I found myself standing on an old battlefield by the Umguza River, near the spot where an enterprising Matabele warrior on that day in 1896 did his level best to have you die a major, instead of Chief Scout, world famous soldier and Lord Baden-Powell—I had just heard in Bulawayo of your latest honour. As I stood looking toward Thabas Induna, my mind is filled with such vivid memories about you that I shall try to get some of them down.

I could see you standing with a group of officers under a dense tree, where you learned the lesson that a scout must look up as well as around and down. Then my thoughts concentrated on that Matabele warrior. He must have been imbued with racial pride, a national patriotism, together with high personal courage in that he—alone among the enemy—must choose certain death, when by silence he could have saved his life. That morning much had happened to him. He had seen the last great attack of the Matabele nation to capture Bulawayo—and destroy the hated white man—come to an end in utter rout and disaster. To avoid the charge of mounted white men, he had climbed with his big gun into this tree. And they all swept by him, but strangely the white indunas incautiously chose his particular tree to stand under while they rested their tired horses and gathered their scattered men.

Suddenly, the thought must have come to him: kill the white man and die. He missed you by a hair. Who knows with what sickening despair he gazed into the muzzles of death as he realized he had missed the great induna. The next instant he lay crumpled at the base of the tree. Let us hope that as his soul sped from the black body, some angel of solace relieved his despair. For if he had killed that induna, he would have destroyed an idea, a great and practical plan that in due time will assuage even such hatred as he and his people have for the whites.

Many other names and faces of those who were with us that day crowded the pages of memory. They all seemed as young and strong as in those days when we were hewing out an empire: Colenbrander, Beal, Spreckley, the Blicks, there are very few of us left now. Some of the old warriors who fought us in 1893 and 1896 are still alive, but I cannot put down their tales in one letter to a very busy Chief Scout.

Next to Rhodes, you probably drew more unjust and untrue comment than any man in South Africa, yet they are now sending their sons to sit at your table and learn wisdom. And the hated Rhodes is almost a god. You are more fortunate than Rhodes, Jameson, Milner, Botha and others, in that you live to know the result of your work and see writ large on the pages of history your deeds and life work.

I am finishing this letter in Kenya Colony. Here I find the end of the trail for the great Selous. He also is enshrined among the immortals, his small human failings forgotten, his genuine life work and final dramatic end will endure for generations in the memory of frontiersmen.

One other thought comes to me—that you should conserve the years and strength still left to you. It must be almost impossible to lay down or pass on the enormous amount of detail of your vast organization reaching all over the world.

I shall be in London in December. If you are not fed up with callers, I should be delighted to see you again. I shall certainly call at Rowland House to see the Scouts there, and at Fulham in Hammersmith to see the troop that have—with your permission—honoured me by calling itself Burnham's Own.

Yours sincerely. F.R. Burnham

The letter was posted in London on November 15, 1929.

• • •

LONDON • NOVEMBER 1929

THE BURNHAMS' STAY in Kenya was cut short. Blanche took a tumble down the grand staircase of that House of Lords — the Hotel Norfolk—and her hip was fractured. As soon as the limb was set in a temporary cast, Fred and Blanche bade farewell to John Blick, King Macomber, Rod, Isabella and young Marta. The couple boarded a ship that took them to England. In London, the Harley Street medics X-rayed the fracture, and replaced the cast. Baden-Powell wrote to Fred inviting him to visit Pax Hill.

November 14, 1929
Dear Burnham,

I hear you are arriving in London tomorrow and am awfully sorry to hear of your short stay here and specially of your wife's accident. Would you possibly have time to run down here to see us on Sunday, either to lunch or to stay the night if you can? If your wife is fit enough, we should of course want her to come too. There is a train leaving Waterloo Station, across Westminster Bridge from Parliament, at 11:10 on Sunday, arriving here 12:45 by which we would meet you if you came by train. Baden-Powell

Fred called on Stephe while Blanche recuperated in the hospital. His visit to the Baden-Powell home produced an article in *The Scout* newspaper under date of December 21. The Chief Scout's weekly column was titled "Stirring adventure in Matabele Land when the M'Limo made a mistake."

Major Burnham, the great American scout, has been staying with me. Long years ago, we met in Matabele Land under exciting circumstances. The Matabele warriors had risen against the British settlers and the white men had banded themselves together in Bulawayo for the protection of their wives and families. General Sir Frederick Carrington was sent out from England to organize their defense and I went with him as his chief staff officer. We reached Bulawayo after an awful journey of ten days and nights in a coach.

Baden-Powell described how Fred and Charles Metcalfe had discovered a Matabele impi camped outside Bulawayo and had ridden into town to warn the settlers. The yarn contained exaggerations that Stephe was noted for.

Burnham seized the bridle of Metcalfe's horse and swung it around with his own and started to gallop back down the road. Not a moment too soon, for out of the bushes on either side there sprang men throwing their assegais and hurriedly firing their guns at the white riders. Luckily, in the darkness they escaped and made their way back to

533

Bulawayo to give the alarm. When Burnham came to me and told me the story, I knew that so good a scout could not be mistaken, so I got my horse and rode out myself. I soon found the enemy were there sure enough. I spent the remainder of the night getting together a force of two hundred mounted men and in the early dawn we sallied forth to attack them.

Baden-Powell related how Colonel Spreckley's force attacked the Matabele, scattering them to the winds and turning the tide of war.

If it had not been for Burnham's sharp ear and his quick thinking and acting, both he and Metcalfe would have been killed, we in Bulawayo would have had no warning, and the Matabele might have come on and caught us unawares and swallowed us up. But Burnham was a scout whose motto was "Be Prepared" at any old time for any old thing.

"Next week there will be another fine yarn from the Chief," the paper said.

• • •

LOS ANGELES • APRIL 1930

IT WAS Fred's turn to write:
Los Angeles, April 21, 1930
Dear General,

Thank you for the articles on the lost civilization of the Yucatan and Mexico. For years it has been a subject of much interest to me. It so happens that twenty years ago, I took the late Professor Charles M. Holder, a cofounder of the Tournament of Roses, on an expedition into the cactus forests of Sonora to decipher some written carvings on a large rock I had found in that country. He declared it to be Mayan and it proved that this ancient people must have sent expeditions and established outposts in the Yaqui Valley a thousand miles north of what is believed to be their national boundaries in Yucatan.

We have now established in Los Angeles the Southwest Museum, the brainchild of the late Charles M. Lummis. Its endowment is devoted to unraveling as far as possible the human history of our western country.

There has just closed here in Los Angeles a Scouts' Exposition entirely of things the Scouts do or make. It is a great success. More than three hundred Tenderfoot Scouts were initiated. My wife has thrown away her crutches and is nearly ready for another long trek. She regrets the accident prevented her visit to your beautiful home and meet Olave Lady Baden-Powell. Regards, F.R. Burnham

Never in a hundred years would Lord Baden-Powell guess what Fred Burnham had up his sleeve.

70

Mount Baden-Powell

Los Angeles • May 1931

ON THE LAST SUNDAY of the month, four hundred automobiles drove into the San Gabriel Mountains north of Los Angeles. All flew flags or were embellished with bunting. The vehicles held a collection of Boy Scouts, Scout officials, parents, politicians, reporters and spectators. Aram, Fred's chauffeur, steered the Overland V-8 touring car along the turns of Highway Two to the mountain ridge at Angeles Forest Crest.

They passed north of the Mount Wilson Observatory and drove along the serpentine Kratka Ridge. Fred, who had turned seventy years old three weeks earlier, would complete a project today that was dear to his heart. He was going to dedicate one of the finest peaks in the San Gabriel Mountains.

The caravan continued for fifty miles until at noon they arrived at what would become the Lodgepole Pine Picnic Area. While a patrol of Eagle Scouts scaled the final five hundred feet of the nine thousand-foot peak, the visitors debarked for an outdoor lunch in the pines.

Then it was two o'clock. The Scouts rose and formed a line on a ridge facing the peak east of them. Stuart French, vice president of the national council of the Boy Scouts of America, was the first to speak.

"It is fitting that the man from whom you are about to hear is a pioneer and frontiersman," French said. He told how Fred's grandparents had followed Daniel Boone into Kentucky, how he counted as his friends Lord Roberts, Theodore Roosevelt and the Chief Scout, Lord Baden-Powell. Then it was Fred's turn.

To all the Scouts of the world, Greetings:

In obedience to your commands, we, your representatives from distant nations and the far-flung frontiers beyond the seas, are assembled here on this lofty mountain to give it the name of our beloved Chief Scout. We feel that this mighty fragment expresses our love and admiration for the chief better than any monument we could erect.

Far back in the pages of recorded history we find that when the nations of mankind wish to confer a special tribute which they desire to last through the ages, they dedicate to their deities and heroes one of the dominating mountains of the world. In this instance, following the custom of our race through a thousand generations, your committee with great care has selected this particular peak because it is as characteristic and outstanding among mountains as our chief is among men.

So today this address will consist of two stories: one of a mountain, one of a man. You are now standing on one of the sentinels of the mighty Sierras, which holds back the frowning desert from all our homes. This mountain closed out the deserts, leaving only a space that made it the Khyber Pass of the West, which held back those three demons: thirst, storms and the creeping dunes. Back in geological time, this desert drove strange monsters down into the valleys below.

Trail Dust

Along the road you traveled today, there once padded softly in the dead of night saber-tooth tigers, long-fanged wolves and lions of enormous size.

High on those crags sat condors and eagles, watching for some animal that might be slain or die of thirst. Herds of camels, horses and many lesser animals passed between those walls of granite, long ages before the first barefoot track of savage man. Then came the soft and silent tread of the moccasined Indian, and ere long the clanking spurs and shining armor of the Spaniard. Then from eastward came the tall, sinewy and skin-clad trapper, and behind him rumbled the heavy wagons of the pioneers. These were soon followed by the iron horse and ribbons of steel. Now you roll on air while overhead those gleaming scouts of the sky, driven by fire, are circling this mountain to pay tribute to the chief. All this pageantry of life down through the centuries could not have been, had this mountain rampart given way.

We have chosen this mountain to symbolize our beloved Chief Scout. In the world of men, he has always been a rampart against the small and mean things of life. For years, he was like this mountain, holding back the endless dunes of savagery that seemed to bury the outposts of civilization.

It so happened that my first meeting with the chief was under the shadow of another mountain in the heart of Africa. Here a handful of pioneers were about to be destroyed by overwhelming numbers of well-armed savages. We had been fighting for months.

He came direct from the bloodstained jungles of the Ashanti. His assistance to us was like one of the knights of King Arthur. Finally, under the strong hand and glowing soul of Cecil Rhodes, a just peace was made. It was at this time in the chief's life that there was planted, as he himself expresses it, an acorn of thought that was to grow into a mighty oak.

Fred described the patrol in June 1896 where he guided Baden-Powell into the World's View area of the Matopo Hills and how the chief had become fascinated with the craft of scouting.

The chief found a way to have the duties of life—its working drudgery—made into a tremendous game. Youth was really a glorious age of joy, growth and accomplishment, of laughter, fun games and sunshine. He saved the puritan virtues, yet stripped them of their dour and deadening don'ts. He reduced the ponderous sermons and endless books of law into the Scout Law. It can be memorized in a few hours. It gives you liberty and freedom. There are only a few don'ts and there are many dos. Your Scout Law preserves courage, truth,

537

strength and mercy.

Now the acorn began to grow. It cast its cool shade over England and almost overnight the entire Empire. Now it leaped the Atlantic and found its original source among the American Indians. Soon it girdled the world. We now, therefore, lay upon this mountain the weight of its name. From this moment forever, it shall be called Mount Baden-Powell.

As aerial skywriters spelled out the initials B P in the sky, a thousand cheers rose. Fred didn't see much of what happened because there were tears in his eyes. There were congratulations, handshaking and posing for pictures. Then everyone got into their cars for the drive back to Los Angeles. The papers wrote up the day's celebration real big. There was only one circumstance to mar the ceremony. The Chief Scout, Baden-Powell, was not there to participate in the christening. In fact, he was half way around the world and didn't learn about plans for the dedication until his travel itinerary was cast in bronze.

• • •

Los Angeles • March 1931

TEN WEEKS before the dedication, Fred had sent a cable to Lord Baden-Powell inviting him to Los Angeles for the dedication of the mountain that would bear his name. Burnham addressed the cable to Baden-Powell's red brick home at Pax Hill on the London-to-Southampton Road.

MARCH 14, 1931
LORD BADEN-POWELL
PAX HILL, BENTLEY, HAMPSHIRE
AM ASKED BY OFFICIALS BOY SCOUTS AMERICA PERSONALLY URGE YOU ACCEPT THEIR INVITATION DEDICATION OF MOUNT BADEN-POWELL MAY 30 STOP THERE IS GREAT ENTHUSIASM STOP I BELIEVE YOUR PRESENCE WOULD MAKE IT A NATIONAL AND EVEN INTERNATIONAL EVENT OF IMPORTANCE STOP PERHAPS YOU CAN RETURN NEW ZEALAND THIS WAY STOP PLEASE REPLY COLLECT TO PETROLEUM LOS ANGELES STOP BURNHAM.

Came this reply from Baden-Powell's secretary, Eileen Nugent Wade, who was vacationing in Paris:

MARCH 19, 1931
PETROLEUM LOS ANGELES
REGRET IT IMPOSSIBLE FOR BADEN-POWELL ATTEND DEDICATION MAY 30TH, OWING TO ENGAGEMENTS IN

SOUTH AFRICA STOP SCOUTCRAFT

Shortly after that cable arrived, Fred received a letter from Stephe sent by boat mail from Christchurch.

Rangitata, New Zealand
18 February 1931
My dear Burnham:

Greetings from our camp on the Rangitata River south of Christchurch. My wife and I are doing a tour of inspection of the Boy Scouts and Girl Guides in this part of the world—New Zealand, Australia and South Africa—taking six months about it. And we shall have a mighty strenuous time while we are at it. But it is well worthwhile. The totals of the two movements combined run this year to three million—and still increasing. There are one hundred fifty thousand more Scouts this year than last.

But this is not what I would want to write to you about. No, I want to tell you once more how delighted we both are with the redwood bole you sent us. It was sending up quite a little forest of green shoots when we left home, and we have handed [it] over to my secretary to care for during our absence. So I expect to see it in a flourishing condition when we get back.

If you are likely to be in Europe after that month, be sure to let us know and keep a few days to spend with us at Pax Hill.

Before I left England, we had a very interesting dinner of old comrades of the Matabele campaign. More than a hundred of them, very cheery and full of reminiscences. I only wish you could have been there to meet them and to swap yarns. Someday perhaps. Meantime, with best of good wishes. Baden-Powell

• • •

Los Angeles • May 1931

FRED BURNHAM celebrated his seventieth birthday at a gathering of Burnhams and Blicks and other members of the Lost White Tribe. Two days later he wrote to Stephe's secretary.

May 13, 1931
Dear Mrs. Wade:

The Chief's letter to me from New Zealand arrived just after my cable [was dispatched to Pax Hill] so we know he will again be in Africa on our Memorial Day. Enclosed is a copy of my speech, which will be broadcast from the speaker's stand at 2 p.m. May 30. The Associated Press will carry news of the ceremonies, but will not quote the address. Perhaps you would like to have a copy for your files.

We who live here think Mount Baden-Powell one of our most majestic mountains when viewed from either the eastern (desert) or western (coastal) side. The north slope is timbered with yellow pine nearly to the summit. Hoping the chief will return in his usual good health and high spirits, and that all in Old England will have a pleasant summer. I am yours sincerely. F.R. Burnham

Burnham then wrote to Baden-Powell in South Africa:

May 13, 1931
My dear General,

I am writing this note with the expectation that it will come before your eye somewhere on the high veld of Africa, the old stomping ground of our youth. One of the Scout officials has a splendid photograph of Mount Baden-Powell, which he is carrying with him to England. All of us here would have been so delighted to have had you with us May 30th, when the mountain is dedicated, yet we would not wish to rob Africa of your visit.

Perhaps at some future time you will come out and join us and we will make the ascent of the mountain a great event for Region Twelve. I think it would be quite in order for the chief to ascend the mountain on wings of steel instead of his own shoe leather, because we would not wish to put a strain upon even such a sturdy heart as yours.

This now is written in advance of the actual ceremony, the synopsis of which will doubtless reach you by wire, followed by personal letters. I am enclosing a copy of my speech, together with the orders for the day. Wishing you and Lady Baden-Powell a successful tour and a joyous homecoming, Yours sincerely, F.R.B.

Four months later—two months behind schedule—Baden-Powell returned to London.

September 16, 1931
The Boy Scouts Association
25, Buckingham Palace Road, London,
My dear Burnham:

I have only today received on my return from Australia and South Africa the details of the great honour done to me in America in the dedication of the mountain to bear my name. I feel overwhelmed by it and more specially by your beautiful address with its far too flattering account of me. It makes me feel that I ought to buck up and really try to deserve the high status you have accorded to me. More specially I feel this because I realize that it is not the empty phrase of a tactful orator, but the opinion of one who knows me personally—and for this I value it all the more and feel the more deeply grateful to you for your very generous and kindly appreciation. Are we never to see you here? Do come again, and soon. Yours sincerely, Baden-Powell.

• • •

LOS ANGELES • 1933

EARLY IN 1933, Burnham became the object of a series of articles in *Boys Life* magazine. The author and editor, James E. West, had been trying for five years to get Fred to write articles for *Boys Life*.

In September, *Boys Life* published "Adventure of the Blue Gum," an article describing how Fred blew up the Boer railway lines near Pretoria. Author West concluded that Burnham's adventures were as fabulous as Daniel Boone, Kit Carson and Jim Bridger. The next month, James West and Peter O. Lamb coauthored "An Old California Ruse," for *Boys Life*, describing Burnham's adventures in Globe, Arizona, during the Apache raid on Cibicue of August 30, 1881.

In 1934, Fred did write an article on his scouting days in the Pinal mountains south of Globe, Arizona. Without boasting, it rehashed in greater detail his activities during the Cibicue uprising.

January 20, 1933
My dear General:

The beautiful Christmas card, Safari in Kenya, makes me so restless that I dare not hang it in the office. I am forwarding it to Troop Twelve, Pasadena Scouts. The scoutmaster is a nephew of mine. His father once served under your command in Rhodesia. I recently had a card from General Aylmer Hunter-Weston from Mombassa as he was going into Kenya.

The Scout movement is still going strong, although there is the ever-present question among the leaders as to who will head the world movement when you pass on. We have the feeling that there are many able generals in your vast organization, but you are the only one who can conquer the world. So here is hoping that you and your good lady will be spared for years to come. Yours most sincerely, F.R.B.

Less than two weeks later, Burnham once again took pen in hand.

February 2, 1933
My dear General:

The summit of your great monument—Mount Baden-Powell—is ten feet taller than it was before the great snowfall of the last few days. This will insure a fine growth of forest trees that have been suffering from three dry years. I enclose a clipping that will bring to your mind the giant peaks of India. Yours sincerely. F.R.B..

A year after that, *Collier's* magazine discovered the old frontiersman. Author W.B. Courtney, in describing Fred as a peer of Davy Crockett, Daniel Boone and Kit Carson, wrote, "The parched sands of Arizona served as his classroom and his teachers were the

Burnham: King of Scouts

best in their profession: the alert and crafty Apaches. At seventy-five, he has the complexion of seven, the glow of seventeen, and the vigor of twenty-seven. His eyes are of an amazing cobalt blue and they fasten upon you and never leave you nor miss a shadow of your expression. They make you feel terribly naked. You'd have to be a consummate actor to lie to this man."

Far more did Fred treasure the regard of friends and peers. Doctor Ira Moore of Skagway wrote in the *Alaska Weekly* that Fred was one of the most loved and distinguished members of the Alaska Brotherhood.

Fritz Duquesne, the Boer scout who had immigrated to America, wrote on the back of a snapshot of himself: "To my friendly enemy: the greatest scout in the world, whose eyes were the vision of an empire. I craved the honor of killing him, but failing that I extend my heartiest admiration."

Walter Howard, the down-and-outer who had volunteered to cross the Shangani to see if there were any survivors from Wilson's Last Stand, wrote of their days on patrol:

I attached myself to Johann Colenbrander. When he noticed this and asked why, I replied that I wanted to learn scouting. He said, "You watch Burnham; he's forgotten more than I shall ever know."

From Willie Posselt on his farm in Rhodesia:

Do you remember when we entered Bulawayo? Bullets, assegais passed your body within a fraction of an inch. The teeth, claws, horns of dangerous wild animals were powerless to harm you. There is one who is of the same stamp as you, who has the same pluck, the same courage, who faced all the hardships and danger, who traveled with you in the wilds of South Africa. That is your wife, Blanche Burnham. Of her I can say a most wonderful, marvelous lady. May the feet of time linger by you, and may death pass your house forgetful.

Also treasured was this note scribbled on the back of a sepia picture by a poet-prospector who helped Fred in the search for manganese during the Great War. Old H.O. Egbert made his home in the Chuckawalla Desert near Indio, California:

Yes, we go into the night as fighters go; we are hard as cats to kill, and our hearts are reckless still, for we've danced with death a dozen times.

• • •

LOS ANGELES • 1934
AFTER FRED resigned from the State Parks Commission, his political schedule slowed, but his other schedules remained active. He took an active role in the California Club, where the all-powerful of Los Angeles met to break bread. In due time he was inducted into the Sunset Club, the inner-sanctum of eighty-five leaders of the California Club. The goals of the Sunset Club centered on choosing who would be the next mayor of Los Angeles and deciding which two names to submit to the voters as the next governor of California.

In the summer of 1934, Fred was elected to the board of trustees of the Southwest Museum. Although it was not a large museum, the institution had distinguished itself by concentrating its attention on the American Indian and on the prehistoric lore of the Southwest.

One of its archaeologists, M.B. Harrington, explored a cave near Las Vegas, Nevada, and upset much of what science knew of the history of man in America. He found human remains and tools lying under a layer of manure from the giant sloth, hitherto believed extinct for centuries before man arrived on this hemisphere.

Pax Hill, Bentley, Hampshire
2 September 1936

Congratulations on your well deserved honor at the hands of the Boy Scouts Association of America. May you live long to wear the Silver Buffalo [Scouting's highest award] and continue to give this example of a true Scout to the oncoming generation. Baden-Powell.

In 1938, Fred was elected president of the Southwest Museum,

Fred and Rod Burnham

succeeding Harvey Mudd, chairman of Cypress Mines Corp. Mudd had endowed the Pomona Colleges, regarded as the Princeton of the West. Fred's new position gained him entree to the inner circle of the academia. The *ex officio* trustees of the Southwest Museum included the president the University of Southern California, the president of Occidental College in Eagle Rock, the president of the Pomona Colleges, and the director of the Huntington Library and Art Gallery in San Marino. The Huntington Library, endowed by railroad magnate Henry E. Huntington, was America's premier repository of *incunabula*—Gutenberg Bibles—as well as the paintings Pinkie and Blue Boy, and hundreds of Thomas Gainsborough originals. For a Minnesota man of log-cabin beginnings who had finished but one year of school, Fred wore the five stars of success. His military rank and decorations attested to his character and bravery. Dominguez Mesa brought him wealth. Sales of *Scouting* brought literary recognition. Membership in the California Club endowed him with social standing. As president of the Southwest Museum, the blessings of academia were now his to savor. All of these gave him the clout he needed to put across his biggest conservation scheme ever.

71

The Bighorns of Arizona

Prescott • 1937

FRED, ROD and John Blick formed a joint venture to buy the Iron King Mine east of Prescott. John had planned to return to Ethiopia, but the Italians in a fit of Fascist imperialism invaded the northeast African country. Hostilities marked an end to Blick's archeological digs in search for the Missing Link. As for Fred, he had known about Iron King from his early days in the territory. In the 1880s, the gold had played out and the mine had laid abandoned waiting for the railroad to arrive. Later the property was operated as a silver and zinc producer. After buying the Iron King, Fred built a mill to concentrate the ore for a copper smelter.

His frequent business trips to Prescott rekindled his interest in Arizona, and he soon became acquainted with George F. Miller of Phoenix, the head of the Theodore Roosevelt Council of the Boy Scouts of America. In time, the Roosevelt Boy Scouts bestowed on Burnham the title Honorary Chief Scout of Arizona.

On one of Burnham's business trips to Arizona, he was accosted by a scruffy desert rat. This sage lizard had seen the chauffeured Overland car with California plates and he made his pitch to Fred. For five hundred dollars in cash, he'd guide Fred into the mountains northeast of Yuma where the distinguished mister from California could shoot a trophy-grade, three hundred-pound bighorn sheep. Fred was aghast. The desert bighorn: majestic master of its harsh mountains, a rare and beautiful animal. In the last forty years, he hadn't given a thought to the desert bighorn. Yet he knew that wild sheep had existed, until the arrival of the white man.

In the 1870s, Fred had seen the bighorns. The pioneers had killed them for food, and Fred recalled seeing ram horns stacked behind stage stations. The banks of the Gila and Colorado Rivers were marked with sheep tracks. While drinking and nibbling grass, the animals were easy prey to the repeating rifle.

The desert bighorn had become as scarce as flamingos in Alaska. To think that wealthy men would pay big money for the privilege of shooting a rare specimen was too much for Fred. After ordering the sage rat to vamoose, he began planning his campaign.

The details of the bighorn slowly began to come back. Fred decided the best way to save the bighorn in Arizona was to create a federal wildlife reserve that forbade all hunting. Fred dimly recalled that the U.S. Biological Survey—later to be the U.S. Fish and Wildlife Service—and the National Park Service had once proposed an immense area of four million acres southwest of Phoenix. This area ran all the way to the Colorado River and south to the Mexican border, making it the largest preserve in the forty-seven states and territory. No action had been taken. Opposition from the livestock owners and mining interests had proved to be unbeatable and the plan died.

By 1937 the very idea of a wildlife preserve was met with skepticism, followed by hostility from hunters—compounded by widespread indifference on the part of the public. The citizens doubted the very existence of the desert bighorn. Honest and well-meaning people wrote derisive letters to the papers. Everyone knew the bighorn's habitat was in the snowy peaks of Montana's Rocky Mountains. The public was opposed to the creation of a refuge on the ground that it was absurd to even think that wild sheep could exist in that dry and barren desert land.

Earlier that year, the National Park Service made an end-run around the question by establishing the Organ Pipe Cactus National Monument. It embraced the site of Fred's old Christmas Gift Mine. That action had locked away part of the land, but it was flat, the kind of land that bighorns shunned.

It proved to be difficult—indeed, almost impossible—to gather information on the horned desert recluses. The surviving sheep had taken refuge in lonely mountains, establishing themselves in the most inhospitable recesses. To gather information, Burnham called on George Miller to enlist the services of the Roosevelt Boy Scouts. The lads scoured attics, mountain cabins and library shelves for evidence of the desert bighorn. In history books they learned Francisco de Coronado had seen the bighorn on his expedition 1540 in search of the Seven Cities of Cibola.

The Scouts produced evidence that Kit Carson had seen the bighorn in 1846 in the Painted Rock Mountains east of Gila Bend. The Scouts even confirmed Burnham's recollection that hunters had shot desert bighorns to provide the mining camps and stage stations with meat. They learned that domestic cattle and sheep drove the bighorn into evermore remote areas.

Biologists revealed that desert bighorn could endure hundred degree heat and go for eight days without water. They said the sheep needed escape terrain, high places where they could feel secure in the ability to escape from an any threat. They coveted sheer crags where they could use their sure-footedness to advantage. Once they found a home, the bighorn developed an amazing loyalty to it. They would stay and die rather than be pushed out.

Major Burnham, using his influence as a museum president, urged the federal authorities to take a census of the bighorn population. The census suggested there were about five hundred of the animals in the mountain retreats of southwest Arizona.

If there was one thing that Fred Burnham had learned during eight decades of life, it was this: Nothing in the world—specially if it is intellectual or cerebral—will capture the attention of the public until someone translates it into a gut issue. It takes an emotional act to make things achieve public acceptance. No matter if the census counted a million bighorns, the people were not going to believe it until politicians sanctioned the census and the newspapers made the findings a matter of public record. That meant Fred had to take the bull by the horns and produce prime bighorn sheep for the news cameras.

To accomplish that task, Burnham rode into the Panamint Mountains where he had shot game as a youth. The Panamints were the southern tip of the Shoshone Nation—one of the eight linguistic tribes in America. There, near the remains of the old Cerro Gordo silver mine, Fred found a grandson of Shacknasty George who had taught him to hunt wild game.

On his return to Phoenix, Fred invited the Boy Scouts, government officials, politicians and news reporters and photographers to meet with him on Wednesday morning on the west side of Castle Dome Peak. It was a rugged mountain that rose to an elevation of nearly four thousand feet. At the appointed hour, everyone had gathered on a little-used trail that ran along the base of Castle Dome Peak. A cowboy breakfast of coffee, eggs and buckwheat cakes was served from a chuckwagon brought there for the occasion. As the guests partook, alert people saw that Castle Dome Mountain was stepped with ledges that rose almost vertically from the sandy desert floor.

At first nothing happened. The photographers and newsmen began to display skepticism when suddenly a hubbub of hideous

547

sounds began to echo off the walls of Castle Dome Peak. It sounded for all the world like a fruit canning plant being trampled by stampeding elephants. The city dwellers looked at one another, mouths agape. Could this be some kind of hoax?

Then, from around the bend, came a woodcutter's cart with two Mexicans standing in the back, rifles at the ready. Roped to the rear of the cart was a motley collection of dented gasoline cans and empty grease drums. When dragged over the rocky trail, the cans made a terrific din.

"What's all this?" demanded a photographer from a Phoenix newspaper.

"Look up at the ledge," Burnham replied, pointing up at the rock wall.

Half a dozen desert bighorn sheep were peering over the ledge, curious as cats as to what was causing all that racket. The sheep had dark, mahogany fur and their horns were a golden color, provoking one learned biologist to declare these bighorns were of a different subspecies than those in the Rocky Mountains.

"Would you like to have a couple of trophies?" Burnham asked the newsmen.

"Sure," replied one of the photographers.

"Not unless you are willing to pay a fine for killing sheep out of season," a stern-faced game warden warned. Armed with telephoto lenses usually reserved for World Series baseball games, the photographers began snapping pictures as the curious sheep peered over the ledge.

A game warden pulled Burnham aside, demanding to know how he had managed to get those sheep to peek over the edges of their ledges and look at the woodcutter's cart.

"These bighorns don't know the crack of a modern rifle," Fred replied. "Like most animals, they have a natural curiosity. The Shoshones had used this trick to lure the bighorns so they could shoot camp meat. With a little cash offering on my part, the son of a Shoshone friend showed me how it is done."

The warden eyed him balefully.

"When I first came out here to try it, the trick didn't work," Burnham continued. "The sheep scampered off at the first sound. I tried it a second time and the sheep ran away again. After several days, the sheep decided the sounds didn't pose a danger. Then their curiosity got the best of them. That's when I knew my experiment was a success."

The next day, the newspapers of Arizona published photos of the rare and beautiful desert bighorn sheep. With their presence firmly established in the public mind, Burnham urged George Miller to make the bighorn sheep the Roosevelt Council's mascot emblem. Fred knew he had to overcome powerful skepticism from Robert Jones, the newly elected governor of Arizona. Jones dismissed Castle Dome as a billy goat pasture and asked derisively if the bighorns ate only the soft rocks.

Despite opposition from the governor-elect, Burnham and company kept up an unrelenting barrage of publicity. When the noise level dulled, Fred called on the lusty Roosevelt Boy Scouts to generate a new explosion of sound in favor of the rare mountain sheep.

They rallied scouts across the state and nation to write to Congress. That coalition swung the tide of battle. On January 25, 1939, President Franklin D. Roosevelt signed a proclamation that established two desert areas—one of a million and another of half a million acres—to be set aside for the preservation of wildlife, principally the desert bighorn. The two preserves were called the Kofa Wildlife Refuge and the Cabeza Prieta Wildlife Refuge.

Tucked away in the hostile mountains fifty miles northeast of Yuma was the abandoned Kofa Gold Mine—Kofa stood for King of Arizona. It was regarded as one of Arizona's all-time gold-mining greats. Everyone agreed the bighorn refuge should be called Kofa.

Few mountains in Arizona compared with those northeast of Yuma for ruggedness, odd freaks of nature and sheer inaccessibility. The Biological Survey picked a site southeast of Quartzite. To Burnham, the place looked like a bizarre caricature of the kopjes of Rhodesia, on a scale magnified by twenty. These peaks weren't just sharp and vertical. They were jagged, angled like Indian arrowheads tilted at grotesque angles. There were enormous globular boulders, three hundred feet tall, perched atop weathered, mesas. The combination of shapes and angles defied human description. It was just the sort of place a bighorn sheep would seek for escape terrain.

Visitors to the bleak desert crossroads at Quartzite are told this conglomeration of rocks is the Kofa National Wildlife Refuge. Callers are free to make a dry camp along one of the three gravel roads that penetrate the Kofa Mountains and the Castle Dome Mountains. North and south, the Kofa Refuge extends forty miles. It ranges thirty miles east and west. If it is big, it is also remote, and well protected. To the west, enclosing the craggy Chocolate Mountains, is the U.S. Army's Yuma Proving Grounds. This military reserve protects the south and east sides of the Kofa Wildlife Refuge from any predators trying to come in from California.

If Kofa seems remote, the Cabeza Prieta Wildlife Refuge is positively difficult to find, to say nothing of getting to. Situated north of a desolate portion of the U.S.-Mexico border, Cabeza Prieta extends sixty miles east and west, crossing Yuma and Pima Counties; it is roughly thirty miles from northern to southern borders. No road of any kind comes within five miles of the refuge. Old timers call it the *despoblado* —the unpopulated wilderness. It is as diverse a piece of real estate as you will find anywhere.

Sand dunes abut lava flows. Rare plants and curious cacti hide in steep canyons. Smooth valleys and parched lake beds abruptly turn into sheer cliffs soaring upward for a thousand feet. The rainfall ranges from a scant three inches a year in the west to a more-lenient nine inches in the east, providing a diversity of plant and animal life. In addition to the mahogany bighorns, these refuges also furnish a stable environment for many other mammals, reptiles, birds and plants that thrive in the desert.

On April 1, 1939, Fred Burnham and George Miller headed a delegation of lads from the Roosevelt Council of Boy Scouts as Roscoe G. Willson of the U.S. Geological Survey delivered a dedication address. Fred was seventy-eight, but he stood ramrod stiff in the spring sun while watching his dream come true. Not one percent of the population in Arizona had ever seen a desert bighorn, but it was important that these sheep be kept alive. Later that year in recognition of his achievement, Fred Burnham was elected to an unprecedented second term as president of the Southwest Museum.

Ritornello • An Interlude
KENYA • 1938

AFTER SERVING thirty years as Chief Scout, Baden-Powell retired from Scouting and moved to Nyere, north of Nairobi. He named his new home Pax Two, with a Swahili twist, Paxtu. Stephe would enjoy only three years in retirement. His neighbor was Sam Steele, formerly of the Royal Canadian Mounted Police. He had been the head of the Mounties in the Yukon during the Klondike Gold Rush.

72

Stabbed in the Back

Pasadena • 1937

THE TITLE OF THE book *The Making of Rhodesia* sounded like the makings for nostalgic reading. Fred couldn't place the author, Hugh Marshall Hole. Actually, Hole was a retired civil servant from Rhodesia. During the 1896 Matabele Rebellion, he had worked as secretary of the Chartered Company at Fort Salisbury, Mashona Land. Years later Hole was transferred to Bulawayo where he spent his time plundering the archives of the Chartered Company. In London, he wrote the history of Rhodesia as he saw it. Among various things, Marshall Hole said the shooting of the M'Limo was an Elaborate Hoax.

On reading that statement, Fred sent the book to his lawyer, who read it and wrote to the publisher in London, demanding on what grounds Hole had made his charges. There was no reply, so Fred took Blanche on a cruise to Panama to see Teddy's Big Ditch.

It was in December 1929 that Jack Hammond had introduced Fred to a Yale classmate, Howell Wright, now a Cleveland lawyer. On his death, Wright willed to the Sterling Memorial Library at Yale a large collection of papers, journals and photos of events in South Africa and Rhodesia. Wright's collection included material on Cecil Rhodes, Doctor L.S. Jameson, Oom Paul Kruger, Jannie Smuts, Louis "Boot" Botha, Barney Barnardo, Jack Hammond and Frederick R. Burnham. Fred agreed that when he died he would leave his papers to the Howell Wright Collection as well.

When Fred and Blanche returned from Panama, they spent the summer at Hockett Meadows. The trip through the giant sequoias brought back memories of more active years. For three months they lived under canvas, fishing for trout and spending the evenings yarning around the campfire. For three decades, Fred had played

551

host to his city friends at Hockett Meadows, men like Art Bent who was now helping to build the Hoover Dam, Teddy Roosevelt Jr., Jack Hammond, western author Charlie Lummis, banker Bill Crocker, Pebble Beach Golf Course developer Sam Morse, the Torrey Everetts and the railroad Harrimans—the list seemed endless.

Summer drew to a close. The days became short and there was a sharp chill in the night air. Squirrels worked overtime and the coyotes registered their displeasure at the end of the hunting season. A flurry of snow sent the campers packing for the trip to the home ranch at La Cuesta. The cattle were herded out and the cooee of the cowmen echoed in the valleys. It was down, down, day and night, until they arrived at Three Rivers.

In the mail Fred found a letter from the British publisher of *The Making of Rhodesia*. It quoted historian Hugh Marshall Hole's source of the accusation that the assassination of the M'Limo was an Elaborate Hoax. Fred recognized the wording.

The native commissioner of Mangwe District, Bonnar W. Armstrong, heard there was a certain cave near Banko's Kraal, close to the Shashi River and within about thirty miles of the Matopo Hills where the Makalaka used to offer up their sacrifices to the ancestral spirit known as the M'Limo.

Hugh Marshall Hole had penned a word-for-word plagiarism of CNC Herb Taylor's secret report to the High Commissioner. The original falsification came from Herb, who had mistaken the Shashi River in Bechuana Land for the Shashani River in Rhodesia.

Fred shook his head with sadness. What was it with these Englishmen? During the 1896 Rebellion, Marshall Hole had been a clerk in Salisbury, three hundred miles from the action. What did he know about the M'Limo?

"You could file a defamation suit," lawyer Wright said. "If Hole did plagiarize a false government document, we might make it hot for the old boy."

"How can we establish the fact the document exists if it's still secret and we cannot gain access to it?" Fred asked.

"If so, he may have you by the short hairs."

Fred decided the matter wasn't worth pursuing. All the pioneers including Jack Hammond were now dead. What matter the opinion of a jiggle-billy crying sour grapes? What counted was rescuing the bighorn sheep, preserving the beaches, protecting the redwoods.

"Let it stand," Fred said. "Hugh Hole wouldn't know Queen Victoria's crown jewels from a baboon's red arse."

● ● ●

BURNHAM STILL HADN'T the faintest notion how dreadfully the record was being altered. Hole, acting on a tip, had written to Jack Carruthers in Bulawayo. The letter asked the former sergeant of scouts if it was true that Burnham had deserted his comrades at Wilson's Last Stand. A month later, Carruthers produced a letter from John Coghlan.

Coghlan said a man had related that Aubrey Woolls-Sampson told him that Trooper George Gooding gave a dying deathbed confession saying that he, Burnham and Ingram had deserted Wilson's Patrol. At best, the information came third hand. Howell Wright learned of the Coghlan letter and wrote to him in Bulawayo. By return mail Wright received a letter from Major Walter Howard, who was now the secretary of the 1893 Pioneer Column Society.

Abercorn Street, Bulawayo
17th January 1938
With regard to the confession you allude to, I very much doubt if what you have heard is a correct version. The people you mention, John Coghlan and Jack Carruthers, can only have retold something that by repetition was much garbled by the time it came to their notice. I would strongly advise you to be very careful of any information you get from Carruthers.

We traveled together to England in 1901 for the coronation of King Edward VII and he showed me an account of the Last Stand of Wilson, which had taken place seven years before. I handed it back after perusal and advised him to destroy it. I told him that of the many accounts I had read of that affair, his was the most inaccurate of the lot. I suggested that we show it to another of our companions who was also on the Shangani Patrol. He did not do it. Carruthers got his information from an old native who claimed that he took part in the affair.

On our return, I was surprised to find out after we left Kimberley that he had taken steps to get it published, but that was not done. If the article had appeared, I should have pointed out how full of errors it was. Possibly he sent you the same account, which is totally incorrect and conveys an entirely wrong impression. Walter Howard, Secretary, 1893 Society.

Wright showed the note to Fred who shrugged.

"I can tell you all about Jack Carruthers," Burnham said. "He wasn't on the Shangani Patrol at all. Later, he pegged Zimbabwe as his farm rights. But Rhodes gave Zimbabwe and Dhlo-Dhlo to Pete Ingram and me."

553

Major Walter Howard's letter to Wright was sent to the Yale Archives where, on Burnham's death, it was sealed for fifty years, until AD 2000. But Hugh Marshall Hole's malicious correspondence ended up on public display in the National Archives at Salisbury, where it became the seed of false revisionist history in Rhodesia.

Counterpoise • Equilibrium

LOS ANGELES • 1938

LATE IN THE 1930s, Rod Burnham and his wife, Isabella Harrah, had a parting of the ways. They were divorced and though each remarried, they remained close friends. Brick Elliott introduced Rod to a striking grand dame named Gayle O'Cranny. A year after they were married, Gayle produced twins: Rick and BeGayle.

Soon after that, while Fred was driving his Packard sedan up to his Hollywood Land mansion, two boys came freewheeling down the switchbacks, their bicycles out of control. Fred swerved to miss them, bounced over the stone guardrail, tumbled down the hill and landed upside down in the yard of David E. Day, a vice president of Richfield Oil.

Though he suffered a fractured neck, he was up and about a month later. But the fates were catching up. While he was still on the mend, Blanche suffered a stroke. She was bedridden and wholly dependent on him. A month later a second stroke extinguished her life. Fred was paralyzed with grief. With tears in his eyes, he wrote a tribute to his mate of fifty-five years.

In boyhood it was my great good fortune to meet a girl who truly believed in me, and that I would carry out the wild schemes and plans which I had confided to her. As fantastic as those dreams were, nearly every one came true. The vision of all she would be called upon to endure amid appalling circumstances was mercifully hidden from her young eyes.

Nor could she foresee how tragedy and sorrow would one day test her soul as by fire. Yet throughout all the hard experiences of our years together, no resentment of destiny ever showed in her manner or crossed her lips. A gentle heart, a pleasant voice, a loyal nature with a wide understanding of life as it is lived; she has indeed met every situation with supreme courage. She was a clear fountain of inspiration to me and to all who knew her.

73

The Last Outspan

LOS ANGELES • 1940

IN THE SUMMER of 1940, Burnham and Baden-Powell exchanged their last letters in an on and off again correspondence that began in South Africa in June 1900. These letters were a brief exchange between two old friends of forty-five years..
Paxtu, Kenya Colony
September 22

What a wonderful old chap you are, for I suppose that as the years roll by you must have been getting older, though I cannot picture you as such. It was a gallant effort of yours to attend the Scout celebration at San Francisco and to be able to give them an address. And what an address it must have been. How I wish I could have been there to hear it. You have the art of making your talk so fully interesting and vivid, in contrast with the usual outpourings of just talk. I was highly flattered by your allusions to myself, and it was so clever of you to adapt our motto of Be Prepared to the greater crisis overhanging the United States today. Yours sincerely, Baden-Powell

While Stephe's letter was still en route, Fred wrote:
September 26
Dear Baden-Powell

Even though in the midst of a great war, I know you have not forgotten the old days in Rhodesia. The enclosed letter is a copy of one just received from Major Walter Howard. It gives the little happenings and personalities of Rhodesia in his inimitable way. I feel sure that you will have several smiles over his comments. I recently visited Canada to speak to eighty Canadian officers where I urged both Canadian and American support of the British cause in the European war. Yours, as ever, Burnham

Shortly after that, Congress increased the top income tax bracket

555

to eighty-one percent. Fred dissolved Burnham Ex and carved out Dominguez Oil Company, which was limited to the collection of royalties and the payment of dividends. At the age of seventy-nine, Fred retired from the oil business. He sold the Iron King Mine in Arizona to the Shattuck-Denn Mining Company.

On January 7, 1941, the Chief Scout, Lord Baden-Powell, died at Paxtu, Kenya, ending a friendship that dated from June 1896. Burnham proposed to the Boy Scouts of America the formation of the Ranger Scouts, which were in fact organized. For Fred's eightieth birthday anniversary on May 11, The Kid hosted The Dad to a whitewater raft ride down the Colorado River.

His third event of 1941 was the disaster called Pearl Harbor which plunged America into the blackness of World War II. Homer Lea's prediction came true. Less than a month later, news came to haunt Fred. On January 2, 1942, the Federal Bureau of Investigation arrested Fritz Duquesne and thirty-two of his accomplices as Nazi spies. In a sensational trial at Brooklyn Federal Court, Duquesne was convicted of passing to the Nazis the secrets of the Norden bombsight, drawings of the shoran bombing concept and plans for the proximity fuse. The former Boer scout was sentenced to twenty years in federal penitentiary.

Fred wrote dry-as-dust reports on his experience in desert fighting, which he forwarded to the U.S. Army for use in battling the Axis forces. An army general took time out to write a note of thanks. The reports were duly filed away. In an era of radar, cryptographic codes and four-engine bombers, there was no place for the opinions of a horse-mounted scout from the nineteenth century.

Living alone in the hilltop mansion rankled. With the greatest war in history raging around him, he felt useless. Rod sensed The Dad's problem and tried to rekindle an interest in his father's life. In a letter from Washington, where he was helping in the war effort, Rod suggested that his father take up a project he had put off for years. After Doubleday had cut *Scouting on Two Continents* to one volume, Fred had vowed to write a second book that would breach the gaps in Kenya, Mexico and the Klondike. Fred gathered paper and pencils and called on Mary Everett for help. It was like the good old days.

The years had dimmed Fred's memory, but he held opinions that were more important than mere facts. From his gazebo, he gazed at the expanse of Los Angeles. When Fred first set eyes on El Pueblo in 1872, no one had listened to a radio. Or talked on a telephone. Movies were unheard of. There was no such thing as an automobile or airplane. As he watched fighter planes take off from Santa Monica and Downey, Fred's mind strayed to Lobengula's Africa. He put down his views:

When World War I turned us all into military robots, the basic facts of life which we had painfully learned from the American Indians and from our own pioneers apparently were discarded. In the 1920s, an army of scientists swarmed over Africa, examining that Dark Continent to bring light. They brought their spectroscopes, stethoscopes and other scopes, backed by awesome -ologies. Then they were gone, leaving behind the roar of the lion and the throb of the drum.

The consensus of European opinion was that Africa should be developed under white leadership, and only then would the black race change from a vast reservoir of a hundred million savages who produce nothing into a mass of intelligent people teeming with power. Then would that great land that is Africa be of value to all the nations and, above all, to the Africans themselves. But an African chief once told me, "When the white man first comes, his powder is dry and he cannot be resisted. Soon that powder becomes damp."

One day in my compound in Nairobi, I sat in the shade of a fig-conquered cedar tree. I began to wonder whether the whites were to be like the cedar tree, to be eventually strangled for invading the African jungle. At first it was slavery and later it was gold—pure and yellow—that lured the other nations of the world to try to wrest Africa's riches from the blacks.

Came the sailors and soldiers of more modern civilizations, and finally Western Europe took a hand in the ageless attempt to conquer the country. Came the Portuguese, the Spanish, the Dutch, fighting first with steel and mail. Later they landed big ships on the shores, fought with guns, built great forts that stand to this day. But the terrible climate of heat and damp disintegrated even the iron rings that held the slaves, leaving only a dark stain on the pages of history.

When I first arrived in Africa, I was imbued with the belief that the civilization of the white man could conquer the globe and that no race could stand against him, that his religion, his laws and customs would eventually supplant and dominate everything else. With my abundant physical energy and strength, I took part in this glorious conquest. Now after many years of the most strenuous experience, I must admit that all the evidence is directly contrary to my original convictions.

I doubt whether our religion, our customs, our laws are beneficial to the black races of Africa, and whether we can ever hold any part of their vast tropics, save by the sword. Africa is one land that the man with blue eyes will never completely possess. He may hold it by the sword for a time, if its riches compensate for the sacrifice of his strongest sons.

For weeks, Fred poured forth his convictions. The pile of yellow paper began to bulk high. Mary Everett wasn't keeping up with the work load. She misplaced pages. She recognized her shortcomings and finally asked to be relieved.

Fred called Brick Elliott, who suggested a competent secretary. Ilo Ferree turned her talents to typing Fred's manuscript. But without Mary to elicit ideas, the fun went out of it. Fred dug out news clippings, magazine articles, old speeches. These he edited for Ilo to type up, which she did. The finished manuscript was a hodgepodge.

New York book publishers, facing a wartime paper shortage, declined to publish. Burnham had it printed privately. The manuscript was set in type and a thousand folios were run off in a print shop. Half of these were bound under the title *Taking Chances*. Few of these books ever found their way into the stacks of a library. None was sold. Fred gave copies to friends. The rest were put into storage where they were forgotten.

On May 11, 1946, there was a gathering of the clan at Burnham Mansion to celebrate Fred's eighty-fifth birthday anniversary. Rod and Gayle were there with Rick and BeGayle. The twins were now in their second year of school, still only dimly aware their grandfather was a hero from another era. The reunion was a happy event with holiday cheer, speeches and singing. Before Rod and Gayle left that day, Fred handed Gayle a letter to hold for his granddaughter until she was old enough to understand. He had written the document three years earlier. He had changed some facts to coincide with the vogue of twentieth century values.

Los Angeles, April 1, 1943
To Blanche Gayle Burnham
Dear BeGayle,

Fifty years ago, the first Matabele War had just ended in Africa, and your Aunt Nada was born. We lived in a native hut with a thatched roof and a hard dirt-floor made of pounded earth, dung and blood. Like all native huts, it swarmed with rats. A gift from the stork was expected so we were rushing a new wood-and-brick house to completion. The house consisted of three small rooms, two of them floored with wood salvaged from whisky cases. Through the diligence of Andrew Main, a fine carpenter and bricklayer, our home was finished on time. Thus your aunt was ushered into the world in a real house instead of a rats' nest.

A few days before we were to move into our new home, Doctor Jameson called on me to carry dispatches beyond the great Belingwe Mountains. It had seemed this journey could be made before we moved, but I was delayed and could not be present when your Grandmother made the change from native hut to our wonderful home. I was further delayed. When your Grandmother's time came, there were only she, your Father and Andrew Main, our bachelor friend. The first thing was to put up a bed. Among our possessions were four boxes of dynamite, used as legs to support the bed. Your Father built a fire to heat water. Andrew Main rode off for a doctor, only to return with news that no doctor was available.

Those days were not even horse-and-buggy days; they were ox-wagon days in a remote and hostile country. When the critical hour drew near, Main realized that he and your Father—then a lad of seven—must bring a new being into the world. Main had a fine record for courage in the war, but this was different. Suffering through it all, your Grandmother told me afterwards that she felt sorry for him as he grew whiter each hour, sometimes walking outside and exclaiming softly "My God. My God."

After Nada's safe arrival, Andrew and Roderick had time to draw deep, thankful breaths. Your Aunt, like your Father, was a husky and active child, fair haired and blue eyed. She was named for Nada the Lily, a novel by Rider Haggard. The most famous of his books, **King Solomon's Mines** and **Allan Quatermain**, were read by millions of persons around the world.

Two years later, when the Matabele Rebellion broke out, we were living in an old Hussar camp about two miles east of Bulawayo: the Matabele place of killing. We had sold the brick house and built a temporary two-room shack of packing cases, canvas and thatch, preparatory to building a real house. We now had ten acres and a water well. Our nearest neighbors were the Cummingses, a pioneer family who operated a dairy farm east of our place. Mr. Cummings had given Nada three newly hatched ostrich chicks. When everyone was moved into town for protection from the rebels, Nada took her chicks along. We settled into a three-room shack on the edge of town and Mrs. Cummings brought a coop of her precious chickens. Her girls led a pet goat, a sheep and three snow-white ducks.

Your Great Uncles, Homer, John and Judd, when not on guard duty or fighting, pastured their horses nearby and ate at an improvised table that Mrs. Cummings supplied with whatever food she could obtain. The food came by ox wagons, each load taking two months for the five-hundred-mile-long trek from railhead. There broke out a terrible disease called rinderpest. Within three weeks, eight thousand oxen died. The Matabele siege grew more terrible. Each night all the pet animals were cooped, while the women and children were compelled to sleep in the market building in the center of town.

One by one all the pets were eaten, except Nada's three ostriches. They had now grown to be large birds, so tall they had to duck their heads to enter the shack where they were cooped at night. Came the day when they were to be issued as rations, and the ostriches were to be seen no more. Mrs. Cummings suggested to an anxious Nada that the savages might have stolen them by night. Nada never knew that her share of soup was made of her much beloved pets.

Those were terrible days. The coarse meal and rotten meat on which we had to live did not keep some of the children from dying, your Aunt Nada among them. She was two years old. She rests under a slab of sandstone brought from the Mountain of the Chiefs. The cemetery was a bare, dry, bullet-shot piece of ground. It was the dream of your Grandmother and me to go back one day to Bulawayo and bring Nada's dust to America and lay it with her ancestors.

The years rolled by. As the Roaring Twenties drew to a close, we stood one day by Nada's grave and talked things over with your Father. Flowers and trees were now growing luxuriantly, and all around were the graves of the Old Pioneers. They all knew her. So we decided that Nada should belong to Africa forever!

With all my love,
Your Grandfather,
Frederick Russell Burnham

• • •

SHORTLY AFTER the birthday party, Ilo suggested—and Fred agreed—that with his eyesight failing, it wasn't a good idea to be living at the edge of a hillside. Fred sold the Hollywood Land mansion and moved to Santa Barbara where he built a home on a gentle knoll overlooking the Pacific Ocean. There he entered into a marriage of convenience with Ilo Ferree—who served primarily as a live-in nurse.

The months passed by. Each day there was only the whisper of the wind and the rustle of the leaves until the sun quenched its flames in the Pacific. There was no one to remember, no one to care, nothing left. Even the memories had faded. Had all these adventures really happened? Was it just a dream? Was all of that another lifetime? Reality began to blur.

On a late summer day, fog descended on the Santa Barbara coast. Fred complained of a chill and went to bed early. During the night, he suffered a stroke and died in his sleep.

It was Monday, September 1, 1947. Death came eighty-six years, three months and twenty days after his birth in Tivoli, Minnesota, on May 11, 1861. He had lived from the time of Abraham Lincoln to Harry Truman, from the musket to the A-bomb, from the Civil War through World War II.

The next day newspapers in Los Angeles, London, Cape Town and Bulawayo published obituary notices for an uncomprehending public. Rod, Gayle, Rick, BeGayle and the widow, Ilo, carried the ashes in a bronze urn to the family cemetery plot at Three Rivers near the La Cuesta Ranch. At a private service, Roderick — acting on behalf of siblings Nada and Bruce — installed a bronze plaque, planted a tree and quoted from the final chapter of *Taking Chances*, The Dad's last published words.

Roaming memories are timeless. They are swifter than light and deeper than the sea, more fragile than gossamer. Expecting them to end is like lying beside a fragrant ironwood campfire, waiting for the last radiant coal to die before closing the eyes to slumber. When the light of dawn casts its shadows, the fire is still warm and glowing, sending almost invisible wreaths of incense-laden smoke to the paling stars. The time to outspan has arrived.

The Kid's Memorial to The Dad

Epilogue

Mount Burnham

LOS ANGELES • MAY 1952

THEY DIDN'T forget you, Fred. Five years after the last outspan, the people of California commemorated your memory. It happened on Saturday, May 10, only a day before you would have been ninety-one years old. A group of business and government leaders traveled to the San Gabriel Mountains north of Los Angeles, just as you had done twenty-one years earlier to dedicate Mount Baden-Powell. They gathered on the pine-clad slopes of a nine thousand-foot peak situated between Mount Throop and Mount Baden-Powell. You recall old Amos Throop? He founded Caltech.

The purpose of the gathering was to honor you by dedicating a third peak as Mount Burnham. The ceremony was solemn and inspiring. Time had healed the pain of your passing and the day's outing afforded an opportunity to recall your achievements. The members of the sponsoring committee were friends and admirers:

• Mary Everett, your coworker in writing *Scouting on Two Continents* and the person who came up with the idea of naming the peak in your honor.

• Roderick Burnham, your loving and devoted son.

• Bill Rosecrans, your neighbor and friend from the Rosecrans Oil Field north of Dominguez Field.

• Dr. Frederick Hodge of the Southwest Museum, who venerated you for your conservation activities and contributions as president of the museum.

• Dr. Robert Millikan, the Nobel Laureate president of Caltech, who said *Scouting* was the Bible of the Boy Scouts.

- Governor Earl Warren, who was about to become Chief Justice of the United States.

Today these three peaks in the San Gabriel Mountains are known as the Baden-Powell Triangle. Each spring Boy Scouts make a pilgrimage to these pinnacles to honor the men who lent their names to these mountains. All of them know Baden-Powell as the Chief Scout. A few recall Amos Throop as the founder of the school that led America into space. Hopefully, this report will help others to remember the third member of the Baden-Powell Triangle, Fred Burnham: the American who inspired Lord Baden-Powell to found the Boy Scout movement.

The Baden-Powell Triangle

Lodgepole Pine Picnic Area

Mount Burnham 8997 Feet

Paradise Springs

Big Pines

Crystal Lake

Mount Baden-Powell 9,399 Feet

Throop Peak 9,138 Feet

San Gabriel River

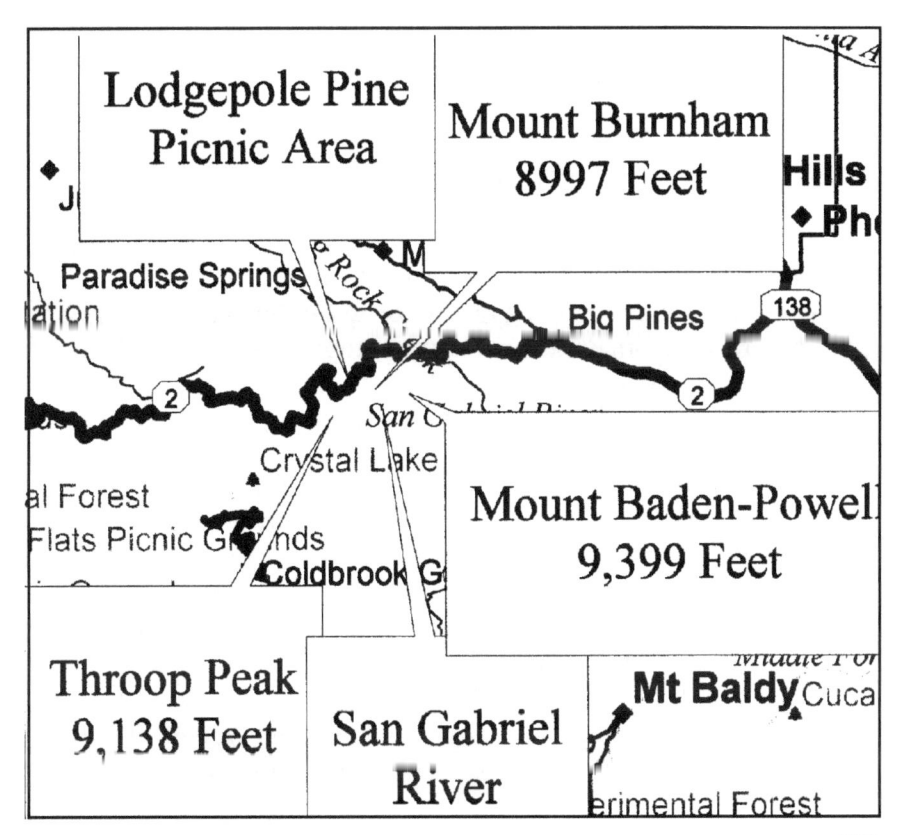

Mt Baldy

Epilogue 2

Cecil B. De Mille

HOLLYWOOD • 1958

PRODUCER Cecil B. De Mille selected David Niven for the title role of his next movie extravaganza: *Baden-Powell of the Boy Scouts*. There was a flurry of planning, followed by story consultations and letters to and from Boy Scout Association headquarters in London.

It was discovered that Olave Lady Baden-Powell had combed through her husband's personal papers and burned anything that didn't positively deify the Chief Scout. That meant time-consuming original research would be needed. Before a script was completed, De Mille died and the project was shelved.

Epilogue 3

Hemingway's Hero

BEVERLY HILLS • OCTOBER 1959

ON THURSDAY, OCTOBER 15, the William Morris Theatrical Agency in Beverly Hills cut a check for three thousand dollars and mailed it to Rod Burnham in Palm Springs, where he was living with his second wife, Gayle, and their twins, Rick and BeGayle.

The cash was paid in exchange for granting a one-year option to Ernest Hemingway's sidekick, A.E. Hotchener, for the literary rights to *Scouting on Two Continents* and *Taking Chances*. Hotchener's goal was to make a Tv series called Hemingway's Hero.

Hotch was Hemingway's biographer and sometimes collaborator. He had learned about Burnham from King Macomber, whom Hemingway had grossly distorted in the fictional story *The Short, Happy Life of Francis Macomber*.

In 1960, Hotch renewed the option on the rights to the two books. The next year Hem hoisted one too many and ended up shaking hands with Saint Peter. Hotch allowed the option to expire.

Epilogue 4

The Return of the Jackal

For Historians

SALISBURY, RHODESIA • 1948

FREDERICK RAMÓN de Bertodano arrived in Salisbury in 1947 to live out his remaining years. De Bertodano was born in 1871 in England to a Navarrese father and an English mother. The Spanish province of Navarre is best known for Pamplona, the town where Ernest Hemingway went to watch the running of the bulls. The De Bertodanos emigrated to Australia where Frederick was educated as a solicitor, a junior lawyer subordinate to a barrister.

De Bertodano first arrived in Bulawayo on Tuesday, May 19, 1896, during the Matabele uprising. At that time, he was using the name Ramón Lopez on a mission to dispose of the mining interests of a British syndicate and scat back to London with the cash. The following evening, he celebrated his twenty-fifth birthday looking down the neck of a bottle at the Bulawayo Club. That was the day Nada Burnham died.

In 1948 while relaxing in the Rhodesian sunshine, De Bertodano came across *Scouting on Two Continents*, written twenty-two years earlier. On reading Burnham's book, De Bertodano was inspired to cobble up a new diary. He fabricated entries for the year 1896 and allowed it to be copied by the National Archives in Salisbury. At age seventy-six, De Bertodano's memory failed to serve him well. He did not check his dates against news clippings or official documents. The poppycock begins two days after his arrival in Bulawayo.

• May 21, 1896—De Bertodano wrote that he met Fred Selous at the Bulawayo Club. That is pure hokum. From May 11 to June 1, Selous and seven hundred fifty other members of the Bulawayo

Column were fifty miles behind enemy lines fighting the Matabele in the Insiza Hills. (Chapter 29) They had been gone for ten days, having left on Burnham's birthday (May 11), six days before De Bertodano arrived in Bulawayo. The date in Moral's diary, May 21, is the day Fred Selous shot a Matabele woman at Insiza, a fact recorded in Chaplain Pelly's Diary, local newspapers and the National Archives.

• May 25—De Bertodano says he wrote a letter to his brother in San Francisco. This was a week before the Bulawayo Column returned from the Insizas on May 31. The letter reads, "Selous says that the indunas seem to have had no organized plan for an uprising."

That statement, written in the past tense, is a paraphrasing, perhaps an outright plagiarism, of Fred Selous's words in his book *Sunshine & Storm in Africa*. That book was published in London on August 22, 1896, three months after it appears in Moral's so-called diary. (The reason Selous included that statement was to try to deflect blame for spilling the beans to the Matabele that the British South Africa Police were in gaol in Pretoria. It was the lack of armed police that emboldened the Matabele to rebel in 1896.)

• June 7—De Bertodano writes that he spoke with Selous in the Bulawayo Club. More balderdash. Selous was serving as a scout for Colonel Spreckley's column, which had departed earlier for Shiloh on a three-week long patrol. (Chapter 30)

• June 9—De Bertodano says General Carrington plans to march on the enemy holding out in the Matopo Hills. Was De Bertodano a fortune teller? It wasn't until June 11 that Colonel Baden-Powell wrote in his diary about "vague rumors of what the Matabele are doing in the Matopo Hills." (Chapter 32)

• June 12 to 14—Burnham and Baden-Powell spent three days and nights together in the Matopo Hills on their inaugural scouting patrol. De Bertodono's diary entry for Sunday, June 14, may be accurate: "Stupendous hangover—ill all day."

• June 17—De Bertodano wrote, "Burnham and Armstrong have found the M'Limo in a cave in the Matopo Hills and are trying to get him." That would have been news to Fred. It wasn't until Friday, June 19, that he was called to Earl Grey's office and told of the M'Limo's presumed whereabouts. (Chapter 32)

• June 21—The entry says, "It is widely rumored that Burnham and Armstrong have shot the M'Limo. Several men don't believe it because they don't trust the yarns of either. Some very outspoken about Burnham's claim that he was with Allan Wilson's Patrol in

1893. They say it is a lie that he left with a dispatch to Forbes. He wasn't there at all." (Chapters 17 & 18)

• June 23—Fact: Burnham shot the M'Limo at Njelele.

• June 24—Fact: Selous returned from his patrol, resigned from the Bulawayo Field Force and departed for London to write *Sunshine & Storm in Africa*. He never returned to Rhodesia. That means De Bertodano had a maximum of two days to get to know Selous and debrief him.

• June 27—This must have been an interesting Saturday at the Bulawayo Club. Alf Taylor, a longtime resident of Mangwe, was at the club where he wrote: "Dear Burnham: It is my opinion that the man killed by you and Armstrong is the M'Limo, and that all the others are only his priests. Yours truly. Alf Taylor." Taylor's letter is in the National Archives. De Bertodano's entry says, "Talk at the Club that Armstrong and Burnham's story of shooting the M'Limo is all balls... . Sergeant Farley of Grey's Scouts says, 'It's a d(amn)d lie—that they shot an old kaffir... .'"

• The first recorded accusation of shooting an unresisting old Negro doesn't appear until a year later, in Frank Sykes' book *With Plumer in Matabele Land*. Any possibility that Sykes was shooting off his mouth at the bar is exceedingly remote. Sykes was a common trooper and the Bulawayo Club was officers country.

• September 13—Six days before leaving Rhodesia, De Bertodano penned, "Judge Watermeyer has made his report to the government. He says the shooting of the M'Limo is a fake and a lie of self-glorification. The M'Limo was an old native working in a kaffir garden. It will probably finish Armstrong as native commissioner."

(Armstrong remained in good graces with the Chartered Company for another two years.)

• Jan. 11, 1897—Four months after De Bertodano left Rhodesia, Percy Inskipp, Secretary, BSA Company, Bulawayo, sent a letter of transmittal to Hugh Marshall Hole, Secretary, BSA Company, Salisbury: "I enclose evidence taken at Mangwe with reference to the shooting of the M'Limo, which I will ask you to be good enough to hand to Judge Watermeyer [in Salisbury]."

That document is on file at the National Archives in Harare.

Despite extensive searches at the National Archives, no record of the evidence sent to Watermeyer was found, only the letter of transmittal. Did it end up in the hands of Hugh Marshall Hole?

The evidence is overwhelming that De Bertodano forged a diary in 1948 and placed this fake document in the National Archives in 1949. In 1955, De Bertodano died of natural causes in Salisbury.

For the record, the secretary of the Bulawayo Club declared in 1976 that De Bertodano was never a member. Burnham joined the club in 1897 shortly before he left for the Klondike.

In the 1960s, Professor Terrence O. Ranger, in writing a pseudo-history of Rhodesia, would quote from De Bertodano's faked diary as his authority to denounce Fred Burnham as a coward and traitor. Burnham's side of the story remained sealed in the Howell Wright archives of the Sterling Memorial Library at Yale University until the year A.D. 2000.

• • •

Pretoria • 1948

JANNIE SMUTS was narrowly defeated for re-election as prime minister of South Africa. Daniel Malan, a Boer, was elected to succeed Jannie. That move ushered in fifty years of Apartheid in South Africa. The cannibal fig had conquered the host cedar and turned it to rot.

— 30 —

Lightning Source UK Ltd.
Milton Keynes UK
UKHW040033221122
412610UK00001B/4